RUSSIAN ECONOMIC HISTORY

ECONOMICS INFORMATION GUIDE SERIES

Series Editor: Robert W. Haseltine, Associate Professor of Economics, State University College of Arts and Science at Geneseo, Geneseo, New York

Also in this series:

CONSUMER EDUCATION—*Edited by Terry A. Darveaux**

HISTORY OF ECONOMIC ANALYSIS—*Edited by William K. Hutchinson*

ECONOMICS OF MINORITIES—*Kenneth L. Gagala*

TRANSPORTATION ECONOMICS—*Edited by James P. Rakowski*

ECONOMIC EDUCATION—*Edited by Catherine Hughes*

HEALTH AND MEDICAL ECONOMICS—*Edited by Ted J. Ackroyd*

LABOR ECONOMICS—*Edited by Ross E. Azevedo*

ECONOMIC HISTORY OF CANADA—*Edited by Trevor J.O. Dick*

MATHEMATICAL ECONOMICS AND OPERATIONS RESEARCH—*Edited by Joseph Zaremba*

MONEY, BANKING, AND MACROECONOMICS—*Edited by James M. Rock*

INTERNATIONAL TRADE—*Edited by Ahmed M. El-Dersh**

ECONOMIC DEVELOPMENT—*Edited by Thomas A. Bieler**

*in preparation

The above series is part of the
GALE INFORMATION GUIDE LIBRARY

The Library consists of a number of separate series of guides covering major areas in the social sciences, humanities, and current affairs.

General Editor: Paul Wasserman, Professor and former Dean, School of Library and Information Services, University of Maryland.

Managing Editor: Dedria Bryfonski, Gale Research Company

RUSSIAN ECONOMIC HISTORY

A GUIDE TO INFORMATION SOURCES

Volume 4 in the Economics Information Guide Series

Daniel R. Kazmer

*Soviet Economic Specialist
Central Intelligence Agency*

Vera Kazmer

M.L.S., Simmons College

Gale Research Company
Book Tower, Detroit, Michigan 48226

Library of Congress Cataloging in Publication Data

Kazmer, Daniel R
Russian economic history.

(Economics information guide series ; v. 4) (Gale information guide library)
Includes index.
1. Russia—Economic conditions—Bibliography.
I. Kazmer, Vera, joint author. II. Title
Z7165.R9K34   [HC333]   016.3309'47   73-17588
ISBN 0-8103--1304-9

Copyright © 1977 by
Daniel R. Kazmer and Vera Kazmer

No part of this book may be reproduced in any form without permission in writing from the publisher, except by a reviewer who wishes to quote brief passages or entries in connection with a review written for inclusion in a magazine or newspaper. Manufactured in the United States of America.

To Our Parents

VITAE

Daniel R. Kazmer, born in Chicago, February 1947, received his B.S. degree in mathematics from the University of Illinois at Chicago Circle and his Ph.D. in economics from the Massachusetts Institute of Technology. He was assistant professor in economics at Eastern Michigan University from 1973-75. He is currently working as a specialist in Soviet economy in the Central Intelligence Agency.

Vera Ulanowski Kazmer, born in Gissen, Germany, September 1946, received her B.A. degree in Russian from the University of Illinois at Champagne-Urbana and her M.L.S. from Simmons College (Boston) in 1973.

CONTENTS

Preface		ix
Chapter 1	- Study of the Soviet Economy	1
Chapter 2	- The Russian Economy in General	5
Chapter 3	- Russian Economic Thought	39
Chapter 4	- Economic Systems and Society in Russia	55
Chapter 5	- Economic Planning and Policy	71
Chapter 6	- War, Defense, and the Russian Economy	97
Chapter 7	- Economic Growth, Development, and Industrialization	107
Chapter 8	- Comparisons Between the Russian and Other Economies	129
Chapter 9	- Economic Fluctuations and Business Cycles	137
Chapter 10	- The Use of Mathematical Models, Econometrics, and Computers in the Soviet Economy	139
Chapter 11	- Soviet Use of Input-Output Analysis	143
Chapter 12	- Economic and Social Statistics	147
Chapter 13	- Russian National Income and Product	163
Chapter 14	- Prices, Price Levels, and Inflation	171
Chapter 15	- Money, Finance, Banking, and Credit	179
Chapter 16	- Government Finance, Budget, Taxation, and Expenditures	189
Chapter 17	- Foreign Trade, Policies, and Relations	195
Chapter 18	- Balance of Payments and International Finance	223
Chapter 19	- International Aid, Business, and Investment	227
Chapter 20	- Economic Organization, Administration, and Reform	237
Chapter 21	- Management and Entrepreneurship	255
Chapter 22	- Soviet Investment Allocation Policies	265
Chapter 23	- Transportation and Communications	269
Chapter 24	- Science, Technology, and the Economy	277
Chapter 25	- Studies of Particular Industries and Sectors	281
Chapter 26	- Russian Agriculture and the Peasantry	299
Chapter 27	- Conservation, Natural Resources, and Pollution in the Soviet Union	361
Chapter 28	- The Economic Geography of the Soviet Union	365
Chapter 29	- Manpower, Labor, Government Policy Towards Labor, and Trade Unions	371
Chapter 30	- Demographic Studies	407
Chapter 31	- Health, Education, and Welfare	415

Contents

Chapter 32 – Women in the Soviet Economy 421
Chapter 33 – The Consumer and Living Standards in the Russian
             Economy 425
Chapter 34 – Housing and the Urban Economy 435
Chapter 35 – Regional Studies 441
Chapter 36 – The Future of the Soviet Economy 455
Author Index 457
Title Index 475
Subject Index 489

PREFACE

It is the hope of the authors that this bibliography will prove both useful and timely. The only other annotated bibliographies on the Soviet economy known to the authors are Harry Schwartz. RUSSIA'S SOVIET ECONOMY; A SELECTED BIBLIOGRAPHY OF MATERIALS IN ENGLISH (Syracuse, N.Y.: Syracuse University Press, 1949); and RUSSIA'S SOVIET ECONOMY. 2d ed. with appendix: THE SOVIET ECONOMY, 1954-58 (Englewood Cliffs, N.J.: Prentice-Hall, 1958). Schwartz's works cover books, pamphlets, and journal articles. They list only works in English and deal only with the Soviet period. The present bibliography covers works in English on the pre-Revolutionary economy of tsarist Russia as well as works dealing with the Soviet economy. It is hoped that this bibliography will prove useful to historians, librarians, students, and economists with an interest in the Soviet economy but who lack a knowledge of Russian.

This bibliography is a classified annotated listing of books, pamphlets, and periodical materials in English only. However, many of the works listed contain references to original sources in Russian. If the reader wishes to make an in-depth study of some aspect of the Russian or Soviet economy, the use of Russian-language materials is essential. Thus, this bibliography cannot meet all the needs of a specialist in the area. Furthermore, it is not an exhaustive listing of all works in English on the subject. We have compiled a selective bibliography covering generally available sources on virtually all aspects of economic activity. Not all sources listed in this bibliography are of the highest quality. Some sources were included because they were the only ones available in English on a particular subject. Thus, the maintenance of minimum quality standards for works included has been sacrificed for more complete and balanced coverage.

Our research was carried out at the Graduate Library of the University of Michigan and Eastern Michigan University Library, with the aid of the interlibrary loan office of the latter. Since our funds were limited, we were unable to make research trips to the Library of Congress or other major libraries. Nevertheless, we were able to obtain about 97 percent of the titles we desired from one of the three sources mentioned above.

In compiling this bibliography, we obtained a preliminary list of sources (for the period 1900-1974) from THE CUMULATIVE BOOK INDEX, NATIONAL UNION

Preface

CATALOG subject listings, the INDEX OF ECONOMIC ARTICLES, and the JOURNAL OF ECONOMIC LITERATURE. This list was supplemented, however, with additional sources which were gleaned from the bibliographies of our preliminary list of sources. We hope that we have thus obtained both the most important works on Russian economic history in general and sources on the various special interest topics of Russian economic history.

This bibliography contains only a selective list of the most important and readily available U.S. government publications because of limitations of time and space. The reader interested in a listing of U.S. government documents dealing with the various aspects of the Russian economy is referred to the CUMULATIVE SUBJECT INDEX TO THE MONTHLY CATALOG OF U.S. GOVERNMENT PUBLICATIONS 1900-1971. 14 vols. (Washington, D.C.: Carrollton Press, 1973-   ). Theses have also been excluded, since they are not easily accessible. Nevertheless, certain sources which are rare and available only in a limited number of libraries have been included because they are classic works on a particular subject and may be available through interlibrary loan. All of the sources listed in this bibliography have been examined by the authors. Sources that could not be obtained by the authors have been excluded with the rationale that if the authors could not obtain them after considerable effort, they are not generally available.

In the annotations we have given a brief description of the scope, content, point of view, and any unique or particularly significant features of each work. Additionally, annotations of journal articles include references to any comments, discussions, or replies to the annotated article. Such cross-referencing is worth the extra work because it alerts the reader that there is further discussion of the annotated article--usually in later issues of the same journal.

This bibliography is classified by subject and organized into thirty-six chapters. This classification roughly approximates the arrangement used in the JOURNAL OF ECONOMIC LITERATURE. We chose this system because it breaks down the major subfields as an economist or economic historian does and because it is familiar to users of either the INDEX OF ECONOMIC ARTICLES or the JOURNAL OF ECONOMIC LITERATURE. Each topic chapter is then divided (where applicable) into four sections. The first section covers works dealing with the topic in general. The other three sections each cover works dealing with the topic in one of the three major periods of Russian economic history: the period up to 1860, the period from 1860 to 1917, and the period after 1917. Within each section the works are listed alphabetically by author.

We would like to extend special thanks to the staff of Eastern Michigan University Library and its interlibrary loan office for their cooperation.

Chapter 1
STUDY OF THE SOVIET ECONOMY

Boulding, Kenneth. "Study of the Soviet Economy: Its Place in American Education." In STUDY OF THE SOVIET ECONOMY, edited by Nicolas Spulber, pp. 104-28. Papers presented at a conference, Bloomington, Ind. Bloomington: Indiana University Press, 1961.

> The following questions were discussed by a panel chaired by the author: (1) should study of Soviet economics be granted a special place in economics curriculums? (2) should "collectivist" or "planning economics" be taught separately from established theory courses? and (3) what is the aim of such courses on the undergraduate and graduate levels?

Campbell, Robert W. "Problems of United States--Soviet Economic Comparisons." In COMPARISONS OF THE U.S. AND SOVIET ECONOMIES, U.S. Congress. Joint Economic Committee, pp. 13-30. Washington, D.C.: Government Printing Office, 1959. Tables.

> This paper deals with the availability and interpretation of statistical data, the index number problem, and the dangers of comparing isolated indicators out of context.

_____. "Research on the Soviet Economy--Achievements and Prospects." In STUDY OF THE SOVIET ECONOMY, edited by Nicolas Spulber, pp. 129-43. Papers presented at a conference, Bloomington, Ind. Bloomington: Indiana University Press, 1961.

> The author discusses current research on the Soviet economy, its relationship to the field of economics, and needed research still to be done. He concludes that more industry and regional studies are necessary.

Campbell, Robert W., et al. "Methodological Problems Comparing the U.S. and USSR Economies." In SOVIET ECONOMIC PROSPECTS FOR THE SEVENTIES, U.S. Congress. Joint Economic Committee, pp. 122-46. Washington, D.C.: Government Printing Office, 1973. Tables.

> This paper provides preliminary estimates of selected U.S./USSR

economic aggregates, interprets them in light of methodological and theoretical considerations, discusses the use of economic comparisons in the analysis of defense policy issues, and comments on the state of the two economies.

Elias, A[ndrew]. SOVIET PRACTICE IN THE CLASSIFICATION OF ECONOMIC ACTIVITY. Bureau of the Census. Foreign Manpower Research Office. Washington, D.C.: Government Printing Office, 1961. 40 p.

This paper examines the Soviet Union's method of classifying various branches of production. Such information facilitates compilation of statistics, economic planning, management, and control.

Gerschenkron, Alexander. "A Neglected Source of Economic Information on Soviet Russia." AMERICAN SLAVIC AND EAST EUROPEAN REVIEW 9 (1950): 1-19.

This article stresses the value of Soviet literature as a source of both factual material and impressions for western economists working in the area of Soviet economy.

Heymann, Hans, Jr. "Problems of Soviet--United States Comparisons." In COMPARISONS OF THE U.S. AND SOVIET ECONOMIES, U.S. Congress. Joint Economic Committee, pp. 1-12. Washington, D.C.: Government Printing Office, 1959.

The author outlines problems of comparing U.S. and Soviet economies, discusses the limitations of data and tools, and mentions some differences over time and space between the two economies.

Jasny, Naum. "On the Wrong Track." SOVIET STUDIES 8 (July 1956): 50-76. Tables.

This article reviews the work of the RAND Corporation in the field of Soviet economy. For further discussion, see: Letter by Oleg Hoeffding. SOVIET STUDIES 8 (October 1956): 215-16 and Reply by Naum Jasny. SOVIET STUDIES 8 (January 1957): 331-33.

_____. "Research on the Soviet Economy." In ESSAYS ON THE SOVIET ECONOMY, edited by Naum Jasny, pp. 1-92. New York: Praeger, 1962.

This lengthy essay covers the topics of obtaining data and of extracting the truth from Soviet statistics, other evidence, and Soviet economists. The author then analyzes (1) the Index of Soviet Industrial Production in studies by western analysts, (2) tie-ins, that is, things like crop utilization vs. production statistics, and (3) price analysis.

_____. "The Summit of Falsehood." In ESSAYS ON THE SOVIET ECONOMY, edited by Naum Jasny, pp. 269-81. New York: Praeger, 1962.

The falsehoods of the "Report on the Fulfillment of the 1948 Plan" are analyzed. The author also unveils the drastic secret revision of the 1940 turnover in kolkhoz trade. He concludes that one generally must be careful when using Soviet statistics.

Knight, Frank H. "The Place of Marginal Economics in a Collectivist System." AMERICAN ECONOMIC REVIEW 26 (March 1936): 255-66.

This article argues (1) that in a collectivist economy the place of marginal economics is not markedly different from their place in an economy of competitive individualism and (2) that problems of collectivism are political problems, not matters of economic theory, and that the economic theorist can thus say little about them. For further discussion, see the following: Calvin B. Hoover et al., "Prices and Valuation in the Soviet System--Discussion." Ibid., pp. 283-90.

Spulber, Nicolas. "Introduction." In STUDY OF THE SOVIET ECONOMY, edited by Nicolas Spulber, pp. vii-xiii. Papers presented at a conference, Bloomington, Ind. Bloomington: Indiana University Press, 1961.

Spulber stresses the need for information on the mainsprings, direction, and impact of Soviet growth in an essay usable by a layman interested in a study of the USSR.

Chapter 2
THE RUSSIAN ECONOMY IN GENERAL

Chirovsky, Nicholas L. THE ECONOMIC FACTORS IN THE GROWTH OF RUSSIA; AN ECONOMIC-HISTORICAL ANALYSIS. New York: Philosophical Library, 1957. 178 p.

> Chirovsky surveys Russian economic history from the twelfth century through 1955-56. In part one he discusses economic factors which shaped the national psychology (i.e., the economic and political consequences of the Mongol invasion and the economic elements in the old Muscovite political growth). Part two deals with the economic factors which led to territorial expansion (i.e., conquest of the Baltic countries, the partition of Poland, and conquests in Central Asia). Part three examines Russian political interests and the economic doctrine of communism. Index and bibliography.

Gerschenkron, Alexander. "An Economic History of Russia." JOURNAL OF ECONOMIC HISTORY 12, no. 2 (1952): 146-59.

> This article reviews P[eter]. I. Liashchenko. ISTORIYA NARODNOGO KHOZYAYSTVA SSSR [History of the national economy of the USSR]. 2 vols. Moscow: Gospolitizdat, 1947-48; and Peter I. Liashchenko. HISTORY OF THE NATIONAL ECONOMY OF RUSSIA TO THE 1917 REVOLUTION. Translated by L. M. Herman. Introduction by Calvin B. Hoover. New York: Macmillan, 1949. xiii, 880 p.

Kochan, Lionel. THE MAKING OF MODERN RUSSIA. London: Jonathan Cape, 1962. 320 p.

> This work attempts to show how the Kievan state of the tenth century developed into the Soviet Union of today. The author has dealt principally with the growth of the state, political developments, economic change, and social problems. Index and five maps.

Treadgold, Donald W. "Russian Expansion in the Light of Turner's Study of the American Frontier." AGRICULTURAL HISTORY 26 (October 1952): 147-52.

The Russian Economy in General

This paper argues that the "frontier approach" as applied by Frederick Jackson Turner to American history is also applicable to the development of Russia both before and after the Revolution. A brief chronicle of Russian expansion into Siberia is given as evidence.

Vernadsky, George. A HISTORY OF RUSSIA. 6th rev. ed. New Haven, Conn.: Yale University Press, 1969. 531 p.

Of particular interest are chapters on "Social and Economic Development, 1700-1850," "Internal Development From the Mid-19th Century to the First World War," and "The New Economic Policy and the Five-Year Plan." Statistical appendix, maps, genealogical tables, bibliography, and index.

THE PERIOD UP TO 1860

Anderson, M.S. "Russia Under Peter the Great and the Changed Relations of East and West." In THE NEW CAMBRIDGE MODERN HISTORY. Vol. 6: THE RISE OF GREAT BRITAIN AND RUSSIA 1688-1715/25, edited by J. S. Bromley, pp. 716-40. London and New York: Cambridge University Press, 1970.

This chapter contains a discussion of Peter's "mercantilism," the successes and failures of industry and labor, the resistance of agriculture to change, the failure of commercial policies, the relationship between landowners and peasants, and the physical and financial burdens of the peasantry.

Davies, R[obert]. "Russia in the Early Middle Ages." ECONOMIC HISTORY REVIEW II 5, no. 1 (1952): 116-27.

After summarizing the accepted historical viewpoints of the early medieval period of Russian history, the author then considers evidence contrary to these viewpoints. He concludes that the viewpoint presented in most general textbooks and Russian histories in English needs to be reexamined.

De Tegoborski, M. Ludvik. COMMENTARIES ON THE PRODUCTIVE FORCES OF RUSSIA. 2 vols. London: Longman, Brown, Green, and Longmans, 1855-56. Vol. 1, xxii, 528 p. Vol. 2, iv, 483 p.

This exhaustive survey of Russia's productive forces includes climate, soil, population, agriculture, industry, commerce, and maritime navigation. Numerous tables.

Fennell, J. L. I. "Russia, 1462-1583." In THE NEW CAMBRIDGE MODERN HISTORY. Vol. 2: THE REFORMATION, 1520-1559, edited by G. R. Elton, pp. 534-61. London and New York: Cambridge University Press, 1968.

This chapter outlines Russian history for the period and devotes a few pages to land tenure and the pomestye system.

The Russian Economy in General

Goldstein, Joseph M. RUSSIA, HER ECONOMIC PAST AND FUTURE. New York: Russian Information Bureau, 1919. 99 p.

    Goldstein discusses economic development under the old regime; agriculture and industrial production; foreign trade and exports and imports; inland water transportation; railway systems; natural systems; and banking. The book contains many charts, graphs, and maps, and substantial statistical information on the prerevolutionary economy.

Grekov, B. D. KIEV RUS. Edited by D. Ogden. Translated by Y. Sdobnikov. Moscow: Foreign Languages Publishing House, 1959. 684 p.

    This translation contains a description of ancient Rus agriculture as well as an account of social relations in Kievan Rus which includes a discussion of the "smerd" movement. Chapter 8 contains a brief account of Eastern Slav trade.

Haxthausen, Baron A. von. THE RUSSIAN EMPIRE, ITS PEOPLE, INSTITUTIONS AND RESOURCES. English ed. 2 vols. London: 1856. Microfilm ed. Ann Arbor, Mich.: University Microfilms, 1964.

    These two volumes give a description of the Russian people, the nature of their institutions, and the form of government in the mid-nineteenth century. Particularly interesting for the economic historian are the chapters dealing with rural institutions.

Henderson, William O. THE INDUSTRIAL REVOLUTION ON THE CONTINENT: GERMANY, FRANCE, RUSSIA, 1800-1914. 2d ed. London: Frank Cars, 1967. ix, 291 p.

    Chapter 5 deals with the industrial revolution in Russia and contains a brief account of industrial expansion, communications, finance and capital, industrial workers, and Russian expansion into Asia.

Kahan, Arcadius. "The Costs of 'Westernization' in Russia: The Gentry and the Economy in the Eighteenth Century." SLAVIC REVIEW 25 (March 1966): 40-66.

    This paper analyzes the income and expenditures of the gentry class in Russia. It concludes that the burden of the drive to "Westernize" was successfully transferred by the gentry to the enserfed peasantry. Nine tables.

Kluichevsky, V. O. A COURSE IN RUSSIAN HISTORY: THE SEVENTEENTH CENTURY. Translated by Natalie Duddington. Chicago: Quadrangle Books, 1968. xi, 400 p.

    This volume is an unabridged translation of volume 3 of A COURSE IN RUSSIAN HISTORY. This famous Russian historian gives an account of the social, political, and economic events in Russia

The Russian Economy in General

during the seventeenth century. The book includes a discussion of the coming of serfdom. Index.

_____. A HISTORY OF RUSSIA. Vol. 2. Translated by C. J. Hogarth. London: J. M. Dent & Sons, 1912. viii, 326 p.

This is a classic general history of Russia. The following chapters are of interest to the economist: 8--pomiestie land tenure; 11--methods of monasterial acquisition of agrarian wealth; and 12--the connection between monasterial landownership and serf law. Index.

Kochan, Miriam. LIFE IN RUSSIA UNDER CATHERINE THE GREAT. European Life Series. Edited by Peter Quennell. London: B. T. Batsford, 1969. x, 182 p.

Kochan describes lifestyles of the nobility and the serfs and gives a brief account of industry and trade during the reign of Catherine the Great. Index.

Lagny, Germain de. THE KNOUT AND THE RUSSIAN. Translated by John Bridgeman. New York: Harper and Brothers, 1854. 266 p. Illustrated.

This book outlines the organization and social structure of Russian society in the mid-nineteenth century. Of particular interest to the economic historian are the chapters on "Finances" and "Slavery" (serfdom).

Liashchenko, Peter I. HISTORY OF THE NATIONAL ECONOMY OF RUSSIA TO THE 1917 REVOLUTION. Translated by L. M. Herman. Introduction by Calvin B. Hoover. New York: Macmillan, 1949. xiii, 880 p.

Written by a Marxist Soviet economic historian, this work is divided into two parts. The first covers the precapitalist economic structures and the second part deals with capitalism in prerevolutionary Russia. In part one the author describes the primitive Slav economy and its decline; the emergence of the feudal serf economy; the feudal economy of the Moscow state and the end of feudal fragmentation; and the feudal economy of Russia during the end of the eighteenth and first half of the nineteenth centuries. Part two gives an account of industrial capitalism; the economy of the "national minority borderlands" and the colonial policy of the tsars during the nineteenth and twentieth centuries; and the era of imperialism during the twentieth century. Bibliographical index. A chronological index of the principal economic events in the history of the USSR. Index and four foldout maps.

Mavor, James. AN ECONOMIC HISTORY OF RUSSIA. 2d ed., rev. 2 vols. New York: Russell and Russell, 1965. Vol. 1, xxxv, 614 p. Vol. 2, xxii, 630 p.

The Russian Economy in General

These two volumes represent a classic study of the Russian economy from earliest times through the revolutionary movement of 1903-7. The volumes are comprised of seven books: book 1 describes the early economic history and the rise of bondage right; book 2 includes the fall of bondage right and agriculture under bondage; book 3 deals with the fall of bondage and industry under bondage; book 4 discusses political and social movements prior to 1903; book 5 covers the agrarian question and its revolutionary phases; book 6 concerns industrial development under capitalism; and book 7 deals with the revolutionary movement in Russia--1903-7. Index and glossary.

Olivia, Lawrence J. RUSSIA IN THE ERA OF PETER THE GREAT. Englewood Cliffs, N.J.: Prentice-Hall, 1969. viii, 184 p.

The author analyzes the alteration in the traditional economic and social patterns during the Petrine period. Of particular interest to the economic historian would be: chapter 1--"Administration and Finance"; chapter 5--"Aristocrat and Serf"; and chapter 6--"Commerce and Industry."

Pokrovsky, M. N. BRIEF HISTORY OF RUSSIA. Translated by D. S. Mirsky. 2 vols. New York: International Publishers, 1933. Vol. 1, 295 p. Vol. 2, 348 p.

The work begins with a congratulatory note from Lenin. It presents the Marxist viewpoint of history from the earliest times to the end of the nineteenth century in volume 1 and from then to the Stolypin regime in volume 2. Economic topics receive considerable attention. Index.

_____. HISTORY OF RUSSIA, FROM THE EARLIEST TIMES TO THE RISE OF COMMERCIAL CAPITALISM. Edited and translated by J. D. Clarkson and M. R. M. Griffiths. New introduction by J. D. Clarkson. 1931. Reprint. Bloomington, Ind.: University Prints and Reprints, 1966. xxviii, 383 p.

This is a Marxist history of early Russia up to Peter the Great, with strong emphasis on economic matters. Maps.

Pushkarev, S[ergei]. THE EMERGENCE OF MODERN RUSSIA, 1801-1917. Translated by R.H. McNeal and Tova Yedlin. New York: Holt, Rinehart, and Winston, 1963. xxiii, 512 p. Illustrated.

This book, although a general history of Russia, discusses economic developments in their historical perspective. Selected bibliography and name and subject indexes.

Raeff, Marc. IMPERIAL RUSSIA 1682-1825; THE COMING OF AGE OF MODERN RUSSIA. Borzoi History of Russia, vol. 4. New York: Alfred Knopf, 1971. xi, 176 p. Illustrated.

The Russian Economy in General

Of particular interest to the economic historian is the chapter on the economy. Maps.

Vyvyan, J. M. K. "Russia in Europe and Asia." In THE NEW CAMBRIDGE MODERN HISTORY. Vol. 10: THE ZENITH OF EUROPEAN POWER 1830-70, edited by J. P. T. Bury, pp. 357-88. London and New York: Cambridge University Press, 1960.

The author briefly accounts local peasant uprisings; changes in economic policy; the emancipation of the serfs; reform of the bank of Russia; economic conditions following the Crimean War; and the economic failure of the agrarian revolution.

_____. "Russia, 1789-1825." In THE NEW CAMBRIDGE MODERN HISTORY. Vol. 9: WAR AND PEACE IN THE AGE OF UPHEAVAL 1793-1830, edited by C. W. Crawley, pp. 495-524. London and New York: Cambridge University Press, 1968.

This chapter considers the population of the empire and the prevalance of serfdom, industry, and trade.

Young, Ian. "Russia." In THE NEW CAMBRIDGE MODERN HISTORY. Vol. 7: THE OLD REGIME 1713-63, edited by J. O. Lindsay, pp. 318-38. London and New York: Cambridge University Press, 1957.

Young notes briefly economic conditions; the development of the iron and other industries; the supply of labor; communications; export trade; Peter's fiscal reforms; the population, social structure, and the conditions of the peasants.

THE PERIOD 1860-1917

Alexinsky, Gregor. MODERN RUSSIA. 2d ed. Translated by Bernard Miall. London: T. Fisher Unwin, 1915. vi, 361 p.

This general history of Russia contains sections on the economic position of Russia in relation to other countries, development and forms of Russian capital, and the rural economy and the agrarian question. Among the topics discussed are foreign trade, peculiarities of Russian capital, importance of foreign capital, Russian industry in comparison with German and Belgian industry (1902), the economic and social life of the peasants, and the decay of the rural commune. Index.

Beable, William H. COMMERCIAL RUSSIA. London: Constable & Co., 1918. 278 p.

Intended as a general guide for businessmen in Russia, this work contains much information useful to the economic historian. The appendix gives equivalents of British and Russian weights and measures. Map.

The Russian Economy in General

Black, Cyril E., ed. THE TRANSFORMATION OF RUSSIAN SOCIETY: ASPECTS OF SOCIAL CHANGE SINCE 1861. Cambridge, Mass.: Harvard University Press, 1960. vii, 695 p.

> The book's essays examine various aspects of Russian society. Of particular interest to the economic historian are the following papers: Theodore H. Von Laue. "The State and the Economy"; Lazar Volin. "The Russian Peasant: From Emancipation to Kolkhoz"; and Jerzy G. Gliksman. "The Russian Urban Worker: From Serf to Proletarian." Index.

Crawford, John M., ed. THE INDUSTRIES OF RUSSIA. 5 vols. in 3. St. Petersburg, Russia: Department of Trade and Manufacture. Imperial Ministry of Finance, 1893.

> Volumes 1 and 2 deal with manufactures and trade and give historical sketches and statistics for many industries. Volume 3 deals with agriculture and forestry. Volume 4 is concerned with mining and metallurgy, and volume 5 describes the great Siberian Railway and Siberia.

Deutscher, Isaac. "The Russian Revolution." In THE NEW CAMBRIDGE MODERN HISTORY. Vol. 12: THE ERA OF VIOLENCE 1898-1945, edited by David Thompson, pp. 386-415. London and New York: Cambridge University Press, 1960.

> The chapters sketch the poverty and backwardness of the peasantry; the growing resentment against the landlords; and industrial backwardness and financial bankruptcy.

Drage, Geoffrey. RUSSIAN AFFAIRS. London: John Murray, 1904. xvi, 738 p.

> Drage explores Russian economic and social conditions on the eve of the Russo-Japanese War. Chapters 2 and 3 discuss agrarian developments (i.e., forms of land tenure and methods of cultivation); famines; and industrial development. Chapters 4 and 5 discuss commerce and finance, past and present. Chapter 7 describes the land and people, agriculture, industry, and commerce of Siberia, Manchuria, and Central Asia. Color foldout maps, tables, and index.

Duff, James D., ed. RUSSIAN REALITIES AND PROBLEMS. Cambridge: At the University Press, 1917. vi, 229 p.

> Included are six lectures delivered at Cambridge in August 1916. One of them, by Peter B. Struve, deals with the Russian economy, "Past and Present of Russian Economics." This lecture outlines the historical foundations of Russian economics, which is of a colonial nature, and discusses the economic prospects of the Russian empire.

The Russian Economy in General

Dyason, J. "Russia, 1900-1936: A Statistical Interpretation." ECONOMIC RECORD 13 (December 1937): 216-23.

This article presents estimates of wheat and rye consumption in Russia and displays graphs showing per capita production of several commodities and animal populations. The author concludes that the prewar period was one of economic advance; the Revolution inflicted bigger losses than the war; and the progressive elimination of private enterprise after 1925 hurt recovery.

First National City Bank of New York. RUSSIA AND THE IMPERIAL RUSSIAN GOVERNMENT: ECONOMIC AND FINANCIAL. New York: 1916. 18 p.

This pamphlet surveys the imperial Russian economy prior to the revolution. It describes the development of resources, economic character of the country, national currency, foreign trade, national debt and wealth, and revenues and expenditures.

Florinsky, Michael T. THE END OF THE RUSSIAN EMPIRE. Economic and Social History of the World War. New Haven, Conn.: Yale University Press, 1931. xvi, 272 p.

This volume aims at a broad description of economic and social processes in Russia during the First World War and introduces the Russian Series of the Economic and Social History of the World War, published by the Carnegie Endowment for International Peace. The book contains chapters on labor and the peasant and a brief description of Russia on the eve of the war. Index.

Gerschenkron, Alexander. EUROPE IN THE RUSSIAN MIRROR: FOUR LECTURES IN ECONOMIC HISTORY. London: Cambridge University Press, 1970. ix, 158 p.

This book, consisting of the Ellen McArthur Lectures delivered at Cambridge University in May 1968, compares Russian and general European economic history. Special attention is given to the Protestant ethic and the spirit of capitalism, mercantilism as a function of economic backwardness, and Russian industrialization (1880-1914) in comparison to European industrialization in the eighteenth and nineteenth centuries.

Goulivitich, Arsene de. CZARISM AND REVOLUTION. Translated by N. J. Couriss. Hawthorne, Calif.: Omni Publications, 1962. 272 p.

The author analyzes the meaning of Czarism to Russia and discusses the following questions: (1) along what lines did the empire of czars develop? (2) what was the international role of the empire? and (3) what led to the collapse of the empire? The book contains chapters on "agriculture," "industry," "trade and the markets," "transport," and "finance."

Gurko, Vladimir I. FEATURES AND FIGURES OF THE PAST; GOVERNMENT AND OPINION IN THE REIGN OF NICHOLAS II. Edited by J. E. Wallace Sterling et al. Translated by Laura Matveev. The Hoover Library on War, Revolution, and Peace. Publication no. 14. Stanford, Calif.: Stanford University Press, 1939. xix, 760 p.

> The book is divided into six parts--one: "The First Years of the Reign of Nicholas II"; two: "The Period of Plehve's Ascendancy, 1902-1904"; three: "The Outbreak of the Russo-Japanese War and the Government's Attempt to Reach an Understanding with the Public, 1904"; four: "The Revolution of 1905"; five: "The World War, 1914-1915." It contains a chapter on Witte as minister of finance; the peasant problem; and peasants and labor questions during Sviatopolk-Mirsky's term of office.

Heyking, A. Baron. "The Economic Resources of Russia, with Special Reference to British Opportunities." ROYAL STATISTICAL SOCIETY. JOURNAL. Ser. A, 80 (March 1917): 187-221.

> This paper covers Russian statistics, transportation and communication, area and population, climate, timber, fur, agriculture, bacon, tobacco, sugar, fruit, wines, tea, fisheries, paper, and minerals. Fifteen tables.

Hourwich, I[saac]. A. "The Economic Condition of Russia." JOURNAL OF POLITICAL ECONOMY 12 (September 1904): 555-63.

> This paper is a review of COMMERCIAL RUSSIA IN 1904. Washington, D.C.: Department of Commerce and Labor, Bureau of Statistics, 1904. Figures on government industrial operations, the government budget, and exports are included.

Hurt, B. "Populists and Industrializers Again." CANADIAN SLAVONIC PAPERS 12 (Spring 1970): 78-85.

> This article is largely a review of Alexander Gerschenkron's "Russia: Agrarian Policies and Industrialization, 1861-1914," in CONTINUITY IN HISTORY AND OTHER ESSAYS. Cambridge, Mass.: Belknap Press, Howard University Press, 1968.

Keep, J. L. H. "Russia." In THE NEW CAMBRIDGE ECONOMIC HISTORY. Vol. 12: MATERIAL PROGRESS AND WORLD-WIDE PROBLEMS 1870-1898, edited by F. H. Hinsley, pp. 352-82. London and New York: Cambridge University Press, 1962.

> Keep outlines the emancipation of the serfs and the reforms of the 1860s, social and economic conditions, and the beginnings of industrialization.

Kozmin, P. A. "Some Features of the Russian Economic Situation." JOURNAL OF POLITICAL ECONOMY 12 (March 1904): 261-70.

The Russian Economy in General

This paper reviews Russian industrial development for the period 1860-1903 and discusses Russia's economic conditions and industrial outlook in 1904. A table provides figures on Russian and U.S. wheat exports to England for five-year periods between 1866-1900.

Lloyd, T. "The Economic Condition of Russia." ECONOMIC JOURNAL 2 (June 1892): 398-403.

Lloyd surveys conditions in Russia in the 1880s and concludes that the country is backward and promises to become even more so.

Malevsky-Malevitch, P., ed. RUSSIA-U.S.S.R.: A COMPLETE HANDBOOK. New York: William Farquhar Payson, 1933. xv, 712 p.

This volume traces development from the early part of the twentieth century in the Russian Empire, to the period prior to the book's publication date. It contains sections on industry, agriculture, transport, money, finance, trade, and labor. Maps.

Monkhouse, Allan. MOSCOW, 1911-1933. Boston: Little, Brown, 1934. 334 p. Illustrated.

Of interest to the economic historian are chapters on industrial development (1911-14), the New Economic Policy (NEP), the Five-Year Plan, agriculture, British firms in the USSR, and transport.

Oberlander, Erwin, et al., eds. RUSSIA ENTERS THE TWENTIETH CENTURY: 1894-1917. New York: Schocken Books, 1971. 352 p.

Twelve previously unpublished essays focus on foreign policy, politics, economics, religion, and philosophy. Three essays would interest the economic historian: "Russia's Economic Development," by Karl C. Thalheim; "The Economic and Cultural Development of Siberia," by Nikolaus Poppe; and "The Agrarian Problem," by Henry T. Willetts. Index.

Pares, Bernard. RUSSIA: BETWEEN REFORM AND REVOLUTION. Edited by Francis B. Rondall. New York: Schocken Books, 1962. xvi, 425 p.

Several chapters discuss the class system, administration and officials, the zemstvo, the peasants, and factory life.

Raffalovich, Arthur, ed. RUSSIA: ITS TRADE AND COMMERCE. London: P. S. King & Son, 1918. ix, 461 p.

This book reviews all aspects of the Russian economy with emphasis on the period 1890-1913. Tables and index.

Villari, Luigi A. RUSSIA UNDER THE GREAT SHADOW. London: T. Fisher Unwin, 1905. 330 p. Illustrated.

The Russian Economy in General

Although this work is a travelog, several chapters (10-12) are of interest. They are concerned with industrial development, the working classes, and the effect of the Russo-Japanese War on the economy. Index.

Von Laue, Theodore H. "The State and the Economy." In THE TRANSFORMATION OF RUSSIAN SOCIETY: ASPECTS OF SOCIAL CHANGE SINCE 1861, edited by Cyril E. Black, pp. 209-25. Cambridge, Mass.: Harvard University Press, 1960.

The author's objective is to determine the unique experiences of Russia during the past hundred years, which resulted in an underdeveloped country's claim to be a great power.

Witte, Sergei. THE MEMOIRS OF COUNT WITTE. Edited and translated by Abraham Yarmolinsky. Garden City, N.Y.: Doubleday, Page & Co., 1921. xi, 445 p.

Several chapters provide a firsthand account of important episodes in Russian economic history up to 1912. Index.

THE PERIOD AFTER 1917

Ames, Edward. SOVIET ECONOMIC PROCESSES. Homewood, Ill.: R. D. Irwin, 1965. 257 p. Illustrated.

Part one deals with microeconomics and discusses plans; enterprises; the theory of output-maximization; and surpluses, shortages, and direct controls. Part two deals with macroeconomics and discusses agriculture; capital formation; monetary and fiscal policy; theories about income and output; planning and the welfare of the state; and international trade. The text is supplemented with tables and diagrams.

Ammende, E. HUMAN LIFE IN RUSSIA. London: Allen & Unwin, 1936. 319 p. Illustrated.

Ammende's stark account of the Russian famine at the end of World War I is supplemented with shocking photographs of famine victims.

Andrews, William G., ed. SOVIET INSTITUTIONS AND POLICIES; INSIDE VIEWS. Princeton, N.J.: Van Nostrand, 1966. xii, 411 p.

Intended for students of political science, this book contains selections by "leaders and official spokesmen of the Soviet Union explaining and defending their own cause." Chapters 37-46 deal with the general economic policy, industry, and agriculture.

Baykov, Alexander M. THE DEVELOPMENT OF THE SOVIET ECONOMIC SYSTEM:

The Russian Economy in General

AN ESSAY ON THE EXPERIENCE OF PLANNING IN THE U.S.S.R. Economic and Social Studies, no. 5. London and New York: Cambridge University Press, 1946. xv, 514 p.

The author discusses industry; agriculture; internal and external trade; public finance, credit and money; labor; and planning during (1) the transitional period and the period of "war communism," (2) the period of the New Economic Policy, (3) the period of extensive industrialization, collectivization of agriculture, and rationing, and (4) the period of intensive endeavor to improve the country's economy and economic systems. Tables, bibliography of sources in Russian only, and index.

——————. "Remarks on the Experiences in the Organisation of 'War Economy' in the USSR." ECONOMIC JOURNAL 51 (December 1941): 422-38.

Presenting massive data on Soviet national income and output for the years 1928-40, this article concludes that "the Soviet government by means of . . . regulations of prices, indirect taxation and State loans--still continues, as in the period of rationing, to control the consumption of the population, and, to a great extent, the disposal of the national income."

Bergson, Abram, and Kuznets, Simon, eds. ECONOMIC TRENDS IN THE SOVIET UNION. Cambridge, Mass.: Harvard University Press, 1963. xiv, 392 p.

This is a collection of articles dealing with trends in national income (Abram Bergson); labor force (Warren W. Eason); capital stock (Norman M. Kaplan); industrial production (Raymond P. Powell); agricultural production (D. Gale Johnson); consumption (Janet G. Chapman); foreign trade (Franklyn D. Holzman); and a comparative appraisal (Simon Kuznets). Most articles make extensive use of statistical tables and discuss techniques used in analyzing the data. Index.

Beriia, L. P. THE 34TH ANNIVERSARY OF THE GREAT OCTOBER SOCIALIST REVOLUTION. Speech delivered at a celebration meeting of the Moscow Soviet, November 6, 1951. Moscow: Foreign Languages Publishing House, 1951. 35 p. Illustrated.

Beriia reviews the successful achievements of the First Postwar Five-Year Plan and states that the plan was fulfilled successfully. One can compare this speech with facts which emerged after the death of Stalin.

Bickermann, Joseph, ed. TEN YEARS OF BOLSHEVIC DOMINATION. Berlin-Schoneberg: Siegfried Scholem, 1928. 260 p.

The book contains two essays dealing with the economy: "Land Policy and Land Conditions in Soviet Russia" by Peter B. Struve and Cyril Zaitzoff and "Economy in Soviet Russia" by S. Sherman.

The Russian Economy in General

The first essay discusses the land policy of the Soviet government and "real land conditions" before large-scale collectivization. The second concerns the Soviet economy, home trade, foreign trade, industry, and currency.

Birmingham University. Bureau of Research on Russian Economic Conditions. "I: New Tendencies. II: Heavy Industry. III: Railway Transport." MEMO-RANDUM no. 11 (December 1935): 1-8.

Part one discusses the Second Five-Year Plan and how it differed from the First Five-Year Plan and NEP. Part two deals with the rapid growth of heavy industry. Part three describes rail transport during the Revolution and after the First World War. Tables.

_____. "I: Remarks on the Five Year Plan. II: Agricultural Collectivization. III: Oil Consumption and Export." MEMORANDUM no. 5 (May 1932): 1-24.

Part one deals with the economic results for 1931 and the control figures for 1932 of the Five-Year Plan in the areas of industry, agriculture, railways, national income, capital investments, and national accumulation. The second section deals with the kolkhoz movement. The third section discusses the internal requirements and export possibilities for oil and examines: the Russian oil market since the revolution; the internal demand for oil products; future production and consumption of oil; and prospects of oil exports in the last year of the plan.

Bolsover, G. H. "Russia in the Modern World." LLOYD'S BANK REVIEW n.s. 20 (April 1951): 1-26.

This article examines factors underlying Russia's position in the modern world. Topics covered include expansion under the tsars, internal development, and Soviet foreign policy.

Bornstein, Morris, and Fusfeld, Daniel, eds. THE SOVIET ECONOMY; A BOOK OF READINGS. Homewood, Ill.: R. D. Irwin, rev. ed., 1966, ix, 389 p. 3d ed., 1970, x, 467 p. 4th ed., 1974, x, 543 p.

Each edition contains mostly different readings suitable for undergraduates interested in the Soviet economy. Topics include operation of the planned economy, the macroeconomics of GNP and growth, reform, and foreign economic relations.

Brailsford, Henry N. RUSSIAN WORKERS' REPUBLIC. New York: Harper & Brothers, 1921. x, 274 p.

Brailsford records his observations during the fall of 1920. He states that he was allowed to go anywhere he wished alone. The book includes his impressions of the provinces and of country life.

The Russian Economy in General

Burns, Emile. RUSSIA'S PRODUCTIVE SYSTEM. New York: E. P. Dutton, 1930. 288 p.

> The organization of the Soviet economy before 1930, including state trusts, syndicates, factories, industry, oil, transports, and agriculture, is discussed. Charts, tables, and index.

Byrne, Terence E. "Recent Trends in the Soviet Economy." In ECONOMIC PERFORMANCE AND THE MILITARY BURDEN IN THE SOVIET UNION, U.S. Congress. Joint Economic Committee, pp. 3-8. Washington, D.C.: Government Printing Office, 1970.

> This paper comments briefly on recent trends in GNP, agricultural and industrial production, defense, investment, consumption, trade, and aid.

Campbell, Robert W. SOVIET ECONOMIC POWER: ITS ORGANIZATION, GROWTH, AND CHALLENGE. Boston: Houghton Mifflin, 1960. xii, 209 p.

> Campbell discusses these aspects of the Soviet economy: ideological and historical background; growth; productivity and efficiency; the problem of rational planning; incentives and motivation; control over resources; technical progress; and future prospects. Index.

──────. SOVIET ECONOMIC POWER: ITS ORGANIZATION, GROWTH, AND CHALLENGE. 2d ed. London: Macmillan and Co. 1967. xiii, 184 p.

> In this revised edition Campbell covers ideological and historical background; planning; strategic and operational decision making; the command principle versus the market approach; growth; allocation and productivity; and the future. Index.

──────. THE SOVIET-TYPE ECONOMIES: PERFORMANCE AND EVOLUTION. 3d ed. Boston: Houghton Mifflin, 1974. xi, 259 p.

> This text consists of three parts: part one is on the Soviet approach to industrialization; part two is on economic performance; and part three is on reform and the future of socialist planning. Paperback.

Carr, Edward H., and Davies, R[obert]. W. FOUNDATIONS OF A PLANNED ECONOMY, 1926-1929. Vol. 1, pts. 1 and 2 of A History of Soviet Russia. New York: Macmillan, 1969. xv, 1,023 p.

> Part one covers various aspects of agriculture and surveys various aspects of industry. Part two deals with labor; trade and distribution; and finance and planning. Tables and index.

Chamberlin, William H. RUSSIA'S IRON AGE. Boston: Little, Brown, 1934. ix, 400 p. Illustrated.

> Chamberlin is concerned with the period which followed NEP,

The Russian Economy in General

which he calls "Russia's Iron Age." The effects of rapid industrialization, widespread use of forced labor, the regimenting of the peasants in collective farms, and the famine of 1932-33 are examined.

Counts, George S. THE SOVIET CHALLENGE TO AMERICA. New York: John Day, 1931. xv, 372 p.

Part one outlines the prominent features of Soviet society and part two discusses the construction of the Five-Year Plan. The third part is concerned with the mobilization of human resources. Bibliography and index.

Cressey, George B. THE BASIS OF SOVIET STRENGTH. New York: McGraw-Hill Book Co., 1945. xi, 285 p.

Cressey sketches the history and political structure of the Soviet Union; the geography and climate of Eurasia; the Soviet people; Soviet mineral wealth; and industrialization. He also describes the various regions making up the USSR. Many maps and photographs. Index.

Davis, Jerome, ed. NEW RUSSIA: BETWEEN THE FIRST AND SECOND FIVE YEAR PLANS. New York: John Day, 1933. xiv, 265 p.

Chapters of interest discuss agriculture, industry, workers' lives, financial structure, and social welfare. Glossary and bibliography.

Day, Richard B. LEON TROTSKY AND THE POLITICS OF ECONOMIC ISOLATION. London: Cambridge University Press, 1973. 221 p.

This work is concerned with Trotsky's views of and roles in Russian social, economic, and political development between 1917 and 1927. Major topics covered include Russia's economic and political isolation, war communism, and the controversy over "socialism in one country." Index.

Dobb, Maurice H. "Some Recent Economic Changes in the Soviet Union." In PATTERNS OF ECONOMIC DEVELOPMENT: A STUDY OF THE ECONOMIC DEVELOPMENT OF THE U.K., THE U.S.A., JAPAN, THE U.S.S.R., AND CHINA, edited by V. B. Singh, pp. 459-72. Bombay, London, and New York: Allied Publishers Private, 1970.

Topics discussed include agriculture, changes in industry, and decentralization in the 1950s.

_____. SOVIET ECONOMIC DEVELOPMENT SINCE 1917. 5th ed. London: Routledge and Kegan, 1960. vi, 494 p.

The book is divided into three parts, with the first one outlining Russian economic development prior to World War I. The second

The Russian Economy in General

part deals with the various periods in the establishment of the Soviet economy: the first eight months, war communism, the NEP, the "scissors crisis," agriculture on the eve of the plan era, and the first six five-year plans. The third part deals with the planning system, location of industry, and trade unions, wages, and conditions of labor. Glossary, indexes, and two maps.

_____. "Soviet Economy: Fact and Fiction." SCIENCE AND SOCIETY 18 (Spring 1954): 123-40.

Topics covered include the reliability of Soviet statistics, the controversy over growth rates, and economic policy. Two tables provide figures on target alterations for 1955 and trends in the output of selected products for selected years, 1940-55.

Dobb, Maurice H., and Stevens, H. C. RUSSIAN ECONOMIC DEVELOPMENT SINCE THE REVOLUTION. New York: E. P. Dutton, 1928. xii, 415 p.

The authors give a general account of the Soviet economy from its beginnings up to 1928 and discuss the economic policy of the first eight months, war communism, the NEP, industrial organization, and the "scissors crisis." Glossary and index.

Dolan, Edwin G. "Structural Interdependence of the Soviet Economy before the Industrialization Drive." SOVIET STUDIES 19 (July 1967): 66-73.

The first part of this paper discusses a pioneering Soviet statistical work, P. I. Popov et al. BALANS NARODNOGO KHOZYAISTVA SOYUZA SSR 1923-24 GODA (1926). The second gives Dolan's conclusions about the structural interdependence of the Soviet economy in the period of the NEP.

Douglas, Paul H., et al. "The Russian Economic Situation: Discussion." AMERICAN ECONOMIC REVIEW 19 (March 1929): 111-30.

Ostensibly, this discussion revolves around a paper by R. T. Bye, "The Central Planning and Coordination of Production in Soviet Russia," which immediately precedes it on pp. 91-110. However, the discussion consists largely of speculation on the immediate future of the Soviet economy.

East, W. Gordon. "The Economic History of the USSR." ECONOMIC HISTORY REVIEW 16, no. 2 (1946): 141-44.

This is a critical essay concerning a book by Alexander Baykov. THE DEVELOPMENT OF THE SOVIET ECONOMIC SYSTEM (see above, this chapter).

Eddy, George S. THE CHALLENGE OF RUSSIA. New York: Farrar and Rinehart, 1931. 64 p.

Two chapters deal with economics--one on Russian agriculture and collectives and the other on industry and labor.

Efimov, Anatolii N., and Anchinhkin, Alexander. ECONOMY, MANAGEMENT, PLANNING. Moscow: Novosti Press Agency Publishing House, 1968. 197 p.

The first part of this book outlines the history of the Soviet economy. The second part deals with management and the way in which it reflects the peculiarities of a socialist economy. The third part discusses planning and analyzes methods of plan calculations.

Fainsod, Merle. HOW RUSSIA IS RULED. Rev. ed. Russian Research Center Studies, 11. Cambridge, Mass.: Harvard University Press, 1965. ix, 698 p.

Two chapters concern the Soviet economy: chapter 15, "Management and Labor in Soviet Industry," and chapter 16, "Controls and Tensions in Soviet Agriculture."

Feiler, Arthur. THE EXPERIMENT OF BOLSHEVISM. Translated by H. J. Stenning. London: Allen and Unwin, 1930. 256 p.

A record of the author's three-month stay in Russia in 1929, the book gives a brief account of Soviet controls over trade, credit, industry and prices; the Five-Year Plan; the red manager and socialist competition; private enterprise; the conditions of workers and peasants; and agrarian communism.

Feiwel, George R., ed. NEW CURRENTS IN SOVIET-TYPE ECONOMIES: A READER. Scranton, Pa.: International Textbook Co., 1968. x, 629 p.

Reprinted articles consider changes and reforms in the Soviet and other Eastern European economies.

Fischer, Ruth. "Background of the New Economic Policy." RUSSIAN REVIEW 7 (Spring 1948): 15-33.

Topics covered in this historical study include the nationalization of industry after the Revolution, relations between the Red Army and the Party, the principle of democratic centralism, the trade unions under war communism, and the Kronstadt revolt.

Florinsky, Michael T. "Soviet Russia." In GOVERNMENTS OF CONTINENTAL EUROPE, edited by James T. Shotwell, pp. 813-936. New York: Macmillan, 1940.

Chapters 5 and 6 discuss economic planning and state control of business function. Planning agencies; the scope and economic program of the first three five-year plans; the cost of industrialization; the elimination of private enterprise; prices and efficiency;

The Russian Economy in General

wages and trade unions; the evolution of agricultural policies; the results of collectivization; and trade, banking, and transportation are covered. Annotated bibliography.

──────. TOWARDS AN UNDERSTANDING OF THE U.S.S.R.: A STUDY IN GOVERNMENT, POLITICS, AND ECONOMIC PLANNING. Rev. ed. New York: Macmillan, 1951. x, 223 p.

Volume updates and revises an earlier edition which was published in 1939. Three out of seven chapters are devoted to the Soviet economy. The following topics are discussed: (1) economic planning, the first four five-year plans, and the cost of industrialization; (2) prices, efficiency, wages, labor discipline, labor legislation, and trade unions; (3) agriculture, trade, banking, transportation, and public utilities.

Freidman, Elisha M. RUSSIA IN TRANSITION: A BUSINESS MAN'S APPRAISAL. New York: Viking Press, 1932. xxxiv, 614 p.

Author gives a firsthand account of industrial efficiency, business administration, banking, accounting, and public finance, and attempts to determine whether or not the revolution can continue in its present phase.

Goldman, Marshall I. "More Heat in the Soviet Hothouse (Special Report)." HARVARD BUSINESS REVIEW 49 (July-August 1971): 4-15, 160.

The author comments on problems in planning and industrial modernization, the unique features of the new plan for 1971-75, the role of the consumer, western technology, and efforts to develop management skills. Four tables.

──────. THE SOVIET ECONOMY: MYTH AND REALITY. Englewood Cliffs, N.J.: Prentice-Hall, 1968. xiii, 176 p.

The author aims at correcting misunderstandings about the economy of the USSR. The book is divided into parts, and the chapters in each part are introduced by some commonly accepted misconceptions concerning the Soviet economy.

Greenslade, Rush V. "The Soviet Economic System in Transition." In NEW DIRECTIONS IN THE SOVIET ECONOMY, U.S. Congress. Joint Economic Committee, pp. 1-17. Washington, D.C.: Government Printing Office, 1966.

Topics discussed include the slowdown in economic growth, the revolution in economic thought, and changes in economic organization.

Gregory, Paul R., and Stuart, Robert C. SOVIET ECONOMIC STRUCTURE AND PERFORMANCE. New York: Harper & Row, 1974. 478 p.

This text first surveys Soviet economic history and then discusses the operation of the present economy, economic reform, growth, and performance. Index. Paperback.

Grigorian, Leon A. SOVIET SOCIETY (ECONOMIC AND SOCIAL STRUCTURE); A HISTORICAL SURVEY. Moscow: Novosti Press Agency Publishing House, 1968. 256 p.

Soviet achievements at the end of five decades are summarized. The author also analyzes aspirations of the Soviet people.

Grossman, Gregory. "The Soviet Economy in the Post-Stalin Decade." In THE REALITIES OF WORLD COMMUNISM, edited by William Petersen, pp. 62-85. Englewood Cliffs, N.J.: Prentice-Hall, 1963.

In discussing the Soviet economy's performance during the first post-Stalin decade, Grossman explains its rapid growth as resulting from two factors: deliberate determination to maximize economic growth, and the large share of the total resources which were devoted to investment.

_____. "The Structure and Organization of the Soviet Economy." SLAVIC REVIEW 21 (June 1962): 203-22.

This article discusses the following topics: the 1961 program of the Communist party, labor, money, decentralization, and agriculture. For further comments, see these papers which follow in the same issue of SLAVIC REVIEW: Henri Chambre. "Rationality in the Soviet Economy," pp. 223-28; David Granick. "The More Answers, The More Questions," pp. 229-36; and Gregory Grossman. "Reply," pp. 237-40.

Haensel, Paul P. ECONOMIC POLICY OF SOVIET RUSSIA. London: P. S. King and Son, 1930. vii, 190 p.

In attempting to inform his readers about economics in the Soviet Union, the author covers agriculture and the economic conditions of the peasantry; industrialization, planning, and the five-year plan; the economic status of the working class; internal trade and monopoly of foreign trade; transportation; and public finance and currency. Tables and index.

Hirsch, Alcan. INDUSTRIALIZED RUSSIA. New York: Chemical Catalog Co., 1934. x, 309 p.

The author gives a firsthand account of, among other things, the iron and steel industry, the fuel industry, agriculture, living standards, finance, and the Second Five-Year Plan. Index.

Holt, Robert T., and Turner, John E., eds. SOVIET UNION--PARADOX AND CHANGE. New York: Holt, Rinehart and Winston, 1962. ix, 240 p.

Of the book's nine nontechnical essays on various aspects of the Soviet Union, three deal with economic topics: (1) F. T. Boddy, "Soviet Economic Growth"; (2) P. M. Raup, "The Farm Problem a la Russe"; and (3) J. W. Buchta, "Soviet Science and Technology."

Holzman, Franklyn D., ed. READINGS ON THE SOVIET ECONOMY. Chicago: Rand, McNally, 1962. xi, 763 p.

This book includes essays on statistics and measurement, the price system, the Soviet industrialization model, economic growth, planning, industrial organization, agriculture, finances, the consumer, the worker, and foreign trade. Selected bibliography.

Hoover, Calvin B. ECONOMIC LIFE OF SOVIET RUSSIA. New York: Macmillan, 1931. vii, 361 p.

This book outlines the Soviet economy and discusses the organization of industry; productivity and capital investment; agriculture; internal and foreign trade; money and banking; and labor and social insurance. Glossary, bibliography, and index.

_____. "The Fate of the New Economic Policy of the Soviet Union." ECONOMIC JOURNAL 40 (June 1930): 184-93.

The article examines evidence that the Soviet leadership intended to do away with the last vestiges of the NEP as soon as it was practical. The fate of the NEP is thus seen as depending on the coming harvest. A good harvest would indicate that the NEP's incentives were no longer necessary to insure grain deliveries.

Iugov, Aron. ECONOMIC TRENDS IN SOVIET RUSSIA. Translated by Eden and Cedar Paul. New York: Richard R. Smith, 1930. 349 p.

The author discusses economic aspects of life in Russia during the first decade of Soviet rule and analyzes the future prospects of the Soviet economy.

Jasny, Naum. ESSAYS ON THE SOVIET ECONOMY. New York: Praeger, 1962. xiv, 247 p.

Included are the following essays: "Research on the Soviet Economy," "Peasant Incomes Under Full-Scale Collectivization," "Soviet 'Perspective' Planning," and "The Summit of Falsehood," comprising essays four through seven, respectively. There is also a list of terms with definitions. Bibliography and index.

_____. THE SOVIET ECONOMY DURING THE PLAN ERA. Food Research Institute, Miscellaneous Publication 11A. Stanford, Calif.: Stanford University Press, 1951. xi, 116 p. Illustrated.

This lengthy essay discusses sources of national income; the allocation of national income in terms of net investment and military expenditures; living-cost indexes; and estimates of private consumption and expenditures on education and health. Naum also remarks on official statistics, terminology, and procedure. Index.

_____. SOVIET INDUSTRIALIZATION, 1928-1952. Chicago: University of Chicago Press, 1961. xviii, 467 p.

The book is divided into two parts, the pre-World War II period and the postwar period. In part one the author details Soviet planning; investment; agriculture; industry; construction; personal incomes; and national income. In part two he discusses factors contributing to recovery; inflation; price structure; investments; agricultural conditions, output, and marketings; retail trade and personal and national income. Tables and index.

Jasny, Naum, et al. THE ECONOMY OF THE U.S.S.R. Proceedings of the Annual Fall Sessions of the National Academy of Economics and Political Science, October 22 and 23, 1957. Washington, D.C.: Special Publications Series, no. 14, 1958. 24 p.

This symposium focused on recent developments in the Soviet economy and included industrial organization and management; productivity and capital formation; the structure and functions of the financial system; international trade and finance; and bloc economic diplomacy. Tables and charts.

Johnson, D. Gale. "Observations on the Economy of the U.S.S.R." JOURNAL OF POLITICAL ECONOMY 64 (June 1956): 185-211.

This paper first presents general impressions about the Soviet economy based on a summer's visit by Johnson and then discusses prospects for expanding agricultural production over the next decade. Six tables.

Kaser, Michael [C.]. SOVIET ECONOMICS. New York: McGraw-Hill Book Co., 1970. 256 p. Illustrated.

This book has three parts. Part one includes chapters on the control of capital, the economic function of the state, and class basis of economic policy. Part two outlines the use of money, the transfers of funds, and the control of production. Part three surveys Soviet economic objectives and deals with economic growth, capital accumulation, and the optimal plan. Tables, graphs, and index.

Kassof, Allen. PROSPECTS FOR SOVIET SOCIETY. New York: Praeger, 1968. x, 586 p.

Of particular interest are the papers on population by Warren W. Eason, agriculture by Arcadius Kahan, and industry by Herbert S. Levine.

The Russian Economy in General

Katkoff, Vladimir. SOVIET ECONOMY 1940-1965. Baltimore: Dangary Publishing Co., 1961. xi, 559 p.

> This book describes the organization and operation of the Soviet economy, examines Soviet industrial and agricultural capabilities, evaluates socioeconomic adjustments under Khruschev, probes Soviet infiltration into underdeveloped areas, and appraises Soviet economic potential. Maps, tables, and bibliographies.

Katz, Zev. "Insights From Emigres and Sociological Studies on the Soviet Union." In SOVIET ECONOMIC PROSPECTS FOR THE SEVENTIES, U.S. Congress. Joint Economic Committee, pp. 87-120. Washington, D.C.: Government Printing Office, 1973.

> Topics discussed include the operation of the economy, statistics, planning, Soviet social structure, dissenters' views, and tendencies toward either a classless or elitist society. Selected bibliography and tables.

Kennan, George. "The Soviet Union 1917-1939." In THE NEW CAMBRIDGE MODERN HISTORY. Vol. 12: THE SHIFTING BALANCE OF WORLD FORCES 1898-1945, edited by C. L. Mowat, pp. 433-72. London and New York: Cambridge University Press, 1968.

> This volume is a second edition of volume 12: THE ERA OF VIOLENCE. Kennan discusses briefly the labor unrest and decline in living standards, the NEP, the famine of 1921-22; recovery, the rich peasant, and the middlemen-traders; collectivization; and the five-year plan.

Khrushchev, Nikita. "The State of the Soviet Economy." In RUSSIA ENTERS THE 1960'S: A DOCUMENTARY REPORT ON THE 22ND CONGRESS OF THE COMMUNIST PARTY OF THE SOVIET UNION, edited by Harry Schwartz, pp. 184-215. Philadelphia and New York: J. B. Lippincott, 1962.

> This report discusses the construction of communism in the Soviet Union, the Seven-Year Plan, efficiency, agriculture, and improvements in welfare. Tables.

Koutaissoff, Elisabeth. THE SOVIET UNION. New York: Praeger, 1971. 288 p. Illustrated.

> The book gives a general description of the Communist party of the Soviet Union; the economy; arts and science; and daily life. Chapters 3-6 deal with the economy and describe planning, industry, agriculture, and demographic trends. Bibliography, index and maps.

Kuibyshev, Valerian V. RESULTS OF THE STRUGGLE FOR THE TECHNICAL RECONSTRUCTION OF NATIONAL ECONOMY. Moscow-Leningrad: Cooperative Publishing Society of Foreign Workers in the U.S.S.R., 1933. 56 p.

The Russian Economy in General

The volume gives an account of a report delivered at the Joint Plenum of the Central Committee and the Central Control Commission of the Communist party of the Soviet Union. The report represents the official Soviet assessment of economic achievements in various industries; transport and communications; and agriculture.

Labedz, Leopold. "The New CPSU Programme." In THE FUTURE OF COMMUNIST SOCIETY, edited by Walter Laquerer and Leopold Labedz, pp. 12-28. New York: Praeger, 1962.

The paper discusses the new program of the Communist party adopted in 1960. The goals of the program are compared and contrasted with the Party program adopted in 1919. Changes in the program are traced historically.

Lamb, Edward. THE PLANNED ECONOMY IN SOVIET RUSSIA. Philadelphia: Dorrance & Co., 1934. 193 p.

This book discusses the mechanics and results of planning; the Soviet legal system; the treatment of minorities; Soviet society under planning; and socialist competition. Selected bibliography.

THE LAND OF SOCIALISM TODAY AND TOMORROW. Moscow: Foreign Languages Publishing House, 1939. 488 p.

This is a collection of reports presented at the Eighteenth Congress of the Communist party of the Soviet Union, March 10-21, 1939. Molotov presented a paper outlining the goals of the Third Five-Year Plan; Andreyev discussed the tasks of agriculture; and Kaganovich spoke on how the Soviets would "outstrip" the capitalists economically.

Lange, Oskar. THE WORKING PRINCIPLES OF THE SOVIET ECONOMY. New York: Research Bureau for Post-War Economics, 1944. 30 p.

A noted Polish socialist describes the way in which the Soviet economy operates.

Lawton, Lancelot. AN ECONOMIC HISTORY OF SOVIET RUSSIA. 2 vols. London: Macmillan and Co., 1932. Vol. 1, ix, 308 p. Vol. 2, viii, 321 p.

The author details outstanding economic ideas and events since the Revolution with at least one chapter devoted to each economic year. Among the topics covered are war communism; measures for the abolition of money; the great famine of 1921; the "scissors" crisis; monetary reform (1922-24); the collectivization of agriculture; and the first, second, and third years of the First Five-Year Plan. The volumes contain analytical tables of contents.

Leites, Kussiel. RECENT ECONOMIC DEVELOPMENTS IN RUSSIA. Edited by H. Westergate. Publications of the Carnegie Endowment for International

Peace. Division of Economics and History. London: Oxford University at the Clarendon Press, 1922. 240 p.

> Part one of this book deals with the Russian economy during the First World War prior to the Bolshevik Revolution and discusses, among other topics, financial effects, loans, industry, the agrarian question, and the role of the cooperative movement. Part two summarizes the results of Bolshevik economic policy and discusses the state of finances, state of industry, the labor question, and the agrarian question. Part three describes economic life in 1920. Index.

Levine, Herbert S. "The Economy, Hard Spots and Soft." In THE SOVIET WORLD IN FLUX: SIX ESSAYS, edited by Clifford M. Foust and Warren Lerner, pp. 63-86. Atlanta: Southern Regional Education Board, 1967.

> This paper analyzes the recent performance (1950-64) of the Soviet economy, discusses planned economic improvements, and appraises prospects for the near future. Two tables.

Lindsay, Franklin A. THE GROWTH OF SOVIET ECONOMIC POWER AND ITS CONSEQUENCE FOR CANADA AND THE UNITED STATES. Washington, D.C.: Canadian-American Committee, 1959. 27 p.

> Topics discussed include trade, aid, agriculture, oil, metals, and international civil aviation.

Lorwin, Lewis L., and Abramson, A. "The Present Phase of Economic and Social Development in the U.S.S.R." INTERNATIONAL LABOUR REVIEW 33 (January 1936): 5-40.

> The authors comment on conditions in Russia in 1935. Topics covered include readjustment, conditions in the kolkhoz, the change from rationing to unified prices, incomes and wage policy, the profit motive, labor shortages and industrial training, planning policy, and living conditions.

Lyons, Eugene. WORKERS' PARADISE LOST; FIFTY YEARS OF SOVIET COMMUNISM: A BALANCE SHEET. New York: Funk & Wagnalls, 1967. 387 p.

> This book is intended to debunk various myths fostered by the Soviets concerning their economy and society. Topics discussed which are of interest to the economist are Marxism-Leninism; classes; the pre-1917 economy; the First Five-Year Plan; industrialization; planning, economic reform; collectivization; living standards; imperialism; science; and Soviet communism as a model for the underdeveloped countries. Index.

Maddison, Angus. "Soviet Economic Performance." BANCA NAZIONALE DEL LAVORO QUARTERLY REVIEW 18 (March 1965): 3-57.

This article outlines the favorable and unfavorable aspects of the economic performance.

Malenkov, G. REPORT TO THE NINETEENTH PARTY CONGRESS ON THE WORK OF THE CENTRAL COMMITTEE OF THE C.P.S.U. Moscow: Foreign Languages Publishing House, 1952. 147 p.

Part two contains a brief discussion of economic progress in industry, agriculture, trade, transport, and communications. The book represents the official Soviet assessment at the close of the Stalin era.

Malevsky-Malevitch, P., ed. THE SOVIET UNION TODAY. New York: Paisley Press, 1936. vii, 102 p.

This supplement to RUSSIA-U.S.S.R. "relies exclusively on official Soviet facts and figures." There are sections on industry, trade, agriculture, transport, finance, and money. It indexes both volumes.

Mazour, Anatole G. RUSSIA, PAST AND PRESENT. New York: Van Nostrand, 1951. v, 785 p.

In this topical, rather than chronological, account of Russian history, the following chapters are useful to the economic historian: 10--"The Development of Agriculture"; 11--"Growth of Industry"; and 23--"The Economic Revolution, 1928-1939." Index.

Miller, J., and Nove, Alec. "Bergson and Jasny on the Soviet Economy." AMERICAN SLAVIC AND EAST EUROPEAN REVIEW 13 (1954): 215-26.

This article contrasts the work on the Soviet economy of Abram Bergson and Naum Jasny. The topics covered are "political economy" ("the study of the structure of the society concerned in its dynamic economic aspect") and statistical work ("the collection, testing, aggregation, and experimental manipulation of economic statistics").

Miller, Jacob. SOVIET RUSSIA: AN INTRODUCTION. London: Hutchinson's University Library, 1955. vii, 190 p.

Of particular interest are chapters on industrialization, farming, and "running the farms and factories." Appendices, bibliography, and index.

Mosley, P. E. "Can Moscow Match Us Industrially?" HARVARD BUSINESS REVIEW 33 (March-April 1955): 101-8.

This general survey of the state of the Soviet economy stresses prospects for future growth.

The Russian Economy in General

Nansen, Fridtjof. RUSSIA AND PEACE. London: Allen & Unwin, 1923. 162 p.

    The author briefly describes social, and especially economic, conditions of Soviet Russia in the early 1920s. The book contains a popular outline of Russian economic development, transport, trade, finance, agriculture, and industry.

National Industrial Conference Board. INDUSTRIAL RUSSIA: THE NEW COMPETITOR. New York: National Industrial Conference Board, 1954. 88 p.

    The conference board has assembled a number of experts to discuss the "industrial and competitive potential of the U.S.S.R." This pamphlet includes discussions of coal and machinery, iron and steel, and chemicals and petroleum industries, as well as discussions of manpower and manpower problems, housing, and consumer goods output.

Nonomura, Kazuo. ESSAYS ON SOVIET ECONOMY. Tokyo: Kinokunija, 1969. iii, 178 p.

    This is a collection of papers which have appeared in other economic publications. Part one deals with economic competition between the United States and the Soviet Union. Part two discusses some of the disputed points relating to economic integration between the Soviet Union and the East European countries. Part three surveys the significance of the 1965 reforms.

Nove, Alec. AN ECONOMIC HISTORY OF THE U.S.S.R. Baltimore: Penguin Books, 1969. 416 p.

    Economic policies, decisions, events, organizations, and conditions, as well as the relative importance of politics in the study of Soviet economic history, are discussed. Nove concludes with an evaluation of Soviet economic growth and a summary of the Brezhnev and Kosygin proposals for streamlining the planning system.

_____. ECONOMIC RATIONALITY AND SOVIET POLITICS--OR WAS STALIN REALLY NECESSARY? New York: Praeger, 1964. 316 p.

    This book discusses political economy, industrial growth, planning, agriculture, labor, welfare, statistics, and ideology. Glossary and index.

_____. THE SOVIET ECONOMY: AN INTRODUCTION. 3d ed., rev. London: Allen & Unwin, 1968. xii, 373 p.

    This is an updated and revised edition of a work which first came out in 1961. This book for the nonspecialist is divided into three parts. The first part outlines institutional arrangements in the USSR. The second part pinpoints problem elements in the system. The third deals with ideas and concepts. Bibliography plus subject and name indexes.

Paarlberg, Don. "The Economic Challenge of the Soviet Union." JOURNAL OF BUSINESS 33 (April 1960): 93-100.

> The potential economic growth of the Soviet Union and its significance as a possible threat to U.S. security are considered.

Polanyi, M. "U.S.S.R. Economics: Fundamental Data, System, and Spirit." MANCHESTER SCHOOL OF ECONOMICS AND SOCIAL STUDIES 6, no. 2 (1935): 67-89.

> Topics covered here include population, food, housing, wages and income, consumption, health, education, heavy industry, planning, marketing, efficiency, poverty, prospects for the individual, and social outlook. Four tables. For a comment on this paper see: Walter Fitzgerald. "U.S.S.R. Economics--A Reply." MANCHESTER SCHOOL OF ECONOMICS AND SOCIAL STUDIES 7, no. 1 (1936): 61-64.

PRODUCTION, ACCUMULATION, AND CONSUMPTION. White Plains, N.Y.: International Arts and Sciences Press, 1967. v, 174 p.

> This is a compendium of five Soviet papers on the relations between production and consumption, the rise in public consumption, capital intensity, structural improvements, and characteristics of the collective-farm economy.

Prokopovitch, Sergei N. THE ECONOMIC CONDITION OF SOVIET RUSSIA. London: P. S. King and Son, 1924. 230 p.

> Topics discussed include the nationalization of industry, the government and the peasants, the NEP, and finance. Several tables.

Putman, George E. "Russian Economic Situation." AMERICAN ECONOMIC REVIEW 21 (March 1931): 37-53.

> Susan M. Kingsbury describes a woolen mill in Moscow; Mildred Fairchild argues that Russia's industrial success has resulted from the efforts of the masses--not from efforts of a few men at the top; Calvin B. Hoover discusses the role of brute force in effecting economic changes; Mabel Newcomer considers the financial side of industrialization; William Adams Brown, Jr., discusses Soviet credit reforms. Paul Haensel examines the theme of force as a means to controlling economic behavior.

Roberts, Henry L., moderator. "Soviet Economic Performance and Reform: Some Problems of Analysis and Prognosis." SLAVIC REVIEW 25 (June 1966): 222-46.

> The topics covered in this round-table discussion include Soviet

economic performance, the possibilities of reform, and the Western economists' views of these reforms.

Rostow, Walt W. "Summary and Policy Implications." In COMPARISONS OF THE U.S. AND SOVIET ECONOMIES, U.S. Congress. Joint Economic Committee, pp. 589-608. Washington, D.C.: Government Printing Office, 1959.

Rostow summarizes Soviet agriculture; working force; capital; transport and power; management incentives; industrial output, productivity, national income and growth rate; standard of living; military expenditures; and foreign aid. The stages of American and Russian growth are outlined, as well as the dimensions of the Soviet challenge.

Rothstein, Andrew. MAN AND PLAN IN SOVIET ECONOMY. London: Frederick Muller, 1948. viii, 300 p.

The first chapter outlines the relationship between planning and foreign policy. The next four chapters consider the role of the individual in the prewar and postwar Soviet economy. The sixth chapter describes the economic and social changes in Soviet Central Asia during World War II. Index and map.

RUSSIA: A CONSIDERATION OF CONDITIONS AS REVEALED BY SOVIET PUBLICATIONS. New York: Commission on Commerce and Marine of the American Bankers Association, 1922? 36 p.

This pamphlet describes, in bleak terms, the condition of the Soviet economy in the early 1920s and concludes that American business would gain little from dealings with Russia.

RUSSIA AFTER TEN YEARS. Report of the American Trade Union Delegation to the Soviet Union. New York: International Publishers, 1927. vi, 96 p.

Representatives of the American Trade Union delegation and a number of experts in economics, sociology, and education visited Russia to observe what had happened in ten years after the Revolution. The book discusses economic progress; Soviet trade unions; wages; labor laws and social insurance; consumers' cooperatives; and agriculture.

Schapiro, Leonard B., ed. THE U.S.S.R. AND THE FUTURE; AN ANALYSIS OF THE NEW PROGRAM OF THE CPSU. Praeger Publications in Russian History and World Communism, no. 124. New York: Praeger, 1962. xix, 324 p.

Of particular interest are papers on the economics of 1980, labor and wages under full communism, Soviet agriculture, and full reprints of the 1919 and 1961 Party Programmes.

Scheffer, Paul. SEVEN YEARS IN SOVIET RUSSIA. London and New York:

The Russian Economy in General

Putman, 1931. xvi, 357 p.

    Part two, on the Soviet economy from NEP to the five-year plan, is particularly valuable.

Schwartz, Harry. THE RED PHOENIX--RUSSIA SINCE WORLD WAR II. New York: Praeger, 1961. xii, 427 p.

    Of particular interest are two chapters on economic growth and scientific development. Index and statistical appendix.

_____. "Reflections on the Economic Race." In COMPARISONS OF THE U.S. AND SOVIET ECONOMIES, U.S. Congress. Joint Economic Committee, pp. 609-16. Washington, D.C.: Government Printing Office, 1959.

    The paper deals with recent and future Soviet industrial growth; Soviet production of key commodities (1955, 1959, and 1960 plan); minimum estimates of Soviet output of key commodities for 1965 and 1970 and Soviet goals for 1965; and some policy implications.

_____. RUSSIA'S SOVIET ECONOMY. 2d ed. New York: Prentice-Hall, 1954. xx, 682 p.

    The text covers various aspects of the Soviet economy in a sector-by-sector approach. The first editions appeared in 1950. Tables, index and maps.

_____. THE SOVIET ECONOMY SINCE STALIN. Philadelphia: J. P. Lippincott, 1965. 256 p.

    This book discusses the economy in general, Malenkov's role, the years 1955-58, the economic factors in Khrushchev's downfall, foreign economic relations, and the prospects for 1980. Map and charts.

Seton, Francis. "Soviet Industry." In THE PREDICTIONS OF COMMUNIST ECONOMIC PERFORMANCE, edited by Peter J. D. Wiles, pp. 287-301. Cambridge: At the University Press, 1971.

    This paper discusses overall performance, individual products, manpower, capital construction and equipment, and reform. Three tables.

Shaffer, Harry G. THE SOVIET ECONOMY: A COLLECTION OF WESTERN AND SOVIET VIEWS. New York: Appleton-Century-Crofts, 1963. xvii, 456 p.

    This book of readings by Western and Soviet authors includes Soviet statistics, comparisons with the U.S. economy, national income and product, the transition to communism, agriculture, industry, labor consumption, growth, value theory, and international economic relations. Glossary.

The Russian Economy in General

Sherman, Howard J. THE SOVIET ECONOMY. Boston: Little, Brown, 1969. xxi, 371 p. Illustrated.

> This text covers Soviet institutions, the economic environment, economic history, planning, and reforms. Index. Paperback.

Shimkin, Dimitri B. "The Structure of Soviet Power." QUARTERLY REVIEW OF ECONOMICS AND BUSINESS 3, no. 3 (1963): 19-24.

> This article looks at Soviet national goals and major resources, the restraints on Soviet policy, and probable future courses of action.

SOVIET ECONOMY TODAY AND TOMORROW (FACTS AND FIGURES). Translated by Leo Lempert. Moscow: Progress Publishers, 1964. 118 p. Illustrated.

> This Soviet booklet gives data on the development of Soviet industry, agriculture, and transport; Soviet science and technology; the country's electrification, mechanization, and automation of production; and the rational location of the productive forces.

SOVIET RUSSIA: LEGAL AND ECONOMIC CONDITIONS OF INDUSTRIAL AND COMMERCIAL ACTIVITY IN SOVIET RUSSIA. Westminster, Eng.: P.S. King & Son, n.d. 174 p.

> Of the book's nine essays on legal and economic conditions, six deal with economic aspects: "The Economic Balance Sheet of Bolshevism," "The Economic Foundations of the Communist Regime," "The Foreign Trade of Soviet Russia," "Financial Situation in Soviet Russia," "Currency Reform in Soviet Russia," and "Private Industry and Foreign Concessions in Soviet Russia."

Spulber, Nicolas. THE SOVIET ECONOMY: STRUCTURE, PRINCIPLES, PROBLEMS. Rev. ed. New York: W. W. Norton, 1969. xiv, 329 p.

> Text is a revised edition of a work which first came out in 1962. Text discusses the operation and planning of the Soviet economic system, industry, agriculture, trade, labor, and finance. Models and theories of socialism, both Western and Soviet, and relations between the capitalist and Soviet systems are also discussed. Tables, charts, bibliography, and index.

_____. SOVIET STRATEGY FOR ECONOMIC GROWTH. Bloomington: Indiana University Press, 1964. 175 p.

> This general study of the Soviet economy covers economic development, efficiency, growth, and planning. Bibliography and index.

_____., ed. STUDY OF THE SOVIET ECONOMY. Papers presented at a conference, Bloomington, Ind. Bloomington: Indiana University Press, 1961. xiii, 169 p.

> This collection of papers on the Soviet economy was prepared by

The Russian Economy in General

experts for use by nonspecialists. The appendix contains outlines
and reading lists for courses on the Soviet economy, including
English-language materials only.

Stalin, Joseph. THE STATE OF THE SOVIET UNION: REPORT ON THE WORK
OF THE CENTRAL COMMITTEE OF THE COMMUNIST PARTY OF THE SOVIET
UNION. New York: International Publishers, 1934. 96 p.

> Soviet foreign relations, the economic development of the USSR,
> and the Communist party are considered.

Stalin, Joseph, et al. FROM THE FIRST TO THE SECOND FIVE-YEAR PLAN.
New York: International Publishers, 1934. 490 p.

> This compendium of speeches and official reports on various aspects
> of the Soviet economy includes the plan, heavy industry, agricul-
> ture, defense, and finance.

Sternberg, Fritz. THE END OF A REVOLUTION; SOVIET RUSSIA--FROM
REVOLUTION TO REACTION. Translated by Edward Fitzgerald. New York:
John Day, 1953. 191 p.

> Topics discussed include industrial development and labor exploita-
> tion in the USSR, the United States, and Western Europe.

Tandon, B. C. THE RUSSIAN ECONOMY. Allahabad, India: Chaitanya Publishing House, 1966. 212 p.

> Topics discussed include the Revolution, the period of 1917-28,
> the period of the plans, the planning system, organization of in-
> dustry and agriculture, transport and communications, the banking
> system, labor, welfare, and trade. Maps.

Treml, Vladimir G., ed. THE DEVELOPMENT OF THE SOVIET ECONOMY:
PLAN AND PERFORMANCE. New York: Praeger, 1968. xiv, 296 p.

> Twelve papers deal with various aspects of the Soviet economy.

Truu, M. L. "Some Reflections on Economic Planning and the Soviet Consumer."
SOUTH AFRICAN JOURNAL OF ECONOMICS 29 (December 1961): 275-87.

> Topics discussed include the planning background; the nature of
> Soviet data; the institutional setting; income; prices; consumption;
> savings; taxes; labor conditions; and social welfare. Six tables.

Turin, S. P. THE U.S.S.R.: AN ECONOMIC AND SOCIAL SURVEY.
London: Methuen, 1944. xiii, 219 p.

> This book covers population; communications; regional economics;
> agriculture; industry; textiles; food; gold; timber; foreign trade;
> development trends; technical research; the artel'; and administra-
> tive and planning organization. Eight maps, sixteen diagrams,

The Russian Economy in General

sixty-three statistical tables. Indexes.

U.S. Congress. Joint Economic Committee. ECONOMIC PERFORMANCE AND THE MILITARY BURDEN IN THE SOVIET UNION. A compendium of papers submitted to the Subcommittee on Foreign Economic Policy. Washington, D.C.: Government Printing Office, 1970. vi, 295 p.

Nineteen papers consider virtually all aspects of the Soviet economy. Tables.

_____. HEARINGS ON DIMENSIONS OF SOVIET ECONOMIC POWER. Washington, D.C.: Government Printing Office, 1962. 185 p.

Subjects covered in these hearings include competition in foreign aid, Soviet foreign trade, the Soviet economic offensive, and political problems of Soviet economic policy. Several papers on planning, the balance of payments, and the machine-building industry are included in the appendix. Tables.

_____. HEARINGS ON SOVIET ECONOMIC OUTLOOK. Washington, D.C.: Government Printing Office, 1973. iv, 270 p.

Statements by witnesses and submissions for the record concerning the Soviet economy are included.

_____. NEW DIRECTIONS IN THE SOVIET ECONOMY. Washington, D.C.: Government Printing Office, 1966. 1,093 p.

This work is a compilation of articles on Soviet economic policy, economic performance, human resources, and economic relations with the outside world. Select bibliography.

_____. SOVIET ECONOMIC PERFORMANCE: 1966-1967. Washington, D.C.: Government Printing Office, 1968. vi, 292 p.

Developments of all aspects of the Soviet economy are discussed in detail. Tables.

_____. SOVIET ECONOMIC PROSPECTS FOR THE SEVENTIES. Washington, D.C.: Government Printing Office, 1973. xvii, 776 p.

This publication contains papers on plan and policy; the military claim on resources; industry; agriculture; consumption; human resources; and foreign trade and aid. Reconstructed input-output tables are included on loose foldout sheets. Foldout diagrams.

_____. STUDIES OF DIMENSIONS OF SOVIET ECONOMIC POWER. Washington, D.C.: Government Printing Office, 1962. xix, 744 p.

This study contains twenty papers on social issues such as the framework of economic policy, the measure and strategy of pro-

The Russian Economy in General

duction, the citizen's share in the economy, and demographic trends and population.

U.S.S.R. Council of Ministers. Central Statistical Board. FORTY YEARS OF SOVIET POWER IN FACTS AND FIGURES. Moscow: Foreign Languages Publishing House, 1958. 319 p.

> This book consists entirely of tables and charts on all aspects of the Soviet economy.

Vinogradov, Vladimir A. SOCIALIST PROPERTY: ITS FORMATION AND ECONOMIC ADVANTAGES. Moscow: "Nauka" Publishing House, 1968. 132 p.

> This Soviet monograph discusses the successes of the Soviet economy, culture, and people's welfare during the first fifty years of its existence.

Walters, Ellery. RUSSIA'S DECISIVE YEAR. New York: G. P. Putnam's Sons, 1932. 282 p. Illustrated.

> This personal account of travel in Russia dwells on economic conditions as perceived by an eyewitness. Maps.

Wiles, Peter J. D., ed. THE PREDICTIONS OF COMMUNIST ECONOMIC PERFORMANCE. Cambridge: At the University Press, 1971. x, 390 p.

> This book of readings has several chapters on Soviet agriculture, industry, the economy in general, and economic growth.

Williams, Albert R. THE SOVIETS. New York: Harcourt, Brace, 1937. xiii, 554 p.

> Part two deals with various aspects of economic life. Bibliography and index.

Zavalani, T. HOW STRONG IS RUSSIA? London: Hollis & Carter, 1951. 244 p.

> This study of the Soviet economy discusses aspects of the economy chronologically by five-year plan periods.

Zhimerin, D. G. ECONOMY OF THE SOVIET UNION, PAST AND PRESENT. Moscow: Foreign Languages Publishing House, 1958. 124 p.

> Topics discussed include planning, industry, agriculture, and management. Tables.

Chapter 3
RUSSIAN ECONOMIC THOUGHT

Ischboldin, Boris. HISTORY OF THE RUSSIAN NON-MARXIAN SOCIAL-ECONOMIC THOUGHT. New Delhi: New Book Society of India, 1971. 328 p.

> This history surveys Russian non-Marxian social economic thought from the sixteenth to the twentieth centuries. Selected bibliography; no index.

THE PERIOD UP TO 1860

Letiche, John M., ed. and trans. A HISTORY OF RUSSIAN ECONOMIC THOUGHT: NINTH THROUGH EIGHTEENTH CENTURIES. Translated with the collaboration of Basil Dmytryshyn and Richard A. Pierce. Berkeley and Los Angeles: University of California Press, 1964. xvi, 690 p.

> This book is an edition of an original Russian work edited by A. I. Pashkov which came out in 1955. It includes essays by distinguished Soviet economists whose research was based on voluminous primary and secondary sources. Each part deals with a particular historical period. Glossary, bibliography, and index.

O'Brien, Carl Bickford. "Ivan Pososhkov: Russian Critic of Mercantilist Principles." AMERICAN SLAVIC AND EAST EUROPEAN REVIEW 14 (1955): 503-11.

> The views and influence of Ivan Pososhkov, a reformer in Russia in the early eighteenth century, are examined.

THE PERIOD 1860-1917

Baron, Samuel H. "Plekhanov on Russian Capitalism and the Peasant Commune, 1883-1885." AMERICAN SLAVIC AND EAST EUROPEAN REVIEW 12 (1953): 463-74.

> This article reviews Plekhanov's thinking on the development of Russian capitalism and the possible sources of a socialist revolution

in Russia. He rejected the Narodnik argument that the Russian peasantry and Russian institutions were the essential elements of future society. He felt that these elements would be destroyed by capitalism, so the only hope for a socialist revolution rested with the proletariat.

Christoff, Peter. "A. S. Khomiakov on the Agricultural and Industrial Problem in Russia." In ESSAYS IN RUSSIAN HISTORY: A COLLECTION DEDICATED TO GEORGE VERNADSKY, edited by Alan D. Ferguson and Alfred Levin, pp. 129-59. Hamden, Conn.: Archon Books, 1964.

Christoff examines Khomiakov's views on agriculture, industry, and the economic aspects of the village commune, which were closely connected with the emancipation question. According to Khomiakov, the primary role of the commune was of an economic-police nature.

Cohen, Stephen F. "Bukharin, Lenin, and the Theoretical Foundation of Bolshevism." SOVIET STUDIES 21 (April 1970): 436-57.

The emphasis here is on the development of Bolshevik thought in the years 1914-16 and on Bukharin's contribution to Lenin's thought.

"Economic Thought in Russia." QUARTERLY JOURNAL OF ECONOMICS 2 (January 1888): 233-43.

This article consists of an anonymous letter written from Kharkov discussing the more important publications in Russian economic thought and the factors limiting economic output in Russia. Journal articles and the field of finance are not discussed.

Enden, M. N. de. "The Roots of Witte's Thought." RUSSIAN REVIEW 29 (January 1970): 6-24.

This paper examines Witte's policies and writings in an effort to determine the principles under which he operated.

Gerschenkron, Alexander. "The Problem of Economic Development in Russian Intellectual History of the Nineteenth Century." In CONTINUITY AND CHANGE IN RUSSIAN AND SOVIET THOUGHT, edited by Ernest J. Simmons, pp. 11-39. Cambridge, Mass.: Harvard University Press, 1955.

This paper sketches Russian economic development and discusses Russian economic thought of the nineteenth century.

Guroff, Gregory. "The Legacy of the Pre-Revolutionary Economic Education: The Saint Petersburg Polytechnic Institute." RUSSIAN REVIEW 31 (July 1972): 272-81.

The development of economic education in Russia from the establishment of the first economics faculty in 1902 up to the Revolution is traced.

Nove, Alec, and Zauberman, Alfred. "A Resurrected Russian Economist of 1900." SOVIET STUDIES 13 (July 1961): 96-101.

    The economist is V. K. Dmitriev, an adherent to the labor theory of value with a mathematical bent.

Page, Stanley W. "The Russian Proletariat and World Revolution: Lenin's Views to 1914." AMERICAN SLAVIC AND EAST EUROPEAN REVIEW 10 (1951): 1-13.

    This article is a summary account of Lenin's view that the Russian proletariat, by overthrowing the tsar, would open the floodgates of revolution in the West.

Radkey, Oliver H. "Chernov and Agrarian Socialism Before 1918." In CONTINUITY AND CHANGE IN RUSSIAN AND SOVIET THOUGHT, edited by Ernest J. Simmons, pp. 63-80. Cambridge, Mass.: Harvard University Press, 1955.

    The ideology and political aspects of agrarian socialism are discussed.

Rogin, Leo. "Marx and Engels on Distribution in a Socialist Society." AMERICAN ECONOMIC REVIEW 35 (March 1945): 137-43.

    Rogin reviews Marxist doctrine on income distribution in a socialist society to attempt to show that income distribution in the Soviet Union does not conform.

Schwarz, Solomon M. "Populism and Early Russian Marxism in Ways of Economic Development of Russia (The 1880's and 1890's)." In CONTINUITY AND CHANGE IN RUSSIAN AND SOVIET THOUGHT, edited by Ernest J. Simmons, pp. 40-62. Cambridge, Mass.: Harvard University Press, 1955.

    This paper discusses the economic background of nineteenth-century Russian thought, the populist notion of noncapitalist development, the views of Marx and Engels on the means to development, and Russian Marxism on capitalist development in Russia.

Simmons, Ernest J., ed. CONTINUITY AND CHANGE IN RUSSIAN AND SOVIET THOUGHT. Cambridge, Mass.: Harvard University Press, 1955. xii, 563 p.

    Of particular interest are four papers on Russian economic thought and two on the peasant commune and the collective farm. Index.

Von Laue, Theodore H. "The Fate of Capitalism in Russia: The Narodnik Version." AMERICAN SLAVIC AND EAST EUROPEAN REVIEW 13 (1954): 11-28.

    This article is concerned with the debate between the Narodniks and the Marxists about the future of Russia. The <u>Narodniks</u> agreed that Russia could not progress under competitive capitalism, but rather that peasant socialist institutions must be allowed to develop fully.

————. "The Industrialization of Russia in the Writings of Sergei Witte." AMERICAN SLAVIC AND EAST EUROPEAN REVIEW 10 (1951): 177-90.

The article comments on Witte's writings on industrialization. The influence of the economist Friedrich List is noted.

THE PERIOD AFTER 1917

Balabkins, Nicholas A. "A Note on the Soviet Evaluation of J. M. Keynes." CANADIAN SLAVONIC PAPERS 12 (Fall 1970): 343-45.

The author presents evidence indicating that "the Soviets have implied that Keynes is pro-fascist."

Baran, Paul A. "New Trends in Russian Economic Thinking?" AMERICAN ECONOMIC REVIEW 34 (December 1944): 862-71.

This is a sympathetic response to, and defense of, the article "Teaching of Economics in the Soviet Union, from the Russian Journal POD ZNAMENEM MARXISMA." AMERICAN ECONOMIC REVIEW 34 (September 1944): 501-30.

Baron, Samuel H. "The Transition from Feudalism to Capitalism in Russia: A Major Soviet Historical Controversy." AMERICAN HISTORICAL REVIEW 77 (June 1972): 715-29.

A review article of PEREHOD OT FEODALIZMA K KAPITALIZMU V ROSSII: MATERIALY VSESOIUZNOI DISKUSII [The transition from feudalism to capitalism in Russia: materials from the all-union discussion]. Akademiia Nauk SSSR, Nauchnyi soviet "zakonomernosti istoricheskogo razvitiia obshchestvo i perekhoda ot odnoi sotsialno-ekonomicheskoi formatsii k drugoi." Edited by V. K. Shunkov et al. Moscow: Izdatel'stvo "Nauka," 1969. 412 p.

The book reviewed is praised as an example of a hoped-for trend among Soviet historians to become more objective and analytical and less dogmatic in their interpretations of Russian history.

Cairncross, Alec. "The Moscow Economic Conference." SOVIET STUDIES 4 (October 1952): 113-32.

This paper presents the author's impressions of the Moscow Economic Conference of April 1952. A table gives prices for selected commodities in state shops.

Campbell, Robert W. "Marx, Kantorovich, and Novozhilov: Stoimost' versus Reality." SLAVIC REVIEW 20 (October 1961): 403-18.

This article describes the search for a new theory of value which has resulted from Soviet research in mathematical economics. Topics covered include deficiencies of the labor theory of value, Kantorovich's early work in linear programming, Novozhilov's work on the problem of capital allocation, and the response of other Soviet economists.

Charles, K. J. "Lenin as Theorist." ECONOMIC AFFAIRS 16 (January-February 1971): 57-72.

The article sketches the development of Lenin's thought on Marxist economic analysis. Some connections are made between this development and Lenin's economic policies.

Chossudowsky, E. M. "The Soviet Conception of Economic Equilibrium." REVIEW OF ECONOMIC STUDIES 6 (February 1939): 127-46.

This article traces the Soviet concept of equilibrium as "a particular form of planned social dynamics" as it evolved from Marx through politics and planning practices of the USSR.

Cohen, Stephen F. "Marxist Theory and Bolshevik Policy: the Case of Bukharin's HISTORICAL MATERIALISM." POLITICAL SCIENCE QUARTERLY 85 (March 1970): 40-60.

This paper examines Bukharin's role in and ideas concerning the development of Soviet Marxist thought.

Davies, R[obert]. W. "Some Soviet Economic Controllers." SOVIET STUDIES 11 (January 1960): 286-306.

The views of Strumilin and Gleb Maksimilianovich Krzhizhanovski are examined.

_____. "Some Soviet Economic Controllers II." SOVIET STUDIES 11 (April 1960): 373-92.

This article discusses the thought and career of Feliks Edmundovich Dzerzhinski (1877-1926).

_____. "Some Soviet Economic Controllers III." SOVIET STUDIES 12 (July 1960): 23-55.

This article outlines the careers and economic thought of Kuibyshev and Grigori Konstantinovich Ordzhonikidze.

Deutscher, L. "Dogma and Reality in Stalin's 'Economic Problems.'" SOVIET STUDIES 4 (April 1953): 349-63.

This paper examines Stalin's last article, "The Economic Problems of Socialism in the USSR."

Dobb, Maurice H. "The Discussions of the Twenties on Planning and Economic Growth." SOVIET STUDIES 17 (October 1965): 198-208.

This paper considers the Soviet industrialization debates of the 1920s and the controversy over the means of transition from capitalism to socialism. Much attention is given to the work of the Soviet economist Preobrazhensky.

──────. "Notes on Recent Economic Discussion." SOVIET STUDIES 12 (April 1961): 342-52.

This article covers recent developments of economic theory in the Soviet Union with special attention given to the interrelatedness of apparently distinct developments. The fact that most theoretical developments are motivated by practical problems is stressed.

──────. "The Revival of Theoretical Discussion Among Soviet Economists." SCIENCE AND SOCIETY 24, no. 4 (1960): 289-311.

This article reviews the development of economic theory among Soviet economists with emphasis on lack of development in the 1930s and 1940s; investment; prices and value theory; mathematical economics; and borrowing from the West.

Dobrin, S. "Lenin on Equality and the Webbs on Lenin: (Some Notes for the History of Ideas)." SOVIET STUDIES 8 (April 1957): 337-57.

This paper is concerned with the question of whether Lenin favored an equal standard of living for all.

Dunayevskaya, Raya. "A New Revision of Marxian Economics." AMERICAN ECONOMIC REVIEW 34 (September 1944): 531-37.

This article is a study of another article, "Teaching of Economics in the Soviet Union, from the Russian journal POD ZNAMENEM MARXISMA," translated by Raya Dunayevskaya. AMERICAN ECONOMIC REVIEW 34 (September 1944): 501-30. The two articles, however, may be read and understood separately. In the present article the Soviet "revisions" of Marxist economics are presented and discussed. A reply to comments on this article by Lange, Rogin, and Baran may be found in Raya Dunayevskaya. "Revision or Reaffirmation of Marxism? A Rejoinder." AMERICAN ECONOMIC REVIEW 35 (September 1945): 660-64.

Erlich, Alexander. "Preobrazhenski and the Economics of Soviet Industrialization." QUARTERLY JOURNAL OF ECONOMICS 64 (February 1950): 57-88.

This paper assembles the disparate elements of E. A. Preobrazhenski's main argument and evaluates its place in the flow of events. Topics covered include the "goods famine," the case for a high rate of economic expansion, his policies, and their relation to the five-year plans.

_____. THE SOVIET INDUSTRIALIZATION DEBATE, 1924-1928. Russian Research Center Studies, 41. Cambridge, Mass.: Harvard University Press, 1960. xxiii, 214 p.

This debate focused on the appropriate pattern and speed for the prospective economic development of the country. Part one describes the different points of view and the changes they underwent. Part two restates the major issues of the debate in terms of Western analysis and analyzes critically the positions of the individual participants. Diagrams.

_____. "Stalin's Views on Soviet Economic Development." In CONTINUITY AND CHANGE IN RUSSIAN AND SOVIET THOUGHT, edited by Ernest J. Simmons, pp. 81-99. Cambridge, Mass.: Harvard University Press, 1955.

Stalin's views on the great industrialization debate of the late 1920s are discussed.

Evenitsky, Alfred. "Preobrazhensky and the Political Economy of Backwardness." SCIENCE AND SOCIETY 30 (Winter 1966): 50-62.

This is a review article of Preobrazhensky's THE NEW ECONOMICS. Translated by Brian Pearce. Introduction by Alec Nove. New York: Oxford University Press, 1965. xx, 310 p.

Goldman, Marshall I. "Economic Controversy in the Soviet Union." FOREIGN AFFAIRS 41 (April 1963): 498-512.

This article analyzes and assesses Liberman's economic objectives and discusses some of the implications of this controversy in Soviet planning.

Grossman, Gregory. "Scarce Capital and Soviet Doctrines." QUARTERLY JOURNAL OF ECONOMICS 67 (August 1953): 311-43.

This article discusses the problem of scarcity of capital as treated by interested engineers and Marxist economic theorists.

Guelfat, Isaac. ECONOMIC THOUGHT IN THE SOVIET UNION: CONCEPTS AND ASPECTS. A COMPARATIVE OUTLINE. The Hague: Martinus Nijhoff, 1969. 163 p.

This book is divided into two parts. Part one discusses important topics such as institutionalism, planning, forecasting, equilibrium, monopoly, location theory, economic laws, value, prices, rent, money, and interest. Part two is concerned with recent developments in economics including mathematical economics, econometrics, and Libermanism. Bibliography and index, but no table of contents.

_____. "Economic Thought in the Soviet Union; Concepts and Aspects." Parts I-IV." ANNALS OF PUBLIC AND CO-OPERATIVE ECONOMY 38 (October-December 1967): 373-412; 39 (January-March 1968): 33-69; (April-June 1968): 251-87; (July-September 1968): 469-505.

This exhaustive historical review of economic thought in the USSR treats the following topics: modern theory, Marxian and Soviet economic theory; genetics and teleology; socialist institutionalism; Soviet planning theory; Soviet economics and compensatory devices; economic forecasting; economic equilibrium; monopoly, monopsony, duopsony; location of economic resources; economic laws and categories; value; prices; income from land; and money and interest. The last section surveys innovations in Soviet economic thought from Bukharin to Kantorovich and from Kantorovich to the Liberman-Trapeznikov school.

Holubnychy, Vsevolod. "Recent Soviet Theories of Value." STUDIES ON THE SOVIET UNION n.s. 1, no. 1 (1961): 47-72.

This review of Soviet value theory treats the stifling impact of Stalin, the debates on the law of value since the late 1950s, the limitations imposed by Marxist doctrine, and prospects for future developments.

Jasny, Naum. SOVIET ECONOMISTS OF THE TWENTIES. NAMES TO BE REMEMBERED. New York and London: Cambridge University Press, 1972. ix, 217 p.

Part one traces developments in the Soviet economy from the October Revolution to 1931 and explores the activities of the opposition in 1922-31. Part two treats persons who were active in the opposition. Part three deals with the lives of V. G. Groman, V. A. Bazarov, A. M. Ginzburg, N. D. Kondrat'ev, and other Mensheviks and neo-Narodniks. Index.

_____. "A Soviet Planner--V. G. Groman." RUSSIAN REVIEW 13 (January 1954): 52-58.

This article discusses an eminent Russian statistician and member of Gosplan who fell into disfavor and has been nearly forgotten.

Kaser, Michael [C.]. "The Soviet Ideology of Industrialization." JOURNAL OF DEVELOPMENT STUDIES 3 (October 1966): 63-75.

This is a review article of Preobrazhenskii's THE NEW ECONOMICS (see below, this chapter). Topics covered include the Soviet concept of industrial priority and the beneficiaries, form, and control of industrialization.

Kaufman, A[dam]. "Origin of 'The Political Economy of Socialism': An Essay on Soviet Economic Thought." SOVIET STUDIES 4 (January 1953): 243-72.

> This article examines the development of Soviet economic theory and its culmination in the acceptance of a political economy of socialism.

Korey, William. "Zinov'ev's Critique of Stalin's Theory of Socialism in One Country, December, 1925-December, 1926." AMERICAN SLAVIC AND EAST EUROPEAN REVIEW 9, no. 4 (1950): 255-67.

> This article summarizes Grigorii E. Zinov'ev's attacks on Stalin's theory and reviews the significance of the attacks.

Kresl, Peter Karl. "Nikolai Bukharin on Economic Imperialism." REVIEW OF RADICAL POLITICAL ECONOMICS 5 (Spring 1973): 3-12.

> This paper argues that Bukharin's work, IMPERIALISM AND WORLD ECONOMY (New York: International Publishers, 1929) is worthy of more attention from Marxist scholars.

Landauer, Carl. "From Marx to Menger: the Recent Development of Soviet Economics." AMERICAN ECONOMIC REVIEW 34 (June 1944): 340-44.

> Author discusses the revisions in the teaching of value theory in Russia. The author feels that the abandonment of the labor theory of value will be advantageous to the Soviet planned economy. For further discussion of Landauer's treatment, see: Otuis, Brooks. "The Communists and the Labor Theory of Value." AMERICAN ECONOMIC REVIEW 35 (March 1945): 134-37.

Lange, Oscar. "Marxian Economics in the Soviet Union." AMERICAN ECONOMIC REVIEW 35 (March 1945): 127-33.

> The article discusses the reasons for the reemergence of the labor theory of value as a planning tool in the Soviet Union and its consequences. The article is largely a commentary on "Teaching of Economics in the Soviet Union" from the Russian journal POD ZNAMENEM MARXIZMA. Translated by Raya Dunayevskaya. AMERICAN ECONOMIC REVIEW 34 (September 1944): 501-30.

Lapidus, Iosif A., and Ostrovityanov, K. [V.]. AN OUTLINE OF POLITICAL ECONOMY: POLITICAL ECONOMY AND SOVIET ECONOMICS. New York: International Publishers, 1932. xi, 546 p.

> This is a textbook on Marxist economics intended for English-speaking students and written by two Soviet economists. Besides discussing Marxist theory, the authors apply the theory in analyzing capitalist and Soviet economies.

Leont'ev, L. A., et al. "Political Economy in the Soviet Union." Translated

Russian Economic Thought

by H. F. Mins, Jr. SCIENCE AND SOCIETY 8 (Spring 1944): 115-25.

This paper discusses the teaching of economics and the Marxist basis of political economy in the Soviet Union. For further discussion, see: "On Misunderstanding Soviet Political Economy." SCIENCE AND SOCIETY 8 (Fall 1944): 342-45.

Leontief, Wassily. "The Decline and Rise of Soviet Economic Science." FOREIGN AFFAIRS 38 (January 1960): 223-36.

Leontief traces the history of Soviet economic thought from its decline in the late 1920s to its rise in the late 1950s and the increasing interest in quantitative economics.

Letiche, John M. "Soviet Views on Keynes: A Review Article Surveying the Literature." JOURNAL OF ECONOMIC LITERATURE 9 (June 1971): 442-58.

Letiche presents an extended review Carl B. Turner. AN ANALYSIS OF SOVIET VIEWS ON JOHN MAYNARD KEYNES. Durham, N.C.: Duke University Press, 1969.

Meek, Ronald L. "Some Conversations with Soviet Economists." SOVIET STUDIES 6 (January 1955): 238-46.

The questions discussed here include those relating to Stalin's last article, "Economic Problems of Socialism in the USSR," the attitudes of Soviet economists toward Western theory, the teaching of economics at Soviet universities, and academic freedom.

_____. "Stalin as an Economist." REVIEW OF ECONOMIC STUDIES 21, no. 56 (1953-54): 232-39.

Selected passages from Stalin's "Economic Problems of Socialism in the U.S.S.R." BOLSHEVIK (October 1952), are discussed.

_____. "The Teaching of Economics in the USSR and Poland." SOVIET STUDIES 19 (April 1959): 339-59.

This article discusses the courses in economics, political economy, and history of economic thought at Moscow University. Four tables are included. An appendix provides a summary of the list of themes recommended for course and thesis work.

Miller, Jacob. "Marxist Economic Theory in the USSR." STUDIES ON THE SOVIET UNION n.s. 7, no. 1 (1967): 35-50.

This paper traces Marxist economic theory through the various periods of Soviet history.

_____. "Some Recent Developments in Soviet Economic Thought." SOVIET STUDIES 1 (October 1949): 119-27.

The major part of this report deals with Stanislav Gustavovich Strumilin's "The Time Factor in the Planning of Capital Investments." IZVESTIA ACADEMIIA NAUK: OTDELENIIA EKONOMIKI I PRAVA 3 (1944): 195-215, and with Soviet reviews of it. For further discussions of Strumilin's analysis, see the following: Alfred Zauberman. "The Prospects for Soviet Investigations into Capital Efficiency." SOVIET STUDIES 1 (April 1950): 328-33, and Warren W. Eason. "On Strumilin's Model." SOVIET STUDIES 1 (April 1950): 334-42.

Montgomery, Arthur. "Production and Ideology in the Soviet Union." SCANDINAVIAN ECONOMIC HISTORY REVIEW 4, no. 2 (1956): 151-77.

Topics covered include production targets, Russian forecasts of development under capitalism, the Party and labor market, and the role of Marxism-Leninism.

Moravcik, Ivo. "Professor Katsenelenbaum and the Optimum Method of Financing Soviet Industrialization: A Note." SOVIET STUDIES 13 (July 1961): 102-7.

The professor was concerned with the problem of capital scarcity in the 1920s.

"The Moscow Institute for Economic Research and its Work." INTERNATIONAL LABOUR REVIEW 17 (February 1928): 231-40.

Discussed are the establishment and work of the Moscow Institute for Economic Research, which was the first institution to examine economic fluctuations and forecasts.

Noah, Harold J. "The 'Underproductive' Labour of Soviet Teachers." SOVIET STUDIES 17 (October 1965): 238-44.

The Marxist view that service labor is "unproductive" is discussed along with its consequences for Soviet national income accounting.

Normano, Joas F. THE SPIRIT OF RUSSIAN ECONOMICS. New York: John Day, 1945. xiv, 170 p.

The author examines the influence of English, French, German, and native currents on the development of Russian economic thought.

Olgin, Constantine. "Ideology and Economics." STUDIES ON THE SOVIET UNION n.s. 3, no. 3 (1964): 98-127.

This article traces the role of ideology in economic theory and policy from the "Critique of the Gotha Program" to Engels' "Revisionism," under Lenin and Stalin, and through de-Stalinization.

_____. "Lenin and the Economics of Socialism." STUDIES ON THE SOVIET UNION n.s. 9, no. 1 (1969): 105-26.

This paper surveys the development of Leninist thought from 1890 through the New Economic Policy.

Preobrazhenskii, Evgenii A. THE NEW ECONOMICS. Translated by Brian Pearce. Introduction by Alec Nove. Oxford: Clarendon Press, 1965. xx, 310 p.

This work by an eminent early Soviet economist discusses the methodology of Soviet economics, the law of primitive socialist accumulation, and the law of value in the Soviet economy. The appendix contains replies to critics. Index. (See also the review of this book by Michael Kaser, above, this chapter.)

Schlesinger, R[udolf]. "Strumilin and Others on the Theory for a New Price Structure." SOVIET STUDIES 9 (July 1957): 92-98.

This article discusses aspects of two of S. G. Strumilin's articles-- "The Law of Value and Measurement of Social Costs of Production in a Socialist Economy." PLANOVOYE KHOZYAISTVO no. 2 (1952); "On the Evaluation of Gratis Gifts of Nature." PROMY-SHLENNO-EKONOMICHESKAYA GAZETA (April 7, 1957).

Scott, N. B. S. "The Soviet Approach to European Economic Integration." SOVIET STUDIES 9 (January 1958): 292-98.

This note reviews treatment of European integration in the Soviet press and scholarly journals.

Stalin, Joseph. ECONOMIC PROBLEMS OF SOCIALISM IN THE U.S.S.R. Moscow: Foreign Languages Publishing House, 1952. 104 p.

This work is of interest primarily as a source in Soviet economic thought.

Strumilin, S[tanislav]. G[ustavovich]. "On the Determination of Value and its Application Under Socialism." PROBLEMS OF ECONOMICS (January 1960): 3-9.

This is a translation from VOPROSY EKONOMIKI no. 8 (1959). Value theory and the need for appropriate prices in planning are discussed.

Suranyi-Unger, Theo. "Metamorphoses of the Soviet Textbook on Economics." AMERICAN ECONOMIC REVIEW 46 (December 1956): 937-46.

This is a review article of the standard Soviet economics textbook, POLITICAL ECONOMY; TEXTBOOK, published by the Soviet Academy of Sciences in 1954. The author discusses the method of the work, presents a critical evaluation, and mentions probable future changes.

Swianiewicz, S. "The Impact of Ideology on Soviet Economic Policy." CANADIAN SLAVONIC PAPERS 11 (Spring 1969): 66-81.

Topics covered include Marxist doctrine, Marxist ideology and economic analysis, the insurrection of October 1917, the New Economic Policy, socialism in one country, economic cooperation with the West, and revisionism.

"Teaching of Economics in the Soviet Union, from the Russian Journal POD ZNAMENEM MARXIZMA." Translated by Raya Dunayevskaya. AMERICAN ECONOMIC REVIEW 34 (September 1944): 501-30.

This article is largely a survey of the "errors" committed previously in the teaching of economics in the USSR. It thus also puts forth guidelines for an "error-free" economics course. There should be heavy reliance on the "classicists of Marxism-Leninism," and topics covered should include a precise definition of the subject of political economy and correct treatments of the primitive communal system, the "historic principle," the fundamental characteristics of the socialist system, and the economic role of the Soviet state.

Treml, Vladimir G. "Interaction of Economic Thought and Economic Policy in the Soviet Union." HISTORY OF POLITICAL ECONOMY 1 (Spring 1969): 187-216.

This paper surveys the development of Soviet economic thought from the Revolution to the Kosygin reforms of 1965.

_____. "Revival of Soviet Economics and the New Generation of Soviet Economists." STUDIES ON THE SOVIET UNION n.s. 5, no. 2 (1965): 10-22.

This article surveys the dismal state of Soviet economics from the late 1920s through the late 1950s, its apparent revival in the 1960s, and the analytical-mathematical-statistical bent which it has taken recently. For further discussion, see the following: Constantine Olgin. "NEP or Back to Stalin?" STUDIES ON THE SOVIET UNION n.s. 5, no. 2 (1965): 56-64.

Treml, Vladimir G., and Gallik, D[imitri]. M. "Teaching the History of Economic Thought in the USSR." HISTORY OF POLITICAL ECONOMY 5 (Spring 1973): 215-42.

The first part of this article outlines the history of teaching economics and of economic thought--especially at Moscow University. Marxist dogma is found responsible for the neglect in the Soviet Union of the history of economic thought. The second part is the translation of a course description in history of economic thought approved by the Soviet Ministry of Higher Education.

Tuckerman, Gustavus, Jr. "Applied Marxism in Soviet Russia." AMERICAN ECONOMIC REVIEW 23 (December 1933): 637-49.

This paper demonstrates how Lenin and Stalin applied Marxist principles in their policies aimed at the foundation of a classless Socialist state. There follows a comment by Karl Scholz and reply by Gustavus Tuckerman, Jr. AMERICAN ECONOMIC REVIEW 24 (March 1934): 90-91.

Turner, Carl B. AN ANALYSIS OF SOVIET VIEWS ON JOHN MAYNARD KEYNES. Durham, N.C.: Duke University Press, 1969. vii, 183 p.

Changes in Soviet views on Keynes are discussed chronologically. Bibliography and index.

Wiles, Peter J.D. "Communist Economics and Our Economics Textbooks." In STUDY OF THE SOVIET ECONOMY, edited by Nicolas Spulber, pp. 83-103. Papers presented at a conference, Bloomington, Ind. Bloomington: Indiana University Press, 1961.

Topics discussed include the study of Marxian practice; the Communist experience and the flow of ideas; and discussion of communism in U.S. economics texts. Extensive notes conclude the paper.

_____. "Scarcity, Marxism, and Gosplan." OXFORD ECONOMIC PAPERS n.s. 5 (September 1953): 288-316.

This article argues that Marxism is incompatible with "scarcity" economics, or the proposition that the essence of economics is choice or the allocation of scarce resources between competing ends. For further discussion, see the following: Ronald L. Meek. "Some Thought on Marxism, Scarcity, and Gosplan." OXFORD ECONOMIC PAPERS n.s. 7 (October 1955): 281-99; and Peter J.D. Wiles. "Some Thoughts on Marxism, Scarcity and Gosplan: A Comment." OXFORD ECONOMIC PAPERS n.s. 8 (February 1956): 108-12.

_____. "Soviet Economics." SOVIET STUDIES 4 (October 1952): 133-38.

This article reports on interviews held with Soviet economists by the British and Canadian economists who were delegates to the Moscow Economic Conference in April 1952.

Wolfe, Bertram D. "Backwardness and Industrialization in Russian History and Thought." SLAVIC REVIEW 26 (June 1967): 177-203.

This article surveys the attitudes of various thinkers (especially Marx, Stalin, and Gerschenkron) toward Russian backwardness and industrialization.

_____. "Valentinov-Volsky on the NEP, An Insider's View." RUSSIAN REVIEW 29 (October 1970): 422-32.

This article surveys the life and works of Nikolai Vladislavovich Volsky, an important writer on Russian affairs, including NEP.

Yanowitch, Murray. "Alienation and the Young Marx in Soviet Thought." SLAVIC REVIEW 26 (March 1967): 29-53.

This article traces Soviet attitudes toward and treatment of the writings of young Marx.

Zauberman, Alfred. "Economic Thought in the Soviet Union: I. Economic Law and the Theory of Value." REVIEW OF ECONOMIC STUDIES 16, no. 39 (1948-49): 1-12.

Topics covered include the contrast between Soviet and Western economics; economic law in Soviet thought; the labor theory of value; interest and amortization; rent; and the division of labor. There is a chart explaining Soviet measures of production.

_____. "Economic Thought in the Soviet Union: II. Economic Planning and Control." REVIEW OF ECONOMIC STUDIES 16, no. 40 (1949-50): 102-16.

Topics covered here include productivity; the roles of prices and profits; money and social product distribution; inflation; savings; the Soviet view of the mixed economy; and international finance.

_____. "Economic Thought in the Soviet Union: III. Economic Heresies at Home and Abroad." REVIEW OF ECONOMIC STUDIES 16, no. 41 (1949-50): 189-200.

Topics covered here include Soviet views on Keynes and others and the Varga heresy and its aftermath.

_____. "Gold in Soviet Economic Theory and Policies." AMERICAN ECONOMIC REVIEW 41 (December 1951): 879-90.

In 1950 the Council of Soviet Ministers put the ruble on a "gold basis" corresponding to its gold content. This article discusses this move in relation to Soviet thought on gold in the last three decades.

_____. "The Soviet and Polish Quest for a Criterion of Investment Efficiency." ECONOMICA n.s. 29 (August 1962): 234-54.

This article is concerned with the problem of investment criteria in Soviet economic thought. The problem is made extremely difficult by the Marxian condemnation of interest charges. The article comments on efforts of Soviet and Polish mathematicians and economists to solve the problem.

_____. "The Soviet Debate on the Law of Value and Price Formation."

Russian Economic Thought

With Comment by Abram Bergson. In VALUE AND PLAN; ECONOMIC CALCULATION AND ORGANIZATION IN EASTERN EUROPE, edited by Gregory Grossman, pp. 17-46. Berkeley and Los Angeles: University of California Press, 1960.

> This paper reviews the efforts of Soviet economists to arrive at a clearcut rule of price formation which would facilitate economic decisions. Some aspects of their debate are interpreted as being non-Marxian. Zauberman discusses the practical impact of the debate on the Soviet economy and speculates on future development of Soviet economic theory.

Zybenko, Roman [O.]. "The Development of Soviet Economic Science." STUDIES ON THE SOVIET UNION n.s. 3, no. 1 (1963): 99-108.

> This paper traces the political fortunes of the science of economics from 1918 to 1962, with emphasis on the post-Stalin era. Important developments in Soviet economic thought are also noted.

Chapter 4
ECONOMIC SYSTEMS AND SOCIETY IN RUSSIA

THE PERIOD UP TO 1860

Fuhrmann, Joseph T. THE ORIGINS OF CAPITALISM IN RUSSIA; INDUSTRY AND PROGRESS IN THE SIXTEENTH AND SEVENTEENTH CENTURIES. Chicago: Quadrangle Books, 1972. viii, 376 p.

> This book deals principally with the history of manufacturing. Topics discussed are the town life, artisanry, and commerce of "early modern Russia"; the history of iron manufacturing; other Russian manufactures of the seventeenth century; state industrial policy; and the activities and influence of foreigners. Russian factories during the sixteenth and seventeenth centuries are summarized in an appendix. Glossary, bibliography, and index.

Ignatieff, Leonid. "Rights and Obligations in Russia and the West." CANADIAN SLAVONIC PAPERS 2 (1957): 26-37.

> Rights and obligations of feudal organization in Russia and Western Europe are examined in an attempt to explain similarities and differences.

Parsons, Steven L. "The Enserfment of the Russian Peasantry: A Reexamination." CANADIAN-AMERICAN SLAVIC STUDIES 6 (Fall 1972): 478-89.

> This is an exhaustive review article of Richard Hellie. ENSERFMENT AND MILITARY CHANGE IN MUSCOVY. Chicago: University of Chicago Press, 1971.

Pethybridge, R. W. "British Imperialists and the Russian Empire." RUSSIAN REVIEW 30 (October 1971): 346-55.

> Victorian visitors to Russia examine and compare two nineteenth-century empires and their imperialist policies.

Tanaka, Masaharu. "The Controversies Concerning Russian Capitalism: An Analysis of the Views of Plekhanov and Lenin." KYKLOS 36 (October 1966): 21-55.

Economic Systems and Society

In the first section of this article Tanaka reviews trends of economic thought in Russia from the middle of the eighteenth century. He then discusses the views of Plekhanov and Lenin concerning the development of capitalism in Russia and Russian society.

Tschebotarioff-Bill, Valentine. "National Feudalism in Muscovy." RUSSIAN REVIEW 9 (July 1950): 209-18.

The adoption of medieval practices and social structure, including that of feudalism, in Muscovy is explored. The author compares these practices in Muscovy with their counterparts in Europe.

Von Loewe, Karl. "Juridical Manifestations of Serfdom in West Russia." CANADIAN-AMERICAN SLAVIC STUDIES 6 (Fall 1972): 390-99.

To illustrate the unreliability of statewide law codes and indices of peasant status in West Russia, this article examines provisions of the major law codes applicable to the entire West Russian state. It shows that nearly a century and a half after de facto enserfment, the West Russian peasant still retained the right of departure.

THE PERIOD 1860-1917

"'Feudalism' in Kazakhstan." CENTRAL ASIAN REVIEW 9, no. 2 (1961): 126-33.

The Soviet classification of the economic and social structure of Kazakh society as "feudal" is examined.

Roosa, Ruth A. "Russian Industrialists and 'State Socialism,' 1906-1917." SOVIET STUDIES 23 (January 1972): 395-417.

This paper recounts the conflict between private industrialists in Russia and the state bureaucracy with regard to control of industrial development. For further discussion, see the following: James D. White. "Moscow, Petersburg and the Russian Industrialists. In Reply to Ruth Amende Roosa." SOVIET STUDIES 24 (January 1973): 421-25.

Tanaka, Masaharu. "The Narodniki and Marx on Russian Capitalism in the 1870's-1880's." KYOTO UNIVERSITY ECONOMIC REVIEW 39 (October 1969): 1-25.

The thoughts of the Narodniki and of Marx and Engels on Russian political economy in the 1870s and 1880s are reviewed. The views of other writers, such as V.P. Vorontsov and Nicholai-on Danielson, on the failures of Russian capitalism are then discussed.

Economic Systems and Society

THE PERIOD AFTER 1917

Anchishkin, I. "The Problem of Abundance and the Transition to Communist Distribution." U.S. JOINT PUBLICATIONS RESEARCH SERVICE 4 (May 1962): 127-46.

> This is a translation from VOPROSY EKONOMIKI, no. 1 (1962). The solution of the problem of scarcity and the implementation of Communist distribution of all goods is discussed.

Artuikhin, N. E. SOCIETY AND ECONOMIC RELATIONS. Moscow: Progress Publishers, 1969. 279 p.

> The goal of this book is an analysis of the role of economic relations in socialist society. Among topics discussed are the relations of production in socialist society, the relations of exchange of labor activity, and the development of distribution relations.

Balabkins, Nicholas A. "Soviet-American Convergence by A. D. 2000? An Analysis of the Trends of Two Social Orders." CANADIAN SLAVONIC PAPERS 10 (Summer 1968): 133-47.

> This article surveys the "convergence" literature and discusses the social order in the two systems, forced economic growth in the Soviet Union, patterns of economic change, and Libermanism. Balabkins concludes that convergence is not yet even a serious possibility.

Balinky, Alexander. "Problems and Issues in Soviet Economic Reform." In PLANNING AND THE MARKET IN THE USSR: THE 1960'S, by Alexander Balinky et al., pp. 3-42. New Brunswick, N.J.: Rutgers University Press, 1967.

> Balinky explores the question of whether the new economic reforms are changing the basic character of the Soviet economy from socialism to capitalism. Terms like profits, bonuses, premium pay, consumer sovereignty, decentralization, and local initiative and what they mean to Soviet economists and planners are discussed.

_____. "The Proclaimed Emergence of Communism in the USSR." SOCIAL RESEARCH 28 (Autumn 1961): 261-82.

> This article discusses the proclaimed Soviet program to achieve communism in the Soviet Union.

Bandera, V. N. "The New Economic Policy (NEP) as an Economic System." JOURNAL OF POLITICAL ECONOMY 71 (June 1963): 265-79.

> The aspects of NEP discussed in this paper include a rapidly changing economy as a system; the law and the legacy from the past as determinants of economic structure; the division of the

economy into private and state sectors; the microeconomic functioning of the economy; and the macroeconomics of the system. Two graphs and two tables.

Banerji, J. ASPECTS OF SOVIET ECONOMY. Calcutta: Samajvadi Sahitya Parishad, 1954. 56 p.

The author deals briefly with many important aspects of the Soviet economy and indicates defects of the Soviet economic system.

Basily, Nikolai A. RUSSIA UNDER SOVIET RULE: TWENTY YEARS OF BOLSHEVIK EXPERIMENT. London: Allen & Unwin, 1938.

Basily gives a firsthand account of the government machinery before the establishment of Bolshevism and bases post-Revolutionary conclusions on information and official statistics issued by the Soviet government. The book considers the economic problems faced by the Soviets. The author discusses the political and economic structure of the USSR, programs and policies pursued on the road to socialism, and their results.

Bauer, Raymond A. HOW THE SOVIET SYSTEM WORKS: CULTURAL, PSYCHOLOGICAL, AND SOCIAL THEMES. Cambridge, Mass.: Harvard University Press, 1956. xiv, 274 p.

Planning and controlling in relation to industry and agriculture are examined. The status of peasants and urban workers are reviewed in chapters 19 and 20. The appendix lists reports and publications of the Harvard project on the Soviet social system; part "D" deals with economic institutions.

Berliner, Joseph S. ECONOMY, SOCIETY, AND WELFARE: A STUDY IN SOCIAL ECONOMICS. Praeger Special Studies in International Economics and Development. New York: Praeger, 1972. xvii, 196 p.

Part three examines the Communist social system by studying the relationships between the economy and the polity. Berliner constructs a model of a totalitarian Communist social system, examines its properties, and considers the extent to which the conclusions derived can explain social change in Soviet society. Bibliography and index.

Best, Harry. SOVIET EXPERIMENT. New York: Richard R. Smith, 1941. vii, 120 p.

This is a brief account, for the lay reader, of the underlying social philosophy of Soviet Russia. Best discusses the economic antecedents of the Revolution, production, and the impact of socialism on the agricultural sector.

Brason, Boris L. THE BALANCE SHEET OF SOVIETISM. New York: Duffield,

1922. ix, 272 p.

The object of this book is "an analysis of the actual 'achievements' of Communism, in the light of economic and social policies enforced by the Bolsheviki during the whole period of their amazing misrule." The author views the land problem as the "keynote to the whole Russian situation." He also sketches Russian industries, trade, and finance.

Brubaker, Earl R. "A Sectoral Analysis of Efficiency under Market and Plan." SOVIET STUDIES 23 (January 1972): 435-49.

This article analyzes the efficiency of the Soviet economy, using Western Europe rather than the United States as the standard of performance. Four tables. The appendix discusses the ambiguity of index numbers.

Brumberg, Abraham. "The Soviet Campaigns Against 'Survivals of Capitalism.' " RUSSIAN REVIEW 12 (April 1953): 65-78.

This article surveys Soviet campaigns against patterns of behavior considered to be indigenous to capitalist society, including the desire for private property, nationalism, pro-Western tendencies, bureaucratic tendencies, and selfishness.

Bukharin, N., and Preobrazhensky, Evengeii A. THE ABC OF COMMUNISM. Edited and introduced by E. H. Carr. Baltimore: Harmondsworth and Ringwood, 1919. Reprint, 1969. 480 p.

First appearing in 1919, the book served as an "elementary textbook of communist knowledge." Part two deals with the practical aspects of the revolutionary process and outlines the organization of industry, agriculture, distribution, banks and monetary circulation, finance and labor production, and social welfare.

Czarnomski, F. B. CAN RUSSIA SURVIVE? AN EXAMINATION OF THE FACTS AND FIGURES OF SOVIET REALITY. London: Melville Press, 1952. 128 p.

The thesis of this book is that the Soviet system will collapse either through war or internal upheaval. The author describes briefly the Soviet land and people; the life, labor, and poverty of the workers; and Soviet planning and finance.

Dean, Vera M. SOVIET RUSSIA, 1917-1936. World Affairs Pamphlets, no. 2. 3d ed., rev. Boston: World Peace Foundation; New York: Foreign Policy Association, 1936. 40 p.

This study of the Soviet political and economic system is intended to be the basis for predicting future developments in the USSR. The Soviet industrial system and agrarian revolution are described.

Devons, E. "The Soviet Economic System." MANCHESTER SCHOOL OF ECONOMICS AND SOCIAL STUDIES 14 (September 1946): 54-59.

This is a review of Alexander Baykov. THE DEVELOPMENT OF THE SOVIET ECONOMIC SYSTEM. National Institute of Economic and Social Research, Economic Studies, no. 5. Cambridge: At the University Press, 1946.

Dobb, Maurice H. PAPERS ON CAPITALISM, DEVELOPMENT, AND PLANNING. New York: International Publishers, 1967. 274 p.

This collection of essays covers the history of capitalism, economic development, the theory of investment planning and economic growth, the priority accorded investment in heavy industry, planning in the Soviet economy, and Marxian economics.

_____. "Transition from Socialism to Communism: Economic Aspects." MARXISM TODAY 5 (November 1961): 340-45.

Soviet economic policy in relation to the goal of a truly Communist society is examined.

Dobbert, Gerhard, ed. RED ECONOMICS. Boston: Houghton Mifflin, 1932. xxiv, 327 p.

Essays deal with the planned economy, industry, agriculture, finance, and housing.

Fallenbuchl, Z. M. "Economic Policy of the Period of Transition from Capitalism to Socialism." CANADIAN SLAVONIC PAPERS 9 (Autumn 1967): 245-69.

This article examines Communist economic policies for this period in the Soviet Union, Central and Eastern Europe, and China. It suggests that some elements in all the policies are universal, while other policies adjust to unique local conditions.

_____. "How Does the Soviet Economy Function Without a Free Market?" QUEEN'S QUARTERLY 70 (Winter 1964): 559-75.

This article examines the roles of planning and planners in Soviet economic decision making.

Fiss, Joan. "Freedom and Occupational Choice in the Soviet Union." SOCIAL RESEARCH 30 (May 1963): 53-76.

This essay points to a need for rethinking about the nature of totalitarianism in Russia and about the West's conception of freedom.

Glovinsky, E[vgeny]. "Soviet Socialism." STUDIES ON THE SOVIET UNION n.s. 2 (September 1959): 71-77.

This work investigates the Soviet view of socialism and its significance for policy.

Gourvitch, Alexander. "The Problem of Prices and Valuation in the Soviet System." AMERICAN ECONOMIC REVIEW 26 (March 1936): 267-82.

The article surveys the various problems of allocation, shortages, surpluses, and criteria of success and efficiency which arise when the Soviets ignore market forces and set prices to achieve certain objectives. The author concludes that "it is the ability to solve in a lasting manner these various price problems rather than any technological accomplishments that will afford the test of adequacy and feasibility of the Soviet program of economic expansion." For a discussion, see: Calvin B. Hoover et al. "Prices and Valuation in the Soviet System--Discussion." AMERICAN ECONOMIC REVIEW 26 (March 1936): 283-90.

Gsovski, Vladimir. "Family and Inheritance in Soviet Law." RUSSIAN REVIEW 7 (Autumn 1947): 71-87.

This paper is a legal and historical analysis of these aspects of Soviet law beginning with the first code of 1918.

Gubsky, N. "Economic Law in Soviet Russia." ECONOMIC JOURNAL 37 (June 1927): 226-36.

This article describes differences in Soviet law and the usual standards of the European codes. Topics covered include the civil code, ownership, buildings, agreements, companies, private industry, inheritance, patents, copyrights, insurance, industrial law, trusts, syndicates, trade, exchanges, banks, cooperatives, mining, land, and cooperative and individual possession.

Guins, George C. "Claims and Realities of Soviet Socialism." RUSSIAN REVIEW 11 (July 1952): 138-47.

This article examines Soviet claims that they have no unemployment or economic crises and considers the costs of eliminating these problems from the Soviet system.

Hendel, Samuel, ed. THE SOVIET CRUCIBLE: THE SOVIET SYSTEM IN THEORY AND PRACTICE. 2d ed. Princeton, N.J.: Van Nostrand, 1963. 706 p. Illustrated.

Included are excerpts from books and journal articles on various social, political, and economic topics. Section seven deals with the Soviet economic system and contains twelve excerpts which discuss the reliability of Soviet statistics, industrialization, recent economic developments, and the Seven-Year Plan.

Hirlekar, K. S., ed. SOVIET RUSSIA, THE SECRET OF HER SUCCESSES.

Rev. ed. Bombay: Padma Publications, 1945. xxiv, 316 p.

> Written by Soviet economists and political leaders, these essays enumerate the successes of the Soviet planned economy during the first fifteen years of the Soviet state. The editor feels that the Soviet system can serve as a model for backward countries like India. Ten statistical appendices which summarize growth during the five-year plans. Four maps.

Hoover, Calvin B. "Some Economic and Social Consequences of Russian Communism." ECONOMIC JOURNAL 40 (September 1930): 422-41.

> The article surveys the Soviet economic system and concludes that a socialist system can survive as a viable economic system.

Jasny, Naum. "A Note on Rationality and Efficiency in the Soviet Economy Part I." SOVIET STUDIES 12 (April 1961): 353-75.

> This paper discusses irrationality and inefficiency with reference to fuel and electric power. Three tables.

―――. "A Note on Rationality and Efficiency in the Soviet Economy. Part II." SOVIET STUDIES 13 (July 1961): 35-68.

> Industries discussed in this part include steel, machinery, timber, artificial fibers, agriculture, construction, transport, and planning in general. Addenda to parts one and two conclude the article. A table provides figures on locomotive production for 1950-60. For further discussion, see: Naum Jasny. "Rationality and Efficiency: A Further Note." SOVIET STUDIES 13 (January 1962): 321-23.

Javits, Benjamin A. "A Comparison of Incentives in the Economic System of the United States and the Soviet Russia." In COMPARISONS OF THE U.S. AND SOVIET ECONOMIES, U.S. Congress. Joint Economic Committee, pp. 341-47. Washington, D.C.: Government Printing Office, 1959.

> Javits outlines similarities in the Soviet and American incentive systems and concludes that the major difference lies in the aim of the underlying philosophies.

Keizer, Willem. THE SOVIET QUEST FOR ECONOMIC RATIONALITY. THE CONFLICT OF ECONOMIC AND POLITICAL AIMS IN THE SOVIET ECONOMY, 1953-1968. Rotterdam, Netherlands: Rotterdam University Press, 1971. vi, 267 p.

> The author analyzes aims of the Soviet economic system, discusses changes in the past fifteen years, and surveys important economic controversies of the past decade.

Khrushchev, Nikita S. "The Future of the Soviet Economy." In RUSSIA ENTERS THE 1960's: A DOCUMENTARY REPORT ON THE 22ND CONGRESS OF

THE COMMUNIST PARTY OF THE SOVIET UNION, edited by Harry Schwartz, pp. 234-78. Philadelphia and New York: J. B. Lippincott, 1962.

This report discusses the prospects for achieving full communism in the Soviet Union.

Kihara, Masao. "Socialism and Political Economy." KYOTO UNIVERSITY ECONOMIC REVIEW 34 (October 1964): 35-56.

The paper probes the relation between the socialist political economy and economic policy from a Marxist viewpoint. Early Soviet policy is discussed.

Lambert, Paul. "A Soviet Co-operator versus the Co-operative Idea." ANNALS OF PUBLIC AND CO-OPERATIVE ECONOMY 38 (January-March 1967): 33-37.

The author defends his version of the cooperative idea against criticisms by Y. Kranarovski, which appeared in the REVIEW OF CENTROSOYUE, the Central Union of Consumers' Cooperatives of the USSR.

Landreth, Harry. "Creeping Capitalism in the Soviet Union? HARVARD BUSINESS REVIEW 45 (September-October 1967): 133-40.

The author argues that the Liberman reforms of 1965 are not evidence of the convergence of socialism and capitalism but of a Soviet trend toward market socialism.

Lovestone, Jay. "Basic Distinctions Between the Soviet Economy and American Economy." In COMPARISONS OF THE U.S. AND SOVIET ECONOMIES, U.S. Congress. Joint Economic Committee, pp. 547-68. Washington, D.C.: Government Printing Office, 1959.

This paper considers the basic distinctions between the U.S. and Soviet economies; gives a description of a totalitarian state economy; notes some recent changes in the administration of the Soviet economy; and views trade union managerial control in the USSR.

Masnata, Albert. "The Soviet Experiment in Collective Economy." ANNALS OF PUBLIC AND CO-OPERATIVE ECONOMY 39 (July-September 1968): 435-68.

The author discusses the bases of the system; reviews the history of the economy; discusses institutions in general and the significance of planning; covers the planning organization and the flow of goods between sectors; and evaluates the economic and social effectiveness of the system.

Meisel, James H., and Kozera, Edward S. MATERIALS FOR THE STUDY OF THE SOVIET SYSTEM: STATE AND PARTY CONSTITUTIONS, LAWS, DECREES,

Economic Systems and Society

DECISIONS AND OFFICIAL STATEMENTS OF THE LEADERS IN TRANSLATION. Ann Arbor, Mich.: George Wahu Publishing Co., 1950. xii, 495 p.

> Included are numerous important administrative codes, laws, and ordinances which have been arranged in chronological order. Particular emphasis has been given to the years 1917-21.

Meyer, Alfred G. "USSR, Incorporated." SLAVIC REVIEW 20 (October 1961): 369-76.

> This informed discussion of the Soviet economic system and industrialization presents some interesting analogies between the Soviet system and the company town or modern corporate structure.

Miller, Jacob. "A Political Economy of Socialism in the Making." SOVIET STUDIES 4 (April 1953): 403-33.

> This article briefly surveys the first stages of socialism as a theory in the USSR since the early 1930s.

Miller, Margaret S. "Markets in Russia." In COMMUNIST ECONOMY UNDER CHANGE--STUDIES IN THE THEORY AND PRACTICE OF MARKETS AND COMPETITION IN RUSSIA, POLAND AND YUGOSLAVIA, edited by Margaret Miller et al., pp. 1-82. London: Andre Deutsch for Institute of Econ-Affairs, 1963.

> The author examines independent, private economic activity in the areas of industry, agriculture, housing, trade, and many commodities and services.

Nearing, Scott, and Hardy, Jack. THE ECONOMIC ORGANIZATION OF THE SOVIET UNION. New York: Vanguard Press, 1927. xxii, 245 p.

> The descriptive and statistical data in the book attempt to answer the following questions: How do the Russians earn their living? Is there private capital in the Soviet Union, and, if so, how much? What are the relations between employer and worker? Are the workers organized? Is the Soviet economic system speeding up or slowing down? Is the Soviet Union moving toward socialism or capitalism? Four charts and index.

Nove, Alec. "The Politics of Economic Rationality: Observations on the Soviet Economy." SOCIAL RESEARCH 25 (July 1958): 127-44.

> This paper considers the growing importance of economic rationality in the Soviet Union and speculates about its possible political implications.

Opie, Redvers. "Soviet Communism: A New Civilization?" QUARTERLY JOURNAL OF ECONOMICS 51 (November 1936): 131-46.

> This article is a review of Sidney and Beatrice Webb. SOVIET

COMMUNISM: A NEW CIVILIZATION? 2 vols. London: Longmans, Green, 1935.

Oxenfeldt, Alfred, and Holubnychy, Vsevolod. ECONOMIC SYSTEMS IN ACTION; THE UNITED STATES, SOVIET UNION AND FRANCE. New York: Holt, Rinehart and Winston, 1965. vii, 264 p.

> This book, intended for nonspecialists, is a text for comparative economic systems. Chapter 3 discusses the Soviet economy and economic problems. Planning, allocation of the factors of production, and the distribution of personal income are examined.

Pasvolsky, Leo. THE ECONOMICS OF COMMUNISM: WITH SPECIAL REFERENCE TO RUSSIA'S EXPERIMENT. New York: Macmillan, 1921. xvi, 312 p.

> Part one of the book describes the Soviet economic system, i.e., nationalized production, cooperative distribution, and the agricultural system. Part two discusses the results and the problems of the system.

Pejovich, Svetozar. "Liberman's Reforms and Property Rights in the Soviet Union." JOURNAL OF LAW AND ECONOMICS 12 (April 1969): 155-62.

> This paper advances the thesis that a theory of economic systems developed around the concept of property rights would aid in understanding the economics of various countries. The analysis suggests that the prevailing property relations in the Soviet Union would seriously hamper the implementation of Liberman's reform.

"The Peoples of Central Asia and Kazakhstan: Their Transition to Socialism." CENTRAL ASIAN REVIEW 11, no. 3 (1963): 224-33.

> The socioeconomic system of this area is discussed, from before the Revolution to prospects for the future.

Pigou, A.C. "The Webbs on Soviet Communism." ECONOMIC JOURNAL 46 (March 1936): 88-97.

> This article is a critical review of Sidney and Beatrice Webb. SOVIET COMMUNISM: A NEW CIVILIZATION? 2 vols. London: Longmans, Green, 1935.

Prybyla, Jan S. "The Convergence of Western and Communist Economic Systems: A Critical Estimate." RUSSIAN REVIEW 23 (January 1964): 3-17.

> This paper reviews four aspects of the convergence hypothesis: disaffiliation or a waning of revolutionary fervor, economic maturity, trends in consumption, and increasing socialization.

_____. "The Quest for Economic Rationality in the Soviet Bloc." SOCIAL

RESEARCH 30 (September 1963): 343-66.

Topics discussed include the economic debates in the Soviet bloc since 1955; the politics of de-Stalinization; the increase in foreign trade; the problems of maintaining a high growth rate; price theory; and mathematical economics.

Raupach, Hans. "Production and Distribution Problems on the Road to Communism." STUDIES ON THE SOVIET UNION n.s. 4, no. 1 (1964): 100-107.

This paper looks at the twenty-year targets set up by the Communist party in 1961 and discusses in Marxist terminology the effects of the implied production relations on the distribution of income in Soviet society.

Roberts, Paul C. ALIENATION AND THE SOVIET ECONOMY: TOWARD A GENERAL THEORY OF MARXIAN ALIENATION, ORGANIZATIONAL PRINCIPLES, AND THE SOVIET ECONOMY. Albuquerque: University of New Mexico Press, 1971. viii, 121 p.

This book discusses alienation and central planning in Marxian literature; war communism; polycentricity and hierarchy; the Soviet economy as polycentric; and Lange's theory of socialist planning.

_____. "Marx's Classification of Economic Systems and the Soviet Economy." SOVIET STUDIES 23 (July 1971): 96-102.

This paper considers the ways in which the material supply system in the Soviet Union resulted from the original Marxian aspirations. For further discussion, see the comment by Alec Nove, pp. 103-5.

_____. "The Polycentric Soviet Economy." JOURNAL OF LAW AND ECONOMICS 12 (April 1969): 163-79.

This paper presents a theoretical framework in which the Soviet economy is studied as an alternative to a centrally planned economy. The author discusses the original socialist intention, intellectual background, the natures of hierarchic and polycentric organizations, and the application to the Soviet economy.

Ronimois, Hans E. "Soviet Experiment with Communist Economy, 1918-20." CANADIAN SLAVONIC PAPERS 2 (1957): 70-85.

This detailed discussion covers the early attempt of the Soviet regime to introduce true communism into Russia after the Revolution. Economically, this meant the physical allocation of resources without money, prices, or other elements of the exchange economy.

Rostow, Walt W. THE DYNAMICS OF SOVIET SOCIETY. New York: W.W. Norton, 1967. xvi, 320 p.

Economic Systems and Society

This book discusses the evolution of Soviet rule, the forces and tensions in Soviet society under Stalin, and prospects for the Khrushchev era and beyond. Select bibliography and index.

Sorlin, Pierre. THE SOVIET PEOPLE AND THEIR SOCIETY, FROM 1917 TO THE PRESENT. Translated by D. Weissbort. New York: Praeger, 1968. x, 293 p. Illustrated.

This book links the economic developments in the Soviet Union with the more general developments of Soviet society. Statistical appendices. Bibliography, index, and maps.

Timasheff, Nicholas S. THE GREAT RETREAT: THE GROWTH AND DECLINE OF COMMUNISM IN RUSSIA. New York: E. P. Dutton, 1946. 470 p.

Of particular interest are chapters on "The Economic Transfiguration" and "Population, Social Classes, Mores, and Morals." Chronological and statistical appendices, bibliography, and index.

Varga, Eugene. TWO SYSTEMS: SOCIALIST ECONOMY AND CAPITALIST ECONOMY. Translated by R. P. Arnot. New York: International Publishers, 1939. 268 p.

Various aspects of the Soviet economy are compared with capitalist economies, with the latter usually suffering in the comparisons. Numerous tables.

Vucinich, Alexander S. SOVIET ECONOMIC INSTITUTIONS: THE SOCIAL STRUCTURE OF PRODUCTION UNITS. Stanford, Calif.: Stanford University Press, 1952. x, 150 p.

The institutions discussed are the factory, the kolkhoz, the sovkhoz, the machine-tractor station, and the industrial and artisan cooperatives.

Ward, Harry F. IN PLACE OF PROFIT: SOCIAL INCENTIVES IN THE SOVIET UNION. New York: Charles Scribner's Sons, 1933. xvi, 460 p.

This book recounts efforts in the Soviet Union to change the incentive system, to introduce initiative among the masses, and yet to maintain control.

Wesson, Robert G. SOVIET COMMUNES. New Brunswick, N.J.: Rutgers University Press, 1963. 275 p.

Topics discussed include Soviet attitudes, the commune movement, the role of the commune in the economy and as a political instrument, its role in collectivization, and its decline. Index.

Wilczynski, Josef. THE ECONOMICS OF SOCIALISM: PRINCIPLES GOVERNING THE OPERATION OF THE CENTRALLY PLANNED ECONOMIES IN THE

USSR AND EASTERN EUROPE UNDER THE NEW SYSTEM. London: Allen and Unwin, 1970. 233 p.

Topics covered in this text include background; plan and market; profit; production; growth; accumulation; consumption; labor; land; pricing; money and banking; fiscal control; and trade. Glossary, graphs, tables, and index.

Wiles, Peter J. D. THE POLITICAL ECONOMY OF COMMUNISM. Oxford: Basil Blackwell, 1962. xv, 404 p.

This work is intended as a graduate level introduction to the Communist economy, but it deals largely with the Soviet economy. Its four parts cover institutions and ideology, planning and resource allocation, growth, and eschatology. Index.

———. "Labour and Wages Under Full Communism." In THE U.S.S.R. AND THE FUTURE; AN ANALYSIS OF THE NEW PROGRAM OF THE CPSU, edited by Leonard B. Schapiro, pp. 114-26. Praeger Publications in Russian History and World Communism, no. 124. New York: Praeger, 1962.

This paper contains a critical discussion of the requirements which must be fulfilled if full communism is to be achieved in Soviet society.

———. "Will Capitalism and Communism Spontaneously Converge?" ENCOUNTER 20 (June 1963): 84-90.

This article examines some of the evidence for "convergence" from three important forces: the adoption of sophisticated mathematical methods of planning; the influence of a professional managerial class; and increasing affluence. The author concludes that the case for convergence on these grounds is weak.

Wiles, Peter J. D., and Markowski, Stefan. "Income Distribution under Communism and Capitalism, Some Facts About Poland, the UK, the USA and the USSR." SOVIET STUDIES 22 (April 1971): 487-511.

The relevant part of this article appears on pp. 501-11. It includes two graphs and five tables on Soviet income distribution with comparisons to other countries.

Zauberman, Alfred. "Value, Price, and Profit." In THE FUTURE OF COMMUNIST SOCIETY, edited by Walter Laquerer and Leopold Labedz, pp. 54-62. Praeger Publications in Russian History and World Communism, no. 101. New York: Praeger, 1962.

The author feels that there is no reason why the Soviet state cannot distribute half the population's real income on a communal basis by 1980. However, even when full communism is finally achieved, real income will still have to be distributed on some kind of wage basis. Hence, there will still be a need to operate a system of incentives. As of yet, the Soviet Union has no definition of economic organization in a fully communistic society.

Zinam, Oleg. "Impact of Modernization on the USSR: Convergence or Divergence?" RUSSIAN REVIEW 32 (July 1973): 254-63.

This article deals with two important relationships: (1) the impact of the growing complexity and sophistication of the Soviet economy caused by forces of modernization on the degree of centralization of both planning and controlling functions and (2) the effect of the revolution of rising expectations on the pattern of consumption in the USSR.

Chapter 5
ECONOMIC PLANNING AND POLICY

THE PERIOD UP TO 1860

Dmytryshyn, Basil. "The Economic Content of the 1767 Nakaz of Catherine II." AMERICAN SLAVIC AND EAST EUROPEAN REVIEW 19 (February 1960): 1-9.

This article reviews and comments on the significance for the Russian economy of the Nakaz or Instruction of Catherine II to the Legislative Commission of 1967-68. The Nakaz serves to show both the backwardness of the Russian economy at that time and how enlightened a ruler Catherine was.

THE PERIOD AFTER 1917

Abramson, A. "The Economic Development of the Soviet Union under the Second and Third Five-Year Plans." INTERNATIONAL LABOUR REVIEW 41 (February 1940): 177-201.

Abramson presents a brief analysis of the Second and Third Five-Year Plans which he has gleaned from Soviet economic literature. The following topics are surveyed: population, agriculture, industry, transportation, and standard of living.

Andres, Enrike. THE NEW ECONOMIC POLICY; ITS ORIGIN AND GOAL. Moscow: Novosti Press Agency Publishing House, 1969. 63 p.

This study attempts to clarify certain aspects of the NEP in the economic development of the USSR which "could be applied in countries engaged in social reconstruction along progressive lines." The book deals with the theoretical and practical aspects of the NEP.

Bakhmetov, Boris. "The NEP in Eclipse." SLAVONIC REVIEW 3, no. 8: 257-71.

Bakhmetov outlines important characteristics of the NEP, especially concessions made to the peasantry, and discusses briefly the dis-

Economic Planning and Policy

sension within the Communist party in late 1923. He feels that there will be a tendency towards decentralization of nationwide control and a consolidation of local government.

Balinky, Alexander, et al. PLANNING AND THE MARKET IN THE USSR: THE 1960'S. New Brunswick, N.J.: Rutgers University Press, 1967. vi, 132 p.

This work investigates Soviet economic reforms of the 1960s. It is intended for a general readership.

Baran, Paul A. "National Economic Planning: The Soviet Experience." In THE SOVIET ECONOMY: A BOOK OF READINGS, edited by Morris Bornstein and Daniel Fusfeld, pp. 3-17. Rev. ed. Homewood, Ill.: R. D. Irwin, 1966.

This article discusses solutions to problems which developed from the limiting of living standards to channel resources into investment and the military. These methods include collectivization of agriculture; wage, price, and tax policies; the distribution of investment; and the use of various "national economic balance sheets" to allocate resources.

Baranov, I. "The Business Contract: An Instrument for Fulfilling the State Plans." SOVIET STUDIES 1 (April 1950): 385-92.

This is a partial translation of an article from I. Baranov. PLANOVOYE KHOZYAISTVO [Planned economy] 5 (September-October 1949): 63-72. It represents an attempt to reconcile central planning with local management efficiency.

Baritz, Joseph. "The Soviet Seven-Year Plan in Industry." STUDIES ON THE SOVIET UNION n.s. 2 (September 1959): 52-70.

This short analysis of the Soviet Seven-Year Plan for 1959-65 gives special attention to metals, chemicals, oil and gas, machine building, light industry, food, power, railroads, and capital construction.

Baykov, Alexander M. "Some Observations on Planning Economic Development in the U.S.S.R." In ECONOMIC PLANNING, edited by L. J. Zimmerman, pp. 21-43. Hauge: Mouton & Co., 1963.

The author summarizes various stages of Soviet economic planning. The initial stage created the prerequisites for introducing planning. The second phase dealt with changes during the period of mixed economy. The third period, which began with the First Five-Year Plan and continued up to 1957, was one of extensive industrialization.

Bergson, Abram. "The Current Soviet Planning Reforms." In PLANNING AND THE MARKET IN THE USSR: THE 1960'S, edited by Alexander Balinky et al., pp. 43-64. New Brunswick, N.J.: Rutgers University Press, 1967.

Economic Planning and Policy

This article traces administrative reforms of 1965, which reversed the 1957 reforms of Khrushchev in which regional authorities were more important. The author assesses that the Soviet government is not dismantling its system of centralized industrial planning but is adapting it in the direction of decentralization and increased use of market-type controls.

_____. THE ECONOMICS OF SOVIET PLANNING. New Haven, Conn.: Yale University Press, 1964. xvii, 394 p.

Bergson discusses Soviet administrative apparatus; the disposition of consumers' goods; managerial motivation in industry; industrial labor recruitment and utilization; supply of industrial materials; price formation of industrial materials; collective farm incentives; management of agriculture; consumption structure; and capital formation.

Bergson, Abram, and Berliner, Joseph S. "Economic Aspects of the Party Program." BULLETIN OF THE ASSOCIATION FOR THE STUDY OF SOVIET-TYPE ECONOMIES 9 (Winter 1962): 20-46.

These are notes of a Russian Research Center (of Harvard University) seminar held on October 26, 1961. Comparative data on the Soviet and U.S. economies appear in four tables.

Berkhin, I. SOVIET ECONOMIC POLICY: EARLY YEARS. Moscow: Novosti Press Agency Publishing House, 1970. 119 p.

This book analyzes Lenin's New Economic Policy as the economic groundwork of socialism and as a model to be followed "for the building of a new society in all socialist countries." It also analyzes policies of the state during the Revolution and the first post-Revolutionary years, when Lenin headed the government.

Berliner, Joseph S. "Marxism and the Soviet Economy." PROBLEMS OF COMMUNISM 13 (September-October 1964): 1-11.

This article examines some of the relationships between Marxist ideology and Soviet economic policy. It concludes that Marxism has had little impact, but it analyzes other factors which the author believes have been influential.

Bernard, Philippe J. PLANNING IN THE SOVIET UNION. Translated by Irene Nove. Oxford and New York: Pergamon Press, 1966. xxv, 309 p.

The author surveys the characteristics of the Soviet system; ideology and planning; the planning process; coordination of plans and the determination of objectives; economic organization and hierarchy; problems of economic administration; regional economic policy; and economic equilibrium and the search for optimization. Bibliography, graphs, tables, and index.

Economic Planning and Policy

Birmingham University. Bureau of Research on Russian Economic Conditions. "Remarks on the Second Five-Year Plan: Prospects of Realisation." MEMO-RANDUM NO. 10 (November 1934): 1-15.

> The authors compare the proposals and their realization in the First Five-Year Plan. The paper examines the following topics: industry and agriculture; general economic indexes; industrialization; the degree of socialization; plans to improve living conditions; Soviet law and the plan; and the exploitation of natural resources. Tables.

Boddy, Francis M. "Ethical Aspects of Current Soviet Economic Policies." REVIEW OF SOCIAL ECONOMY 23 (March 1965): 1-8.

> Ethical considerations related to the Soviet constitution and the Communist party program are evaluated. See the comments which follow by F. J. Mueller, pp. 9-13, and Leon Smolinski, pp. 14-16.

Bor, Mikhail Z. AIMS AND METHODS OF SOVIET PLANNING. London: Lawrence and Wishart, 1967. 255 p.

> This is an extensive study of Soviet planning, with discussions of how national economic plans are drafted; methods and techniques of planning; and the state economic plan for development 1966-70. It has a concluding section on economic planning versus economic programming. Tables.

Brutskus, Boris D. ECONOMIC PLANNING IN SOVIET RUSSIA. London: Routledge & Sons, 1935. xvii, 234 p.

> The book contains a foreword by F. A. Hayek. The first part deals with the relation of Marxism to the Russian revolutions and discusses the following topics: the calculation of labor value in the socialist society; labor costs and the market price; the problem of distribution under socialism; and socialism and agriculture. Part two surveys the results of economic planning in Russia and discusses some of the following topics: war communism and the NEP, economic development and policy under the five-year plan, and the results of the planned economy.

Bush, Keith. "Soviet Economic Priorities, 1968-1970: The Supreme Soviet Session of October 1967." BULLETIN OF THE ASSOCIATION FOR THE STUDY OF SOVIET-TYPE ECONOMIES 10 (Spring 1968): 3-12.

> Topics covered include plan and performance in 1967, the plan for 1968, and the Eighth Five-Year Plan. Tables.

Bye, Raymond T. "The Central Planning and Coordination of Production in Soviet Russia." AMERICAN ECONOMIC REVIEW 19 (March 1929): 91-110.

Economic Planning and Policy

This detailed examination of bureaucratic planning and coordination of the Soviet Union up to 1928 evaluates specific policies up to that time. A table shows target and actual output increases for selected industries in 1927-28. A discussion ostensibly based on the article follows on pp. 111-30.

Chamberlin, William H. "The Planned Economy." In RED ECONOMICS, edited by Gerhard Dobbert, pp. 3-22. Boston: Houghton Mifflin, 1932.

The author discusses planning in industry and agriculture and the differences between the first and second five-year plans.

---------. SOVIET PLANNED ECONOMIC ORDER. Boston: World Peace Foundation, 1931. vii, 258 p.

Chamberlin discusses the origin of Soviet economic planning; the way in which a five-year plan is carried out; the remolding of agriculture; and the results and prospects of economic planning. The appendices, which comprise almost half the book, contain translations of documents relating to the five-year plan, labor, and agriculture.

Coates, William P., and Coates, Zelda K. SECOND FIVE-YEAR PLAN OF DEVELOPMENT OF THE U.S.S.R. New York: Methuen, 1934. xxvi, 129 p.

The first chapter summarizes the results of the First Five-Year Plan and discusses the metallurgical industry, electrification, machine construction, agriculture, and conditions of workers. The second chapter deals with the goals of the Second Five-Year Plan, considering the same topics as in chapter 1. The third chapter consists of tables which summarize five-year plan estimates for industrial output, agriculture, finance, labor, and population. Index and three maps.

Cook, A. C. "Current Developments in Soviet Economic Planning." ECONOMIC RECORD 39 (September 1963): 305-23.

This paper describes some recent changes in the organization of economic planning in the USSR. Topics covered include the roles of the various government levels and agencies, the planning procedures, use of material balances, agricultural planning, reforms, capital investment, and supervision and control.

Counts, George S. "The Soviet Planning System and the Five Year Plan." In BOLSHEVISM, FASCISM, AND CAPITALISM: AN ACCOUNT OF THE THREE ECONOMIC SYSTEMS, edited by George S. Counts et al., pp. 1-54. New Haven, Conn.: Yale University Press, 1932.

The author gives an outline of the structure of Soviet planning. According to Counts, the two principal goals of the Five-Year

Economic Planning and Policy

Plan are rapid industrialization and socialistic reconstruction of the countryside.

Cross, Samuel H. "The Outlook for the Five-Year Plan." HARVARD BUSINESS REVIEW 9 (January 1931): 169-77.

This article provides a partial evaluation of the First Five-Year Plan midway through its execution.

Davies, R[obert]. W. "Economic Aspects of the XX Congress." SOVIET STUDIES 8 (October 1956): 172-84.

Topics discussed here include policy changes, appraisals of past performance, economic competition with the West, the Sixth Five-Year Plan (1956-60), and planning problems. Three tables.

──────. "Industrial Planning Reconsidered." SOVIET STUDIES 8 (April 1957): 426-36.

This note discusses two aspects of the Soviet controversy over industrial planning: diagnosis of problems and price-setting difficulties.

──────. "Planning a Mature Economy in the USSR." ECONOMICS OF PLANNING 6, no. 2 (1966): 138-53.

This article attempts to place the Soviet economic system in the context of traditional economics. It also discusses the problems of Soviet-type central planning in a mature economy.

──────. "Planning for Rapid Growth in the USSR." ECONOMICS OF PLANNING 5, nos. 1-2 (1965): 74-86.

This article examines the Soviet environment in the 1920s; the models of industrialization proposed at that time; and the principal features of planned industrialization, 1928-55. Tables present data on GNP, uses of GNP, output of major sectors, and the relative contribution of the factors of production to economic growth.

──────. "The Reappraisal of Industry." SOVIET STUDIES 7 (January 1956): 308-31.

Topics discussed include planning, management, and labor.

──────. "The Soviet Planning Process for Rapid Industrialization." ECONOMICS OF PLANNING 6, no. 1 (1966): 53-67.

This article presents an outline of the system and discussions of the planning process, financial planning, labor and labor controls, and strengths and weaknesses of the planning system. Diagrams of the organization of the planning system are included.

Economic Planning and Policy

Degras, Jane, and Nove, Alec, eds. SOVIET PLANNING: ESSAYS IN HONOUR OF NAUM JASNY. Oxford: Basil Blackwell, 1964. xi, 225 p.

These essays consider various aspects of planning, including priorities and shortfalls, urbanization plans, the role of the State Bank, welfare criteria, and planning theory. The book includes a bibliography of the principal works of Naum Jasny.

Dobb, Maurice H. "Economic Planning in the Soviet Union." SCIENCE AND SOCIETY 6 (Fall 1942): 305-14.

This article discusses in general terms the mechanism, organization, and problems of Soviet central planning.

──────. "Kantorovich on Optimal Planning and Prices." SCIENCE AND SOCIETY 31, no. 2 (1967): 186-202.

This article deals with proposals by L. V. Kantorovich and is largely a review of his THE BEST USE OF ECONOMIC RESOURCES. English edition edited by G. Morton. Translated by P. F. Knightsfield. London and New York: Pergamon Press and Harvard University Press, 1965. This is a translation of EKONOMICHESKII RASCHET NAILUCHAHEGO ISPOLZOVANIA RESORSOV. Moscow: Academy of Sciences Press, 1959.

──────. "The Significance of the Five Year Plan." SLAVONIC REVIEW 10 (June 1931): 80-89.

The author feels that the successes of the five-year plan outweigh its failures and that Soviet Russia can serve as a model of an alternative, rival social system.

Dolan, Edwin G. "The Teleological Period in Soviet Economic Planning." YALE ECONOMIC ESSAYS 10 (Spring 1970): 3-42.

This paper first discusses the historical context and intellectual origins of teleological planning and then uses a model of a teleological planning system to analyze Soviet planning. Plan performance and tautness are then discussed.

Edie (Lionel D.) & Co., Inc. Economics Division. SOVIET ECONOMIC INTENTIONS: AN ANALYSIS OF THE SEVEN-YEAR PLAN, 1959-1965; A SPECIAL REPORT. New York: 1960. 59 p.

The goals of the Seven-Year Plan in various areas of industry, industry investment, agriculture, and transportation are examined. The conclusion is that the part of the plan dealing with industry will probably be attained. Output of capital goods will be higher than of consumer goods; however, heavy capital investment will hamper production of consumer durables. This book argues that there is little chance that the Seven-Year Plan for agriculture will be fulfilled. Tables.

Economic Planning and Policy

Efimov, Anatolii N. NATIONAL ECONOMIC PLANNING IN USSR. Moscow: Economics Publishing House, 1967. 55 p.

This book represents a popular account of the "scientific foundations of socialist planning, its development in the USSR, the results of realization of Soviet plans . . . and . . . the content of the Soviet five-year plan for 1966-1970." The author outlines the initial steps in planning; scientific planning; proportional development of socialist economics; contemporary forms of organization of planning; and new targets of economic development.

_____. STATE PLANNING; AIMS, WAYS, RESULTS. Moscow: Novosti Press Agency Publishing House, 196?. 226 p.

This book contrasts socialist planning and capitalist programming in terms of functions, organization, methodology, and aims.

Ellman, Michael [J.]. "The Consistency of Soviet Plans." SCOTTISH JOURNAL OF POLITICAL ECONOMY 16 (February 1969): 50-74.

This paper discusses both the theoretical and organizational aspects of the consistency of Soviet plans, including material balance and input-output. Two tables and an input-output planning organization chart are included. An appendix lists input-output tables compiled in the USSR.

_____. SOVIET PLANNING TODAY; PROPOSALS FOR AN OPTIMALLY FUNCTIONING ECONOMIC SYSTEM. Cambridge: At the University Press, 1971. xv, 219 p.

This study seeks to analyze the current Soviet work on the theory of an optimally functioning socialist economy. Tables, glossary, and list of references.

Evenko, I. A. PLANNING IN THE U.S.S.R. Moscow: Foreign Languages Publishing House, 1962? 249 p.

In dealing with the organization of planning in the Soviet Union at the present stage, this book explores functions of planning agencies, the general principles of drafting long-term and annual national economic plans, and the system of their targets. The book also describes the methods of drafting plans and analyzing and controlling their outcomes using industry as an illustration.

Farbman, Michael S. PIATILETKA: RUSSIA'S 5-YEAR PLAN. New York: New Republic, 1931. xii, 220 p.

In the first part, Farbman sketches Russia in 1930. The second part discusses the industrial revolution under the Soviets and gives an account of the internal market, the problem of labor, inflation, and the key industries. The agrarian revolution is outlined in the third part. Farbman discusses the amount of land under cultivation, the state farms, collectivization, the livestock crisis, agricultural capital, and the geographic redistribution of crops.

Feiwel, George R. "Toward a Model of Soviet Planning." ECONOMIA INTERNAZIONALE 20 (November 1967): 709-19.

This article defines general characteristics of Soviet planning as a first step toward the development of a model of Soviet planning.

"The Fourth Five-Year Plan of the U.S.S.R." INTERNATIONAL LABOUR REVIEW 54 (July-August 1946): 45-58.

This article covers background of the plan; the general directives; and plans for industry, agriculture, transport, and material and cultural advancement during the period 1946-50.

Frank, Z., and Waelbroeck, J. "Soviet Economic Policy since 1953: A Study of its Structure and Changes." SOVIET STUDIES 17 (July 1965): 1-43.

The study is an attempt to apply the E. Kirschen-L. Morissens approach (which emphasizes institutions) to a planned economy. Attention is centered on developments in the USSR in 1953-62. Results are summarized in several tables.

FROM THE FIRST TO THE SECOND FIVE-YEAR PLAN. A symposium by J. Stalin, V. Molotov, L. Kaganovich, K. Voroshilov, G. Orjonikidze, V. Kuibyshev, Y. Yakovlev, G. Grinko. New York: International Publishers, 1933? 490 p.

These reports were delivered at the Joint Plenum of the Central Committee and Central Control Commission of the CPSU. Some of the topics dealt with are (1) "The Results of the First Five-Year Plan," (2) "The Advance of Heavy Industry," and (3) "Consolidating the Collective Farms."

Gallik, Dimitri M. "The Soviet Eighth Five-Year Plan for 1966-1970." BULLETIN OF THE ASSOCIATION FOR THE STUDY OF SOVIET-TYPE ECONOMIES 8 (Summer 1966): 18-25.

This series of tables compiled by the author details the targets of the Eighth Five-Year Plan.

Glovinsky, Evgeny. "Economic Policy." STUDIES ON THE SOVIET UNION n.s. 2, no. 3 (1963): 50-56.

This review of economic policy, 1953-63, highlights deviations from Stalinist economic policy.

Grinko, Grigorii F. THE FIVE-YEAR PLAN OF THE SOVIET UNION: A POLITICAL INTERPRETATION. New York: International Publishers, 1930. 340 p.

Economic Planning and Policy

The author was vice-chairman of Gosplan and played an important role in preparing the Five-Year Plan for the industrial reconstruction of the Soviet Union. The book attempts to show "not only the goal set by the plan, but the actual process by which it is being accomplished. In this connection the actual experiences of the already-completed first year and the second, now in progress, are used." Map.

Grossman, Gregory. "A Note on the Fulfilment of the Fifth Five-Year Plan in Industry." SOVIET STUDIES 8 (April 1957): 358-68.

This note examines Khrushchev's claims that the industrial portion of the Fifth Five-Year Plan was substantially overfulfilled. Tables.

Hallaraker, Harold, comp. "Soviet Discussion on Enterprise Incentives and Methods of Planning." ECONOMICS OF PLANNING 3 (April 1963): 53-68.

The short papers here include excerpts: "From the Report of N.S. Khrushchev"; "The Plan, Profits, and Bonuses" by Evsei G. Liberman; "The Chief Problem is Rationalization" by O. Gromyko; "Material Incentives Should be Based on Lowering Production Costs" by B. Smekhov; "Enterprises Should be Interested in a More Intensive Plan" by V.S. Nemchinov; "On Perfection of the Plan Indices and Coordination of the Scientific Research Activities" by Mikhail Z. Bor; "The Problem of Planning and Management of the Industry by the Help of Electronic Computing Techniques" by A. Dorodmitsyn; and "Previous Experiences" by I. Kasitsky.

Hardt, John P. "Strategic Alternatives in Soviet Resource Allocation Policy." In DIMENSIONS OF SOVIET ECONOMIC POWER, U.S. Congress. Joint Economic Committee, pp. 1-31. Washington, D.C.: Government Printing Office, 1962.

This article deals with the economic aspects of Soviet national policy. Hardt considers how Soviet leaders will use their growing economic strength to satisfy their rapidly expanding requirements. Soviet strategy can be determined by the way resources are allocated in each annual plan.

Hardt, John P., et al. "Institutional Stagnation and Changing Economic Strategy in the Soviet Union." In NEW DIRECTIONS IN THE SOVIET ECONOMY, U.S. Congress. Joint Economic Committee, pp. 19-62. Washington, D.C.: Government Printing Office, 1966.

Topics discussed include changes in Soviet economic strategy, problems with old institutions, Khrushchev's policies, and trends and prospects for the future.

Herman, Leon M. "The Cult of Bigness in Soviet Economic Planning." In

Economic Planning and Policy

ECONOMIC CONCENTRATION, U.S. Congress. Senate Committee on the Judiciary. Subcommittee on Antitrust and Monopoly. Hearings. 90th Cong., 2d sess., pp. 4346-58. Washington, D.C.: Government Printing Office, 1969.

Topics covered include ideological background; economic concentration in Russian history; industrial organization under Lenin and Stalin and the scale of economic enterprises; giantism in enterprises; the illusion of the superior productivity of giant enterprises; and the neglect of the development of smaller towns.

Hirsch, Hans. QUANTITY PLANNING AND PRICE PLANNING IN THE SOVIET UNION. Translated by Karl Scholz. Philadelphia: University of Pennsylvania Press, 1961. 272 p.

This work is concerned with the way in which choices are made-- what is produced, how much is produced, whether to produce for the short-term or long-term--as opposed to the organization of the planning mechanism. The study treats quantity planning, financial planning, the relation between quantity and financial planning, and price planning.

Hoeffding, Oleg. "State Planning and Forced Industrialization." PROBLEMS OF COMMUNISM 8 (November-December 1959): 38-46.

This article explores the relevance of Soviet experience with centralized economic planning and forced industrialization to the specific problems faced by underdeveloped countries in Asia. A short table compares outputs of certain commodities in Russia of 1913 with those of India in 1956.

Holzman, Franklyn D. "Some Notes on Over-full Employment Planning, Short-run Balance, and the Soviet Economic Reforms." SOVIET STUDIES 22 (October 1970): 255-61.

This paper explores the implications of over-full employment through input-output analysis and discusses possible advantages. For further discussion, see: Henry Schaefer. "A Note on Over-full Employment Planning, Priorities and Prices." SOVIET STUDIES 23 (July 1971): 106-8.

Hulicka, Karel. "Political and Economic Aspects of Planning of the National Economy in U.S.S.R. and the Soviet Bloc." SOUTH AFRICAN JOURNAL OF ECONOMICS 29 (March 1961): 3-34.

This paper seeks to present the Soviet theory of economic planning; show the relation between political and economic aspects of planning; demonstrate how these aspects influence the transition for a capitalistic to a socialistic system; outline planning methods and control; and discuss the challenge of Soviet planning for the Western world.

Hunter, Holland. "The Overambitious First Soviet Five-Year Plan." SLAVIC

Economic Planning and Policy

REVIEW 32 (June 1973): 237-57.

This article applies plan-testing methods developed in the study of Soviet planning to the First Five-Year Plan and concludes that the plan was not achievable. Alternative growth paths are also explored. The article contains three charts and five tables. It is extensively discussed in the following comments, all in the same issue of SLAVIC REVIEW: Campbell, Robert. "What Makes a Five-Year Plan Feasible?"; Cohen, Stephen F. "Stalin's Revolution Reconsidered"; Lewin, Moshe. "The Disappearance of Planning in the Plan"; and Hunter, Holland. "Reply."

_____. "The Planning of Investments in the Soviet Union." REVIEW OF ECONOMICS AND STATISTICS 31 (February 1949): 54-62.

This is an abbreviated translation of Khachaturov's analysis of the allocation of investment by equalizing the marginal net productivity of capital throughout the economy. It also relates the Soviet approach to familiar capitalist concepts and assesses proposals made and their feasibility.

_____. "Priorities and Shortfalls in Prewar Soviet Planning." In SOVIET PLANNING: ESSAYS IN HONOUR OF NAUM JASNY, edited by Jane Degras and Alec Nove, pp. 1-31. Oxford: Basil Blackwell, 1964.

The author examines Soviet planning during the prewar period and compares it to actual performance on a yearly basis. He focuses on whether the plan relaxed or intensified efforts for growth.

Iugov, A[ron]. RUSSIA'S ECONOMIC FRONT FOR WAR AND PEACE: AN APPRAISAL OF THE THREE FIVE-YEAR PLANS. Translated by N. I. and M. Stone. New York: Harper & Bros., 1942. ix, 279 p.

The Soviet economy during the first three five-year plans is discussed. The first chapter outlines the underlying ideas of the plans, and chapter 11 discusses state planning of the national economy. Other chapters survey industrialization, the reconstruction of agricultural economy, internal commerce and rationing of consumer goods, foreign trade, finance, geographical distribution of industry, labor, and standards of living.

Jasny, Naum. "A Close-up of the Soviet Fourth Five-Year Plan." QUARTERLY JOURNAL OF ECONOMICS 66 (May 1952): 139-71.

This paper examines the Fourth Five-Year Plan and discusses in detail prices and wages in the 1946-50 period. Specific attention is given to the price and wage basis of the Fourth Five-Year Plan. Three tables.

_____. "Plan and Superplan." In THE SOVIET ECONOMY: A COLLECTION OF WESTERN AND SOVIET VIEWS, edited by Harry G. Shaffer, pp. 90-105.

New York: Appleton-Century-Crofts, 1963.

>Jasny discusses the unrealistic goals set by the new general Twenty-Year Plan (1960-80). In this plan only a few figures are given, and they are given only in round numbers. The economic provisions have been incorporated into the program of the XXII Congress of the CPSU. The author includes a table of projected percentages of growth of some sectors of the economy for the Twenty-Year Plan.

──────. "The Secret 1941 Uzbek Economic Plan." SOVIET STUDIES 13 (April 1962): 407-13.

>This plan is contrasted with the all-Union plan. Two tables.

──────. "Soviet 'Perspective' Planning." In ESSAYS ON THE SOVIET ECONOMY, pp. 159-268. New York: Praeger, 1962.

>In this extensive study of Soviet planning and the five-year plans, the author discusses the stages of Soviet economic development and planning, as well as some of its major features. The general plan is reviewed along with some individual long-range plans (railway traction and electric power). Seven tables.

Kachaturov, T. S. "Long-Term Planning and Forecasting in the U.S.S.R." AMERICAN ECONOMIC REVIEW 62 (May 1972): 444-55.

>A distinguished member of the Soviet Academy of Sciences discusses the necessity of long-term planning in the Soviet Union and gives some optimistic estimates of the economic strides which the Soviet Union will make in the years to come.

Kaplan, Norman M. THE LAW OF VALUE AND SOVIET ECONOMIC PLANNING. Santa Monica, Calif.: RAND Corp., 1950. 30 p.

>The author argues (1) that the meaning of the proposition that the law of value operates in the Soviet economy is demonstrated by the fact that money, prices, and commodity relationships have been preserved; (2) these institutions must be preserved because there is heterogeneity of labor; and (3) there really is no conflict between the law of value and the law of planning.

Karmiloff, G. "Soviet Economic Models, Investment Criteria and Prices." KYKLOS 16 (1963): 83-109.

>This article discusses the use of input-output analysis in the USSR, methods and criteria used in making investment decisions, and the implications of all these analytical techniques. The author summarizes fundamental problems. The appendix sketches research projects that are underway.

Kaser, Michael [C.]. "Changes in Planning Methods During the Preparation of the Soviet Seven-Year Plan." SOVIET STUDIES 10 (April 1959): 321-38.

Economic Planning and Policy

Topics discussed here include the central planning mechanism; Gosplan and industrial planning; the system of supply and trade; construction planning; agricultural planning; transport planning; regional development and autarky; and ownership.

_____. "The Nature of Soviet Planning: A Critique of Jasny's Appraisal." SOVIET STUDIES 14 (October 1962): 109-31.

This article is a commentary on Naum Jasny's appraisal of Soviet planning in SOVIET INDUSTRIALIZATION 1928-1952. Chicago: University of Chicago Press, 1961. A table presents several net industrial output indexes.

_____. "Welfare Criteria in Soviet Planning." In SOVIET PLANNING: ESSAYS IN HONOUR OF NAUM JASNY, edited by Jane Degras and Alec Nove, pp. 144-72. Oxford: Basil Blackwell, 1964.

This essay analyzes the extent of awareness by Soviet planning officials and economists about the shortcomings of their theories and policies and describes the current lines of change. It examines the concept of welfare in the absence of consumer sovereignty and the Soviet criteria of "welfare" and "proportionality." Kaser also identifies Soviet techniques and failures in producing output-mixes in conformity with these criteria.

Kluck, Mary van. "Planning and Reconstruction." In U.S.S.R. IN RECONSTRUCTION, pp. 35-44. New York: American Russian Institute, 1944.

Kluck discusses the technological and scientific bases of Soviet planning, the three five-year plans, the restoration of coal mining in the Donbas region, and a 1943 plan for the reconstruction of the liberated areas.

Knickerbocker, Hubert R. THE SOVIET FIVE-YEAR PLAN AND ITS EFFECT ON WORLD TRADE. London: John Lane the Bodley Head, 1931. xx, 245 p. Illustrated.

The author, who was sent to Russia by the New York Evening Post, studied the industrial conditions under the Five-Year Plan and the potential repercussions of the plan on world trade. He explores the food situation; railroads; steel, chemical, and tractor plants; convict labor; Baku oil reserves; and production costs, bookkeeping, and financial problems.

Kohn, Martin J. "The Soviet Economy in 1961: Plan, Performance, and Priorities." In DIMENSIONS OF SOVIET ECONOMIC POWER, U.S. Congress. Joint Economic Committee, pp. 215-32. Washington, D.C.: Government Printing Office, 1962.

Economic Planning and Policy

This paper reveals changes in Soviet economic priorities by comparing the performance of the Soviet economy with the goals of the plan laid down before the year began. The data are based on statistics released by the Soviets.

Kuibyshev, Valerian V., et al. THE SECOND FIVE-YEAR PLAN. Moscow-Leningrad: Co-operative Publishing Society of Foreign Workers in the USSR, 1934. 126 p.

This Soviet economist outlines the "key tasks" of the Second Five-Year Plan; discusses the prospects for raising the standards of living; describes the decisive condition for fulfilling the plan; and examines regional development during the plan. The author cites Lenin and Stalin.

Kurskii, Aleksandr D. THE PLANNING OF THE NATIONAL ECONOMY OF THE U.S.S.R. Moscow: Foreign Languages Publishing House, 1949. 216 p.

The tasks of planning, the development of planning, the principles of plan construction, and efforts to fulfill the plan are considered.

Kuvshinov, I. S. " 'Planning Procedures': Union of Soviet Socialist Republics." In AGRICULTURE AND ITS TERMS OF TRADE, pp. 425-34. Proceedings of the Tenth International Conference of Agricultural Economists, Mysore, India 1958. London: Oxford University Press, 1960.

This Soviet economist states that plans are the major instruments which insure a well-balanced development of the Soviet national economy. He describes how the state determines the economic objectives in each part of the country and in each sector of the economy. In particular, the article deals with planning in the agricultural sector and the new system of planning in agriculture in 1955.

Lambert, Paul. "Planning in the U.S.S.R.: Signs of a Changeover from Rigid to Flexible Methods: Introduction." ANNALS OF PUBLIC AND CO-OPERATIVE ECONOMY 35 (October-December 1964): 276-78.

This is followed by V. Trapeznikov. "Towards a Flexible Economic Control of Undertakings." Lambert provides an introductory comment to the article by Trapnikov, which calls for extended use of material incentives in the Soviet economy so that managers, by acting in their own interests, further the interests of society as a whole.

Lange, Oskar. "Fundamentals of Economic Planning." In ESSAYS ON ECONOMIC PLANNING, pp. 1-32. Calcutta: Asia Publishing House, 1960.

General principles of economic planning as developed in the Soviet Union and in the People's Democracies are briefly explored. Lange attributes the methods and forms of economic planning to the particular historical situation of each country and the choice of a

Economic Planning and Policy

socialist road to development.

Leontief, Wassily W. "Soviet Planning: The Problem of Economic Balance." RUSSIAN REVIEW 6 (Autumn 1946): 26-36.

> This paper examines the first three five-year plans and compares the plans with the actual results. Two tables give planned and actual output of selected products for the plan periods and per capita production of selected products in 1937.

Levine, Herbert S. "The Centralized Planning of Supply in Soviet Industry." In COMPARISONS OF THE U.S. AND SOVIET ECONOMIES, U.S. Congress. Joint Economic Committee, pp. 151-76. Washington, D.C.: Government Printing Office, 1959.

> This paper deals with organizations in supply planning; the coverage of the supply plan; chronology of plan construction; material bases; weaknesses of supply planning; and mathematical methods and electronic computers. Two charts.

──────. "Pressure and Planning in the Soviet Economy." In INDUSTRIALIZATION IN TWO SYSTEMS: ESSAYS IN HONOR OF ALEXANDER GERSCHENKRON, edited by Henry Rosovsky. New York, London, Sydney: John Wiley & Sons, 1966. 289 p.

> In this paper Levine argues that pressure to fulfill the plan in the Soviet economy, rather than central planning itself, accounts for the nature of the economy.

──────. "Recent Developments in Soviet Planning." In DIMENSIONS OF SOVIET ECONOMIC POWER, U.S. Congress. Joint Economic Committee, pp. 49-65. Washington, D.C.: Government Printing Office, 1962.

> The author describes the May 1957 reorganization of the structure of Soviet industrial administration and planning and comments on the effects of these changes. He concludes that the Soviets will continue to experiment with various mathematical methods and that improvements in their planning system will result.

Lubimtsev, N. A. BASIC PRINCIPLES AND EXPERIENCE OF INDUSTRIAL DEVELOPMENT PLANNING IN THE SOVIET UNION. New York: United Nations, 1965. iv, 136 p.

> The author discusses (1) the development and organization of planning in the Soviet Union; (2) the planning of industrial production and geological surveys; (3) investment planning; (4) the planning of labor, manpower, and wages; (5) the planning of production costs and prices; and (6) the planning of material-supply and machinery.

Manove, Michael. "A Model of Soviet-Type Economic Planning." AMERICAN ECONOMIC REVIEW 61 (June 1971): 390-406.

A model of the material-supply planning procedure of the Autonomous Soviet Republic of Morozhevoe is used to demonstrate that, theoretically at least, the Soviet-type planning procedure can produce a consistent plan. The abstract procedure used in the article is demonstrated to be operationally equivalent to a succession of three kinds of iterations in which supply targets are tentatively set equal to estimates of demand. The usefulness of the iterative technique is increased by the fact that the effects of the iterations accumulate over time. The analysis is highly mathematical with an appendix containing the derivation of the solution of the model. For further comments, see: J. M. Montias. "A Model of Soviet-Type Economic Planning: Comment." AMERICAN ECONOMIC REVIEW 62 (September 1972): 685-88; and Michael Manove. "A Model of Soviet-Type Economic Planning: Reply." AMERICAN ECONOMIC REVIEW 62 (September 1972): 689-91.

Marshak, I. I. NEW RUSSIA'S PRIMER: THE STORY OF THE FIVE-YEAR PLAN. Translated by G. S. Counts and N. P. Lodge. Boston: Houghton Mifflin, 1931. xii, 162 p.

This book is a translation of a Russian text designed for children twelve to fourteen years old. It acquaints Soviet students with the Five-Year Plan. The book presents a clear account of the major provisions of the Five-Year Plan and can be readily understood by the general reader.

Meyendorff, A[lexander]. F. "Some Notes on the Five Year Plan." SLAVONIC REVIEW 9 (June 1930): 22-28.

This article collates "some of the more important facts relating to the execution of the Five-Year Plan by the various departments and subdivisions of production."

Miller, Jacob. "The 1941 Economic Plan: A Confidential Administrative Document." SOVIET STUDIES 3 (April 1952): 365-86.

This article is a description of the 1941 plan, not as intended for publication but for confidential use by administration. Two tables.

———. "Soviet Planners in 1936-37." In SOVIET PLANNING: ESSAYS IN HONOUR OF NAUM JASNY, edited by Jane Degras and Alec Nove, pp. 116-43. Oxford: Basil Blackwell, 1964.

This essay attempts to convey a picture of the people who staff the planning offices of Gosplan. The author worked and studied at the Economic Research Institute of Gosplan during 1936 and 1937 and some of the information is based on interviews of department heads and assistants of Gosplan.

———. "Soviet Planning Organisations." SLAVONIC REVIEW 14 (April 1938): 586-600.

This article analyzes two parts of the Soviet planning system: horizontal planning--the planning of each administrative area of the country; and vertical planning--planning economic activity by individual industries.

_____, ed. "The Planning of Industry and Investment." SOVIET STUDIES 3 (April 1952): 341-58.

This article consists of partial translations of the following: B. Miroshnichenko. "The Planning of Industrial Production." PLANOVOYE KHOZYAISTVO 3 (1951): 82-91; B. Smekhov. "The Planning of Capital Works." PLANOVOYE KHOZYAISTVO 4 (1951): 82-90.

Miller, Margaret S. "The Planning System in Soviet Russia." SLAVONIC REVIEW 9 (December 1930): 449-56.

Miller surveys the structure of the planning system to determine whether it is superior to capitalist methods as "justified by present achievements and future possibilities."

Molotov, V. M. THE FULFILMENT OF THE FIRST FIVE YEAR PLAN. New York: International Pamphlets, 1932? 88 p.

This pamphlet contains two speeches by V. M. Molotov, chairman of the Council of People's Commissars, which deal with the accomplishments of the Five-Year Plan up to 1931 and an outline of the national economic plan for 1932.

_____. SECOND FIVE-YEAR PLAN. Moscow: Co-operative Publishing Society of Foreign Workers in the USSR, 1932. 80 p.

This Communist party leader gives a brief account of the successes of the First Five-Year Plan, along with the goals of the Second Five-Year Plan.

_____. SUCCESS OF THE FIVE-YEAR PLAN. London: Modern Books, 1931. 77 p.

This book contains two speeches by Molotov, chairman of the Council of People's Commissars, which were delivered before the sixth All-Union Soviet Congress in 1931. He speaks on the progress of the First Five-Year Plan during the first two years.

_____. TASKS OF THE SECOND FIVE-YEAR PLAN. Moscow: Co-operative Publishing Society of Foreign Workers in the USSR, 1934. 141 p.

This pamphlet contains the amended, or revised, goals of the Second Five-Year Plan as put forth by Molotov and Kuibyshev.

Economic Planning and Policy

Montias, J[ohn]. M. "An Additional Note on Iterative Procedures Used in Planning Material Balances." BULLETIN OF THE ASSOCIATION FOR THE STUDY OF SOVIET-TYPE ECONOMIES 3 (November 1960): 12-20.

   The first part of this note is a clarification of some points in the author's article "Planning with Material Balance in Soviet-Type Economies." AMERICAN ECONOMIC REVIEW 49 (December 1959): 963-85. In the second part additional evidence on the relation of the model to actual planning procedures is presented.

_____. "Planning with Material Balance in Soviet-Type Economies." AMERICAN ECONOMIC REVIEW 49 (December 1959): 963-85.

   This paper is confined to technical aspects of drawing up a consistent set of interlocking balances of material resources, an important part of overall Soviet economic planning. Topics covered include the administrative framework, theoretical models of administrative planning, a comparison of the models with actual planning methods, and discussion of the chief obstacles to accurate planning with material balances.

Moravcik, I[vo]. "The Marxian Model of Growth and the 'General Plan' of Soviet Economic Development." KYKLOS 14 (1961): 548-71.

   This paper discusses the derivation of the general Soviet planning model from Marx's model of expanded reproduction, the ensuing problems of unrealistic targets, and the failure to heed the warnings from within the Soviet Union that the targets were unrealistic. The paper deals chiefly with the 1920s.

_____. "The Priority of Heavy Industry as an Objective of Soviet Economic Policy." SOVIET STUDIES 17 (October 1965): 245-51.

   The Marxist theoretical basis for this priority is discussed.

Morozov, Petr Tarasovich. FUNDAMENTALS OF ECONOMIC PLANNING. Translated by Ivanov-Mumjiev. Moscow: Progress Publishers, 1966. 158 p.

   This Soviet work discusses the following topics: (1) prerequisites and organization of economic planning; (2) planning of industrial production, agricultural output, investments, increase in labor productivity; (3) higher living and cultural standards; and (4) production costs.

Mueller, Charles E. "Antitrust and Centralization: A Look at the 'Planned' Economy." In ECONOMIC CONCENTRATION, pp. 4371-86. Washington, D.C.: Government Printing Office, 1969.

   This article examines the history of Soviet economic policy. Topics covered include the peasantry, the "scissors crisis," the decline in growth, the new Soviet economics, and economic competition in the Soviet Union. It concludes that Soviet policy-makers are moving toward decentralization and "administered competition."

Narkiewicz, O[lga]. A. "Stalin, War Communism and Collectivization." SOVIET STUDIES 18 (July 1966): 20-37.

This paper discusses the effect of war communism on later Stalinist policies, collectivation, and grain procurements. A table reports degrees of collectivation of various districts by December 15, 1929.

Nemchinov, V. S. "The Use of Statistical and Mathematical Methods in Soviet Planning." In STRUCTURAL INTERDEPENDENCE AND ECONOMIC DEVELOPMENT, by Tibor Barna et al., pp. 171-88. Proceedings of the Third International Conference on Input-Output Techniques, Geneva 1961. New York: St. Martin's Press, 1963.

In this technical discussion of the statistical and mathematical methods used in the planning of the Soviet national economy, some mathematical models of the planned economy are included.

Noren, James H., and Whitehouse, F. Douglas. "Soviet Industry in the 1971-75 Plan." In SOVIET ECONOMIC PROSPECTS FOR THE SEVENTIES, U.S. Congress. Joint Economic Committee, pp. 206-45. Washington, D.C.: Government Printing Office, 1973.

Topics discussed include the five-year plans in general, the 1971-75 plan for industry, consistency, feasibility, productivity plans, regional aspects, plans for particular branches of industry, policy implications, and progress toward the plan goals. Tables.

Nove, Alec. "The Industrial Planning System: Reforms in Prospect." SOVIET STUDIES 14 (July 1962): 1-15.

Nove seeks to analyze the weak spots (of the sovnarkhoz reform of 1957) and assess their importance.

_____. "Planners' Performance, Priorities and Reforms." ECONOMIC JOURNAL 76 (June 1966): 267-77.

Practical issues being debated in the Soviet Union in the course of the search for new and more efficient forms of managing the economy are examined. Topics discussed include planners' preferences, consumers' preferences, and the Liberman reforms.

_____. "Towards a Theory of Planning." In SOVIET PLANNING: ESSAYS IN HONOUR OF NAUM JASNY, edited by Jane Degras and Alec Nove, pp. 193-204. Oxford: Basil Blackwell, 1964.

The law of planned (proportional) development, said to be an economic law valid in the USSR, is examined critically.

Obolensky-Ossinsky, V. O., et al. SOCIAL ECONOMIC PLANNING IN THE UNION OF SOVIET SOCIALIST REPUBLICS. Report of a Delegation from the U.S.S.R. to the World Social Economic Congress, Amsterdam, August 1931. New York: International Industrial Relations Association, 1932. 126 p.

    Four papers concern the planned economy: "The Premises, Nature and Forms of Social-Economic Planning," by V. O. Obolensky-Ossinsky; "The Plan in Action," by S. L. Ronin; "The Planning and Development of Agriculture in the USSR," by A. Gayster; and "Labour in the Planned Economy of the USSR," by I. A. Kraval.

Paquet, Gilles. "The Structuration of a Planned Economy." CANADIAN SLAVONIC PAPERS 8 (1966): 250-59.

    The work done by Eugene Zaleski, particularly in the last decade, is examined. Attention is given to his book, PLANIFICATION DE LA CROISSANCE ET FLUCTUATIONS ECONOMIQUES EN U.R.S.S. TOME I: 1918-32. Paris: Societe d'edition d'enseignement superieur, 1962.

Preece, P. F. W. "The Priority Given to Heavy Industry in Socialist Economic Planning." SCIENCE AND SOCIETY 32 (Summer 1968): 288-99.

    Preece sets up a simple three-sector model of the economy to investigate the effects of giving different degrees of priority to the machine-tool sector or the growth of output of consumption goods. Applications to the Soviet Union are discussed.

Prociuk, Stephan G. "Russian Intervention in Early Ukrainian Planning." SOVIET STUDIES 15 (April 1964): 443-58.

    The development of the organizational structure of Ukrainian industry, 1917-21, is traced.

Prokopovich, Sergius. "The Crisis of the Five-Year Plan." SLAVONIC REVIEW 10 (December 1931): 317-27.

    The results of production in 1931 are compared with the estimates mapped out in the plan for 1931. The article also discusses how the discrepancy has affected the accumulation of national capital.

Pshelyaskovskiy, V. I. "Elements of the Theory of Growth in Lenin's Plan for the Electrification of Russia." MATEKON 6 (Fall 1969): 98-118.

    This paper translates the GOELRO plan for the electrification of Russia into mathematical terms.

Richman, B[arry]. M. "Formulation of Enterprise Operating Plans in Soviet Industry." SOVIET STUDIES 15 (July 1963): 48-71.

    Aspects discussed include the structure of industrial planning, enterprise authority with regard to the enterprise plan, and the procedures of annual plan formulation. The appendix lists the base plan indexes used in several plans.

Roberts, Paul C. "War Communism: A Re-examination." SLAVIC REVIEW 29 (June 1970): 238-61.

This article investigates the historical and political roots of war communism and argues that the policies of that period were not merely temporary expedients.

Ronimois, Hans E. SOVIET PLANNING AND ECONOMIC THEORY. Vancouver: University of British Columbia, 1950. 337 p.

This work discusses the economic problems of the Soviet economy; Soviet allocation of capital; the Soviet exchange economy; industrial production; capital formation; money; personal income; and price determination. Graphs and tables.

Schlesinger, Rudolf. "A Note on the Context of Early Soviet Planning." SOVIET STUDIES 16 (July 1964): 22-44.

Topics considered include the impact of Soviet economists on planning theory in the 1920s and the timing of the decision in favor of the first plan. For further discussion see: Herbert J. Ellison. "Comment on 'The Concept of Early Soviet Planning.'" SOVIET STUDIES 16 (January 1965): 326-27; Schlesinger's reply follows, pp. 327-29. Also see: J. L. H. Keep. "Comment on 'The Context of Early Soviet Planning.'" SOVIET STUDIES 16 (April 1965): 467-70.

Schroeder, Gertrude E. "Recent Developments in Soviet Planning and Incentives." In SOVIET ECONOMIC PROSPECTS FOR THE SEVENTIES, U.S. Congress. Joint Economic Committee, pp. 11-38. Washington, D.C.: Government Printing Office, 1973.

This paper focuses on changes in planning methods in relation to the Ninth Five-Year Plan and changes in incentive arrangements introduced with the current Five-Year Plan.

Sherman, Howard J. "Marxist Economics and Soviet Planning." SOVIET STUDIES 18 (October 1966): 169-88.

Conflict between Marxist theory and modern planning theories and practices is explored.

_____. "The 'Revolution' in Soviet Economics." In SOCIAL THOUGHT IN THE SOVIET UNION, edited by Alex Simirenko, pp. 222-68. Chicago: Quadrangle Books, 1969.

This article concentrates on three interrelated debates on planning: growth strategies; achievement of balance and full employment; and optimal planning or programming.

Smolinski, Leon. "Grinevetskii and Soviet Industrialization." SURVEY 64 (April 1968): 100-15.

This paper asserts that V. Grinevetskii drew up the first long-term economic plan for Russia and published it in 1919 in THE POST-WAR OUTLOOK FOR RUSSIAN INDUSTRY. Aspects of this plan are discussed.

──────. "Planning Without Theory, 1917-1967." SURVEY 64 (July 1967): 108-28.

This paper sees the history of Soviet planning as one of pragmatic solving of problems rather than the application of theory to design the planning system.

──────. "What Next in Soviet Planning?" In THE SOVIET ECONOMY; A BOOK OF READINGS, edited by Morris Bornstein and Daniel Fusfeld, pp. 329-38. Rev. ed. Homewood, Ill.: R. D. Irwin, 1966.

This article analyzes the information problems in Soviet planning and changes proposed to overcome them.

Smolinski, Leon, and Wiles, Peter J.D. "The Soviet Planning Pendulum." PROBLEMS OF COMMUNISM 12 (November-December 1963): 21-34.

This article discusses the increasing complexity of planning, reformers versus bureaucrats, differences in the degree of centralization, and the creation of sovnarkhozes in 1957.

SOVIET SEVEN-YEAR PLAN, 1959-1965. London: Todd Reference Books, 1959. 248 p.

Topics discussed include the plan in general, foreign trade, technical progress, science, Eastern Siberia, management, and agriculture.

Stalin, Joseph. "Industrialization of the Country and the Right Deviation in the CPSU." In WORKS, vol. 2, pp. 256-66. Moscow: Foreign Languages Publishing House, 1964.

This speech, presented at the Plenum of the Central Committee on November 19, 1928, is concerned with the First Five-Year Plan.

Stolte, Stefan C. "The Soviet Plan to Overtake the Economy of the United States." STUDIES ON THE SOVIET UNION n.s. 2 (September 1959): 34-51.

This paper considers Khrushchev's ambitious program to overtake the U.S. economy, the great efforts which would be needed to accomplish this aim, and the consequences for Russia's COMECON trading partners in Eastern Europe. Tables.

Economic Planning and Policy

Strumilin, Stanislav G[ustavovich]. PLANNING IN THE SOVIET UNION. Soviet News Booklet, no. 17. London: Soviet News, 1957. 55 p.

> A Soviet economist discusses the organization and methodology of planning.

Thornton, Judith [G.]. "Differential Capital Changes and Resource Allocation in Soviet Industry." JOURNAL OF POLITICAL ECONOMY 79 (May-June 1971) 545-61.

> Estimates are made of the magnitude of the output loss that can be attributed to differential capital charges in Soviet industry. Three tables and a graph.

──────. "The New Soviet Two-Year Plan." SLAVIC REVIEW 23 (September 1964): 537-62.

> This paper is concerned with the Two-Year Plan for 1964-65, which superseded the Seven-Year Plan. It discusses the reasons for the interim plan, the implied changes in national economic goals, and the prospects and problems of the new plan. Statistical appendix.

Turin, S. P. "The Second Five-Year Plan." SLAVONIC REVIEW 11 (July 1932): 58-64.

> Turin notes the Party's attitude toward the "success" of the First Five-Year Plan and demonstrates the actual condition of industry as described by heads of different branches of industry.

Volin, Lazar. "Khrushchev's Economic Neo-Stalinism." AMERICAN SLAVIC AND EAST EUROPEAN REVIEW 14 (1955): 445-64.

> This article surveys the economic policies and political tactics used by Soviet leaders. The emphasis is on Khrushchev and the agricultural sector.

──────. "The Malenkov-Khrushchev New Economic Policy." JOURNAL OF POLITICAL ECONOMY 62 (June 1954): 187-209.

> Changes made in Soviet economic policy with the end of the Stalin epoch are considered. Five tables provide figures on production and production goals for selected products, sown area, and numbers of livestock. Volin's correction to this article may be found in JOURNAL OF POLITICAL ECONOMY 62 (December 1954): 538.

Voznesenski, Nikolai A. FIVE-YEAR PLAN FOR THE REHABILITATION OF THE NATIONAL ECONOMY OF THE USSR, 1946-50. London: Soviet News, 1946. 39 p.

> This is a translation of a report made at the first session of the Supreme Soviet of the USSR on March 15, 1946.

Economic Planning and Policy

Vvedensky, George. "The New Five-Year Plan." STUDIES ON THE SOVIET UNION n.s. 6, no. 1 (1966): 20-25.

    This is a discussion of the plan for 1966-70. Two tables present figures on output of selected commodities in the USSR and United States in 1965 and planned Soviet output in 1961 and 1970.

──────. "The Political Significance and the Immediate Goals of the New Soviet Seven-Year Plan." STUDIES ON THE SOVIET UNION n.s. 4, no. 4 (1965): 141-42.

    This short paper notes the lower output targets in this plan as compared to the Five-Year Plan which it replaced.

──────. "The Twenty-Year Plan for Soviet Heavy Industry." STUDIES ON THE SOVIET UNION n.s. 2, no. 4 (1963): 35-49.

    This article is a study of the long-term Soviet plan for 1961-80. Two tables compare actual (1960 and 1961) with planned (1970 and 1980) production for selected commodities and compare U.S. and Soviet cement production for selected years between 1940-62.

Weitzman, Phillip. "Soviet Long-Term Consumption Planning: Distribution According to Rational Need." SOVIET STUDIES 26 (July 1974): 305-21.

    Long-term planning for nutritional needs, clothing requirements, and services and consumer durables are discussed. Six tables.

Wootton, Barbara. PLAN OR NO PLAN. New York: Farrar & Rinehart, 1935. 360 p.

    Of particular interest is chapter 2, "The Nature of the Russian Planned Economy." Index.

Zaleski, Eugene. PLANNING FOR ECONOMIC GROWTH IN THE SOVIET UNION, 1918-1932. Translated and edited by Marie-Christine MacAndrew and G. Warren Nutter. Chapel Hill: University of North Carolina Press, 1971. xxxviii, 425 p.

    This study deals with the goals and fulfillment of the First Five-Year Plan (1928-32) and the goals of the Second Five-Year Plan (1933-37). Soviet planning is studied through analysis of the revisions of the plan, the system of priorities and the first attempts at coordination, the annual plans, and the emergency measures. Seventy-seven tables and fifteen charts.

──────. "Planning for Industrial Growth." STUDIES ON THE SOVIET UNION n.s. 6, no. 4 (1967): 55-77.

    Types of planning discussed here include flexible, integral, and administrative. Reform proposals are also discussed. Three tables.

Zauberman, Alfred. "New Winds in Soviet Planning." SOVIET STUDIES 12 (July 1960): 1-13.

This article focuses on two Soviet works: L. V. Kantorovich, EKONOMICHESKI RASCHET NAILUCHAHEVO ISPOLZOVANIYA RESURSOV [Economic calculation of the best use of resources]. Moscow: Akademiia Nauk, 1959 and V. S. Nemchinov, ed. PRIMENENIYE MATEMATIKI V EKONOMICHESKIKH ISSLEDOVANIYAKH [Application of mathematics in economic investigations]. Moscow: Sotsal' no-Ekonomicheskaia Leteratyra, 1959. A short postscript reports on a discussion of Kantorovich's book in a Soviet periodical.

⎯⎯⎯⎯. "Recent Developments in Soviet Planning Techniques." ECONOMIA INTERNAZIONALE 20 (May 1967): 255-74.

This article reviews the development of important tools of Soviet planning, including "the balance-approach" and "variant approximation."

Chapter 6

WAR, DEFENSE, AND THE RUSSIAN ECONOMY

THE PERIOD 1860-1917

Apostol, P. N. "Credit Operations of the Russian Government during the War." In RUSSIAN PUBLIC FINANCE DURING THE WAR, pp. 233-333. New Haven, Conn.: Yale University Press, 1928.

> In the introductory chapter the author discusses the government debt, the development of an investment market, and conditions for war loans in Russia prior to World War I. The remaining chapters survey domestic loans and foreign credits opened to Russia during the war from France, Britain, the United States, Japan, and Italy. The author comments on the total Russian government debt and credit operations during the war.

Bernatsky, M. W. "Monetary Policy of the Russian Government." In RUSSIAN PUBLIC FINANCE DURING THE WAR, pp. 337-456. New Haven, Conn.: Yale University Press, 1928.

> Bernatsky covers the following: (1) Russian transition to a gold standard and the state of the currency on the eve of the war; (2) changes in the currency system caused by the war; (3) inflation and government measures to combat it; and (4) the Russian gold reserve.

Kadomtsev, Boris. THE RUSSIAN COLLAPSE: A POLITICO-ECONOMIC ESSAY. New York: Russian Mercantile and Industrial Corp., 1919. 63 p.

> The author outlines economic disintegration in Russia during the war, the Bolshevik Revolution, and Bolshevik rule.

Kohn, Stanislav, and Meyendorff, Alexander F. THE COST OF THE WAR TO RUSSIA. New Haven, Conn.: Yale University Press, 1932. xv, 219 p.

> Kohn wrote part one: "The Vital Statistics of European Russia during the World War, 1914-1917." Meyendorff wrote part two: "Social Cost of the War." Kohn discusses the physical influences

of the war on Russian society and Meyendorff outlines the war's effects on the peasantry, industrial labor, and investments. Index.

Nol'de, Boris E. RUSSIA IN THE ECONOMIC WAR. New Haven, Conn.: Yale University Press, 1928. xvi, 232 p.

Topics discussed include Russia in the economic war of 1914-17, the blockade of Russia, the embargo and tariff war, treatment of enemy property within the Russian Empire, financial blockade, foreign trade, and Russia at the Paris Economic Conference of 1916. Index.

Nordman, N. PEACE PROBLEMS: RUSSIA'S ECONOMICS. London: Putney Press, 1919. xiii, 127 p.

This four-part book analyzes Russian economics during World War I. Part one outlines the prewar economic conditions. Part two explains the war's influence on the Russian economy. Parts three and four deal with the Revolution and the economic aims of the Bolsheviks.

Raffalovich, Arthur. "Some Effects of the War on the Economic Life of Russia." ECONOMIC JOURNAL 27 (March 1917): 103-9.

The article surveys problems of the Russian economy during World War I. The emphasis is on war materials and consumer goods.

Struve, Peter B., ed. FOOD SUPPLY IN RUSSIA DURING THE WORLD WAR. New Haven, Conn.: Yale University Press, 1930. xxviii, 469 p.

In this detailed study of food supply in Russia during World War I, part one: "Organization and Policy," is authored by K. I. Zaitsev and N. V. Dolensky. Part two: "Food Prices and the Market in Foodstuffs," is by S. S. Demosthenov. Index.

Zagorskii, S. O. STATE CONTROL OF INDUSTRY IN RUSSIA DURING THE WAR. New Haven, Conn.: Yale University Press, 1928. xix, 351 p.

Aspects of the Russian economy during World War I discussed here include the influence of the war, the organization of resources, forms and methods of control, and policy after the Revolution of March 1917. Tables and index.

THE PERIOD AFTER 1917

Alexandorva, Vera. "The Revival of Liberated Cities in the Soviet Union." RUSSIAN REVIEW 4 (Spring 1945): 62-71.

This paper uses eyewitness quotes to show the degree of damage done by the war and discusses plans for rebuilding.

War, Defense, and Russian Economy

Allen, Robert L[oring]. SOVIET ECONOMIC WARFARE. Washington, D.C.: Public Affairs Press, 1960. x, 293 p.

Topics discussed include economic warfare; state trading; economic motivation; political goals; Soviet capabilities; commercial policy; credit; and policies in various regions of the world. Statistical appendices, bibliography, and index.

Baykov, Alexander M. "Internal Trade During the War and Its Post-War Development." BULLETINS ON SOVIET ECONOMIC DEVELOPMENT 4 (September 1950): 1-9.

Internal trade in the Soviet Union during the war was mobilized along the lines followed during peace-time rationing (1929-35) so that scarce goods could be distributed to facilitate rapid industrialization. However, after the war, the Soviets had to abolish rationing as soon as possible because of its undesirable effects on trade and production. Tables list prices of some goods and reductions of prices in 1949.

──────. "Russia's Economic Losses." OXFORD UNIVERSITY. INSTITUTE OF ECONOMICS AND STATISTICS. BULLETIN 4 (September 1942): 245-47.

This is a brief summary of the economic significance of the geographic area the Soviet Union lost to Axis armies in World War II up to 1942.

Becker, Abraham S. SOVIET MILITARY OUTLAYS SINCE 1955. Santa Monica, Calif.: RAND Corp., 1964. xiii, 106 p.

This report is concerned with the growth of Soviet military outlays since 1955 during the period of the Seven-Year Plan. It critically reviews what is and is not known from open sources about Soviet military outlays. Tables and graphs.

Block, Herbert. "Value and Burden of Soviet Defense." In SOVIET ECONOMIC PROSPECTS FOR THE SEVENTIES, U.S. Congress. Joint Economic Committee, pp. 175-204. Washington, D.C.: Government Printing Office, 1973.

Topics covered include plan failures; the Soviet Defense Ministry budget; official Soviet data on "science" outlays; defense as a share of the budget and national income; Western estimates of Soviet defense outlays; and Soviet defense priorities and prospects. A table provides annual data on Soviet defense and space expenditures, 1960-73.

Boretsky, Michael. "The Technological Base of Soviet Military Power." In ECONOMIC PERFORMANCE AND THE MILITARY BURDEN IN THE SOVIET UNION, U.S. Congress. Joint Economic Committee, pp. 189-231. Washington, D.C.: Government Printing Office, 1970.

Topics discussed include the output of machinery-producing industries, the technological base of Soviet military power, and the problem of quality. Seven tables.

Brubaker, Earl R. "The Opportunity Costs of Soviet Military Conscripts." In SOVIET ECONOMIC PROSPECTS FOR THE SEVENTIES, U.S. Congress. Joint Economic Committee, pp. 163-74. Washington, D.C.: Government Printing Office, 1973.

This work discusses the disparity between money and real Soviet manpower costs; numbers of draft-eligible personnel; payments to conscripts; value of conscripts' income; civilian opportunity costs; attributes of conscripts; distribution of civilian wages; and foregone earnings of conscripts. Seven tables.

Carter, Edward C. "Russian War Relief." SLAVONIC AND EAST EUROPEAN REVIEW 22 (August 1944): 61-74.

This general discussion covers the quantity, nature, and significance of U.S. aid to Russia during the Second World War.

Cohn, Stanley H. "Economic Burden of Defense Expenditure." In SOVIET ECONOMIC PROSPECTS FOR THE SEVENTIES, U.S. Congress. Joint Economic Committee, pp. 147-62. Washington, D.C.: Government Printing Office, 1973.

This paper discusses the concept of opportunity cost; defense expenditure time series; defense and the composition of GNP; an econometric estimate of defense opportunity cost; input-output structure; and sectoral distribution of high quality human inputs. Tables.

_____. "The Economic Burden of Soviet Defense Outlays." In ECONOMIC PERFORMANCE AND THE MILITARY BURDEN IN THE SOVIET UNION, U.S. Congress. Joint Economic Committee, pp. 166-88. Washington, D.C.: Government Printing Office, 1970.

This study evaluates, in quantitative fashion, the economic impact of trends in Soviet defense expenditures since 1950. Many tables.

Colm, Gerhard, and Darmstadter, Joel. "Evaluation of the Soviet Economic Threat." In COMPARISONS OF THE U.S. AND SOVIET ECONOMIES, U.S. Congress. Joint Economic Committee, pp. 529-43. Washington, D.C.: Government Printing Office, 1959.

This paper summarizes U.S.-Soviet economic growth, the so-called Soviet economic offensive, and future economic threat. Tables.

"Conditions in the Baltic Republics and White Russia under German Occupation: Economic and Labour Measures in 1941-1942." INTERNATIONAL LABOUR REVIEW 49 (February 1944): 171-90.

This article uses available legal texts to describe changes made by
the Germans in the economic and social structure of the region.
The information came entirely from official German sources and
therefore reflects the German point-of-view.

Dobb, Maurice H. "Post-War Economic Prospects in the U.S.S.R." OXFORD
UNIVERSITY. INSTITUTE OF ECONOMICS AND STATISTICS. BULLETIN 8
(June 1946): 190-98.

This article summarizes the prewar position, the effects of the war,
the problems of restoration, and the significance of the Five-Year
Plan.

_____. SOVIET ECONOMY AND THE WAR. New York: International Publishers, 1943. 99 p.

In the first part the author summarizes the first three five-year
plans. The second section is concerned with the war potential of
the USSR, the location of industry, collective farms, the role of
trade unions, and the plan and the budget.

_____. SOVIET PLANNING AND LABOUR IN PEACE AND WAR. London:
Routledge & Sons, 1942. 126 p.

Dobb is concerned primarily with the presentation of essential facts
and not with theoretical generalizations. Planning, the financial
system, work and wages, and the economic effects of the war are
surveyed.

_____. "Soviet Post-War Reconstruction." SCIENCE AND SOCIETY 15 (Spring
1951): 122-28.

This paper reviews plans for reconstruction and discusses the reconstruction already accomplished. A short table provides figures of
1949 estimated output and 1950 planned output for coal, steel, and
grain.

Godaire, J. M. "The Claim of the Soviet Military Establishment." "In DIMENSIONS OF SOVIET ECONOMIC POWER, U.S. Congress. Joint Economic
Committee, pp. 35-46. Washington, D.C.: Government Printing Office, 1962.

Godaire examines Soviet defense and space systems procurement
during the 1950s and includes graphs which represent both "published" and "possible" levels of Soviet military expenditure for the
twelve-year period (1950-62). He notes that when military expenditures have increased, Soviet overall economic growth has
decelerated.

Grajdanzev, A. "Labor in the Post-War Reconstruction of the Soviet Union."
In U.S.S.R. IN RECONSTRUCTION, pp. 126-35. New York: American
Russian Institute, 1944.

In discussing the problem of labor the author notes the size of the population; the status of women; the training of workers in factories; the establishment of special labor schools; and the Soviet school system.

──────. "Soviet Public Finances on the Eve of the War." SLAVONIC AND EAST EUROPEAN REVIEW 21 (March 1943): 89-95.

This article uses the Soviet Union's budget as approved in 1941 as a guide to how the financing of Soviet involvement in World War II would be met. Tables provide data on growth of the Soviet budget, expenditures, changes in important budget items, expenditures directly related to the economy, and revenue.

Gregory, Paul R. "Economic Growth, U.S. Defence Expenditures and the Soviet Defence Budget: A Suggested Model." SOVIET STUDIES 26 (January 1974): 72-80.

Gregory offers a model of Soviet defense expenditures and tests it. For further discussion, see: Franz Walter. "Once More: Economic Growth, U.S. Defence Expenditures and the Soviet Defence Budget." SOVIET STUDIES 26 (July 1974): 441-45.

Grossman, Gregory. "Steel, Planning, and War Preparation in the USSR." EXPLORATIONS IN ENTREPRENEURIAL HISTORY 9 (April 1957): 231-38.

This is ostensibly a review of M. Gardner Clark. THE ECONOMICS OF SOVIET STEEL. Cambridge, Mass.: Harvard University Press, 1956. The article does, however, provide much information and touches on the works of other authors. The tables include "Industrial Production in the USSR, 1936-1940"; "Economic Indicators of Military Preparations in the USSR, 1934-1941"; and "Indicators of Construction Activity, USSR, 1934-1940."

Haensel, Paul [P.]. "Soviet Finance." OPENBARE FINANCIEN 1, no. 1 (1946): 38-51.

This paper reviews Soviet taxes and government expenditures in the early years of World War II. Two tables.

Harvey, Mose L., and Ruggles, Melville J. "The Eastward Course of Soviet Industry and the War." RUSSIAN REVIEW 1 (April 1942): 10-26.

This paper surveys Soviet efforts to locate industry in the East before the war and discusses possibilities for a further eastward shift of industry during the war. A table compares output of selected commodities in the East with total Soviet output.

──────. "Lend-Lease to Russia. A Story That Needs to Be Told Like It Was." RUSSIAN REVIEW 29 (January 1970): 81-86.

This article reviews two books: Jones, Robert Huhn. THE ROADS TO RUSSIA: UNITED STATES LEND-LEASE TO THE SOVIET UNION. Norman: University of Oklahoma Press, 1969; and Kimball, Warren F. THE MOST UNSORDID ACT: LEND-LEASE, 1939-1941. Baltimore: Johns Hopkins University Press, 1969.

Kazakevich, Vladimir D. "Financing War and Reconstruction." In U.S.S.R. IN RECONSTRUCTION, pp. 136-54. New York: American Russian Institute, 1944.

The author gives an elementary account of the distinguishing features of Soviet finance.

Kerner, Robert J., ed. U.S.S.R. ECONOMY AND THE WAR. New York: Russian Economic Institute, 1943. 110 p.

In this book several papers consider various aspects of the Soviet economy and their relation to the war effort. The individual papers are annotated elsewhere and are listed under the appropriate subject sections.

Kershaw, Joseph A. "The Economic War Potential of the USSR." AMERICAN ECONOMIC REVIEW 41 (May 1951): 475-82.

This paper considers conceptual problems of economic war potential, compares Soviet economic war potential to that of the United States, and discusses problems of precise measurements. For further discussion, see: E. D. Domar et al. "The Economy of the Soviet Union--Discussion." AMERICAN ECONOMIC REVIEW 41 (May 1951): 483-94.

Mandel, William [M.]. "Wartime Changes in Soviet Industry." In U.S.S.R. IN RECONSTRUCTION, pp. 83-97. New York: American Russian Institute, 1944.

This article summarizes the relocation of industry during the Nazi invasion, the reconstruction of industries destroyed by the Germans, improvements in the functioning of industry, the reconstruction of railroads, and the Fifteen-Year Plan for after the war.

Milstein, Jeffrey. "Soviet and American Influences on the Arab-Israeli Arms Race: A Quantitative Analysis." PEACE RESEARCH SOCIETY INTERNATIONAL PAPERS 15 (June 1970): 6-27.

This article includes a regression analysis of U.S. and Soviet trade and aid on Arab-Israeli arms expenditures. Tables.

Ofer, Gur. "The Economic Burden of Soviet Involvement in the Middle East." SOVIET STUDIES 24 (January 1973): 329-47.

Ofur concentrates on the economic burden of military aid to the Middle East and compares it with the corresponding burden on the

United States. Four tables.

Pasvolsky, Leo, and Moulton, Harold G. RUSSIAN DEBTS AND RUSSIAN RECONSTRUCTION: A STUDY OF THE RELATION OF RUSSIA'S FOREIGN DEBTS TO HER ECONOMIC RECOVERY. New York: McGraw-Hill, 1924. xiii, 247 p.

> This book studies investment credit analysis, a problem in public finance. It analyzes Russia's capacity to meet both war and prewar debts.

Pethybridge, R. W. "The Bolsheviks and Technical Disorder, 1917-1918." SLAVONIC AND EAST EUROPEAN REVIEW 49 (July 1971): 410-24.

> This paper discusses the breakdown of communications, transport, and production in Russia after the Revolution.

Reitz, J. T. "Soviet Defense-Associated Activities Outside the Ministry of Defense." In ECONOMIC PERFORMANCE AND THE MILITARY BURDEN IN THE SOVIET UNION, U.S. Congress. Joint Economic Committee, pp. 133-65. Washington, D.C.: Government Printing Office, 1970.

> Topics discussed include KGB and MVD troops, police and firefighters of the MVD, Soviet transport enterprises, and counterintelligence and security activities of the KGB.

Schwartz, Harry. "Prices in the Soviet War Economy." AMERICAN ECONOMIC REVIEW 4 (December 1946): 872-82.

> Soviet price behavior during World War II is considered. The author's findings are based on fragmentary available materials. The article includes tables on (1) ration and free-market prices for certain foods, 1942-44; (2) commercial store food prices, 1944-46; and (3) reductions in prices of unrationed goods, 1946.

_____. RUSSIA'S POST-WAR ECONOMY. Syracuse, N.Y.: Syracuse University Press, 1947. 119 p.

> Schwartz describes various spheres of the postwar Soviet economy, including industrial expansion; transportation reconstruction; the catastrophe in agriculture; the Soviet labor force; international economic relations; and Soviet economic strength.

_____. "Soviet Economic Reconversion, 1945-46." AMERICAN ECONOMIC REVIEW 37 (May 1947): 611-23.

> The author states that in general reconversion was completed in 1946. Tables summarize budget expenditures for defense and other main branches of the national economy for the years 1944 and 1946; percentage of plan fulfillment by Soviet industries in 1946; and percentage increase over 1945 output of certain commodities.

These statistics are based on Russian sources, such as Pravda. For further discussion, see: Paul A. Baran. "The Economy of the USSR: Discussion." AMERICAN ECONOMIC REVIEW 37 (May 1947): 646-48.

Schwarz, Solomon M. "Economic Reconstruction in the Soviet Union." RUSSIAN REVIEW 4 (Spring 1945): 49-61.

This paper discusses reconstruction of those areas which either suffered direct battle damage or were occupied by the Germans. Two tables outline livestock losses and restoration.

Sheren, Andrew. "Structure and Organization of Defense-Related Industries." In ECONOMIC PERFORMANCE AND THE MILITARY BURDEN IN THE SOVIET UNION, U.S. Congress. Joint Economic Committee, pp. 123-32. Washington, D.C.: Government Printing Office, 1970.

This paper surveys the various defense-related ministries. Two charts and a table.

Sumberg, Theodore. "The Soviet Union's War Budgets." AMERICAN ECONOMIC REVIEW 36 (March 1946): 113-26.

Sumberg details, for the first time, the Russian wartime budgets based on estimates by Finance Commissar A. G. Zverev. Such information enables one to study the economic basis of the Russian war effort. Article includes tables on state budget expenditures for 1938, 1940-45, and state budget revenues for 1938, 1940-45. For further discussion, see: Earl Rolph. "Mr. Sumberg's Interpretation of the Soviet Turnover Tax." AMERICAN ECONOMIC REVIEW 36 (September 1946): 661-62.

Volin, Lazar. "German Invasion and Russian Agriculture." RUSSIAN REVIEW 3 (Autumn 1943): 75-88.

Major problems of food supply and agricultural policy during World War II are explored.

Volin, Lazar, and Goodstein, Sylvia. "Problems of Agricultural Rehabilitation in the Liberated Regions of the Soviet Union." In U.S.S.R. IN RECONSTRUCTION, pp. 98-110. New York: American Russian Institute, 1944.

The authors briefly describe the extent of German destruction of Russia's agricultural sector. Tables summarize figures on livestock and tractors.

_____. SOVIET ECONOMY DURING THE SECOND WORLD WAR. New York: International Publishers, 1949. 160 p.

This book discusses virtually all aspects of the Soviet economy during the war. Index. A previous work deals with virtually the same material: Nikolai A. Voznesensky. THE ECONOMY OF THE USSR DURING WORLD WAR II. Washington, D.C.: Public Affairs Press, 1948. 115 p.

Wieczynski, Joseph L. "Economic Consequences of Disarmament: The Soviet View." RUSSIAN REVIEW 27 (July 1968): 275-85.

This paper surveys the view of Soviet strategists regarding the consequences of disarmament for capitalist and socialist economies.

Yugow, Aron. "Reconversion and Reconstruction in the U.S.S.R." INTERNATIONAL LABOUR REVIEW 55 (January-February 1947): 62-76.

This article is drawn from Soviet reports from various factories and branches of industry, journal articles on economic reconstruction, the report of the president of the State Planning Commission, and the text of the Fourth Five-Year Plan.

Chapter 7
ECONOMIC GROWTH, DEVELOPMENT, AND INDUSTRIALIZATION

THE PERIOD UP TO 1860

Blackwell, W[illiam]. L. THE BEGINNINGS OF RUSSIAN INDUSTRIALIZATION, 1800-1860. Princeton, N.J.: Princeton University Press, 1968.

>This detailed, scholarly survey covers the following topics: industry in Russia prior to 1860; the role of the state in industrial development; private enterprise; a survey of transportation; and the role of technology in industrialization. Tables in the appendices, glossary of Russian terms, extensive bibliography, and index.

Ellison, Herbert J. "Economic Modernization in Imperial Russia: Purposes and Achievements." JOURNAL OF ECONOMIC HISTORY 25 (December 1965): 523-40.

>This article examines Russian economic growth in the nineteenth and early twentieth centuries in detail, with attention to qualitative economic changes as well as quantitative.

Falkus, Malcolm E. THE INDUSTRIALIZATION OF RUSSIA, 1700-1914. London: Macmillan and Co., 1972. 96 p.

>Falkus outlines the course of Russian industrialization, discussing the beginnings of industrialization; economic development after Peter the Great; industrial development, 1800-1861 and 1861-1913; the emancipation of the serfs and economic development; industrial growth before the 1890s; the boom of the 1890s; and stagnation and boom, 1900-1913. Bibliography.

Henderson, William O. THE INDUSTRIAL REVOLUTION IN EUROPE, 1815-1914. Chicago: Quadrangle Books, 1961. ix, 287 p.

>Chapter 5 deals with the industrial revolution in Russia. The author discusses the course of industrial expansion beginning with eighteenth-century factories; the development of a communications system; finance and capital; the evolution of industrial workers;

and Russian expansion into Asia. A map of the coal and iron industries in South Russia (1900) is included.

———. THE INDUSTRIAL REVOLUTION ON THE CONTINENT: GERMANY, FRANCE, RUSSIA 1800-1914. 2d ed. London: Cass, 1967. ix, 291 p.

The book briefly accounts industrial expansion, communications, finance and capital, industrial workers, and Russian expansion in Asia. Nine maps.

Kahan, Arcadius. "Continuity in Economic Activity and Policy During the Post-Petrine Period in Russia." JOURNAL OF ECONOMIC HISTORY 25 (March 1965): 61-85.

Three subjects are discussed: the durability of the industrial development that occurred in Russia during the Petrine period; the significance of the economic slump which occurred after Peter's death; and whether or not the post-Petrine period should be considered as a major discontinuity in Russia's economic growth. Eleven tables.

Wieczynski, Joseph L. "The Frontier in Early Russian History." RUSSIAN REVIEW 31 (April 1972): 110-16.

This article applies Frederick Jackson Turner's "frontier thesis" to the frontier in eleventh- and twelfth-century Russia.

———. "Toward a Frontier Theory of Early Russian History." RUSSIAN REVIEW 33 (1974): 284-95.

This is a further elaboration of an earlier article, see directly above.

Yatsunsky, V. K. "Main Features of Industrialization in Russia Before 1917." In CONTRIBUTIONS ON INDUSTRIALIZATION AS A FACTOR IN ECONOMIC GROWTH AFTER 1700, pp. 297-307. First International Conference of Economic History, Stockholm, 1960. Paris: Mouton & Co., 1960.

This is a sketchy account of Russian industrialization. The author traces big enterprise back to the seventeenth century in salt-making and metallurgical industries. Written by a Soviet economist, the article is based on Soviet sources.

THE PERIOD 1860-1917

Blackwell, W[illiam]. L. THE INDUSTRIALIZATION OF RUSSIA; AN HISTORICAL PERSPECTIVE. New York: Crowell, 1970. x, 198 p.

The transformation of the Russian economy from agriculture to industry in the past century is examined. Blackwell focuses on social and political history, not economic analysis. Glossary of Russian terms, bibliographical essay, and index.

DaCosta, Eric P. W. THE ECONOMIC PROGRESS OF RUSSIA, 1860-1948. Eastern Economic Pamphlets 4. New Delhi: Eastern Economist, 1952. x, 61 p.

Various periods in the history of the development of the Soviet economy are surveyed. Only the first chapter deals with the economy under the tsars, 1860-1917.

Gerschenkron, Alexander. "The Early Phases of Industrialization in Russia: After Thoughts and Counterthoughts." In THE ECONOMICS OF TAKEOFF INTO SUSTAINED GROWTH, edited by Walt W. Rostow, pp. 151-69. New York: St. Martin's Press, 1963.

This paper summarizes Russian industrialization, 1885-1915, and discusses Rostow's approach to industrial history.

_____. "The Early Phases of Industrialization in Russia and Their Relationship to the Historical Study of Economic Growth." In THE EXPERIENCE OF ECONOMIC GROWTH; CASE STUDIES IN ECONOMIC HISTORY, edited by Barry E. Supple, pp. 426-44. New York: Random House, 1963.

The first part of this paper summarizes Gerschenkron's view of Russian industrialization from 1885 to 1914 and presents six propositions concerning industrialization in backward countries. The second part compares these six propositions with Walt W. Rostow's THE STAGES OF ECONOMIC GROWTH.

_____. ECONOMIC BACKWARDNESS IN HISTORICAL PERSPECTIVE: A BOOK OF ESSAYS. Cambridge, Mass.: Belknap Press, Harvard University Press, 1962. 456 p.

This volume contains essays first published in various journals and symposia between 1951 and 1961. The first eight essays deal with Gerschenkron's hypothesis that interspatial variations in the process of industrialization are functionally related to the degree of economic backwardness that prevailed in the countries, including Russia, on the eve of their great spurts of industrial growth. The remaining six chapters discuss economic and social change in Russia. Index.

_____. "Problems and Patterns of Russian Economic Development." In THE TRANSFORMATION OF RUSSIAN SOCIETY: ASPECTS OF SOCIAL CHANGE SINCE 1861, edited by Cyril E. Black, pp. 42-72. Cambridge, Mass.: Harvard University Press, 1960.

The author examines Russian economic development from the emancipation of the serfs to the present.

_____. "The Rate of Industrial Growth in Russia Since 1885." JOURNAL

Economic Growth

OF ECONOMIC HISTORY 7 (1947): 144-74.

This paper compares the rates of industrial growth in various periods of Russian history, from the mid-1880s until the end of the interwar period and describes factors which promoted or obstructed industrialization.

Goldsmith, Raymond W. "The Economic Growth of Tsarist Russia 1860-1913." ECONOMIC DEVELOPMENT AND CULTURAL CHANGE 9 (April 1961): 441-75.

This highly informative study details periods and sectors in which growth occurred and explores the reasons for the patterns. The first section is a useful summary of conclusions; the second section treats the growth of agricultural output; the third examines growth of industrial output; the fourth considers growth of total output; and the fifth analyzes the economic growth of Russia before the Revolution in international comparison. A wealth of data is presented in numerous tables.

Gregory, Paul R. "Economic Growth and Structural Change in Tsarist Russia: A Case of Modern Economic Growth?" SOVIET STUDIES 23 (January 1972): 418-34.

This article examines six aspects of the tsarist economy during 1860-1917 for signs of modern economic growth: population growth; demographic trends; growth of product and efficiency; trends in industrial structure and sector efficiency; trends within industry; and patterns of consumption. Nine tables.

Miller, Margaret S. THE ECONOMIC DEVELOPMENT OF RUSSIA 1905-1914: WITH SPECIAL REFERENCE TO TRADE, INDUSTRY, AND FINANCE. London: P. S. King & Son, 1926. xviii, 311 p.

This book contains a helpful analytical table of contents and is divided into four parts. Part one includes a geographical survey and a discussion of the sociological bases of economic development. Part two deals with trade balance and tariff policy. However, internal trade is not covered. Part three outlines the financial system and discusses banking, currency, and the state budget. Part four analyzes the communications system--roads, waterways and railway system. Each part contains an appendix comprised of tables. Bibliography, index, and two foldout maps.

Popluiko, A. "The Economic Development of Pre-revolutionary Russia." STUDIES ON THE SOVIET UNION n.s. 1 (July 1957): 20-25.

The article highlights the contents of Edmond Thery's LA TRANSFORMATION ECONOMIQUE DE LA RUSSIE (Paris, 1914). Tables present data on population; trade in foodstuffs; production of coal, iron, and steel; consumption of lead and copper; and budget expenses for 1898-1912.

Portal, Roger. "The Industrialization of Russia." In THE CAMBRIDGE ECONOMIC HISTORY OF EUROPE, vol. 6, pp. 801-74. Cambridge: At the University Press, 1965.

Portal describes five periods of Russian industrialization from mid-nineteenth century through war and revolution, covering railways, balance of trade, decline of domestic industry, artisan industry, petroleum industry, and the role of foreign capital.

Singh, V. B., and Reddy, V. V. "Soviet Economic Development." In PATTERNS OF ECONOMIC DEVELOPMENT: A STUDY OF THE ECONOMIC DEVELOPMENT OF THE U.K., THE U.S.A., JAPAN, THE U.S.S.R., AND CHINA, edited by V. B. Singh, pp. 349-458. Bombay, London, and New York: Allied Publishers Private, 1970.

This paper traces Russian economic development from the abolition of serfdom to the 1960s. Tables.

Sinzheimer, G. P. G. "Reflections on Gerschenkron, Russian Backwardness and Economic Development." SOVIET STUDIES 17 (October 1965): 209-25.

This paper extensively analyzes Gerschenkron's ECONOMIC BACKWARDNESS IN HISTORICAL PERSPECTIVE. Cambridge, Mass.: Harvard University Press, 1962.

Thalheim, Karl C. "Russia's Economic Development." In RUSSIA ENTERS THE TWENTIETH CENTURY: 1894-1917, edited by Edwin Oberlander et al., pp. 85-110. New York: Schocken Books, 1971.

This article outlines the enormous difficulties faced by advocates of modernization and industrialization and recounts the results of modernization, which were inadequate on the eve of World War I.

Tompkins, Stuart R. "Witte as Minister of Finance." SLAVONIC REVIEW 11 (April 1933): 590-606.

Witte's role in the industrialization of Russia is examined. Tompkins considers (1) did Witte actually design a plan for the industrialization of Russia and (2) did the industrial development of the 1890s stem from Witte's policies or did they "come from the operation of forces that lay beyond (Witte's) control?"

Von Laue, Theodore H. "The High Cost and the Gamble of the Witte System: A Chapter in the Industrialization of Russia." JOURNAL OF ECONOMIC HISTORY 13, no. 4 (1953): 425-48.

This article discusses Witte's policies and their consequences, especially political.

_____. "Problems of Industrialization." In RUSSIA UNDER THE LAST TSAR, edited by T. Stavrou, pp. 117-53. Minneapolis: University of Minnesota Press, 1969.

This paper discusses Russian industrialization in the period preceding World War I.

———. SERGEI WITTE AND THE INDUSTRIALIZATION OF RUSSIA. New York: Columbia University Press, 1963. x, 360 p.

This book recounts Witte's crucial role in Russian development efforts before World War I. Glossary, bibliography, and index.

Yurievsky, E. "The Development of Russia Before 1917." STUDIES ON THE SOVIET UNION o.s. 1 (July 1957): 12-19.

This article reviews the industrial development of Russia before the Revolution and suggests that Russia might have developed even more rapidly without the Revolution.

THE PERIOD AFTER 1917

Adler-Larlsson, Gunner. "The Semi-developed Soviet Economy: A Foreign Trade Illustration." ECONOMICS OF PLANNING 6, no. 1 (1966): 83-87.

This paper uses the commodity pattern of foreign trade as a defining factor to show how Soviet foreign trade figures confirm Paul A. Samuelson's thesis that the Soviet Union belongs in the group of "semideveloped" nations. A table and a diagram provide figures on the net commodity structure of Soviet trade with non-Communist countries in 1963.

Ali, A[gha].[S.]. ECONOMIC DEVELOPMENT OF THE SOVIET UNION. Dacca: Ideal Library, 1966. vi, 127 p.

Ali, in this short survey of the history of the Soviet economy, discusses (1) economic development prior to 1917; (2) the period of war communism and the NEP; (3) economic recovery and the "scissors crisis" of 1923; (4) five-year plans before and after the Second World War; (5) trade unions; (6) wage system, labor incentive, labor discipline, and social security; (7) planning; and (8) taxation.

Barker, G[eoffrey]. R. "Industry and Construction." BULLETINS ON SOVIET ECONOMIC DEVELOPMENT ser. 3, 9-10 (September 1956): 1-28.

Barker examines industrial growth since the end of the Fourth Five-Year Plan in 1950.

Basseches, Nikolaus. "Industry." In RED ECONOMICS, edited by Gerhard Dobbert, pp. 93-110. Boston: Houghton Mifflin, 1932.

The author outlines the process of Soviet industrialization, which was based on the foundation of Imperial Russian industrialization.

Economic Growth

Baykov, Alexander M. "Development of Industrial Production in the U.S.S.R." ECONOMICA n.s. 8 (February 1941): 94-103.

This is a concise statement of the negative and positive factors affecting industrial production in the USSR. Emphasis is on Soviet mistakes and hopes for avoiding them in the future. Tables covering selected years between 1913-38 provide data on total production by industry and iron, steel, and coal production by region.

_____. "The Economic Development of Russia." ECONOMIC HISTORY REVIEW 11 (December 1954): 137-49.

Baykov foresees that the industrial sector of the Soviet economy will continue to grow but that the rate of growth will slow down after about twenty years. Agricultural production will lag behind and will probably never return to levels of agricultural exports of the pre-Revolutionary period.

_____. "Industrial Development in the U.S.S.R." BULLETINS ON SOVIET ECONOMIC DEVELOPMENT 1 (May 1949): 3-27.

This article examines trends of industrial development in the USSR between 1913 and 1940; the effect of World War II on industry; the aims of the Five-Year Plan for 1946-50; and actual postwar industrial developments based on rare Soviet statistical information. Tables.

_____. "Industry." BULLETINS ON SOVIET ECONOMIC DEVELOPMENT. ser. 2, 8 (May 1953): 8-28 (notes on pp. 46-47).

The author discusses new information that has become available since the publication of previous bulletins on the following topics: construction, labor, production, the new Five-Year Plan (1951-55), and some of the major construction projects. Tables.

_____. "Post-War Economic Development in the U.S.S.R." BULLETINS ON SOVIET ECONOMIC DEVELOPMENT ser. 2, 8 (May 1953): 1-48.

In reviewing issues which were discussed in previous bulletins, the author provides additional information based on "material which has since become available." He also considers the reliability of the data and furnishes additional information on industry and agriculture.

Bergson, Abram. "Future Growth Strategy for the Soviet Economy." ASSOCIATION FOR COMPARATIVE ECONOMIC STUDIES BULLETIN 14 (Spring 1972): 2-13.

This article reviews Soviet growth strategy and its past performance and concludes that Stalin's strategy for growth is in need of change. Tables summarize estimates of growth rates for 1950-69 and give figures for 1970 with hypothetical projections for 1975 and 1980.

_____. "Soviet Economic Perspectives: Toward a New Growth Model."
PROBLEMS OF COMMUNISM 22 (March-April 1973): 1-9.

    This paper argues that increased costs of forced-draft growth are
compelling the Soviet regime to shift from the traditional Stalinist
model to a more balanced approach to economic development.
Tables.

_____, ed. SOVIET ECONOMIC GROWTH: CONDITIONS AND PERSPEC-
TIVES. Evanston, Ill.: Row, Peterson, 1953. viii, 376 p.

    This collection of papers focuses on the conditioning factors and
long-range prospects for future Soviet economic growth. Many
of the conclusions are tentative, since they are based on incom-
plete Soviet data.

Birmingham University. Bureau of Research on Russian Economic Conditions.
"I: Foreign Trade; II: Monetary Conditions; III: Indices of Wholesale
Prices; IV: State Budget." MEMORANDUM NO. 7. (October 1932):
1-24.

    Part one deals with foreign trade during the depression; exports and
imports; and trade activities with foreign countries. Part two examines the volume of circulation of money in relation to the value
of money. Part three summarizes wholesale prices for the period
1900-1930. Part four discusses peculiarities of the Soviet state
budget. Tables.

Boddy, Francis M. "Soviet Economic Growth." In SOVIET UNION--PARADOX
AND CHANGE, edited by Robert T. Holt and John E. Turner, pp. 62-89.
New York: Holt, Rinehart & Winston, 1962.

    This paper concerns growth rates; determinates of growth; the lo-
cation of the decision-making power in capitalism and Soviet communism; a simple input-output table; administrative organization in
a planned economy; and the search for a pricing system.

Bornstein, Morris. "The Role of Economic Growth in the Sino-Soviet Bloc."
In NATIONAL SECURITY: POLITICAL, MILITARY, AND ECONOMIC STRATE-
GIES IN THE DECADE AHEAD, edited by David M. Abshire and Richard V.
Allen, pp. 119-47. Proceedings of a conference sponsored by the Center for
Strategic Studies, Georgetown University, January 23-25, 1963. New York:
Praeger, 1963.

    The author examines the patterns of economic growth in the Sino-
Soviet bloc and appraises the implications for each nation's strategic
objectives. Tables.

Bron, Saul G. SOVIET ECONOMIC DEVELOPMENT AND AMERICAN BUSI-
NESS: RESULTS OF THE FIRST YEAR UNDER THE FIVE-YEAR PLAN AND
FURTHER PERSPECTIVES. New York: Liveright, 1930. xiii, 147 p.

Bron discusses the economic conditions in the Soviet Union in 1929 and measures the results of the first year of the plan against its goals. Indicators of the national economy and Soviet foreign trade are summarized in the appendices. Tables.

Brubaker, Earl R. "Synthetic Factor Shares, the Elasticity of Substitution, and the Residual in Soviet Growth." REVIEW OF ECONOMICS AND STATISTICS 52 (February 1970): 100-104.

This paper analyzes data on growth of labor and capital and on synthetic factor shares to obtain a range of implied values for the elasticity of substitution. It then uses the values to obtain further implications about output which is explained by combined input of capital and labor and the part left to be explained by other factors. Four tables.

Campbell, Robert W. "The Post-War Growth of the Soviet Economy." SOVIET STUDIES 16 (July 1964): 1-16.

Soviet economic growth from 1950 to 1963 is analyzed. Three tables.

Chakrabarti, S. C., et al. ECONOMIC DEVELOPMENT OF THE SOVIET UNION. 2d rev. ed. Calcutta: Nababharat Publishers, 1965. xi, 151 p.

The authors discuss economic development prior to 1917; early months of the Soviet regime and the period of war communism; the New Economic Policy; economic recovery and the "scissors crisis" of 1923; collectivization of agriculture; the five-year plans; trade unions; wages and incentives; the planning system; the system of taxation; and the Soviet economy in transition.

Cohn, Stanley H. ECONOMIC DEVELOPMENT IN THE SOVIET UNION. Lexington, Mass.: Heath, 1970. xiv, 135 p.

This study examines the evolution and performance of the Soviet economic development model. It stresses resource endowment and allocation policies, which are the economic core of the development strategy.

_____. "The Soviet Economy: Performance and Growth." STUDIES ON THE SOVIET UNION n.s. 6, no. 4 (1967): 24-54.

This study seeks to evaluate quantitatively the performance of the Soviet economy during its first half century. Fourteen tables are included. Two appendices discuss historical trends in GNP and derivation of combined factor inputs and productivity.

_____. "Soviet Growth Retardation: Trends in Resource Availability and Efficiency." In NEW DIRECTIONS IN THE SOVIET ECONOMY, U.S. Congress. Joint Economic Committee, pp. 99-132. Washington, D.C.: Government

Printing Office, 1966.

    Topics discussed include comparative trends in GNP, resource utilization, economic structure, trends in factor availability and productivity, and future growth prospects. Many tables.

Colton, Ethan. "The Test of Communist Economic Resources." SLAVONIC REVIEW 11 (July 1932): 37-58.

    Soviet economic achievements and failures during the first fifteen years of Soviet rule, especially during the First Five-Year Plan, are reviewed.

Datta, Amlankusum. A CENTURY OF ECONOMIC DEVELOPMENT OF RUSSIA AND JAPAN. Calcutta: World Press, 1963. ix, 187 p.

    The first part outlines economic development in Russia, especially during the Soviet period. The book covers: war communism; the New Economic Policy; the "scissors crisis" and alternative roads to industrialization; collective farming; the five-year plans; and the reforms of the post-Stalin period. Maps.

Deane, Phyllis. "Measuring Soviet Economic Growth." SOVIET STUDIES 14 (October 1962): 132-37.

    Problems of measuring Soviet economic growth are discussed.

Denton, Frederick G. "A Recent Soviet Study of Economic Growth 1951-63." SOVIET STUDIES 19 (April 1968): 501-9.

    This note briefly describes the fitting of a modified version of the Cobb-Douglas production function to aggregate Soviet growth data for the period 1951-63 by two Soviet economists. Their work is compared with similar studies by Western economists. Two tables.

Dobb, Maurice H. "Comparative Rates of Growth in Industry: A Comment on Strumilin's Article on 'Expanded Reproduction.'" SOVIET STUDIES 7 (July 1955): 52-58.

    The article discussed here is "Balance of the National Economy as an Investment of Socialist Planning." VOPROSY EKONOMIKI no. 11 (1954): 22-39. An appendix presents Strumilin's table of the reproduction of the social product of the USSR. For further discussion, see: Andre Gabor. "Comparative Growth Rates: A Note." SOVIET STUDIES 7 (October 1955): 161-63; Maurice H. Dobb. "Comparative Growth Rates: A Reply." SOVIET STUDIES 7 (January 1956): 274; Andre Gabor. "Comparative Growth Rates: A Rejoinder." SOVIET STUDIES 7 (April 1956): 408.

_____. "Rates of Growth Under the Five Year Plans." SOVIET STUDIES 4 (April 1953): 364-85.

Economic Growth

This paper looks at growth rates for the metal, fuel, and power industries and compares them with growth rates in other countries. The Fifth Five-Year Plan for 1951-55 is discussed.

_____. SOVIET ECONOMIC DEVELOPMENT SINCE 1917. 6th ed. London: Routledge & Kegan Paul, 1966. viii, 515 p.

In this three-part book, the first portion discusses reasons for studying the Soviet economy and Russian economic development prior to 1917. The second part deals with the periods of war communism; the New Economic Policy; the "scissors crisis" of 1923; problems of industrialization; the agrarian situation before the five-year plans; and the first five five-year plans. The third part covers the planning system; the financial system; the location of industry; and trade unions, wages, and the conditions of labor.

Dockstader, Robert A. "Development in Soviet Industry." In ECONOMIC PERFORMANCE AND THE MILITARY BURDEN IN THE SOVIET UNION, U.S. Congress. Joint Economic Committee, pp. 18-25. Washington, D.C.: Government Printing Office, 1970.

Topics discussed include industrial production; industrial materials; civilian machinery; consumer nondurables; industrial productivity; and the outlook for 1970. Five tables.

Efimov, Anatolii N. SOVIET INDUSTRY. Moscow: Progress Publishers, 1968. 267 p.

This Soviet publication contains information on rates and scale of production; technological progress; organization of industrial production; pattern and intersectoral links of industry; and raw material base and territorial distribution. Two maps.

Erlich, Alexander. "Development Strategy and Planning: The Soviet Experience." In NATIONAL ECONOMIC PLANNING, edited by Max Millikan, pp. 233-71. New York: Columbia University Press, 1967.

This paper explores development strategy and the role of planning in development. A table of NNP, factor input, and productivity figures, 1928-58, is included. A comment by Abram Bergson follows.

Fallenbuchl, Z. M. "The Communist Pattern of Industrialization." SOVIET STUDIES 21 (April 1970): 458-84.

This is an extensive analysis of industrialization patterns in Eastern Europe, as well as the Soviet Union. Emphasis is on the 1950s and early 1960s. Tables.

Fischer, Louis. MACHINES AND MEN IN RUSSIA. New York: Smith, Harris, 1932. xv, 283 p. Illustrated.

In the first part the author describes Soviet reasons for rapid industrialization and discusses two giants of Soviet industry: Dnieperstroi--the biggest dam in the world at that time--and the Kharkov tractor factory. In the second part he analyzes human elements in industry and wages in Russia. Black and white photographs.

Gerschenkron, Alexander. "A Note on Russian Industry in 1947." AMERICAN SLAVIC AND EAST EUROPEAN REVIEW 7 (1948): 139-43.

This note concerns that portion of the Gosplan report of January 18, 1948, which deals with the development of Russian industry during 1947.

──────. "Notes on the Rate of Industrial Growth in Soviet Russia." In ECONOMIC BACKWARDNESS IN HISTORICAL PERSPECTIVE: A BOOK OF ESSAYS, pp. 254-69. Cambridge, Mass.: Belknap Press, Harvard University Press, 1962.

Estimates of the rate of industrial growth in Soviet Russia from 1928-60 are given, and the problems of obtaining the estimates are discussed. Tables.

Gisser, Micha, and Jonas, Paul. "Soviet Growth in Absence of Centralized Planning: A Hypothetical Alternative." JOURNAL OF POLITICAL ECONOMY 82 (March-April 1974): 333-52.

The study speculates on whether the Soviet Union would be richer or poorer if it had adopted a decentralized, agriculture-propelled, market-oriented economic policy.

Goldman, Marshall I. "Economic Growth and Institutional Change in the Soviet Union." In SOVIET POLICYMAKING: STUDIES OF COMMUNISM IN TRANSITION, edited by P. H. Juviler and H. W. Morton, pp. 63-80. New York: Praeger, 1967.

Growth problems, planning, and the debates over reforms are discussed.

Greenslade, Rush V., and Wallace, P. "Industrial Production in the U.S.S.R." In DIMENSIONS OF SOVIET ECONOMIC POWER, U.S. Congress. Joint Economic Committee, pp. 119-36. Washington, D.C.: Government Printing Office, 1962.

This article reviews Soviet industrial production from 1950 to 1961 and compares it with Western countries, as well as with other Soviet indexes of industrial production. The authors also examine the future prospects for industrial growth. Tables.

Grossman, Gregory. "National Income." In SOVIET ECONOMIC GROWTH: CONDITIONS AND PERSPECTIVES, edited by Abram Bergson, pp. 1-36. Evanston, Ill.: Row, Peterson, 1953.

This essay summarizes rates and patterns of growth of the Soviet economy preceding and following the Second World War and examines possibilities for the 1950s and 1960s. Comments by Alexander Gerschenkron, Wassely W. Leontief, and Abram Bergson follow.

_____. "Soviet Growth Routine, Inertia, and Pressure." AMERICAN ECONOMIC REVIEW 50 (May 1960): 62-72.

This article concerns forces initiating growth in the Soviet economy; channels for the transmission of that initiative to economic units; response of these units; and incentive systems designed to make the units respond correctly. For further discussion, see: Joseph S. Berliner et al. "Incentives and Economic Growth--Discussion." AMERICAN ECONOMIC REVIEW 50 (May 1960): 84-92.

_____. "Thirty Years of Soviet Industrialization." SOVIET SURVEY 26 (October-December 1958): 15-21.

In attempting to assess Soviet industrial growth during the first three decades, Grossman cites three impediments to making such an evaluation: (1) gaps in available information, (2) the unevenness of Soviet economic growth, and (3) the "index number problem."

Gurevich, S. M., and Partigul, S. THE NEW ECONOMIC UPSWING OF THE U.S.S.R. IN THE POST-WAR FIVE-YEAR PLAN PERIOD. Moscow: Foreign Languages Publishing House, 1950. 256 p.

This Soviet publication discusses the state of industry, transport, and agriculture after the Second World War. Tables.

Hansen, Alvin H. "The Economics of the Soviet Challenge." ECONOMIC RECORD 36 (March 1960): 5-12.

Reasons for the high level of Soviet growth rate are discussed.

Hardt, John P. "Soviet Economic Development and Policy Alternatives." STUDIES ON THE SOVIET UNION n.s. 6, no. 4 (1967): 1-23.

This survey of fifty years of Soviet economic development appraises performance "in the light of developmental and doctrinal alternatives."

Hardt, John P., and Modig, Carl. THE INDUSTRIALIZATION OF SOVIET RUSSIA IN THE FIRST HALF CENTURY. McLean, Va.: Research Analysis Corp., 1968. 20 p.

This paper briefly surveys economic performance over the period and explains the basic planning mechanism.

_____. "Stalinist Industrial Development in Soviet Russia." In THE SOVIET

UNION: A HALF-CENTURY OF COMMUNISM, edited by Kurt London, pp. 295-322. Baltimore: Johns Hopkins University Press, 1968.

The industrial-development process in Russia for the first half-century of Soviet rule is traced. Six tables.

Heller, A.A. THE INDUSTRIAL REVIVAL IN SOVIET RUSSIA. New York: Thomas Seltzer, 1922. xv, 241 p.

This is a firsthand account of the "constructive stage" of development, which began in 1921. Discussed are: Siberia under the Soviet government; the period of military communism; early industrial problems; economic reconstruction; the New Economic Policy in practice; and industries and resources.

Hutchings, Raymond [F.] [D.]. SEASONAL INFLUENCES IN SOVIET INDUSTRY. London: Oxford University Press, 1971. xii, 321 p.

This study sheds light on Soviet growth processes and planning; supplements input-output analysis; and throws light on seasonal influences on economic development. Statistical appendices, select bibliography, general index, and index of industries.

_____. SOVIET ECONOMIC DEVELOPMENT. Oxford: Basil Blackwell, 1971. xii, 314 p. Illustrated.

This book deals with the sequence of events, origins, and characteristic features of Soviet economic development. Agriculture is considered only in a summary manner. Growth of industrial output for the years 1913 through 1967 is summarized in an appendix. Tables and subject and name indices.

"The Industrial Conference." SOVIET STUDIES 7 (October 1955): 201-13.

This paper discusses the proceedings of the industry conference of May 16-18, 1955.

Jasny, Naum. "Soviet Economic Growth." SOCIAL RESEARCH 21 (April 1954): 11-42.

This article is largely a commentary on the paper appearing in Bergson, Abram, ed. SOVIET ECONOMIC GROWTH: CONDITIONS AND PERSPECTIVES. Evanston, Ill.: Row, Peterson, 1953. The paper stresses forecasts of future economic growth. Tables. The article is not a book review and may be read separately from the book.

Kaplan, Norman M. THE RECORD OF SOVIET ECONOMIC GROWTH, 1928-1965. Santa Monica, Calif.: RAND Corp., 1969. vii, 238 p.

This study focuses on the data dealing with Soviet economic growth, which showed a marked retardation since 1950 and rates of growth for the USSR markedly exceeding the long-run rates of growth for the United States. Tables.

———. "Retardation in Soviet Growth." REVIEW OF ECONOMICS AND STATISTICS 50 (August 1968): 293-303.

This paper establishes that a retardation in the Soviet growth rate occurred in 1958-63 and considers possible explanations for it. Four tables and a graph. For a discussion of the sensitivity of Kaplan's results to variations in the elasticity of substitution, see: Charles R. Blitzer. "Elasticity of Substitution and the Retardation of Soviet Growth Rates." REVIEW OF ECONOMICS AND STATISTICS 52 (February 1970): 104-8.

Kato, Hiroshi, and Niwa, Haruki. "The Prospect of Soviet Economic Policy." KEIO ECONOMIC STUDIES 3 (1965): 122-41.

This article discusses reasons for change in Soviet economic policy, presents a model of Soviet economic growth, and uses it to predict patterns of Soviet growth. Tables.

Kazakevich, Vladimir D. "The Economic Strength of the Soviet Union." SCIENCE AND SOCIETY 5 (Fall 1941): 385-89.

This short article discusses growth of industrial output. A table presents value of industrial production and national income for selected years, 1900-1940.

Kershaw, Joseph A. "Directions for Future Growth of the Soviet Economy." In STUDY OF THE SOVIET ECONOMY, edited by Nicolas Spulber, pp. 3-16. Papers presented at a conference, Bloomington, Ind. Bloomington: University of Indiana Press, 1961.

Kershaw discusses comparative rates of growth and the competition for resources. He concludes that, in spite of the many successful achievements of the Soviet economy, the new affluence has created some problems, especially in planning and the computation of vast input-output tables.

Khrushchev, Nikita S. CONTROL FIGURES FOR THE ECONOMIC DEVELOPMENT OF THE U.S.S.R., 1959-1965. Theses of N. S. Khrushchev's report to the Twenty-first Congress of the CPSU. Moscow: Foreign Languages Publishing House, 1958. 130 p.

Topics covered include results of past development efforts, development targets for 1959-65, economic development of union republics, general welfare, education, and the international significance of the Seven-Year Plan.

Kim, M. P. "U.S.S.R. Industrial Development." In CONTRIBUTIONS ON INDUSTRIALISATION AS A FACTOR IN ECONOMIC GROWTH AFTER 1700, pp. 287-96. Comparative Study of Large-Scale Agricultural Enterprise in Post-Medieval Times; and Communications of the First International Conference of Economic History, Stockholm, 1960. Paris: Mouton & Co., 1960.

    Five stages in the history of Soviet industrialization are outlined and difficulties of industrialization are discussed.

Koshelev, F. P. SOVIET INDUSTRY. Moscow: Foreign Languages Publishing House, 1957. 53 p. Illustrated.

    This Soviet pamphlet outlines economic growth in the areas of heavy industry, consumer goods, industry in the national republics, and transport.

Kuibyshev, Valerian V. INDUSTRIAL DEVELOPMENT UNDER THE SECOND FIVE-YEAR PLAN. Moscow: Co-operative Publishing Society of Foreign Workers in the USSR, 1932. 80 p.

    Topics discussed include fulfillment of the first plan; socialism, economic tasks connected with the economy as a whole, specific sectors, and specific regions; living standards; and the requirements of the second plan.

Lalan, M. Yves, ed. PROSPECTS FOR SOVIET ECONOMIC GROWTH IN THE 1970'S. Main findings of symposium held April 14-16, 1971 in Brussels. Brussels: NATO Information Service, 1971. 156 p.

    Of the eight papers included in this volume, six are in English and two are in French. Paperback.

Levine, Herbert S. "Industry." In PROSPECTS FOR SOVIET SOCIETY, edited by Allen Kassof, pp. 291-317. New York: Praeger, 1968.

    This paper discusses the record of economic growth, the slowdown in growth in the mid-1960s, the reforms, and their implications. Tables.

Lokshin, Efraim. INDUSTRY IN THE U.S.S.R. Moscow: Foreign Languages Publishing House, 1948. 170 p.

    This is a Soviet account of Russian industry in the pre-revolutionary era, during the early years of Soviet rule, during the first three five-year plans, and during and after the Second World War.

_____. SOVIET INDUSTRY. Allahabad: Kitabistan, 1946. 81 p.

    This book reviews Russian industrial development and the role of industry in World War II.

Mazour, Anatole G. SOVIET ECONOMIC DEVELOPMENT: OPERATION OUTSTRIP, 1921-1965. Princeton, N.J.: Van Nostrand, 1967. 191 p.

The book's first part outlines the Soviet economy from war communism to the Eighth Five-Year Plan (1966-70). The second part is a collection of thirty-eight Soviet documents which have been translated into English. Bibliography and index.

Millar, James R. "Soviet Rapid Development and the Agricultural Surplus Hypothesis." SOVIET STUDIES 22 (July 1970): 77-93.

This paper discusses the hypothesis of agricultural surplus and measurement of that surplus; it then develops an alternative framework for appraising the role of agriculture in the rapid development of the Soviet Union. For further discussion, see: Alec Nove. "The Agricultural Surplus Hypothesis: A Comment on James R. Millar's Article." SOVIET STUDIES 22 (January 1971): 394-401; James R. Millar. "The Agricultural Surplus Hypothesis: A Reply to Alec Nove." SOVIET STUDIES 23 (October 1971): 302-6; and Alec Nove. "A Reply to the Reply." SOVIET STUDIES 23 (October 1971): 307-8.

Miller, Margaret S. "The Financing of Industry in Soviet Russia." SLAVONIC REVIEW 9 (June 1930): 13-21.

Miller examines the Soviet methods used to achieve industrial development in the shortest possible time. The article deals with the role of agriculture, capital accumulation, the credit system, capital market, and industrial profits.

Niwa, Haruki. "An Econometric Analysis and Forecast of Soviet Economic Growth." In THE PREDICTIONS OF COMMUNIST ECONOMIC PERFORMANCE, edited by Peter J. D. Wiles, pp. 339-72. Cambridge: At the University Press, 1971.

This paper presents a simplified econometric model of Soviet economic growth and discusses prospects for the future. Charts and tables.

Noren, James H. "Soviet Industry Trends in Output, Inputs, and Productivity." In NEW DIRECTIONS IN THE SOVIET ECONOMY, U.S. Congress. Joint Economic Committee, pp. 271-325. Washington, D.C.: Government Printing Office, 1966.

This article analyzes trends in output, input, and productivity in the period 1951-65 and the reasons for the decline in Soviet industrial growth. Methodology is discussed in the appendices. Nine tables and three charts.

Nove, Alec. COMMUNIST ECONOMIC STRATEGY; SOVIET GROWTH AND CAPABILITIES. Washington, D.C.: National Planning Association, 1959. 82 p.

The probable effectiveness of the Soviet bloc's effort to win the battle of "peaceful coexistence" is examined. A major portion is devoted to economic growth in the near future.

──────. "The Pace of Soviet Economic Development." LLOYD'S BANK REVIEW n.s. 40 (April 1956): 1-23.

Topics covered include Soviet statistics and problems of measurement, growth and efficiency, future trends and prospects, and implications for the West. Three tables.

──────. "Prospects for Economic Growth in the USSR." AMERICAN ECONOMIC REVIEW 53 (May 1963): 541-54.

Nove speculates on the prospects for future growth. He includes a table showing the annual increase in some important indicators of the USSR economy. For further discussion, see: G. Warren Nutter et al. "Trends and Prospects in Eastern Europe--Discussion." AMERICAN ECONOMIC REVIEW 53 (May 1963): 572-77.

──────. "Soviet Economic Progress." LLOYD'S BANK REVIEW n.s. 78 (October 1965): 15-33.

Soviet economic growth since the mid-1950s is analyzed. Topics covered include the decline of investment and growth rates, labor shortages, increased consumption, the need for reforms, and the role of prices. Three tables.

──────. "2½ Per Cent and All That." SOVIET STUDIES 16 (July 1964): 17-21.

This article discusses the evidence that the Soviet economy grew at an annual rate of only 2.5 percent or less in 1962-63. For further discussion, see: Stanley H. Cohn et al. "Comment on '2½ Per Cent and All That.'" SOVIET STUDIES 16 (January 1965): 302-25.

──────. WAS STALIN REALLY NECESSARY? SOME PROBLEMS OF SOVIET POLITICAL ECONOMY. London: Allen & Unwin, 1964. 316 p.

Papers which first appeared in various journals explore whether or not the ruthless Stalinist economic policy was necessary for rapid industrialization.

Nutter, G. Warren. "The Effects of Economic Growth on Sino-Soviet Strategy." In NATIONAL SECURITY: POLITICAL, MILITARY, AND ECONOMIC STRATEGIES IN THE DECADE AHEAD, edited by David M. Abshire and Richard V. Allen, pp. 149-68. Proceedings of a conference sponsored by the Center for Strategic Studies, Georgetown University, January 23-25, 1963. New York: Praeger, 1963.

Nutter examines the record of Soviet economic growth and its implications for future strategy. He stresses the Soviet concern for retarded growth in 1960-61 and the need for reforms in the economic system.

_____. GROWTH OF INDUSTRIAL PRODUCTION IN THE SOVIET UNION. A study by the National Bureau of Economic Research. Princeton, N.J.: Princeton University Press, 1962. xxvii, 706 p.

This study seeks to describe the history of Soviet industrial production, but its scope is limited by the shortcomings of Soviet statistics. Tables, charts, bibliography, and index.

_____. "Industrial Growth in the Soviet Union." AMERICAN ECONOMIC REVIEW 48 (May 1958): 398-411.

Several indexes of Soviet industrial production are examined. Tables and graphs. For further discussion, see: Hans Heymann, Jr., and Holland Hunter. "Measuring Production in the USSR--Discussion." AMERICAN ECONOMIC REVIEW 48 (May 1958): 422-27; Rush V. Greenslade and Phyllis A. Wallace. "Industrial Growth in the Soviet Union: Comment." AMERICAN ECONOMIC REVIEW 49 (September 1959): 687-95; and G. Warren Nutter. "Industrial Growth in the Soviet Union: Reply." AMERICAN ECONOMIC REVIEW 49 (September 1959): 695-701.

_____. "Some Observations on Soviet Industrial Growth." AMERICAN ECONOMIC REVIEW 47 (May 1957): 618-30.

This article measures the lag of the Soviet Union behind the United States in industrial achievement. Four tables. For further discussion, see: Gregory Grossman et al. "Soviet Economic Development--Discussion." AMERICAN ECONOMIC REVIEW 47 (May 1957): 643-52.

_____. "Some Reflections on the Growth of the Soviet Economy." STUDIES ON THE SOVIET UNION n.s. 7, no. 1 (1967): 144-50.

Economic performance since the Revolution and its costs are discussed.

Peterson, Howard C. "Soviet Economic Growth and U.S. Policy." In COMPARISONS OF U.S. AND SOVIET ECONOMIES, U.S. Congress. Joint Economic Committee, pp. 517-27. Washington, D.C.: Government Printing Office, 1959.

The author analyzes the possible affects of Soviet economic expansion, Soviet military strength, aid and trade with underdeveloped countries, and its ability to conduct an offensive economic policy against industrial nations.

Poplyuyko, Anatoli. "The Tempo of Soviet Economic Growth." STUDIES ON THE SOVIET UNION n.s. 7, no. 3 (1968): 54-69.

> The Soviet reponse to problems associated with high growth rates is discussed. A table provides figures on actual and planned output for selected industrial commodities.

Powell, Raymond P. "Industrial Production." In ECONOMIC TRENDS IN THE SOVIET UNION, edited by Abram Bergson and Simon Kuznets, pp. 150-202. Cambridge, Mass.: Harvard University Press, 1963.

> This paper is concerned with the sources of Soviet growth and the manner in which the Soviet Union industrialized.

Prybyla, Jan S. "The Economic Problems of Soviet Russia in Transition." INDIAN JOURNAL OF ECONOMICS 45 (October 1964): 133-51.

> The article outlines Stalin's strategy for economic growth and states that at Stalin's death "the USSR had arrived near the payoff stage," which necessitated some fundamental changes in economic strategy. The author concludes that most problems of the current Soviet economy relate to adapting the strategy of economic growth to a new pattern of dynamic resource variables.

———. "Soviet Economic Growth: Perspectives and Prospects." QUARTERLY REVIEW OF ECONOMICS AND BUSINESS 4, no. 1 (1964): 57-67.

> In analyzing factors affecting the rate of Soviet economic growth, this article examines the labor force; natural resources; technological progress; quality in addition to quantity of output; and competition in resource allocation among consumption, military programs, foreign aid, and investment for future growth. The author concludes that, as the Soviet economy matures, the role of economic science in decision making must increase at the expense of political, bureaucratic, and ideological forces.

Seton, Francis. "An Estimate of Soviet Industrial Expansion." SOVIET STUDIES 7 (October 1955): 128-42.

> This article discusses indexes of Soviet economic growth and presents compounds of them. Two tables. For further discussion, see: Donald R. Hodgman. "Measuring Soviet Industrial Expansion: A Reply." SOVIET STUDIES 8 (July 1956): 34-45; Francis Seton. "Measuring Soviet Industrial Expansion: A Reply in Question." SOVIET STUDIES no. 2 (October 1956): 144-47.

———. "Production Functions in Soviet Industry." AMERICAN ECONOMIC REVIEW 49 (May 1959): 1-14.

> Topics covered include identification of growth factors, measurement of the impact of growth factors, the Soviet data available, and prewar and postwar findings. Tables. For further discussion,

see: Raymond P. Powell et al. "Soviet Economic Trends and Prospects--Discussion." AMERICAN ECONOMIC REVIEW 49 (May 1959): 43-49.

_____. "Soviet Progress in Western Perspective." SOVIET STUDIES 12 (October 1960): 126-44.

This paper discusses Soviet growth statistics and Western estimates of Soviet growth. Six tables.

_____. "The Tempo of Soviet Industrial Expansion." OXFORD UNIVERSITY. INSTITUTE OF ECONOMICS AND STATISTICS. BULLETIN 20 (February 1958): 1-28.

This paper estimates the rate of increase of Soviet industrial output since the beginning of full-scale planning in 1928. Soviet claims, criticisms of them, and alternative estimates advanced in the West are also reviewed. Graphs and tables. For further discussion, see: L. R. Klein. "Measuring Soviet Industrial Growth." OXFORD UNIVERSITY. INSTITUTE OF ECONOMICS AND STATISTICS. BULLETIN 20 (November 1958): 373-77; Francis Seton. "Measuring Soviet Industrial Growth: A Rejoinder." 378-80 of same issue of journal.

Spulber, Nicolas, ed. FOUNDATION OF SOVIET STRATEGY FOR ECONOMIC GROWTH: SELECTED SOVIET ESSAYS, 1924-1930. Bloomington: Indiana University Press, 1964. xii, 530 p.

This book presents thirty-six Soviet articles and documents grouped under three headings: "Macro-economic Models"; "Economic Growth-Strategies of Development, Pace, and Efficiency"; and "Planning Theories and Methods." Guide to Soviet sources and index.

Thornton, Judith [G.]. "Factors in the Recent Decline in Soviet Growth." SLAVIC REVIEW 25 (March 1966): 101-19.

This paper analyzes the decline in Soviet economic growth between 1958 and 1965 and attributes it to stagnation in agriculture and the slowing of industrial growth. The low growth in industry is attributed to decline in the growth rate of inputs, while the decline in agricultural growth is seen as resulting from failure of factor productivity to increase. Statistical tables.

Thorpe, Willard L. "Soviet Economic Growth and Its Policy." In COMPARISONS OF THE U.S. AND SOVIET ECONOMIES, U.S. Congress. Joint Economic Committee, pp. 571-88. Washington, D.C.: Government Printing Office, 1959.

This paper deals with Russia's economic growth, the economic significance of Soviet growth, and the American image of Soviet economic growth.

Vvedensky, George. "Industrial Developments." STUDIES ON THE SOVIET UNION n.s. 2, no. 3 (1963): 57-61.

This is a survey of successes and failures in industrial development.

Weitzman, Martin L. "Soviet Postwar Economic Growth and Capital Labor Substitution." AMERICAN ECONOMIC REVIEW 60 (September 1970): 676-92.

For further discussion on the estimation techniques used, see the following, all of which are in the AMERICAN ECONOMIC REVIEW: Earl R. Brubaker. "Soviet Postwar Economic Growth and Capital-Labor Substitution: Comment." 62 (September 1972): 675-78; Mitchell Kellman and Lorenzo L. Perez. "Soviet Postwar Economic Growth and Capital-Labor Substitution: Comment." 62 (September 1972): 679-81; Martin L. Weitzman. "Soviet Postwar Economic Growth and Capital-Labor Substitution: Reply." 62 (September 1972): 682-84; Krishna T. Kumar and Ephraim Asher. "Soviet Postwar Economic Growth and Capital-Labor Substitution." 64 (March 1974): 240-42; and Martin L. Weitzman. "Reply." 64 (March 1974): 243.

Wilber, Charles K. "A Nonmonetary Index of Economic Development." SOVIET STUDIES 17 (April 1966): 408-16.

The index is constructed and applied to Soviet Central Asia and selected countries in four tables.

Winterton, Paul. "Soviet Economic Development Since 1928." ECONOMIC JOURNAL 43 (September 1933): 442-52.

This survey of Soviet economic development under the First Five-Year Plan concludes that the most important developments were the provision of a vast industrial plant based on modern techniques; technical advance in agriculture; more equal income distribution; and creation of a basis for future advances.

Zhdanko, T. "Sedentarisation of the Nomads of Central Asia, Including Kazakhstan, Under the Soviet Regime." INTERNATIONAL LABOUR REVIEW 93 (June 1966): 600-620.

Zhdanko outlines characteristics of the nomadic peoples of Central Asia and the official policy adopted towards them prior to 1917. He then describes the measures taken by the Soviet state to modernize the social structure along socialist lines. He stresses in his analysis agrarian reform, collectivization, sedentarization, the diversification of agriculture, and industrialization.

Chapter 8

COMPARISONS BETWEEN THE RUSSIAN AND OTHER ECONOMIES

THE PERIOD UP TO 1860

Dow, Roger. "Seichas: A Comparison of Pre-Reform Russia and the Ante-Bellum South." RUSSIAN REVIEW 7 (Autumn 1947): 3-15.

This paper compares the institutions of serfdom and bonded labor in pre-1861 Russia with those of slavery in the pre-Civil War American South.

THE PERIOD AFTER 1917

Balassa, Bela. "The Dynamic Efficiency of the Soviet Economy." AMERICAN ECONOMIC REVIEW 54 (May 1964): 490-505.

This article compares growth rates in the U.S. and Soviet economies at similar levels of economic development to provide an indication of their relative dynamic efficiencies, once adjustment for disparate changes in the quantity of inputs and in static efficiency have been made. For further discussion, see: Judith Thornton et al. "Efficiency of the Soviet Economy--Discussion." AMERICAN ECONOMIC REVIEW 54 (May 1964): 516-22.

Bergson, Abram. "Comparative Productivity and Efficiency in the USA and the USSR." In COMPARISON OF ECONOMIC SYSTEMS: THEORETICAL AND METHODOLOGICAL APPROACHES, edited by Alexander Eckstein, pp. 161-218. Berkeley and Los Angeles: University of California Press, 1971.

This paper discusses methodology, compares productivity and efficiency in the United States and USSR, and considers how much of the difference is due to the nature of economic systems. Thirteen tables.

_____. PLANNING AND PRODUCTIVITY UNDER SOVIET SOCIALISM. New York: Columbia University Press, 1968. 95 p.

Bergson compares economic productivity in the USSR and Western capitalist countries and considers the sources of "static" inefficiency under socialism in the USSR and how they compare with those under Western capitalism. Tables.

Berliner, Joseph S. "The Static Efficiency of the Soviet Economy." AMERICAN ECONOMIC REVIEW 54 (May 1964): 480-89.

An index of comparative efficiency for the United States and the Soviet Union is developed in this article. An appendix supplies data and sources for GNP, and capital stock, labor, and input weight estimates. For further discussion, see: Judith Thornton et al. "Efficiency of the Soviet Economy--Discussion." AMERICAN ECONOMIC REVIEW 54 (May 1964): 516-22.

Blumenfeld, Hans. "Growth Rate Comparisons: Soviet Union and German Democratic Republic." LAND ECONOMICS 49 (May 1973): 122-32.

This paper includes eight tables presenting statistics concerning the two countries involved. It concludes that "only highly centralized decision making can bring about spatial decentralization of population and activities."

Campbell, Robert W. "A Comparison of Soviet and American Inventory-Output Ratios." AMERICAN ECONOMIC REVIEW 48 (September 1958): 549-65.

This article presents some measure of inventory holdings and of output in the Soviet Union, to be compared with similar data for the United States, to determine which economic system is really the more economical of inventories. Numerous data are presented in six tables. For further discussion reinforcing Campbell's conclusions, see: Boris P. Pesek. "Soviet and American Inventory-Output Ratios Once Again." AMERICAN ECONOMIC REVIEW 49 (December 1959): 1030-33; and David Granick. "The Problem of Pricing in Comparisons of International Ratios." SOVIET STUDIES 10 (April 1959): 370-74.

Cohn, Stanley H. "General Growth Performance of the Soviet Economy." In ECONOMIC PERFORMANCE AND THE MILITARY BURDEN IN THE SOVIET UNION, U.S. Congress. Joint Economic Committee, pp. 9-17. Washington, D.C.: Government Printing Office, 1970.

Soviet growth performance in 1950-70 is compared with that of the United States, Western Europe, and Japan. Seven tables.

──────. "The Gross National Product in the Soviet Union: Comparative Growth Rates." In DIMENSIONS OF SOVIET ECONOMIC POWER, U.S. Congress. Joint Economic Committee, pp. 69-89. Washington, D.C.: Government Printing Office, 1962.

The author's objective is to compare the economic growth of the

USSR and six leading market-oriented economies (European Common Market, Japan, United Kingdom, and the United States) during the period 1950-60. The author compares overall national products and changes in the structure and distribution of GNPs. Tables.

"Different Systems-Different Results." PROBLEMS OF ECONOMICS 3 (February 1961): 12-16.

This is a translation from TRUD, February 10, 1961. U.S. and Soviet economic performance in the 1950s is compared. Several tables.

Dodge, Norton T., and Wilber, Charles K. "The Relevance of Soviet Industrial Experiences for Less Developed Economies." SOVIET STUDIES 21 (January 1970): 330-49.

This paper emphasizes the concentrated efforts on heavy industry and unbalanced growth; the Soviet economizing on the use of capital and skilled labor, and the Soviet stress on technical education and use of the factory in the educational process. A table presents indicators of an unbalanced growth strategy.

Dulles, Allen W. "United States and Soviet Union Economies--A Comparison." In COMPARISONS OF THE U.S. AND SOVIET ECONOMIES, U.S. Congress. Joint Economic Committee, pp. 1-28. Washington, D.C.: Government Printing Office, 1959.

Dulles summarizes the growth of the Soviet economy in the postwar period and concludes that the way economic resources are directed determines the measure of national power.

Fallenbuchl, Z. M. "The Relevance of the Communist Experience for the Development of Underdeveloped Countries." CANADIAN SLAVONIC PAPERS 6 (1964): 44-58.

The article first reviews previous studies of the Soviet economy. Planning, growth policy, and organization are then discussed with a view to their application in underdeveloped countries.

Hansen, Alvin H. "The Economics of the Soviet Challenge." ECONOMIC RECORD 36 (March 1960): 5-12.

The article predicts that the Soviet Union's GNP will catch up to that of the United States by 1980 and suggests reasons for the anticipated high growth rate. For a rebuttal to this article, see: K. Bieda. "Professor Hansen and the Economics of the Soviet Challenge." ECONOMIC RECORD 37 (June 1961): 157-70. Bieda's article is rebutted in turn by B. McFarlane. "Soviet Investment Policy." ECONOMIC RECORD 38 (June 1962): 198-208.

Harris, Leon. "Some Comparisons of Socialist and Capitalist Agriculture."
SCIENCE AND SOCIETY 10 (Spring 1946): 159-71.

> This article compares the agricultural sectors in the United States and
> USSR before World War II. Five tables. For further discussion,
> see: Stephen Wellington. "Soviet Agriculture: A Discussion.
> I. Queries." SCIENCE AND SOCIETY 11 (Summer 1947): 270-
> 71; Leon Harris. "II. Reply," which follows Wellington's comments on pp. 272-78.

Hoeffding, Oleg. SOVIET STATE PLANNING AND FORCED INDUSTRIALIZATION AS A MODEL FOR ASIA. Santa Monica, Calif.: RAND Corp., 1958. 30 p.

> The paper concentrates on the reality, not the planned version,
> of economic development in the USSR and considers its "lessons
> for Asia."

Inkeles, Alex. "The Soviet Union: Model for Asia?--The Social System."
PROBLEMS OF COMMUNISM 8 (November-December 1959): 30-38.

> Inkeles examines Soviet society--its structure, ethos, and values--
> in terms of its applicability, in both practical and moral terms, to
> underdeveloped countries.

Kasdan, Saul. "The Relationship Between Machinery and Steel Production in Russia and the United States." REVIEW OF ECONOMICS AND STATISTICS 34 (February 1952): 57-66.

> This paper first comments on previous work done by Alexander
> Gerschenkron and Maurice H. Dobb. It then presents figures in
> an attempt to determine which period in U.S. economic history
> is most similar to the period of the Soviet five-year plans. Five
> charts and three tables.

Kershaw, Joseph A. THE ECONOMIC STRENGTH OF THE SOVIET UNION. Santa Monica, Calif.: RAND Corp., 1949. i, 33 p.

> This paper examines the current literature (secondary sources) of
> the time to determine the position of the Soviet economy relative
> to its own past, other economies of the world, and, in particular,
> the United States.

Krengel, Rold. "Soviet, American and West German Basic Industries: A Comparison." SOVIET STUDIES 12 (October 1960): 113-25.

> Three tables are included. The emphasis is on the 1950s.

Kuznets, Simon. "A Comparative Appraisal." In ECONOMIC TRENDS IN THE SOVIET UNION, edited by Abram Bergson and Simon Kuznets, pp. 333-82. Cambridge, Mass.: Harvard University Press, 1963.

Comparisons of Russian and Other Economies

This comparative appraisal of Soviet economic performance with that of other nations, including the United States, Western Europe, and Japan, covers overall growth rates, industrial structure, capital formation, consumption expenditures, and foreign trade. Extensive data are presented in the numerous statistical tables.

Litoshenko, L. N. "The National Income of the Soviet Union." QUARTERLY JOURNAL OF ECONOMICS 42 (November 1927): 70-93.

National income of the Russian Soviet Union is compared to that of other countries, as is the distribution of income in Russia to that in the United States. Ten tables.

Long, Neal B., Jr. "An Input-Output Comparison of the Economic Structure of the U.S. and the U.S.S.R." REVIEW OF ECONOMICS AND STATISTICS 52 (November 1970): 434-41.

These tables compare a 200-sector input-output table for the United States in 1947 and one for the USSR in 1959, derived by Valdimir G. Treml.

Maddison, Angus. ECONOMIC GROWTH IN JAPAN AND THE USSR. New York: W. W. Norton, 1969. xxviii, 174 p.

Russian and Japanese experiences over the past century are compared with those in the other major industrial countries. Tables, bibliography, and index.

_____. "Soviet Economic Performance." BANCA NAZIONALE DEL LAVORO REVIEW 18 (March 1965): 3-57.

A comparison is made of the economic performances of the Soviet Union with those of Western Europe and Japan. Tables.

Miyashita, Tadao. "The Red Chinese and Soviet Economies in Comparison." KOBE UNIVERSITY ECONOMIC REVIEW 7 (1961): 45-65.

This paper focuses on economic conditions in the two countries at the beginning of their development and on the means used by them to further development. A table gives values of indicators of levels of development in the two countries.

Montias, John M. "The Soviet Economic Model and the Underdeveloped Nations." In STUDY OF THE SOVIET ECONOMY, edited by Nicolas Spulber, pp. 57-80. Papers presented at a conference, Bloomington, Ind. Bloomington: Indiana University Press, 1961.

This article surveys impact of Soviet development models on underdeveloped countries, decentralization in developing economies, and the Soviet model and questions of size and efficiency.

Nutter, G. Warren. "The Structure and Growth of Soviet Industry: A Comparison with the United States." JOURNAL OF LAW AND ECONOMICS 2 (October 1959): 147-74.

>Six tables and three charts present data covering selected years between 1870 and 1955.

Spulber, Nicolas. "Contrasting Economic Patterns: Chinese and Soviet Development Strategies." SOVIET STUDIES 15 (July 1963): 1-16.

>This paper reviews the history of economic growth strategies in the two countries, contrasts them, and discusses future options.

Starovskii, V. N. "On the Methodology of Computing Economic Indices of the USSR and the USA." PROBLEMS OF ECONOMICS 3 (July 1960): 14-24.

>This is a translation from VOPROSY EKONOMIKI no. 4 (1960): 103-17. It discusses comparisons of industrial production, agricultural output, labor productivity, national income, and living standards.

Tarn, Alexander. "A Comparison of Dollar and Ruble Values of the Industrial Output of the USA and the USSR." SOVIET STUDIES 19 (April 1968): 482-500.

>Methods of computing the index of industrial output and the significance of the results are discussed. Figures for 1955-67 are given in eight tables.

――――. "Dollar Value of Soviet Industrial Production, 1955-1960." REVIEW OF ECONOMICS AND STATISTICS 46 (November 1964): 406-12.

>This study is an extension of a previous paper: Alexander Tarn and Robert W. Campbell. "A Comparison of U.S. and Soviet Industrial Output." (See below). It extends the comparison to the years 1958 and 1960. Eight tables.

――――. "The Soviet Union May Soon Surpass the United States in Total Industrial Output." ASSOCIATION FOR COMPARATIVE ECONOMIC STUDIES BULLETIN 16 (Spring 1974): 33-44.

>Methods of analysis are discussed and findings are presented. Three tables.

Tarn, Alexander, and Campbell, Robert W. "A Comparison of U.S. and Soviet Industrial Output." AMERICAN ECONOMIC REVIEW 52 (September 1962): 703-37.

>The article explores methods used in arriving at estimates of U.S. and Soviet industrial output, discusses the results, and makes a final evaluation. Numerous data tables. The appendix consists of a table of Soviet-U.S. output relatives by four-digit Standard Indus-

trail Classification categories.

U.S. Congress. Joint Economic Committee. COMPARISONS OF THE U.S. AND SOVIET ECONOMIES. Washington, D.C.: Government Printing Office, 1959. 376 p.

    The major topics of this study are (1) problems of Soviet-United States comparisons, (2) population and labor force, (3) industry, (4) transportation, (5) agriculture, (6) levels of living and incentives in the Soviet and U.S. economies, (7) national income and product, (8) foreign economic activities, and (9) evaluation of the Russian economic threat by private policymakers. Tables.

U.S. Library of Congress. Legislative Reference Service. SOVIET ECONOMIC GROWTH: A COMPARISON WITH THE UNITED STATES. New York: Greenwood Press, 1968. xi, 149 p.

    Comparisons are made in many areas, including industry, transportation, agriculture, population, labor force, living standards, and national income and product. Twenty-eight tables.

_____. TRENDS IN ECONOMIC GROWTH: A COMPARISON OF THE WESTERN POWERS AND THE SOVIET BLOC. Washington, D.C.: Government Printing Office, 1955. xiii, 339 p.

    This work, although dealing with the Soviet bloc and the Western powers, contains a wealth of information on many aspects of the Soviet economy. Tables and charts.

Whitehouse, F. Douglas, and Havelka, Joseph F. "Comparisons of Farm Output in the U.S. and the USSR,--1950-1971." In SOVIET ECONOMIC PROSPECTS FOR THE SEVENTIES, U.S. Congress. Joint Economic Committee, pp. 340-74. Washington, D.C.: Government Printing Office, 1973.

    Topics covered include the role of agriculture in the U.S. and Soviet economies, crop and livestock production 1950-71, relative levels of farm technology, and the outlook for the mid-1970s. Sixteen tables and five charts.

Chapter 9
ECONOMIC FLUCTUATIONS AND BUSINESS CYCLES

THE PERIOD UP TO 1860

Crouzet, F., et al. ESSAYS IN EUROPEAN ECONOMIC HISTORY, 1789-1914. London: Edward Arnold; New York: St. Martin's, 1969. viii, 280 p.

> This volume contains an essay by Stanislav G. Strumilin, "Industrial Crises in Russia 1847-67," pp. 155-78. Strumilin gives a brief account of the industrial crisis in Russia prior to 1847, and he discusses the worldwide industrial crisis of 1847 and its effects on Russian foreign trade. He also considers the effects on Russia of world crises in 1857 and 1866.

THE PERIOD 1860-1917

Pervushin, S. A. "Cyclical Fluctuations in Agriculture and Industry in Russia 1869-1926." QUARTERLY JOURNAL OF ECONOMICS 42 (August 1928): 564-92.

> This paper discusses the importance to Russia of the relation between agricultural and industrial cycles; the characteristics of the Russian economic system; the economically important events in the period 1869-1914; similarities and differences in relation to other countries' cycles; and the correlation between crops and cycles. The period 1913-26 is then treated separately.

THE PERIOD AFTER 1917

Feller, Arthur. "The Soviet Union and the Business Cycle." SOCIAL RESEARCH 3 (August 1936): 282-303.

> This article discusses whether the absence of business cycles in the Soviet Union is a transitional phenomenon or is permanent.

Goldman, Marshall I. "The Reluctant Consumer and Economic Fluctuations in the Soviet Union." JOURNAL OF POLITICAL ECONOMY 73 (August 1965): 366-80.

This paper surveys the new problems (and the reasons for them) which the Soviet planner faces at the present stage of development: consumer unpredictability, inventory accumulation, production cutbacks, factory closings, and diminishing growth rates. Seven tables and a graph provide data, mostly on consumer behavior.

Chapter 10

THE USE OF MATHEMATICAL MODELS, ECONOMETRICS, AND COMPUTERS IN THE SOVIET ECONOMY

Bartol, Kathryn M. "Soviet Computer Centers: Network or Tangle?" SOVIET STUDIES 23 (April 1972): 608-18.

> This study examines the origin of the government-agency debate and traces the progress which has been made in creating a network, particularly exploring the effect of the debate and other administrative difficulties on work quality. The possibilities for carrying out the plan suggested in 1966 are assessed.

Belkin, V. D. "Soviet Co-ordination Plan Concerning the Application of Mathematical Methods and Electronic Computers in Economic Calculations." ECONOMICS OF PLANNING 2 (December 1962): 159-83.

> Most of this article consists of tables summarizing steps in which use of mathematical methods and computers will be introduced into the economy.

Hardt, John P., et al. MATHEMATICS AND COMPUTERS IN SOVIET ECONOMIC PLANNING. New Haven, Conn.: Yale University Press, 1967. xxii, 298 p.

> The four major papers are: (1) "Information Control, and Soviet Economic Management," by R. W. Judy; (2) "Input-Output Analysis and Soviet Planning," by Vladimir G. Treml; (3) "Linear Programming and Soviet Planning," by Benjamin Ward; and (4) "Soviet Optimizing Models for Multiperiod Planning," by John M. Montias. Index.

Johansen, Leif. "Soviet Mathematical Economics." ECONOMIC JOURNAL 76 (September 1966): 593-601.

> This article is a review of THE USE OF MATHEMATICS IN ECONOMICS, edited by V. S. Nemchinov: English edition edited by Alec Nove. Edinburgh: Oliver and Boyd, 1964. In reviewing the book, the article presents a capsule survey of Soviet mathematical economics.

Kovalev, N. "Introducing Mathematical Methods and Computers in Planning Practice." PROBLEMS OF ECONOMICS 5 (May 1962): 32-39.

This is a translation from PLANOVOE KHOZIAISTVO no. 8 (1961): 15-25.

"Linear Economics in Soviet Planning." BULLETIN OF THE ASSOCIATION FOR THE STUDY OF SOVIET-TYPE ECONOMIES 1 (May 1959): 2-5.

This is a note concerning the growing areas of linear programming and input-output in Soviet application and the increasing sophistication of Soviet electronic equipment.

Miller, Katherine. "Computers in the Soviet Economy." In NEW DIRECTIONS IN THE SOVIET ECONOMY, U.S. Congress. Joint Economic Committee, pp. 327-37. Washington, D.C.: Government Printing Office, 1966.

The demand for computers in economic planning and at the enterprise level and computer production are discussed. A table compares U.S. and Soviet computer production for 1958-65.

Montias, John M. "Soviet Optimizing Models for Multiperiod Planning." In MATHEMATICS AND COMPUTERS IN SOVIET ECONOMIC PLANNING, by John P. Hardt el al., pp. 201-60. New Haven, Conn.: Yale University Press, 1967.

This paper analyzes some of the mathematical methods and models of Kantorovich and Novozhilov; transition models; aggregate models; dynamic programming models; and suboptimization (the location of investment projects and the selection of technological variants). A comment by E. Ames follows.

Morton, George, and Zauberman, Alfred. "Von Neumann's Model and Soviet Long-Term (Perspective) Planning." KYKLOS 22, no. 1 (1969): 45-61.

This highly mathematical article is concerned with the impact of John Von Neumann's model on the model of "dynamic planning" designed by Kantorovich and V.L. Makarov. Specific topics covered include "the nexus between the pace of the economy's growth and investment efficiency . . . the problems of efficiency and profit rates . . . [and] the quest for an optimality criterion."

Nemchinov, V. [S.]. "Mathematics and Electronics in the Service of Planning." PROBLEMS OF ECONOMICS 4 (November 1961): 3-9.

Current breakthroughs and problems in this area are discussed.

Olgin, Constantine. "Cybernetics in the Soviet Economy." STUDIES ON THE SOVIET UNION n.s. 10, no. 4 (1970): 41-67.

The history and the role of cybernetics in the modern Soviet economy are analyzed.

"Recommendations of the All-Union Scientific-Technical Conference on Problems of Determining the Economic Effectiveness of Capital Investments and New Techniques in the USSR National Economy." PROBLEMS OF ECONOMICS 1 (January 1959): 86-90.

> Problems in measuring the returns from investment and technical innovations are discussed.

Ward, Benjamin. "Kantorovich on Economic Calculation." JOURNAL OF POLITICAL ECONOMY 68 (December 1960): 545-56.

> This article is a review of Kantorovich's book in Russian. ECONOMIC CALCULATION OF THE BEST USE OF RESOURCES. Moscow: Akademiia Nauk, SSR, 1959.

―――. "Linear Programming and Soviet Planning." In MATHEMATICS AND COMPUTERS IN SOVIET ECONOMIC PLANNING, by John P. Hardt et al., New Haven, Conn.: Yale University Press, 1967.

> This paper discusses Soviet plan making; transport planning; long-run planning and the location of enterprises; enterprise and intermediate level studies; and centralized planning.

Zauberman, Alfred. "A Few Remarks on a Discovery in Soviet Economics." OXFORD UNIVERSITY. INSTITUTE OF ECONOMICS AND STATISTICS. BULLETIN 24 (November 1962): 437-45.

> This article is concerned largely with the work of V. K. Dmitriev, a little-known Russian mathematical economist who wrote at the turn of the century. His work is found to be related to that of Leontief.

―――. "A Few Remarks on Trends in Soviet Plan-Programming." ECONOMICS OF PLANNING 7, no. 3 (1967): 270-79.

> These loosely organized remarks cover the following topics, among others: use of the programming approach in Soviet planning; attempts to make the programming dynamic; efforts to develop a methodology of decomposition; problems of linear programming; the shift to nonlinear programming; and "intensive work on multi-external and integer and mixed-integer programming."

―――. "On the Objective Function for the Soviet Economy." ECONOMICA n.s. 32 (August 1965): 323-29.

> First attempts by Soviet mathematical economists "to formalize the objective function and that of social time-preference for a centrally-planned command system" are surveyed. The article uses some calculus.

―――. "The Present State of Soviet 'Planometrics.'" SOVIET STUDIES 14 (July 1962): 62-74.

Use of Mathematical Models

Topics discussed include data gathering, aggregation problems, and input-output techniques.

_____. "Soviet Attempts to Dynamize Interindustry Analysis: A Survey." ECONOMIA INTERNAZIONALE 21 (May 1968): 258-77.

This is a survey of the Soviet effort in this field.

Chapter 11

SOVIET USE OF INPUT-OUTPUT ANALYSIS

Becker, Abraham S. INPUT-OUTPUT AND SOVIET PLANNING; A SURVEY OF RECENT DEVELOPMENTS. Santa Monica, Calif.: RAND Corp., 1963. ix, 27 p.

This study summarizes the stages in the development of Soviet input-output studies and discusses planning issues such as centralization versus decentralization.

Ellman, Michael J. "The Use of Input-Output in Regional Economic Planning: The Soviet Experience." ECONOMIC JOURNAL 78 (December 1968): 855-67.

This survey of Soviet uses of input-output tables in regional planning concludes that Soviet economists are ahead of those in other countries, that the work has been largely experimental, and that problems remain, but that the technique will eventually increase the efficiency of planning.

Freeman, J. Fisher. "The Soviet Interindustry Table for 1959." BULLETIN OF THE ASSOCIATION FOR THE STUDY OF SOVIET-TYPE ECONOMIES 9 (Fall 1962): 11-14.

The article attempts to reconstruct the entire 1959 input-output table for the Soviet economy from the available data.

Jasny, Naum. "The Russian Economic 'Balance' and Input-Output Analysis: A Historical Comment." SOVIET STUDIES 14 (July 1962): 75-80.

This note comments on the treatment of this subject in several other works. The idea of "balance" is placed in historical context. For further discussion, see: Herbert S. Levine. "The Russian Economic 'Balance' and Input-Output Analysis: A Reply." SOVIET STUDIES 15 (January 1964): 352-56.

Kaplan, Norman M., et al. A TENTATIVE INPUT-OUTPUT TABLE FOR THE USSR, 1941 PLAN. Santa Monica, Calif.: RAND Corp., 1952. i, 153 p.

The authors have attempted to reproduce an input-output table for the USSR which is implied by, or consistent with, the 1941 plan structure of the Soviet economy.

Kossov, V. V. "Regional Input-Output Analysis in the USSR." REGIONAL SCIENCE ASSOCIATION. PAPERS AND PROCEEDINGS 14 (1965): 175-81.

>Kossov provides a Soviet account of the construction of Soviet input-output tables.

Levine, Herbert L. "Input-Output Analysis and Soviet Planning." AMERICAN ECONOMIC REVIEW 52 (May 1962): 127-37.

>The paper discusses input-output analysis and its possible application in the construction of short-term economic plans. The discussion is restricted to the problem of attaining internal consistency in the annual plan. The appendix presents a mathematical model which combines the material balance and input-output methods. For a further discussion, see: Lloyd G. Reynolds et al. "Soviet Economic Planning--Discussion." REGIONAL SCIENCE ASSOCIATION. PAPERS AND PROCEEDINGS 14 (1965): 158-64.

Modin, Anatoly. "Developing Interbranch Balance for Economic Simulation." ECONOMICS OF PLANNING 3 (September 1963): 104-16.

>This article discusses the use of input-output matrices in economic simulations to facilitate planning.

Serck-Hanssen, J. "Input-Output Tables in the USSR and Eastern Europe." ECONOMICS OF PLANNING 2 (July 1962): 65-72.

>This is a brief review of input-output tables in the Soviet Union from the 1920s to 1959. The use of input-output tables in the USSR is also discussed.

Treml, Vladimir G. "Input-Output Analysis and Soviet Planning." In MATHEMATICS AND COMPUTERS IN SOVIET ECONOMIC PLANNING, edited by John P. Hardt et al., pp. 68-120. New Haven, Conn.: Yale University Press, 1967.

>The author examines Soviet explorations of the input-output concept and the efforts to adopt it to the needs of central planning. The paper deals with empirical work on ex-post models and planning input-output models. A comment by Abraham S. Becker follows, pp. 121-35.

_____. "A New Tool for Soviet Optimal Planning?" BULLETIN OF THE ASSOCIATION FOR THE STUDY OF SOVIET-TYPE ECONOMIES 11 (Spring 1969): 1-5.

>This article is concerned with a Soviet input-output table for 1966 and its significance for the future of Soviet planning.

Soviet Use of Input-Output Analysis

———. "The 1959 Soviet Input-Output Table (As Reconstructed)." In NEW DIRECTIONS IN THE SOVIET ECONOMY, U.S. Congress. Joint Economic Committee, pp. 257-70. Washington, D.C.: Government Printing Office, 1966.

> This paper presents the original 1959 Soviet input-output table, reconstructs it in value terms, and compares the results with Soviet national income and product statistics. Several tables, the reconstructed input-output table, and an annex table of commodity classifications used in the reconstruction are included.

———. "A Note on Soviet Input-Output Tables." SOVIET STUDIES 21 (July 1969): 21-34.

> This article provides an introduction to Soviet input-output statistics generally and to the newly published 1966 table in particular. Two tables.

———. "A Tabulation of Soviet Input-Output Tables." BULLETIN OF THE ASSOCIATION FOR THE STUDY OF SOVIET-TYPE ECONOMIES 11 (Fall 1969): 13-16.

> This is a complete list of all input-output tables compiled by the Soviets, including national, regional, and industry tables.

Treml, Vladimir G., et al. "Interindustry Structure of the Soviet Economy: 1959 and 1966." In SOVIET ECONOMIC PROSPECTS FOR THE SEVENTIES, U.S. Congress. Joint Economic Committee, pp. 246-69. Washington, D.C.: Government Printing Office, 1973.

> This paper discusses the development of input-output analysis in the USSR, the reconstruction of the 1959 and 1966 tables, and the comparability of the two tables. Information on the tables is given in the appendices.

———. THE STRUCTURE OF THE SOVIET ECONOMY: ANALYSIS AND RECONSTRUCTION OF THE 1966 INPUT-OUTPUT TABLE. New York and London: Praeger, 1972. xxiv, 660 p.

> Topics given particular attention include input-output analysis in the USSR, the 1966 table itself, sector and commodity classification, Soviet statistics, foreign trade, labor input, output by sectors, capital, employment, and consumption. Tables and data appendices.

Zauberman, Alfred. "A Note on the Soviet Inter-Industry Labour Input Balance." SOVIET STUDIES 15 (July 1963): 53-57.

> The use of input-output techniques in planning is discussed.

Chapter 12
ECONOMIC AND SOCIAL STATISTICS

THE PERIOD 1860-1917

Hutt, W. H. "Two Studies in the Statistics of Russia." SOUTH AFRICAN JOURNAL OF ECONOMICS 13 (March 1945): 18-42.

> This paper presents statistics on "The Progressiveness of Russia Before 1917" and "Soviet Standards of Living Before the War." Many tables. For further discussion, see: C. A. Friedmann. "A Critique of Professor Hutt's 'Two Studies in the Statistics of Russia.'" SOUTH AFRICAN JOURNAL OF ECONOMICS 13 (December 1945): 332-43; W. H. Hutt. "Reply: Further Aspects of Russian Statistics." SOUTH AFRICAN JOURNAL OF ECONOMICS 13 (December 1945): 344-63.

Wheatcroft, S. G. "The Reliability of Russian Prewar Grain Output Statistics." SOVIET STUDIES 26 (April 1974): 157-80.

> This paper examines a long controversy on the reliability of these statistics. It discusses the applications of corrections, their justification, and the significance of the corrections made. The statistical appendix includes a foldout table of various estimates of grain total corrections.

THE PERIOD AFTER 1917

American-Russian Chamber of Commerce. ECONOMIC HANDBOOK OF THE SOVIET UNION. New York: American-Russian Chamber of Commerce, 1931. 151 p.

> This book contains statistical information on area and population; the government; the national economy--development, state planning system, and the Five-Year Plan; a number of industries; electrification; agriculture; transportation; finance; foreign trade and education and health. Many tables and two foldout maps. The data come from official Soviet sources.

Economic and Social Statistics

Baykov, Alexander M. "Reliability of Data." BULLETINS ON SOVIET ECONOMIC DEVELOPMENT Ser. 2, 8 (May 1953): 1-7.

    The reliability and availability of Soviet data in the postwar period are discussed.

Bergson, Abram. "A Problem in Soviet Statistics." REVIEW OF ECONOMICS AND STATISTICS 29 (November 1947): 234-42.

    This paper examines an apparent inconsistency in the targets of the Fourth Five-Year Plan for 1950. Workers times average salary is significantly less than the stated payroll. A table presents data on employment and earnings for selected years 1932-50. For further discussion, see: Maurice H. Dobb. "Further Appraisal of Russian Economic Statistics: A Comment on Soviet Statistics," pp. 34-38; and Harry Schwartz. "A Critique of Appraisals of Russian Economic Statistics," pp. 38-41; both in REVIEW OF ECONOMICS AND STATISTICS 30 (February 1948).

_____. "Reliability and Usability of Soviet Statistics: A Summary Appraisal." AMERICAN STATISTICIAN 7 (June-July 1953): 19-23.

    The author outlines Soviet statistical procedures.

Berliner, Joseph S. "Real Income and Consumption Statistics: Summary and Assessment." In SOVIET ECONOMIC STATISTICS, edited by Vladimir G. Treml and John P. Hardt, pp. 348-52. Durham, N.C.: Duke University Press, 1972.

    Berliner comments on questions raised in papers presented by Gertrude Schroeder, "An Appraisal of Soviet Wage and Income Statistics," and Marshall I. Goldman, "Consumption Statistics." (See below.)

Campbell, Robert W. "The Changing Role of Statistics in the Soviet Economic System." In SOVIET ECONOMIC STATISTICS, edited by Vladimir G. Treml and John P. Hardt, pp. 21-44. Durham, N.C.: Duke University Press, 1972.

    The author aims at discerning how well the statistical system used in the USSR serves the needs of the economic policymakers. This need, in turn, influences the kind and volume of Soviet statistics produced.

_____. "A Shortcut Method for Estimating Soviet GNP." ASSOCIATION FOR COMPARATIVE ECONOMIC STUDIES BULLETIN 14 (Fall 1972): 31-34.

    This short article presents a makeshift method for estimating Soviet GNP from the data contained in the Soviet annual statistical handbook, NARODNOYE KHOZIAISTVO SSR. Table 1 presents a calculation of Soviet NNP for 1970; Table 2, a comparison of RAND Corporation GNP estimates with the simplified method. A further simplification of the method can be found in Gregory Grossman. "A Simplified Method." ASSOCIATION FOR COMPARATIVE

Economic and Social Statistics

ECONOMIC STUDIES BULLETIN 14 (Winter 1972-73): 9-10.

Central Statistical Administration. THE NATIONAL ECONOMY OF THE USSR; A STATISTICAL COMPILATION. Moscow: State Statistical Publishing House, 1956. 271 p.

    Statistical tables are provided on virtually all aspects of the Soviet economy. The period 1940-55 receives the greatest emphasis, but some pre-Revolutionary figures are provided to allow comparison.

_____. THE NATIONAL ECONOMY OF THE U.S.S.R.: A STATISTICAL COMPILATION. Moscow: State Statistical Publishing House, 1957. 364 p.

    A compilation of statistical tables on the Soviet economy. 1940-56 is stressed, but pre-Revolutionary figures are provided for the sake of comparison. This volume has since been updated and reissued annually.

_____. SOVIET TRADE: A STATISTICAL COMPILATION. Moscow: State Statistical Publishing House, 1956. 345 p.

    This handbook contains data on state and cooperative retail trade and the collective farm market, which characterized Soviet trade from 1924 to 1955. A series of basic Soviet trade indices provides information according to the union republics and according to krays, oblasts, and ASSR's.

_____. THE U.S.S.R. ECONOMY: A STATISTICAL ABSTRACT. London: Lawrence & Wishart, 1957. 264 p.

    Essential statistics, illustrating the present level of the Soviet economy in comparison with 1913, 1928, and 1940 are provided. Figures for the separate union republics are sometimes included.

_____. USSR INDUSTRY; A STATISTICAL COMPILATION. Moscow: State Statistical Publishing House, 1957. 434 p.

    Statistical tables are provided on the principal industrial sectors including regional figures, with emphasis on 1940-56.

Clark, Colin. CRITIQUE OF RUSSIAN STATISTICS. London: Macmillan and Co., 1939. v, 76 p.

    This book collates and tests Russian statistics, using tests of internal consistency and comparisons with statistics of the outside world. Many tables.

_____. "Some Statistical Comparisons." In SOVIET PLANNING: ESSAYS IN HONOUR OF NAUM JASNY, edited by Jane Degras and Alec Nove, pp. 205-10. Oxford: Basil Blackwell, 1964.

    This paper presents some of Clark's thoughts on some statistics concerning the Soviet economy, especially those in Naum Jasny's works. Attention is also given to estimates made by Abram Bergson, G. Warren Nutter, and others.

Clarke, Roger A. SOVIET ECONOMIC FACTS 1917-1970. New York: John Wiley, 1972.

The author's purpose "is to present under one cover as nearly as possible complete annual series for the main aggregate economic magnitudes, a list of industrial and agricultural products . . . and certain other more general data related to economic performance." The data are based exclusively on original Soviet sources.

De Pauw, John W. THE SOVIET STATISTICAL SYSTEM: THE CONTINUOUS SAMPLE BUDGET SURVEY. International Population Reports Series P-95, no. 62. Washington, D.C.: Government Printing Office, 1965. iii, 95 p.

This report details the organization, program, and special features of the continuous sample budget survey. Many tables. Bibliography.

Desai, Padma. "Soviet Industrial Production: Estimates of Gross Output by Branches and Groups." OXFORD BULLETIN OF ECONOMICS AND STATISTICS 35 (May 1973): 153-71.

The author presents a technique for deriving Soviet industrial output data by branches and also a method for aggregating these estimates into heavy and consumer goods sectors. Tables

"The Development of Soviet Statistics." OST OKONOMI 2 (July 1962): 120-35.

Papers included are "Social Responsibility of the Economist," by Stanislav G. Strumilin; "New Tasks of the Statistical Service," by A. Yezhov; "The Basis of Scientific Planning," by I. Evenko; "But What Will the Machines Calculate?," by P. Maslov; and " 'Pure' Science and the Facts of Life," by N. Druzhinin.

"The Discussion of Statistics Summed Up." SOVIET STUDIES 6, no. 3 (1955): 321-31.

This is a translation of K. V. Ostrovitianov. "The Result of the Discussion of Statistics." VESTNIK AKADEMII NAUK SSSR, no. 8 (1954). It seeks to distinguish between "statistics," dealing with socioeconomic matters, and "mathematical statistics," dealing with natural and technical phenomena.

Dobb, Maurice H. "Comment on Soviet Economic Statistics." SOVIET STUDIES 1 (June 1949): 18-27.

Problems in the interpretation of Soviet economic statistics, including accuracy, prices, and measurement of national income, are considered.

Economic and Social Statistics

Eckstein, Alexander, and Gutmann, Peter. "Capital and Output in the Soviet Union, 1928-1937." REVIEW OF ECONOMICS AND STATISTICS 38 (November 1956): 436-44.

This paper develops measurements of the aggregate and industrial incremental capital-output in the Soviet Union, points out factors which may account for the comparatively low ratios observed, and discusses the implications for measurements in general. A table estimates capital stock in the USSR, 1928-45.

Feshbach, Murray. "Soviet Industrial Labor and Productivity Statistics." In SOVIET ECONOMIC STATISTICS, edited by Vladimir G. Treml and John P. Hardt, pp. 195-228. Durham, N.C.: Duke University Press, 1972.

This chapter is concerned primarily with the availability of official statistical data on Soviet industrial labor. Tables.

_____. THE SOVIET STATISTICAL SYSTEM: LABOR FORCE RECORDKEEPING AND REPORTING. International Population Statistics Reports, Series P-90, no. 12. Washington, D.C.: Government Printing Office, 1960. vi, 151 p.

This study describes agencies concerned with collecting data, examines the collection of employment statistics, traces the flow of data, and discusses the methodology of some of the most important labor statistics. Tables, appendices, bibliography, and index.

_____. THE SOVIET STATISTICAL SYSTEM: LABOR FORCE RECORDKEEPING AND REPORTING SINCE 1957. International Population Statistics Reports, Series P-90, no. 17. Washington, D.C.: Government Printing Office, 1962. vi, 99 p.

This report traces the impact of the Soviet administrative reorganization of mid-1957 on structure and operations of the Soviet statistical agencies which gathered data on the labor force. Tables and bibliography.

Freeman, J. Fisher, and Lee, W. T. "Establishment of an Absolute Ruble Value for the Soviet Statistical Concept, the 'Gross Out-put of Industry.'" SOVIET STUDIES 13 (October 1961): 172-86.

Seven tables provide data on the 1950s, while the text discusses derivation of the estimates.

_____. "Soviet Industrial Statistics: Use of Cost Data in Relation to Gross and Net Output." SOVIET STUDIES 13 (April 1962): 362-82.

The derivation of the statistics is discussed in the text. Ten tables provide data for the 1950s.

Gerschenkron, Alexander. "Soviet Heavy Industry: A Dollar Index of Output, 1927/28-1973." REVIEW OF ECONOMICS AND STATISTICS 37 (May 1955): 120-30.

Gerschenkron computes an index of output, covering machine-building, iron and steel, petroleum, coal, and electric power. Tables.

_____. "The Soviet Indices of Industrial Production." REVIEW OF ECONOMICS AND STATISTICS 29 (November 1947): 217-26.

This paper describes the indexes, looks at performance claims, and analyzes biases in the indexes. Tables. For further discussion, see: Maurice H. Dobb, "Further Appraisal of Russian Economic Statistics: A Comment on Soviet Statistics," pp. 34-38; and Harry Schwartz, "A Critique of 'Appraisals of Russian Economic Statistics,' " pp. 38-41; both in REVIEW OF ECONOMICS AND STATISTICS 30 (February 1948).

_____. "Use and Misuse of Russian Statistics." REVIEW OF ECONOMICS AND STATISTICS 33 (February 1951): 76-78.

This paper is a review of Charles Bettelheim. L'ECONOMIE SOVIETIQUE. Paris (1950).

Giffler, Milton. "Industrial Statistics of the State Planning Committee of the U.S.S.R. (Gosplan)." AMERICAN STATISTICIAN 24 (April 1970): 10-16.

This paper examines the Gosplan system of statistics and its potential use to analysts. Covered are data collection for Gosplan; the flow of Gosplan data; methodological instructions; Gosplan's national accounts; material balances; pricing standards; and the aggregate value of industrial output. Three organizational charts and a table of alternative measurements of gross industrial activity, 1958-68, are included.

Goldman, Marshall I. "Consumption Statistics." In SOVIET ECONOMIC STATISTICS, edited by Vladimir G. Treml and John P. Hardt, pp. 315-47. Durham, N.C.: Duke University Press, 1972.

This paper attempts to discover the kinds of consumption data which are and are not collected and made available by the authorities. Appropriate uses of this material are considered. Tables.

Greenslade, Rush V. "Industrial Production Statistics." In SOVIET ECONOMIC STATISTICS, edited by Vladimir G. Treml and John P. Hardt, pp. 155-94. Durham, N.C.: Duke University Press, 1972.

This paper presents a value-added weighted index of civilian industrial production which can be compared with the official gross-value index. Tables.

Greenslade, Rush V., and Robertson, Wade E. "Industrial Production in the USSR." In SOVIET ECONOMIC PROSPECTS FOR THE SEVENTIES, U.S. Congress. Joint Economic Committee, pp. 270-82. Washington, D.C.: Government Printing Office, 1973.

> Topics discussed include indexes of civilian industrial production with 1968 weights, productivity, and the methodology of constructing the indexes. Eleven tables.

Grossman, Gregory. SOVIET STATISTICS OF PHYSICAL OUTPUT OF INDUSTRIAL COMMODITIES; THEIR COMPILATION AND QUALITY. Princeton, N.J.: Princeton University Press, 1960. 151 p. Illustrated.

> The reliability and usability of Soviet statistics of the physical output of industrial commodities are discussed. The period beginning with the five-year plans is stressed. Bibliography and index.

Harris, Seymour E. "Appraisals of Russian Economic Statistics." REVIEW OF ECONOMICS AND STATISTICS 29 (November 1947): 213-14.

> This introductory note discusses the need for assessing the accuracy and usefulness of Russian economic statistics and the problems involved in making such judgments. For further discussion, see: Maurice H. Dobb. "Further Appraisal of Russian Economic Statistics: A Comment on Soviet Statistics," pp. 34-38; and Harry Schwartz, "A Critique of 'Appraisals of Russian Economic Statistics,' " pp. 38-41; both in REVIEW OF ECONOMICS AND STATISTICS 30 (February 1948).

Herman, Leon M. VARIETIES OF ECONOMIC SECRECY IN THE SOVIET UNION. Santa Monica, Calif.: RAND Corp., 1963. 28 p.

> This paper discusses the origin of Soviet "statistical blackout"; the secret system of taxation; trade union finances; price formation; foreign travel by Soviet citizens; and the fear of losing economic secrets.

Hodgman, Donald R. "Industrial Production." In SOVIET ECONOMIC GROWTH: CONDITIONS AND PERSPECTIVES, edited by Abram Bergson, pp. 225-45. Evanston, Ill.: Row, Peterson, 1953.

> Hodgmen discusses the problems of obtaining reliable data for computing Soviet industrial production. The revised index of Soviet industrial production used in this paper is computed using Soviet value relationships and physical production data. The article is followed with a comment by Dimitri B. Shimkin, pp. 244-45.

_____. SOVIET INDUSTRIAL PRODUCTION, 1928-1951. Cambridge, Mass.: Harvard University Press, 1954. xix, 241 p.

> The first three chapters concern official measures and value-added weights for Soviet industry, as well as statistical procedures in computing the production index. Chapters 4 and 5 summarize production figures for large-scale industry from 1927-28 through 1951.

Chapter 7 concludes with a discussion of Soviet industrial development. Charts, tables, bibliography, and index.

Holubnychy, Vsevolod. "Government Statistical Observation in the USSR: 1917-1957." AMERICAN SLAVIC AND EAST EUROPEAN REVIEW 19 (February 1960): 28-41.

This article reviews the history of the organization of the Soviet statistics-collecting apparatus from the experience acquired before the Revolution to 1957.

Hunter, Holland. "Recent Soviet Industrial Output in Rubles." BULLETIN OF THE ASSOCIATION FOR THE STUDY OF SOVIET-TYPE ECONOMIES 5 (Winter 1963): 22-27.

This article manipulates available Soviet data to obtain ruble estimates of Soviet industrial output for the years 1958-62.

_____. "Soviet Economic Statistics: An Introduction." In SOVIET ECONOMIC STATISTICS, edited by Vladimir G. Treml and John P. Hardt, pp. 3-20. Durham, N.C.: Duke University Press, 1972.

This paper deals with five topics: (1) a comparison of Soviet statistics for 1947 and 1969; (2) the new conditions and new tasks for Soviet statistics; (3) Soviet problems of measuring and managing economic growth; (4) the optimum amount of statistics; and (5) future statistical concepts and extensions.

_____. "Soviet Industrial Growth: The Early Plan Period." JOURNAL OF ECONOMIC HISTORY 15 (September 1955): 281-87.

This article is a discussion of two works: Donald R. Hodgman. SOVIET INDUSTRIAL PRODUCTION, 1928-1951. Cambridge, Mass.: Harvard University Press, 1954; and Oleg Hoeffding. SOVIET NATIONAL INCOME AND PRODUCTION IN 1928. New York: Columbia University Press, 1954.

Jasny, Naum. INDICES OF SOVIET INDUSTRIAL PRODUCTION, 1928-1954. Washington, D.C.: Council for Economic and Industry Research, 1955. iii, 53 p.

This paper contains a discussion of the various indices of Soviet industrial production for the years 1928-54; a comment on Donald R. Hodgman's index for industrial consumers' goods; and a comment on the machinery output indices (1927-28 to 1937) calculated by Alexander Gerschenkron and Donald R. Hodgman.

_____. "International Organization and Soviet Statistics." AMERICAN STATISTICAL ASSOCIATION. JOURNAL 45 (March 1950): 48-64.

The article discusses the problems which various international organizations have had with Soviet statistics, including the International Institute of Agriculture in Rome, the League of Nations, the International Labour Office, the United Nations, and the Food and Agriculture Office of the United Nations. Two charts estimate industrial production for the Soviet Union and other industrial countries.

───── . THE SOVIET 1956 STATISTICAL HANDBOOK: A COMMENTARY. East Lansing: Michigan State University Press, 1957. xii, 212 p.

This commentary examines "the impossibly large rates of growth" shown in official Soviet statistics to reduce them to their real proportions, to determine major growth periods, and to determine where the largest rates of growth have occurred (heavy industry, transports, and investment). Tables and index.

───── . "The Soviet Statistical Yearbooks for 1955 'Through 1960.' " SLAVIC REVIEW 21 (March 1962): 121-56.

This review article analyzes the deficiencies of the statistical information provided by the Central Statistical Office. The article concludes that serious research is difficult, if not impossible, with the data from Soviet sources.

───── . "Soviet Statistics." REVIEW OF ECONOMICS AND STATISTICS 32 (February 1950): 92-99.

This article treats the history, completeness, and reliability of Soviet economic statistics and gives specific attention to territorial, demographic, agricultural, and consumption statistics. For further discussion, see: Alexander Gerschenkron and Daniel Marx. "Comments on Naum Jasny's 'Soviet Statistics.' " REVIEW OF ECONOMICS AND STATISTICS 32 (August 1950): 250-55.

Johnson, Albert A. PROGRESS IN THE SOVIET UNION: PAST, PRESENT, FUTURE. Springfield, Mass.: A. A. Johnson and Associates, 1931. 52 p.

The booklet is comprised entirely of charts, which summarize data dealing with the characteristics of the national economy, industry and transportation, labor, agriculture, and trade and finance.

Kaplan, Norman M. "Capital Stock." In ECONOMIC TRENDS IN THE SOVIET UNION, edited by Abram Bergson and Simon Kuznets, pp. 96-149. Cambridge, Mass.: Harvard University Press, 1963.

Kaplan presents and interprets data from the 1959 Soviet revaluation of its capital stock. Extensive data are presented in the tables, some with comparisons to U.S. figures.

Economic and Social Statistics

Kaplan, Norman M., and Moorsteen, Richard H. "An Index of Soviet Industrial Output." AMERICAN ECONOMIC REVIEW 50 (June 1960): 295-318.

> This article first presents an index of Soviet industrial output and discusses its nature and limitations. The second part compares the index with some others, discusses dynamic aspects of Soviet industrial growth, explores probable future rates of growth, presents an index of the output of final products, and estimates changes in productivity. Tables.

──────. INDEXES OF SOVIET INDUSTRIAL OUTPUT. 2 vols. Santa Monica, Calif.: RAND Corp., 1960. xv, 284 p.

> The four sections of volume one deal with individual output series, explain the benchmark indexes, explain the annual indexes, and summarize the resulting indexes. Volume two consists of fifty tables.

Kaser, Michael [C.]. "The Publication of Soviet Statistics." In SOVIET ECONOMIC STATISTICS, edited by Vladimir G. Treml and John P. Hardt, pp. 45-65. Durham, N.C.: Duke University Press, 1972.

> This paper examines the practices of TsSU (Tsentral' noye Statisticheskoe Upravlenie) in publishing statistics and how they have been influenced by the personal attitude of Vladimir N. Starovskii, who has been the ministerial head of TsSU for thirty-one years.

──────. "Soviet Statistics of Wages and Prices." SOVIET STUDIES 7 (July 1955): 31-51.

> Studied here are household budget data, retail prices, cost of living; services, money wages, free services in real wages, and real income. Eight tables. Two appendices discuss non-Soviet computations of retail price indexes and sources and methods.

Kolpakov, B. "The Tomorrow of Our Statistics." THE SOVIET ECONOMIC SYSTEM: STRUCTURE AND POLICY. U.S. Joint Publications Research Service 1 (March 1962): 312-31.

> This is a translation from EKONOMICHESKAYA GAZETA, no. 1 (1962). Topics discussed include the role of accounting, the use of computers, and central control.

Matko, D. J. I., and Ticktin, H. H. "Some Notes on the 1965 [Statistical] Yearbook." SOVIET STUDIES 19 (July 1967): 122-26.

> Topics discussed are industry, income, and agriculture. A table provides figures on profitability in selected sectors.

Mickiewicz, Ellen, ed. HANDBOOK OF SOVIET SOCIAL SCIENCE DATA. New York: The Free Press; London: Collier-Macmillan, 1973. xxvi, 225 p.

This work consists largely of data tables on demography, agriculture, production, health, housing, education, elite recruitment and mobilization, communications, and international interactions. Data on each topic have been compiled by a specialist in that area.

Moore, John H. "Soviet Industry Statistics." In SOVIET ECONOMIC STATISTICS, edited by Vladimir G. Treml and John P. Hardt, pp. 229-33. Durham, N.C.: Duke University Press, 1972.

The author comments briefly on the papers by Rush V. Greenslade, "Industrial Production Statistics in the USSR," pp. 155-94; and Murray Feshbach, "Soviet Industrial Labor and Productivity Statistics," pp. 195-228.

Moorsteen, Richard H., and Powell, Raymond P. THE SOVIET CAPITAL STOCK, 1928-1962. Homewood, Ill.: R. D. Irwin, 1966. xxiii, 671 p.

The book is comprised of two parts: Part one deals with capital estimates and part two with capital and growth. Part one explains the procedures used in calculating the data and presents the findings. In part two, the capital estimates are used in an analysis of Soviet growth. This detailed study contains many tables and graphs and name and subject indexes.

Nash, Edmund. "U.S.S.R. Economic and Labor Data for 1971." MONTHLY LABOR REVIEW 95 (October 1972): 61.

A table provides figures on production of selected commodities in 1971. General economic and labor data are given in the text.

National Bureau of Economic Research. STATISTICAL ABSTRACT OF INDUSTRIAL OUTPUT IN THE SOVIET UNION, 1913-1955. 5 vols. New York: National Bureau of Economic Research, 1956.

These five volumes represent the official output statistics of the Soviet government. Statistics for some important industrial sectors--like those relating to military production--are missing. A bibliography is in volume five.

Newth, J. A. "The Sovnarkhozy and the Central Statistical Administration." SOVIET STUDIES 9 (October 1957): 242-43.

This paper reports Soviet discussion of the problems and technical apparatus of the Central Statistical Administration.

_____. "The Statisticians' Conference." SOVIET STUDIES 9 (April 1958): 435-45.

The conferees discussed were the draft program for the 1959 census of population and the draft set of tables for the balances of the national economy.

Economic and Social Statistics

Nove, Alec. "A Note on the Availability and Reliability of Soviet Statistics." In THE SOVIET ECONOMY; A BOOK OF READINGS, edited by Morris Bornstein and Daniel Fusfeld, pp. 267-74. Rev. ed. Homewood, Ill.: R. D. Irwin, 1966.

> Nove considers the availability and credibility of Soviet statistics. Special attention is given to physical output figures, index numbers, and national income.

Powell, Raymond P. "Monetary Statistics." In SOVIET ECONOMIC STATISTICS, edited by Vladimir G. Treml and John P. Hardt, pp. 397-432. Durham, N.C.: Duke University Press, 1972.

> In this paper the author traces the history of the release of balance-sheet data for Gosbank, the State Bank. He also discusses existing data, indicating, for various categories, "what is available and what its characteristics are." Tables.

Rice, Stuart A. "Statistical Conceptions in the Soviet Union Examined from Generally Accepted Scientific Viewpoints." REVIEW OF ECONOMICS AND STATISTICS 34 (February 1952): 82-86.

> This paper looks at conceptual premises of Soviet statistical science which have been discarded to determine the reasons for discarding them and the implications for other practitioners. For further discussion, see: Mahesh Chand. "Some Observations on 'Statistical Conceptions in the Soviet Union.' " REVIEW OF ECONOMICS AND STATISTICS 35 (February 1953): 97-99.

Ropes, E. C. "The Statistical Publications of the U.S.S.R." RUSSIAN REVIEW 1 (November 1941): 122-25.

> This short paper surveys the most important publications of the Central Statistical Administration from the first one in 1923.

Schinke, Eberhard. "Soviet Agricultural Statistics." In SOVIET ECONOMIC STATISTICS, edited by Vladimir G. Treml and John P. Hardt, pp. 237-62. Durham, N.C.: Duke University Press, 1972.

> The paper briefly discusses: (1) the history of Soviet agricultural statistics; (2) the organization of agricultural statistics; (3) land area, yields, livestock, animal products, and output; (4) the labor force; (5) material inputs; and (6) production costs and labor inputs. The author concludes that major gaps exist in the limited available data, as well as in that used for planning which is not available to the general public.

Schroeder, Gertrude E. "An Appraisal of Soviet Wage and Income Statistics." In SOVIET ECONOMIC STATISTICS, edited by Vladimir G. Treml and John P. Hardt, pp. 287-314. Durham, N.C.: Duke University Press, 1972.

This paper discusses the availability and quality of statistics on money wages in nonagricultural sectors; on money "wages" for state farm workers and collective farmers; on money incomes; and on real wages and incomes.

Schwartz, Harry. "On the Use of Soviet Statistics." AMERICAN STATISTICAL ASSOCIATION. JOURNAL 42 (September 1947): 401-6.

Topics covered include the gaps in Soviet data, its reliability, and the method of valuation used in calculating Soviet national income.

_____. "The Renaissance of Soviet Statistics." REVIEW OF ECONOMICS AND STATISTICS 40 (May 1958): 122-26.

This article surveys the availability of Soviet statistics after the Twentieth Party Congress decided to drop the veil of secrecy on economic statistics in February 1956.

_____. "Soviet Postwar Industrial Production." JOURNAL OF POLITICAL ECONOMY 56 (October 1948): 438-41.

This article attempts to approximate the absolute Soviet postwar gross industrial production by means of an elementary algebraic analysis of official Soviet statements. Two tables. For further discussion, see: Russell T. Nichols. "Soviet Production Estimates." JOURNAL OF POLITICAL ECONOMY 57 (June 1949): 249-50; Harry Schwartz. "Comments." Same journal 57 (June 1949): 250.

_____, trans. STATISTICAL HANDBOOK OF THE U.S.S.R. New York: National Industrial Conference Board, 1957. vi, 122 p. Russian ed. NARODNOYE KHOZIAISTVO SSSR Moscow, 1956.

This is a compendium of tables on virtually all aspects of the Soviet economy. Glossary, bibliography, and index.

Segal, Louis, and Santalov, A. A., comps. and eds. COMMERCIAL YEARBOOK OF THE SOVIET UNION, 1925. London: Allen & Unwin, 1925. xxiv, 428 p.

This handbook provides data on virtually all aspects of the Soviet economy. Tables, graphs, index, and maps.

Snodgrass, John H. RUSSIA: A HANDBOOK ON COMMERCIAL AND INDUSTRIAL CONDITIONS. Washington, D.C.: Government Printing Office, 1913. 255 p.

Information on all aspects of the Soviet economy is provided. Many tables. Bibliography.

SOVIET UNION YEAR-BOOK, 1930. 6th ed. London: Allen & Unwin, 1930. 670 p.

Economic and Social Statistics

This statistical compilation presents a wealth of information on the Soviet economy. Maps and index.

Staller, George J. "The Soviet Input-Output Table and Measures of Growth: Industrial Weights." SOVIET STUDIES 16 (April 1965): 422-31.

This paper uses the 1959 Soviet input-output table to derive a weighting system to indexes of Soviet industrial output. The reliability of the system is then discussed. Three tables.

Starovskii, V. N. "The Tasks of Soviet Statistics." THE SOVIET ECONOMIC SYSTEM: STRUCTURE AND POLICY. Washington, D.C.: U.S. Joint Publications Research Service 2 (April 1962): 207-41.

This is a translation of an article by the director of the Central Statistical Administration which appeared in VESTNIK STATISTIKI no. 1 (1962): 3-15.

Thornton, Judith [G.]. "Estimation of Value Added and Average Returns to Capital in Soviet Industry from Cross-Section Data." JOURNAL OF POLITICAL ECONOMY 73 (December 1965): 620-35.

This study reconstructs the Soviet financial accounts of industry for 1960 to estimate the average return to capital by industry at nominal Soviet prices. Nine tables. For further discussion, see: G. Warren Nutter. "The Relative Size of Soviet Industry: A Comment." JOURNAL OF POLITICAL ECONOMY 74 (October 1966): 526-28.

──────. "Value-Added and Factor Productivity in Soviet Industry." AMERICAN ECONOMIC REVIEW 60 (December 1970): 863-71.

This article develops estimates of Soviet industrial value-added at current and constant prices for the period 1955-67. The major conclusion is that the share of capital in Soviet industrial value-added is larger than has been estimated previously and is rising during the period. Capital's share in value-added rises from 0.32 to 0.53 from 1955 to 1967. Many tables.

Treml, Vladimir G. "New Soviet Capital Data." SOVIET STUDIES 18 (January 1967): 290-95.

Treml attempts to make Soviet published data more usable by supplying the necessary gross output data and by converting the coefficients into capital stock data. A table on Soviet gross output and capital data by industry in 1959 is included.

Treml, Vladimir G., and Hardt, John P., eds. SOVIET ECONOMIC STATISTICS. Durham, N.C.: Duke University Press, 1972. xii, 457 p.

This book consists of eighteen articles and summary comments which present a general evaluation of the state of Soviet statistics in the beginning of the 1970s. Topics covered are statistics in the Soviet Union; national income statistics; industry statistics; agricultural statistics; real income and consumption statistics; and statistics on prices and money.

Turgeon, Lynn. "On the Reliability of Soviet Statistics." REVIEW OF ECONOMICS AND STATISTICS 34 (February 1952): 75-76.

> This short paper discusses the reliability of Soviet statistics in general and 1941 plan statistics in particular. A table compares figures from two sources on the 1941 plan.

U.S. Central Intelligence Agency. INDEX OF CIVILIAN INDUSTRIAL PRODUCTION IN THE USSR, 1950-1961. Washington, D.C.: 1963. viii, 60 p.

> This report gives an index of Soviet industrial production that includes the most important product groups omitted from the officially announced sample. The index given here is thus more comparable in coverage with the United States. Tables and index.

U.S. Congress. Joint Economic Committee. ANNUAL ECONOMIC INDICATORS FOR THE U.S.S.R. Washington, D.C.: Government Printing Office, 1964. 218 p.

> This book consists almost entirely of data tables on such areas as population, agriculture, industry, investment, employment, wages, education, transportation, national income accounts, national budget, and foreign trade and aid. Selected bibliographies are included.

U.S. Joint Publications Research Service. THE NATIONAL ECONOMY OF THE USSR IN 1960 (Statistical Yearbook). Washington, D.C.: 1962. xlviii, 937 p.

> Statistical tables on territory, population, the economy as a whole, industry, agriculture, transportation, communications, capital construction, workers, trade, science, culture, public health, finance, and credit are included.

Veverka, Jindrich. "Long-Term Measures of Soviet Industrial Output." SOVIET STUDIES 16 (January 1965): 285-301.

> This is a review of G. Warren Nutter. THE GROWTH OF INDUSTRIAL PRODUCTION IN THE SOVIET UNION. Princeton, N.J.: Princeton University Press, 1962 and Richard H. Moorsteen. PRICES AND PRODUCTION OF MACHINERY IN THE SOVIET UNION 1928-1958. Cambridge, Mass.: Harvard University Press, 1962. It deals with problems of calculating measures of long-term changes in output. Three tables.

Wadekin, Karl-Eugen. "Soviet Agricultural Statistics: Summary and Assessment." In SOVIET ECONOMIC STATISTICS, edited by Vladimir G. Treml and John P.

Economic and Social Statistics

Hardt, pp. 279-84. Durham, N.C.: Duke University Press, 1972.

> The author comments briefly on the papers presented by Eberhard Schinke, "Soviet Agricultural Statistics," pp. 236-62; and Philip M. Raup, "Some Consequences of Data Deficiencies in Soviet Agriculture," pp. 263-78. Wadekin believes that "the urge to conceal the weak sides of the [Soviet] economic and social system" and ideological peculiarities are responsible for the unreliability and incompleteness of the available data.

Wiles, Peter J. D. "Statistics on the Soviet Economy." BULLETIN OF THE ASSOCIATION FOR THE STUDY OF SOVIET-TYPE ECONOMIES 9 (Fall 1967): 3-29.

> This article first discusses the value and significance of these statistics. The rest of it consists of ten tables which collect data from a number of sources on the Russian economy from 1897 to the 1960s. For further discussion, see: Raymond P. Powell. "Comment on Peter Wiles, 'Statistics on the Soviet Economy,' " and Peter J. D. Wiles. "Rejoinder." BULLETIN OF THE ASSOCIATION FOR THE STUDY OF SOVIET-TYPE ECONOMIES 19 (Spring 1968): 22-24.

Yugov, A[ron]. "Economic Statistics in the USSR." REVIEW OF ECONOMICS AND STATISTICS 29 (November 1947): 242-46.

> Soviet statistics in general are discussed. For further discussion, see: Maurice H. Dobb. "Further Appraisal of Russian Economic Statistics: A Comment on Soviet Statistics," pp. 34-38; and Harry Schwartz. "A Critique of 'Appraisals of Russian Economic Statistics,' " pp. 38-41, both in REVIEW OF ECONOMICS AND STATISTICS 30 (February 1948).

Chapter 13

RUSSIAN NATIONAL INCOME AND PRODUCT

THE PERIOD 1860-1917

Falkus, Malcolm E. "Russia's National Income, 1913: A Revolution." ECONOMICA n.s. 35 (February 1968): 52-73.

This article details estimates of Russia's national income advanced by S. N. Prokopovich and suggests that Prokopovich understated the national income. New estimates, derived by employing the procedures adopted by Prokopovich, are presented. The tables include a great deal of data, and an appendix details the estimation techniques used.

THE PERIOD AFTER 1917

Baran, Paul A. "National Income and Product of the USSR in 1940." REVIEW OF ECONOMICS AND STATISTICS 29 (November 1947): 226-34.

This author examines official Soviet statistics, proposes his own income and product estimates, presents valuation in U.S. dollars, and discusses allocation of national income. Four tables present data, and an appendix discusses technical aspects of the problem. For further discussion, see: Maurice H. Dobb. "Further Appraisal of Russian Economic Statistics: A Comment on Soviet Statistics," pp. 34-38; and Harry Schwartz. "A Critique of 'Appraisals of Russian Economic Statistics,'" pp. 38-41; both in REVIEW OF ECONOMICS AND STATISTICS 30 (February 1948).

Becker, Abraham S. "National Income Accounting in the USSR." In SOVIET ECONOMIC STATISTICS, edited by Vladimir G. Treml and John P. Hardt, pp. 69-119. Durham, N.C.: Duke University Press, 1972.

Becker considers the concepts, procedures, and numerical estimates of national income and product adopted by the Central Statistical Administration of the Soviet Union (TsSU). Section one deals with current accounting practices; section two with the published data;

and section three with some problem areas. Tables.

———. SOVIET NATIONAL INCOME AND PRODUCT IN 1965; THE GOALS OF THE SEVEN YEAR PLAN. Santa Monica, Calif.: RAND Corp., 1963. xii, 237 p.

The author discusses gross national product by use at prevailing prices; investment and the capital stock; and the Soviet definition of income and product. Tables.

———. SOVIET NATIONAL INCOME AND PRODUCT, 1958-1962: PART I-NATIONAL INCOME AT ESTABLISHED PRICES. Santa Monica, Calif.: RAND Corp., 1965. xvii, 203 p.

This study analyzes estimates of Soviet national income at actual current prices for each of the years 1958-62. The accounting system used is basically the one devised by Abram Bergson.

———. SOVIET NATIONAL INCOME AND PRODUCT, 1958-1962: PART II-NATIONAL INCOME AT FACTOR COST AND CONSTANT PRICES. Santa Monica, Calif.: RAND Corp., 1966. xv, 201 p.

This study adjusts the estimates for distortions in the Soviet price system and revalues them at constant prices. Tables.

———. SOVIET NATIONAL INCOME 1958-1964: NATIONAL ACCOUNTS OF THE USSR IN THE SEVEN YEAR PLAN PERIOD. A RAND Corp. Study. Berkeley and Los Angeles: University of California Press, 1969. xvii, 608 p.

This book presents an independently constructed set of national accounts for each of the years in the period indicated. Part two analyzes the major findings and part three compares the author's calculations with those of Soviet and non-Soviet estimates. Much quantitative information is presented in tables and charts. Bibliography and index.

Bergson, Abram. "National Income." In ECONOMIC TRENDS IN THE SOVIET UNION, edited by Abram Bergson and Simon Kuznets, pp. 1-37. Cambridge, Mass.: Harvard University Press, 1963.

This article is concerned with the techniques of estimating the growth in Soviet national income and Soviet factor productivity and with comparing the results with U.S. figures. An appendix discusses the derivation of NNP estimates from Soviet data. Extensive statistical tables.

———. THE REAL NATIONAL INCOME OF SOVIET RUSSIA SINCE 1928. Cambridge, Mass.: Harvard University Press, 1961.. Pp. xix, 472.

This volume presents calculations of Soviet real national income for the period 1928-55. Part one discusses methodology; part two, national income in prevailing rubles; part three, national income in adjusted rubles; part four, conclusions. Bibliography, index, and many tables.

_____. SOVIET NATIONAL INCOME AND PRODUCT IN 1937. New York: Columbia University Press, 1953. viii, 156 p.

This volume is a revised, elaborated version of a two-part study which first appeared in the QUARTERLY JOURNAL OF ECONOMICS (see next two citations below). In part, it is an attempt to apply to the Soviet Union a novel methodology of national income calculation that had been applied to numerous Western countries. The book, concerned primarily with the estimation techniques used in constructing the figures, is well documented. The national income and product figures are in twelve major tables spread throughout the text.

_____. "Soviet National Income and Product in 1937. Part I: National Economic Accounts in Current Rubles." QUARTERLY JOURNAL OF ECONOMICS 64 (May 1950): 208-41.

This paper first discusses methodology and covers the income and outlay categories under the following headings: general, household, and government. It then breaks down national product by sector and discusses the government budget. There is an addendum discussing official Soviet income statistics. Five tables provide the figures.

_____. "Soviet National Income and Product in 1937. Part II: Ruble Prices and the Valuation Problem." QUARTERLY JOURNAL OF ECONOMICS 64 (August 1950): 408-41.

The particular aspects of the valuation problem treated here are prices and "real" costs, wages and retail prices, collective farm incomes, Soviet GNP in adjusted rubles, and ruble versus dollar valuations. Seven large tables and several smaller ones are included.

_____. SOVIET NATIONAL INCOME AND PRODUCT, 1940-48. New York: Columbia University Press, 1954. xii, 249 p. Illustrated.

Bergson has compiled data for Soviet national income accounts for the years 1940, 1944, and 1948. The text examines the techniques and assumptions used in arriving at the estimates. Map.

_____. "Soviet National Income Statistics: Summary and Assessment." In SOVIET ECONOMIC STATISTICS, edited by Vladimir G. Treml and John P. Hardt, pp. 148-52. Durham, N.C.: Duke University Press, 1972.

Bergson comments briefly on the papers by Abraham Becker, "National Income Accounting in the USSR," and Stanley H. Cohn, "National Income Growth Statistics," in the same book.

Birmingham University. Bureau of Research on Russian Economic Conditions. "The National Income of the U.S.S.R." MEMORANDUM NO. 3 (November 1931): 1-16.

Many tables supplement the text.

Russian National Income and Product

Boddy, Francis M. "National Income and Product of the U.S.S.R.; Recent Trends and Prospects." In COMPARISONS OF THE U.S. AND SOVIET ECONOMIES, U.S. Congress. Joint Economic Committee, pt. 2: 397-401. Washington, D.C.: Government Printing Office, 1959.

> This paper outlines growth in selected national income data of the USSR, 1949-58, and includes Soviet predictions of future growth, 1958-65. Five tables.

Bornstein, Morris. "A Comparison of Soviet and United States National Product." In COMPARISONS OF THE U.S. AND SOVIET ECONOMIES, U.S. Congress. Joint Economic Committee, pt. 2: 377-95. Washington, D.C.: Government Printing Office, 1959.

> The structure of national product by end use, national income by sector of origin, the comparative size of national product and the growth of national product are discussed. Five tables summarize statistical data.

_____. "Soviet National Income Accounts for 1955." REVIEW OF ECONOMICS AND STATISTICS 44 (November 1962): 446-57.

> This paper presents a concise summary of a detailed estimate of the national income and product of the Soviet Union in 1955. Problems involved in the construction of such accounts are considered also.

Campbell, Robert W. "The Growth of Soviet Output." SLAVIC REVIEW 21 (September 1962): 520-26.

> This is a review article of Abram Bergson. THE REAL NATIONAL INCOME OF SOVIET RUSSIA SINCE 1928. (See p. 164). Cambridge, Mass.: Harvard University Press, 1961.

Clark, Colin. "Russian Income and Production Statistics." REVIEW OF ECONOMICS AND STATISTICS 29 (November 1947): 215-17.

> A table presents estimates of some uses of Russian national income for the years 1913, 1928, 1934, and 1938. Problems of obtaining such estimates are discussed. For further discussion, see: Maurice H. Dobb. "Further Appraisal of Russian Economic Statistics: A Comment on Soviet Statistics," pp. 34-38; and Harry Schwartz. "A Critique of 'Appraisals of Russian Economic Statistics,'" pp. 38-41, both in REVIEW OF ECONOMICS AND STATISTICS 30 (February 1948).

Cohn, Stanley H. "National Income Growth Statistics." In SOVIET ECONOMIC STATISTICS, edited by Vladimir G. Treml and John P. Hardt, pp. 120-47. Durham, N.C.: Duke University Press, 1972.

> This paper deals with the following: (1) technical deficiencies, relevance, and concern for validity of Soviet national income

growth statistics; (2) the divergence between official and Western-computed indexes; (3) the statistical significance of the use of the Marxist concept of national product; (4) effect of Soviet pricing and weights; (5) deflators; (6) differences in component origination-sector trends; (7) unofficial Soviet national income indexes; (8) validity of official Soviet investment indexes; and (9) the operational role of GNP-type indicators.

Gol'tsev, Aleksandr, and Ozerov, Sergey. "Distribution of the National Income of the USSR." ASSOCIATION FOR COMPARATIVE ECONOMIC STUDIES BULLETIN 15 (Summer-Fall 1973): 79-102.

This work seeks to determine the true dimensions and distribution of the national income of the USSR, and particularly the proportion allocated for defense. Two tables. Two appendices compare Soviet and Western methodologies of calculating national income and criticize official economic comparisons of the United States and USSR. For further discussion, see: Victor Perlo. "Two Misleading Articles in THE ACES BULLETIN." THE ASSOCIATION FOR COMPARATIVE ECONOMIC STUDIES BULLETIN 16 (Spring 1974): 59-66.

Hoeffding, Oleg. SOVIET NATIONAL INCOME AND PRODUCT IN 1928. A Research Study by the RAND Corp. New York: Columbia University Press, 1954. 156 p.

This study estimates the national income and production of the Soviet Union in 1928, in a form comparable to the data produced by Abram Bergson and Hans Heymann, Jr., for 1940-48. (See p. 165). The book is concerned largely with the estimation techniques used in constructing the figures and is well documented. The national income and product figures are in eleven major tables spread throughout the text.

Holesovsky, Vaclav. "Karl Marx and Soviet National Income Theory." AMERICAN ECONOMIC REVIEW 51 (June 1961): 325-44.

This article is concerned only with "the extent of the area of economic activity to be covered by the national income and product aggregates." Topics covered include confrontation of the Soviet and Marxian theory and between Marxian and dissenters' theory.

Jasny, Naum. "Intricacies of Russian National-Income Indexes." JOURNAL OF POLITICAL ECONOMY 55 (August 1947): 299-322.

This paper analyzes the intricate ways in which official Soviet figures are prepared. In addition, it presents a computation of the national income from agriculture and tentative approximations to other items, including the aggregate national income, in the period 1928-38. Ten tables and two charts.

_____. "A Short Cut to Growth Rates in Soviet National Income." SOVIET STUDIES 15 (July 1963): 38-42.

    This article uses the correctly calculated official index for farm production and the falsified official index of Soviet national income to derive a more accurate index for national income. For further discussion, see: Francis Seton. "Consistency Tests on Soviet Output Indices." SOVIET STUDIES 15 (October 1963): 182-86.

Kaplan, Norman M. "Arithmancy, Theomancy, and the Soviet Economy." JOURNAL OF POLITICAL ECONOMY 61 (April 1953): 93-116.

    This article reexamines the estimates of Soviet national income and industrial output provided by Naum Jasny in three of his works: THE SOVIET ECONOMY DURING THE PLAN ERA. Stanford, Calif.: Stanford University Press, 1951; THE SOVIET PRICE SYSTEM (Stanford University Press, 1951); and SOVIET PRICES OF PRODUCERS' GOODS (Stanford University Press, 1952). The article also contains two tables on investment costs and national product, according to Jasny, with accompanying notes.

Kaser, Michael C. "Estimating the Soviet National Income." ECONOMIC JOURNAL 67 (March 1957): 83-104.

    This article surveys and criticizes commentary on the estimates of Soviet national income advanced by various economists. Four tables.

Koropechyj, I[van]. S. "Methodological Problems of Calculating National Income for Soviet Republics." JOURNAL OF REGIONAL SCIENCE 12 (December 1972): 387-400.

    Methodology used in preparing national income estimates for these republics is analyzed. Most of the paper describes concepts and approaches adopted by Soviet economists and statisticians in obtaining these estimates. The paper discusses deficiencies in Soviet estimates and their usefulness for regional planning.

Kudrov, V. "Anti-Scientific Methods Employed by Bourgeois Economists to Compare the National Incomes of the USSR and the US." PROBLEMS OF ECONOMICS 4 (August 1961): 37-42.

    This is a translation from VOPROSY EKONOMIKI, no. 2 (1961).

Nimitz, Nancy. SOVIET NATIONAL INCOME AND PRODUCT, 1956-1958. Santa Monica, Calif.: RAND Corp., 1962. x, 179 p.

    This study estimates the national income and product of the USSR at current actual prices for the years 1956-58 and at current adjusted prices (ruble factor cost) for the years 1949-58. The study supplements and extends a previous study by Abram Bergson. THE REAL NATIONAL INCOME OF SOVIET RUSSIA SINCE 1928. (See p. 164).

Nove, Alec. "Some Notes on Soviet National Income Statistics." SOVIET STUDIES 6 (January 1955): 247-80.

Subjects discussed include the Soviet definition of national income; the turnover tax; profits; prices; "factor cost"; price categories; and national income accounting. Three tables.

―――. "Statistical Puzzles Continue." SOVIET STUDIES 18 (July 1966): 83-85.

This paper examines some anomalies in the official Soviet national income accounts.

Nove, Alec, and Zauberman, Alfred. "A Dollar Valuation of Soviet National Income?" SOVIET STUDIES 10 (October 1958): 146-50.

This paper discusses efforts to estimate Soviet GNP in 1955. A table presents estimates of per capita GNP for selected countries in 1955.

―――. "A Soviet Disclosure of Ruble National Income." SOVIET STUDIES 11 (October 1959): 195-202.

Three tables present figures on Soviet national income in 1957.

Seton, Francis. "The Social Accounts of the Soviet Union in 1934." REVIEW OF ECONOMICS AND STATISTICS 36 (August 1954): 290-308.

A detailed reconstruction is made of the Soviet national income and social accounts of 1934. Thirteen tables.

Studenski, Paul, and Wyler, Julius. "National Income Estimates of Soviet Russia: Their Distinguishing Characteristics and Problems." AMERICAN ECONOMIC REVIEW 37 (May 1947): 595-610.

The author discusses some of the methods employed by the Soviets in computing the national income.

Thornton, Judith G. "The Index Number Problem in the Measurement of Soviet National Income." JOURNAL OF ECONOMIC HISTORY 22 (September 1962): 379-89.

This paper is a review of Abram Bergson. THE REAL NATIONAL INCOME OF SOVIET RUSSIA SINCE 1928. (See p. 164). Cambridge, Mass.: Harvard University Press, 1961. It is primarily concerned with the methodological and practical issues raised by Bergson's use of index numbers. It examines the relationship of Bergson's formal discussion of index number theory to his empirical treatment of it. It makes extensive use of graphs.

Russian National Income and Product

Wyler, Julius. "The National Income of Soviet Russia." SOCIAL RESEARCH 13 (December 1946): 501-18.

This paper discusses the reliability and complexities of Soviet national income figures in general. Topics covered include the value of the ruble, trends, structure of the accounts, and a comparison with the United States. Four tables.

Chapter 14
PRICES, PRICE LEVELS, AND INFLATION

THE PERIOD UP TO 1860

Blum, Jerome. "Prices in Russia in the Sixteenth Century." JOURNAL OF ECONOMIC HISTORY 16, no. 2 (1956): 182-99.

　　The most important factors affecting price levels in Russia in the late sixteenth century are investigated.

Pintner, Walter M. "Inflation in Russia during the Crimean War Period." AMERICAN SLAVIC AND EAST EUROPEAN REVIEW 18 (February 1959): 81-87.

　　Although comprehensive data on the Russian economy during the Crimean War are not available, this article summarizes and interpretes the available data. Five tables.

THE PERIOD 1860-1917

Turin, S. P. "Market Prices and Controlled Prices of Food in Moscow." ROYAL STATISTICAL SOCIETY. JOURNAL. Ser. A 83 (May 1920): 478-79.

　　This short note presents food prices in Moscow for November 1, 1919, and the years 1915 and 1920.

THE PERIOD AFTER 1917

Becker, Abraham S. "The Price Level of Soviet Machinery in the 1960's." SOVIET STUDIES 26 (July 1974): 363-79.

　　Inflation of ruble prices in the Soviet machinery industry in the 1960s is examined. Two tables.

Bergson, Abram, et al. BASIC INDUSTRIAL PRICES IN THE USSR, 1928-1950: TWENTY-FIVE BRANCH SERIES AND THEIR AGGREGATION. Santa Monica,

Calif.: RAND Corp., 1956. iv, 125 p.

Part one is a compendium of index numbers of the series that have been compiled for different industrial branches. Part two is an aggregate compilation of the branch series into corresponding series for major industries and industry groups. Tables.

_____. "Prices of Basic Industrial Products in the USSR, 1928-50." JOURNAL OF POLITICAL ECONOMY 64 (August 1956): 303-28.

Five tables and two charts present the price figures, and the article discusses their derivation.

Bornstein, Morris. "The 1963 Soviet Industrial Price Revision." SOVIET STUDIES 15 (July 1963): 43-52.

The price revisions discussed are for fuels, power, transport, and heavy industry products. One table shows percentage changes in prices for these commodities.

_____. "The Soviet Price Reform Discussion." QUARTERLY JOURNAL OF ECONOMICS 78 (February 1964): 15-48.

This paper discusses the 1963 Soviet industrial price revision. Covered are the background of the debate, deficiencies in industrial wholesale prices identified during the debate, and leading proposals for price reform.

_____. "Soviet Price Statistics." In SOVIET ECONOMIC STATISTICS, edited by Vladimir G. Treml and John P. Hardt, pp. 355-96. Durham, N.C.: Duke University Press, 1972.

This paper evaluates the major official Soviet price statistics, with emphasis on those published by the Soviet government and available to outside scholars. Bornstein focuses on the coverage, collection procedures, statistics, and publication practices of price statistics.

_____. "The Soviet Price System." AMERICAN ECONOMIC REVIEW 52 (March 1962): 64-103.

The role of prices in the Soviet planned economy is examined. After a summary of the various functions of prices in the Soviet economy, the article deals with three major subsystems of the Soviet price system: industrial wholesale prices, agricultural procurement prices, and retail prices.

_____. "Soviet Price Theory and Policy." In NEW DIRECTIONS IN THE SOVIET ECONOMY, U.S. Congress. Joint Economic Committee, pp. 63-98. Washington, D.C.: Government Printing Office, 1966.

This paper summarizes the various functions of prices in the Soviet economy and then deals with the three major subsystems of the

Soviet price system: industrial wholesale prices, agricultural procurement prices, and retail prices. Seven tables.

Chapman, Janet G. RETAIL PRICES OF MANUFACTURED CONSUMER GOODS IN THE USSR, 1937-1948. Rev. ed. Santa Monica, Calif.: RAND Corp., 1952. viii, 120 p.

This study calculates an index of the change in retail prices of manufactured goods between 1937 and 1948. The index's main purpose is to deflate the consumer outlay component of the Soviet national income accounts compiled by Abram Bergson and Hans Heymann, Jr. Tables and two appendices.

Dobb, Maurice H. "Some Further Comments on the Discussion About Socialist Price-Policy." In his PAPERS ON CAPITALISM, DEVELOPMENT, AND PLANNING, pp. 191-207. New York: International Publishers, 1967.

This article discusses the development of Socialist price policy, with emphasis on that in the Soviet Union.

Fearn, Robert M. "Controls Over Funds and Inflationary Pressures in the USSR." INDUSTRIAL AND LABOR RELATIONS REVIEW 18 (January 1965): 186-95.

This article examines the problem of Soviet labor market policy, caused by overexpenditure of wage funds, which has resulted in "wage creep" and repressed inflation. Evidence presented here suggests that, given continuation of current policies concerning labor mobility, social services, and production priorities, the Soviet Union will probably experience continued inflation.

Gekker, Paul. "Statistics on Prices and Money: Summary and Assessment." In SOVIET ECONOMIC STATISTICS, edited by Vladimir G. Treml and John P. Hardt, pp. 433-45. Durham, N.C.: Duke University Press, 1972.

The author comments on the papers by Morris Bornstein, "Soviet Price Statistics"; and Raymond P. Powell, "Monetary Statistics."

Grossman, Gregory. "Industrial Prices in the USSR." AMERICAN ECONOMIC REVIEW 49 (May 1959): 50-64.

This work examines the role of prices in the Soviet economy during the plan era, especially from the administrative and financial reforms of 1929-34 to the reorganization of industry and construction in 1957. It is concerned primarily with prices at the enterprise level, as contrasted with the planning level, and "with only one of the four transaction areas of the Soviet economy, namely, that in which state entities deal with each other." For further discussion, see: Robert W. Campbell and David Granick. "Soviet Economic Planning--Discussion." AMERICAN ECONOMIC REVIEW 49 (May 1959): 78-83.

Holubnychy, Vsevolod. "The Soviet Price System, Based on a New Method." STUDIES ON THE SOVIET UNION n.s. 2, no. 2 (1962): 51-65.

> A statistical analysis is made of certain aspects of the economic rationale of Soviet consumer goods prices. An accompanying explanation of the method used is given. Relative price data on selected similar goods in the USSR and the United States are presented.

Holzman, Franklyn D. "Soviet Inflationary Pressures; 1928-1957: Causes and Cures." QUARTERLY JOURNAL OF ECONOMICS 74 (May 1960): 167-88.

> This article explains the peculiar price trends which developed in the 1928-47 period; presents some hypotheses concerning the causal factors of the Soviet inflation; and considers factors responsible for the end of price inflation in the postwar period. Two tables.

Hutchings, R[aymond]. F. D. "The Origins of the Soviet Industrial Price System." SOVIET STUDIES 13 (July 1961): 1-22.

> This paper concentrates on the organizational basis of price formation from the NEP through the Third Five-Year Plan. Price discrimination and the turnover tax are also discussed.

Jasny, Naum. "The Soviet Price System." AMERICAN ECONOMIC REVIEW 40 (December 1950): 845-63.

> This discusses price and price-wage relationships, factors contributing to high prices of consumer goods, effects of the price system, and the real worth of the budgetary and other expenditures. Many tables.

_____. SOVIET PRICE SYSTEM. Stanford, Calif.: Stanford University Press, 1951. ix, 179 p.

> This essay deals with wages, prices of producers' and consumers' goods, farm prices and the distinction between producers' and consumers' goods. The effects of the price system, turnover taxes, and profits and subsidies are also examined. The author concludes with a discussion of the use of prices, "phantom" prices, and national-income indexes. Index.

_____. SOVIET PRICES OF PRODUCERS' GOODS. Stanford, Calif.: Stanford University Press, 1952. vii, 180 p.

> This essay discusses prices of capital goods, 1926-27, prices in general, railway costs and rates, fuel products, metal products, construction costs, and machinery as part of capital investments. Many tables.

Kaplan, Norman M., and Wainstein, Eleanor S. "A Comparison of Soviet and

Prices, Price Levels, and Inflation

American Retail Prices in 1950." JOURNAL OF POLITICAL ECONOMY 64 (December 1956): 470-91.

> Five tables and a chart present the price figures, while the text discusses their derivation and significance.

Kaplan, Norman M., and White, William L. A COMPARISON OF 1950 WHOLESALE PRICES IN SOVIET AND AMERICAN INDUSTRY. Santa Monica, Calif.: RAND Corp., 1955. iv, 352 p.

> This study compiles price ratios, a comparison of ruble and dollar prices for about 2,000 commodities produced in both the Soviet Union and the United States.

Kaser, Michael C. "Soviet Planning and the Price Mechanism." ECONOMIC JOURNAL 60 (March 1950): 81-91.

> This article is a study of prices and price distortions in the Soviet economy and their consequences for planning.

Kishimoto, Shigenobu. "A Note on Pricing Mechanism in the Industrialization of the U.S.S.R." DEVELOPING ECONOMIES 6 (March 1968): 40-59.

> This paper examines price policy of the Soviet Union during the process of industrialization and also considers the actual function of the planned prices fixed by such policy. Tables.

Krovis, Irving B., and Mintzes, Joseph. "Food Prices in the Soviet Union, 1936-50." REVIEW OF ECONOMICS AND STATISTICS 32 (May 1950): 164-68.

> This paper computes index numbers and discusses the problems involved. Tables.

Lavelle, Michael J. "The Soviet 'New Method' Pricing Formulae." SOVIET STUDIES 26 (January 1974): 81-97.

> This article uses mathematics to present the 1969 pricing method and discusses proposed changes in the method.

Minnich, Barbara. "Soviet Price Reform of July 1967." BULLETIN OF THE ASSOCIATION FOR THE STUDY OF SOVIET-TYPE ECONOMIES 10 (Fall 1968): 12-19.

> Most of this article is a table showing average percent change in industrial wholesale prices by a given industry or product group.

Moskoff, William. "A Note on the Soviet State Retail Price Index." BULLETIN OF THE ASSOCIATION FOR THE STUDY OF SOVIET-TYPE ECONOMIES 12 (Spring 1970): 20-24.

> This article attempts to reconstruct the index to answer two questions

which are of importance to the Western scholar: (1) whether the traditional stability of the State Retail Price Index reflects planners' desideratum or is an actual achievement and (2) whether the scholar can accept, with confidence, the index as it is published in NARODNOYE KHOZIAISTVO SSSR.

Newth, J. A. "Soviet Periodical Prices 1964-73." SOVIET STUDIES 25 (October 1973): 271-73.

Three tables present figures on the rising costs of Soviet books and periodicals.

Niwa, Haruki. "Retail and Real Wages in the USSR, 1928-59." JOURNAL OF ECONOMIC BEHAVIOR 1 (October 1961): 93-111.

This article discusses the computation of a retail price index and index numbers of real wages. Tables.

Nove, Alec. "The Changing Role of Soviet Prices." ECONOMICS OF PLANNING 3 (December 1963): 185-95.

This article discusses the secondary role played by prices in the Stalin era and contrasts it with the more important role accorded to prices under the Liberman reforms.

_____. "The New Planning Prices." SOVIET STUDIES 5 (July 1953): 84-89.

This paper summarizes two articles by Soviet economists describing the new price basis of 1949.

_____. " '1926/7' and All That." SOVIET STUDIES 9 (October 1957): 117-30.

This paper discusses the weaknesses and peculiarities of the 1926-27 price series. Three tables.

Rao, Subba. "Determination of Prices in Soviet Russia." INDIAN JOURNAL OF ECONOMICS 21 (April 1941): 497-510.

According to the author, the "basic principle of pricing is 'cost plus.' " The nature of the pricing process is illustrated by a detailed analysis of wholesale and retail agricultural and industrial prices.

Seton, Francis. "Pre-War Soviet Prices in the Light of the 1941 Plan." SOVIET STUDIES 3 (April 1952): 351-64.

This article examines volume and value data, planned gross output, and sales targets at current wholesale prices for most important industries to obtain price information. Tables.

Turgeon, Lynn. "Cost-Price Relationships in Basic Industries During the Soviet Planning Era." SOVIET STUDIES 9 (October 1957): 143-77.

> Trends of prices and production costs in Soviet basic industries from 1928 to 1955 are examined. One chart and two tables.

Ware, Henry H. "The Function and Formation of Commodity Prices in the USSR." BULLETINS ON SOVIET ECONOMIC DEVELOPMENT 4 (September 1950): 21-31.

> This article considers the relationship of prices to supply and demand on the retail markets, the nature of the various planned prices and free prices, the formation of retail prices and their functions in relation to national economic planning.

Wiles, Peter J. D. "Are Adjusted Rubles Rational?" SOVIET STUDIES 7 (October 1955): 143-60.

> This article discusses the question of the degree to which Soviet prices reflect true scarcity. Two tables. For further discussion, see: Joan Robinson. "Mr. Wiles' Rationality: A Comment." SOVIET STUDIES 7 (January 1956): 269-73; Donald R. Hodgman. "Measuring Soviet Industrial Expansion: A Reply." SOVIET STUDIES 8 (July 1956): 34-45; David Granick. "Are Adjusted Rubles Rational? A Comment." SOVIET STUDIES 8 (July 1956): 46-49; Peter J. D. Wiles. "A Rejoinder to All and Sundry." SOVIET STUDIES 8 (October 1956): 134-43; K. W. Rothschild. "A Note on the Rationality Controversy." SOVIET STUDIES 9 (July 1957): 28-31; and Franklyn D. Holzman. "The Adjusted Factor Cost Standard of Measuring National Income: Comment." SOVIET STUDIES 9 (July 1957): 32-36.

Chapter 15
MONEY, FINANCE, BANKING, AND CREDIT

THE PERIOD UP TO 1860

Garvy, George. "Banking Under the Tsars and the Soviets." JOURNAL OF ECONOMIC HISTORY 32 (December 1972): 869-93.

This article discusses the role of the tsarist regime in introducing banking into Russia and, after the liberation of the serfs, to foster commercial banking on the pattern of Western Europe. Views of Russian economists who advocated a monetary and banking system, many elements of which can be found in the credit system of the Soviet Union, are also reviewed.

McGraw, Roderick E. "The Politics of Absolutism: Paul I and the Bank of Assistance for the Nobility." CANADIAN-AMERICAN SLAVIC STUDIES 7 (Spring 1973): 15-38.

This article deals largely with the Bank of Assistance for the Nobility created in 1797 to aid the nobility in paying off their debts and reestablishing themselves financially.

Miklashevsky, Alex. "Monetary Reform in Russia." ECONOMIC JOURNAL 6 (December 1896): 632-39.

The article surveys Russian handling of coin and currency from 1768, when Catherine II introduced paper money, to the legislation of 1896 regarding the relative values of paper and metallic money.

THE PERIOD 1860-1917

Barkai, Haim. "The Macro-Economics of Tsarist Russia in the Industrialization Era: Monetary Developments, the Balance of Payments and the Gold Standard." JOURNAL OF ECONOMIC HISTORY 33 (June 1973): 339-71.

The period covered here extends from about 1860 to 1913. Five tables provide data, and some use is made of mathematical analysis.

Money, Finance, Banking, and Credit

Crisp, Olga. "Russia 1860-1914." In BANKING IN THE EARLY STAGES OF INDUSTRIALIZATION: A STUDY IN COMPARATIVE ECONOMIC HISTORY, edited by Rondo Cameron, pp. 183-238. New York: Oxford University Press, 1967.

The evolution and structure of the financial system is outlined, along with the functions of the main institutions of commercial credit. The author describes the State Bank, joint-stock commercial banks, municipal banks, mutual credit societies, other banks of private commercial credit, small credit institutions, state savings banks, and mortgages. Tables.

──────. "Russian Financial Policy and the Gold Standard at the End of the 19th Century." ECONOMIC HISTORY REVIEW. 2d Ser. 6, no. 2 (1953): 156-72.

Russia's financial problems during the period and the policies used by various ministers of finance to combat them are reviewed.

Dehn, Wladimir. "The Russian Currency Reform." ECONOMIC JOURNAL 8 (June 1898): 225-33.

The article gives a historical account of the paper circulation in Russia. The balance of the article concerns the Russian currency reform which had its origins in 1887 and was largely completed by 1897.

Frederiksen, D. M. "Mortgage Banking in Russia. 1894." AMERICAN ACADEMY OF POLITICAL AND SOCIAL SCIENCE 5 (1894-95): 242-56.

This summarizes loans made by thirty-six public, private, and mutual banks. It shows that 41 percent of the acres belonging to private individuals to be subject to a debt of 51.5 percent of their value.

Johnston, Charles. "State Advances on Corn in Russia." ECONOMIC JOURNAL 4 (1894): 133-36.

This article reveals that as a result of a tariff war with Germany, Russia lost one of her chief markets for cereals. It thus became necessary for the state to support the price of grain by buying large supplies for the military and making loans directly to cultivators with their grain as collateral.

Katzenellenbaum, Sakharii S. RUSSIAN CURRENCY AND BANKING, 1914-24. London: P. S. King & Son, 1925. x, 198 p.

This book contains a brief section on the economic condition and financial position of Russia before the war. Succeeding chapters deal with currency during the period of war and revolution, the reestablishment of currency, the monetary reform of 1924 and the liquidation of the Soviet ruble, banking before 1923, the State

Bank in its role as bank of issue, and other credit institutions. Tables.

Kayden, Eugene M. "Central Co-operative Banking in Russia." JOURNAL OF POLITICAL ECONOMY 32 (February 1924): 15-55.

Topics covered include the Moscow Narodny Bank, the period of Communist control, the Bank of Consumers' Co-operation, and the All-Russian Co-operative Bank. Sixteen tables provide data for the years 1912-23.

Laughlin, J. L. "Specie Resumption in Russia." JOURNAL OF POLITICAL ECONOMY 5 (March 1897): 241-44.

This note discusses the background of the ukase of February 1897 concerning the redemption in specie of Russian paper money.

Willis, H. Parker. "Monetary Reform in Russia." JOURNAL OF POLITICAL ECONOMY 5 (June 1897): 277-315.

This paper reviews the events leading up to the 1897 monetary reform. The historical survey goes back to the seventeenth century. Tables. A note on further monetary developments in 1899 may be found in H. Parker Willis. "The Russian Monetary Reform." JOURNAL OF POLITICAL ECONOMY 7 (September 1899): 550-51.

THE PERIOD AFTER 1917

Alexandrov, B. "The Soviet Currency Reform." RUSSIAN REVIEW 8 (January 1949): 56-61.

This paper looks at the Soviet currency reform of 1947, the way in which it was carried out, and its effectiveness.

Ames, Edward. "Soviet Bloc Currency Conversions." AMERICAN ECONOMIC REVIEW 44 (June 1954): 339-53.

This article studies currency conversions in the consumer sector and the enterprise sector and relates the conversions to changes in exchange rates. Three tables.

Andreassen, Knut. "Features of Banking Organization, Monetary and Credit Policy in the Soviet Union." ECONOMICS OF PLANNING 3 (April 1963): 41-52.

Topics covered include the banking system, short-term credit, long-term credit, interest, credit planning, control of enterprises through the banking mechanism, and the planning of money circulation.

Arnold, Arthur Z. BANKS, CREDIT AND MONEY IN SOVIET RUSSIA. New

Money, Finance, Banking, and Credit

York: Columbia University Press, 1937. xix, 559 p.

> The following topics are covered in this book: (1) the nationalization and liquidation of the credit system, 1917-21; (2) the monetary system, 1918-21; (3) the reestablishment of banks and currency in 1921-22; (4) the bipaper standard and hyper-inflation; (5) the monetary reform of 1924; (6) the state bank, 1924-28; (7) the evolution of specialized banks; (8) the state bank and the Credit Reform of 1930; and (9) money, prices, and gold since 1928. There is a bibliography of both English and Russian sources.

Baran, Paul A. "Currency Reform in the USSR." HARVARD BUSINESS REVIEW 26 (March 1948): 194-206.

> This article examines the background, details, and economic implications of the currency reform of 1947-48.

Beermann, R. "Gosbank Procedures in the Case of Economic Difficulties." SOVIET STUDIES 12 (January 1961): 273-87.

> Procedures discussed include credit sanctions, accounting sanctions, sanctions against goods and chattels, and other measures.

Berliner, Joseph S. "Monetary Planning in the USSR." AMERICAN SLAVIC AND EAST EUROPEAN REVIEW 9, no. 4 (1950): 237-54.

> Soviet planning is examined in the light of the alternatives open to planners. The planning of the monetary system is the focus.

Bernatsky, M. "The Problem of Soviet Finance." SLAVONIC REVIEW 9 (January 1933): 288-303.

> This article explores the "problem of the finances of the U.S.S.R., namely: What is their real money volume, what are their sources, and to what extent can they be considered as stabilised?" For further discussion, see: Maurice H. Dobb. "Problems of Soviet Finance." SLAVONIC REVIEW 10 (April 1933): 522-29.

Bogoliepov, Mikhail I. SOVIET FINANCIAL SYSTEM; WHAT IT IS AND HOW IT WORKS. London: Lindsay Drummond, 1945. 64 p.

> The source of state funds, the structure of the Soviet financial system, development of finance, finance in war time, and the supervision of state finance are discussed by this Soviet economist.

Bornstein, Morris. "The Reform and Revaluation of the Ruble." AMERICAN ECONOMIC REVIEW 51 (March 1961): 117-23.

> The Soviet currency reform and exchange rate change, effective on January 1, 1961, is analyzed. A table gives ruble-dollar ratios for gross national product and its principal components.

Money, Finance, Banking, and Credit

Campbell, Malcolm. "Money, Credit, and Banking." In RED ECONOMICS, edited by Gerhard Dobbert, pp. 156-82. Boston: Houghton Mifflin, 1932.

> The author investigates the Party's attitude toward money, credit, and banking and how it fluctuates between two extremes of negation and affirmation. The Strumilin and other plans for the abolition of money are reviewed. The effects of the NEP on money, credit, and banking; the role of the State Bank; the role of banking in the plan; the credit reform of 1930; and the main features of the credit system are discussed.

Campbell, Robert W. "The Problem of Financial Equilibrium." In THE SOVIET ECONOMY; A BOOK OF READINGS, edited by Morris Bornstein and Daniel Fusfeld, pp. 97-100. Rev. ed. Homewood, Ill.: R. D. Irwin, 1966.

> This article explains how the Soviets maintained a high rate of saving while preserving work incentives and minimizing the threat of inflation.

Comstock, Alzada. "Soviet Finance." In SOVIET RUSSIA IN THE SECOND DECADE, pp. 165-88. American Trade Union Delegation. New York: John Day, 1928.

> In part one the author discusses taxation and the budget. Part two deals with currency and banking.

Condoide, Mikhail V. SOVIET FINANCIAL SYSTEM: ITS DEVELOPMENT AND RELATIONS WITH THE WESTERN WORLD. Columbus: Ohio State University Press, 1951. xiii, 230 p.

> This study analyzes the operations and significance of the Soviet financial system and its role in the collectivistic economy of the Soviet Union. The weaknesses and strength of the Soviet financial system are explored. Soviet publications are the basic source of information. Bibliography and index.

Davies, Robert W. "Finance." BULLETINS ON SOVIET ECONOMIC DEVELOPMENT. Ser. 3, 9-10 (September 1956): 57-78.

> This article outlines the major characteristics of Soviet finance during the period 1953-56. Davis discusses the results of the Five-Year Plan and the financial provisions of the Sixth Five-Year Plan and the changes made in the financial system.

_____. "Short-term Credit in the USSR: Some Post-war Problems." SOVIET STUDIES 5 (July 1953): 18-31.

> This paper discusses several aspects of short-term credit, including payments between enterprises, supervision of industry via the State Bank, and current practice in preparation and use of the overall credit plan.

Money, Finance, Banking, and Credit

DeMaris, E. Joe. "Lenin and the Soviet 'Control by the Ruble' System." SLAVIC REVIEW 22 (September 1963): 523-29.

> This note discusses the political and historical development of the use of financial limits rather than direct controls to limit resource use by economic enterprises.

Dobbert, Gerhard. "State Finance." In RED ECONOMICS, edited by Gerhard Dobbert, pp. 134-55. Boston: Houghton Mifflin, 1932.

> Dobbert discusses how steady growth influenced the country's finances; the relationship between the administration of the nation's finances and economic development; the fourfold program of the state budget and the budgetary system; taxes in the collectivized sector and in the private sector; and the role of the financial system during the world economic crisis.

Einzig, Paul. "The Monetary Economy of Bolshevism." ECONOMIC JOURNAL 30 (March 1920): 123-26.

> This article is a criticism of the Bolshevist attempt to replace the system of paper money with a system of labor-tickets.

Garvy, George. "The Role of the State Bank in Soviet Planning." In SOVIET PLANNING: ESSAYS IN HONOUR OF NAUM JASNY, edited by Jane Degras and Alec Nove, pp. 46-76. Oxford: Basil Blackwell, 1964.

> The author discusses the Gosbank after Stalin, two principal activities of Gosbank, the control function of Gosbank, and the future of monetary planning. Tables and bibliography.

Gekker, Paul. "The Banking System of the USSR." In THE SOVIET ECONOMY; A BOOK OF READINGS, edited by Morris Bornstein and Daniel Fusfeld, pp. 101-8. Rev. ed. Homewood, Ill.: R. D. Irwin, 1966.

> This article explains how the Soviet banking system is organized and how it acts as a financial intermediary between the state budget and state enterprises and also supervises the operations of the state enterprises in fulfilling the plan.

Goldweiser, Alexis. "Banking and Currency Reforms in Russia." JOURNAL OF POLITICAL ECONOMY 33 (April 1925): 234-43.

> Topics covered include the establishment of the State Bank, the bank's customers, currency reform, kinds of money used in Russia, 1924 currency legislation, and the situation and prospects as they were in 1924. Five tables.

Grinko, Grigorii F. FINANCIAL PROGRAM OF THE U.S.S.R. FOR 1936. Moscow: Co-operative Publishing Society of Foreign Workers in the USSR, 1936. 72 p.

Part one summarizes the financial results of 1935. Part two discusses the Stakhanov movement, trade and budget receipts, the organization of savings, the work of the Savings Banks, and quality of tax collection work. Part three surveys budget expenditures in 1936. Part four briefly discusses the republic and local budgets.

Grossman, Gregory. "Gold and the Sword: Money in the Soviet Command Economy." In INDUSTRIALIZATION IN TWO SYSTEMS: ESSAYS IN HONOR OF ALEXANDER GERSCHENKRON, edited by Henry Rosovsky, pp. 204-36. New York: John Wiley, 1966.

The paper discusses the role of financial controls in the operation of the Soviet economy.

_____. "Union of Soviet Socialist Republics." In BANKING SYSTEMS, edited by Benjamin H. Beckhart, pp. 733-68. New York: Columbia University Press, 1954.

This chapter is devoted to monetary stability and financial organization; the functions of Gosbank; banks for long-term investment; savings banks; the banking system during and after the Second World War; control by the ruble; and banking and planning.

Haensel, Paul. "Soviet 'Inflation' Reform." PUBLIC FINANCE 3, no. 2 (1948): 107-8.

This short note explains the purpose of the 1947 currency reform.

Hodgman, Donald R. "Soviet Monetary Controls Through the Banking System." In VALUE AND PLAN; ECONOMIC CALCULATION AND ORGANIZATION IN EASTERN EUROPE, edited by Gregory Grossman, pp. 105-30. Berkeley and Los Angeles: University of California Press, 1960.

The author examines how the Soviets maintain monetary stability.

Holzman, Franklyn D. "An Estimate of the Tax Element in Soviet Bonds." AMERICAN ECONOMIC REVIEW 47 (June 1957): 390-96.

The article estimates the amount of tax in the case of Soviet forced loans and concludes that the decline in the tax element in Soviet bonds may be responsible for a reduced Soviet reliance on bond sales. A table shows the tax element of a Soviet bond as a percent of the compulsory purchase price. For further discussion, see: Morris Bornstein. "An Estimate of the Tax Element in Soviet Bonds: Comment." AMERICAN ECONOMIC REVIEW 48 (September 1958): 665-67.

_____. "Financing Soviet Economic Development." In CAPITAL FORMATION AND ECONOMIC GROWTH, edited by Moses Abramovitz, pp. 229-87. Princeton, N.J.: Princeton University Press, 1955.

This paper seeks to explain Soviet choice among sources of finance, analyze the relevant data, and evaluate the fiscal and monetary policies pursued. Tables.

Hubbard, L[eonard]. E. SOVIET MONEY AND FINANCE. London: Macmillan and Co., 1936. xix, 339 p.

The book can be divided into three parts. The first surveys the evolution of money under socialism and discusses the organization of industrial administration. The second describes present methods and organization of banking and credit. It gives an explanation of financial policy and theory, with an outline of the organization of distribution, transport, and collection of agricultural produce. The third part is a critical study of Soviet financial theory and practice. Index.

Kamins, Robert M. " 'Democratic Centralism': Local Finance in the Soviet Union." NATIONAL TAX JOURNAL 15 (December 1962): 353-67.

This paper examines republican and local finance institutions within the national fiscal structure, as reflected in Russian publications and in conversations with Soviet administrators during a month's travel in the USSR in 1961. Tables.

Miller, Margaret S. "Financial Reform in Soviet Russia. II." SLAVONIC REVIEW 10 (April 1932): 547-56.

This article deals with the sphere of industrial financing and how the state has tightened its control through a series of decrees on credit reform passed in January of 1930 and later.

Nonomura, Kazuo. "The Problem of Rouble." HITOTSUBASHI JOURNAL OF ECONOMICS 2 (March 1962): 81-89.

This paper concerns the economic effects of the 1961 change in the value of the ruble. Change in the foreign exchange value are included.

Pardigon, Vladimir. "The Role of the Gosbank in the Economy of the USSR." ANNALS OF PUBLIC AND CO-OPERATIVE ECONOMY 35 (April-September 1964): 211-15.

This article discusses the role of Gosbank as a provider on a relatively large scale of credits to build up fixed funds for technical improvements and capacity increases. Tables provide data on Gosbank's credit activities for the years 1955, 1961, and 1962.

Pavlovsky, G[eorge]. A. "Russia's Current Monetary Problems." ECONOMIC JOURNAL 33 (December 1923): 496-508.

This article surveys the monetary problems of Russia in 1923 brought

Money, Finance, Banking, and Credit

on by Soviet attempts to replace the capitalist-tainted paper money system, the great increases in the amount of currency in circulation, and the consequent inflation.

Pereslegin, V. I. FINANCE AND CREDIT. Moscow: Progress Publishers, 1965. 141 p.

This book discusses the state financial system, the Soviet budget system, and the organization of the credit system. Tables.

Pickersgill, Joyce E. "Hyperinflation and Monetary Reform in the Soviet Union, 1921-26." JOURNAL OF POLITICAL ECONOMY 76 (September-October 1968): 1037-48.

This study is concerned with the specification of the demand function for money in the Soviet Union during two periods, 1921-23, and 1924-26. Six tables.

――――. "A Long-run Demand Function for Money in the Soviet Union: Comment." JOURNAL OF MONEY, CREDIT AND BANKING 2 (February 1970): 123-31.

This paper analyzes data for the years 1922-28 and 1928-38 to derive a demand function for money during a time when the economy evolved from an essentially free market system into a command economy. A model is presented in equation form, and three tables contain the data and results.

Powell, Raymond P. "Recent Developments in Soviet Monetary Policy." In READINGS ON THE SOVIET ECONOMY, edited by Franklyn D. Holzman, pp. 571-81. Chicago: Rand-McNally, 1962.

This article compares and contrasts Soviet monetary policy and institutions in 1932-39 with those in 1948-57.

Reddaway, W. B. THE RUSSIAN FINANCIAL SYSTEM. London: Macmillan and Co., 1935. x, 106 p.

This essay investigates the monetary and financial system and its place in the rest of the economy.

Rybczynski, T. M. "Banking in the U.S.S.R." In COMPARATIVE BANKING, edited by H. W. Auburn, pp. 157-67. Dunstable, Eng.: Waterlow & Sons, 1966.

The author reviews parts of the Soviet financial structure and their relationship to the banking mechanism. The article discusses the functions of the state bank of the USSR (Gosbank) and four special-purpose banks.

Money, Finance, Banking, and Credit

SOVIET FINANCIAL SYSTEM. Moscow: Progress Publishers, 1966. 352 p.

> This Soviet work deals with the nature and functioning of financial institutions. Subjects discussed include the Soviet budgeting system and methods of budgetary planning; state revenue and expenditure; state loans and state insurance; the finance of socialist enterprises and of branches of the economy; and state financial control.

Spring Rice, D. "The North Russian Currency." ECONOMIC JOURNAL 29 (September 1919): 280-89.

> This article describes the origin and operation of the issue of the currency made in 1918, at the suggestion and with the cooperation of the British treasury in London, by an appendage of the Russian government which established itself in North Russia after the flight of the Bolshevik authorities.

THE STATE BANK OF THE U.S.S.R. U.S.S.R.: 1925. 35 p.

> This brief Soviet publication describes the formation of the State Bank.

Usoskin, M. "Soviet Banking System." PUBLIC FINANCE 2, no. 4 (1947): 348-53.

> This short article surveys the various types of banks in the USSR and their functions.

Yurovsky, Leonid N. CURRENCY PROBLEMS AND POLICY OF THE SOVIET UNION. London: Leonard Parsons, 1925. 152 p.

> The book describes the Russian monetary system which prevailed in Russia prior to August 1914, the changes in this system produced by the war and by the Revolution of 1917, the attempts by the government to introduce a state economy on Communist lines and to do away with money, the work of financial reconstruction which started in 1921, and, finally, the measures which brought the monetary circulation of Soviet Russia to its present stage.

Zybenko, Roman O. "Gold Hoarding and Illegal Speculation in the USSR." STUDIES ON THE SOVIET UNION n.s. 4, no. 4 (1965): 150-53.

> Concern with these problems as reported in the Soviet press is reviewed.

Chapter 16
GOVERNMENT FINANCE, BUDGET, TAXATION, AND EXPENDITURES

THE PERIOD UP TO 1860

Duran, James A., Jr. "The Reform of Financial Administration in Russia During the Reign of Catherine II." CANADIAN SLAVIC STUDIES 4 (Fall 1970): 485-96.

> According to Duran, when Catherine assumed power in 1762, the financial administration was in such bad shape that "nobody knew what the revenue of the State actually was." By 1781, the new financial administration could estimate the state budget.

Kashtanov, S. M. "The Centralized State and Feudal Immunity in Russia." SLAVONIC AND EAST EUROPEAN REVIEW 49 (April 1971): 235-54.

> This paper is concerned with immunity from taxes in Russia from the fourteenth to the sixteenth centuries.

Pintner, Walter M. "Government and Industry During the Ministry of Count Kankrin, 1823-1844." SLAVIC REVIEW 23 (March 1964): 45-62.

> This essay considers what effect government policy during the twenty-one year term (1823-44) of Count Egor Kankrin as minister of finance had on the long-standing "mercantilist" tradition. Three tables.

THE PERIOD 1860-1917

Harper, Samuel N. "The Budget Rights of the Russian Duma." JOURNAL OF POLITICAL ECONOMY 16 (March 1908): 152-56.

> This paper discusses the involvement of the state Duma in setting the Russian government budget for the years 1906-8.

Kahan, Arcadius. "Government Policies and the Industrialization of Russia." JOURNAL OF ECONOMIC HISTORY 27 (December 1967): 460-77.

Government Finance

This article discusses four features of Russian economic policies: (1) fiscal policy and its impact on domestic demand for industrial goods; (2) government borrowings and their impact on private industrial investment; (3) tariff policy; and (4) monetary policy. Seven tables provide data for the years 1885-1913.

Michelson, Alexander M. "Revenue and Expenditure on the Russian Government." In RUSSIAN PUBLIC FINANCE DURING THE WAR, pp. 3-229. New Haven, Conn.: Yale University Press, 1928.

The author covers the following topics: (1) direct taxation; (2) duties; (3) indirect taxation; (4) royalties; (5) property and funds owned by the state; and (6) expenditures on the eve of the war and in 1914. In addition, there are summaries of revenue and expenditure for 1915-17. The text and appendices contain many tables which summarize revenues and expenditures.

Raffalovich, Arthur. "The Financial Situation in Russia." ECONOMIC JOURNAL 14 (December 1904): 625-32.

The article surveys the state of Russian finances from the 1880s on. Tables present data on the government budget, gold stock, and balance of payments.

_____. "Russian Financial Policy (1862-1914)." ECONOMIC JOURNAL 26 (December 1916): 528-32.

This article surveys the policies of the successive ministers of finance in Russia and finds a surprising continuity of views.

THE PERIOD AFTER 1917

Baykov, Alexander M., and Barker, G[eoffrey]. R. "Financial Developments in the U.S.S.R." BULLETINS ON SOVIET ECONOMIC DEVELOPMENT 3 (August 1950): 1-24.

The authors outline the main characteristics of the prewar Soviet financial system, finance during the war, and some postwar financial developments. Tables.

Coogan, James. "Bread and the Soviet Fiscal System." REVIEW OF ECONOMICS AND STATISTICS 35 (May 1953): 161-67.

This paper discusses assessment and collection techniques that apply to the bread-grain economy, lists costs, tax, and price for bread for selected years, and quantifies the importance of the bread-grain economy in the fiscal structure of the Soviet Union for selected years. Tables.

_____. "Finance." BULLETIN ON SOVIET ECONOMIC DEVELOPMENT 7, Ser. 2 (December 1952): 1-21.

Government Finance

The author discusses how the ministry of finance acted in controlling plan fulfillment in the Postwar Five-Year Plan. The following subjects are reviewed: capital investments; circulating capital; allocations to industry; and allocations to transport, communications, and trade. Many tables.

Davies, Robert W. THE DEVELOPMENT OF THE SOVIET BUDGETARY SYSTEM. London: Cambridge University Press, 1958. xxi, 372 p.

This book attempts to outline the development of the Soviet budgetary system prior to World War II. Emphasis is on the role played by economic policy and development in shaping the Soviet budgetary system. Two foldout charts and a bibliography.

Gallik, Daniel. THE SOVIET FINANCIAL SYSTEM: STRUCTURE, OPERATION, AND STATISTICS. U.S. Department of Commerce. Bureau of the Census. Washington, D.C.: Government Printing Office, 1968. xi, 416 p.

This report provides a detailed description of the organization and administration of the Soviet financial system and of the plans, accounts, reports, and control procedures employed, as well as the statistics produced. Figures and tables.

Gerashchenko, V. S., and Lavrov, V. V. "The Budget and Credit Methods of Increasing the Efficiency of Public Expenditure on the National Economy." PUBLIC FINANCE 22, nos. 1-2 (1967): 139-54.

Topics covered here include economic reforms and the use of credit ration resources and budget controls. Two tables.

Glovinsky, E. "Abolition of Income Tax and the Soviet Tax Structure." STUDIES ON THE SOVIET UNION n.s. 4, no. 4 (1965): 75-82.

This paper discusses the effects of the abolition of the income tax on workers' income and state revenues. Whether or not workers will be free of the tax by 1965 is also discussed. Two tables.

Holzman, Franklyn D. "The Burden of Soviet Taxation." AMERICAN ECONOMIC REVIEW 43 (September 1953): 548-71.

The article discusses the general methodology of measuring the tax burden, covers the major assumptions and problems in measuring income and taxation, provides numerical estimates of the burden of taxation, and compares the burden in the Soviet Union with that in the United States. Numerous tables providing data on consumer income and taxes in both the United States and USSR.

_____. "Commodity and Income Taxation in the Soviet Union." JOURNAL OF POLITICAL ECONOMY 58 (October 1950): 425-33.

This paper explores approaches open to the Soviet authorities to

Government Finance

solve the inflation problem. A short table provides sample average tax rates by income level in 1934.

_____. "Equity of the Livestock Tax of Outer Mongolia." AMERICAN SLAVIC AND EAST EUROPEAN REVIEW 15 (December 1956): 506-10.

This article uses the livestock tax on Outer Mongolia as an example of the relation between equitable and rational taxation methods and Soviet ideology. Tables provide information on tax rates per head, livestock equivalents, and exemptions for herd increases.

_____. "Income Taxation in the Soviet Union: A Comparative View." NATIONAL TAX JOURNAL 11 (June 1958): 99-113.

This paper briefly describes the history of the Soviet personal income tax and compares its provisions (rate structure, dependency provisions, exemptions) with the personal income taxes of the United States and Great Britain. Eight tables.

_____. "The Soviet Budget, 1928-1952." NATIONAL TAX JOURNAL 6 (September 1953): 226-49.

Topics discussed include budget size and structure, expenditures, and statistical trends. Eight tables.

_____. SOVIET TAXATION: THE FISCAL AND MONETARY PROBLEMS OF A PLANNED ECONOMY. Cambridge, Mass.: Harvard University Press, 1955. xix, 376 p.

This book includes a theoretical discussion of functions and structure, an historical account of Soviet taxes, a statistical analysis of trends in Soviet finance, and an evaluation of Soviet tax policy. Tables and index.

_____. "Taxes and Standard of Living in the USSR: Postwar Developments." NATIONAL TAX JOURNAL 10 (June 1957): 138-47.

This paper studies the effects of consumer goods taxes on consumers' standards of living. Four tables.

Hutchings, R[aymond]. F. D. "Some Behavior Patterns of the Soviet Post-War Budget." BULLETIN OF THE ASSOCIATION FOR THE STUDY OF SOVIET-TYPE ECONOMIES 4 (Fall 1962): 2-10.

Revenues and spending patterns are analyzed statistically. Tables include Soviet budget revenues and expenditures, 1946-60; increments in planned expenditures, 1953-62; and planned budget expenditures, 1953-62.

Kokovtsev, Vladimir, Count. "The Financial Embarrassments of the Soviet Government." SLAVONIC REVIEW 6 (June 1927): 1-11.

> The author, who was minister of finance in Russia during 1903-5 and 1906-14, gives an analysis of the 1926-27 Soviet budget.

Marer, Paul. SELECTED COMPARISONS OF THE FINANCIAL SYSTEMS OF THE USSR, CZECHOSLOVAKIA, HUNGARY AND POLAND. New York: Columbia University Press, 1971. xi, 70 p.

> This report deals with the state budget, its role in the economy, principles of finance which link various enterprise and public expenditures to the state budget, and budget revenues and expenditures.

Miller, Margaret S. "Financial Reform in Soviet Russia." SLAVONIC REVIEW 10 (December 1931): 328-37.

> Miller examines changes in the sphere of finance in taxation, banking, the financing of industry, and budget organization.

——. "Taxation in Soviet Russia." SLAVONIC REVIEW 5 (March 1927): 494-514.

> This article is based on a revised and updated version of THE SYSTEM OF TAXATION IN SOVIET RUSSIA by Paul Haensel. Miller deals only with alterations and new tendencies which have appeared since 1923-24.

——. "Taxation in Soviet Russia I." SLAVONIC REVIEW 4 (December 1925): 124-36.

> This paper contains a brief discussion of the period during which there was a disintegration of the monetary economy (1918-21) and the NEP and financial reconstruction (1921-28), as well as descriptions of the industrial and income-property taxes. See below.

——. "Taxation in Soviet Russia. II." SLAVONIC REVIEW 4 (March 1926): 418-32.

> This article contains an appended estimate of income from taxes and other sources (for 1922-23) which is based on Gosplan figures. See above.

Morrison, Rodney J. "The Liberman Reforms, the Turnover Tax, and Negative Non-Neutralities." NATIONAL TAX JOURNAL 21 (June 1968): 141-46.

> In looking at the relation between the Liberman reforms and the turnover tax, this paper concludes that the turnover tax structure as it exists is theoretically inconsistent with the new goal of consumers', as opposed to planners', sovereignty. Indifference curve analysis is used. For further discussion, see: John S. McConnell.

Government Finance

"The Liberman Reforms, the Turnover Tax, and Negative Non-Neutralities: Reply." Ibid. 23, no. 3 (September 1970). p. 357.

Nove, Alec. "Soviet Budgets After Stalin." REVIEW OF ECONOMICS AND STATISTICS 36 (November 1954): 415-24.

> This paper compares the post-World War II budgets of the Stalin era with the budgets for 1953 and 1954 after Stalin's death. Tables.

Pettibone, Peter J. "The Soviet Turnover Tax." PUBLIC FINANCE 19, no. 4 (1964): 361-79.

> Descriptions are given of how the Soviet financial system collects the turnover tax, who pays the tax, which transfers are taxed, how the amount of tax in each taxable transfer is defined, how the tax is paid, and how the Ministry of Finance and its subordinate organs supervise the process. Two tables.

Slusser, Robert M. "The Budget of the OGPU and the Special Troops from 1923-24 to 1928-29." SOVIET STUDIES 10 (April 1959): 375-83.

> This paper covers several aspects of the security police budget: (1) the total annual budget and its relation to the state budget as a whole; (2) the internal allocation of credits within major sectors of the budget; and (3) the geographical distribution of budgetary sources. Tables.

Sokolnikov, Grigory. SOVIET POLICY IN PUBLIC FINANCE 1917-1928. Stanford, Calif.: Stanford University Press, 1931. xiv, 470 p.

> Eleven chapters, written by different authors, examine the financial system of prewar Russia; finances during the Civil War; the NEP; comparisons of the prewar and 1927-28 financial systems; budgets; and the finance system in the late 1920s. Many tables. Index.

Steele, Rodney E. "The State Budget for 1970." In ECONOMIC PERFORMANCE AND THE MILITARY BURDEN IN THE SOVIET UNION, U.S. Congress. Joint Economic Committee, pp. 54-59. Washington, D.C.: Government Printing Office, 1970.

> Article contains two tables: one on expenditures and one on revenues. The significance of the numbers in the tables is discussed.

Chapter 17

FOREIGN TRADE, POLICIES, AND RELATIONS

Ronimois, H[ans]. E. RUSSIA'S FOREIGN TRADE AND THE BALTIC SEA. London: Boreas Publishing Co., c. 1946. 51 p.

> This booklet discusses the role of the Baltic Sea route in Russian foreign trade from ancient times up to World War II. Twelve tables.

Sladkovskii, M. I. HISTORY OF ECONOMIC RELATIONS BETWEEN RUSSIA AND CHINA. Translated by M. Roublev. Sinological editor: G. Grause. Jerusalem: Israel Program for Scientific Translations, 1966. xii, 299 p.

> This work examines China's economic relations with Russia over nearly three hundred years. Numerous tables; statistical appendices; chronology of events; bibliography.

THE PERIOD UP TO 1860

"British and Russian Trade in Sinkiang, 1819-1851." CENTRAL ASIAN REVIEW 13, no. 2 (1965): 149-56.

> The major concern here is on policy and maneuvering by the governments of Britain, Russia, and China, rather than on quantity and types of goods traded.

Entner, M. L. RUSSO-PERSIAN COMMERCIAL RELATIONS, 1828-1914. University of Florida Monographs. Social Sciences, no. 28. Gainesville: University of Florida Press, 1965. 80 p.

> The author examines: (1) business conditions and treaty relations; (2) economics and politics from mid-century up to 1890; and (3) ruble imperialism. Tables.

Foust, Clifford M. MUSCOVITE AND MANDARIN; RUSSIA'S TRADE WITH CHINA AND ITS SETTING, 1727-1805. Chapel Hill: University of North Carolina Press, 1969. x, 424 p. Illustrated.

Foreign Trade, Policies, and Relations

Foust discusses the relations of Russian and Chinese diplomats and courts and how they "at times dictated the circumstances, condition, and size of trade." The book can be viewed as a study of Russian entrepreneurial and economic history of the eighteenth century. Bibliography, index, and maps.

Frederiksen, Oliver J. "Virginia Tobacco in Russia Under Peter the Great." SLAVONIC AND EAST EUROPEAN REVIEW 21 (March 1943): 40-56.

This article recounts the introduction of tobacco into Russia on a large scale by Peter the Great. Both the initiative for the trade and the tobacco came largely from America.

Gopal, Surendra. "Trading Activities of Indians in Russia in the Eighteenth Century." INDIAN ECONOMIC AND SOCIAL HISTORY REVIEW 5 (June 1968): 141-48.

A survey of the role of the Indians of Astrakhan in Russian trade in the eighteenth century. A table compares Russian trade with Persia handled by Indians, Armenians, Russians, and Persians.

Kahan, Arcadius. "Observations on Petrine Foreign Trade." CANADIAN-AMERICAN SLAVIC STUDIES 8 (Summer 1974): 222-36.

Russian foreign trade is examined and compared to other economic activities. Several tables.

Kirchner, Walter. COMMERCIAL RELATIONS BETWEEN RUSSIA AND EUROPE, 1400 TO 1800; COLLECTED ESSAYS. Indiana University Publications. Russian and East European Series, vol. 33. Bloomington: Indiana University Press, 1966. x, 332 p.

The following essays are of particular interest to an economic historian: "On Russia's Foreign Trade in Early Modern Times," pp. 26-42; "The Beginnings of Franco-Russian Economic Relations, 1550-1650," pp. 90-119; "Entrepreneurial Activity in Russian-Western Trade Relations During the Sixteenth Century," pp. 120-31; "Franco-Russian Economic Relations in the Eighteenth Century," pp. 132-75; "Ukrainian Tobacco for France," pp. 176-91; and "Western Businessmen in Russia: Practices and Problems," pp. 231-46. Bibliographical and name indexes. Map.

Macmillan, David S. "The Scottish-Russian Trade: Its Development, Fluctuations, and Difficulties 1750-1796." CANADIAN SLAVIC STUDIES 4 (Fall 1970): 426-42.

Both the politics and economic significance of Scottish-Russian trade are covered. Two tables.

Ohberg, Arne. "Russia and the World Market in the Seventeenth Century: A Discussion of the Connection Between Prices and Trade Routes." SCANDINAVIAN

ECONOMIC HISTORY REVIEW 3, no. 2 (1955): 123-62.

> This detailed study of Russian trade routes in the seventeenth century includes five tables and six charts.

Rich, E. E. "Russia and the Colonial Fur Trade." ECONOMIC HISTORY REVIEW 7, no. 3 (1955): 307-28.

> This detailed study of trade in furs from both Russia and the New World in the seventeenth and eighteenth centuries discusses competition and interaction between these two major sources of furs. Of note is the author's discussion of Russia as a significant importer of beaver furs from the New World.

Thompson, James W. "Early Trade Relations Between Germans and the Slavs." JOURNAL OF POLITICAL ECONOMY 30 (August 1922): 543-58.

> This article investigates the trade relations between the Hanseatic League and the Slavs prior to the thirteenth century.

Valiliev, A. "Economic Relations Between Byzantium and Old Russia." JOURNAL OF ECONOMIC AND BUSINESS HISTORY 4 (February 1932): 314-34.

> This paper covers the trade--usually down the Dnieper--between Rus' and Byzantium, including articles traded, social relations, alternatives to the Dnieper route, and the Byzantine influence on Russian coinage.

Willan, T. S. "The Russia Company and Narva, 1558-81." SLAVONIC REVIEW 31 (June 1953): 405-519.

> This paper discusses the struggle between the Russia Company, which had a legal monopoly of English trade with Narva, and interlopers who sought "free trade" in the sixteenth century meaning of the term.

Yakobson, S. "Early Anglo-Russian Relations." SLAVONIC REVIEW 13 (April 1935): 597-610.

> Early diplomatic and commercial relations between Russia and England are described.

THE PERIOD 1860-1917

Brutzkus, Boris. "Russia's Grain Exports and their Future." Translated by W. J. Roth. JOURNAL OF FARM ECONOMICS 16 (October 1934): 662-79.

> Topics discussed here include grain exports before World War I, between 1914 and 1922, under the NEP, during collectivization, and prospects after 1934.

Foreign Trade, Policies, and Relations

Dihkala, Erkki. "Finnish Iron and the Russian Market, 1880-1913." SCANDINAVIAN ECONOMIC HISTORY REVIEW 12, no. 2 (1964): 121-44.

   This paper investigates the reasons for the deterioration of Finland's iron exports to Russia. Covered are the tariff policy, Finnish iron production and exports to Russia, the Russian iron industry, and a comparison of the Russian and Finnish industries. Two tables and four charts. Five appendices contain more tables.

Falkus, M[alcolm]. E. "Russia and the International Wheat Trade, 1861-1914." ECONOMICA n.s. 33 (November 1966): 416-29.

   Russia's wheat exports are examined. The 1880s and 1890s were a turning point when foreign competition and changes in demand for particular qualities of wheat produced a new pattern. Specialization with regard to both qualities of wheat produced and the markets to which they were sent emerged.

Gay, J. E. "Anglo-Russian Economic Relations." ECONOMIC JOURNAL 27 (June 1917): 213-37.

   The article surveys Russian and English trade from 1870 to 1913, concluding that further expansion is to be expected. Tables present data on Russian imports and exports by country and values of various goods exported to Russia from Great Britain and Germany.

Hourwich, Isaac A. "Russia in the International Market." JOURNAL OF POLITICAL ECONOMY 2 (March 1894): 284-90.

   This short paper summarizes the most important statements of the reports of the Statistical Bureau of the Russian Customs Department. Many figures, including three tables, concern Russian foreign trade in 1891-92.

Johnston, Charles. "The Russo-German Tariff War." ECONOMIC JOURNAL 4 (March 1894): 136-39.

   The article surveys the circumstances surrounding Germany's Differential Tariff of February 1892 and Russia's Retaliatory Tariff of July 1893.

Just, C. F. REPRINT OF ARTICLES DEALING WITH RUSSIAN TRADE. Ottawa: Department of Trade and Commerce, 1916. 97 p.

   This pamphlet surveys Russian trade and trade by regions (i.e., Petrograd, the Caucasus, Siberia) with maps and an account of trade methods of competing countries. Numerous appendices give trade statistics and Russian markets for hardware specialties.

McRoberts, Samuel. RUSSIA. An address before the Boston chapter, American Institute of Banking, January 16, 1917. New York: National City Bank of

New York, 1917. 18 p.

> The author outlines the prospects of Russian-American trade prior to the Bolshevik Revolution.

Taylor, Alonzo E. "The Commercial Importance of Russia." AMERICAN ECONOMIC REVIEW 12 (September 1922): 447-59.

> Taylor surveys the commercial importance of Russia to Europe prior to World War I as a supplier of agricultural products and raw materials. Short tables on Russian foreign trade in general and agricultural exports in particular are included.

Tuve, Jeanette E. "Changing Directions in Russian-American Economic Relations, 1912-1917." SLAVIC REVIEW 31 (March 1972): 52-70.

> This article deals more with general history and politics than with the economics of U.S.-Russian trade relations.

THE PERIOD AFTER 1917

Aboltin, V. "Economic Aspects of Peaceful Coexistence of Two Social Systems." AMERICAN ECONOMIC REVIEW 48 (May 1958): 385-92.

> An eminent Soviet economist argues that the potential for fruitful economic relations between the Soviet Union and the United States supports peaceful coexistence between the two social systems of the two nations. For further discussion, see: Holland Hunter and Frank H. Golay. "Capital Investment Decisions in the USSR--Discussion." AMERICAN ECONOMIC REVIEW 48 (May 1958): 393-97.

Alison, Colin A. "The Second Russian Five-Year Plan and the Australian Primary Producer." ECONOMIC RECORD 9 (June 1933): 108-12.

> The author sees the Russian Second Five-Year Plan with its determination to improve living conditions as an important factor in increasing the demand and thus in raising the prices for Australian raw materials, especially wool, and foodstuffs.

Alkhimov, V., and Mordvinov, V. FOREIGN TRADE OF THE U.S.S.R. Soviet Booklet, 37. London: Soviet Booklets, 1958. 38 p. Illustrated.

> The following aspects of Soviet foreign trade are examined by two Soviet economists; principles and features of Soviet foreign trade; growth of Soviet foreign trade; trade with the people's democracies and Western capitalist countries; and economic relations with underdeveloped countries.

Allen, Robert L[oring]. "Economic Motives in Soviet Foreign Trade Policy."

Foreign Trade, Policies, and Relations

SOUTHERN ECONOMIC JOURNAL 25 (October 1958): 189-201.

This paper examines recent development, trends, relative costs, terms of trade, and official statements in Soviet foreign trade and concludes that both economic and political considerations are operative. Two tables.

———. "An Interpretation of East-West Trade." In COMPARISONS OF THE U.S. AND SOVIET ECONOMIES, U.S. Congress. Joint Economic Committee, pt. 2, pp. 403-26. Washington, D.C.: Government Printing Office, 1959.

Allen sketches the value and volume; growth and trends; geographic direction of trade; commodity composition; prices and terms of trade; commercial policy; bloc motives for trade; trade experience; evaluation and prospects; and the implications for U.S. policy of East-West trade. Eight tables and bibliography.

———. "A Note on Soviet Foreign Trade Statistics." SOVIET STUDIES 10 (April 1959): 360-69.

This note discusses recently published statistics. Two tables.

———. "Soviet Foreign Trade Pricing Policy." WESTERN ECONOMIC ASSOCIATION, PROCEEDINGS, pp. 15-19 (1960). Stanford, 1960; Seattle, 1961. Salt Lake City: Western Economic Association, 1960, 1961.

Allen considers whether or not Soviet commercial policies have a favorable effect on the terms of trade. The article contains a brief outline of trade organization and commercial policy of the Soviet Union, as well as the official pricing policy.

Ames, Edward. "Economic Integration in the European Soviet Bloc?" AMERICAN ECONOMIC REVIEW 49 (May 1959): 113-24.

After a mathematical presentation, the paper concludes that the criteria of ordinary market analysis fail in analyzing economic relations within the Soviet bloc because they do not start from premises appropriate to Soviet bloc conditions. "A restatement of equilibrium conditions, plans, and price controls yields a different (if tentative) formulation of equilibrium which would explain the volume of output and trade within the bloc," the author concludes. For further discussion, see: Nicholas Spulber, William W. Hollister, and Thad P. Alton. "The Non-Russian Communist Economies--Discussion." AMERICAN ECONOMIC REVIEW 49 (May 1959): 125-33.

Anderson, Edgar. "The USSR Trades with Latvia: The Treaty of 1927." SLAVIC REVIEW 21 (June 1962): 296-321.

The history and politics of the Latvian-Soviet commercial treaty of 1927 are explored.

Andrew, I. "USSR-Largest Exporter of Machines and Equipment." SOVIET AND EASTERN EUROPEAN FOREIGN TRADE 3 (September-October 1967): 3-23.

    This is a translation of an article from VNESHNIAIA TORGOVLIA no. 6 (1966): 3-39. The emphasis is on the period 1955-65. Six tables.

Aubrey, Henry G. "Soviet Trade, Price Stability, and Economic Growth." KYKLOS 12, fasc. 3 (1959): 290-99.

    The emergence of the Sino-Soviet group as a major seller and buyer of certain commodities on the world market is traced. The effect of stabilization policies in industrial countries on primary producers is examined.

Baykov, Alexander M. SOVIET FOREIGN TRADE. Princeton University Department of Economics and Social Institutions. International Finance Section. Publication no. 10. Princeton, N.J.: Princeton University Press, 1946. 100 p.

    The author discusses: the development of foreign trade in tsarist Russia (1803-1913); the evolution of the Soviet foreign trade system; the organization of Soviet foreign trade prior to the Second World War; general trends in Soviet foreign trade; and Soviet trade with the more important foreign countries. Appendix tables cover the period 1913-38.

Becker, Abraham S. OIL AND THE PERSIAN GULF IN SOVIET POLICY IN THE 1970'S. Santa Monica, Calif.: RAND Corp., 1972. 45 p.

    The pamphlet discusses Soviet economic interests in Persian Gulf oil and outlines the Soviet oil balance in 1970 and 1980. Becker concludes that by the end of the decade the Soviet Union will be in the market for Persian Gulf oil. The second part of the paper examines the political implications. Tables.

Berliner, Joseph S. "Soviet Foreign Economic Competition." AMERICAN ECONOMIC REVIEW 49 (May 1959): 33-42.

    The article looks at Soviet economic relations with other countries to determine the patterns of trade and aid and the reasons for them. For further discussion, see: Raymond P. Powell; Francis Seton; Robert Loring Allen; and Chauncy D. Harris. "Soviet Economic Trends and Prospects--Discussion." AMERICAN ECONOMIC REVIEW 49 (May 1959): 43-49.

Berman, H. J. "A Reappraisal of US-USSR Trade Policy." HARVARD BUSINESS REVIEW 42 (July-August 1964): 139-51.

    This article assesses the political and economic advantages of increased U.S. trade with the Soviet Union.

Bernard, Jean. SOVIET COLONIALISM. Calcutta: Institute of Political and Social Studies, 1961. 51 p.

    This pamphlet gives a brief account of "Soviet Colonialism" today, which the author feels is more dangerous than the older Western colonial systems. Economic consequences are discussed.

Bilimovich, Aleksandr. "The Common Market and COMECON." STUDIES ON THE SOVIET UNION n.s. 2, no. 2 (1962): 40-50.

    The most interesting part of this paper is the survey of the Soviet press concerning attitudes toward COMECON in the 1950s and early 1960s. Two tables compare growth of production in the West with growth of selected industries in the USSR.

Birmingham University. Bureau of Research on Russian Economic Conditions. "The Foreign Trade of the U.S.S.R." MEMORANDUM NO. 2 (July 1931): 1-24.

    This memorandum discusses the monopoly of foreign trade, the development of Soviet foreign trade, agricultural and industrial exports, imports, and trade with various countries. The text contains numerous tables and graphs which were compiled from official Soviet sources.

_____. "Foreign Trade of the U.S.S.R." (July 1934): 1-23.

    This memorandum discusses the foreign trade monopoly; the official data on Soviet exports and imports; and the economic consequences of the foreign trade monopoly and the planning of foreign trade. Tables.

Boles, John J. "The Soviet System of Foreign Trade." REVIEW OF SOCIAL ECONOMY 12 (September 1954): 135-46.

    This paper traces the evolution of the Soviet foreign trade system from its pre-Revolutionary origins to the post-World War II period.

Boltho, Andrea. FOREIGN TRADE CRITERIA IN SOCIALIST ECONOMIES. Soviet and East European Studies. London and New York: Cambridge University Press, 1971. viii, 176 p.

    This book contains one chapter on the Soviet model of foreign trade planning which discusses practical and economic shortcomings. Statistical tables, bibliography, and index.

Bowers, Robert E. "American Diplomacy, the 1933 Wheat Conference, and Recognition of the Soviet Union." AGRICULTURAL HISTORY 40 (January 1966): 39-52.

    This political and historical study is intended to point out the relationship of the wheat trade and wheat conference to the establishment of diplomatic relations between the United States and the Soviet Union in 1933.

Brada, Josef C., and King, Arthur E. "The Soviet-American Trade Agreements: Prospects for the Soviet Economy." RUSSIAN REVIEW 32 (October 1973): 345-59.

This article examines certain post-World War II economic and noneconomic strategies which either have failed or outlived their usefulness; gives a detailed account of some of the more important trade agreements between the United States and the USSR; and attempts to assess the potential impact of the developing trade on the Soviet economy.

Braeker, Hans. "Soviet Policy Towards the Communist Countries with Special Reference to Its Economic Aspects." STUDIES ON THE SOVIET UNION n.s. 1, no. 2 (1961): 96-114.

This study concerns ideological principles; cooperation between Eastern bloc Communist parties; the Council of Mutual Economic Co-operation as a Soviet policy tool; and Soviet attempts to "guide" the long-term economic development of COMECON members.

Budish, Jacob M., and Shipman, Samuel S. SOVIET FOREIGN TRADE. New York: Liviright, 1931. xii, 276 p.

This study, sponsored by the Amtorg Trading Corp., attempts to present a well-rounded survey of Soviet foreign trade and, in particular, its trade with the United States. The book deals principally with the major commodities imported by the United States. Many tables.

Cheng, Chu-Yuan. ECONOMIC RELATIONS BETWEEN PEKING AND MOSCOW: 1949-63. Praeger Special Studies in International Economics. New York: Praeger, 1964. 119 p.

This book examines four integral aspects of Sino-Soviet economic relations: (1) Soviet aid to China's industrialization program; (2) Sino-Soviet commercial relations; (3) the nature and amount of Soviet financial aid; and (4) prospects for the future. The appendix contains a chronology of basic events in Sino-Soviet economic relations, 1949-62. Tables.

Committee on Russian-American Relations. THE UNITED STATES AND THE SOVIET UNION. New York: American Foundation, 1933. 279 p.

Section eight deals with trade and discusses the Soviet theory of social-economic planning; the nature and extent of Soviet foreign trade; trade between the USSR and the United States; and USSR trade with other countries.

Foreign Trade, Policies, and Relations

Condoide, Mikhail V. RUSSIAN-AMERICAN TRADE, A STUDY OF THE SOVIET FOREIGN-TRADE MONOPOLY. Columbus: The Bureau of Business Research, College of Commerce and Administration, Ohio State University, 1946. xiii, 160 p.

> This study surveys trade relations between the United States and Russia, particularly between the First and Second World Wars. Tables and bibliography.

Conolly, Violet. SOVIET ECONOMIC POLICY IN THE EAST: TURKEY, PERSIA, AFGHANISTAN, MONGOLIA AND TANA TUVA. London: Oxford University Press, 1933. ix, 168 p.

> The author discusses the "special trading system which more or less ignored the Soviet foreign trade monopoly," which has been in operation for more than a decade. Tables, index, and foldout map of communications in Asiatic Russia.

_____. SOVIET TRADE FROM THE PACIFIC TO THE LEVANT: WITH AN ECONOMIC STUDY OF THE SOVIET FAR EASTERN REGION. London: Oxford University Press, 1935. x, 238 p.

> The book is a continuation and conclusion of a study of the previously cited study. This volume discusses Soviet economic relations with China, Manchuria, Japan, the Chinese Eastern Railway, India, the Pacific Tropics, Egypt and the Levant, and the Red Sea Basin. Tables, appendix containing legal documents, and bibliography.

De Alessi, Louis. "The Sale of Wheat to the USSR: a Change in US Policy?" KYKLOS 18, fasc. 1 (1965): 116-29.

> This paper examines two alternative hypotheses which can explain the decision of the United States to sell wheat to the USSR: (1) the economic gains available to the United States through trade exceed the damage which might be done to the USSR by not trading; and (2) U.S. policy is shifting toward a willingness to share trade gains with the USSR. Two tables give figures on U.S. and Canadian wheat sales to the USSR.

Debo, Richard K. "Dutch-Soviet Relations, 1917-1924: The Role of Finance and Commerce in the Foreign Policy of Soviet Russia and the Netherlands." CANADIAN SLAVIC STUDIES 4 (Summer 1970): 199-217.

> This study traces the breakdown of Dutch-Soviet relations in 1918 and the failure of reconciliation between the two states.

Dewar, Margaret. SOVIET TRADE WITH EASTERN EUROPE, 1945-1949. London and New York: Royal Institute of International Affairs, 1951. vii, 123 p.

> This study collects available data on the nature and extent of the exchange of goods between Eastern Europe and the USSR. Various trade agreements-treaties are included in the appendices. Index.

Foreign Trade, Policies, and Relations

Drummond, Ian M. "Empire Trade and Russian Trade: Economic Diplomacy in the Nineteen-Thirties." CANADIAN JOURNAL OF ECONOMICS 5 (February 1972): 35-47.

> This article outlines trade relations between the British Empire and Russia in the 1930s, largely from the political viewpoint.

Dudinskii, I. "Some Features of the Development of the World Socialist Market." PROBLEMS OF ECONOMICS 4 (September 1961): 55-62.

> This is a translation from VOPROSY EKONOMIKI no. 2 (1961): 40-50. The gains from trade to the Soviet Union and its trading market are discussed.

Duimulen, I. "The Soviet Union in the System of International Economic Relations." SOVIET AND EASTERN EUROPEAN FOREIGN TRADE 1 (January-February 1965): 39-51.

> This is a translation of an article from MIROVAIA EKONOMIKA I MEZHDUNARODNYE OTNOSHENIIA no. 3 (1964). One graph and five tables.

Duncan, M. W. "Selling the Soviets: A Story of Problems and Profits." SOVIET AND EASTERN EUROPEAN FOREIGN TRADE 3 (March-April 1967): 38-53.

> Various aspects and problems of selling U.S. goods to the Soviets are discussed.

Duranty, Walter. "The United States of America and the Union of Socialist Soviet Republics." In RED ECONOMICS, edited by Gerhard Dobbert, pp. 311-27. Boston: Houghton Mifflin, 1932.

> Duranty discusses trade relations between the United States and the USSR and outlines the U.S. attitude toward tsarist Russia and the Bolsheviks. In conclusion, he speculates on the future of Russian-American economic cooperation.

"Economic Cooperation with Iran: the Immediate Future." CENTRAL ASIAN REVIEW 16, no. 4 (1968): 338-41.

> A Soviet writer comments on problems and prospects of Soviet-Iranian trade.

Fallenbuchl, Z. M. "COMECON Integration." PROBLEMS OF COMMUNISM 22 (March-April 1973): 25-39.

> This paper surveys the postwar economic development of the COMECON countries, the development of economic cooperation, and the position of the USSR in COMECON. Several tables.

Foreign Trade, Policies, and Relations

Fituni, L. A. THE SOVIET UNION AND INTERNATIONAL ECONOMIC CO-OPERATION. Moscow: Foreign Languages Publishing House, 1952. 46 p.

This booklet discusses the official Party line concerning international economic cooperation under Stalin. Fituni concludes that the restoration of normal economic relations between countries would lessen tensions in international relations.

Fokin, D. "Soviet Foreign Trade in 1963." SOVIET AND EASTERN EUROPEAN FOREIGN TRADE 1 (May-June 1964): 39-68.

This is a translation of an article from VNESHNIAIA TORGOVLIA, no. 11 (1964): 9-20. A table and fifteen illustrative charts are included.

"Foreign Trade of the USSR in the Postwar Years." SOVIET AND EASTERN EUROPEAN FOREIGN TRADE 3 (January-February 1967): 39-64.

This is a translation from a supplement to VNESHNIAIA TORGOVLIA no. 11 (1965). The entire article consists of tables on Soviet foreign trade for selected years, 1946-64.

Foster, E. D. "The Trend of Soviet-German Commercial Relations and its Significance." HARVARD BUSINESS REVIEW 11 (April 1933): 376-85.

Topics covered include Russian trade before and during World War I; Soviet-German trade agreements; growth and potential of Soviet-German trade; and the political significance of that trade.

Galenson, Walter. "Economic Relations Between the Soviet Union and Communist China." In STUDY OF THE SOVIET ECONOMY, edited by Nicolas Spulber, pp. 32-56. Papers presented at a conference, Bloomington, Ind. Bloomington: Indiana University Press, 1961.

The following topics are reviewed: (1) Sino-Soviet aid and trade; (2) mutual advantages and Communist value theory; (3) Chinese requirements and Soviet investment for growth; and (4) the impact of Chinese industrialization on Soviet growth. The article includes tables as well as sources from which statistical data were obtained and extensive notes.

Garrison, Mark J., and Crawford, Morris H. "Soviet Trade With the Free World in 1961." In DIMENSIONS OF SOVIET ECONOMIC POWER, U.S. Congress. Joint Economic Committee, pp. 443-56. Washington, D.C.: Government Printing Office, 1964.

The article outlines Soviet foreign trade policy during and after the Stalin era. The current trends in Soviet foreign trade are reviewed: volume of trade; geographic distribution; commodity composition; and balance of trade and balance of payments. The article contains many tables and appendix data on foreign trade by country for 1960 and 1961.

Gerschenkron, Alexander. "Russia and the International Trade Organization." AMERICAN ECONOMIC REVIEW 37 (May 1947): 624-42.

> Gerschenkron discusses certain provisions of the International Trade Organization charter, which would have relevance to Russia should she decide to adhere to them. Comments on this article are in Paul A. Baran. "The Economy of the USSR: Discussion." AMERICAN ECONOMIC REVIEW 37 (May 1947): 646-48.

Giffen, James H. THE LEGAL AND PRACTICAL ASPECTS OF TRADE WITH THE SOVIET UNION. Praeger Special Studies in International Economics and Development. New York: Praeger, 1969. xxii, 373 p.

> The author discusses U.S. export and import regulations; legislation to increase East-West trade; the process of negotiating with the Soviets; financial aspects of trade; and industrial property rights. Tables. The book contains forty-three appended documents. No index.

Gillette, Philip S. "American Capital in the Context for Soviet Oil, 1920-23." SOVIET STUDIES 24 (April 1973): 477-90.

> This paper first reviews the petroleum picture before 1917 and then concentrates on relations between American oil companies, the American government, and the Soviet government regarding concessionary rights to Russian petroleum.

Ginsburgs, George. "The Kremlin and the Common Market: A Conspectus." SOCIAL RESEARCH 37 (Summer 1970): 296-305.

> This paper discusses the responses of the Soviet leaders to the establishment of the Common Market, especially COMECON.

Glovinsky, Evgeny. "The Economic Relations of the USSR with Latin America." STUDIES ON THE SOVIET UNION n.s. 1, no. 3 (1962): 64-79.

> Expansion of economic relations is seen as a means of political penetration and expansion. Trade data are presented in eleven tables.

_____. "Soviet-Albanian Economic Relations." STUDIES ON THE SOVIET UNION n.s. 2, no. 2 (1962): 66-79.

> Glovinsky provides a survey of Soviet-Albanian economic relations since July 1947. Trade data are included in ten short tables.

Goldman, Marshall I. "Who Profits More From U.S.-Soviet Trade?" HARVARD BUSINESS REVIEW 51 (November-December 1973): 79-87.

> This paper discusses Soviet interest in U.S. goods, U.S. interest in Soviet trade, the risk of granting credits to the Soviets, and the Soviet need for credit. Several tables.

Foreign Trade, Policies, and Relations

Grossman, Gregory. "Prospects and Policy for U.S.-Soviet Trade." AMERICAN ECONOMIC REVIEW 64 (May 1974): 289-93.

    This paper discusses, in general terms, reasons for Soviet trade with the United States and its prospects.

_____. "U.S. Soviet Trade and Economic Relations: Problems and Prospects." ASSOCIATION FOR COMPARATIVE ECONOMIC STUDIES BULLETIN 15 (Spring 1973): 3-22.

    This article discusses the Soviet readiness to import from the United States and the types of goods that the two countries are likely to trade.

Grzybowski, Kazimierz. "United States-Soviet Union Trade Agreement of 1972." LAW AND CONTEMPORARY PROBLEMS 37 (Summer 1972): 395-428.

    This article provides a general survey and then discusses the mechanism of trade and the legal aspects of U.S.-Soviet trade.

Hanson, Philip. "Soviet Imports of Primary Products: A Case Study of Cocoa." SOVIET STUDIES 23 (July 1971): 59-77.

    The size, growth and stability of Soviet imports of cocoa beans during 1955-67 are compared with U.S. and U.K. imports. Hanson then reviews purchasing terms and estimates and compares indirect tax burdens on cocoa products. Seven tables.

Heiss, Hertha W. "The Soviet Union in the World Market." In NEW DIRECTIONS IN THE SOVIET ECONOMY, U.S. Congress. Joint Economic Committee. Subcommittee on Foreign Economic Policy, pp. 917-33. Washington, D.C.: Government Printing Office, 1966.

    Current trends in Soviet foreign trade are discussed. Ten tables.

Herman, Leon M. "A Dollar Estimate of Soviet Foreign Trade, 1947-1951." REVIEW OF ECONOMICS AND STATISTICS 36 (November 1954): 437-43.

    This paper presents estimates and discusses their significance. Five tables. A short appendix discusses foreign trade of the Soviet bloc and contains a table on trade of the Soviet bloc in 1951.

_____. "The Promise of Economic Self-Sufficiency under Soviet Socialism." STUDIES ON THE SOVIET UNION n.s. 7, no. 1 (1967): 67-102.

    Foreign trade and attempts at self-sufficiency are traced from the Revolution to the 1960s. Eight tables provide data on foreign trade.

_____. "Soviet Foreign Trade and the United States Market." In NEW DIRECTIONS IN THE SOVIET ECONOMY, U.S. Congress. Joint Economic Committee. Subcommittee on Foreign Economic Policy, pp. 935-46. Washington,

D.C.: Government Printing Office, 1966.

The attraction of trade with the West and the role of the United States in Soviet foreign trade are discussed. Five tables.

Heymann, Hans, Jr. "Oil in Soviet-Western Relations in the Interwar Years." AMERICAN SLAVIC AND EAST EUROPEAN REVIEW 7, no. 4 (1948): 303-16.

This article chronicles the history and politics of Soviet oil in the worldwide struggle for petroleum between the First and the Second World Wars.

Hoeffding, Oleg. "East-West Trade Possibilities: An Appraisal of the Moscow Economic Conference." AMERICAN SLAVIC AND EAST EUROPEAN REVIEW 12 (1953): 350-59.

At a conference in Moscow in April 1952, the Soviet bloc countries argued that East-West trade would be greater if the "artificial barriers" to trade erected by the West were removed. This paper contends that a hypothetical program of expanded trade advanced at Moscow implies only a modest revival of East-West trade in comparison to its levels before World War II or in 1948. The Moscow trade targets are translated into an index of East-West trade volume on a 1938 base. Four tables present data on trade, and an appendix contains notes to one of the tables.

_____. RECENT TRENDS IN SOVIET TRADE. Santa Monica, Calif.: RAND Corp., 1955. iii, 28 p.

This study deals with Soviet foreign trade with the free world and with the Soviet bloc during the postwar period, particularly 1953-55.

_____. SINO-SOVIET ECONOMIC RELATIONS. Santa Monica, Calif.: RAND Corp., 1963. vii, 23 p.

Sino-Soviet economic relations during the early 1960s are reviewed against the background of economic troubles in Chinq and political conflicts between Moscow and Peking.

_____. "Soviet Economic Relations with the Orbit." In SOVIET ECONOMIC GROWTH: CONDITIONS AND PERSPECTIVES, edited by Abram Bergson, pp. 320-37. Evanston, Ill.: Row, Peterson, 1953.

This paper offers a qualitative appraisal of current economic developments in Eastern Europe which relate to the general attempt to appraise the economic perspectives of the USSR. Comments by Nicolas Spulber, Janet G. Chapman, Hans Heymann, Jr., and Leon M. Herman follow the paper "East-West Trade," by Harry Schwartz, which is in the same volume.

Foreign Trade, Policies, and Relations

Hoeffding, W. "German Trade with the Soviet Union." SLAVONIC REVIEW 14 (January 1936): 473-94.

The article describes: Germany's pioneering efforts in the establishment of trade relations with Russia; the credit agreement of April 1935; the main trends of Soviet-German trade in 1925-35; credit relations; and political and economic prospects of Soviet-German trade.

Holzman, Franklyn D. "East-West Trade and Investment Policy Issues: Past and Future." In SOVIET ECONOMIC PROSPECTS FOR THE SEVENTIES, U.S. Congress. Joint Economic Committee, pp. 660-89. Washington, D.C.: Government Printing Office, 1973.

Topics discussed include export controls, high technology commodities, embargoes on China and Cuba, extension of credits, restrictions on imports, dumping, gains from trade liberalization, and international monetary problems.

_____. "Foreign Trade." In ECONOMIC TRENDS IN THE SOVIET UNION, edited by Abram Bergson and Simon Kuznets, pp. 283-332. Cambridge, Mass.: Harvard University Press, 1963.

The two purposes of this paper are to explain the major trends in Soviet international trade and to assess the importance of international commodity and capital flows for Soviet industrial growth. Concern is chiefly with the period of the five-year plans. Extensive data are presented in the tables.

_____. "More on Soviet Bloc Trade Discrimination." SOVIET STUDIES 17 (July 1965): 44-65.

Holzman critically reviews arguments on the Soviet bloc price discrimination issues and presents statistical material. Eleven tables.

_____. "Soviet Foreign Trade Pricing and the Question of Discrimination." REVIEW OF ECONOMICS AND STATISTICS 44 (May 1962): 134-47.

This paper is a detailed analysis of two works by Horst Mendershausen --"Terms of Trade between the Soviet Union and Smaller Communist Countries, 1955-57." REVIEW OF ECONOMICS AND STATISTICS 41 (May 1959): 106-18; and "The Terms of Soviet-Satellite Trade: A Broadened Analysis." REVIEW OF ECONOMICS AND STATISTICS 42 (May 1960): 152-63. It concludes that Mendershausen's price discrimination is a natural consequence of the "customs union" of the Soviet bloc. Four tables and an addendum on Polish foreign trade in 1959 are included. For further discussion of Holzman's paper, see: Horst Mendershausen. "Mutual Price Discrimination in Soviet Bloc Trade." REVIEW OF ECONOMICS AND STATISTICS 44 (November 1962): 493-96; Franklyn D. Holzman. "Soviet Bloc Mutual Discrimination: Cement." REVIEW OF ECONOMICS

AND STATISTICS 44 (November 1962): 496-99; and Horst Mendershausen. "A Final Comment." REVIEW OF ECONOMICS AND STATISTICS 44 (November 1962): 499.

Huntingdon, W. Chapin. "The Prospects of American Trade with the Soviet Union." SLAVONIC REVIEW 14 (July 1935): 222-45.

Huntingdon discusses Soviet-American trade during the decade before the Five-Year Plan; trade under the Five-Year Plan; and the prospects of resolving the "deadlock in American-Soviet negotiations over debts and credits."

Kaser, Michael C. "A Volume Index of Soviet Foreign Trade." SOVIET STUDIES 20 (April 1969): 523-26.

One table provides an index of exports plus imports for 1938 and 1956-67. The second table provides index numbers based on various years for value and volume of foreign trade in 1913 and 1917-67.

Kasparek, Jiri. "Soviet Russia and Czechoslovakia's Uranium." RUSSIAN REVIEW 11 (April 1952): 97-105.

This article presents the political history of the Soviet-Czech uranium supply relations immediately after World War II.

Kato, Hiroshi. "Soviet-East European Trade Relations." KEIO ECONOMIC STUDIES 1 (1963): 134-56.

Topics covered here include changes in Soviet trade over time, the 1957 COMECON settlement agreement, a Communist bloc trade matrix for 1958, and discriminatory pricing. Eighteen tables give trade-related statistics.

Kerblay, B. H. "The Economic Relations of the U.S.S.R. with Foreign Countries During the War and in the Post-War Period." BULLETINS ON SOVIET ECONOMIC DEVELOPMENT 5, Ser. 2 (March 1951): 1-27.

This article deals with the effect of World War II on Soviet foreign trade and reparations policy and changes in the organization of economic relations with foreign countries after the war.

Kitagawa, Tokusuke. "Legal Aspects of Soviet-Japanese Trade." LAW AND CONTEMPORARY PROBLEMS 37 (Autumn 1972): 557-70.

This paper discusses the legal status of Soviet foreign trade organizations, the most-favored-nation clause, payments, settlement of commercial disputes, navigation, and aviation.

Klein, Sidney. THE ROAD DIVIDES--ECONOMIC ASPECTS OF THE SINO-SOVIET DISPUTE. Hong Kong: International Studies Group, 1966. ix, 178 p.

Foreign Trade, Policies, and Relations

Klein examines the economic relations between Moscow and Peking since 1949. The study deals with the terms of trade, technical assistance, and aid.

Knickerbocker, H[ubert]. R. "Foreign Trade." In RED ECONOMICS, edited by Gerhard Dobbert, pp. 291-310. Boston: Houghton Mifflin, 1932.

The author discusses the Soviet foreign trade monopoly and why the Soviet government considered it necessary.

Kovach, Robert S., and Farrell, John T. "Foreign Trade in the U.S.S.R." In ECONOMIC PERFORMANCE AND THE MILITARY BURDEN IN THE SOVIET UNION, U.S. Congress. Joint Economic Committee, pp. 100-116. Washington, D.C.: Government Printing Office, 1970.

This paper discusses trends in trade, the distribution and composition of trade, and trade by region. Thirteen tables.

Kovner, Milton. THE CHALLENGE OF COEXISTENCE; A STUDY OF SOVIET ECONOMIC DIPLOMACY. Washington, D.C.: Public Affairs Press, 1961. vi, 130 p.

This book considers some political determinants of Soviet foreign economic policy within the context of the existing global competition between the Communist and non-Communist worlds. Index.

Lubell, Harold. "The Soviet Oil Offensive." QUARTERLY REVIEW OF ECONOMICS AND BUSINESS 1 (November 1961): 7-18.

This paper briefly discusses the future prospects for increased Soviet oil exports and then cites several examples in examining in some detail and aims and techniques of the USSR in penetrating non-Soviet oil markets. It concludes with a discussion of some of the implications for the West of the Soviet oil export drive.

_____. THE SOVIET OIL OFFENSIVE AND INTER-BLOC ECONOMIC COMPETITION. Santa Monica, Calif.: RAND Corp., 1961. 82 p.

This paper summarizes available data on Soviet oil production and exports and assesses the effects of those exports on the West as both consumer and producer of oil. Tables.

McKitterick, T. E. M. RUSSIAN ECONOMIC POLICY IN EASTERN EUROPE: ALBANIA, BULGARIA, CZECHOSLOVAKIA, HUNGARY, JUGOSLAVIA, POLAND, ROUMANIA AND AUSTRIA. Research Series no. 128. London: Fabian Publications, 1948. 41 p.

The trading policy of the USSR toward the East European countries is discussed.

McMillan, Carl H. "Factor Proportions and the Structure of Soviet Foreign Trade." ASSOCIATION FOR COMPARATIVE ECONOMIC STUDIES BULLETIN 15 (Spring 1973): 57-81.

This study uses Soviet input-output data for 1959 to investigate the factor proportions in Soviet foreign trade. The two-factor, two-country model (the USSR and the rest of the world) was extended to include additional factors and to account for the direction of Soviet trade. For further discussion of McMillan's methodology, see: Steven Rosefielde. "The Embodied Factor Content of Soviet International Trade: Problems of Theory, Measurement and Interpretation." ASSOCIATION FOR COMPARATIVE ECONOMIC STUDIES BULLETIN 15 (Summer-Fall 1973): 3-12.

_____. "Some Recent Developments in Soviet Foreign Trade Theory." CANADIAN SLAVONIC PAPERS 12 (Fall 1970): 243-72.

This paper reviews the substance of recent (1958-68) Soviet theoretical contributions on major foreign trade questions. The role of foreign trade in a socialist economy is considered, and indexes of foreign trade effectiveness are presented.

_____. "Soviet Specialization and Trade in Manufactures." SOVIET STUDIES 24 (April 1973): 522-32.

Patterns of specialization in Soviet trade are compared with those of several industrial market economies. It analyzes the extent to which a rational pattern of production specialization has been the basis of trade expansion. The conclusion is that COMECON efforts to foster intraspecialization have largely been unsuccessful. Three tables.

Malish, Anton F., Jr. "An Analysis of Tariff Discrimination on Soviet and East European Trade." ASSOCIATION FOR COMPARATIVE ECONOMIC STUDIES BULLETIN 15 (Spring 1973): 43-56.

The article first provides a brief legislative history of tariff discrimination in the United States and then discusses Malish's conclusions about the effects of this discrimination on Soviet and East European foreign trade.

Marer, Paul. SOVIET AND EAST EUROPEAN FOREIGN TRADE, 1946-1969. STATISTICAL COMPENDIUM AND GUIDE. Studies on Development, no. 4. London and Bloomington: Indiana University Press, 1972. xviii, 408 p.

This compendium presents comprehensive data on the value of foreign trade of individual East European countries during 1946-69. The data are variously arranged by country or region of origin and destination, or by structure according to a number of commodity classifications. The USSR is among nine East European countries which are documented individually.

Foreign Trade, Policies, and Relations

Mendershausen, Horst. "The Terms of Soviet-Satellite Trade: A Broadened Analysis." REVIEW OF ECONOMICS AND STATISTICS 42 (May 1960): 152-63.

This paper looks for evidence of Soviet price discrimination in its foreign trade by analyzing data for the years 1955-58. Nine tables and six charts are included. For further discussion, see: Franklyn D. Holzman. "Soviet Foreign Trade Pricing and the Question of Discrimination." REVIEW OF ECONOMICS AND STATISTICS 44 (May 1962): 134-47; Horst Mendershausen. "Mutual Price Discrimination in Soviet Bloc Trade." REVIEW OF ECONOMICS AND STATISTICS 44 (November 1962): 496-99; and Horst Mendershausen. "A Final Comment." REVIEW OF ECONOMICS AND STATISTICS 44 (November 1962): 499.

_____. "Terms of Trade between the Soviet Union and Smaller Communist Countries 1955-1957." REVIEW OF ECONOMICS AND STATISTICS 41 (May 1959): 106-18.

This paper discusses the new Soviet data for 1955-57; estimates costs of Soviet imports and exports to Eastern and Western Europe; and looks for evidence of price discrimination on the part of the Soviet Union. Six tables and seven charts. For further discussion, see: Franklyn D. Holzman. "Soviet Foreign Trade Policy and the Question of Discrimination." REVIEW OF ECONOMICS AND STATISTICS 44 (May 1962): 134-47; Horst Mendershausen. "Mutual Price Discrimination in Soviet Bloc Trade." REVIEW OF ECONOMICS AND STATISTICS 44 (November 1962): 493-96; Franklyn D. Holzman. "Soviet Bloc Mutual Discrimination: Comment." REVIEW OF ECONOMICS AND STATISTICS 44 (November 1962): 496-99; and Horst Mendershausen. "A Final Comment." REVIEW OF ECONOMICS AND STATISTICS 44 (November 1962): 499.

Moravcik, I[vo]. "Prospects for Soviet and East European Purchases of Canadian Wheat." CANADIAN SLAVONIC PAPERS 7 (1965): 159-72.

This paper discusses shortrun and longrun prospects for Soviet and East European purchases of Canadian wheat. In so doing, it estimates actual output, per capita requirements, and production potential in the USSR and Eastern Europe. Eleven tables.

Moskoff, William. "The USSR and Developing Countries: Politics and Export Prices, 1955-69." SOVIET STUDIES 24 (January 1973): 348-63.

In this article the author attempts to demonstrate that definite patterns of discrimination exist within the LDC (less developed countries) group and, in relation to the East European satellites, the Soviet Union blatantly discriminates against its closest political allies in the Third World. Four tables.

Neuberger, Egon. "International Division of Labor in CEMA: Limited Regret

Strategy." AMERICAN ECONOMIC REVIEW 54 (May 1964): 506-15.

This paper analyzes the "limited regret strategy," a conservative strategy that describes Council for Economic Mutual Assistance efforts. Neuberger concludes it nevertheless can be considered a reasonable strategy when full account is taken of conflicting objectives, political, economic, and ideological constraints, and the lack of satisfactory theory of division of labor in the East or the West. For further discussion, see: Judith Thornton, Evsey D. Domar, and Frederic L. Pryor. "Efficiency of the Soviet Economy --Discussion." AMERICAN ECONOMIC REVIEW 54 (May 1964): 516-22.

_____. THE USSR AND THE WEST AS MARKETS FOR PRIMARY PRODUCTS: STABILITY, GROWTH, AND SIZE. Memorandum no. RM 3341-PR. Santa Monica, Calif.: RAND Corp., 1963. xviii, 150 p.

This RAND memorandum evaluates two Soviet claims: (1) first, that the USSR is an ideal market for primary-product exports of underdeveloped countries and (2) that the markets of capitalist countries are "extremely unsatisfactory due to the chaos and stagnation."

Nove, Alec. "Soviet Trade and Soviet Aid." LLOYD'S BANK REVIEW n.s. 51 (January 1959): 1-19.

Topics covered here include trade within the Soviet bloc, pattern and motivation of trade with nonbloc countries, and bloc country aid to underdeveloped countries. Four tables.

Ostlund, Lyman E., and Halvorsen, Kjell M. "The Russian Decision Process Governing Trade." JOURNAL OF MARKETING 36 (April 1972): 3-11.

The authors examine the decision-making structure for formal and informal trade in the USSR and offer alternative approaches to trade negotiations with the Russians. Three organization charts.

Owen, G. L. "The Metro-Vickers Crisis: Anglo-Soviet Relations Between Trade Agreements, 1932-1934," SLAVONIC AND EAST EUROPEAN REVIEW 49 (January 1971): 92-112.

This paper discusses the political and economic significance of the arrest and conviction of six British engineers for espionage in the Soviet Union. Tables in appendices.

Prybyla, Jan S. "Eastern Europe and Soviet Oil." JOURNAL OF INDUSTRIAL ECONOMICS 13 (March 1965): 154-67.

In this paper cooperation among the Soviet bloc countries as it relates to petroleum production and trade is examined. Topics covered include growing East European dependence on Soviet petroleum, obstacles to economic integration caused by lack of an integrated price system, and alleged exploitation by the Soviet Union of East European oil importers through price discrimination. Three tables.

Pryor, Frederic L. "Foreign Trade Theory in the Communist Bloc." SOVIET STUDIES 14 (July 1962): 41-61.

The three topics discussed here are the domestic profitability of foreign trade, pure trade theory, and theoretical issues in intra-bloc pricing.

Pubantz, Jerry. "Marxism-Leninism and Soviet-American Economic Relations Since Stalin." LAW AND CONTEMPORARY PROBLEMS 37 (Autumn 1972): 535-47.

Topics discussed include Soviet foreign economic policy, the history of U.S.-Soviet bilateral relations, summit talks, and the future of these relations.

Quigley, John. "Soviet Foreign Trade Agencies Abroad: A Note." LAW AND CONTEMPORARY PROBLEMS 37 (September 1972): 465-73.

This note outlines development of such agencies and their chief characteristics.

Rachkov, B. "The Soviet Union--A Major Exporter of Petroleum and Petroleum Products." SOVIET AND EASTERN EUROPEAN FOREIGN TRADE 1 (January-February 1965): 26-38.

This is a translation of an article from VNESHNIAIA TORGOVLIA, no. 3 (1964). Six tables.

Ronimois, Hans E. "The Baltic Trade of the Soviet Union: Expectations and Probabilities." AMERICAN SLAVIC AND EAST EUROPEAN REVIEW 4 (December 1945): 174-78.

This article reviews Russian trade with the Baltic countries from 1913 with a view toward estimating the probability of expansion. Trade figures in tons for the years 1913 and 1935 are given in a table.

Ropes, E. C. "American-Soviet Trade Relations." RUSSIAN REVIEW 3 (Autumn 1943): 89-94.

This article discusses and presents figures concerning U.S.-USSR trade between 1918 and 1942.

──────. "The Future of American-Soviet Trade Relations." In U.S.S.R. IN RECONSTRUCTION, pp. 155-60. New York: American Russian Institute, 1944.

The paper outlines U.S. trade with the USSR under lend-lease and speculates on the future of Soviet-American trade relations. Ropes reviews both export and import possibilities with the USSR.

_____. "The Shape of United States-Soviet Trade, Past and Future." SLAVONIC AND EAST EUROPEAN REVIEW 22 (August 1944): 1-15.

This article reviews the method of organization and control of Soviet foreign trade, the creation of the Amtorg Trading Corporation in the United States lend-lease, and the prospects for future U.S.-Soviet trade. There are lists of Soviet export-import combines and of American technical assistance contracts with Soviet organizations. Tables.

Rosefielde, Steven. "Factor Proportions and Economic Rationality in Soviet International Trade 1955-1968." AMERICAN ECONOMIC REVIEW 64 (September 1974): 670-81.

This article investigates the factor proportions of Soviet trade to determine the degree to which those proportions are rational according to Eli F. Heckscher-Bertil G. Ohlin criteria. Graphs and tables.

_____. SOVIET INTERNATIONAL TRADE IN HECKSCHER-OHLIN PERSPECTIVE: AN INPUT-OUTPUT STUDY. Lexington, Mass.: Lexington Books, D. C. Heath, 1973. xxv, 173 p.

The economic rationality of Soviet foreign trade is assessed according to modern economic theory. Graphs, bibliography, and index.

Rubinshtein, G. "Some Problems in the Development of Foreign Trade." SOVIET AND EASTERN EUROPEAN FOREIGN TRADE 3 (March-April 1967): 54-67.

This is a translation of an article from VOPROSY EKONOMIKI no. 9 (1966). The emphasis is on Soviet foreign trade in the decade 1955-64.

Schwartz, Harry. "East-West Trade." In SOVIET ECONOMIC GROWTH: CONDITIONS AND PERSPECTIVES, edited by Abram Bergson, pp. 338-68. Evanston, Ill.: Row, Peterson, 1953.

The author argues that the Soviet Union will have to engage in a "moderate level of trade with what it considers the enemy nations." Comments by Nicolas Spulber, Janet G. Chapman, Hans Heymann, Jr., Leon M. Herman, G. B. Cressey, and Oleg Hoeffding follow.

Scott, N. B. [S.]. "Sino-Soviet Trade." SOVIET STUDIES 10 (October 1958): 151-61.

Foreign Trade, Policies, and Relations

This review and discussion of Sino-Soviet trade is especially concerned with the period since World War II, although even the pre-World War I period is touched on briefly. Thirteen tables.

Smirnov, G., et al. "Evaluating the Economic Effectiveness of Foreign Trade." SOVIET AND EASTERN EUROPEAN FOREIGN TRADE 1 (January-February 1965): 3-15.

This is a translation of a paper on the theory of foreign trade from PLANOVOE KHOZIAISTVO, no. 8 (1964). Two tables.

Smith, Glen Alden. SOVIET FOREIGN TRADE: ORGANIZATION, OPERATIONS, AND POLICY, 1918-1971. New York: Praeger, 1973. xviii, 370 p.

This book analyzes Soviet foreign trade organizations, operations, and policies from 1918-72, including various long-term trends in Soviet foreign trade. Tables, charts, and bibliography. No index.

Spulber, Nicholas, and Gehrek, Franz. "The Operations of Trade Within the Soviet Bloc." REVIEW OF ECONOMICS AND STATISTICS 40 (May 1958): 140-48.

This discussion evaluates the efficiency of the mechanism of trade among the Eastern European countries. A table reports shares of the Soviet Union, the Soviet bloc, and the rest of the world in each country's trade for 1937, 1948, and 1954.

Starr, Kenneth M. "The Framework of Anglo-Soviet Commercial Relations: The British View." LAW AND CONTEMPORARY PROBLEMS 37 (Summer 1972): 448-64.

Topics discussed include Anglo-Soviet trade agreements, state trading activities, diplomatic immunity, contracts, legal conflicts, and counterclaims.

Stolte, Stefan [C.]. "COMECON Through Soviet Eyes." STUDIES ON THE SOVIET UNION n.s. 5, no. 3 (1966): 37-45.

This paper discusses Soviet views of the use of COMECON. Four tables.

_____. "Moscow's COMECON Empire-Colonialism or Liberation?" STUDIES ON THE SOVIET UNION n.s. 1, no. 2 (1961): 115-26.

This paper considers whether the "people's democracies" are equal partners of the Soviet Union, or, as is usually accepted in the West, its satellites. It also considers whether such concepts as "imperialism" and "colonialism" can be applied to relations between the Soviet Union and the people's democracies. A table concerning machinery output is included.

Strba, Jan. "On Prospects of Promoting Economic Cooperation with the Soviet Union." CZECHOSLOVAK ECONOMIC DIGEST 8 (December 1971): 3-14.

The author cites three major tendencies of economic cooperation with the Soviet Union: (1) the Soviet Union will develop stronger economic ties with the CEMA countries; (2) economic cooperation will continue on both bilateral and multilateral bases; and (3) there will be an increase in the rate of exchange of finished products.

Szawlowski, Richard. "The International Economic Organizations of the Communist Countries." CANADIAN SLAVONIC PAPERS 10 (Autumn 1968): 254-77.

This paper deals with the system of the international economic organizations of the Communist countries as it exists in 1968.

_____. "The International Economic Organization of the Communist Countries: II." CANADIAN SLAVONIC PAPERS 11 (Spring 1969): 82-107.

This article is concerned largely with the organization of COMECON, and its relations with the Western European Economic Community, and the Organization for Economic Cooperation and Development.

Szu-k'ai, C., and King, V. "Sino-Soviet Trade and Payment Balance, 1960-1961." CONTEMPORARY CHINA 5 (1961-62): 57-64.

This article attempts to answer the questions of what was the outstanding trade deficit during the period and what was the reduction in trade resulting from the decline in agricultural production? Tables.

Tabacek, Jan. "Trade Relations between Czechoslovakia and the Soviet Union." NEW TRENDS IN CZECHOSLOVAK ECONOMICS 7 (November 1969): 37-64.

This paper first gives an historical survey and then discusses price fixing and problems, the present structure of Czech imports from and exports to the Soviet Union, and prospects.

Terada, Yataro. "The System of Trade Between Japan and the East European Countries, Including the Soviet Union." LAW AND CONTEMPORARY PROBLEMS 37 (Summer 1972): 429-47.

The chief concern here is the period 1967-71. Three tables are included. Appendices present an organization chart of the Japan-USSR Economic Committee and a list of exchange delegations.

Tereshtenko, Valery J. AMERICAN-SOVIET TRADE RELATIONS: PAST AND FUTURE, pp. 1-17. New York: Russian Economic Institute, 1945.

The author discusses the organization of Soviet foreign trade; the extent of American-Soviet trade; the effects of World War II on the Soviet economy; Soviet programs of postwar reconstruction

Foreign Trade, Policies, and Relations

and import needs; and future trade with the USSR for the United States.

Thumberg, Penelope H. "The Soviet Union in the World Economy." In DIMENSIONS OF SOVIET ECONOMIC POWER, U.S. Congress. Joint Economic Committee, pp. 413-38. Washington, D.C.: Government Printing Office, 1962.

> This paper gives details on Soviet foreign trade with Eastern Europe, China, and the free world. The author uses many tables in discussing economic assistance and trade with bloc countries, problems of finance with the free world, and various institutions of the Socialist market.

Timoshenko, V[ladimir]. P. ECONOMIC BACKGROUND FOR THE POST-WAR INTERNATIONAL TRADE OF THE USSR, pp. 18-26. New York: Russian Economic Institute, 1945.

> Timoshenko examines the development of Soviet trade during the period between the Revolution of 1917 and the Second World War; contrasts Soviet trade with trade in pre-revolutionary Russia; and scrutinizes the basic principle of Soviet trade policy.

Treml, Vladimir G. "A Note on Soviet Foreign Trade Statistics." ASSOCIATION FOR COMPARATIVE ECONOMIC STUDIES BULLETIN 14 (Spring 1972): 24-27.

> This note deals with a feature of Soviet official foreign trade statistics as published by the Ministry of Foreign Trade of the USSR --the "complete industrial plants" shown in Soviet exports. This item, significant in magnitude, distorts analysis of the commodity composition of Soviet foreign trade in many respects, the author argues. A table estimates exports of selected commodities included in the category of "complete industrial plants" for 1960, 1966, and 1968.

Turin, S. P. "The Foreign Trade of the U.S.S.R." SLAVONIC REVIEW 10 (December 1931): 338-43.

> Turin focuses on features of Russian foreign trade which are of greatest importance to Russia, the world, and the United States in particular.

U.S. Joint Publications Research Services. FOREIGN TRADE OF THE USSR, 1957; STATISTICAL SURVEY. New York: 1959. 291 p.

> This book consists of statistical tables of USSR exports by commodity, imports by commodity, and exports and imports by commodity and country for the years 1956 and 1957.

_____. FOREIGN TRADE OF THE USSR, 1958; STATISTICAL SURVEY. New York: 1958. 240 p.

Foreign Trade, Policies, and Relations

This is a compendium of tables of official Soviet trade statistics. Totals are broken down by commodity and country with emphasis on the years 1955-56.

"The U.S.-Soviet Agreement on Trade and Three Interpretations." ASSOCIATION FOR COMPARATIVE ECONOMIC STUDIES BULLETIN 15 (Spring 1973): 83-113.

This article includes the text of the U.S.-Soviet Agreement on Trade signed on May 29, 1972 and commentaries by an official of the State Department, from the Soviet journal FOREIGN TRADE, and from a Hungarian journal.

Vernon, Raymond. "Apparatchiks and Entrepreneurs; U.S.-Soviet Economic Relations." FOREIGN AFFAIRS 52 (January 1974): 249-62.

Prospects for further trade are discussed in the light of detente.

Vladimirov, IU. V. "The Question of Soviet-Chinese Economic Relations in 1950-1966." CHINESE ECONOMIC STUDIES 3 (Fall 1969): 3-32.

This article was translated by A. Schultz from VOPROSY ISTORII [Problems of history] no. 6 (1969). It is a denunciation of the Maoists, who are held responsible for the breakdown of Sino-Soviet relations. The article presents a wealth of data on Soviet trade and aid with China in the course of its argument.

Ward, Richard J. "Soviet Competition in Western Markets: a Commodity Case and its Implications." JOURNAL OF INDUSTRIAL ECONOMICS 8 (March 1960): 133-50.

This paper examines Soviet activities in the Western European petroleum market. Eight tables provide data. Two appendices give figures on oil production by the various Soviet republics for selected years 1950-60.

Watstein, Joseph. "Role of Foreign Trade in Financing Soviet Modernization." AMERICAN JOURNAL OF ECONOMICS AND SOCIOLOGY 29 (July 1970): 305-19.

This paper deals with the costs of the economic transformation imposed upon Russia by a coercive state and the pivotal role of Soviet foreign trade in securing the transformation. Tables provide data on imports and exports of selected products and a breakdown of Soviet exports into agricultural and industrial product categories.

Wilson, Edward T., et al. "U.S.-Soviet Commercial Relations." In SOVIET ECONOMIC PROSPECTS FOR THE SEVENTIES, U.S. Congress. Joint Economic Committee, pp. 638-59. Washington, D.C.: Government Printing Office, 1973.

Foreign Trade, Policies, and Relations

This paper discusses the historical background of commercial relations, the 1972 commercial and technical agreements, and the role of the Joint U.S.-USSR Commercial Commission and its future prospects. Ports open to calls upon notice from each country are listed.

Wilson, J. H. "American Business and the Recognition of the Soviet Union." SOCIAL SCIENCE QUARTERLY 52 (September 1971): 349-68.

This paper traces the complications of the question of U.S. recognition of the Soviet government in the period 1923-31.

Yanson, J. D. FOREIGN TRADE IN THE U.S.S.R. The New Soviet Library, no. 8. London: Victor Gollancz, 1934. 176 p.

Topics discussed include the structure of foreign trade and its role in the Soviet economy, Soviet trade relations, Soviet trade laws, and the chartering of foreign ships for Soviet trade.

Zabijaka, Valentine. "The Soviet Grain Trade 1961-1970: A Decade of Change." ASSOCIATION FOR COMPARATIVE ECONOMIC STUDIES BULLETIN 15 (Spring 1974): 3-16.

This paper outlines USSR activities in the world grain trade in the decade preceding the massive purchases of the early 1970s. It focuses on transshipments as a possible explanation for some confusion with the Soviet grain data.

Zdziechowski, Stanislas. "The Impact of the Common Market on the Soviet Union." STUDIES ON THE SOVIET UNION n.s. 2, no. 4 (1963): 50-59.

This paper looks at Soviet attitudes toward the formation of the Common Market and trade between the EEC and the Soviet Union and her satellites. Two tables.

Zolotarev, V. I. "Main Stages of Development of USSR Foreign Trade, 1917-1967." SOVIET AND EASTERN EUROPEAN FOREIGN TRADE 4 (Summer 1968): 3-34.

This article is translated from VOPROSY ISTORII, no. 8 (1967). Six tables.

Zybenko, Roman [O.]. "The Economic Problems of COMECON Integration." STUDIES ON THE SOVIET UNION n.s. 2, no. 4 (1963): 60-70.

This paper discusses political relations and planning emphasis within COMECON with emphasis on the early 1960s.

Chapter 18
BALANCE OF PAYMENTS AND INTERNATIONAL FINANCE

THE PERIOD UP TO 1860

Anderson, Olive. "The Russian Ivan of 1855: An Example of Economic Liberalism." ECONOMICA n.s. 27 (November 1960): 368-71.

> This short article corrects a misapprehension among historians that the United Kingdom, in the midst of the Crimean War, allowed the Russian government to float loans on the London market. Further comment on this article may be found in the following: Frank W. Fetter. "The Russian Loan of 1855: A Postscript." ECONOMICA n.s. 28 (November 1961): 421-26. Olive Anderson's "Comment" follows.

THE PERIOD 1860-1917

Hermonius, E. "Russia's Agriculture and the Repayment of Foreign Loans." ECONOMIC JOURNAL 28 (September 1918): 333-36.

> The article deals with whether or not Russia could achieve a sufficiently favorable balance of trade to be able to repay her foreign debts. The question was made moot by the Bolshevik Revolution.

Miller, Margaret S. "The Trade Balance of Russia: A Critical Analysis of the Methods in the Collection of Trade Statistics." SLAVONIC REVIEW 1, no. 2: 401-18.

> The meaning of the term "trade balance" and the way in which the figures on exports and imports are determined are discussed. She then deals with the trade balance problem as applied to Russia.

T'ang, L. L., and Miller, Margaret S. "The Political Aspect of International Finance in Russia and China." ECONOMICA 1st ser. 5 (March 1925): 69-88.

The section dealing with Russia covers motives of international financing, markets in which Russia had borrowed, and political factors.

THE PERIOD AFTER 1917

Altman, Oscar L. "Russian Gold and the Ruble." INTERNATIONAL MONETARY FUND 7 (April 1960): 416-38.

Altman evaluates the possible repercussions of the introduction of a convertible gold ruble. He considers Russian gold production, sales, and stocks; ruble coins and deposit balances; and the potential threat of Soviet gold reserves.

Bednarik, Mojmir K. "The Moscow Bank: The International Bank for Economic Cooperation." SOVIET AND EASTERN EUROPEAN FOREIGN TRADE 2 (January-February 1966): 3-8.

The role of the bank in COMECON is discussed.

Birmingham University. Bureau of Research on Russian Economic Conditions. "The Balance of Payments and the Foreign Debt of the U.S.S.R." MEMORANDUM NO. 4 (February 1932): 1-23.

The memorandum gives a general survey of the balance of trade; movements of capital; foreign labor and technical assistance; noncommercial transactions and services; and the influence of the Depression.

Caiola, Marcello. "Balance of Payments of the U.S.S.R., 1955-1958." INTERNATIONAL MONETARY FUND 9 (March 1962): 1-34.

This paper assembles the available information on the transactions of the USSR with Soviet countries and with the rest of the world during 1955-58. Fourteen tables.

_____. "The Balance of Payments of the USSR, 1959-60." In DIMENSIONS OF SOVIET ECONOMIC POWER, U.S. Congress. Joint Economic Committee, pp. 147-63. Washington, D.C.: Government Printing Office, 1962.

This statistical account of Soviet transactions with other countries covers the period 1959-60. Methods of estimation can be found in an article published in the March 1962 issue of the INTERNATIONAL MONETARY FUND (pp. 1-34) staff papers.

_____. "Balance of Payments of the USSR, 1959-60." INTERNATIONAL MONETARY FUND 10 (July 1963): 321-43.

Transactions of the USSR with Soviet and non-Soviet countries during 1959-60 are studied. The article includes ten tables and concludes with appendices on economic and technical assistance agreements.

International Finance

Edwards, Stephen. "Soviet Exchange Rates: A Study in Disequilibrium." AMERICAN ECONOMIST 16 (Fall 1972): 129-32.

External and internal conditions which have hindered the effective operation of an exchange rate system are examined. The future of these rates is then considered.

Farrell, John T. "Soviet Payments Problems in Trade with the West." In SOVIET ECONOMIC PROSPECTS FOR THE SEVENTIES, U.S. Congress. Joint Economic Committee, pp. 690-711. Washington, D.C.: Government Printing Office, 1973.

Topics discussed include recent trends in commodity trade with the West; Soviet hard currency trade problems; developments in 1972-73; and prospects for hard currency trade. Commodity trade data are given in the appendix.

Gekker, Paul. "The Soviet Bank for Foreign Trade and Soviet Banks Abroad: A Note." ECONOMICS OF PLANNING 7, no. 2 (1967): 183-97.

This article appraises the balance sheet data for the Soviet Bank for Foreign Trade published in the monthly journal of the State Bank of the USSR. Tables.

Holzman, Franklyn D. "The Ruble Exchange Rate and Soviet Foreign Trade Pricing Policies, 1929-1961." AMERICAN ECONOMIC REVIEW 58 (September 1968): 803-25.

This paper reviews Soviet practices on export and import pricing and the ruble exchange rate. Topics covered include the procedure of analysis; average trends in the value of the foreign trade ruble; the history of exchange rate policy; and price ratio variance. Four tables.

_____. "Some Financial Aspects of Soviet Foreign Trade." In COMPARISONS OF THE U.S. AND SOVIET ECONOMIES, U.S. Congress. Joint Economic Committee, pp. 427-43. Washington, D.C.: Government Printing Office, 1959.

This paper deals with trends in the official ruble exchange rate; the overvalued ruble and exchange rate; Soviet international price policy and the foreign trade accounts; foreign trade and internal financial stability; the Soviet gold policy; and the payments agreement. Tables.

Marer, Paul. "Foreign Trade Prices in the Soviet Bloc." ASSOCIATION FOR COMPARATIVE ECONOMIC STUDIES BULLETIN 10 (Fall 1968): 1-11.

Soviet bloc foreign trade prices are compared with prices on the world market. Tables.

International Finance

Poliakov, M. "USSR Bank for Foreign Trade." SOVIET AND EASTERN EUROPEAN FOREIGN TRADE 1 (January-February 1965): 63-67.

This is a translation of an article from ECONOMICHESKAIA GAZETA (February 29, 1964).

Prince, Charles. "The USSR's Role in International Finance." HARVARD BUSINESS REVIEW 25, no. 1 (1946): 111-28.

This paper summarizes Soviet attitudes reflected in the Soviet government's views on the Bretton Woods Articles of Agreement. Probable future actions by the Soviets are assessed.

Wyczalkowski, Marcin R. "The Soviet Price System and the Ruble Exchange Rate." INTERNATIONAL MONETARY FUND. Staff Papers 1 (September 1950): 203-23.

This paper is concerned with the economic significance of the 1950 revaluation of the ruble exchange rate, the simultaneous adjustment of retail prices, and their relation to the international functions of the ruble.

Chapter 19
INTERNATIONAL AID, BUSINESS, AND INVESTMENT

Kirchner, Walter. "Western Businessmen in Russia: Practices and Problems." BUSINESS HISTORY REVIEW 38, no. 3 (1964): 315-27.

> Cultural differences encountered by Western businessmen in Russia which significantly shaped their conduct of trade are explored. The article goes as far back as the dealings of Western merchants with Tsar Ivan the Terrible.

THE PERIOD UP TO 1860

Macmillan, David S. "Paul's 'Retributive Measures' of 1800 Against Britain: The Final Turning-Point in British Commercial Attitudes Towards Russia." CANADIAN-AMERICAN SLAVIC STUDIES 7 (Spring 1973): 68-77.

> The article reviews the often stormy commercial relations between Britain and Russia in the 1790s and the tsar's forbidding of timber exports in 1800. The friction between the two countries is attributed to their social and political differences and to Russia's desire for economic self-sufficiency.

Okun', S. B. THE RUSSIAN-AMERICAN COMPANY. Translated by C. Ginsburg. Cambridge, Mass.: Harvard University Press, 1951. viii, 311 p.

> This study of the Russian-American Company emphasizes its history and its role in North America. Index.

Willan, T. S. THE EARLY HISTORY OF THE RUSSIAN COMPANY, 1553-1603. Manchester, Eng.: Manchester University Press, 1956. ix, 295 p.

> This is a general history of the company's activities. Index.

_____. THE MUSCOVY MERCHANTS OF 1555. Manchester, Eng.: Manchester University Press, 1953. viii, 141 p.

> Topics discussed include the economic environment, the Russian Company, trading activity, and wealth. Index.

International Aid

THE PERIOD 1860-1917

"A British Factory in Kazakhstan 1914-1919." CENTRAL ASIAN REVIEW 12, no. 2 (1964): 108-13.

> This article summarizes a Russian writer's survey of the evils of the Spasskiy copper works and presents a reply by a British engineer who was employed there. A table on wage rates is included.

Crisp, Olga. "French Investment in Russian Joint-stock Companies, 1894-1914." BUSINESS HISTORY 2 (June 1960): 75-90.

> This article surveys the reasons for French investment and its timing, the nature (mostly bonds), and significance of that investment for both Russia and France.

_____. "Russo-Chinese Bank: An Episode in Franco-Russian Relations." SLAVONIC AND EAST EUROPEAN REVIEW 52 (April 1974): 197-212.

> This article discusses the bank, its international finances, and Count Witte's attempts to use it to further Russian interests in the Far East in the late 1890s.

_____. "Some Problems of French Investments in Russian Joint-Stock Companies, 1894-1914." SLAVONIC REVIEW 25 (December 1956): 223-40.

> Crisp sketches the size of French capital in Russia and attempts to determine the degree of control and power over Russia's economy attained by French capitalists.

Fisher, Richard B. "American Investments in Pre-Soviet Russia." AMERICAN SLAVIC AND EAST EUROPEAN REVIEW 8 (1949): 90-105.

> Types of investments covered include United States Treasury loans; insurance investments; noninsurance investments in Russian state bonds; commercial investments; and industrial investments. A final section discusses the outlook for further investment in 1918 after such investment was attacked by the Soviets. Eleven tables.

McKay, John P. "John Cockerill in Southern Russia, 1885-1905: A Study of Aggressive Foreign Entrepreneurship." BUSINESS HISTORY REVIEW 41, no. 3 (1967): 243-56.

> A case study of two ventures undertaken by a Belgian company in Russia focuses on major problems experienced by foreign entrepreneurs under the tsars at the turn of the century. Tables provide data on the growth of the two companies.

Queen, George S. "American Relief in the Russian Famine of 1891-1892." RUSSIAN REVIEW 14 (April 1955): 140-50.

International Aid

This article is concerned largely with the accounts of the famine relief carried in American newspapers.

———. "The McCormick Harvesting Machine Company in Russia." RUSSIAN REVIEW 23 (April 1964): 164-81.

This article discusses the commercial and political aspects of export of McCormick's equipment to Russia from 1858, when the first machine reached Russia, to World War I.

Sontag, John P. "Tsarist Debts and Tsarist Foreign Policy." SLAVIC REVIEW 27 (December 1968): 529-41.

This article surveys Russian commercial and financial relations before World War I and suggests that economics had comparatively little influence on diplomacy in the last years of tsarist rule. Tables present data on trade with Europe.

THE PERIOD AFTER 1917

Allen, Robert L[oring]. "The Soviet and East European Foreign Credit Program." AMERICAN SLAVIC AND EAST EUROPEAN REVIEW 16 (1957): 433-49.

Soviet and East European foreign credit programs for underdeveloped countries, 1953-57, are discussed. Attention also is given to credits to individual countries--Afghanistan, Egypt, India, Indonesia, and Yugoslavia. The impact, motivation, and capabilities of the program are then discussed.

Aubrey, Henry G. "Sino-Soviet Economic Activities in Less Developed Countries." In COMPARISONS OF THE U.S. AND SOVIET ECONOMIES, U.S. Congress. Joint Economic Committee, pp. 445-66. Washington, D.C.: Government Printing Office, 1959.

This paper deals with various political and economic aspects of Sino-Soviet aid and trade. Tables.

Berliner, Joseph S. SOVIET ECONOMIC AID: THE NEW AID AND TRADE POLICY IN UNDERDEVELOPED COUNTRIES. New York: Praeger, 1958. xv, 232 p.

Berliner discusses the politics of Soviet economic aid; the character and size of the aid program; Soviet aid and Western aid; the expansion of commercial trade; Soviet capacity to extend economic aid; and Soviet economic gains from the aid program.

Bowles, Chester. "America and Russia in India." FOREIGN AFFAIRS 49 (July 1971): 636-51.

In this political analysis of American and Russian policy toward

International Aid

India, some attention is given to the significance of trade and aid between the two powers and India.

Carnett, George S., and Crawford, Morris H. "The Scope and Distribution of Soviet Economic Aid." In DIMENSIONS OF SOVIET ECONOMIC POWER, U.S. Congress. Joint Economic Committee, pp. 461-74. Washington, D.C.: Government Printing Office, 1962.

> The article covers interest rates, repayment terms, technical and military assistance, and Soviet administration of foreign economic aid. Soviet credits and grants to less developed countries are sketched in an appendix.

Carter, James R. THE NET COST OF SOVIET FOREIGN AID. New York: Praeger, 1969. xiv, 134 p.

> Carter discusses Soviet foreign policy; her economic aid program; the cost of economic aid; Soviet foreign trade; the relationship between Soviet aid and the volume of Soviet foreign trade; gains from trade and the increased volume of Soviet trade caused by Soviet foreign aid; and the net cost of Soviet foreign aid, 1955-68. Selected bibliography.

Cleinow, Georg. "Foreign Technical Assistance." In RED ECONOMICS, edited by Gerhard Dobbert, pp. 270-90. Boston: Houghton Mifflin, 1932.

> Cleinow outlines foreign technical assistance from the time of Peter the Great to the Five-Year Plan.

Cooper, Orah. "Soviet Economic Assistance to the Less Developed Countries of the Free World." In ECONOMIC PERFORMANCE AND THE MILITARY BURDEN IN THE SOVIET UNION, U.S. Congress. Joint Economic Committee, pp. 117-22. Washington, D.C.: Government Printing Office, 1970.

> This paper discusses shifts in the aid program, the amount of aid, implementation of aid, and the future outlook. Four tables.

Datar, Asha L. INDIA'S ECONOMIC RELATIONS WITH THE USSR AND EASTERN EUROPE, 1953-1969. London and New York: Cambridge University Press, 1972. xiv, 278 p.

> The following topics are explored: the role of external finance, the terms and conditions of aid, and advantages and disadvantages of economic relations with the centrally planned economies. Many tables, bibliography, and index.

Desai, Padma. THE BOKARO STEEL PLANT: A STUDY OF SOVIET ECONOMIC ASSISTANCE. New York: American Elsevier, 1972. xviii, 108 p.

> The book describes and analyzes the Bokaro steel plant in India, an Indo-Soviet project.

Fisher, Harold H. FAMINE IN SOVIET RUSSIA, 1919-1923. New York: Macmillan, 1927. x, 609 p.

> The first fifteen chapters describe the activities of the American Relief Administration in Russia, 1919-23. A chapter summarizes the causes of the famine of 1921-22, which was vastly more devastating than previous crop failures. Documents and statistical tables are included in the appendices.

Gerschenkron, Alexander. "Soviet Policies Versus International Cartels: Four Historical Case Studies." SLAVIC REVIEW 33 (March 1974): 69-90.

> This article examines Soviet relations with international cartels in the 1930s. The commodities involved are matches, phosphates, potash, and platinum. Tables.

Glovinsky, Evgeny. "Soviet Economic Expansion in the Developing Countries." STUDIES ON THE SOVIET UNION n.s. 1, no. 2 (1961): 173-92.

> With sixteen tables, this article is brimming over with factual material on Soviet trade and aid to the developing countries, 1954-60. Glovinsky is chiefly concerned with the political and strategic significance of economic relations.

Goldman, Marshall I. "A Balance Sheet of Soviet Foreign Aid." FOREIGN AFFAIRS 43 (January 1965): 348-60.

> This article recounts the successes and failures of ten years of Soviet foreign aid and concludes that "they have encountered almost all of the problems which have frustrated us, plus some that we have been spared."

_____. SOVIET FOREIGN AID. New York: Praeger, 1967. xiv, 265 p.

> In this analysis of Soviet foreign aid, the material is arranged on a country-by-country or continent-by-continent basis. Each chapter concerns a particular issue. Tables, bibliography, and index.

Herman, Leon M. "The Political Goals of Soviet Foreign Aid." In DIMENSIONS OF SOVIET ECONOMIC POWER, U.S. Congress. Joint Economic Committee, pp. 477-85. Washington, D.C.: Government Printing Office, 1962.

> The article establishes that the Soviets are attempting to influence the world political situation in favor of socialism by urging the less developed and underdeveloped nations to follow the Soviet model to economic development.

Holbik, Karel. THE UNITED STATES, THE SOVIET UNION, AND THE THIRD WORLD. Hamburg, Germany: Verlag Weltarchiv, 1968. 110 p.

International Aid

This monograph investigates the structure of U.S. and Soviet foreign aid programs. The author argues that these programs not only determine but are also the products of these countries' national interests and international economic policy objectives. Select bibliography and index. Paperback.

Horvath, Janos. "Economic Aid Flow from the USSR: A Recount of the First Fifteen Years." SLAVIC REVIEW 29 (December 1970): 613-32.

This study enumerates Soviet aid projects, arranges the findings so that they are usable for further study, and explores possible reasons for fluctuations in the program. Many tables.

_____. "Grant Elements in Intra-Bloc Aid Programs." BULLETIN OF THE ASSOCIATION FOR THE STUDY OF SOVIET-TYPE ECONOMIES 13 (Fall 1971): 1-17.

This article deals extensively with grant-like transfers between the USSR and Communist countries, 1945-69. Tables.

Kanet, Roger E. "Soviet and American Behavior Toward the Developing Countries: A Comparison." CANADIAN SLAVONIC PAPERS 15, no. 4 (1973): 439-61.

The article compares Soviet and American behavior toward the states of Africa, Asia and Latin America, most of which have achieved independence within the last thirty years. Soviet and American behavior toward these states is found to be remarkably similar. Topics of economic interest include trade and aid, military assistance, and educational assistance. Tables.

_____. "Soviet Economic Policy in Sub-Saharan Africa." CANADIAN SLAVIC STUDIES 1 (Winter 1967): 566-86.

Covered are Soviet trade and assistance in Africa and the success of Soviet policy in Africa. Seven tables and two charts present data on Soviet exports to and imports from Africa, Soviet credits, and Soviet aid.

Klages, Walter J. "Soviet Economic Thought and Economic Development: The Case of Foreign Aid." CANADIAN SLAVONIC PAPERS 12 (Winter 1970): 417-30.

The article reviews Soviet foreign aid to underdeveloped countries from its beginnings in 1953 and concludes that the aid program is now more flexible since the Soviets no longer require that underdeveloped countries emulate the Soviet growth model.

Klatt, Werner. "Development Aid for Development's Sake." In SOVIET PLANNING: ESSAYS IN HONOUR OF NAUM JASNY, edited by Jane Degras and Alec Nove, pp. 173-92. Oxford: Basil Blackwell, 1964.

Klatt discusses changes in Soviet foreign economic relations since
the death of Stalin. The author compares Sino-Soviet economic
aid with Western aid. Tables and bibliography.

Knorr, Klaus E. RUBLE DIPLOMACY: CHALLENGE TO AMERICAN FOREIGN
AID. Princeton, N.J.: Princeton University Press, 1956. 42 p.

This paper discusses the role of trade and aid in the foreign policies
of the Soviet bloc, its effectiveness, and its significance for American policy.

Nag, Daga S. FOREIGN ECONOMIC POLICY OF SOVIET RUSSIA. Agra,
India: Lakshmi Narain Agarwal, 1964. 111 p.

The author examines ideological motivation of Soviet technical and
economic aid to poor nations, linking the present to the historical,
from Marx to Khrushchev.

Naleszkiewicz, Vladimir. "Technical Assistance of the American Enterprises to
the Growth of the Soviet Union, 1929-1933." RUSSIAN REVIEW 25 (January
1966): 54-76.

The extent and the strategic importance of the technological aid
given by U.S. private enterprise to Soviet industry during its First
Five-Year Plan, are assessed. A map shows the location of
assistance contracts.

Prybyla, Jan S. "Soviet and Chinese Economic Competition Within the Communist World." SOVIET STUDIES 15 (April 1964): 464-73.

The relative importance of Soviet and Chinese aid and trade with
Communist underdeveloped countries is discussed.

Scott, N. B. [S.]. "Soviet Economic Relations with the Under-Developed
Countries." SOVIET STUDIES 10 (July 1958): 36-53.

This article reviews Soviet trade, aid, and policies toward the
underdeveloped countries. Five tables.

Stokke, B. R. SOVIET AND EASTERN EUROPEAN TRADE AND AID TO
AFRICA. New York: Praeger, 1967. xx, 326 p.

The book seeks to provide the reader with a perspective on African-
Soviet bloc economic interchange, apply newly available material
in examining each pertinent African country and its relations with
the centrally planned economies, and evaluate the primary effects
of this interchange on the African economies. Tables, bibliography,
and index.

Tansky, Leo. "Soviet Foreign Aid: Scope, Direction and Trends." In SOVIET
ECONOMIC PROSPECTS FOR THE SEVENTIES, U.S. Congress. Joint Economic

Committee, pp. 766-76. Washington, D.C.: Government Printing Office, 1973.

> The author discusses ideological bases, the economic aid program, technical assistance, military assistance, Moscow's economic benefits, and prospects. Four tables.

──────. "Soviet Foreign Aid to the Less Developed Countries." In NEW DIRECTIONS IN THE SOVIET ECONOMY, U.S. Congress. Joint Economic Committee, pp. 947-74. Washington, D.C.: Government Printing Office, 1966.

> Aspects discussed include the economic aid program, aid to Cuba, the military aid program, successes and failures, and the outlook for Soviet aid. Four tables.

──────. U.S. AND U.S.S.R. AID TO DEVELOPING COUNTRIES--A COMPARATIVE STUDY OF INDIA, TURKEY AND THE UAR. New York: Praeger, 1967. xvii, 192 p.

> This book discusses the objectives, magnitude, and character of aid programs of the two countries and then the specific programs in India, Turkey, and the United Arab Republic.

Taylor, George E. "Sino-Soviet Trade and Aid." In NATIONAL SECURITY: POLITICAL, MILITARY, AND ECONOMIC STRATEGIES IN THE DECADE AHEAD, edited by David M. Abshire and Richard V. Allen, pp. 95-118. New York: Praeger, 1963.

> This article details the economic aid which the Sino-Soviet bloc extends to former colonial peoples of the world.

U.S. House of Representatives. Committee on Banking and Currency. THE FIAT-SOVIET AUTO PLANT AND COMMUNIST ECONOMIC REFORMS. Washington, D.C.: Government Printing Office, 1967. v, 99 p.

> This is a study of the Fiat-Soviet auto plant and the Soviet auto program in general with some attention given to Communist economic reforms. Tables. Some reprinted articles included.

Watstein, Joseph. "Soviet Economic Concessions: The Agony and the Promise." ASSOCIATION FOR COMPARATIVE ECONOMIC STUDIES BULLETIN 16 (Spring 1974): 17-32.

> Soviet economic concessions to foreign investors under the NEP are discussed. Two tables.

Weissman, Benjamin M. "The Aftermath of the American Relief Mission to Soviet Russia." RUSSIAN REVIEW 29 (October 1970): 411-21.

> This paper surveys official Soviet efforts to denigrate the efforts of the American Relief Mission in the early 1920s.

Yalowitz, Kenneth. "U.S.S.R.-Western Industrial Cooperation." In SOVIET ECONOMIC PROSPECTS FOR THE SEVENTIES, U.S. Congress. Joint Economic Committee, pp. 712-18. Washington, D.C.: Government Printing Office, 1973.

    Industrial cooperation, the perspective of the Soviet Union, and possible obstacles are examined.

Zevin, L. "The Mutual Advantage of Economic Cooperation Between the Socialist and Developing Countries." SOVIET AND EASTERN EUROPEAN FOREIGN TRADE 1 (July-August 1965): 30-50.

    This article is a translation from VOPROSY EKONOMIKI, no. 2 (1965): 71-80.

Chapter 20

ECONOMIC ORGANIZATION, ADMINISTRATION, AND REFORM

THE PERIOD UP TO 1860

Tugan-Baranovsky, Mikhail I. THE RUSSIAN FACTORY IN THE 19TH CENTURY. Translated by A. Levin and C. C. Levin. 3d ed. 1922. Reprint. Homewood, Ill.: R. D. Irwin, 1970. xvii, 474 p.

 This is a classic detailed study of the Russian factory system up to the end of the nineteenth century. Indexes and tables.

THE PERIOD 1860-1917

Giffin, F[rederick]. C. "I. I. Yanzhul, Russia's First District Factory Inspector." SLAVONIC AND EAST EUROPEAN REVIEW 49 (January 1971): 80-91.

 This paper recounts the frustrating experiences of a Russian factory inspector between 1882-87.

Rimlinger, Gaston V. "Autocracy and the Factory Order in Early Russian Industrialization." JOURNAL OF ECONOMIC HISTORY 20 (March 1960): 67-92.

 This article integrates new evidence and earlier data to analyze methods used by the tsarist government to cope with internal government of industry in an era of growing labor unrest. The period between the Emancipation and the 1905 Revolution is the focus.

THE PERIOD AFTER 1917

Abouchar, Alan. "Inefficiency and Reform in the Soviet Economy." SOVIET STUDIES 25 (July 1973): 66-76.

 This paper summarizes the reforms and examines those features of the traditional system which may make some of the reforms unnecessary. For further discussion, see: Roger A. Clarke. "Dr. Abouchar and Levels of Inefficiency." SOVIET STUDIES 25 (July 1973): 177-87; and R. W. Davies. "A Note on Defence Aspects of the Ural-Kuznetsk Combine." SOVIET STUDIES 26 (April 1974): 272-73.

Adam, Jan. "The Incentive System in the USSR: The Abortive Reform of 1965." INDUSTRIAL AND LABOR RELATIONS REVIEW 27 (October 1973): 84-92.

This paper discusses reforms in the incentive system in Soviet industry in 1965 and reasons for their failure.

Bandera, V. N. "Market Orientation of State Enterprises During NEP." SOVIET STUDIES 22 (July 1970): 110-21.

This paper examines the economic autonomy of the trusts, market conduct, and allocative efficiency in a concentrated industrial organization.

Blackman, James H. "The Kosygin Reforms: New Wine in Old Bottles?" STUDIES ON THE SOVIET UNION n.s. 7, no. 1 (1967): 103-43.

This study focuses on reforms introduced by Kosygin in his speech to the Central Committee of the Soviet Communist Party on September 27, 1965. His policies are compared to those of his predecessors.

Campbell, Robert W. "Accounting for Cost Control in the Soviet Economy." REVIEW OF ECONOMICS AND STATISTICS 40 (February 1958): 59-67.

This article describes some problems of cost accounting in the settling of the Soviet economy and evaluates the effectiveness of Soviet cost accounting as an instrument of control.

_____. "Accounting for Depreciation in the Soviet Economy." QUARTERLY JOURNAL OF ECONOMICS 70 (November 1956): 481-506.

This study concentrates within the state sector of the economy on the khozraschet organizations, i.e., organizations in which outlays are covered primarily by revenues from the sale of goods and services. Tables.

_____. ACCOUNTING IN SOVIET PLANNING AND MANAGEMENT. Cambridge, Mass.: Harvard University Press, 1963. 315 p.

Campbell discerns how accounting information is used in the process of planning and management. The book deals primarily with the industrial sector. Source materials are Soviet. Glossary and index.

_____. "Economic Reform in the U.S.S.R." AMERICAN ECONOMIC REVIEW 58 (May 1968): 547-58.

This paper considers whether or not the economic reforms begun in

the Soviet Union in 1965 are serious and far-reaching in their
effects, whether or not the Soviet leaders are moving toward a
kind of system distinct from both the command economy and market
socialism, and what the political implications of the reforms might
be. For further discussion, see: Abram Bergson and John M.
Montias. "Economic Reform in Eastern Europe--Discussion." AMERICAN ECONOMIC REVIEW 58 (May 1968): 580-85.

_____. "Economics: Roads and Inroads." PROBLEMS OF COMMUNISM 14
(November-December 1965): 23-33.

This paper deals with topics such as "how to reform the planning
and supervision of enterprise behavior," the Liberman proposals,
new experiments in management of economy, and priorities given
to consumption in relation to other claims on national resources."

_____. "The Mechanization of Accounting in the Soviet Union." AMERICAN
SLAVIC AND EAST EUROPEAN REVIEW 17 (1958): 59-80.

This article describes Soviet efforts in accounting mechanization
and discusses the results of the low level of mechanization achieved
in terms of the quality of the accounting job and the size of the
accounting labor force. Tables.

_____. "Soviet Accounting and Economic Decisions." In VALUE AND PLAN;
ECONOMIC CALCULATION AND ORGANIZATION IN EASTERN EUROPE,
edited by Gregory Grossman, pp. 76-101. Berkeley and Los Angeles: University of California Press, 1960.

The author is concerned with whether Soviet accounting practices
enable Soviet planners to make correct economic decisions or
whether they represent an obstacle to economic efficiency. A
comment by H. S. Levine follows.

Cattell, David T. "Local Government and the Sovnarkhoz in the USSR, 1957-1962." SOVIET STUDIES 15 (April 1964): 430-42.

This study concludes that the role of local government in local
industry was severely reduced during the period.

Chase, Stuart. "Industry and the Gosplan." In SOVIET RUSSIA IN THE
SECOND DECADE, American Trade Union Delegation, pp. 14-54. New York:
John Day, 1928.

Soviet industrial organization is described as being in a flux.

Conklin, David [W.]. "A Note on Soviet Profit Maximization." CANADIAN
JOURNAL OF ECONOMICS 2 (August 1969): 452-55.

Conklin explains why each of four maximization criteria which
have been advocated may lead to inefficient production. He is

concerned with profit per unit of labor, capital, total production costs, and revenue.

"Consumer Goods and the Manufacturers." SOVIET STUDIES 5 (January 1954): 312-16.

> This is a translation of Y. Miletsky. "From the Chamber of Commerce to the Counter." OGONYOK, no. 35 (1953). It discusses administrative snags in the conversion to consumer goods production.

Cook, Paul K. "The Administration and Distribution of Soviet Industry." In DIMENSIONS OF SOVIET ECONOMIC POWER, U.S. Congress. Joint Economic Committee, pp. 183-210. Washington, D.C.: Government Printing Office, 1962.

> Cook sketches the administrative structure of the Soviet Union from the Communist Party to enterprise administration, along with an account of their problems and prospects. Tables, diagram, and map.

_____. "Party, State, and Economic Reorganization in the USSR." BULLETIN OF THE ASSOCIATION FOR THE STUDY OF SOVIET-TYPE ECONOMIES 5 (Winter 1963): 2-11.

> Topics covered include the Communist Party reorganization, government reorganization, and the economic administrative structure under Khrushchev.

Davies, R[obert]. W. "The Decentralization of Industry: Some Notes on the Background." SOVIET STUDIES 9 (April 1958): 353-67.

> This paper notes important factors relating to Soviet planning at different periods before 1957, which generally have been neglected in Western discussion about the background to Khrushchev's 1957 reform of industrial administration.

Davletshin, Tamurbek. "Centralization of Industrial Management in Turkestan." STUDIES ON THE SOVIET UNION n.s. 5, no. 2 (1965): 82-88.

> This paper recounts the reasons for the reimposition of Stalinist centralization in Turkestan after eight years at attempted reform.

Diakonoff, V. A. "Industry and Accounting in the U.S.S.R." HARVARD BUSINESS REVIEW 11 (January 1933): 205-16.

> After noting the organization of Soviet industry, the author gives a detailed discussion of a Soviet balance sheet.

Dobb, Maurice H. "A Comment on the Discussion about Price Policy." SOVIET STUDIES 9 (October 1957): 131-42.

Economic Organization

Special attention is given to central planning versus decentralized decision making by autonomous enterprises, use of market prices as signals for consumer goods production, and managerial incentives.

———. "Operational Aspects of Soviet Economy." STATSOKONOMISK TIDDSKRIFT 74 (December 1960): 297-312.

Allocational aspects of planning and of the consumer goods markets are discussed.

"Economic Incentives--I." SOVIET STUDIES 7 (April 1956): 451-62.

This article summarizes articles in Russian on economic cost calculations, Liberman's bonus fund, capital and costs, and government policy measures.

"Economic Reorganization in Central Asia." CENTRAL ASIAN REVIEW 5, no. 4 (1957): 389-97.

This article concerns the all-Union economic reorganization and decentralization scheme as applied in Central Asia and Kazakhstan.

Ellman, Michael [J.]. ECONOMIC REFORM IN THE SOVIET UNION. London: Political and Economic Planning, 1969. iii, 89 p.

This book contains a brief history of the Soviet economy; gives an account of the 1965 reforms; and provides a description of Soviet and optimal planning, the allocation of resources, and future prospects. Broadsheet.

"Extracts from the Newspaper 'Trud,' Organ of U.S.S.R. Trade Unions." ANNALS OF PUBLIC AND CO-OPERATIVE ECONOMY 37 (July-August 1966): 309-11.

The extracts are concerned with autonomous enterprises operated on the profit principle and the need for improvements in the system for distributing goods.

Federov, A. "Reorganization of Industrial Administration in the U.S.S.R." STUDIES ON THE SOVIET UNION n.s. 1, no. 2 (1958): 99-105.

This article traces the events leading up to the decision in 1957 to reorganize industrial administration along regional rather than industry lines. It also surveys the discussion of the proposed reorganization in the Soviet press.

———. THE SOVIET QUEST FOR ECONOMIC EFFICIENCY: ISSUES, CONTROVERSIES, AND REFORMS. Expanded and updated ed. New York: Praeger, 1972. xxiv, 790 p.

In this inquiry into the causes, nature, and direction of the economic reform movement in the Soviet Union, the author also evaluates the Soviet planning system. Tables and bibliography.

Felker, Jere L. SOVIET ECONOMIC CONTROVERSIES; THE EMERGING MARKETING CONCEPT AND CHANGES IN PLANNING, 1960-1965. Cambridge, Mass.: M.I.T. Press, 1966. x, 172 p.

Felker explores the reasons for the recent shift in emphasis toward the consumer in Soviet industrial planning and the emergence of the "marketing concept" as a basic guide in formulating new Soviet economic and welfare policies. Bibliography and name and subject indexes.

Gerschenkron, Alexander. "Industrial Enterprise in Soviet Russia." In THE CORPORATION IN MODERN SOCIETY, edited by Edward S. Mason, pp. 277-300. Cambridge, Mass.: Harvard University Press, 1959.

The author examines industrial enterprise and management in Soviet Russia. He looks at the ideological antecedents of policies which have shaped Soviet Russia's industrial organization.

Gindin, Sam. "A Model of the Soviet Firm." ECONOMICS OF PLANNING 10, no. 3 (1970): 145-57.

A mathematical and graphical microeconomic theory of the Soviet firm is presented.

Goldman, Marshall I. "Economic Revolution in the Soviet Union." FOREIGN AFFAIRS 45 (January 1967): 319-31.

The Liberman reforms are discussed.

Gorlin, Alice C. "Socialist Corporations: The Wave of the Future in the USSR?" In THE SOVIET ECONOMY: A BOOK OF READINGS, edited by Morris Bornstein and Daniel Fusfeld, pp. 522-35. 4th ed. Homewood, Ill.: R. D. Irwin, 1974.

The author examines alternative possible organizational arrangements and reviews previous mergers in the USSR and consolidations in several East European countries. A chart of management schemes is included.

_____. "The Soviet Economic Association." SOVIET STUDIES 26 (January 1974): 3-27.

This paper explains the 1973 reorganization of industry administration, summarizes the background and development of the merger movement, assesses its significance in improving economic performance, and discusses the prospects of the reform.

Economic Organization

Granick, David. "An Organizational Model of Soviet Industrial Planning." JOURNAL OF POLITICAL ECONOMY 67 (April 1959): 109-30.

Prospects for change in the organization of the Soviet economy are analyzed. Two alternative types of change are discussed: movements toward the competitive market model and administrative reorganization.

_____. "Technological Policy and Economic Calculation in Soviet Industry." In VALUE AND PLAN; ECONOMIC CALCULATION AND ORGANIZATION IN EASTERN EUROPE, edited by Gregory Grossman, pp. 271-91. Berkeley and Los Angeles: University of California Press, 1960.

The author examines Soviet decision making to determine whether it is consistent with rational economic calculation. The article deals with the metal-working industries. It includes many tables which are based on Soviet sources. A comment by Richard H. Moorsteen follows, pp. 288-91.

Hoeffding, Oleg. "The Soviet Industrial Reorganization of 1957." AMERICAN ECONOMIC REVIEW 49 (May 1959): 65-77.

This article is a commentary on selected aspects of the reorganization of industrial administration and planning in the Soviet Union in 1957. The objectives of the reform are a major concern. For further discussion, see: Robert W. Campbell and David Granick. "Soviet Economic Planning--Discussion." AMERICAN ECONOMIC REVIEW 49 (May 1959): 78-83.

Horwitz, Bertrand N. ACCOUNTING CONTROLS AND THE SOVIET ECONOMIC REFORMS OF 1966. Evanston, Ill.: American Accounting Association, 1970. ix, 74 p.

The decentralization movement in the Soviet Union is examined. The study focuses on accounting and financial controls, and Horwitz discusses the new economic reforms, bonuses, and pricing.

Johnson, E. L. "Commercial Arbitration in the USSR Since the Decentralization of Industrial Management." SOVIET STUDIES 11 (October 1959): 134-42.

Special attention is paid to state and sovnarkhoz arbitration.

_____. "Planning and Contract Law." SOVIET STUDIES 12 (January 1961): 263-72.

Discussed are contract and specific performance, execution of awards, and changes in planning and prices.

_____. "Reforms in Arbitration Procedure." SOVIET STUDIES 14 (October 1962): 179-83.

Economic Organization

Reforms promulgated on July 23, 1959, and the cases which prompted them are discussed.

Jonas, Hans. "The Economic Organization." In RED ECONOMICS, edited by Gerhard Dobbert, pp. 23-50. Boston: Houghton Mifflin, 1932.

The author sketches Soviet economic organization.

Kaser, Michael C. "Kosygin, Liberman, and the Pace of Soviet Industrial Reform." WORLD TODAY 21 (September 1965): 375-88.

The article discusses the Liberman proposals and the ways in which they fall short of free-enterprise capitalism.

──────. "The Reorganization of Soviet Industry and Its Effects on Decision Making." In VALUE AND PLAN; ECONOMIC CALCULATION AND ORGANIZATION IN EASTERN EUROPE, edited by Gregory Grossman, pp. 213-40. Berkeley and Los Angeles: University of California Press, 1960.

The paper deals with the following aspects of decision making: (1) the apparatus of executive control; (2) decisions internal to a sovnarkhoz; (3) local influences on sovnarkhoz decisions; (4) limits to sovnarkhoz decisions; and (5) decision making by the enterprise.

Katz, Abraham. THE POLITICS OF ECONOMIC REFORM IN THE SOVIET UNION. New York: Praeger, 1972. viii, 230 p.

Written by a scholar and career foreign service officer, this work examines political aspects of managing the Soviet economy from the period of war communism up to a few years after the 1965 reforms. Half of the book is devoted to the Kosygin reforms. Lengthy bibliography.

Koropeckkj, Ivan S. "Soviet Industrial Location in Practice." STUDIES ON THE SOVIET UNION n.s. 1, no. 1 (1961): 38-46.

This article compares the location of industry in each of the five-year plans to Soviet theory on industrial location. It concludes that the application of theory has been only moderately successful. A table presents figures on population and industrial output for the Russian and the non-Russian Soviet Union for 1913 and 1955.

──────. "Soviet Theory on Industrial Location." STUDIES ON THE SOVIET UNION 3, no. 5 (1960): 72-82.

In reviewing Soviet thinking about industrial location, the author finds that both economic and political considerations are important.

Kosiachenko, G. "Important Condition for Improvement of Planning." PROBLEMS OF ECONOMICS 5 (April 1963): 21-23.

Economic Organization

A Soviet economist criticizes the Liberman proposals for reform.

Kvasha, Ya. "Concentration of Production and Small Scale Industry." In ECONOMIC CONCENTRATION, U.S. Senate. Committee on the Judiciary, pp. 4358-62. Washington, D.C.: Government Printing Office, 1969.

> Kvasha compares the size distribution of enterprises in the USSR with that in other countries and argues that there is still a significant role for the small enterprise in the Soviet economy. Tables.

Laskovsky, Nikolas. "Reflections on Soviet Industrial Reorganization." AMERICAN SLAVIC AND EAST EUROPEAN REVIEW 17 (February 1958): 47-58.

> This article concerns the nature and probable effects of the Soviet industrial reorganization which began in 1957.

Leeman, Wayne A. "An Analysis of Proposals for Reform in the Soviet-type Economy." RIVISTA INTERNAZIONALE DI SCIENZE ECONOMICHE E COMMERCIALI 17 (January 1970): 63-71.

> The proposals discussed include reduction in output directives, reduction in inputs subject to rationing, price reform, rewards for sales, profit incentives, and reductions in subsidies.

Liberman, Evsei G. ECONOMIC METHODS AND THE EFFECTIVENESS OF PRODUCTION. White Plains, N.Y.: International Arts and Sciences Press, 1971. x, 180 p.

> This book gives a general description of the economic reform in the USSR; analyzes the operation of the law of value; considers the shortcomings of Soviet planning and discusses the optimality of centralized planning; and outlines Liberman's views on further reforms aimed at "the simplification and rationalization of success criteria for Soviet enterprise."

_____. "Liberman's Reply to Critics." In THE SOVIET ECONOMY; A BOOK OF READINGS, edited by Morris Bornstein and Daniel Fusfeld, pp. 359-68. Rev. ed. Homewood, Ill.: R. D. Irwin, 1966.

> In this reply, Liberman argues that profitability is the superior measure of enterprise performance, asserts that "material incentives" are necessary, contends that his plan would not entail a dangerous surrender of central control, and urges that even though major changes in the price system are needed, adoption of his proposals should not be delayed until these changes are made. This article originally appeared as "The Plan, Profits, and Bonuses" in EKONOMICHESKAYA GAZETA (November 10, 1962).

_____. "The Plan, Profits, and Bonuses." In THE SOVIET ECONOMY; A BOOK OF READINGS, edited by Morris Bornstein and Daniel Fusfeld, pp. 352-58. Rev. ed. Homewood, Ill.: R. D. Irwin, 1966.

Economic Organization

This article presents Liberman's statement of his proposals for reforms in the planning and management of the Soviet economy. It originally appeared in PRAVDA (September 9, 1972).

──────. "The Role of Profits in the Industrial Incentive System of the U.S.S.R." INTERNATIONAL LABOUR REVIEW 97 (January 1968): 1-14.

Topics covered include the function of profits in the new system, principles underlying the system, and some results of the reform.

──────. "The Soviet Economic Reform." In ECONOMIC CONCENTRATION, U.S. Senate. Committee on the Judiciary, pp. 4366-71. Washington, D.C.: Government Printing Office, 1969.

Liberman defends his reform on ideological grounds and discusses the early results of the reform, the key role of profit, and the problems presented by the reform.

Liberman, Evsei G., and Dobb, Maurice H. THEORY OF PROFIT IN SOCIALIST ECONOMY: A DISCUSSION ON THE RECENT ECONOMIC REFORMS IN THE USSR. New Delhi: D. P. Sinha (for People's Publishing House Private), 1966. 96 p.

The nine brief essays in this book attempt to present an objective picture of the dialogue that has followed the 1965 economic reforms.

Lonsdale, Richard E. "The Soviet Concept of the Territorial-Production Complex." SLAVIC REVIEW 24 (September 1965): 466-78.

This article traces the development of the concept of the territorial-production complex from 1920 to the early 1960s.

Lydolph, Paul E. "The Soviet Reorganization of Industry." AMERICAN SLAVIC AND EAST EUROPEAN REVIEW 17 (October 1958): 293-301.

Events leading up to the 1957 reorganization of industry and its probable significance are discussed.

McFarlane, B. J., and Gordijew, I. "Profitability and the Soviet Firm." ECONOMIC RECORD 40 (December 1964): 554-68.

This article draws heavily on Soviet sources to produce a detailed discussion of the Liberman reforms and their possible significance for the Soviet economy and for socialist economics in general.

──────. "Profitability and the Soviet Firm: A Note on the 1964 Discussions." ECONOMIC RECORD 41 (December 1965): 617-25.

This is a followup note to the authors article cited above, but it may be read independently. Topics covered include these aspects

Economic Organization

of the Liberman reforms: the techniques of measuring enterprise performance; the reforms and planning techniques; and the reactions of the Communist economies.

Melnyk, Z[inowij]. L. "Measurement and Analysis of Profitability of Soviet Enterprises." RIVISTA INTERNAZIONALE DI SCIENZE ECONOMICHE E COMMERCIALI 18 (September 1971): 867-90.

This essay reviews the development of the concept and the techniques of measuring profitability in the Soviet Union. Melnyk also evaluates micro- and macroeconomic implications of the 1965-66 revisions. Two tables provide figures on returns to capital in the United States and the USSR.

Merrett, Stephen. "Capital, Profit and Bonus In Soviet Industry." ECONOMICA n.s. 31 (November 1964): 401-7.

This article treats the Liberman reforms in relation to the introduction of capital changes in Soviet industry; linking of bonuses to profit rates on capital; use of profits as a success indicator; and "the payment of bonuses to management by multiplying the incentive rate per unit of capital by the quantity of capital used within a plant." For further comment, see: C. A. Knox Lovell. "Capital, Profit and Bonus in Soviet Industry: A Comment." ECONOMICA 33 (February 1966): 88-91.

Mieczkowski, A. "The Reforms in Soviet Economic Regionalization." SLAVIC REVIEW 24 (September 1965): 479-96.

This paper examines the structure of economic regions resulting from the 1962-63 reforms at three levels: rural administrative districts, middle-level economic administrative regions, and major economic regions. The districts are outlined in tables and maps.

Miller, Jacob. "The Decentralization of Industry." SOVIET STUDIES 9 (July 1957): 65-83.

This account covers the Central Committee orders of December 1956 and February 1957, working notes for decentralization, the discussion in PRAVDA, and the role of the Supreme Soviet.

Narkiewicz, Olga [A.]. THE MAKING OF THE SOVIET STATE APPARATUS. New York: Humanities; Manchester, Eng.: Manchester University Press, 1970. ix, 328 p. Illustrated.

Several economic works and agricultural treatises are the bases of this book, which accounts the problems faced by ordinary people, especially the peasantry, during the period of the New Economic Policy.

Economic Organization

Nemchinov, V. S. "The Plan Target and Material Incentive." PROBLEMS OF ECONOMICS 7 (July 1965): 9-13.

    A respected Soviet economist comments on the Liberman reforms.

Neuberger, Egon. "Libermanism, Computopia, and Visible Hand: The Question of Informational Efficiency." AMERICAN ECONOMIC REVIEW 56 (May 1966): 131-44.

    This paper examines alternatives which are open to Soviet leaders if they should choose to follow Libermanism with other, more radical changes. A review of recent reforms is followed by a discussion of government planning and guidance mechanisms and the uses of computers and other means to process information. For further discussion, see: Alexander Eckstein and Joseph S. Berliner. "Soviet Economy--Discussion." AMERICAN ECONOMIC REVIEW 56 (May 1966): 154-58.

Norman, Conrad. "Liberman, Russian Prophet." AMERICAN ECONOMIST 11 (Fall 1967): 23-33.

    This paper discusses the role of Liberman's reform in the operation of the Soviet economy. Topics covered include the economic distortions caused by quantitative production targets, the recognition of these economic inadequacies, the theoretical departure from centralized control, the practical applications of Liberman's theory, and ideological conclusions.

Nove, Alec. "The Liberman Proposals." SURVEY no. 47 (April 1963): 112-18.

    This article discusses the Liberman proposals, the reasons for them, and their likely consequences.

_____. "The Problem of 'Success Indicators' in Soviet Industry." ECONOMICA n.s. 25 (February 1958): 1-13.

    This article discusses the problem of motivating the enterprise manager to do what the planning authorities desire and the difficulty of discovering what the manager should be motivated to do, since prices set by the state do not reflect true costs. Remedies to these problems are considered.

_____. "The U.S.S.R.: The Reform That Never Was." In REFORMS IN THE SOVIET AND EASTERN EUROPEAN ECONOMIES, edited by C. A. D. Dellin and Hermann Gross, pp. 19-38. Lexington, Mass.: D. C. Heath, 1972.

    This paper discusses the so-called reforms of the 1960s and contrasts the Soviet and the Hungarian experiences.

Oliver, James H. "Turnover and 'Family Circles' in Soviet Administration."

Economic Organization

SLAVIC REVIEW 32 (September 1973): 527-45.

This article is concerned with the high turnover rates and the short terms of office of middle and lower ranking Soviet Party and governmental officials. Interpretations of the significance of this phenomenon, the disruptiveness of such turnover rates, attempts to measure turnover rates and lengths of terms in the same job, and career associations and patterns are covered. Tables.

Oppenheim, Samuel A. "The Supreme Economic Council 1917-21." SOVIET STUDIES 25 (July 1973): 3-27.

This paper discusses the organizational development of the council, difficulties which it encountered, and its role within the Soviet system.

"Optimal Sizes for Enterprises." In ECONOMIC CONCENTRATION, U.S. Senate. Committee on the Judiciary, pp. 4362-66. Washington, D.C.: Government Printing Office, 1969.

This paper summarizes the discussions at a meeting of Soviet economists concerned with determining the factors affecting the optimal sizes of enterprises in the USSR.

Palubinskas, Feliksas. "The Role of Marketing Research in the Soviet Economy." BUSINESS AND GOVERNMENT REVIEW 10 (September-October 1969): 17-24.

In surveying the state of marketing research in the Soviet Union, the author concludes that its role must increase. Topics covered include consumer goods planning, research on consumer demand, the Liberman reforms, and marketing research. Tables. A diagram shows the interrelationship of statistical information and planning.

Pardigon, Vladimir. "Recent Developments in the Soviet Union's Experiments with Autonomous Enterprises Operated on a Profit-earning Basis." ANNALS OF PUBLIC AND CO-OPERATIVE ECONOMY 37 (April-June 1966): 133-44.

The article outlines discussions among Soviet economists of enterprises operated on a profit-earning basis, briefly compares enterprise conduct before and after the introduction of the profit-earning criteria, and concludes that the results warrant further study.

Pecker, Boris. "The Soviet Accounting and Credit Systems." HARVARD BUSINESS REVIEW 11 (October 1932): 14-22.

Topics covered include organization of accounting, effects of government policy, recent changes in accounting methods, and organization and problems of the credit system.

"Plan and Contract in Transactions Between Soviet State Enterprises." SOVIET STUDIES 5 (July 1953): 89-96.

Economic Organization

This paper translates part of section three of R. O. Halfina. "Administrative Act and Contract." SOVETSKOYE GOSUDARSTVO I PRAVO, no. 1 (1952).

Pogosov, I. "Questions of the Economic Effectiveness in Concentrating Industrial Production." In ECONOMIC CONCENTRATION, U.S. Senate. Committee on the Judiciary, pp. 4395-404. Washington, D.C.: Government Printing Office, 1969.

> After presenting a great deal of data on the concentration of production by industry groups, Pogosov concludes that large enterprises are advantageous and that the growth of output per employee is more intensive at the large enterprises.

Poliakov, V., and Silin, A. "Personnel Management in Soviet Undertakings Under the Economic Reform." INTERNATIONAL LABOUR REVIEW 106 (December 1972): 527-42.

> This article is particularly concerned with the increased participation by trade unions in decision making; the procedure for incentives and educational work; social planning; and the growth of industrial associations and their councils of directors. Special reference is made to the practical experience of the Moscow Carburetor Works. An organizational chart of the enterprise is included.

Probst, A. "Optimal Dimensions of an Enterprise and Regional Factors." In ECONOMIC CONCENTRATION, U.S. Senate. Committee on the Judiciary, pp. 4404-12. Washington, D.C.: Government Printing Office, 1969.

> In this article specific industries are used to demonstrate that regional factors are essential in determining the selection of the economically most effective dimensions of the enterprise.

Ronimois, Hans E. "The Soviet Economic Machine." SLAVONIC REVIEW 30 (December 1951): 112-38.

> The author discusses the interrelatedness of two elements of the Soviet economic machine, the targets and the administrative offices.

Scaperlanda, Anthony E. "The Political Economy of Liberman-Type Reforms." JOURNAL OF ECONOMIC ISSUES 5 (March 1971): 77-85.

> This article presents an analytical framework which emphasizes the interaction of institutional resistances and technology and discusses the evolution of the reform movement, the bureaucratic resistance to reform, and the reforms and the power structure.

Schroeder, Gertrude E. "The 1966-67 Soviet Industrial Price Reform: A Study in Complications." SOVIET STUDIES 20 (April 1969): 462-77.

"The theses of this paper are (1) that Soviet planners, having eschewed the use of markets in the reforms, are in effect attempting instead to solve millions of equations and (2) that these attempts are leading to a further 'bureaucratization of economic life.'" Three tables.

_____. "Soviet Economic 'Reforms': A Study in Contradictions." SOVIET STUDIES 20 (July 1968): 1-21.

This paper sketches the background of the reforms, their provisions, and their effects.

Schwarz, Solomon M. "The Industrial Enterprise in Russia." HARVARD BUSINESS REVIEW 23 (May-June 1945): 265-76.

This article discusses the organization of Soviet industry, stressing the means of controlling the enterprise.

Selucky, Radoslav. ECONOMIC REFORMS IN EASTERN EUROPE: POLITICAL BACKGROUND AND ECONOMIC SIGNIFICANCE. Translated by Zdenek Elias. New York: Praeger, 1972. x, 179 p.

Of particular interest are the chapters on the prereform system in Eastern Europe, the alternative types of reform, and the reforms in the Soviet Union.

Sharpe, M. E., ed. PLANNING, PROFIT AND INCENTIVES IN THE USSR. VOL. I. THE LIBERMAN DISCUSSION: A NEW PLACE IN SOVIET ECONOMIC THOUGHT. White Plains, N.Y.: International Arts and Sciences Press, 1965. xiii, 314 p.

This book consists of translations from the Soviet press and journals concerning the Liberman reforms.

Sheehy, Ann. "Phases in the Economic Organization of Soviet Central Asia: Central, Regional, and Republican Interests in Conflict." CENTRAL ASIAN REVIEW 16, no. 4 (1968): 278-93.

The background, operation, and abolition of joint Central Asian economic agencies are discussed.

Smolinski, Leon. "The Scale of Soviet Industrial Establishments." AMERICAN ECONOMIC REVIEW 52 (May 1962): 138-48.

This article characterizes Soviet policy on the scale of industrial establishments as one of giantism. A further appraisal of this policy compares it with Chinese policy. Two tables. For further discussion, see: Lloyd G. Reynolds et al. "Soviet Economic Planning--Discussion." AMERICAN ECONOMIC REVIEW 52 (May 1962): 158-64.

Economic Organization

Spechler, Martin C. "Decentralizing the Soviet Economy: Legal Regulation of Price and Quality." SOVIET STUDIES 22 (October 1970): 222-54.

Topics discussed include socialist contract law; law and the administration of price and quality; the enforcement of quality; reform and decentralization; bars to change; and law and lawyers as a source of change.

Swearer, Howard R. "Administration of Local Industry after the 1957 Industrial Reorganization." SOVIET STUDIES 12 (January 1961): 217-30.

The impact of the reorganization of industrial management on local industry is examined from a political and public administration perspective.

_____. "Decentralization in Recent Soviet Administrative Practice." SLAVIC REVIEW 21 (September 1962): 456-70.

Topics covered include problems of decentralization, the territorial organization, administrative consolidation, central controls, current trends, and bureaucracy in flux.

Tahir, Pervez. "Soviet Economic Reform: Progress and Problems." PAKISTAN DEVELOPMENT REVIEW 12 (Spring 1973): 62-67.

This is a review article of Group of Economists (author reference given), SOVIET ECONOMIC REFORM: PROGRESS AND PROBLEMS. Moscow: Progress Publishers, 1972.

Tereshtenko, V[alery]. J. "Industrial Cooperatives in the Post-War Ukraine." AMERICAN SLAVIC AND EAST EUROPEAN REVIEW 10 (1951): 26-37.

The organization and operations of an industrial cooperative which Tereshtenko visited in 1947 are described. Topics covered include primary cooperatives, regional unions, work methods, planning, financing, taxation, and education.

Timacheff, N[icholas]. S. "The Organization of State Industry in Soviet Russia." INTERNATIONAL LABOUR REVIEW 19 (March 1929): 338-57.

Some earlier phases in the development of the Soviet economy are examined.

Treml, Vladimir G. "The Politics of 'Libermanism.'" SOVIET STUDIES 19 (April 1968): 567-72.

This paper examines the role of Evsei Liberman in the theory and application of what has come to be called the "Liberman reforms."

Turner, Carl B. "The Liberman Proposals and the Soviet Economy." QUARTERLY REVIEW OF ECONOMICS AND BUSINESS 6, no. 2 (1966): 17-24.

This paper traces these proposals from the debate invited in the
PRAVDA article to their adoption in 1965.

Vedishchev, A. "Three Years of Work Under New Conditions--An Economic
Survey." PROBLEMS OF ECONOMICS 3 (January 1961): 52-61.

This is a translation from PLANOVOE KHOZIAISTVO, no. 7
(1960). It discusses three years under the territorial system of
economic organization.

Walden, M., ed. and trans. "Enterprise Incentives and Methods of Planning."
ECONOMICS OF PLANNING 5, nos. 1-2 (1965): 95-105.

This article contains extracts of a PRAVDA article by V. Trapeznikov
and Evsei G. Liberman. Also included are excerpts from articles
by two Soviet enterprise directors, I. Manvelov and I. Iljushin,
concerning management and planning problems in the light of new
economic trends.

Zaleski, Eugene.. PLANNING REFORMS IN THE SOVIET UNION, 1962-1966:
AN ANALYSIS OF RECENT TRENDS IN ECONOMIC ORGANIZATION AND
MANAGEMENT. Translated by Marie-Christine MacAndrew and G. Warren
Nutter. Chapel Hill: University of North Carolina Press, 1967. viii, 203 p.

Topics discussed include permanent features of Soviet administrative
planning, administrative reforms, obstacles to reform, and administrative experiments. Index and charts.

Zauberman, Alfred. "Liberman's Rules of the Game for Soviet Industry."
SLAVIC REVIEW 22 (December 1963): 734-44.

This article discusses the Liberman reforms with emphasis on enterprise performance indexes and the profit incentives.

Zverev, A. G. "Against Oversimplification in Solving Complex Problems."
PROBLEMS OF ECONOMICS 5 (April 1963): 15-18.

A former minister of finance criticizes the Liberman reform proposals.

Chapter 21
MANAGEMENT AND ENTREPRENEURSHIP

THE PERIOD UP TO 1860

Bendix, Reinhard. WORK AND AUTHORITY IN INDUSTRY. New York: John Wiley, 1956. 466 p.

> Chapter 3 deals with entrepreneurial ideologies in eighteenth and nineteenth-century Russia. The author discusses the preconditions of industrialization in the West and in Russia, social classes and economic change in eighteenth-century Russia, and the management of labor and industry.

[Tschebotarioff-] Bill, Valentine. THE FORGOTTEN CLASS: THE RUSSIAN BOURGEOISIE FROM THE EARLIEST BEGINNINGS TO 1900. New York: Praeger, 1959. 229 p.

> Bill traces the history of the Russian bourgeoisie and presents a detailed account of the Morozov family, which is the representative type of the Russian bourgeoisie. The book discusses the beginnings of this class during the Kievan period, the contribution of Old Belief to the rise of capitalism and the emergence of the bourgeoisie, and the appearance of entrepreneurs in railroad construction during the 1860s.

Blackwell, William L. "The Old Believers and the Rise of Private Industrial Enterprise in Early Nineteenth Century Moscow." SLAVIC REVIEW 24 (September 1965): 407-24.

> This paper presents a detailed discussion of the role of the Old Believers as entrepreneurs in Moscow, their problems, and the effects of their commercial success on their religious and social lives.

Kirchner, Walter. "Entrepreneurial Activity in Russian-Western Trade Relations During the Sixteenth Century." EXPLORATIONS IN ENTREPRENEURIAL HISTORY 8 (April 1956): 245-52.

This article calls for further study of the Russian entrepreneur and his counterpart in Western Europe after reviewing the economic importance of the tsar and his government and foreign entrepreneurs in Russia.

Lewitter, L. R. "Ivan Tikhonovich Pososhkov (1652-1726) and 'The Spirit of Capitalism.'" SLAVONIC AND EAST EUROPEAN REVIEW 51, no. 125 (1973): 524-553.

The relation between religion and the Weberian Protestant or Capitalist Ethic in seventeenth and eighteenth-century Russia is explored through the career of an early entrepreneur.

Rosovsky, Henry. "The Serf Entrepreneur in Russia." EXPLORATIONS IN ENTREPRENEURIAL HISTORY 6 (May 1954): 207-33.

This paper is concerned with the serfs from 1700 to 1850. Contributions by serfs to business enterprise are considered. The author criticizes economists' natural predispositions to think of entrepreneurship only in terms of free societies. Tables provide data on numbers and types of serfs and obrok payments. For further discussion, see: Peter Gutmann. "The Serf Entrepreneur in Russia: A Comment." EXPLORATIONS IN ENTREPRENEURIAL HISTORY 7 (October 1954): 48-50. A rejoinder by Rosovsky follows.

Tschebotarioff-Bill, Valentine. "The Morozovs." RUSSIAN REVIEW 14 (April 1955): 109-16.

This note chronicles the rise of this entrepreneurial peasant family during the nineteenth century.

THE PERIOD 1860-1917

McKay, John P. PIONEERS FOR PROFIT: FOREIGN ENTREPRENEURSHIP AND RUSSIAN INDUSTRIALIZATION 1855-1913. Chicago: University of Chicago Press, 1970. xiii, 442 p.

McKay considers three distinct problems: (1) the pattern of enterprise and investment as practiced by business leaders of the advanced countries of Western Europe; (2) foreign participation in Russian industry and its influence on accelerated Russian growth; and (3) the nature of economic relations between Russia and more technologically advanced foreigners.

Roosa, R. A. THE ASSOCIATION OF INDUSTRY AND TRADE, 1906-1914: AN EXAMINATION OF THE ECONOMIC VIEWS OF ORGANIZED INDUSTRIALISTS IN PREREVOLUTIONARY RUSSIA. New York: ?, 1967. 699 p.

Part one of this book discusses the Russian business community, 1905-18, and the Association of Industry and Trade. Part two reviews the industrialists' views of the future. Part three considers growth patterns in industry, agriculture, transport, and communications. Part four deals with finances, living standards, and Russia in the world market.

Shimkin, Dimitri B. "The Entrepreneur in Tsarist and Soviet Russia." EXPLORATIONS IN ENTREPRENEURIAL HISTORY 2 (November 1949): 24-34.

The author discusses some unique aspects of Russian entrepreneurial activity, i.e., its persistent dependence upon foreign capital and technical skill.

Tschebotarioff-Bill, Valentine. "The Dead Souls of Russia's Merchant World." RUSSIAN REVIEW 15 (October 1956): 245-58.

This paper looks at the attitudes of Russian writers toward Russian entrepreneurs, merchants, and industrialists.

Watstein, Joseph. "Ivan Sytin--An Old Russian Success Story." RUSSIAN REVIEW 30 (January 1971): 43-53.

The career of a very successful book publisher in Russia in the second half of the nineteenth century is recounted.

THE PERIOD AFTER 1917

Arakelian, A. INDUSTRIAL MANAGEMENT IN THE USSR. Translated by E. L. Raymond. Washington, D.C.: Public Affairs Press, 1950. 168 p.

The author discusses (1) the development of forms of management for Soviet industry; (2) management principles of Soviet industry; (3) organization and structure of Soviet industry; (4) administration of Socialist enterprise; (5) conversion to peacetime construction; and (6) the Party's role in management of trade unions and industrial production.

Azrael, Jeremy R. MANAGERIAL POWER AND SOVIET POLITICS. Cambridge, Mass.: Harvard University Press, 1966. ix, 258 p.

The author discusses the management doctrine that emerged from the writings of Marx, Engles and Lenin before the Revolution: the role of the technical intelligentsia in industrialization and growth; the role of "red-directors" appointed by the Party to managerial posts after the Revolution; the position of the managerial elite after the purge; and the emergence of the new managerial elite recruited from the ranks of engineers and retrained in Western-type "business administration" programs.

Berliner, Joseph S. FACTORY AND MANAGER IN THE USSR. Cambridge, Mass.: Harvard University Press, 1957. xv, 386 p.

Management and Entrepreneurship

Among the aspects of management discussed are the economic milieu of the Soviet manager; the goals of managers; the role of premiums and profits; plan fulfillment through deceptive manipulation and deliberate deterioration of the quality of production; falsification of reporting and "blat" (usage of personal influence to obtain favors); and various controls over management.

_____. "The Informal Organization of the Soviet Firm." QUARTERLY JOURNAL OF ECONOMICS 66 (August 1952): 342-65.

After discussing the sources of information and their reliability, this study treats the goals of managerial behavior, informal management practices, factors encouraging these informal practices, and the consequences for the economic system.

_____. "Managerial Incentives and Decisionmaking: A Comparison of the United States and the Soviet Union." In COMPARISONS OF THE U.S. AND SOVIET ECONOMIES, U.S. Congress. Joint Economic Committee, pp. 349-76. Washington, D.C.: Government Printing Office, 1959.

This paper deals with managerial incentives and recruitment; material incentives; and production, procurement, and investment decisions.

Bienstock, Gregory, et al. MANAGEMENT IN RUSSIAN INDUSTRY AND AGRICULTURE. Ithaca, N.Y.: Cornell University Press, 1944. xxxii, 198 p.

Part one deals with management in industry and the organs of management; management and the Party; management and employees; the planning of production; procurement and sale; output, cost, profit and price; incentives and a discussion of plant managers. Part two deals with the management of collective farms and surveys planning and accounting, incomes and incentives, private versus cooperative interests, and the status and selection of kolkhoz officials. Glossary.

Campbell, Robert W. "Management Spillovers From Soviet Space and Military Programmes." SOVIET STUDIES 23 (April 1972): 586-607.

Several areas of innovation in planning and management in the Soviet economy are examined, with the goal of ascertaining to what extent space and military experience can be discerned as the source. The diffusion process is also described.

Dulles, Allen W. "Incentives that Drive Soviet Managers." In INCENTIVES FOR EXECUTIVES, edited by David W. Ewing and Dan H. Genn, pp. 165-79. New York: McGraw-Hill, 1962.

This paper discusses popular incentives, managerial incentives, the political environment, discipline, and reforms.

Management and Entrepreneurship

Granick, David. "Initiative and Independence of Soviet Plant Management." AMERICAN SLAVIC AND EAST EUROPEAN REVIEW 10 (1951): 191-201.

Areas in which initiative by plant management personnel is required by the Soviet system are outlined. The considerable degree of independent decision making which is left to these plant managements is analyzed. Emphasis is on heavy industry in 1934-41.

_____. MANAGEMENT OF THE INDUSTRIAL FIRM IN THE USSR; A STUDY OF SOVIET ECONOMIC PLANNING. New York: Columbia University Press, 1954. xiii, 346 p.

The role of plant executives in Soviet economic planning is analyzed. This study covers the period 1934-41. Bibliography and index.

_____. MANAGERIAL COMPARISONS OF FOUR DEVELOPED COUNTRIES: FRANCE, BRITAIN, UNITED STATES, AND RUSSIA. Cambridge, Mass.: M.I.T. Press, 1972. viii, 394 p.

This study of management practices in large-scale comparative manufacturing enterprises is based on in-depth interviews. Index.

_____. THE RED EXECUTIVE--A STUDY OF THE ORGANIZATION MAN IN RUSSIAN INDUSTRY. Garden City, N.Y.: Doubleday, 1960. 334 p.

The book presents a popular account of Soviet management and discusses similarities between Soviet and American managers (their organizational problems and some of the ways that they solve them); the training of managers; a description of their way of life; a comparison of factories--East and West; and the way in which the factories are run.

_____. "Soviet-American Management Comparisons." In COMPARISONS OF THE U.S. AND SOVIET ECONOMIES, U.S. Congress. Joint Economic Committee, pp. 143-50. Washington, D.C.: Government Printing Office, 1959.

Granick compares education, management incentives, the bureaucracy, and the problems of communication upwards of Soviet and American managers. The paper includes a chart of the ratio of white-collar to manual workers in industry and mining in the USSR and the United States.

Guillebaud, Philomena. "The Role of Honorary Awards in the Soviet Economic System." AMERICAN SLAVIC AND EAST EUROPEAN REVIEW 12 (1953): 486-505.

This article reviews the use of awards in the Soviet Union as a part of the incentive system for workers. Several trends are noted: numbers of awards given annually have increased over time; and the behavior characteristics are no longer energy, innovation, or experiment but persistence, punctuality, and conscientiousness.

Harcourt, G. C. "The Measurement of the Rate of Profit and the Bonus Scheme for Managers in the Soviet Union." OXFORD ECONOMIC PAPERS 18 (March 1966): 58-63.

> The author discusses the implications of the bonus scheme as used in the Soviet Union and concludes that the size of expected bonuses influences the choice of investment projects. However, the profit rate has an arbitrary impact on the decisions.

Hardt, John P., and Frankel, Theodore. "The Industrial Managers." In INTEREST GROUPS IN SOVIET POLITICS, edited by Gordon H. Skilling and Franklyn Griffits, pp. 171-76, 189-208. Princeton, N.J.: Princeton University Press, 1971.

> Topics discussed include the statistical model of planning and management, changes made after Stalin, and management autonomy, professionalism, and status.

Horwitz, Bertrand N. "Profit Responsibility in Soviet Enterprise." JOURNAL OF BUSINESS 41 (January 1968): 47-55.

> This article describes changes in the central management of Soviet enterprises and analyzes the possible effects on capital investment of the introduction of a new scheme for awarding bonuses to enterprise directors.

Judy, Richard W. "Information, Control, and Soviet Economic Management." In MATHEMATICS AND COMPUTERS IN SOVIET ECONOMIC PLANNING, edited by John P. Hardt et al, pp. 1-48. New Haven, Conn.: Yale University Press, 1967.

> This paper contains a model of a management system, outlines the existing Soviet economic information system, and discusses Soviet economic cybernetics, Soviet computer science, and the future of Soviet computer science. A comment by Robert W. Campbell follows, pp. 49-60.

Kabaj, M. "Evolution of the Incentive System in U.S.S.R. Industry." INTERNATIONAL LABOUR REVIEW 94 (July 1966): 22-38.

> Topics discussed include economic development and success indicators, the shift toward qualitative goals, the debate on incentives, experiments with incentive systems, and reforms. Five diagrams.

Khrushchev, Nikita S. ON THE FURTHER IMPROVEMENT OF MANAGEMENT IN INDUSTRY AND CONSTRUCTION IN THE U.S.S.R. Materials of the Seventh Session of the Supreme Soviet of the U.S.S.R. May 7-10, 1957. London: Soviet News, 1957? 76 p.

> This booklet contains Khrushchev's report and reply to the discussion of the Seventh Session of the Supreme Soviet, as well as the text of the new law. He discusses the growth of the national

economy and the need for improving organizational forms in the management of industry and construction.

Kosygin, Alexei. "On Improving Management of Industry." In NEW METHODS OF ECONOMIC MANAGEMENT IN THE USSR, pp. 26-49. Moscow: Novosti Press Agency Publishing House, n.d.

This speech was concerned with new planning methods, incentives, and administrative relations, including abolition of the territorial organization introduced by Khrushchev in 1957.

Krynski, George I. "Management Problems in Soviet Public Enterprise as Indicated by Arbitration Awards." AMERICAN SLAVIC AND EAST EUROPEAN REVIEW 12 (1953): 175-87.

This article reviews commercial disputes in the Soviet Union in the late 1930s.

Leeman, Wayne A. "Bonus Formulae and Soviet Managerial Performance." SOUTHERN ECONOMIC JOURNAL 36 (April 1970): 434-45.

The objectives of this paper are: the algebraic expression of pecuniary rewards for managers; a demonstration that prices are implicit in schemes which reward output and efficiency; a demonstration that input plans are less efficient than using prices; a demonstration that something close to net income or profit is implicit in a system which rewards efficiency; and a demonstration that behavior motivated by an output plan differs from that motivated by profit. For further discussion, see: Francis W. Rushing. "Bonus Formulae and Soviet Managerial Performance: Comment." SOUTHERN ECONOMIC JOURNAL 38 (April 1972): 569-72; Michael Ellman. "Bonus Formulae and Soviet Managerial Performance: A Further Comment." SOUTHERN ECONOMIC JOURNAL 39 (April 1973): 652-53.

Miller, Jack. "Tomorrow's Industrialists." STUDIES ON THE SOVIET UNION n.s. 5, no. 2 (1965): 23-28.

This article discusses the important effects of the age of policymakers on economic policy in the Soviet Union. For further discussion, see: Constantine Olgin. "NEP or Back to Stalin?" STUDIES ON THE SOVIET UNION n.s. 5, no. 2 (1965): 56-64.

Miller, Jacob, ed. "Budgetary Control in Soviet Factories." SOVIET STUDIES 2 (July 1950): 94-108.

The article translated here by Miller is: A. Vorobyova. "More Khozraschot within the Enterprise." VOPROSY EKONOMIKI 7 (1949): 3-15.

Management and Entrepreneurship

Miller, Margaret S. "Management Reforms in Industry." CENTRAL ASIAN REVIEW 15, no. 2 (1967): 99-113.

This is a review of comments on reforms culled from the Central Asian and Kazakh press in 1965-66. The aim is to reveal local feelings and actions.

Nuti, D. M. "Material Incentive Schemes and the Choice of Techniques in Soviet Industry." AUSTRALIAN ECONOMIC PAPERS 5 (December 1966): 183-98.

The article summarizes incentive schemes, examines the actual criteria used in the Soviet Union for the choice of production techniques, and reconsiders possible divergences between the socially optimum technique and the bonus-maximizing technique.

"Party Organizations and Management." SOVIET STUDIES 6 (April 1955): 458-62.

This paper reports on articles in the Soviet press to illustrate "the way in which the supervising function of party organizations in public enterprises was supposed to work in the autumn of 1954."

Polakov, Walter N. "Myths and Realities About Soviet Russia." HARVARD BUSINESS REVIEW 11 (October 1932): 1-13.

This article surveys some misconceptions about Soviet Russia, notes the business effects of these views, and compares Soviet and U.S. management and their problems.

Poppelmann, Heinrich. "The Captains of Industry and Trade." In RED ECONOMICS, edited by Gerhard Dobbert, pp. 75-92. Boston and New York: Houghton Mifflin, 1932.

The author describes his impressions of important Soviet industrial leaders.

"The Powers of Industrial Managers." SOVIET STUDIES 9 (October 1957): 239-42.

This note reviews Soviet discussions about the division of power between managers and the central planners after the decentralization of industrial administration.

Richman, Barry M. MANAGEMENT DEVELOPMENT AND EDUCATION IN THE SOVIET UNION. Lansing: Michigan State University Press, 1967. xviii, 308 p.

Topics discussed include Soviet management development, the managerial job, the prototype Soviet manager, management education and training, and changing needs. Tables.

_____. SOVIET MANAGEMENT--WITH SIGNIFICANT AMERICAN COMPARISONS. Englewood Cliffs, N.J.: Prentice-Hall, 1965. vii, 279 p.

> Discussed are management levels, organization of industry, the enterprise, enterprise management, planning, incentives, behavior, innovation, and controls. Tables and map.

Ryapolov, Gregory. "I was a Soviet Manager." HARVARD BUSINESS REVIEW 44 (January-February 1966): 117-25.

> A first-person account of the problems, practices, and attitudes of a Soviet factory director.

Ryavec, Karl W. "Soviet Industrial Management: Challenge and Response, 1965-1970." CANADIAN SLAVIC STUDIES 5 (Summer 1971): 151-77.

> In analyzing the present state and dynamics of Soviet industrial management, the author stresses economic reform and political implications.

_____. "Soviet Industrial Managers, Their Superiors and the Economic Reforms: A Study of an Attempt at Planned Behavioral Change." SOVIET STUDIES 21 (October 1969): 208-29.

> This paper presents "a comparison of authoritative statements defining the 'model' of 'ideal' behavior intended by the reform with the actual behavior of managers and their superiors after the reform was implemented."

Schwarz, Solomon M. "Heads of Russian Factories: A Sociological Study." SOCIAL RESEARCH 9 (September 1942): 315-33.

> This paper is concerned with the questions of the environment from which managers are drawn, how they attain their positions, their social standing, relations with the government, and whether or not they form a distinct class. Two tables.

Sellakaerts, Willy. "The Soviet Managerial Evolution." MARQUETTE BUSINESS REVIEW 17 (Summer 1973): 84-97.

> This paper discusses the desired qualifications of the new type of manager needed in the Soviet Union and the managerial characteristics most likely to emerge in the future.

Shaffer, Harry G. "A New Incentive Plan for Soviet Managers." RUSSIAN REVIEW 22 (October 1963): 410-16.

> This article discusses the role of the Liberman reforms in making the interests of Soviet managers more consistent with those of the economy as a whole.

Management and Entrepreneurship

Sharpe, M. E., ed. PLANNING PROFIT AND INCENTIVES IN THE USSR--VOL. II, REFORM OF SOVIET ECONOMIC MANAGEMENT. White Plains, N.Y.: International Arts and Sciences Press, 1966. viii, 337 p.

    This book consists of translations of articles from the Soviet press and journals concerned with the reforms of 1965-66.

Soboleva, Galina D. "The New Soviet Incentive System: A Study of its Operation in Kiev." INTERNATIONAL LABOUR REVIEW 101 (January 1970): 15-33.

    Concentrating on industry in Kiev, the author demonstrates how the new system is improving efficiency and productivity. Tables.

Valentinov (Volsky), Nikolai. "Non-Party Specialists and the Coming of the NEP." RUSSIAN REVIEW 30 (April 1971): 154-63.

    This excerpt from Valentinov's work represents his observations about why non-Party intellectuals accepted the coming of the NEP and how it affected their attitudes toward and activities within the Soviet regime.

Chapter 22
SOVIET INVESTMENT ALLOCATION POLICIES

Abouchar, Alan. "The New Soviet Standard Methodology for Investment Allocation. SOVIET STUDIES 24 (January 1973): 402-10.

This article investigates the new standard methodology introduced in 1969 and compares it with its predecessor, which had been in effect since 1959.

Bush, Keith. "Resource Allocation Policy: Capital Investment." In SOVIET ECONOMIC PROSPECTS FOR THE SEVENTIES, U.S. Congress. Joint Economic Committee, pp. 39-44. Washington, D.C.: Government Printing Office, 1973.

Two tables provide figures on the percentage distribution by sector of cumulative gross fixed investment, 1961-75.

_____. "Soviet Capital Investment Since Khrushchev; A Note." SOVIET STUDIES 24 (July 1972): 91-96.

This paper presents two tables: cumulative gross fixed investment from all sources of financing by industry branch and sector and its percentage distribution, 1961-75.

Butler, Scot. "The Soviet Capital Investment Program." In ECONOMIC PERFORMANCE AND THE MILITARY BURDEN IN THE SOVIET UNION, U.S. Congress. Joint Economic Committee, pp. 43-53. Washington, D.C.: Government Printing Office, 1970.

Investment performance and the 1970 plan are discussed. Eleven tables.

Dobb, Maurice H. "A Note on the Discussion of the Problem of Choice Between Alternative Investment Projects." SOVIET STUDIES 2 (January 1951): 289-95.

This note answers critics of Strumilin's work on choice of investment projects.

Soviet Investment Allocation Policies

Fallenbuchl, Z. M. "Some Structural Aspects of Soviet-Type Investment Policy." SOVIET STUDIES 16 (April 1965): 433-47.

> This paper examines the aspects of Soviet-type investment policy; the balance between aggregate demand and aggregate supply; the effects of producer and consumer goods sector growth on overall growth; and the possible bad effects from over-stressing a particular sector such as heavy industry.

Gregory, Paul R., et al. "New Soviet Investment Rules: A Guide to Rational Investment Planning?" SOUTHERN ECONOMIC JOURNAL 40 (January 1974): 500-504.

> This short paper evaluates the new investment rules in terms of static efficiency criteria.

Grossman, Gregory. "Some Current Trends in Soviet Capital Formation." In CAPITAL FORMATION AND ECONOMIC GROWTH, pp. 171-228. Conference on Capital Formation and Economic Growth, New York, November 6-8, 1953. Princeton, N.J.: Princeton University Press, 1955.

> This paper discusses the implications of the Fifth Five-Year Plan with respect to capital formation, especially the trend toward more capital intensive investment. Five tables. Comments by Norman M. Kaplan, Alexander Erlich, and Abram Bergson follow.

Hardt, John P. "Industrial Investment in the U.S.S.R." In COMPARISONS OF THE U.S. AND SOVIET ECONOMIES, U.S. Congress. Joint Economic Committee, pp. 121-41. Washington, D.C.: Government Printing Office, 1960.

> This paper contains chapters on maximum industrial growth; the Stalinist plan for industrial investment; Khrushchev's revision of the Stalinist investment formula for the Seven-Year Plan (1958-65); and investment for future industrial growth. Tables.

_____. "Investment Policy in the Soviet Electric-Power Industry." In VALUE AND PLAN; ECONOMIC CALCULATION AND ORGANIZATION IN EASTERN EUROPE, edited by Gregory Grossman, pp. 295-318. Berkeley and Los Angeles: University of California Press, 1960.

> This study is concerned with rationality in Soviet industrial investment.

"The Investment Discussion Summed Up." SOVIET STUDIES 6 (October 1954): 201-17.

> This is a translation of "The Results of the Discussion on Determination of Capital Effectiveness in the Industry of the USSR," which appeared in VOPROSY EKONOMIKI no. 3 (1954): 99-113.

Jackson, Marvin R. "Information and Incentives in Planning Soviet Investment Projects." SOVIET STUDIES 23 (July 1971): 3-25.

This article contains a description of the major elements of organization of Soviet investment decision making in recent years. It also explores several kinds of dysfunctions which have characterized Soviet investment decision making in recent years.

Kaplan, Norman M. "Capital Formation and Allocation." In SOVIET ECONOMIC GROWTH: CONDITIONS AND PERSPECTIVES, edited by Abram Bergson, pp. 37-100. Evanston, Ill.: Row, Peterson, 1953.

The first section discusses Soviet capital formation. The second deals with the relationship between capital formation and industrial output. The paper is supplemented with tables and followed with comments by Evsey D. Domar, Alexander Erlich, and M. Millikan.

──────. CAPITAL INVESTMENT IN THE SOVIET UNION, 1924-51. Santa Monica, Calif.: RAND Corp., 1951. v, 218 p.

The first of four papers which study Soviet capital formation, this one is concerned only with investment flows in current rubles. Many statistical tables.

──────. "Investment Alternatives in Soviet Economic Theory." JOURNAL OF POLITICAL ECONOMY 60 (April 1951): 133-44.

This paper summarizes rules for investment choice proposed by eleven Soviet economists.

Khachaturov, T. S. "Choice Between Investments." SOVIET STUDIES 2 (January 1951): 317-22.

This is a summary of T. S. Khachaturov. "Methods of Economic Comparison of Investment Varients." IZV. AKAD. NAUK, OTDEL, EK. I PRAVA. 4 (1950): 252-68.

──────. "The Economic Effectiveness of Capital Investments in the USSR." AMERICAN ECONOMIC REVIEW 48 (May 1958): 368-84.

The relationships between Soviet economic plans, capital investments, and increases in output are examined. For further discussion, see: Holland Hunter and Frank H. Golay. "Capital Investment Decisions in the USSR--Discussion." AMERICAN ECONOMIC REVIEW 48 (May 1958): 393-97.

McFarlane, B. [J.]. "Soviet Investment Policy." ECONOMIC RECORD 38 (June 1962): 198-208.

Topics covered include criteria of investment choice, the role of capital "effectiveness" indicators, and the grounds for rejecting marginal analysis in investment decision making.

Miller, Jacob. "The Discussion on Choice Between Investments Within the Plan." SOVIET STUDIES 4 (January 1953): 338-48.

> This article summarizes the following three articles: A. I. Baumgolts. "On the Question of the Effectiveness of Capital Investments." IZVESTIA AKAD. NAUK, OTDEL. EK. I PRAVA 6 (1950): 440-52; P. Oslov and I. Romanov. "On the Methodology of Comparing Varients of a Projected Construction." VOPROSY EKONOMIKI no. 1 (1951): 104-11; and P. Denisov. "The Best Test of a Method is to Try It Out in Practice." VOPROSY EKONOMIKI no. 1 (1951): 112-19.

──────, ed. "Three Articles on the Effectiveness of Investments, from Soviet Periodicals." SOVIET STUDIES 1 (April 1950): 356-82.

> Discussed and summarized here are: D. E. Chernomordik. "Effectiveness of Capital Investments and the Theory of Reproduction: Towards A Statement of the Problem." VOPROSY EKONOMIKI 6 (1949): 78-95; P. Mstislavsky. "Some Questions of the Effectiveness of Capital Investments in the Soviet Economy." VOPROSY EKONOMIKI 6 (1949): 96-115; and A. Emelyanov. "On Methods of Ascertaining the Economic Effectiveness of the Employment of Machines in the Soviet Economy." VOPROSY EKONOMIKI 11 (1949): 104-14. Many tables.

Nove, Alec. "A Note on the Volume of Soviet Investment." REVIEW OF ECONOMICS AND STATISTICS 36 (February 1954): 74-80.

> This paper considers the probable increases in the volume of Soviet investment since 1940. Existing official figures are subjected to critical analysis, as are the attempts made outside Russia to throw light on this problem. A table presents data on Soviet investment, 1946-52.

Wohlmuth, Karl. "The Growth of the Capital Stock in the Soviet Union." KYKLOS 23, no. 1 (1970): 122-32.

> This paper is a review of Richard Moorsteen and Raymond P. Powell. THE SOVIET CAPITAL STOCK, 1928-1962. New Haven, Conn.: Yale University Press, 1966.

Chapter 23
TRANSPORTATION AND COMMUNICATIONS

Ames, Edward. "A Century of Russian Railroad Construction, 1837-1936." AMERICAN SLAVIC AND EAST EUROPEAN REVIEW 6 (December 1947): 57-74.

Topics covered include total railroad construction, cycles in construction, regional distribution of construction, and economic functions as a factor in construction. Three tables provide data on lengths of track laid and peak years for construction.

THE PERIOD UP TO 1860

Haywood, Richard M. THE BEGINNINGS OF RAILWAY DEVELOPMENT IN RUSSIA IN THE REIGN OF NICHOLAS I, 1835-1842. Durham, N.C.: Duke University Press, 1969. xvii, 270 p.

The book deals with problems in the building of Russia's first railway (the Tsarskoe Selo Railway and the St. Petersburg-Moscow Railway). Bibliography, index, and map.

_____. "The Question of a Standard Guage for Russian Railways, 1836-1860." SLAVIC REVIEW 28 (March 1969): 72-80.

The history of the decision to set a standard guage on Russian railways different from that of neighboring countries is traced.

Tarsaidze, Alexander. "American Pioneers in Russian Railroad Building." RUSSIAN REVIEW 9 (October 1950): 286-95.

This paper discusses the roles of some American entrepreneurs and engineers in Russian railroad building in the period 1840-60.

Tschebotarioff-Bill, Valentine. "The Early Days of Russian Railroads." RUSSIAN REVIEW 15 (January 1956): 14-28.

This paper looks at the politics and important personalities involved in the building of Russian railroads from the 1840s to the 1880s.

Transportation and Communications

THE PERIOD 1860-1917

"The Building of the Bukhara Railway, 1914-16." CENTRAL ASIAN REVIEW 11, no. 1 (1963): 46-50.

    The concern here is with labor problems encountered during construction.

Garbutt, Paul E. THE RUSSIAN RAILWAYS. London: Sampson Low, Marston & Co., 1949. ix, 95 p.

    The book gives the history of the development of Russian railways before and after the Revolution, outlines its organization and staff, describes the technical features, and discusses rail traffic, including passenger traffic. Tables, bibliography, and index.

Le Fleming, H. M., and Price, J. H. RUSSIAN STEAM LOCOMOTIVES. New York: Kelley, 1960. 140 p.

    This book is concerned with the types and technical aspects of steam locomotives in Russia both before and after the Revolution.

Metzer, Jacob. "Railroad Development and Market Integration: The Case of Tsarist Russia." JOURNAL OF ECONOMIC HISTORY 34 (September 1974): 529-50.

    Market development and gains from trade and the evolution of a national grain market in tsarist Russia are evaluated. Tables.

Westwood, J. N. A HISTORY OF RUSSIAN RAILWAYS. London: Allen and Unwin, 1964. 326 p. Illustrated.

    The author discusses railway construction during the boom years (1866-99); railways into Asia; rail construction during the war, during the NEP, and during the period of five-year plans (1928-59). Bibliography, index, maps, photographs, and diagrams.

_____. "The Vladikavkaz Railway: A Case of Enterprising Private Enterprise." SLAVIC REVIEW 25 (December 1966): 669-75.

    This article outlines the history and economic significance of this privately owned railway which connected the northern Caucausus with Rostov in the second half of the nineteenth century.

THE PERIOD AFTER 1917

Athay, Robert E. THE ECONOMICS OF SOVIET MERCHANT SHIPPING POLICY. Chapel Hill: University of North Carolina Press, 1971. xiii, 150 p.

    This book recounts the growth of the Soviet merchant fleet and analyzes the economic reasons for and against the expansion of the fleet. Prospects for further growth in the Soviet merchant fleet and its significance for world shipping are also considered. Index.

Blackman, James H. "Transportation." In SOVIET ECONOMIC GROWTH: CONDITIONS AND PERSPECTIVES, edited by Abram Bergson, pp. 126-57. Evanston, Ill.: Row, Peterson, 1953.

Development of traffic and production in the USSR, with a view to appraising the long-range transportation requirements, is analyzed. Tables. Comments by Holland Hunter, pp. 157-61, and Dimitri B. Shimkin, pp. 161-62, follow.

_____. TRANSPORT DEVELOPMENT AND LOCOMOTIVE TECHNOLOGY IN THE SOVIET UNION. Columbia: Bureau of Business and Economic Research, School of Business Administration, University of South Carolina, 1957. iv, 64 p.

Blackman traces the development of diesel and electric traction on the Soviet railroad network in relation to growth of the Soviet economy and its expanding transport requirements.

Central Statistical Administration. USSR, TRANSPORT AND COMMUNICATIONS. A STATISTICAL COMPILATION. Moscow: State Statistical Publishing House, 1957. 218 p.

This volume contains numerous tables on general transport, railroad, maritime, river, motor, air, and pipeline transport. The tables also provide data on postal service, telegraph, telephone, and radio. Many graphs.

Dobb, Maurice H. "Practice and Theory of Railway Rates." SOVIET STUDIES 1 (April 1950): 313-18.

This paper is a discussion of D. E. Chernomordik. "Towards a Theory of Railway Rates." VOPROSY EKONOMIKI, no. 9 (1948). Table of rates.

Edwards, Imogene U. "Automotive Trends in the USSR." In SOVIET ECONOMIC PROSPECTS FOR THE SEVENTIES, U.S. Congress. Joint Economic Committee, pp. 291-314. Washington, D.C.: Government Printing Office, 1973.

This paper discusses the overall goals of the Ninth Five-Year Plan, the passenger car, truck, and bus production programs and implications for the road system. Many tables.

Hanson, Philip. "The Soviet Union and World Shipping." SOVIET STUDIES 22, no. 1 (July 1970): 44-60.

This article reviews Soviet merchant shipping policy, using evidence mainly from Soviet sources, to gauge the nature of the Soviet shipping threat. Nine tables.

Hopkins, J. A., and Alexander, Melinda. "Russia's Transportation System." In SOVIET RUSSIA IN THE SECOND DECADE, by the American Trade Delegation, pp. 334-40. New York: John Day, 1928.

    This article discusses how Russian railroads have been run since the Revolution and, in particular, the freight and passenger rates.

Hunter, Holland. "Costs, Freight Rates, and Location Decision in the USSR." In VALUE AND PLAN; ECONOMIC CALCULATION AND ORGANIZATION IN EASTERN EUROPE, edited by Gregory Grossman, pp. 322-43. Berkeley and Los Angeles: University of California Press, 1960.

    After examining some of the recent Soviet transportation literature, Holland notes that the Soviets are concerned with whether freight rates should be determined by cost of service or by value of service. Tables.

_____. "Soviet Railroads Since 1940." BULLETINS ON SOVIET ECONOMIC DEVELOPMENT 4 (September 1950): 10-20.

    Based on Soviet data, the author attempts to answer the following questions: Was rail transport a bottleneck during the postwar recovery? How do the railroads compare to their prewar status? What are the immediate and long-range prospects for the rail system? Tables.

_____. "Soviet Transportation Policies--A Current Review." In COMPARISONS OF THE U.S. AND SOVIET ECONOMIES, U.S. Congress. Joint Economic Committee, pp. 189-99. Washington, D.C.: Government Printing Office, 1959.

    The author discusses the major policy issues and summarizes transportation prospects up to 1965. Ten tables.

_____. SOVIET TRANSPORTATION POLICY. Cambridge, Mass.: Harvard University Press, 1957. xxiii, 416 p.

    This essay deals mainly with the period 1928-55 and examines Soviet economic policies toward the transport sector. Part one presents a historical and geographic overview and a sketch of government objectives. Part two analyzes transportation developments during 1928-55. Part three analyzes aspects of the railroad sector's relations with the rest of the economy. Charts, tables, and bibliography.

_____. SOVIET TRANSPORT EXPERIENCE: ITS LESSONS FOR OTHER COUNTRIES. Washington, D.C.: The Brookings Institution, 1968. xiii, 194 p.

    Holland examines three basic Soviet policy decisions--national self-sufficiency, dispersed development, and the primacy of industry which have influenced Soviet transport development. Factors which have limited and influenced transport development are also discussed,

Transportation and Communications

including railroads, trucks, and passenger transport in the Soviet Union. In his conclusion Hunter cites implications of Soviet transport policy for other countries. Tables and index.

_____. "The Soviet Transport Sector." In NEW DIRECTIONS IN THE SOVIET ECONOMY, U.S. Congress. Joint Economic Committee, pp. 569-91. Washington, D.C.: Government Printing Office, 1966.

This paper discusses policies and problems in both passenger and freight transport, as well as the implications for developed and underdeveloped economies. Ten tables.

_____. "Transport in Soviet and Chinese Development." ECONOMIC DEVELOPMENT AND CULTURAL CHANGE 14 (October 1965): 71-84.

Data on transport and transport capacity are presented in tables and a graph.

Kaplan, Norman M. "The Growth of Output and Inputs in Soviet Transport and Communications." AMERICAN ECONOMIC REVIEW 57 (December 1967): 1154-67.

Part one shows indexes revealing growth rates and compares the output increases with increases in capital and employment; U.S. data for similar sectors are assembled as a framework for appraising USSR performance. Part two explores retardation in output growth by distinguishing between changes in the rate of increase of factor inputs and changes in the rate of increase of combined factor productivity. Many tables. See also: Earl R. Brubaker. "Growth in Soviet Transport and Communications: Note." AMERICAN ECONOMIC REVIEW 59 (September 1969): 622-24.

_____. SOVIET TRANSPORT AND COMMUNICATIONS: OUTPUT INDEXES, 1928-1962. Santa Monica, Calif.: RAND Corp., 1965. v, 11 p.

This is a supplement to SOVIET TRANSPORT AND COMMUNICATIONS: OUTPUT INDEXES, 1928-1962. It extends the Soviet output indexes to 1963 and makes some corrections in the original study.

Lebed, Andrei I. "Party Calls for Increased Labor Productivity on Soviet Railroads." STUDIES ON THE SOVIET UNION n.s. 4, no. 4 (1965): 154-57.

The reasons for the timing of this call, as well as labor productivity, are discussed.

Mitchell, Earl L., and Painter, Priscilla. "Freight Transportation in the U.S.S.R." In ECONOMIC PERFORMANCE AND THE MILITARY BURDEN IN THE SOVIET UNION, U.S. Congress. Joint Economic Committee, pp. 38-42. Washington, D.C.: Government Printing Office, 1970.

Transportation and Communications

This outline of Soviet transport in the 1960s includes three tables.

Mirski, Michael S. "The Soviet Railway System: Policy and Operation." RUSSIAN REVIEW 13 (January 1954): 18-32.

This surveys Russian railroad construction and operation before and after the Revolution. A short table provides figures on expenditures for industry and communications in the first three five-year plans.

Obraztsov, V., et al. SOVIET TRANSPORT: RAIL, AIR, AND WATER. London: Soviet News, 1946. 63 p.

This booklet outlines the development of Soviet railways, air transport, the merchant fleet, and inland water transport.

Petrov, Vsevolod I., and Ushakov, Serafim. TRANSPORT IN THE USSR. Moscow: Novosti Press Agency Publishing House, n.d. 64 p.

This booklet surveys transport from before the Revolution and outlines the development of the various modes of transport.

Redding, David A. "Employment and Labour Productivity in USSR Railroads, 1928-1950." SOVIET STUDIES 5 (July 1953): 32-43.

This paper presents and annotates certain railroad time series culled from numerous official Soviet sources. Three tables.

Saller, H. "Communications." In RED ECONOMICS, edited by Gerhard Dobbert, pp. 183-207. Boston: Houghton Mifflin, 1932.

The author discusses the development of transportation systems in the Soviet Union, particularly railroads. Russian transport policy after the Civil War; transportation in the Five-Year Plan; the importance of transportation in developing natural resources; difficulties in maintaining and extending rail transport systems; electrification of transportation; and waterways are reviewed briefly.

Shadrin, Nicholas G. "The Soviet Merchant Marine, A Late Developing Economic Growth Sector." In SOVIET ECONOMIC PROSPECTS FOR THE SEVENTIES, U.S. Congress. Joint Economic Committee, pp. 719-65. Washington, D.C.: Government Printing Office, 1973.

Topics discussed include the stages of development, the need for an expanding merchant marine, aspects of Soviet merchant marine expansion, organization, efficiency, and fishing. Tables.

Tverskoi, K. N. THE UNIFIED TRANSPORT SYSTEM OF THE U.S.S.R. London: Victor Gollancy, 1935. 176 p.

Topics discussed include transport planning, the inheritance from tsarist Russia, and transport networks by region. Index and map.

Westwood, J. N. "Soviet Railway Development." SOVIET STUDIES 11 (July 1959): 22-48.

> Westwood reviews railways not under the Ministry of Transport, general history, technical base, freight traffic, and passenger service. Four tables.

_____. SOVIET RAILWAYS TODAY. New York: The Citadel Press, 1963. 192 p. Illustrated.

> This detailed account of Soviet railways concerns the infrastructure; electric, diesel, and steam locomotives; and freight and passenger services. There are many photographs of engines and stations and sketches of elevators and plans of railcars. Index.

Williams, Ernest W. "Some Aspects of the Structure and Growth of Soviet Transportation." In COMPARISONS OF THE U.S. AND SOVIET ECONOMIES, U.S. Congress. Joint Economic Committee, pp. 177-87. Washington, D.C.: Government Printing Office, 1959.

> The author discusses some of the unusual features in Soviet transportation development; Soviet-American freight traffic comparisons; Soviet rail operations; and postwar intensification of railway operations. Three tables.

_____. "Soviet Transportation Development: A Comparison With the U.S." AMERICAN ECONOMIC REVIEW 48 (May 1958): 412-21.

> This is a discussion of the development of the Soviet transportation system with tables. The emphasis is on railroads. For further discussion, see: Hans Heymann, Jr., and Holland Hunter. "Measuring Production in the USSR--Discussion." AMERICAN ECONOMIC REVIEW 48 (May 1958): 422-27.

Williams, Ernest, et al. FREIGHT TRANSPORTATION IN THE SOVIET UNION-- INCLUDING COMPARISONS WITH THE UNITED STATES. Princeton, N.J.: Princeton University Press, for National Bureau of Economic Research, 1962. xxi, 221 p.

> The first chapter traces the composition and growth of Soviet and U.S. freight transportation. The remainder of the book discusses Soviet rail traffic, the factors affecting rail traffic, and railway operation. Many tables, bibliography, and index.

Chapter 24

SCIENCE, TECHNOLOGY, AND THE ECONOMY

THE PERIOD UP TO 1860

Home, R. W. "Science as a Career in Eighteenth Century Russia: The Case of F. U. T. Aepinus." SLAVONIC AND EAST EUROPEAN REVIEW 51, no. 122 (1973): 75-94.

> This survey of a scientist's career provides an informative view of the problems and institutional framework of research and development in eighteenth-century Russia.

THE PERIOD AFTER 1917

Baritz, Joseph. "Problems of Mechanization and Automation in the USSR." STUDIES ON THE SOVIET UNION n.s. 3 (December 1960): 58-71.

> This article reviews the degree of automation in Soviet industry in the late 1950s, finds it wanting, and attributes the failure to automate as quickly as possible to red tape, bureaucracy, lack of interest, and unwillingness to accept the risks of innovation. A table presents the percentages of mechanization in selected branches of industry.

Boretsky, Michael. "Comparative Progress in Technology, Productivity, and Economic Efficiency: U.S.S.R. vs. U.S.A." In NEW DIRECTIONS IN THE SOVIET ECONOMY, U.S. Congress. Joint Economic Committee, pp. 133-256. Washington, D.C.: Government Printing Office, 1966.

> This paper first discusses methodology and findings; presents comparisons of technological progress and factor productivity; and, finally, discusses implications of the findings and sources of inefficiency in the Soviet economy. Many tables.

Brubaker, Earl R. "The Age of Capital and Growth in the Soviet Nonagricultural Nonresidential Sector." SOVIET STUDIES 21 (January 1970): 350-59.

Science, Technology, and the Economy

   This article focuses on the nonagricultural sector of the Soviet economy and explores the possible quantitative importance of the contribution to growth made by technical change related to investment in fixed capital. Tables.

_____. "Embodied Technology, the Asymptotic Behavior of Capital's Age, and Soviet Growth." REVIEW OF ECONOMICS AND STATISTICS 50 (August 1968): 304-11.

   This paper explores the usefulness of the hypothesis of embodied technical change for providing insight into sources of the growth in output. Two tables.

Campbell, Robert W. "Problems of Technical Progress in the USSR." In THE SOVIET ECONOMY; A BOOK OF READINGS, edited by Morris Bornstein and Daniel Fusfeld, pp. 348-64. 4th ed. Homewood, Ill.: R. D. Irwin, 1974.

   This paper discusses research and development in the Soviet economy and lower-level initiative and cooperation.

Cohn, Viktor, and Buchta, J. W. "Soviet Science and Technology." In SOVIET UNION--PARADOX AND CHANGE, edited by Robert T. Holt and J. W. Buchta, pp. 118-37. New York: Holt, Rinehart and Winston, 1962.

   The author recounts the secret of rapid development in science and technology; "regimentation of science--Stalinist style"; the influence of Stalin's death and Sputnik's success; a comparison of Soviet science and technology with their U.S. counterpart; and the future trends.

Davies, R[obert]. W. "Science and the Soviet Economy." In ECONOMIC CONCENTRATION, U.S. Senate. Committee on the Judiciary, pp. 4332-45. Washington, D.C.: Government Printing Office, 1969.

   This paper is an historical sketch of the organization of Russian science and research and development institutions from Peter the Great up to the 1960s.

Dobrov, Gennady M. "Science Policy and Assessment in the Soviet Union." INTERNATIONAL SOCIAL SCIENCE JOURNAL 25, no. 3 (1973): 305-25.

   This article examines science policy and outlines the structure of the discipline which aims to formulate the theory behind it. Graphs and tables.

Gibson, Roland. "Recent Technological Progress in the Soviet Union." SOCIAL RESEARCH 22 (July 1955): 183-98.

   Recent technical progress as reported in the Soviet press is surveyed in such areas as iron and steel, electric power, automatic machine tools, coal mining, excavators, and tractors.

Grossman, Gregory. "Innovation and Information in the Soviet Economy." AMERICAN ECONOMIC REVIEW 56 (May 1966): 118-30.

　　Topics covered include uniform technological policy and plans for the development and introduction of new technology. For further discussion, see: Alexander Eckstein and Joseph S. Berliner. "Soviet Economy--Discussion." AMERICAN ECONOMIC REVIEW 56 (May 1966): 154-58.

Hughes, Francis F. "Incentive for Soviet Initiative." ECONOMIC JOURNAL 56 (September 1946): 415-25.

　　This article is a study of the "Act Governing Inventions and Technical Improvements," ratified by the Council of Commisars on March 5, 1941.

_____. "Soviet Inventions Awards." ECONOMIC JOURNAL 55 (June-September 1945): 291-97.

　　The provisions of the "Act Governing Inventions and Technical Improvements," published by the Central Committee in April 1931, are reviewed.

Hutchings, Raymond [F.] [D.]. "Soviet Technology Policy." In SOVIET ECONOMIC PROSPECTS FOR THE SEVENTIES, U.S. Congress. Joint Economic Committee, pp. 71-86. Washington, D.C.: Government Printing Office, 1973.

　　Topics discussed include the general directions of technical progress, the location of capital investments, technical progress in particular sectors of the economy, policy changes, obstacles, opportunities, motivations for technical progress, and measurement of its effects.

Kantorovitch, V. "U.S.S.R.: An Essay in Self-criticism. The Problem of Technical and Scientific Supervisory and Managerial Staff." ANNALS OF PUBLIC AND CO-OPERATIVE ECONOMY 39 (April-June 1968): 295-96.

　　A noted Soviet economist surveys shortcomings in the technical and scientific aspects of the Soviet economy.

Kas'ianenko, Vasilii I. HOW THE SOVIET ECONOMY WON TECHNICAL INDEPENDENCE. Moscow: Progress Publishers, 1966. 183 p.

　　This Soviet book contains four chapters on how the USSR achieved economic independence. Chapter 1 discusses Lenin's plan for achieving economic independence; chapter 2 deals with the struggle for technical progress; chapter 3 examines how foreign technical assistance was used; and chapter 4 describes the great socialist industrial state.

Korsakov, E. "Technological Progress and Its Effect on Soviet Dockworkers." INTERNATIONAL LABOUR REVIEW 105 (June 1972): 531-42.

The experience in Soviet ports in cargo handling and how the introduction of new technology altered the organization of dock work is reviewed.

Leontief, Wassily W. "Scientific and Technological Research in Russia." AMERICAN SLAVIC AND EAST EUROPEAN REVIEW 4 (December 1945): 70-79.

This is a review of scientific and technological research in the USSR, 1917-39. Topics covered include development, organization, and the roles of the Academy of Sciences, industry, and agriculture. Six tables.

Organisation for Economic Co-operation and Development. Directorate for Scientific Affairs. SCIENCE POLICY IN THE USSR. Paris: O.E.C.D., 1968. xxx, 738 p.

This study discusses the planning of research and development, scientific manpower in the early 1960s, research in the academies, and the relations between science and industry.

Sutton, Antony C. WESTERN TECHNOLOGY AND SOVIET ECONOMIC DEVELOPMENT: 1917 TO 1930. Stanford, Calif.: Hoover Institution Press, 1968. xx, 381 p.

This book discusses the history of foreign concessions and technological transfers and their significance in the Soviet economy. Many tables, charts, glossary, and maps.

_____. WESTERN TECHNOLOGY AND SOVIET ECONOMIC DEVELOPMENT: 1930-1945. Stanford, Calif.: Hoover Institution Press, 1971. xxiv, 401 p.

This is a detailed sector-by-sector study of Western technical assistance to the Soviet Union. Particular chapters are also devoted to methodology, expropriation of foreign concessions, the technical transfer process, technical assimilation, and sectoral growth rates. Graphs and tables.

"The Technological Gap in Russia." In ECONOMIC CONCENTRATION, U.S. Senate. Committee on the Judiciary, pp. 4507-9. Washington, D.C.: Government Printing Office, 1969.

This article reports that the Soviets have found their system short on incentives for technological innovation and are working on a remedy.

Voronitsyn, Sergei. "The Social Consequences of Automation in the USSR." STUDIES ON THE SOVIET UNION n.s. 3, no. 1 (1963): 56-63.

This paper surveys the official Soviet attitude toward automation and discusses problems involved in implementing automation.

Chapter 25

STUDIES OF PARTICULAR INDUSTRIES AND SECTORS

THE PERIOD UP TO 1860

Baron, Samuel H. "Vasilii Shorin: Seventeenth Century Russian Merchant Extraordinary." CANADIAN-AMERICAN SLAVIC STUDIES 6 (Winter 1972): 503-48.

    The life history of this merchant is used to highlight the realities of economic life in Russia during the third quarter of the seventeenth century.

Fisher, Alan W. "Muscovy and the Black Sea Slave Trade." CANADIAN-AMERICAN SLAVIC STUDIES 6 (Winter 1972): 575-94.

    This is an exhaustive study of the role of Russia in the Islamic slave trade around the Black Sea. A table gives collected estimates of numbers of captives from Tartar raids by location for selected years between 1468 and 1694.

Fisher, Raymond H. THE RUSSIAN FUR TRADE 1550-1700. Berkeley and Los Angeles: University of California Press, 1943. xi, 275 p. Illustrated.

    This book contains chapters on the following topics: the fur trade and the opening up and conquest of Siberia; the acquisition of furs by the Muscovite state; the preservation of the state's fur trade; the fur income of the state; the disposal of furs by the state; the private trade in furs; and the export of furs to Europe and Asia. Bibliography, index, and foldout map.

Goldman, Marshall I. "The Relocation and Growth of the Pre-revolutionary Russian Ferrous Metal Industry." EXPLORATIONS IN ENTREPRENEURIAL HISTORY 9 (October 1956): 19-36.

    This paper discusses the decline and stagnation of the Urals ferrous metal industry (1825-70) and the regeneration of the industry when it was transferred to the Ukraine (1870-90). Tables. A map shows the development of Krivoi Rog and the Donets Basin regions.

Studies of Particular Industries

Kahan, Arcadius. "Entrepreneurship in the Early Development of Iron Manufacturing in Russia." ECONOMIC DEVELOPMENT AND CULTURAL CHANGE 10 (July 1962): 395-422.

   Topics covered include prehistory and government attitudes toward the iron industry; origins and behavior of entrepreneurs; geographical shifts in industry; government attitudes toward private entrepreneurs; and entrepreneurial relations with labor, management, and technical personnel.

_____. "A Proposed Mercantilist Code in the Russian Iron Industry, 1734-36." EXPLORATIONS IN ENTREPRENEURIAL HISTORY II 2, no. 2 (1965): 75-89.

   This article reviews several articles in Russian on such topics as monopoly versus competition; motivation for entering industry; problems of product mix; uniformity in quality and prices; wages; finance; welfare and child labor; and supervision.

Koutaissoff, Elisabeth. "The Ural Metal Industry in the Eighteenth Century." ECONOMIC HISTORY REVIEW II 4, no. 2 (1951): 252-55.

   This review essay is based on the following works: Roger Portal. L'OURAL AU XVIII SIECLE. Etude d'historie economique et sociale. Paris: Collection historique de l'Institut d'Etudes Slaves, 1950. xiv, 434 p.; and B. B. Kafengauz. ISTORIYA KHOZIAISTVA DEMIDOVYKH V XVIII-XIX vv. Vol. 1. Moscow-Leningrad: Academy of Sciences of the USSR, 1949. 524 p.

THE PERIOD 1860-1917

Faas, Vladimir V. RUSSIA'S EXPORT TRADE IN TIMBER AND THE IMPORTANCE OF THE FORESTS OF NORTH EUROPEAN RUSSIA. New York: Youroveta Home and Foreign Trade Co., 1919. 35 p.

   Faas discusses the importance of Russian trade in timber on the world market; timber export from Russia between 1904-13; the timber industry of north European Russia; the administration of forest areas; and the prospects for developing other wood industries. Tables.

Raffalovich, Alexis. "The State Monopoly of Spirits in Russia, and Its Influence on the Prosperity of the Population." ROYAL STATISTICAL SOCIETY JOURNAL. Ser. A 64 (March 1901): 1-30.

   The liquor industry in Russia and the state spirit monopoly introduced in 1895 are explored. An appendix consisting of eleven tables presents data, and a discussion of the paper follows.

Westwood, J. N. "John Hughes and Russian Metallurgy." ECONOMIC HISTORY REVIEW. 2d ser. 17 (April 1965): 564-69.

Studies of Particular Industries

This is a biographical sketch of a Welsh ironmaster who played an important role in the development of metal-working in Russia in the late nineteenth century. General information on Russian metal-working is also included.

THE PERIOD AFTER 1917

Abouchar, Alan. "Rationality in the Prewar Soviet Cement Industry." SOVIET STUDIES 19 (October 1967): 211-31.

This paper examines the impact of the hydraulic cement industry on the demand for transportation services to determine whether growth in the demand for rail transport was a necessary part of development or the result of poor marketing, poor product mix, and misallocation of investment. Four tables.

_____. SOVIET PLANNING AND SPATIAL EFFICIENCY: THE PREWAR CEMENT INDUSTRY. Bloomington and London: Indiana University Press for the International Affairs Center, 1971. x, 134 p.

This book discusses the product mix, raw materials, costs, management, operation, and locational efficiency of the Soviet cement industry before 1941. Index.

"Agitation Amongst the Shop Assistants." SOVIET STUDIES 5 (July 1953): 99-102.

This is a partial translation of N. Chigirin. "Exemplary Service for Shoppers." BLOKNOT AGITATORA, no. 13 (1952).

Algvere, Karl V. FOREST ECONOMY IN THE U.S.S.R.: AN ANALYSIS OF SOVIET COMPETITIVE POTENTIALITIES. Stockholm: Royal College of Forestry, 1966. 449 p.

This exhaustive study of forestry in the Soviet Union first covers vegetation zones, natural conditions, statistics of forest resources, population and settlement, forest industries, and transport facilities. Part two analyzes management of forest land in tsarist Russia and the Soviet Union; compares management under the two regimes; and even discusses the application of Marxist doctrine to forest management. Part three analyzes potentials for production in the USSR by region. Part four analyzes Soviet foreign trade in forest products. Many tables, maps, selected bibliography, and index.

Bauer, Raymond A., and Field, Mark G. "Ironic Contrast: U.S. and U.S.S.R. Drug Industries." HARVARD BUSINESS REVIEW 40 (September-October 1962): 89-97.

This article compares the strengths and weaknesses of the American and Soviet drug industries and concludes that U.S. reliance on

Studies of Particular Industries

private firms and research has important advantages.

_____. "The Soviet and the American Pharmaceutical Systems: Some Paradoxical Contrasts." In DRUG INDUSTRY ACT OF 1962, pp. 344-55. Washington, D.C.: Government Printing Office, 1962.

> The authors are attempting to discern why the retail prices of pharmaceuticals in the Soviet Union have increased while the unit cost of production has gone down. Soviet noncommercial drug research and the control of quality and supply of drugs are examined.

Bernstein, S. A. THE FINANCIAL AND ECONOMIC RESULTS OF THE WORKING OF THE LENA GOLDFIELDS CO., LTD. London: Blackfriars Press, 1930. 36 p.

> The author discusses the activities of the Lena Goldfields Company during a four-and-a-half year period and presents a detailed account of factors which led to the failure of an enterprise "calculated to last many years."

Boretsky, Michael. "The Soviet Challenge to U.S. Machine Building; A Study in Production and Technological Policy." In DIMENSIONS OF SOVIET ECONOMIC POWER, U.S. Congress. Joint Economic Committee, pp. 71-143. Washington, D.C.: Government Printing Office, 1962.

> The study is divided into four parts: (1) the methodology employed; (2) comprehensive summary of U.S. and Soviet machine-building industries in 1958; (3) Soviet strategy to implement their challenge; and (4) data on development of industries in the United States and Soviet Union since 1958.

Bowles, W. Donald. "Cost-Price Relationships and the Location of Soviet Industry: A Case Study (Timber)." INTERNATIONAL ECONOMIC REVIEW 9 (October 1968): 273-93.

> The state of the Soviet timber industry is surveyed, producer and consumer locational preference is considered, and problems of planning and efficiency in the logging industry are explored. Four tables.

_____. "The Logging Industry: A Backward Branch of the Soviet Economy." AMERICAN SLAVIC AND EAST EUROPEAN REVIEW 17 (December 1958): 426-38.

> This article surveys the development of the Soviet logging industry, 1928-57. A table provides index numbers.

_____. "Pricing in Soviet Timber Sales." SOVIET STUDIES 13 (July 1961): 23-34.

Studies of Particular Industries

The Soviet practice of establishing charges for timber transferred to enterprises and institutions is examined since the inception of national economic planning in 1928. Emphasis is placed on current policies. Four tables.

_____. "Soviet Timber: Two Steps Forward, One Step Back." SOVIET STUDIES 16 (April 1965): 377-405.

This paper concerns the resource problems, labor force, investment, productivity, wages, prices, profitability, administration, and short-run prospects. Five tables.

Brubaker, Earl R. "Some Effects of Policy on Productivity in Soviet and American Crude Petroleum Extraction." JOURNAL OF INDUSTRIAL ECONOMICS 18 (November 1969): 33-52.

This paper traces features of Soviet and American economic organization and petroleum production policies and stresses how they conform to or deviate from the normative model. Tables.

Bush, Keith. "Soviet Gold Production and Reserves Reconsidered." SOVIET STUDIES 17 (April 1966): 490-93.

The problems of estimating gold production and reserves are discussed. A table gives estimates for 1946-64.

Campbell, Robert W. THE ECONOMICS OF SOVIET OIL AND GAS. Baltimore: Johns Hopkins University Press, 1968. xv, 279 p.

The book is a detailed economic study of the Soviet petroleum industry, which discusses recent developments and future possibilities. Campbell examines the USSR's future as an oil exporter. Tables, index, and maps.

_____. "Some Issues in Soviet Energy Policy for the Seventies." In SOVIET ECONOMIC PROSPECTS FOR THE SEVENTIES, U.S. Congress. Joint Economic Committee, pp. 45-55. Washington, D.C.: Government Printing Office, 1973.

Topics discussed include reserves, location, technological demand, domestic demand, and projections of supply and demand.

Clark, M. Gardner. "Economics and Technology: The Case of Soviet Steel." In STUDY OF THE SOVIET ECONOMY, edited by Nicolas Spulber, pp. 17-31. Bloomington: Indiana University Press, 1961.

The paper is concerned with the factors which have contributed to the outstanding success of the Soviet steel industry.

_____. THE ECONOMICS OF SOVIET STEEL. Cambridge, Mass.: Harvard University Press, 1956. xiv, 400 p.

Studies of Particular Industries

The growth of production and investment in the iron and steel industry and its main branches is discussed in part one. Part two is concerned with specialization and the scale of both plant and equipment. Part three deals with location and development, and part four discusses the changing pattern of productivity, with emphasis on productivity as a substitute for capital investment. Seven statistical appendices.

_____. "The Soviet Steel Industry." JOURNAL OF ECONOMIC HISTORY 12, no. 4 (1952): 396-410.

This paper describes the administrative organization and planning system of the typical large Soviet steel plant and then shows how the plant director carries out one of his essential functions within the institutional framework. Some data on salaries and productivity of Magnitogorsk blast furnaces are given in tables.

Daukas, Anthony. "Machine Tool Production in the United States and USSR." In DIMENSIONS OF SOVIET ECONOMIC POWER, U.S. Congress. Joint Economic Committee, pp. 165-80. Washington, D.C.: Government Printing Office, 1962.

The article covers the patterns of growth, problems of comparisons with the United States, product mix, organization of production, inventories, foreign trade, and research in the machine tool industry.

Davies, R[obert]. W. "The Builders' Conference." SOVIET STUDIES 6 (April 1955): 443-57.

This article summarizes discussions at the Builders' Conference (November 31-December 7, 1954). Discussed were the industry in general, new materials, labor, administration, planning, finance, and architecture.

_____. "The Building Reforms and Architecture." SOVIET STUDIES 7 (April 1956): 418-29.

This note reports on recent orders issued to the building industry. A table on wages for building workers is included.

De Felice, Frank. "Productivity Changes in Soviet Distribution." ECONOMIC JOURNAL 79 (March 1969): 185-87.

This is a short digest of a paper studying changes in productivity in the distribution sector of the USSR economy, 1950-64.

_____. "Soviet Distribution Policy." RIVISTA INTERNAZIONALE DI SCIENZE ECONOMICHE E COMMERCIALI 15 (June 1968): 573-85.

Aspects of distribution policy discussed include continuation of pre-Soviet policies, the influence of rapid industrialization, and the effects of military and political factors.

"Developments in the Oil Industry of Central Asia and Kazakhstan, 1956-57." CENTRAL ASIAN REVIEW 6, no. 2 (1958): 180-89.

This article reports on oil and natural gas exploration, producing areas and refining in Central Asia and Kazakhstan.

Dobb, Maurice H. "Soviet Agriculture and the Chemical Industry." SLAVONIC REVIEW 24 (January 1946): 127-32.

This paper describes the Soviet chemical industry during the Third Five-Year Plan, which is sometimes referred to as the Chemical Plan. Dobb speculates on possible influence of the chemical industry on Russian agriculture.

Dodge, Norton T., and Dalrymple, Dana G. "The Stalingrad Tractor Plant in Early Soviet Planning." SOVIET STUDIES 18 (October 1966): 164-68.

This paper (1) reviews "source material on the general steps taken by the Soviet planners to develop a tractor industry" and (2) assesses the transition from plan to reality at Stalingrad.

Douglas, Paul H. "The Consumers' Cooperative Movement." In SOVIET RUSSIA IN THE SECOND DECADE, American Trade Union Delegation, pp. 253-67. New York: John Day, 1928.

This article analyzes the governing of the consumer cooperative movement; the price policy of the cooperatives; and the distributive system.

Ebel, Robert E. COMMUNIST TRADE IN OIL AND GAS: AN EVALUATION OF THE FUTURE EXPORT CAPABILITY OF THE SOVIET BLOC. New York: Praeger, 1970. xx, 447 p.

Part one surveys the oil and gas industry from tsarist times; expansion and contraction between 1918 and 1940; postwar exports of oil; the pricing policy of the Soviet Union; and trade projections up to 1975. Part two contains a cross-section of pertinent material that has appeared in the Soviet and Eastern European press during the last several years. Many tables, charts, and maps.

_____. THE PETROLEUM INDUSTRY OF THE SOVIET UNION. New York: American Petroleum Institute, 1961. 167 p.

The author discusses energy in the USSR; organization and control; capital investment, pricing, and wages; petroleum research; exploration, production, and refining; and consumption, storage, transport, and trade. Tables, charts, maps, and photographs.

Studies of Particular Industries

"Food Trade and Public Catering in Central Asia." CENTRAL ASIAN REVIEW 8, no. 2 (1960): 151-59.

>Topics discussed include changes in eating habits; food consumption, supply, and distribution; supply and sale of alcohol; and public catering.

Gallik, Dimitri [M.]. "Soviet Machine Building--A Critical Review." BULLETIN OF THE ASSOCIATION FOR THE STUDY OF SOVIET-TYPE ECONOMIES 3 (March 1961): 8-13.

>A critical review of G. Smirnov and N. Yasnovskiy. "The Prospects for Competition Between the USSR and the United States in the Sphere of Machine Building." PLANOVOE KHOZIAISTVO [Planned economy] no. 8 (1960): 81-91. This article purports to show that Soviet machine-building will soon catch up with that of the United States. Tables.

Gerschenkron, Alexander, and Erlich, Alexander. A DOLLAR INDEX OF SOVIET MACHINERY OUTPUT, 1927-28 TO 1937. Santa Monica, Calif.: RAND Corp., 1951. v, 357 p.

>This study contains a description of procedures used, the results obtained, and an appraisal of the results and methods used. Numerous appendices.

Gerschenkron, Alexander, and Nimitz, Nancy. A DOLLAR INDEX OF SOVIET IRON AND STEEL OUTPUT. Santa Monica, Calif.: RAND Corp., 1953. 266 p.

>This is a recomputation of output of the Soviet iron and steel industry in U.S. dollars of 1939 purchasing power for the period 1927/28-37.

Goldman, Marshall I. "The Cost and Efficiency of Distribution in the Soviet Union." QUARTERLY JOURNAL OF ECONOMICS 76 (August 1962): 437-53.

>This paper compares Russian and American distribution markups and considers the lower costs of distribution in the Soviet Union as an indicator of higher productivity. Six tables. For further discussion, see: Myron H. Ross. " 'The Cost and Efficiency of Distribution in the Soviet Union': Comment." QUARTERLY JOURNAL OF ECONOMICS 77 (August 1963): 503-4; Marshall I. Goldman. " 'The Cost of Efficiency of Distribution in the Soviet Union': Reply." QUARTERLY JOURNAL OF ECONOMICS 78 (February 1964): 177-78.

_____. "Marketing: A Lesson for Marx." HARVARD BUSINESS REVIEW 38 (January-February 1960): 79-86.

>This article traces the development of marketing techniques in the Soviet Union.

Studies of Particular Industries

_____. "The Marketing Structure in the Soviet Union." JOURNAL OF MARKETING 25 (July 1961): 7-14.

> The state-owned and controlled marketing structure of the Soviet Union, the largest in the world, is discussed. Three organization charts are included.

_____. "Retailing in the Soviet Union." JOURNAL OF MARKETING 24 (April 1960): 9-15.

> This article describes the Soviet retail network and the pattern of merchandising and examines some innovations in trade and distribution. A table provides figures on retail sales volume for selected years, 1940-58.

_____. SOVIET MARKETING; DISTRIBUTION IN A CONTROLLED ECONOMY. New York: Free Press of Glencoe, 1963. 229 p.

> This study is concerned only with the domestic sale of consumer goods. It contains descriptions of the organization of the distribution system; the trade-planning mechanism; pricing procedures, the system of financial controls, the effects on management incentives; and the costs of distribution in the Soviet Union. Tables, bibliography, and index.

Granick, David. "Economic Development and Productivity Analysis: The Case of Soviet Metal-Working." QUARTERLY JOURNAL OF ECONOMICS 71 (May 1957): 205-33.

> The article deals with the problem of factor proportions, specifically, with capital intensity and the substitution of labor for capital. It also considers problems of introducing modern methods without prior local experience.

_____. "On Patterns of Technological Choice in Soviet Industry." AMERICAN ECONOMIC REVIEW 52 (May 1962): 149-57.

> Granick examines the interlinked aspects of the technological development of the metal-fabricating industries during the first two five-year plans. Actual development is compared to alternative development paths which were clearly known to Soviet planners. For a further discussion, see: Lloyd G. Reynolds et al. "Soviet Economic Planning--Discussion." AMERICAN ECONOMIC REVIEW 52 (May 1962): 158-64.

_____. "Organization and Technology in Soviet Metalworking: Some Conditioning Factors." AMERICAN ECONOMIC REVIEW 47 (May 1957): 631-42.

> The effects of Soviet social-economic institutions upon the Soviet economic development process is examined. The article concludes with some comments on future prospects. For further discussion,

Studies of Particular Industries

see: Gregory Grossman et al. "Soviet Economic Developments-- Discussion." AMERICAN ECONOMIC REVIEW 47 (May 1957): 643-52.

_____. SOVIET METAL-FABRICATING AND ECONOMIC DEVELOPMENT-- PRACTICES VERSUS POLICY. Madison: University of Wisconsin Press, 1967. xiv, 367 p.

    The book's first part considers the positive investment in tangible capital, worker training, and new technology and the organizational aspects of Soviet metal-fabricating development. Tables and index.

Hajenko, Fedor. "Public Services in the USSR." STUDIES ON THE SOVIET UNION n.s. 2, no. 3 (1963): 75-82.

    This article discusses Soviet concern with public services and presents evidence that these services are poorly provided.

Hanson, Philip. "The Assortment Problem in Soviet Retail Trade." SOVIET STUDIES 14 (April 1963): 347-64.

    This article explains how the Soviet economic system gets a particular assortment of consumer goods into the shops and examines suggestions by various Soviet writers about how this process can be improved. Two tables.

_____. "The Structure and Efficiency of Soviet Retailing and Wholesaling." SOVIET STUDIES 16 (October 1954): 186-208.

    This article considers the statistical evidence that in this sector, planning is less successful than a market system. Eleven tables.

Hassmann, Heinrich. OIL IN THE SOVIET UNION: HISTORY, GEOGRAPHY, PROBLEMS. Edited and translated by Alfred M. Leeston. Princeton, N.J.: Princeton University Press, 1953. xvi, 173 p.

    The author discusses the Russian oil industry against the background of world politics and economics. He considers the basis of the Russian oil industry, the development of both the tsarist and Soviet oil industries, characteristics of the oil production regions, and the demand and the satisfaction of demand for oil in the Soviet Union. Charts, bibliography, index, and maps.

Haugland, Anton. "Notes on the Soviet Fishing Industry." ECONOMICS OF PLANNING 4, no. 3 (1964): 165-74.

    A review of the organization and operation of the Soviet fishing industry. Tables.

Studies of Particular Industries

Hemy, Geoffrey. THE SOVIET CHEMICAL INDUSTRY. London: Leonard Hill; New York: Barnes and Noble, 1971. 382 p.

> The author describes capital construction and depreciation; manpower; costs and materials; profits and incentives as well as the makeup of an individual factory. The text is based on information in Soviet sources. Bibliography and index.

Herman, Leon M. "Russian Manganese and the American Market." AMERICAN SLAVIC AND EAST EUROPEAN REVIEW 10 (1951): 272-81.

> This article attempts to assess the relationship between Soviet production, consumption, and exports of manganese, based on prewar data. Tables.

Hodgkins, Jordan A. SOVIET POWER: ENERGY RESOURCES, PRODUCTION AND POTENTIALS. Englewood Cliffs, N.J.: Prentice-Hall, 1961. xviii, 190 p.

> This book discusses production and consumption of coal, oil shale, oil, and natural gas. Tables and statistical appendices.

Hodgman, Donald R. "Soviet Machinery Output." AMERICAN SLAVIC AND EAST EUROPEAN REVIEW 12 (1953): 57-71.

> This article is a review of the conclusions and methodology of Alexander Gerschenkron. A DOLLAR INDEX OF SOVIET MACHINERY OUTPUT, 1927-28 TO 1937. Santa Monica, Calif.: RAND Corp., 1951.

Hubbard, Leonard E. SOVIET TRADE AND DISTRIBUTION. London: Macmillan and Co., 1938. xiii, 381 p.

> Part one describes the early phases in the organization of distribution; parts two and three outline planned distribution during the first and second five-year plans; part four presents a detailed account of the organization of distribution; part five deals with the economic aspects of Soviet trade; and part six discusses the "social dividend." Appendices, glossary, and index.

Jasny, Naum. "Prospects of the Soviet Iron and Steel Industry." SOVIET STUDIES 14 (January 1963): 275-94.

> Prospects from 1960 to 1980 are discussed, with emphasis on the difficulties of fulfilling the Twenty-Year Plan. Three tables.

Kaufman, Adam. SMALL-SCALE INDUSTRY IN THE SOVIET UNION. New York: National Bureau of Economic Research, 1962. xvi, 95 p.

> Chapter one gives a historical sketch of the role of small-scale industry. Chapter two discusses the nature of statistics on small-scale industry. Chapter three outlines the state of small-scale

Studies of Particular Industries

industry on the eve of the Revolution. Chapter four focuses on the condition of small-scale industry during the pre-plan period. Chapter five describes the absorption of small-scale industry during the plan period. Chapter six deals with indexes of small-scale production. Many tables, appendix, and bibliography.

Lamet, Stefan. "Soviet Fuel and Power." SOVIET STUDIES 4 (July 1952): 1-14.

This article recounts the growth in the Soviet fuel and power industry from the Revolution to 1950. Seven tables.

⎯⎯⎯⎯. "A Survey of the Soviet Engineering Industries." SOVIET STUDIES 5 (April 1954): 335-56.

Topics covered in this paper include the foundation of the modern industry; growth in output; manpower; the Third Five-Year Plan; war effects; postwar development; machine tools; motor vehicles; agricultural machinery; power equipment; railway equipment; and machinery for light industry. Eight tables.

Lee, J. Richard. "The Fuels Industries." In ECONOMIC PERFORMANCE AND THE MILITARY BURDEN IN THE SOVIET UNION, U.S. Congress. Joint Economic Committee, pp. 33-37. Washington, D.C.: Government Printing Office, 1970.

Four tables are included in this review of the fuel industries in the 1960s.

⎯⎯⎯⎯. "The Soviet Petroleum Industry: Promise and Problems." In SOVIET ECONOMIC PROSPECTS FOR THE SEVENTIES, U.S. Congress. Joint Economic Committee, pp. 283-90. Washington, D.C.: Government Printing Office, 1973.

Reserves and production of oil and natural gas are discussed. Seven tables.

Littlepage, John D., and Demaree, Bess. IN SEARCH OF SOVIET GOLD. New York: Harcourt, Brace & World, 1937.

This book recounts the experience of an American expert hired to increase Soviet gold output in the period 1928-37.

Markham, James W. "Is Advertising Important in the Soviet Economy?" JOURNAL OF MARKETING 28 (April 1964): 31-37.

Topics covered include the orthodox Communist view of advertising; early forms; recent developments; advertising copy; the selection of media and policy of advertisements; attitudes toward advertising; and lessons for the West.

Studies of Particular Industries

Moorsteen, Richard H. PRICES AND PRODUCTION OF MACHINERY IN THE SOVIET UNION: 1928-1958. Cambridge, Mass.: Harvard University Press, 1962. xi, 498 p.

> This study measures trends in the prices and output of machinery in the USSR from fiscal year 1927/28 through fiscal year 1958. Many tables.

Moskoff, William. "Retail-Wholesale-Manufacturing Relationships in the Soviet Leather Footwear Industry." QUARTERLY REVIEW OF ECONOMICS AND BUSINESS 12 (Summer 1972): 39-52.

> This article examines the relationship of the retail, wholesale, and manufacturing sectors to determine the factors which led to a dramatic fall in the sales-inventory ratio in the post-Stalin period. Four tables.

Nazaroff, Alexander. "The Soviet Oil Industry." RUSSIAN REVIEW 1 (November 1941): 81-89.

> This general survey of the Soviet oil industry before Germany attacked Russia on June 22, 1941, covers its growth since 1938 and its processing capacity.

Nodel', V. A. SUPPLY AND TRADE IN THE U.S.S.R. London: Victor Gollancz, 1934. 176 p.

> The following topics are discussed: the standard of living; characteristics of Soviet trade; consumers' cooperatives and workers' supply departments; the system of state collections; and vegetable gardens and their importance in the workers' supplies. Index.

Ofer, Gur. THE SERVICE SECTOR IN SOVIET ECONOMIC GROWTH. Cambridge, Mass.: Harvard University Press, 1973. xiv, 202 p.

> In this book the author tries to explain why the service industries occupy such a small place in the Soviet economy. The discussion considers general theories of economic development and industrial structure and the nature of the socialist economic system and its growth strategy. Many tables and graphs.

"The Oil Resources of Central Asia and Kazakhstan." CENTRAL ASIAN REVIEW 4, no. 3 (1956): 276-86.

> This article explores current oil production in Central Asia and Kazakhstan, with some description of oil resources and their prospects. Tables listing the major oilfields in each republic, and giving available details of each, are appended.

Palubinskas, Feliksas. "The Growing Importance of Marketing in Soviet Russia." WESTERN ECONOMIC JOURNAL 3 (Summer 1965): 274-87.

Studies of Particular Industries

Aspects discussed include marketing and ideology, merchandising, preparation of goods for marketing, handling, financing, risk, incentive, and dispersion of goods.

Phelps, D. M. "Soviet Marketing, Stronger Than We Think." HARVARD BUSINESS REVIEW 39 (July-August 1961): 69-80.

This paper surveys the effectiveness of the Soviet marketing system.

Poplyniko, Anatoli. "Chemical Fertilizer Production." STUDIES ON THE SOVIET UNION n.s. 4, no. 3 (1965): 59-65.

Four tables provide data as far back as 1928.

Powell, Raymond P. "An Index of Soviet Construction, 1927/28 to 1955." REVIEW OF ECONOMICS AND STATISTICS 41 (May 1959): 170-77.

The results of an effort to compare a constant-price index of Soviet construction are reported, and reliability is discussed. Two tables and a chart.

Rodin, Nicholas W. PRODUCTIVITY IN SOVIET IRON MINING 1890-1960. Santa Monica, Calif.: RAND Corp., 1953. 49 p.

This paper discusses the data, labor productivity for the entire industry, resource conditions, technological progress, personnel problems, geographic shifts, and the impact of these factors on labor productivity. Twelve tables.

Rosen, J. "Soviet Retail Trade: Turnover and Price Reductions in 1947-51." KYKLOS 5, no. 3 (1951-52): 181-96.

This paper covers the four retail price reductions during 1947-51, their significance, the volume of retail turnover, price reductions as a percentage of turnover, and the related change in saving. Seven tables.

Rushing, Francis W. "Growth, Capital-Output Ratios, and the Soviet Chemical Industry." ECONOMIA INTERNAZIONALE 25 (November 1972): 731-42.

This paper presents a model relating capital-output ratios to the growth rate, shows that the ratio has been rising for the chemical industry for a decade, and discusses the causes of this rise. Three tables.

Schroeder, Gertrude E. "The 'Reform' of the Supply System in Soviet Industry." SOVIET STUDIES 24 (July 1972): 97-119.

This article analyzes recent attempts to solve the problem of supply by a complex set of changes launched in 1965 as part of the general economic reform. Three tables.

Studies of Particular Industries

Shabad, Theodore. BASIC INDUSTRIAL RESOURCES OF THE U.S.S.R. New York: Columbia University Press, 1969. xiv, 393 p.

> Part one briefly discusses the general production trade and locational patterns of each resource sector and stresses changes in the last two decades. Part two is a regional survey of specific mining centers and other resource complexes by major regions, with information on start of operations, output, and development problems.

Shimkin, Dimitri B. THE SOVIET MINERALS-FUELS INDUSTRIES, 1928-1958: A STATISTICAL SURVEY. U.S. Department of Commerce. Bureau of the Census. International Population Statistics Report, Series P-90, no. 19. Washington, D.C.: Government Printing Office, 1963. 183 p.

> This study represents a comprehensive study of the major statistical series bearing on the mineral-fuels industries during 1928-58. It includes a detailed account of the growth of Soviet mineral-fuels production, as well as some comparisons with the United States. Bibliography.

Skurski, Roger. "The Factor Proportions Problem in Soviet Internal Trade." SOVIET STUDIES 23 (January 1972): 450-64.

> This paper estimates the inputs of labor and capital into Soviet trade, combines them, and then computes the share of each factor in the total. The results are compared with factor shares in other sectors of the Soviet economy. Similar estimates are made for the U.S. economy and comparisons made. Six tables.

_____. "Wholesaling of Consumer Goods in the USSR." QUARTERLY REVIEW OF ECONOMICS AND BUSINESS 12 (Spring 1972): 53-68.

> This article examines Soviet wholesaling to present information on the effects of a major shift from a sellers' to a buyers' market for most nonfood consumer goods on the behavior of Soviet wholesalers. The differences found between U.S. and USSR wholesaling are also analyzed and explained. Two tables present data on warehouse capacity and use.

Smith, Willard [S.]. "The 1970 Estimate Costs for Soviet Construction." BULLETIN OF THE ASSOCIATION FOR THE STUDY OF SOVIET-TYPE ECONOMIES 12 (Winter 1970): 12-22.

> This article is a discussion of the upward revision in 1970 of "estimate" unit costs of construction in the USSR in the form of indexes of the new unit cost compared with 1956 unit costs. Numerous construction cost data are included in the tables.

Solecki, J. "Policy Decisions and the Fuel Source Pattern in the USSR." CANADIAN SLAVONIC PAPERS 5 (1961): 98-113.

Studies of Particular Industries

This is a review of energy policy in the USSR from the Revolution to 1965 (projected). Statistical tables.

"The Stalingrad and Minsk Building Contest." SOVIET STUDIES 5 (July 1953): 96-99.

This article discusses some interesting points from a book in Russian on the contest between two cities to rebuild after World War II.

Thompson, A. B. OIL FIELDS OF RUSSIA AND THE RUSSIAN PETROLEUM INDUSTRY. London: C. Lockwood and Son, 1904. xviii, 504 p. Illustrated.

This is a practical handbook on the exploration, exploitation, and management of Russian oil properties, including notes on the origin of petroleum in Russia, a description of the theory and practice of liquid fuel extraction, and a translation of the rules and regulations concerning Russian oil properties. Map.

Union of Soviet Socialist Republics. Committee for International Scientific and Technical Conferences. ELECTRIC POWER DEVELOPMENT IN THE U.S.S.R. Moscow: INRA Publishing Society, 1936. xvi, 496 p.

This exhaustive study covers construction of the electric power system; electrification and the fuel supply; steam-electric stations and electric networks; heat and power stations and networks; hydroelectric stations; fundamental problems of power systems; the structure and location of generating plants; high-voltage networks; and principal hydroelectric developments in the Soviet Union.

U.S. Bureau of the Census. THE SOVIET LOGGING INDUSTRY: ITS RESOURCES, EMPLOYMENT, PRODUCTION, AND PRODUCTIVITY. International Population Reports Series P-95, no. 54. Washington, D.C.: Government Printing Office, 1959. ii, 101 p.

This report deals primarily with employment in the logging industry --its recruitment, size, composition, and productivity. Also covered are the national resources available to the logging industry. The data are based primarily on Soviet sources published since 1954. Tables and bibliography.

Vennard, Edwin. "Evaluation of the Russian Threat in the Field of Electric Power." In COMPARISONS OF THE U.S. AND SOVIET ECONOMIES, U.S. Congress. Joint Economic Committee, pp. 467-87. Washington, D.C.: Government Printing Office, 1959.

This paper describes the Soviet electric power system; forecasts construction plans and the goals for 1965; discusses the economics of the Soviet electric power industry; and presents an evaluation of the Russian system. Charts.

Studies of Particular Industries

Vietorisz, Thomas. "Alternative Approaches to Metal-Working Process Analysis." In STUDIES IN PROCESS ANALYSIS. ECONOMY-SIDE PRODUCTION CAPABILITIES, edited by Alan S. Manne and Harry M. Markowitz, pp. 364-76. New York: John Wiley, 1963.

    This paper compares two alternative approaches to metal-working process analysis: (1) the Markowitz-Rowe study of metal-working and (2) the Soviet Machinery Industry Study of the University of North Carolina. The author derives a general model, which is a synthesis between the two approaches.

Vvedensky, George. "The Soviet Aluminium Industry." STUDIES ON THE SOVIET UNION n.s. 5, no. 3 (1966): 79-83.

    This is a short history of the industry. A table lists plants in operation in 1965.

_____. "The Soviet Chemical Fertilizer Industry." STUDIES ON THE SOVIET UNION n.s. 3, no. 4 (1964): 183-92.

    The emphasis here is on the period from 1958 to 1965. Four tables.

_____. "The Soviet Chemical Fertilizer Industry." In SOVIET AGRICULTURE: THE PERMANENT CRISIS, edited by Roy D. Laird and Edward L. Crowley, pp. 183-92. New York: Praeger, 1965.

    The decline in productivity of the virgin lands have led Party leaders to seek a remedy for the crisis in the development of the chemical fertilizer industry. The author discusses the measures taken to increase productivity in this area, i.e., expanding programs in agricultural chemistry and creating a permanent base for providing raw materials for the fertilizer industry in Siberia and the Far East.

Ware, Henry H. "Costs of Distribution in Soviet Domestic Trade." JOURNAL OF MARKETING 15 (July 1950): 21-32.

    Topics covered include costs of distribution in terms of Soviet aims, the structure of these costs, and the way in which conflicting aims preserve high costs.

_____. "Incentives for Soviet Store Personnel." AMERICAN SLAVIC AND EAST EUROPEAN REVIEW 9 (1950): 20-32.

    This article first describes the economic environment in which the Soviet retail worker is employed and then discusses specific wage-payment schemes applicable to retail trade.

_____. "The Procurement Problem in Soviet Retail Trade." JOURNAL OF MARKETING 15 (October 1950): 167-81.

Studies of Particular Industries

This article is concerned with the problems of state and cooperative enterprise in obtaining merchandise for sale. Topics covered include local supplies and government controls.

Wesolowski, Zdzislau P. "The Role of Marketing in a Soviet Type Economy." MARQUETTE BUSINESS REVIEW 13 (Spring 1969): 15-21.

This paper examines the basic theory and practices general to all marketing procedures of the Soviet Bloc. Topics covered include the philosophy of Soviet-type marketing, the national organization of trade, production and channels of distribution, marketing functions, and the role of the consumer.

Chapter 26

RUSSIAN AGRICULTURE AND THE PEASANTRY

Chamberlin, William H. "The Ordeal of the Russian Peasantry." RUSSIAN REVIEW 14 (October 1955): 295-300.

This article surveys the Russian policies toward the peasantry which tended to frustrate the peasants' desires to accumulate their own wealth in private property.

Koslow, Jules. THE DESPISED AND THE DAMNED: THE RUSSIAN PEASANT THROUGH THE AGES. New York: Macmillan, 1972. 174 p. Illustrated.

Koslow describes the village, the mir, the landowner, the economy and work, the condition of the peasantry, the peasant in the city, emancipation and after, the years prior to 1917, the collectivization drive, the collective and state farms, and the "new Soviet peasant." Bibliography, index, and map.

Tchayanov, A. "The Organization and Development of Agricultural Economics in Russia." JOURNAL OF FARM ECONOMICS 12 (April 1930): 270-77.

This article provides an historical sketch of the field from its beginnings in 1737 to 1925 and discusses the teaching of farm management and research around 1930.

Treadgold, Donald W. "Soviet Agriculture in the Light of History." In SOVIET AGRICULTURE AND PEASANT AFFAIRS, edited by Roy D. Laird, pp. 3-8. Lawrence: University of Kansas Press, 1963.

The author gives a very brief account of the role of the peasantry from the seventeenth century through the twentieth century and concludes that a major concern of Khrushchev's is that close to half the population is still engaged in agriculture.

THE PERIOD UP TO 1860

Blum, Jerome. "The Early History of the Russian Peasantry." JOURNAL OF ECONOMIC HISTORY 11, no. 2 (1951): 153-58.

Russian Agriculture and the Peasantry

This article is a discussion of Boris Dmitrievich Grekov. KRESTIANE NA RUSI I DREVNEISHIKH VREMEN DO XVII VEKA [Peasants in Russia from earliest times to the xviith century]. Moscow: Akademiia Nauk SSSR, 1946.

_____. LORD AND PEASANT IN RUSSIA, FROM THE NINTH TO THE NINETEENTH CENTURY. Princeton, N.J.: Princeton University Press, 1961. x, 656 p.

The first section covers the Kievan period of Russian history and discusses peasant communes, private landowners, estate organizations, and the labor force. The second section deals with the Mongol era. The third section covers the sixteenth and seventeenth centuries and a new era of economic expansion. The final section is a detailed account of the last 150 years of serfdom. Glossary, extensive list of works cited, index, and maps.

_____. "Russian Agriculture in the Last 150 Years of Serfdom." AGRICULTURAL HISTORY 34 (January 1960): 3-12.

The paper discusses the development of Russian agriculture generally from the end of Peter the Great's reign (1725) to that of Alexander II (1881). Possible reasons for the retarded development of Russian agriculture are discussed. Types of crops and estimates of their magnitudes are also analyzed. A table of estimated annual average harvests for periods between 1800-1863 is included.

De Madariaga, I. "Catherine II and the Serfs: A Reconsideration of Some Problems." SLAVONIC AND EAST EUROPEAN REVIEW 52 (January 1974): 34-62.

This paper reexamines the generally accepted hypothesis that the reign of Catherine II was the high point of serfdom in Russia. Four tables.

Drew, Ronald F. "The Emergence of an Agricultural Policy for Siberia in the XVII and XVIII Centuries." AGRICULTURAL HISTORY 33 (January 1959): 29-39.

This paper considers efforts of the Muscovite state to establish a permanent basis of support for its agricultural interests in Siberia when mere dependence on native husbandmen no longer seemed feasible. A map of Siberia showing the principal agricultural areas is included.

Dunn, Stephen P., and Dunn, Ethel. THE PEASANTS OF CENTRAL RUSSIA. New York: Holt, Rinehart and Winston, 1967. xiv, 139 p.

The following are among the topics discussed: land tenure and social organization before 1861; land and agriculture; nonagricultural wage labor and crafts; socioeconomic structure; the public versus the private economy; the standard of living; consumer services; and wages and social security.

Kachorovsky, K. R. "The Russian Land Commune in History and To-day." SLAVONIC REVIEW 7 (March 1929): 565-76.

This paper is divided into three sections: (1) a discussion of opinions about the "land commune" before emancipation, (2) the results of research on the land commune (1861-1905), and (3) a scientific chronicle of the land commune during the revolution.

Leroy-Beaulieu, Anatole. THE EMPIRE OF THE TSARS AND THE RUSSIANS. Edited and translated by Z. A. Ragozin. 2 vols. New York: G. P. Putnam's Sons, 1893.

The book contains a classic account of Russian society under the tsars. Of interest to the economic historian are the sections on the peasant and emancipation; land tenure after emancipation; the commune in theory and practice; and the role of the rural commune. Foldout maps.

Melia, Martin E. "Herzen and the Peasant Commune." In CONTINUITY AND CHANGE IN RUSSIAN AND SOVIET THOUGHT, edited by Ernest Simmons, pp. 197-217. Cambridge, Mass.: Harvard University Press, 1955.

Herzen's views on agrarian communism are discussed.

O'Brien, Carl B[lickford]. "Agriculture in Russian War Economy in the Late Seventeenth Century." AMERICAN SLAVIC AND EAST EUROPEAN REVIEW 8 (1949): 167-74.

This article is concerned with the relation between the needs of the military and the development and organization of agriculture in seventeenth-century Russia. Land tenure practices and the chain of authority are also discussed.

Robinson, Geriod T. RURAL RUSSIA UNDER THE OLD REGIME. London: Longmans, Green, 1932. x, 342 p. Illustrated.

The worlds of the landlord and the peasant before and after the emancipation of the serfs are studied. Appendices provide data on landholding. Bibliography, index, and maps.

Skerpan, A. "The Russian National Economy and Emancipation." In ESSAYS IN RUSSIAN HISTORY, edited by A. Ferguson and A. Levin, pp. 161-230. Hamden, Conn.: Archon, 1964.

Topics discussed here include the problems of the Russian state; Russian thought on labor; the role of government in the economy; economic expectations of the reform; limitations on reform for economic development; the effect of the emancipation on economic development; and misconceptions about serfdom and economic development.

Smith, Robert E. F. THE ENSERFMENT OF THE RUSSIAN PEASANTRY. Cambridge: At the University Press, 1968. xii, 180 p.

    The book contains translations of fifty-six documents from the twelfth to the mid-seventeenth century which document the process of the legal enserfment of the peasantry. Glossary and index.

──────. "Medieval Agrarian Society in its Prime: Russia." In THE CAMBRIDGE ECONOMIC HISTORY OF EUROPE, edited by M. M. Postan. Vol. 1: THE AGRARIAN LIFE OF THE MIDDLE AGES, 2d ed., pp. 506-47. London and New York: Cambridge University Press, 1966.

    The author describes the layout of settlements and large estates; farming implements and methods; animal husbandry and hunting and fishing; and social relations and land ownership.

Tretheway, R. "The Establishment of Serfdom in Eastern Europe and Russia." AMERICAN ECONOMIST 18 (Spring 1974): 36-41.

    This article discusses the establishment of serfdom and the manorial system in the light of the land-to-labor ratio in agriculture.

Vernadsky, George. "On Feudalism in Kievan Russia." AMERICAN SLAVIC AND EAST EUROPEAN REVIEW 7 (1948): 3-14.

    This article is an excerpt from Vernadsky's book KIEVAN RUSSIA. New Haven, Conn.: Yale University Press, 1966. It is concerned with the question of "to what stage of social and economic development . . . Kievan Russia belongs." Political feudalism is also discussed.

Vernadsky, George, and Cherepnin, L. V. "Feudalism in Russia." In READINGS IN RUSSIAN CIVILIZATION, edited by Thomas Riha. Vol. I: RUSSIA BEFORE PETER THE GREAT, 900-1700, pp. 75-91. Chicago and London: University of Chicago Press, 1964.

    Vernadsky examines the institution of feudalism in Russia, and Cherepnin discusses Western historiography on Russian feudalism.

Volin, Lazar. "The Russian Peasant and Serfdom." AGRICULTURAL HISTORY 17 (January 1943): 41-61.

    This article discusses the reactions of the various classes to the institution of serfdom, peasant attempts to lessen the burdens of serfdom, and the reasons for the final official abolition of serfdom in 1861.

Vucinich, Wayne S., ed. THE PEASANT IN NINETEENTH-CENTURY RUSSIA. Stanford, Calif.: Stanford University Press, 1968. xx, 314 p.

This volume includes ten papers by various authors on various aspects of peasant life. Of particular interest are papers on the emancipation, the commune, and the factory. Index.

Zaitsev, Cyril. "Economic Aspects of the Agrarian Question in Russia Before and After the Bolshevik Revolution." JOURNAL OF ECONOMIC AND BUSINESS HISTORY 3 (August 1931): 499-528.

This article surveys the relations of the Russian peasant with the landlord from the seventeenth century to collectivization. At times the landlord was the nobleman, the commune, briefly, under Stolypin, the peasant himself, and now the state.

THE PERIOD 1860-1917

Antsiferov, Alexis N. "Credit and Agricultural Cooperation." In THE COOPERATIVE MOVEMENT IN RUSSIA DURING THE WAR, pp. 233-420. New Haven, Conn.: Yale University Press, 1929.

The author discusses the three periods of credit cooperation before the war; cooperative credit societies and the war; cooperative credit unions and national cooperative banks; cooperation for supply and marketing; and agricultural cooperation in Siberia. Tables.

Antsiferov, Alexis N., et al. "Rural Economy." In RUSSIAN AGRICULTURE DURING THE WAR, pp. 1-300. New Haven, Conn.: Yale University Press, 1930.

The following are discussed: (1) Russian agriculture at the beginning of the twentieth century; (2) the progress of agriculture in the years preceding the war; (3) the balance of production and consumption of agricultural produce before the war; (4) changes in the conditions of agriculture during the war; (5) changes in crops and agricultural industry during the war; (6) changes in the condition of the market; (7) exploitation of forests before and during the war; and (8) the Revolution's effects upon agriculture. Appendices provide data.

Baykalov, A. "A Brief Outline of the Russian Co-operative Movement." SLAVONIC REVIEW 1 (June 1922): 130-43.

The article briefly sketches the history of the cooperative movement in Russia during the following periods: up to 1905; 1905-14; during the war and the beginning of the Revolution; and 1919-20.

Bilimovich, Alexander D. "The Land Settlement in Russia and the War." In RUSSIAN AGRICULTURE DURING THE WAR, pp. 303-88. New Haven, Conn.: Yale University Press, 1930.

The author discusses the defects of Russia's agrarian organization before the reforms of 1906, the effects of the war on land settlement, and the effects of the Revolution on land settlement. Appendices are included.

Borodaewsky, S. W. "Co-operation in Russia During the War." INTERNATIONAL LABOUR REVIEW 10 (August 1924): 263-76.

This article surveys the development of consumers' and producers' cooperatives during the war. The author discusses cooperative credit societies, consumer's cooperatives, agricultural cooperatives, producers' cooperatives, and government policy toward cooperative unions.

Dalrymple, Dana G. "Joseph A. Rosen and Early Russian Studies of American Agriculture." AGRICULTURAL HISTORY 38 (July 1964): 157-60.

This article sketches the life and work of a Russian emigre to the United States who, through his writings, acquainted Russian agriculturalists with the developments taking place in U.S. agriculture from 1908 to World War I. A list of his major publications is included.

De Lestrade, Combes. "Present Conditions of Peasants in Russian Empire." ANNALS OF THE AMERICAN ACADEMY OF POLITICAL AND SOCIAL SCIENCE 2 (September 1891): 225-35.

This article discusses the emancipation of the serfs and the ill effects of the mir on peasant enterprise.

Ely, Richard T. "Russian Land Reform." AMERICAN ECONOMIC REVIEW 6 (March 1916): 61-68.

This summarizes the Stolypin land reform in Russia and is based largely on a German publication: K. A. Wieth-Knudsen. BAUERNFRAGE UND AGRARREFORM IN RUSSLAND. Munich: Verlag von Dunckev & Mumbost, 1913.

Gerschenkron, Alexander. "Agrarian Polices and Industrialization: Russia 1861-1917." In THE CAMBRIDGE ECONOMIC HISTORY OF EUROPE. Vol. 4, pt. 2: THE INDUSTRIAL REVOLUTION AND AFTER, pp. 706-800. Cambridge: At the University Press, 1966.

The author discusses the causes and purposes of serfdom; the abolition of serfdom as a prerequisite to industrialization; the Emancipation Act and its effect on the peasantry; and the aftermath of emancipation.

Gubsky, N. "The Land Settlement of Russia." ECONOMIC JOURNAL 31 (December 1921): 472-81.

This article is a critical treatment of communal landholding in Russia.

Hourwich, Isaac A. THE ECONOMICS OF THE RUSSIAN VILLAGE. Studies in History, Economics and Public Law, vol. 2. Edited by Columbia College. New York: Columbia College, 1892. vi, 182 p.

> The following are among the subjects covered: a sketch of the development of landholding; forms of land ownership; the productive forces of the peasantry; taxation of the peasant; communal tenure and small holdings; the evolution of the farmer into the agricultural laborer; wages in the rural districts; the rural surplus population; individual ownership and agrarian communism; the redivision of the communal land; and agriculture on a large scale. Many statistical tables.

_____. "Wheat-Growing in Russia." JOURNAL OF POLITICAL ECONOMY 12 (March 1904): 256-61.

> This paper is a review of DER WEIZENBAU IM SUDWESTLICHEN UND CENTRALEN RUSSLAND UND SEINE RENTABILITAT. Berlin, 1902. Two tables provide data on agricultural wages and the cost of farmlands.

Kennard, Howard P. RUSSIAN PEASANT. London: T. Werner Laurie, 1907. xv, 302 p. Illustrated.

> The book is divided into three parts: part one describes village life; part two contains an account of the history of the peasantry; and part three discusses the Russian bureaucracy and church.

Kravchinskii, Sergei M. [Stepniak]. THE RUSSIAN PEASANTRY: THEIR AGRARIAN CONDITION, SOCIAL LIFE, AND RELIGION. 2d ed. 2 vols. London: Swan Sonnenschein, 1888.

> The author's goal is to acquaint the English reader with the main features of the "double process of growth and decay" within the rural classes. The book deals with economic, social, and political crises faced by the Russian peasantry during the 1880s.

Lee, Frederic E. RUSSIAN COOPERATIVE MOVEMENT. Washington, D.C.: Government Printing Office, 1920. 83 p.

> This monograph discusses producers' societies, consumers' societies, credit societies, cooperatives in Siberia, and the economic status of the movement. Tables.

Leroy-Beaulieu, Anatole. THE RUSSIAN PEASANT. Edited by H. J. Tobias. Sandoval, N.M.: Coronado Press, 1962. xi, 286 p.

> The book is divided into three parts: part one deals with the emancipation of the serfs and the role it played in changing the old social and economic order; parts two and three deal with the peasant, peasant institutions, and peasant relations with the rest

of Russian society. The commune is examined from two perspectives —as a system of land tenure and as an administrative agency.

Levasseur, E. "The Russian Famine." ROYAL STATISTICAL SOCIETY. JOURNAL. Ser. A 55 (March 1892): 80-87.

This paper, which is a translation from the JOURNAL DE LA SOCIETE DE STATISTIQUE DE PARIS, presents an estimate of the seriousness of the Russian famine by comparing agricultural output for the years 1883-91. Six tables.

Maklakov, V. "The Agrarian Problem in Russia before the Revolution." RUSSIAN REVIEW 9 (January 1950): 3-15.

This paper looks at the reasons for Russia's apparent land shortage, despite its large expanse, and for the apparently revolutionary temper which developed in the peasant class by 1905.

_____. "The Peasant Question and the Russian Revolution." SLAVONIC REVIEW 2 (December 1923): 225-48.

Maklakov describes how the "peasant question" in Russia (or status of the peasant) differed from that of the European peasant and outlines the main characteristics and the position of the peasant at the time of the Revolution. The article also traces the way in which the institution of serfdom emerged.

Morse, W. E. "Stolypin's Villages." SLAVONIC AND EAST EUROPEAN REVIEW 43 (June 1965): 257-74.

The article contains a "definitive assessment of Stolypin's agrarian reform, its achievements and its limitations."

Owen, L. A. "The Russian Agrarian Revolution of 1917." SLAVONIC REVIEW 12 (July 1933): 155-66.

This article summarizes the main features of the peasant risings of 1917.

_____. "The Russian Agrarian Revolution of 1917: II." SLAVONIC REVIEW 12 (January 1934): 368-86.

This article gives an account of peasant risings in the Central Agricultural and Middle Volga regions. It is a continuation of "The Russian Agrarian Revolution of 1917: I." SLAVONIC REVIEW 34 (July 1933): 155-66.

_____. THE RUSSIAN PEASANT MOVEMENT, 1906-1917. New York: Russell & Russell, 1937. xix, 267 p.

Chapters are organized along the following lines: the Stolypin agrarian policy; the controversy of Stolypin's policy in the Duma; Lenin and the peasant movement; and the role played by social dissolution in the villages in the October Revolution.

Pavlovsky, George. AGRICULTURAL RUSSIA ON THE EVE OF THE REVOLUTION. 1930. Reprint. New York: Howard Fertig, 1968. x, 340 p.

The book is divided into three parts. Part one contains a sketch of the agricultural geography of European Russia, as it had been shaped by natural conditions, historical and economic factors and other influences. Part two deals with a study of the organization and conditions of Russian farming. Part three discusses Russia's characteristics as an agricultural producer and the origins and disposal of her available surpluses of agricultural products. Statistical appendices, index, and three maps.

Pushkarev, Sergei G. "The Russian Peasants' Reaction to the Emancipation of 1861." RUSSIAN REVIEW 27 (April 1968): 199-214.

This paper examines the peasants' expectations regarding the results of the 1861 emancipation and their reactions, sometimes violent, when those expectations were not fulfilled.

Robbins, Richard G., Jr. "Russia's System of Food Supply Relief on the Eve of the Famine of 1891-92." AGRICULTURAL HISTORY 45 (October 1971): 259-69.

Robbins provides a detailed historical account of measures taken by the tsarist government to supply famine relief. The government's failure to institute needed reforms in the administration of famine relief is also noted.

Shanin, Teodor. "Socio-Economic Mobility and the Rural History of Russia 1905-1930." SOVIET STUDIES 23 (October 1971): 222-35.

This paper discusses peasant socioeconomic mobility and its relation to rural economic policies under both regimes. Three tables.

Timoshenko, Vladimir P. "The Agrarian Policies of Russia and the Wars." AGRICULTURAL HISTORY 17 (October 1943): 192-210.

This article discusses the agrarian policies of Russia from 1861 to 1917 as they were affected by the abolition of serfdom and the various wars in which Russia was engaged.

Tokmakoff, George. "Stolypin's Agrarian Reform: An Appraisal." RUSSIAN REVIEW 30 (April 1971): 124-38.

This paper argues "that Stolypin's agrarian reform was neither a success nor a failure; no final conclusion can be drawn because the reform was never completed."

Russian Agriculture and the Peasantry

Totomiantz, V. T. "Co-operation in Russia before the War." INTERNATIONAL LABOUR REVIEW 7 (January 1923): 15-24.

> The spread of the Russian cooperative movement before the war is traced. The study is intended to serve as an introduction to a future study of cooperation in Russia since the Revolution. The article also discusses the cooperative movement from 1900 onwards.

Treadgold, Donald W. "Was Stolypin in Favor of Kulaks?" AMERICAN SLAVIC AND EAST EUROPEAN REVIEW 14 (1955): 1-14.

> This article examines Stolypin's speeches and policies to determine whether or not he favored the economic success of the richer peasants or kulaks at the expense of the poorer ones.

Tschuprow, A. A. "The Break-up of the Village Community in Russia." ECONOMIC JOURNAL 22 (June 1912): 173-97.

> This article surveys the reasons for the Stolypin land reform beginning in 1906 and assesses the success of the reform up to 1912.

"Vygurs Settlers in the Murgab Oasis 1885-1905." CENTRAL ASIAN REVIEW 11, no. 3 (1963): 274-79.

> Tsarist government policy and the migration of this group into the Transcaspian area is discussed. Map.

Volin, Lazar. A CENTURY OF RUSSIAN AGRICULTURE: FROM ALEXANDER II TO KHRUSHCHEV. Russian Research Center Studies, no. 63. Cambridge, Mass.: Harvard University Press, 1970. viii, 644 p.

> This is a comprehensive study of Russian agriculture from 1860 to the 1960s. The three parts discuss the peasant and the landlord, the peasant under communism, and collectivized agriculture under Khrushchev. Tables and index.

_____. "Land Tenure and Land Reform in Modern Russia." AGRICULTURAL HISTORY 27 (April 1953): 48-55.

> The article discusses the history of land tenure and reform in Russia since the abolition of serfdom as largely a series of conflicts between the peasants and whomever happens to be in power--the nobility, the tsar, or the Soviets.

_____. "The Russian Peasant Household Under the Mir and the Collective Farm System." FOREIGN AGRICULTURE 4, no. 3 (March 1940): 133-46.

> The essential characteristics of mir and kolkhoz organization are compared.

_____. "The Russian Peasant: From Emancipation to Kolkhoz." In THE

TRANSFORMATION OF RUSSIAN SOCIETY: ASPECTS OF SOCIAL CHANGE SINCE 1861, edited by Cyril E. Black, pp. 292-311. Cambridge, Mass.: Harvard University Press, 1960.

> The author notes that the peasant question has not been resolved in Russia in the past hundred years, in spite of the fact that the agrarian sector of the economy has shrunk. However, significant changes have taken place, i.e., literacy of the peasant population and new farm technology. The one outstanding break in historic continuity has been the reversal by collectivization of the trend toward independent peasant farming.

Whitman, John [T.]. "Turkestan Cotton in Imperial Russia." AMERICAN SLAVIC AND EAST EUROPEAN REVIEW 15 (April 1956): 190-205.

> This article traces the development of cotton culture in Turkestan and its significance for Russia from the earliest cultivation to the early 1920s. Tables provide information on sown area and harvests for selected periods between 1870 and 1925.

Willetts, Harry T. "The Agrarian Problem." In RUSSIA ENTERS THE TWENTIETH CENTURY: 1894-1917, edited by Erwin Oberlander, pp. 111-37. New York: Schocken, 1971.

> Willetts deals with the agrarian problem during the last decades of the Russian empire. He describes the official attitudes towards serfdom, notes the condition of the countryside, recounts Witte's plans for reform, analyzes the agrarian problem in the First Duma, and outlines the Stolypin reforms.

Williams, D. S. M. "Russian Peasant Settlement in Semirechye." CENTRAL ASIAN REVIEW 14, no. 2 (1966): 110-22.

> Tsarist government policy regarding Russian peasant settlement in the approximate period 1883-1906 is considered.

Wolfe, Bertram D. "Lenin, Stolypin, and the Russian Village." RUSSIAN REVIEW 6 (Spring 1947): 44-54.

> This article examines the policies of Lenin and Stolypin toward the peasantry and finds them similar in some respects.

Yaney, George L. "The Concept of the Stolypin Land Reform." SLAVIC REVIEW 23 (June 1964): 275-93.

> This essay presents a description of the series of actions taken by the Russian Imperial government during the years 1905-17 "to cope with the social and economic problems of the European peasants." Topics covered include general interpretation, problems of the reform, the outline of its evolution, and the role of force in its execution.

Zenkovsky, Serge A. "The Emancipation of the Serfs in Retrospect." RUSSIAN REVIEW 20 (October 1961): 280-93.

This paper discusses several aspects of the institution of serfdom in Russia, including its regional distribution, the attempts of the nobility to ameliorate the effects of emancipation, and the average losses suffered by peasants in the emancipation.

THE PERIOD AFTER 1917

Abramov, Viktor. THE BASIC PRINCIPLES OF THE ORGANIZATION OF SOVIET AGRICULTURE. Moscow: Progress Publishers, 1971. 122 p.

This Soviet economist gives a brief discussion of the system of socialist agriculture; organization and productivity; labor remuneration; planning agricultural production; and finance and credit. Tables and index.

_____. THE ECONOMICS OF AGRICULTURE. Moscow: Progress Publishers, 1960. 111 p.

The author discusses the tasks and specific features of agricultural production; kolkhozes and sovkhozes; structure and specialization of agricultural production; organization of crop farming and animal husbandry; production assets and capital investment in agricultural enterprise; productivity, organization, and remuneration of farm labor; production costs and cost accounting; and the planning of agricultural production.

Adams, Arthur E. "Educated Specialists and Change in Soviet Agriculture." AGRICULTURAL HISTORY 40 (January 1966): 1-10.

Article discusses the quality of agricultural specialists and how it has changed over the past twenty-five years. Author suggests some effects of these changes. Tables.

_____. MEN VERSUS SYSTEMS; AGRICULTURE IN THE USSR, POLAND AND CZECHOSLOVAKIA. New York: Free Press, 1971. viii, 327 p. Illustrated.

The first part (pp. 3-96) discusses the effects of collectivization in the Soviet Union. Tables and bibliography.

Anderson, Jeremy. "A Historical-Geographical Perspective on Khrushchev's Corn Program." In SOVIET AND EAST EUROPEAN AGRICULTURE, edited by Jerzy Karcz, pp. 104-34. Berkeley and Los Angeles: University of California Press, 1967.

Four aspects of Khrushchev's corn program are reviewed in this article.

Anisimov, Nikolai I. SOVIET AGRICULTURE. Moscow: Foreign Languages Publishing House, 1957. 53 p. Illustrated.

> A Soviet economist discusses socialist reorganization of agriculture, state and collective farms, machine-tractor stations (MTS), the planned economy, machines in agriculture, and the main branches of agriculture.

Arkhimovich, A. "The 1960 Soviet Harvest." STUDIES ON THE SOVIET UNION n.s. 1, no. 1 (1961): 73-82.

> This careful review of the 1960 Soviet harvest concludes that even if allowances are made for the weather, the harvests fell below expectations and the virgin lands program and other investments in agriculture did not pay off. Tables.

_____. "Soviet Agriculture in 1962." STUDIES ON THE SOVIET UNION n.s. 3, no. 1 (1963): 64-71.

> This paper carefully analyzes harvest and sown area statistics to compare performance in 1962 with that of previous years. Six tables.

_____. "A Survey of Soviet Agriculture." STUDIES ON THE SOVIET UNION n.s. 1, no. 3 (1962): 51-63.

> Topics covered include sown area, average harvests, and grain yields and production. Responsibility for the status of agriculture is placed on the Soviet regime. Tables.

Auhagen, Otto. "Agriculture." In RED ECONOMICS, edited by Gerhard Dobbert, pp. 111-33. Boston: Houghton Mifflin, 1932.

> This article discusses the Russian agrarian situation after the Revolution, under the New Economic Policy, and in collectivization under Stalin.

Australia Bureau of Agricultural Economics. THE ECONOMICS OF THE SOVIET WHEAT INDUSTRY. Canberra, Australia: 1966. 82 p.

> This is an extensive study of the Soviet wheat industry, including trends in production, factors influencing long-run production trends, consumption, utilization, trade, recent developments, and future prospects. Tables.

Baikalov, Anatole. "Bolshevist Agrarian Policy." SLAVONIC REVIEW 8 (March 1930): 533-47.

> Baikalov deals with the following questions: (1) Have the Bolsheviks solved the agrarian problem? (2) Have they been successful in overcoming the agrarian crisis? (3) What has been the agrarian policy during the first twelve years of Bolshevik rule? (4) How

will they direct agriculture in the future?

Bakalo, Ivan. "Mass Training of Skilled Agricultural Workers in the USSR." STUDIES ON THE SOVIET UNION n.s. 3, no. 1 (1963): 83-98.

> On December 24, 1958, the Supreme Soviet enacted a decree which required secondary students to work for two years before continuing their education. This paper traces the effects of this policy on the supply of agricultural specialists. Four tables.

Baker, C. B., and Swanson, E. R. "The Training of Agricultural Economists in the USSR." JOURNAL OF FARM ECONOMICS 46 (August 1964): 47-55.

> The authors' visits to training institutions for agricultural economists in Moscow, Leningrad, and Kiev are described. They list undergraduate course requirements at Timiryazev Agricultural Academy and recount graduate programs and procedures for obtaining thesis approval.

Ballard, Allen B., Jr. "Problems of State Farm Administration." SOVIET STUDIES 17 (January 1966): 339-52.

> The four areas discussed are administrative apparatus, political apparatus, management of sovkhozy, and organization of sovkhoz workers.

Bass, Robert H. FORCE VERSUS FOOD; A SHORT HISTORY OF AGRICULTURE IN THE SOVIET SPHERE. New York: Free Europe Press, 1957. 72 p. Illustrated.

> The first part summarizes the characteristics of Soviet agriculture, development of agricultural institutions under war communism, the New Economic Policy, and collectivization. The second part describes agriculture since the collectivization drive of the 1930s. The third part deals with agricultural production, peasant income, and the political consequences of collectivization.

Batra, Raveendra N. "Technological Change in the Soviet Collective Farm." AMERICAN ECONOMIC REVIEW 64 (September 1974): 594-603.

> This paper presents a mathematical model incorporating technical change into a microeconomic model of the collective farm.

Baykov, Alexander M. "Agricultural Development in the USSR." BULLETINS ON SOVIET ECONOMIC DEVELOPMENT 2 (December 1949): 3-28.

> The author surveys some of the main problems and trends of agriculture since 1917, agricultural development during the war, the plans for postwar restoration and development of agriculture, and the actual development of agriculture. Tables. A map in Russian is included.

_____. "Agriculture." BULLETINS ON SOVIET ECONOMIC DEVELOPMENT. Ser. 2, 8 (May 1953): 29-45.

> Baykov considers the reliability of indices of agricultural production and summarizes postwar developments of agricultural production. Many tables.

Belov, Fedor. THE HISTORY OF A COLLECTIVE FARM. Praeger Publications in Russian History and World Communism, no. 36. New York: Praeger, 1955. xiii, 237 p.

> The author gives a firsthand account of life on a collective farm based on diaries he maintained while in Russia. Tables and index.

Bennett, M. K. "Food and Agriculture in the Soviet Union, 1917-48." JOURNAL OF POLITICAL ECONOMY 57 (June 1949): 185-98.

> The topics discussed include growth in output, population growth, the food supply, grain output, crop statistics, and the organization of agriculture.

Bergamini, John D. "Stalin and the Collective Farm." In CONTINUITY AND CHANGE IN RUSSIAN AND SOVIET THOUGHT, edited by Ernest J. Simmons, pp. 218-36. Cambridge, Mass.: Harvard University Press, 1955.

> This paper discusses Stalin's approach to the peasant problem, his views on collective farms and on mass collectivization, and the results.

Birmingham University. Bureau of Research on Russian Economic Conditions. "Communist Policy Towards the Peasant and the Food Crisis in the U.S.S.R." MEMORANDUM NO. 8 (December 1932): 1-24.

> The memorandum contains brief accounts of the agrarian revolution of 1917; the period of war communism, 1918-21; the New Economic Policy and its reversal, 1921-29; and the period of collectivization from 1930 onwards.

Boev, V. R. "Agricultural Production and the Rural Standard of Living in the U.S.S.R. Since 1917." INTERNATIONAL LABOUR REVIEW 87 (June 1963): 520-50.

> Covered here are mechanization, collective and state farms, work organization, development of virgin lands, productivity, living standards, and vocational training. Thirteen tables.

Borders, Karl. VILLAGE LIFE UNDER THE SOVIETS. New York: Vanguard Press, 1927. xxii, 191 p.

> The author's description of village life covers the village and the villager; the land; the commune; artels and the collective under the NEP; government education and aid in agriculture; the market-

place; consumers' cooperatives and agricultural cooperatives; politics; and social and cultural activities.

Bornstein, Morris. "The Soviet Debate on Agricultural Price and Procurement Reforms." SOVIET STUDIES 21 (July 1969): 1-20.

This paper analyzes criticisms and reform suggestions for the system of agricultural prices, examines the related debate over "economic" versus "administrative" methods of regulating agricultural production and marketing, and offers some comparisons with Eastern Europe. A table provides ratios of price to production costs for selected commodities.

Bradley, Michael E. "Incentives and Labor Supply on Soviet Collective Farms." CANADIAN JOURNAL OF ECONOMICS 4 (August 1971): 342-52.

This analysis of the shortrun labor supply on collectives considers implications of current Soviet agricultural policies and reforms for member incentives and performance of collective farms. For further discussion, see: Michael E. Bradley. "Incentives and Labour Supply on Soviet Collective Farms: Reply." CANADIAN JOURNAL OF ECONOMICS 6 (August 1973): 438-42; Norman Cameron. "Incentives and Labour Supply on Soviet Collective Farms: Rejoinder." CANADIAN JOURNAL OF ECONOMICS 6 (August 1973): 442-44.

Bradley, Michael E., and Clark, M. Gardner. "Supervision and Efficiency in Socialized Agriculture." SOVIET STUDIES 23 (January 1972): 465-73.

This paper is concerned with low labor productivity and high costs of production on collective and state farms in the Soviet Union. A small table compares average size and labor force of Soviet and American farms.

Braginskii, B. I., and Dumov, D. "Labor Productivity in Agriculture in the USSR and the USA." PROBLEMS OF ECONOMICS 4 (May 1961): 3-9.

This is a translation of "Proizvoditel'nost truda v sel'skom Rhoziaistve SSSR i SShA." VESTNIK STATISTIKI, no. 2 (1961): 23-33. The concern here is with the late 1950s.

Bronson, David W., and Krueger, Constance B. "The Revolution in Soviet Farm Household Income, 1953-1967." In THE SOVIET RURAL COMMUNITY: A SYMPOSIUM, edited by James R. Millar, pp. 214-58. Urbana: University of Illinois Press, 1971.

Eleven tables.

Brubaker, Earl R. "Development of Soviet Agriculture under a Vintage Model of Production." AMERICAN JOURNAL OF AGRICULTURAL ECONOMICS 51 (November 1969): 882-902.

Within the framework provided by a vintage model of productive activity this paper examines the pertinent evidence on output, inputs, and the age of fixed capital to further understanding of the sources of growth (1928-62) in Soviet agricultural output. For further discussion, see: Dana G. Dalrymple. "Comment on the Development of Soviet Agriculture." AMERICAN JOURNAL OF AGRICULTURAL ECONOMICS 52 (May 1970): 337-38.

Bush, Keith. "Agricultural Reforms Since Khrushchev." In NEW DIRECTIONS IN THE SOVIET ECONOMY, U.S. Congress. Joint Economic Committee, pp. 451-72. Washington, D.C.: Government Printing Office, 1966.

Topics discussed include procurement targets, prices, investments, machinery, fertilizers, land improvement, direct marketing of produce, kolkhozes, sovkhozes, the private sector, economic concessions to the peasants, and budgetary redistributions. Eleven tables.

Carey, David W. "Soviet Agriculture." In ECONOMIC PERFORMANCE AND THE MILITARY BURDEN IN THE SOVIET UNION, U.S. Congress. Joint Economic Committee, pp. 26-32. Washington, D.C.: Government Printing Office, 1970.

This paper discusses current developments in policy and the outlook for 1970. Four tables.

Chaianov, A. V. THE THEORY OF PEASANT ECONOMY. Edited by D. Thorner et al. Homewood, Ill.: R. D. Irwin, 1966. lxxv, 317 p.

The major portion of the book consists of a translation from the Russian PEASANT FARM ORGANIZATION (1925). This book presents a detailed, theoretical account of peasant economy based on Russian agriculture. Glossary, bibliography of author's works with locations, list of tables, and index.

"Changes in State Agricultural Purchasing Policy." SOVIET STUDIES 5 (April 1954): 446-50.

This paper discusses the decision to pay higher prices for agricultural products in September 1953. Four tables.

Churchward, L. G. "The Agricultural Reorganization and the Rural District Soviets." SOVIET STUDIES 10 (July 1958): 94-98.

This note reviews the reactions of local officials to the sale of machine-tractor station equipment to collective farms.

Clarke, Roger A. "Soviet Agricultural Reforms since Khrushchev." SOVIET STUDIES 10 (October 1968): 159-78.

This article discusses the principal reform measures instituted since 1965 and the performance of the agricultural sector since 1964. Four tables.

"The Collectivization Campaign in Uzbekistan, 1927-33." CENTRAL ASIAN REVIEW 12, no. 1 (1964): 40-52.

> The kolkhoz movement and Uzbek reaction to it are reviewed from roughly 1917 to 1935. A table shows percentages of livestock in the socialized sector in 1929 and 1932.

"The Collectivization of Agriculture in the U.S.S.R." INTERNATIONAL LABOUR REVIEW 26 (September 1932): 386-409.

> Methods of collectivization and the organization of the predominant type of collective farm are described. The article also gives statistical and other information showing the results of the first two years.

Conklin, David W. AN EVALUATION OF THE SOVIET PROFIT REFORMS, WITH SPECIAL REFERENCE TO AGRICULTURE. New York: Praeger, 1970. xiii, 192 p. Illustrated.

> The author discusses the shortcomings of Stalinist economic policies as maintained up to 1965 and post-Stalinist reforms in the agricultural sector. He then analyzes three economic frameworks for central planning which combine central planning with decentralized decision making.

Conquest, Robert. AGRICULTURAL WORKERS IN U.S.S.R. London and Sydney: Badley Head, 1968. 139 p.

> The first chapter outlines the historical development of collectivization up to the death of Stalin; the second and third chapters describe Soviet agriculture during and after the Khrushchev period; and the final chapter gives an account of living and working conditions on the farms.

Dalrymple, Dana G. "American Technology and Soviet Agricultural Development, 1924-1933." AGRICULTURAL HISTORY 40 (July 1966): 187-206.

> The article focuses on the Soviet organizational framework for obtaining American agricultural technology, the American contributions, major problem areas, and the economic significance of the technology transfer. Tables.

_____. "Higher Education and Soviet Agriculture." JOURNAL OF FARM ECONOMICS 42 (February 1960): 160-74.

> Developments in higher education in agriculture in the Soviet Union are related to needs and prospects for Soviet agriculture. Two tables.

_____. MARX AND AGRICULTURE: THE SOVIET EXPERIENCE. East Lansing: Michigan State University Press, 1961. 22 p.

Karl Marx's views on agriculture and their relationship to subsequent development in the Soviet Union are traced.

_____. "The Soviet Famine of 1932-1934." SOVIET STUDIES 15 (January 1964): 250-84.

> The extent of the famine, its immediate and longrun causes, and the way in which the famine was hidden are discussed. Tables. For further discussion, see: Dana G. Dalrymple. "The Soviet Famine of 1932-1934; Some Further Reference." SOVIET STUDIES 16 (April 1965): 471-74.

Davletshin, Tamurbek. "Property Law in the Soviet Union." STUDIES ON THE SOVIET UNION n.s. 2, no. 4 (1963): 11-22.

> This article surveys the changes in Soviet property law and private ownership from the period of war communism to 1962.

"The Decision on Grain Production." SOVIET STUDIES 6 (July 1954): 101-5.

> This note discusses Khrushchev's report "On the Further Increase of Grain Production and on the Bringing into Cultivation of Virgin Lands" to the Communist Party Plenum in 1954 and the decisions which it precipitated.

De Pauw, John W. MEASURES OF AGRICULTURAL EMPLOYMENT IN THE U.S.S.R.: 1950-1966. U.S. Department of Commerce. Bureau of the Census. Washington, D.C.: Government Printing Office, 1968. vi, 78 p.

> Methodology and data collection are discussed. Nineteen tables provide figures on employment in the three agricultural sectors: collective, state, and private.

_____. "The Private Sector in Soviet Agriculture." SLAVIC REVIEW 28 (March 1969): 63-71.

> This article concludes that the private sector is an important supplier of agricultural products to state and families, that it helps to keep farmers on the farm, and that it will not be eliminated in the near future. A table provides figures on the private sector's share of agriculture, 1958-66.

Diamond, Douglas B. "Trends in Output, Inputs, and Factor Productivity in Soviet Agriculture." In NEW DIRECTIONS IN THE SOVIET ECONOMY, U.S. Congress. Joint Economic Committee, pp. 339-81. Washington, D.C.: Government Printing Office, 1966.

> This paper is concerned with the period 1950-64 and includes many tables.

Diamond, Douglas B., and Krueger, Constance B. "Recent Developments in Output and Productivity in Soviet Agriculture." In SOVIET ECONOMIC PROSPECTS FOR THE SEVENTIES, U.S. Congress. Joint Economic Committee, pp. 316-39. Washington, D.C.: Government Printing Office, 1973.

> Topics discussed include trends in the 1960s, the Brezhnev Program II and its implementation, and output performance in 1971-72. Many tables.

Dibb, Paul. SOVIET AGRICULTURE SINCE KHRUSHCHEV; AN ECONOMIC APPRAISAL. Occasional Paper no. 4. Canberra: Department of Political Science, Research School of Social Sciences, Australian National University, 1969. 51 p.

> The purpose of this paper is to assess the progress in the agricultural sector since 1965 in relation to performance during the Khrushchevian period. An appendix contains a brief outline of the 1971-75 plan for agriculture.

Dinerstein, Herbert S. COMMUNISM AND THE RUSSIAN PEASANT. Goure, Leon, and Dinerstein, Herbert S. MOSCOW IN CRISIS. Two Studies in Soviet Controls. 2 in 1 vol. Glencoe, Ill.: Free Press, 1955. xviii, 254 p.

> Of interest to the economic historian is COMMUNISM AND THE RUSSIAN PEASANT, a study of the Soviet controls over the peasantry.

Djalilov, K. M. "Country Experiences: Uzbek SSR." In THE ROLE OF AGRICULTURE IN ECONOMIC DEVELOPMENT, pp. 236-45. Proceedings of the Eleventh International Conference of Agricultural Economists held at Cuernavaca, Morelos, Mex. London: Oxford University Press, 1963.

> The author briefly outlines the economic development of Uzbek SSR before and after the Revolution. He discusses the basic changes that agriculture underwent, especially the consequences of the organization of collective and state farms.

Dobrovolsky, Alexander. ECONOMIC ADMINISTRATION AND LABOR PRODUCTIVITY ON A SOVIET STATE FARM. New York: Research Program on the USSR, 1953. 35 p.

> This pamphlet deals with the structure of the industrial and financial plan of a state farm; the distribution of funds; wage fund and level of material security of agricultural workers; and the setting of norms.

Dodge, Norton T. "Recruitment and the Quality of the Soviet Agricultural Labor Force." In THE SOVIET RURAL COMMUNITY: A SYMPOSIUM, edited by James R. Millar, pp. 180-213. Urbana: University of Illinois Press, 1971.

> Aspects discussed include sex composition, age structure, education, and recruitment and retention. Charts and tables are included.

Dodge, Norton T., and Feshbach, Murray. "The Role of Women in Soviet Agriculture." In SOVIET AND EAST EUROPEAN AGRICULTURE, edited by Jerzy Karcz, pp. 265-305. Berkeley and Los Angeles: University of California Press, 1967.

> This study examines the participation of women in the agricultural labor force and Soviet policy on the utilization of women in agriculture.

Domar, Evsey D. "The Soviet Collective Farm as a Producer Cooperative." AMERICAN ECONOMIC REVIEW 56 (September 1965): 734-57.

> This paper presents a microeconomic theory of a producer cooperative analogous to the theory of the farm. The author first presents the pure model of the cooperative and then the model with a supply schedule of labor. The effects of price increases on magnitudes of outputs and inputs of the capitalist and cooperative farms and of the effects of changes in rent, tax rates, and prices on employment in the cooperative farm are presented in tables. For further discussion, see: Joan Robinson. "The Soviet Collective Farm as a Producer Cooperative: Comment." AMERICAN ECONOMIC REVIEW 57 (March 1967): 222-23; Evsey D. Domar. "Reply." AMERICAN ECONOMIC REVIEW 57 (March 1967): 223.

Dovring, Folke. "Progress on Mechanization in Soviet Agriculture." In THE SOVIET RURAL COMMUNITY: A SYMPOSIUM, edited by James R. Millar, pp. 259-75. Urbana: University of Illinois Press, 1971.

> The emphasis is on the period 1950-68. Eight tables.

_____. "Soviet Farm Mechanization in Perspective." SLAVIC REVIEW 25 (June 1966): 287-302.

> "The problem here is: given the collectivist ideology which found expression in the collective-farm and state-farm systems, what will mechanization ultimately do to the farm system?" A table provides data on use of labor in agriculture in 1958.

Durgin, Frank A., Jr. "The Growth of Inter-Kolkhoz Cooperation." SOVIET STUDIES 12 (October 1960): 183-89.

> This cooperation has been significant only since the middle 1950s. Reasons for cooperation and the types, numbers, and distribution of inter-kolkhoz enterprise are discussed.

_____. "Monetization and Policy in Soviet Agriculture since 1952." SOVIET STUDIES 15 (April 1964): 375-407.

> This paper describes the gradual shifting, over the past decade, from direction of agriculture based on administrative concerns to direction based on economic and financial concerns. Stressed are

the attempts since 1958 to institute a system of free sales, i.e., a system in which administrative sanctions are replaced by sanctions of financial profits and losses.

──────. "Toward the Abolition of the RTS." SOVIET STUDIES 12 (July 1960): 83-86.

The relations between the RTS (repair tractor stations) and the collective and state farms are discussed.

──────. "The Virgin Lands Programme 1954-1960." SOVIET STUDIES 13 (January 1962): 255-80.

This paper covers Soviet efforts at plowing up virgin land prior to 1954, background of the 1954 program, year-by-year progress in plowing and grain production, impact of the program on agricultural output since 1953, and difficulties encountered to date. Eleven tables.

Eason, Warren W. THE AGRICULTURAL LABOR FORCE AND POPULATION OF THE USSR: 1926-41. Santa Monica, Calif.: RAND Corp., 1954. vii, 210 p.

This study documents the decrease of Soviet agricultural labor force during the first three five-year plans. Many statistical tables.

Ellison, Herbert J. "The Decision to Collectivize Agriculture." AMERICAN SLAVIC AND EAST EUROPEAN REVIEW 20 (April 1961): 189-202.

The article criticizes the official explanation of the need to collectivize agriculture and the unquestioned adoption of this Soviet view by Western scholars.

Feiwel, George R. "The Vicissitudes of Soviet Agriculture. I." RIVISTA INTERNAZIONALE DI SCIENZE ECONOMICHE E COMMERCIALE 19 (August 1972): 748-64.

This discussion of Soviet agriculture emphasizes the 1960s. Table. (See below.)

──────. "The Vicissitudes of Soviet Agriculture. II." RIVISTA INTERNAZIONALE DI SCIENZE ECONOMICHE E COMMERCIALE 19 (September 1972): 906-20.

The emphasis here is on the late 1960s and plans for the 1970s. Two tables. (See above.)

Finegold, I. M. "A Critical Analysis of some Prevailing Concepts Concerning Soviet Agriculture." SOVIET STUDIES 4 (July 1952): 15-31.

This article is essentially a review of Naum Jasny. THE SOCIALIZED AGRICULTURE OF THE USSR: PLANS AND PERFORMANCE.

Stanford, Calif.: Stanford University Press, 1949.

Frank, Andrew G. "Labor Requirements in Soviet Agriculture." REVIEW OF ECONOMICS AND STATISTICS 41 (May 1959): 178-82.

> This paper presents estimates of man days of actual labor inputs in the Ukraine in 1913, 1928, 1937, 1950, and 1955. It then uses 1925/26 and 1922-24 labor use coefficients to compare with "hypothetical" inputs for 1937, 1950, and 1955.

Gaev, A. G. "The Kolkhoz and the Kolkhoz Worker in Soviet Literature." STUDIES ON THE SOVIET UNION n.s. 3, no. 4 (1964): 20-26.

> This article discusses the significance of passages commenting on the peasantry from various literary sources of the 1960s. For a discussion, see the commentary by Boris Wjunow. STUDIES OF THE SOVIET UNION n.s. 3, no. 4 (1964): 26-27.

Gararin, Grigon. "Development of Soviet Agronomy." STUDIES ON THE SOVIET UNION n.s. 7, no. 3 (1968): 36-57.

> In this historical survey data are given on crop yields for selected years, 1913-64.

──────. "Varietal Seed-Breeding in the Soviet Union." STUDIES ON THE SOVIET UNION n.s. 4, no. 3 (1965): 47-58.

> This article discusses seed production and selection in the Soviet Union. A table provides figures on area sown with varietal seeds for various crops in 1958, 1961, and 1962.

Gerschenkron, Alexander. "An Analysis of Soviet Agriculture." JOURNAL OF ECONOMIC HISTORY 11, no. 1 (1951): 42-49.

> This article is a discussion of Naum Jasny. THE SOCIALIZED AGRICULTURE OF THE USSR: PLANS AND PERFORMANCE. Stanford, Calif.: Stanford University Press, 1949.

Goldman, Marshall I. "Commission Trade and the Kolkhoz Market." SOVIET STUDIES 10 (October 1958): 136-45.

> This article discusses the introduction of commission trade in October 1953. Cooperatives were then allowed to market surpluses for the members and collect a percentage of the sale price as commission.

Grossman, Philip. "A Note on Agricultural Employment in the USSR." SOVIET STUDIES 19 (January 1968): 398-404.

> This note summarizes the Nove-Feshbach exchange over the magnitude of Soviet agricultural employment, describes the methods used

to construct the "Balance of Labour Resources," and discusses the validity and significance of official figures.

Hahn, Werner G. THE POLITICS OF SOVIET AGRICULTURE, 1960-1970. Baltimore and London: Johns Hopkins University Press, 1972. xviii, 311 p.

Part one of this study deals with the Khrushchev era and is concerned primarily with intra-agricultural issues. Part two deals with the Brezhnev period and centers on the priorities question, and the problem of resources for agriculture. Eight appendices and an index.

Harris, Chauncy D. "Soviet Agricultural Resources Reappraised." JOURNAL OF FARM ECONOMICS 38 (May 1956): 258-73.

This paper discusses the effect of climate on the possibilities for expanding the cultivated area, the possibilities of increasing yields per acre, and corn production. Thirteen maps and charts. For further discussion, see: Otto Schiller. "Discussion: The Resources and Performance of Soviet Agriculture." JOURNAL OF FARM ECONOMICS 38 (May 1956): 296-308.

Hindus, Maurice. BROKEN EARTH. New York: International Publishers, 1926. 288 p.

The author gives an account of the condition of the Russian peasant obtained from interviews in the Central Russian village of his birth.

Honigsheim, Paul. "The Roots of the Soviet Rural Social Structure: Where and Why It Has Spread." AGRICULTURAL HISTORY 25 (July 1951): 104-14.

Soviet collectivization policies are discussed not as the logical result of Marxian analysis but as "a return to slavophile Greek Orthodox czarism."

Horwitz, Bertrand [N.]., and Whitehouse, F. Douglas. "Soviet Land Value and Enterprise Location." LAND ECONOMICS 49 (May 1973): 233-37.

Topics covered include the effects of the 1966 reforms, concepts of land rent and land value, rent for site value, and suggested solutions for the determining of land values.

Hough, Jerry F. "The Changing Nature of the Kolkhoz Chairman." In THE SOVIET RURAL COMMUNITY: A SYMPOSIUM, edited by James R. Millar, pp. 103-20. Urbana: University of Illinois Press, 1971.

The personnel policies of the Soviet leadership in its selection of kolkhoz chairmen and regional agricultural and Party officials are outlined.

Hubbard, Leonard E. THE ECONOMICS OF SOVIET AGRICULTURE. London: Macmillan and Co., 1939. xii, 315.

> The first nine chapters deal with peasants and agriculture before the Revolution. The remaining fifteen chapters concern the Soviet period. Subjects discussed include the New Economic Policy and the peasantry; forced collectivization; administration and organization of labor; domestic economy of collective farms; and the effects of collectivization on the peasant. Appendices, glossary, and index.

Hultquist, Warren E. "Soviet Sugar-beet Production: Some Geographical Aspects of Agro-industrial Coordination." In SOVIET AND EAST EUROPEAN AGRICULTURE, edited by Jerzy Karcz, pp. 135-55. Berkeley and Los Angeles: University of California Press, 1967.

> This essay considers some geographic problems resulting from the Soviet drive for a larger store of sugar.

"Irrigation: Progress Since 1960." CENTRAL ASIAN REVIEW 2, no. 2 (1963): 138-54.

> This article reviews development in inter-republican irrigation schemes and projects in Uzbekistan, Turkmenistan, Kirgizia, and Tadzhikistan.

Jackson, William A. Douglas. THE NATURE AND STRUCTURE OF SOVIET AGRICULTURE. New York: Institute of International Education, 1963. 33 p.

> This paper discusses natural conditions, crops, livestock, organization, management, agricultural research, and U.S. research on Soviet agriculture. Several tables and bibliographical appendices.

_____. "The Soviet Approach to the Good Earth: Myth and Reality." In SOVIET AGRICULTURE AND PEASANT AFFAIRS, edited by Roy D. Laird, pp. 171-89. Lawrence: University of Kansas Press, 1963.

> The author surveys the assumptions which underlie Soviet agricultural policy, the myth of unlimited agricultural resources, and the problem of agricultural regionalization.

Jacobs, Everett M. "Ownership and Planning in Soviet and East European Agriculture." In THE PREDICTIONS OF COMMUNIST ECONOMIC PERFORMANCE, edited by Peter J. D. Wiles, pp. 39-86. Cambridge: At the University Press, 1971.

> This questionaire-type study provides easy-to-use material for the assessment of the agricultural sectors of the Soviet and East European economies. Four tables.

Jasny, Naum. "The Failure of the Soviet Animal Industry. I." SOVIET STUDIES 15 (October 1963): 187-218.

Inefficiencies in the Soviet animal industry are discussed. Part A discusses the animal industry in selected countries outside the USSR; part B, in the USSR. Four tables. For further discussion, see: Enid Smith. "Comparing Soviet Agriculture." SOVIET STUDIES 15 (July 1964): 82-89. (See below.)

———. "The Failure of the Soviet Animal Industry. II." SOVIET STUDIES 15 (January 1964): 285-307.

Inefficiency in the Soviet animal industry is discussed further. Eight tables. (See above.)

———. KHRUSHCHEV'S CROP POLICY. Glasgow: G. Outram, 1965. 243 p.

The author examines low-yielding and high-yielding crops (such as maize and sugar beets) and compares Soviet agricultural statistics and production with those in the West. He compares, in detail, maize cultivation in the USSR and United States. Tables, glossary, and maps.

———. "Labor Productivity in Agriculture in USSR and USA." JOURNAL OF FARM ECONOMICS 27 (May 1945): 419-32.

Topics covered include output, farm population and labor, land, capital and draft animals, worker productivity, and various crops. Data on farm product output in 1938 and labor inputs are provided in two tables.

———. "Low- and High-Yielding Crops in the USSR." In SOVIET AGRICULTURE AND PEASANT AFFAIRS, edited by Roy D. Laird, pp. 215-65. Lawrence: University of Kansas Press, 1963.

The author discusses Khrushchev's new agronomy, which attempts to bring the output per hectare of land to a maximum.

———. "Peasant Incomes Under Full Scale Collectivization." In his ESSAYS ON THE SOVIET ECONOMY, pp. 93-157. New York: Praeger, 1962.

This essay covers the periods 1927-28 and 1937-40. Jasny discusses material and procedure; income in kind in the form of farm products; purchases of farm products; industrial consumer goods; nonmoney and total money incomes; addition to the fixed capital stock; and total expenditures. Tables.

———. "The Plight of the Collective Farms." JOURNAL OF FARM ECONOMICS 30 (May 1948): 304-21.

The topics treated here include the Marxist preference for big farms; collectivization; the procurement system; the effect on output; labor productivity; the rewards of the collective farm laborer; and the means used to make him work for meager rewards.

———. "Production Costs and Prices in Soviet Agriculture." In SOVIET AND EAST EUROPEAN AGRICULTURE, edited by Jerzy Karcz, pp. 212-64. Berkeley and Los Angeles: University of California Press, 1967.

> The author deals principally with production cost since there is a scarcity of data on prices of individual farm products. He also attempts to compare the value of farm output as a whole for the USSR with the corresponding item for the United States.

———. "Prospects for Soviet Farm Output and Labor." REVIEW OF ECONOMICS AND STATISTICS 36 (May 1954): 212-19.

> This paper reviews farm output in the past and looks at factors which will influence output in 1954-60.

———. THE SOCIALIZED AGRICULTURE OF THE USSR: PLANS AND PERFORMANCE. Stanford, Calif.: Stanford University Press, 1949. xv, 837 p.

> Part one deals with marketings and consumption. Part two analyzes preceding developments in agriculture dating back to the beginning of this century. Part three is concerned with socialized organization and control. Part four surveys mechanization and outputs. Part five deals primarily with the methods of estimating output. Four maps.

———. "Soviet Agriculture and the Fourth Five-Year Plan." RUSSIAN REVIEW 8 (April 1949): 135-41.

> This paper looks at the possibilities for the agricultural sector to meet its planned targets of doubling the 1945 output by 1950.

Jensen, Robert G. "The Soviet Concept of Agricultural Regionalization and Its Development." In SOVIET AND EAST EUROPEAN AGRICULTURE, edited by Jerzy Karcz, pp. 77-103. Berkeley and Los Angeles: University of California Press, 1967.

> Jensen examines the aim of agricultural regionalization and its theoretical significance; regionalization as part of a Russian intellectual tradition; agricultural regionalization during the Soviet period; regionalization and the territorial planning of agriculture; and agricultural regionalization and price zonation.

Johnson, Alvin. "The Communist Farmer." SOCIAL RESEARCH 25 (July 1958): 228-33.

> This paper discusses the conflict between Communist theory and peasant or farmer practicality and need for material incentives.

Johnson, D. Gale. "Agricultural Production." In ECONOMIC TRENDS IN THE SOVIET UNION, edited by Abram Bergson and Simon Kuznets, pp. 203-34. Cambridge, Mass.: Harvard University Press, 1963.

The article interprets a large amount of data on agricultural inputs, outputs, and factors associated with increased agricultural output. Some of the data go back to the tsarist period.

_____. "The Environment for Technological Change in Soviet Agriculture." AMERICAN ECONOMIC REVIEW 56 (May 1966): 145-53.

Topics covered include farm size, supply of new inputs, lack of confidence by collective farm workers, lack of extension services, and irrational planning. For further discussion, see: Alexander Eckstein and Joseph S. Berliner. "Soviet Economy--Discussion." AMERICAN ECONOMIC REVIEW 56 (May 1966): 154-58.

_____. "Eye-Witness Appraisal of Soviet Farming, 1955." JOURNAL OF FARM ECONOMICS 38 (May 1956): 287-96.

This paper is an appraisal of Soviet agriculture based on a five-week visit. For further discussion, see: Otto Schiller. "Discussion: The Resources and Performance of Soviet Agriculture." JOURNAL OF FARM ECONOMICS 38 (May 1956): 296-308.

_____. "Soviet Agriculture Revisited." AMERICAN JOURNAL OF AGRICULTURAL ECONOMICS 53 (May 1971): 257-64.

Topics covered include input changes, investment, the private plots, changes in labor requirements, agricultural price policy, and returns to labor. Tables. For further discussion, see comments by D. E. Hathaway, Roy D. Laird, James S. Plaxico, and W. Neill Schaller. AMERICAN JOURNAL OF AGRICULTURAL ECONOMICS 53 (May 1971): 264-68.

_____. "The Soviet Livestock Sector: Problems and Prospects." ASSOCIATION FOR COMPARATIVE ECONOMIC STUDIES BULLETIN 16 (Fall 1974): 41-62.

Johnson examines policies in the feed and livestock sector, considers plans for raising output by improving the feed mix, and examines the interaction of pricing incentives with the cost of meat production.

Johnson, D. Gale, and Kahan, Arcadius. THE SOVIET AGRICULTURAL PROGRAM: AN EVALUATION OF THE 1965 GOALS. Santa Monica, Calif.: RAND Corp., 1962. xi, 111 p.

This study evaluates the feasibility of the Seven-Year Plan goals for eleven basic agricultural commodities.

_____. "Soviet Agriculture: Structure and Growth." In COMPARISONS OF THE U.S. AND SOVIET ECONOMIES, U.S. Congress. Joint Economic Committee, pp. 201-37. Washington, D.C.: Government Printing Office, 1959.

The paper contains discussions of the growth of agricultural output; changes in inputs and average productivity; an explanation of long-run changes in output; Khrushchev's pronouncement that the USSR will overtake the United States in per capita output of butter, milk, and meat; and progress made during the Sixth Five-Year Plan. Many tables.

Joravsky, David. "Ideology and Progress in Crop Rotation." In SOVIET AND EAST EUROPEAN AGRICULTURE, edited by Jerzy Karcz, pp. 156-74. Berkeley and Los Angeles: University of California Press, 1967.

The author attempts to determine whether the Soviet policy of "squeezing the peasants" was tantamount to a rejection of rational agronomy and whether this policy generated gains as well as losses for Soviet agriculture.

Kabysh, Simon. "The Agricultural Scene." STUDIES ON THE SOVIET UNION n.s. 5, no. 1 (1965): 55-64.

This paper examines the agricultural scene in Siberia and the Far East broken down by districts. Tables.

─────. "Agriculture." STUDIES ON THE SOVIET UNION n.s. 8, no. 1 (1968): 14-21.

Agricultural output of Soviet Central Asia is discussed. Tables.

─────. "Mechanization of Agriculture." STUDIES ON THE SOVIET UNION n.s. 5, no. 3 (1966): 72-78.

Acquisition and maintenance of agricultural machinery is discussed. A table provides figures on machinery in service for selected years, 1953-63.

─────. "The Merging of Sovkhozes with Kolkhozes." STUDIES ON THE SOVIET UNION n.s. 3, no. 4 (1960): 91-98.

This paper surveys the history of sovkhozes in the USSR from the original decision to organize them in 1917 to the late 1950s. The author evaluates the decision in the mid-1950s to convert unprofitable kolkhozes into sovkhozes or to merge them with sovkhozes as a mistake as far as increasing production is concerned.

─────. "New Policy on the Private Plots." STUDIES ON THE SOVIET UNION n.s. 6, no. 1 (1966): 26-34.

This article discusses the liberalization of restrictions on use of private plots in 1965. A table presents figures on livestock in public and private ownership in 1965.

——. "The Permanent Crisis in Soviet Agriculture." STUDIES ON THE SOVIET UNION n.s. 3, no. 4 (1964): 164-82.

> Topics discussed include cultivation of the virgin lands; obligatory corn planting; gross yields and exports and imports of grain; machinery; chemical fertilizers; capital investment; the private sector and payments to kolkhoz workers; and irrigation. Tables. For further discussion, see below.

——. "The Permanent Crisis in Soviet Agriculture." STUDIES ON THE SOVIET UNION n.s. 4, no. 4 (1965): 126-40.

> See above.

——. "Problems Faced by Soviet Agriculture." STUDIES ON THE SOVIET UNION n.s. 7, no. 3 (1968): 27-35.

> Topics discussed include post-Stalin policies, livestock-breeding, and mechanization.

——. "Soviet Agriculture." STUDIES ON THE SOVIET UNION n.s. 2, no. 3 (1963): 62-70.

> This survey of agricultural policies deals largely with the period 1953-63. Tables.

——. "Soviet Agriculture and the Programme." In THE U.S.S.R. AND THE FUTURE; AN ANALYSIS OF THE NEW PROGRAM OF THE CPSU, edited by Leonard B. Schapiro, pp. 127-44. New York: Praeger, 1962.

> The problems of the agricultural sector in the Party program to achieve full communism in the Soviet Union are discussed. Several tables.

——. "Soviet State Farms." STUDIES ON THE SOVIET UNION n.s. 3, no. 1 (1963): 72-82.

> The article chronicles the political and production ups and downs of the Soviet state farms from World War II to 1962. Three short tables are included. The final two pages provide further data on collective, state, and other state-owned agricultural enterprises for 1961.

Kahan, Arcadius. "Agriculture." In PROSPECTS FOR SOVIET SOCIETY, edited by Allen Kassof, pp. 263-90. New York: Praeger, 1968.

> This paper discusses resource allocation; the efficiency of the planning process in agriculture; farm organization; specialization by region and by farm; the changing composition of inputs; and farm prices and farm incomes. Table.

_____. "Changes in Labor Inputs in Soviet Agriculture." JOURNAL OF POLITICAL ECONOMY 67 (October 1959): 451-62.

Effects of Soviet policy on the agricultural labor force are examined. Kahan traces the impact upon the volume of labor inputs in agriculture of recent changes in agricultural policy. Six tables.

_____. "The Collective Farm System in Russia: Some Aspects of its Contribution to Soviet Economic Development." In AGRICULTURE IN ECONOMIC DEVELOPMENT, edited by Carl Eicher and Lawrence Witt, pp. 251-71. New York: McGraw-Hill, 1964.

This paper discusses socialization of agriculture, the collective system between 1928 and 1962, agricultural contribution to the economy, and taxation. Six tables.

_____. "A Note on Estimates of Soviet Grain Output, 1934-38." JOURNAL OF POLITICAL ECONOMY 64 (June 1956): 259-60.

This note looks at available figures and discusses their consistency and reliability. Two tables provide estimates of yields per hectare and total short output.

_____. "Soviet Statistics of Agricultural Output." In SOVIET AGRICULTURE AND PEASANT AFFAIRS, edited by Roy D. Laird, pp. 134-68. Lawrence: University of Kansas Press, 1963.

Soviet agricultural statistics are discussed as: (1) a means of describing a particular economic reality, reporting past performance, and conveying information; (2) a tool of analysis, planning, and control; and (3) shorthand for administrative decisions and as a guide for management.

Kalvoda, Josef. "Soviet Agricultural Reform and the Future of the Collective Farms." RUSSIAN REVIEW 19 (October 1960): 384-95.

Kalvoda considers the managing of the collective farm sector, Khrushchev's reforms (including the disbanding of the machine-tractor stations), and their chances of success.

Karcz, Jerzy F. "Back on the Grain Front." SOVIET STUDIES 22 (October 1970): 262-94.

This paper discusses in detail the reliability of Soviet grain statistics and then examines statistics on grain output during 1909-13 and grain marketings. Tables.

_____. "Farm Marketings and State Procurements: Definitions and Interpretations." SOVIET STUDIES 15 (October 1963): 152-66.

This article explores the coverage of Soviet data on market output of agriculture and defines more precisely the officially published series on the volume of state procurements (now also called state purchases) of various farm products. A table shows shares of USSR state procurement in market output, 1953-61.

_____. "From Stalin to Brezhnev: Soviet Agricultural Policy in Historical Perspective." In THE SOVIET RURAL COMMUNITY: A SYMPOSIUM, edited by James R. Millar, pp. 36-70.

Three tables are included.

_____. "Khrushchev's Impact on Soviet Agriculture." AGRICULTURAL HISTORY 40 (January 1966): 19-38.

Karcz assesses the changes in Soviet agriculture during the Khrushchev era. A table of performance indicators (1958-64) and a table showing trends in sown areas and livestock holdings in the private sector (1959-63) are included.

_____. "The New Soviet Agricultural Programme." SOVIET STUDIES 17 (October 1965): 129-61.

This paper describes measures of agricultural policy undertaken by Khrushchev's successors. Six tables. A short appendix presents an index of net agricultural output.

_____. "Quantitative Analysis of the Collective Farm Market." AMERICAN ECONOMIC REVIEW 54 (June 1964): 315-34.

The author discusses market statistics, their interpretation, and presents a series of estimates of extra-village market prices as well as of quantities sold on this market during the years 1940, 1950-62. Tables.

_____. "Seven Years on the Farm: Retrospect and Prospects." In NEW DIRECTIONS IN THE SOVIET ECONOMY, U.S. Congress. Joint Economic Committee, pp. 383-450. Washington, D.C.: Government Printing Office, 1966.

This paper discusses agricultural policy from 1953 to 1964, agriculture and plan targets, and the MTS reform. An appendix discusses Soviet income elasticities of demand. Tables.

_____. "Soviet Agriculture: A Balance Sheet." In THE DEVELOPMENT OF THE SOVIET ECONOMY: PLAN AND PERFORMANCE, edited by Vladimir G. Treml, pp. 108-46. New York: Praeger, 1968.

This paper evaluates the performance of the agricultural sector since the Revolution. Derivation of a deflator for peasant incomes is discussed in the appendix. Tables.

_____. "Soviet Inspectorates for Agricultural Procurements in 1961." CALIFORNIA SLAVIC STUDIES 3 (1964): 149-72.

This article sets into historical perspective the recent activities of the lowest units of this administrative pyramid (governing the agricultural sector).

———. "Thoughts on the Grain Problem." SOVIET STUDIES 18 (April 1967): 399-434.

Topics covered include the Stalin-Nemchinov data on grain marketings in the 1920s and the 1928 crisis. Tables. For further discussion, see: R. Beermann. "The Grain Problem and Anti-Speculation Laws." SOVIET STUDIES 19 (July 1967): 127-29.

Karcz, Jerzy F., and Timoshenko, V[ladimir]. P. "Soviet Agricultural Policy, 1953-1962." STANFORD UNIVERSITY. FOOD RESEARCH INSTITUTE. STUDIES 4, no. 2 (1964): 123-63.

There is a brief discussion of the state of agriculture after Stalin, an evaluation of the virgin lands program, and coverage of the years 1953-57 and 1958-62. A map shows value of gross agricultural output by region in 1953 and 1961. Tables.

Karpov, K. "Some Problems Relating to the Economic Recovery of Backward Kolkhozes." ANNALS OF PUBLIC AND COOPERATIVE ECONOMY 35 (April-September 1964): 181-95.

This is a complete translation of an article published in KOMMUNIST, no. 2 (January 1964): 48-57. It is concerned with administrative means of adjusting economic relations between the state and the individual kolkhoz so that backward enterprises will be given the means and motivation to become efficient producers.

Katkoff, Vladimir. "Agricultural Labor Force in the USSR." JOURNAL OF FARM ECONOMICS 39 (February 1957): 128-39.

The size and composition of the agricultural labor force, mostly in the years 1940-55 are examined. Tables.

———. "Financing of Agriculture in Russia." JOURNAL OF FARM ECONOMICS 22 (August 1940): 640-46.

This note surveys the development of Soviet financing of agriculture through the Agricultural Bank from 1928-40.

———. "The Price System in Socialized Agriculture." JOURNAL OF MARKETING 16 (July 1951): 43-50.

Topics covered include market fees on peasant to consumer sales, the relationship between state and market prices, rationing and prices during and after World War II, and the outlook for future prices.

_____. "The Soviet Citrus Industry." SOUTHERN ECONOMIC JOURNAL 18 (January 1952): 374-80.

> This article surveys the development of the Russian citrus fruit industry since 1914. The emphasis, however, is on the 1940s. Tables.

_____. "The Soviet Dairy Industry." JOURNAL OF FARM ECONOMICS 34 (August 1952): 378-86.

> Topics discussed include sources of milk production in 1939, ice cream production, the butter industry, the effects of World War II, and recovery from the war. Tables.

_____. "Soviet Grain Production: 1940-1950." LAND ECONOMICS 26 (August 1950): 207-21.

> This detailed discussion of the level and geographic distribution of Soviet grain productions includes ten tables and a map.

_____. "The Soviet Livestock Industry." JOURNAL OF FARM ECONOMICS 32 (February 1950): 128-34.

> This note surveys the livestock population and its distribution roughly between 1940 and 1950. Tables.

Kershaw, Joseph A. "Agricultural Output and Employment." In SOVIET ECONOMIC GROWTH: CONDITIONS AND PERSPECTIVES, edited by Abram Bergson, pp. 294-319. Evanston, Ill.: Row, Peterson, 1953.

> Kershaw discusses the labor-land ratio and its significance; the dual nature of the agricultural problem; the release of farm labor to industry; and the volume of farm output. The article is followed by comments by Abram Bergson, Richard H. Moorsteen, and Edward Ames, pp. 315-19.

"The Khrushchev Livestock Plan." SOVIET STUDIES 7 (July 1955): 117.

> This note describes the livestock plan published on February 3, 1955.

Klatt, Werner. "Output and Utilization of Foodstuffs in the Soviet Union." STUDIES ON THE SOVIET UNION n.s. 3, no. 4 (1964): 99-109.

> This paper discusses supply and demand for foodstuffs in the Soviet Union in 1963-64. Tables. See the commentaries by Jerzy F. Karcz, pp. 110-16, and Luba Richter, pp. 116-22.

_____. "Soviet Agriculture." In THE PREDICTIONS OF COMMUNIST ECONOMIC PERFORMANCE, edited by Peter J. D. Wiles, pp. 309-22. Cambridge: At the University Press, 1971.

Topics discussed include the influence of ideology, food consumption data, supply and demand 1966-67, and prospects for 1967-70. Three tables.

Kraev, M. "The Collective Farm Labour Day. Pt. I - II." SOVIET STUDIES 1 (October 1949; January 1950): 166-71; 261-68.

This report consists of a translation from "O Kolkhoznom Trudodne." VOPROSY EKONOMIKI [Questions of economics] no. 3 (1949): 33-44. It discusses the problems in arriving at an economic definition of the labor day.

Krueger, Constance B. "A Note on the Size of Subsidies on Soviet Government Purchases of Agricultural Products." ASSOCIATION FOR COMPARATIVE ECONOMIC STUDIES BULLETIN 16 (Fall 1974): 63-72.

The calculations involved are shown in the table and notes, while the text discusses the significance of the subsidies.

Krylov, K. "Some Recent Problems in Soviet Agriculture." STUDIES ON THE SOVIET UNION n.s. 1, no. 2 (December 1958): 87-98.

This article examines the reasons for the reforms of the kolkhoz system and the abolition of the machine-tractor stations in 1958. The effects of these reforms are seen as minimal. Tables.

Kucherov, Samuel. "The Future of the Soviet Collective Farm." AMERICAN SLAVIC AND EAST EUROPEAN REVIEW 19 (April 1960): 180-201.

This article reviews the various steps taken by the Soviet government in its efforts to turn the peasant class into an agricultural proletariat and to bring the kolkhozes closer to the status of sovkhozes. Topics covered include the nature of socialist property, the sale of MTS machinery to the kolkhozes, sovkhozes versus kolkhozes, kolkhoz life, and fixed wages for peasants.

Kutt, Aleksander. "Tractive Power for Field Work in Soviet Agriculture." STUDIES ON THE SOVIET UNION n.s. 3, no. 3 (1964): 158-71.

This paper presents a mechanical power count of tractive power for field work, compares U.S. and Soviet agriculture in horses versus tractors, in a hypothetical tractor count, and in self-propelled grain combines. Tables.

Kuvshinov, I. S. "The Experience to Large-scale Collective and State Farms of the U.S.S.R." In THE ROLE OF AGRICULTURE IN ECONOMIC DEVELOPMENT, pp. 307-30. Proceedings of the Eleventh International Conference of Agricultural Economists held at Cuernavaca, Morelos, Mex., 1961. London: Oxford University Press, 1963.

A Soviet economist discusses the achievements made by collective and state farms.

Labsvirs, Janis. "The Effect of Collectivization on Latvian Agriculture." SLAVIC REVIEW 22 (March 1963): 121-25.

>This article compares "the data reflecting agricultural production in the LSSR with those on prewar Latvia to see if the comparison supports official Soviet claims about the superiority of socialist agriculture in Latvia. Four tables.

Laird, Roy D. COLLECTIVE FARMING IN RUSSIA: A POLITICAL STUDY OF THE SOVIET KOLKHOZY. Lawrence: University of Kansas Publications, 1958. v, 176 p.

>Part one of the book gives a summary of the agrarian revolution (1861-1918); part two deals with Bolshevik agricultural policy from 1917-27; part three outlines the kolkhoz system; and part four discusses the Soviet agricultural revolution during the third decade. Bibliography and index.

_____. "Collectivization: New and Old Myths." STUDIES ON THE SOVIET UNION n.s. 6, no. 4 (1967): 78-88.

>The views of Marx, Lenin, Stalin, Khrushchev, and his successors are discussed, as well as the post-1966 commitment to collectivization.

_____. "The Demise of the Machine Tractor Station." AMERICAN SLAVIC AND EAST EUROPEAN REVIEW 17 (December 1958): 418-25.

>This article discusses the machine-tractor stations as an essential feature of forced collectivization and control, the dissolution of the stations under Khrushchev, and the remaining problems.

_____. "The Dilemma of Soviet Agricultural Administration: The Short and Unhappy Life of the TPA." AGRICULTURAL HISTORY 40 (January 1966): 11-18.

>This chronicles the brief history of the Territorial Production Administration, created by Khrushchev in 1962 to further control agricultural production.

_____. "Khrushchev's Administrative Reforms in Agriculture: An Appraisal." In SOVIET AND EAST EUROPEAN AGRICULTURE, edited by Jerzy Karcz, pp. 29-56. Berkeley and Los Angeles: University of California Press, 1967.

>The first part is concerned with the major changes in Russian agriculture, the second with an account of the agricultural scene by 1964, and the third with agriculture after 1965.

_____. "The Politics of Soviet Agriculture." In SOVIET AGRICULTURE: THE PERMANENT CRISIS, edited by Roy D. Laird and Edward L. Crowley, pp. 147-58. New York: Praeger, 1965.

The author discusses the importance of the political factor in Soviet agriculture, Soviet agricultural theory, the theory in practice, and advantages and disadvantages of the system.

———. "Soviet Agriculture in 1973 and Beyond in Light of United States Performance." RUSSIAN REVIEW 33 (October 1974): 372-85.

Soviet agricultural output and policies are discussed. Ten tables.

———. "Soviet Goals for 1965 and the Problems of Agriculture." SLAVIC REVIEW 20 (October 1961): 454-64.

This article discusses the backwardness and neglect of the agricultural sector and the consequences for the economy-wide goals for 1965. Tables.

———, ed. SOVIET AGRICULTURE AND PEASANT AFFAIRS. Lawrence: University of Kansas Press, 1963. xi, 335 p.

The papers in this volume consider the following questions: How different is rural Russia under Khrushchev from the situation under Stalin? What is the impact of the new incentives, both material and psychic, on the peasants and on the administration? What is the present level of Soviet agricultural science and practice?

Laird, Roy D., and Crowley, Edward L., eds. SOVIET AGRICULTURE: THE PERMANENT CRISIS. Symposium held in Munich, Ger., 1964. New York: Praeger, 1965.

The essays in this volume are concerned with the following questions: (1) Are some of the fundamental changes in agriculture (1962) marking the advent of a revolutionary situation in agriculture? (2) Will a new era of rational decision making make the intensification of agriculture more successful? (3) What benefits can be expected from increased usage of fertilizers, cultivation of new lands, and an increase in wages for agricultural workers? (4) How have kolkhozes been affected by Territorial Production Administration controls? (5) What can one expect from future advances in Soviet agriculture?

Laird, Roy D., and Laird, Betty A. SOVIET COMMUNISM AND AGRARIAN REVOLUTION. Baltimore: Penguin, 1970. 158 p.

Part one deals with forced collectivization, Stalinist kolkhozy, and Soviet commitment to collectivization in the 1960s and beyond. Part two covers science and Soviet agriculture, Soviet technical potential in 1980, and the price of collectivization. Part three discusses the spreading worldwide agrarian revolution, which was initiated by the Bolshevik Revolution in Russia. Bibliography. Paperback.

Russian Agriculture and the Peasantry

Laird, Roy D., et al. THE RISE AND FALL OF THE MTS AS AN INSTRUMENT OF SOVIET RULE. Lawrence: University of Kansas Press, 1960. 97 p.

> This study constitutes an analysis of the MTS in its political context. The authors examine the controlling function of the MTS over the peasants and their product. Bibliography.

Lewin, Moshe. "The Immediate Background of Soviet Collectivization." SOVIET STUDIES 17 (October 1965): 162-97.

> Topics discussed include the New Economic Policy; weaknesses in Party policy; the role of the 15th Congress; the grain crisis; the right-wing of the Party; the Five-Year Plan; and Stalin's attitude. For further discussion, see: Rudolf Schlesinger. "On the Scope of Necessity and Error. Some Observations on Dr. Lewin's Article." SOVIET STUDIES 17 (January 1966): 353-67.

_____. RUSSIAN PEASANTS AND SOVIET POWER: A STUDY OF COLLECTIVIZATION. Translated by Irene Nove. Evanston, Ill.: Northwestern University Press, 1968. 539 p.

> This book examines the period between the grain crisis of the winter of 1927-28 and the onset of intensive and ruthless collectivization during the winter of 1929-30. However, the author also discusses peasant society during the period 1925-27, prior to collectivization.

_____. "Who was the Soviet Kulak?" SOVIET STUDIES 18 (October 1966): 189-212.

> This paper discusses the defining of the kulaks, their economic potential, and their social position. See also: R. Beerman. "Comment on Who was the Soviet Kulak?" SOVIET STUDIES 18 (January 1967): 371-75.

Liastchenko, Peter I. "Technical Reconstruction and the Growth of Production in the Agriculture of the USSR." JOURNAL OF FARM ECONOMICS 16 (July 1934): 539-43.

> This short note surveys planned and actual growth in crops between 1928 and 1932. Four tables.

Lovell, C. A. Knox. "The Role of Private Subsidiary Farming During the Soviet Seven Year Plan; 1959-65." SOVIET STUDIES 20 (July 1968): 46-66.

> Achievements of the private agricultural sector during the Seven-Year Plan are examined as responses to the changing attitudes and policies of the state. Eleven tables.

Luxenburg, Norman. "Soviet Agriculture Since Khrushchev." RUSSIAN REVIEW 30 (January 1971): 64-68.

This short article surveys Soviet agricultural output in the 1960s. Seven tables.

McAuley, Alastain N. D. "Kolkhoz Problems in Recent Literary Magazines." SOVIET STUDIES 15 (January 1964): 308-30.

Problems covered include rural conditions, the kolkhoznik, the kolkhoz chairman, and interference by the Party and the state.

Maggs, Peter B. "The Law of Farm-Farmer Relations." In THE SOVIET RURAL COMMUNITY: A SYMPOSIUM, edited by James R. Millar, pp. 139-56. Urbana: University of Illinois Press, 1971.

This paper discusses farm law governing the relations between the worker and the state farm and the member and the collective farm.

Male, D. J. RUSSIAN PEASANT ORGANIZATION BEFORE COLLECTIVIZATION. A STUDY OF COMMUNE AND GATHERING, 1925-1930. London and New York: Cambridge University Press, 1971. viii, 253 p.

The twofold nature of the commune--as land holding organ and unit of local administration--is examined. Its response to the pressures for change in the late 1920s is also stressed. Part one deals with the function and organization of the commune in its agricultural perspective. Part two examines the relationship of the commune to Soviet society. Bibliography and index.

_____. "The Village Community in the USSR: 1925-1930." SOVIET STUDIES 14 (January 1963): 225-48.

Forms of self-government among the peasants to the end of the NEP period are considered. Six tables.

Maynard, John. "Collective Farming in the USSR." SLAVONIC REVIEW 15 (July 1936): 47-69.

The author describes the effects of collectivization on the peasantry, as well as the condition of the peasant under collectivization.

Mertsalov, V. "Collectivisation in the USSR." STUDIES ON THE SOVIET UNION n.s. 1, (July 1957): 37-57.

This extensive survey of Soviet efforts to collectivize agriculture is divided into the following sections: war communism, the New Economic Policy, the establishment of collective farms, collective farm policy after Stalin, and the situation in early 1957. Tables.

Millar, James R. "Financial Innovation in Contemporary Soviet Agricultural Policy." SLAVIC REVIEW 32 (March 1973): 91-114.

This article reviews changes made in finances of the agricultural sector since the 1950s. Topics covered include financing in the collective farm sector and innovations in financing in the state farm sector and in other agricultural organizations. Tables.

_____. "Financing the Modernization of Kolkhozy." In THE SOVIET RURAL COMMUNITY: A SYMPOSIUM, edited by James R. Millar, pp. 276-303. Urbana: University of Illinois Press, 1971.

This paper focuses on how the increased access of the kolkhoz sector to the Soviet main money circuit has been financed since 1953 and on the problems that have characterized this process. Tables.

_____, ed. THE SOVIET RURAL COMMUNITY: A SYMPOSIUM. Urbana: University of Illinois Press, 1971. xv, 420 p.

This book includes fifteen papers on Soviet agriculture by noted specialists under four headings: (1) agricultural policy in historical perspective; (2) rural administration, law, and farm management; (3) recent trends in the rural economy; and (4) the texture of rural life. Selected bibliography and index.

Miller, Jacob. "The Reorganization of the MTS." SOVIET STUDIES 10 (July 1958): 84-94.

This article reviews the subject as treated in Soviet publications and by the Central Committee. A table shows numbers of farms buying machines and paying for them quickly in selected districts.

_____, ed. "The Agricultural Planning Order." SOVIET STUDIES 7 (July 1955): 93-102.

This article presents a translation and discussion of an order published on March 11, 1955, changing the practice of agricultural planning.

_____, ed. "Collective Farm Policy, Conditions and Incentives." SOVIET STUDIES 2 (July 1950): 70-94.

This article consists of three translations from Soviet periodicals.

Miller, Margaret S. "Notes on Agricultural Development." CENTRAL ASIAN REVIEW 16, no. 2 (1968): 122-35.

These notes are based on materials from the Central Asian press from late 1966 and May, November, and December 1967. Cotton, other crops, labor, management, livestock, and soil erosion are discussed.

Miller, Robert F. "Continuity and Change in the Administration of Soviet Agriculture Since Stalin." In THE SOVIET RURAL COMMUNITY: A SYMPOSIUM, edited by James R. Miller, pp. 73-102. Urbana: University of Illinois

Press, 1971.

> Administrative policies are treated in chronological order.

_____. ONE HUNDRED THOUSAND TRACTORS: THE MTS AND THE DEVELOPMENT OF CONTROLS IN SOVIET AGRICULTURE. Cambridge, Mass.: Harvard University Press, 1970. xv, 423 p.

> This work discusses the historical and ideological background of the machine-tractor stations, their relation to agricultural administration and the system of Party controls at the village level, and their final disbanding. Tables and index.

Mills, Richard M. "The Formation of the Virgin Lands Policy." SLAVIC REVIEW 29 (March 1970): 58-69.

> This paper surveys the political background of this policy.

Narkiewicz, Olga A. "Soviet Administration and the Grain Crisis of 1927-28." SOVIET STUDIES 20 (October 1968): 235-41.

> This paper discusses the circumstances of the decision to collectivize and its immediate effects.

Nazartsev, N. "The Farms Set Their Own Labour-day Minima." SOVIET STUDIES 6 (January 1955): 332-36.

> This is a translation from SELSKOYE KHOZYAISTVO (August 31, 1954). A table shows average input of labor days by time of year.

Neetz, Roger E. "Inside the Agriculture Index of the U.S.S.R." In NEW DIRECTIONS IN THE SOVIET ECONOMY, U.S. Congress. Joint Economic Committee, pp. 483-93. Washington, D.C.: Government Printing Office, 1966.

> In this paper two sets of Soviet agricultural price weights are compared. Their applicability in the construction of an index is made. Tables.

"New Norms in Livestock Farms." SOVIET STUDIES 6 (July 1954): 107-8.

> This note discusses the new norms published on January 20, 1954.

"The New State Farms: Party Organization and Relations With Local Government." SOVIET STUDIES 7 (October 1955): 233-35.

> This note recounts a report concerning a successful state farm established in Kazakhstan.

Newth, J. A. "Kolkhoz Capital Assets 1952-56." SOVIET STUDIES 10 (July 1958): 98-99.

Two tables provide the data.

———. "The Kolkhoz Household: Ukraine, 1950-1955." SOVIET STUDIES 11 (January 1960): 307-16.

Nine tables.

———. "Kolkhoz Trade in April, 1957." SOVIET STUDIES 10 (October 1958): 206-10.

This note reports on an investigation of agricultural trade in the free peasant market conducted by the Central Statistical Administration.

———. "Soviet Agriculture: The Private Sector 1950-1959." SOVIET STUDIES 13 (October 1961): 160-71.

Data on sown area, yields, and share of total output produced in the private sector are provided in eleven tables.

———. "Soviet Agriculture: The Private Sector 1950-1959--Animal Husbandry." SOVIET STUDIES 13 (April 1962): 414-32.

Many tables comprise this study.

Nicholaevsky, Boris I. "The New Soviet Campaign Against the Peasants." RUSSIAN REVIEW 10 (April 1951): 81-98.

This article is concerned with Soviet efforts to enlarge both the collective farm and the work brigade within the collective farm structure in the early 1950s. The history of this policy is also discussed.

Nimitz, Nancy. "Agriculture Under Khrushchev: The Lean Years." PROBLEMS OF COMMUNISM 14 (May-June 1965): 10-22.

This essay "offers a critique which in some ways parallels Brezhnev's criticism of Khrushchev's agricultural policies, while attempting also to assess Khrushchev's personal responsibility for the poor record in agriculture under the Seven-Year Plan."

———. "Farm Employment in the Soviet Union, 1928-1963." In SOVIET AND EAST EUROPEAN AGRICULTURE, edited by Jerzy F. Karcz, pp. 175-211. Berkeley and Los Angeles: University of California Press, 1967.

The article contains, in table form, an account of Soviet farm employment (1928-63) for the private sector as well as for collective and state farms. The author discusses the derivation of her estimates and compares her estimates with official Soviet series and with Western estimates.

_____. FARM EMPLOYMENT IN THE SOVIET UNION, 1928-1963. Santa Monica, Calif.: RAND Corp., 1965. ix, 155 p.

> Nimitz estimates employment on private, collective, and state farms from 1928-63, excluding the war years, in man days and in annual averages or equivalents. Many statistical tables.

_____. "Soviet Agricultural Prices and Costs." In COMPARISONS OF THE U.S. AND SOVIET ECONOMIES, U.S. Congress. Joint Economic Committee, pp. 239-84. Washington, D.C.: Government Printing Office, 1959.

> This paper deals with the pattern of output and marketings, procurement prices, average realized prices, and collective farm costs of production. Many tables.

_____. SOVIET GOVERNMENT GRAIN PROCUREMENTS, DISPOSITIONS, AND STOCKS, 1945-1963. Santa Monica, Calif.: RAND Corp., 1964. xi, 113 p.

> The memorandum estimates the allocation of government grain resources among domestic uses, exports, and stockpiling in 1940 and all postwar years. Tables.

Nonomura, Kazuo. "The Soviet Agriculture Today." HITOTSUBASHI JOURNAL OF ECONOMICS 3 (October 1962): 34-48.

> This survey of Soviet agriculture has data ranging from 1909 to 1966 in eleven tables.

Novak-Decker, Nikolai. "The Fate of the Grass-Arable System." STUDIES ON THE SOVIET UNION n.s. 2, no. 3 (1963): 71-74.

> This short paper traces the rise and fall of academician Vilyams and his theories, which dominated Soviet soil science and were predominant in Stalin's agricultural policies. The period discussed stretches from 1927-62.

_____. "Soviet Efforts to Introduce Intensive Farming." STUDIES ON THE SOVIET UNION n.s. 3, no. 4 (1964): 193-99.

> This paper discusses recent efforts to increase yields per acre.

_____. "Soviet Soil Resources." STUDIES ON THE SOVIET UNION n.s. 4, no. 4 (1965): 120-25.

> This paper discusses Soviet estimates of available agricultural land. A table shows land area figures by type of soil.

Nove, Alec. "Collectivization of Agriculture in Russia and China." In SYMPOSIUM ON ECONOMIC AND SOCIAL PROBLEMS OF THE FAR EAST, edited by Edward Szczepanik, pp. 16-24. Proceedings of a meeting held in September

1961 as part of the Golden Jubilee Congress of the University of Hong Kong. Hong Kong: Hong Kong University Press, 1962.

Policies toward the peasantry pursued by the Communist regimes of the Soviet Union and of China are contrasted.

_____. "The Decision to Collectivize." In AGRARIAN POLICIES AND PROBLEMS IN COMMUNIST AND NON-COMMUNIST COUNTRIES, edited by William A. D. Jackson, pp. 69-105. Seattle: University of Washington Press, 1971.

This paper explores the stages in the decision to collectivize and its implementation. It is followed by comments by T. P. Berstein and George L. Yaney, pp. 99-105.

_____. "Epilogue: Summary Remarks (on Shortcomings of Soviet Agriculture)." In SOVIET AGRICULTURE: THE PERMANENT CRISIS, edited by Roy D. Laird and Edward L. Crowley, pp. 143-45. New York: Praeger, 1965.

In considering some of the shortcomings of Soviet agriculture, the author distinguishes between two types of defects: those inherent in the system and those resulting from shortages.

_____. "Ideology and Agriculture." SOVIET STUDIES 17 (April 1966): 397-407.

The effect of ideology on Soviet agricultural policy is discussed.

_____. "Incentives for Peasants and Administrators." In SOVIET AGRICULTURE AND PEASANT AFFAIRS, edited by Roy D. Laird, pp. 51-75. Lawrence: University of Kansas Press, 1963.

The author states that not only are incentives required to motivate peasants to work, but that they are also necessary to stimulate and direct the work of management and Party and state officials.

_____. "Jasny's 'Agriculture' Revisited." SOVIET STUDIES 12 (October 1960): 190-92.

This is a discussion of Naum Jasny. THE SOCIALIZED AGRICULTURE OF THE USSR. Stanford, Calif.: Stanford University Press, 1949.

_____. "Peasants and Officials." In SOVIET AND EAST EUROPEAN AGRICULTURE, edited by Jerzy F. Karcz, pp. 57-76. Berkeley and Los Angeles: University of California Press, 1967.

The relationship between the local officials and the peasants is examined. The author notes attitudes toward the kolkhozes; attitudes towards kolkhozniks; the status of chairmen of kolkhozes; and the future of Soviet agriculture.

_____. "Rural Taxation in the USSR." SOVIET STUDIES 5 (October 1953): 159-66.

The weight of taxation borne by the collectivized sector of the Soviet rural economy is assessed. Three tables.

_____. "Some Notes on the 1953 Budget and the Peasants." SOVIET STUDIES 5 (January 1954): 227-33.

Nove here discusses the peasants and agricultural policy and general financial policy.

_____. "Some Problems in Soviet Agricultural Statistics." SOVIET STUDIES 7 (January 1956): 248-68.

This paper is concerned with output statistics in physical and monetary terms, gross and net; productivity; and costs of production.

_____. "Some Thoughts on Soviet Agricultural Administration." STUDIES ON THE SOVIET UNION n.s. 3, no. 4 (1964): 1-12.

This article discusses various aspects of administration including organization, the position of the peasant, the sizes of the kolkhoz and sovkhoz, planning, prices, and general history. For further discussion, see: commentaries by William B. Ballis, pp. 12-15, and Boris Wjunow, pp. 16-19.

_____. "Soviet Agriculture Marks Time." FOREIGN AFFAIRS 4 (July 1962): 576-94.

Soviet agriculture in the late 1950s and early 1960s is covered. Discussed are production, peasants, administration, and planning. Tables.

_____. "Soviet Agriculture Under Brezhnev." SLAVIC REVIEW 29 (September 1970): 379-410.

Topics covered include Khrushchev's policies; Brezhnev's new policies; implementation of Brezhnev's policies; pricing policies; peasant income; consumption; agricultural investment; production; and costs. Tables. For further discussion, see the following (all of which are in the SLAVIC REVIEW): William A. D. Jackson. "Wanted: An Effective Land Use Policy and Improved Reclamation." 29 (September 1970): 411-16; Jerzy F. Karcz. "Some Major Persisting Problems in Soviet Agriculture." 29 (September 1970): 417-26; Alec Nove. "Reply." 29 (September 1970): 427-28; Alan Abouchar (with comment by Alec Nove). "The Private Plot and the Prototype Collective Farm Charter." 30 (June 1971): 355-60.

Nove, Alec, and Laird, Roy D. "Kolkhoz Agriculture in the Moscow Oblast." AMERICAN SLAVIC AND EAST EUROPEAN REVIEW 13 (1954): 549-65.

This article discusses the relationships between the advanced and backward sectors of agriculture and between the peasantry and the town workers. Seven tables.

———. "A Note on Labour Utilization in the Kolkhoz." SOVIET STUDIES 4 (April 1953): 434-42.

This paper looks at labor utilization and productivity in two operations: combine-harvesting and threshing. Two tables.

Oi, Walter Y., and Clayton, Elizabeth M. "A Peasant's View of a Soviet Collective Farm." AMERICAN ECONOMIC REVIEW 58 (March 1968): 37-59.

This paper modifies previous models of cooperative enterprises to reflect the influences of private plots and quota constraints.

Osofsky, Stephen. "The Soviet Grain Problem in Perspective." RUSSIAN REVIEW 32 (April 1973): 152-57.

The author examines the dimensions of the current grain problem in the context of the two five-year plans implemented so far by the Brezhnev regime.

"Ovechkin on Material and Moral Incentives." SOVIET STUDIES 5 (January 1954): 289-98.

This is a translation of a sketch involving some machine-tractor station workers which appeared in PRAVDA in 1953.

Pares, Bernard. "The New Crisis in Russia." SLAVONIC REVIEW 11 (April 1933): 489-502.

The author feels that the Soviets are having more difficulties in the agricultural sector than in other sectors of the economy.

"The Party and the Farms." SOVIET STUDIES 6 (October 1954): 172-79.

This note translates excerpts from an article concerning rural district party work relating to the collective farms and the machine-tractor stations.

Ploss, Sidney. CONFLICT AND DECISION-MAKING IN SOVIET RUSSIA: A CASE STUDY OF AGRICULTURAL POLICY, 1953-1963. Princeton, N.J.: Princeton University Press, 1965. 312 p.

This study reconstructs from the official record the disputes over agricultural policy in the post-Stalin period. Bibliography and index.

Pospielovsky, Dimitry. "The 'Link System' in Soviet Agriculture." SOVIET STUDIES 21 (April 1970): 411-35.

> The "link" referred to here is an informal team of several peasants who are given a plot of land and all the necessary implements and seed by the parent kolkhoz or sovkhoz. They are then allowed to run their plot autonomously and are rewarded only in payment for their final produce. Emphasis is on the 1960s.

Prokopovitch, M. "Co-operation in Soviet Russia." INTERNATIONAL LABOUR REVIEW 10 (September 1924): 411-34.

> The author discusses the history of the cooperative movement under the Soviets and divides it into three periods. During the first period (1917 to beginning of 1919) the cooperative system existed as an independent organization. During the second period (1919-20) the movement became a state institution. In the third period, beginning in 1921 (NEP), autonomy was gradually restored.

Prybyla, Jan S. "Private Enterprise in the Soviet Union." SOUTH AFRICAN JOURNAL OF ECONOMICS 29 (September 1961): 218-24.

> This paper surveys private enterprise from 1917 to 1960. A short table shows the shares of state farms in state procurements of selected products, 1956 and 1960. For further discussion, see: Jan. S. Prybla. "Communication Regarding Private Enterprise in the Soviet Union." SOUTH AFRICAN JOURNAL OF ECONOMICS 29 (December 1961): 315-16.

_____. "Problems of Soviet Agriculture." JOURNAL OF FARM ECONOMICS 44 (August 1962): 820-36.

> This paper deals mostly with the period 1956-61 and discusses the problems, reasons for those problems, and the reforms. Four tables provide figures on crop yields, milk and wool production, and labor productivity.

Raup, Philip M. "The Farm Problem A La Russe." In SOVIET UNION--PARADOX AND CHANGE, edited by Robert T. Holt and John E. Turner, pp. 90-117. New York: Holt, Rinehart & Winston, 1962.

> The authors outline post-Stalin reforms in agricultural policy; the current objectives of Soviet agriculture; the "physical plant" (land and agricultural capital) of Soviet agriculture; incentives; politics and the Soviet farm problem; and the future of Soviet agriculture. Maps.

_____. "Some Consequences of Data Deficiencies in Soviet Agriculture." In SOVIET ECONOMIC STATISTICS, edited by Vladimir G. Treml and John P. Hardt, pp. 263-78. Durham, N.C.: Duke University Press, 1972.

>This paper explores data deficiencies and their consequences for agricultural policies and farm management. The author discusses the structure and function of Soviet farm prices; data deficiencies and the evolution of management goals; and some policy consequences of accounting practices and data reporting systems.

Raupach, Hans. "Epilogue: Summary Remarks." In SOVIET AGRICULTURE: THE PERMANENT CRISIS, edited by Roy D. Laird and Edward L. Crowley, pp. 145-46. New York: Praeger, 1965.

>The author remarks on the papers and comments presented at a symposium held in Munich in 1964.

"Recent Agricultural Orders." SOVIET STUDIES 6 (October 1954): 170-72.

>This note reviews several decisions made by the Central Committee about agriculture in 1954.

"Recruitment of Kolkhoz Organizers from the Towns." SOVIET STUDIES 7 (October 1955): 230-32.

>Reports in the Soviet press of efforts to recruit kolkhoz chairmen are noted.

"Re-organization of the MTS." SOVIET STUDIES 9 (April 1958): 446-47.

>This note discusses reasons for the sale of machine-tractor stations' machinery to the collective farms. A table shows various prices and costs for selected agricultural products.

"The Rules of the Collective Farms." SOVIET STUDIES 8 (April 1957): 461-64.

>This note discusses proposed changes in the rules governing collective farms, from private plots to work norms.

Russell, E. John. "The Farming Problem in Russia: How it is Being Met." SLAVONIC REVIEW 16 (January 1938): 320-40.

>Russell gives a firsthand account of the peasant situation under collectivization.

"The Russian Cooperative News." BULLETIN OF THE AMERICAN COMMITTEE OF RUSSIAN COOPERATIVE UNIONS 1 (June 1919) to 2 (February-March 1920).

>This shortlived serial contains notes on the scope of the Russian cooperative movement.

Schiller, Otto. "Structural Changes in Soviet Agriculture." In THE SOVIET UNION: A HALF-CENTURY OF COMMUNISM, edited by Kurt London, pp. 277-94. Baltimore: Johns Hopkins University Press, 1968.

This paper discusses agricultural policy changes chronologically.

Schinke, Eberhard. "Some Peculiarities of the Employment of Factors in Soviet Agriculture." In AGRARIAN POLICIES AND PROBLEMS IN COMMUNIST AND NON-COMMUNIST COUNTRIES, edited by William A. D. Jackson, pp. 142-58. Seattle: University of Washington Press, 1971.

The author analyzes the development of productivity and per capita production by examining some particularities of expenditure in Soviet agriculture. The paper is followed by a comment by Elizabeth M. Clayton, pp. 156-58.

Schlesinger, Rudolf. "The Decisions on Agriculture." SOVIET STUDIES 5 (January 1954): 234-45.

This paper discusses agricultural policy decisions made at the Central Committee plenary session of September 3-7, 1953.

_____. "The New Structure of Soviet Agriculture." SOVIET STUDIES 10 (January 1959): 228-51.

This paper discusses the significance of the sale of machine-tractor station equipment to the farms. Three tables. For further discussion, see the correspondence from Otto Schiller and Rudolf Schlesinger in SOVIET STUDIES 11 (October 1959): 223-25.

_____. "Some Problems of Present Kolkhoz Organization." SOVIET STUDIES 2 (April 1951): 325-55.

The problems discussed here include grain shortages; stabilization of the artel; attitudes toward work; transforming the artel into an enterprise; organization; and kolkhoz versus sovkhoz. For further discussion, see the following: Naum Jasny. "Kolkhozy, the Achilles' Heel of the Soviet Regime." SOVIET STUDIES 3 (October 1951): 150-63; Alec Nove. "The Kolkhoz--Some Comments on Dr. Schlesinger's Article." SOVIET STUDIES 3 (October 1951): 163-72; Rudolf Schlesinger. "The Kolkhoz System: A Reply." SOVIET STUDIES 3 (January 1952): 288-315; Alec Nove. "The Kolkhoz System--A Rejoinder." SOVIET STUDIES 4 (July 1952): 48-52.

"Sheep Breeding and Wool Production." CENTRAL ASIAN REVIEW 3, no. 2 (1955): 113-22.

This article is concerned with Tadzhikistan, Uzbekistan, Kirgizia, and Turkmenistan. A table gives total head for selected years 1941-55. Two maps.

Shimkin, Dimitri B. "Current Characteristics and Problems of the Soviet Rural Population." In SOVIET AGRICULTURE AND PEASANT AFFAIRS, edited by Roy D. Laird, pp. 79-133. Lawrence: University of Kansas Press, 1963.

This paper identifies demographic, social, and economic features of the Soviet rural population as revealed by the 1959 census and other currently relevant materials and outlines major problems affecting the welfare of Soviet peasants and other rural folk.

Shuman, Charles B. "An Agricultural View of the Soviet Threat." In COMPARISONS OF U.S. AND SOVIET ECONOMIES, U.S. Congress. Joint Economic Committee, pp. 489-507. Washington, D.C.: Government Printing Office, 1959.

The author discusses why the USSR is a threat to the United States, compares agriculture in the United States and USSR, examines the developing trends in Soviet international trade in farm products, and considers the implications of the Soviet economic offensive to U.S. policies.

Smith, R[obert]. E. F. "Agriculture." BULLETINS ON SOVIET ECONOMIC DEVELOPMENT 9-10, Ser. 3 (September 1956): 29-55.

The author discusses new measures in agriculture which have created changes in the pattern of agricultural development in the USSR. Many tables.

―――. "The Amalgamation of Collective Farms: Some Technical Aspects." SOVIET STUDIES 6 (July 1954): 16-32.

The aspects discussed include personnel, the machine-tractor stations, livestock farming, and funds for investment. Four tables.

"Soviet Agricultural Legislation." SLAVONIC REVIEW 10 (June 1931): 201-13.

Verbatim translations are given of important laws and regulations on agriculture passed by the Soviet government.

"Soviet Agricultural Legislation. II." SLAVONIC REVIEW 10 (December 1931): 344-56.

These translations of Soviet decrees and documents inform readers as to how the Soviets have achieved rapid collectivization.

"Soviet Agriculture, 1962." BULLETIN OF THE ASSOCIATION FOR THE STUDY OF SOVIET-TYPE ECONOMIES 4 (Spring 1962): 14-17.

This is a concise outline of the state of Soviet agriculture in 1962.

"Special Issue on Agriculture in the USSR." STUDIES ON THE SOVIET UNION n.s. 2, no. 1 (1962): 1-160.

Topics covered in part one include the March 1962 Plenum; reorganization; the future of collective and state farms; agricultural administration; causes of problems; military aspects; labor problems;

mechanization; and price increases in meat and dairy products. Part two contains ninety-six pages of data on Soviet agriculture.

"Stabilization of the Nomads." CENTRAL ASIAN REVIEW 7, no. 3 (1959): 221-29.

> Soviet policies to settle and collectivize the nomads of Central Asia are discussed.

Strauss, Erich. SOVIET AGRICULTURE IN PERSPECTIVE: A STUDY OF ITS SUCCESSES AND FAILURES. New York: Praeger, 1969. 328 p.

> This work discusses the problems of Soviet agriculture in general terms and history of Soviet agriculture from 1917 to 1968. Tables and index.

──────. "The Soviet Dairy Economy." SOVIET STUDIES 21 (January 1970): 269-96.

> This article reviews the history of the dairy industry since Stalin, its condition in 1969, and its future prospects. Ten tables.

Strausz, David A. THE HOP INDUSTRY OF EASTERN EUROPE AND THE SOVIET UNION. Pullman: Washington State University Press, 1969. 242 p.

> This book includes a discussion of the history of hop culture, the industry structure, output, yields, and technology in the Soviet Union. Index.

Strong, Anna L. THE SOVIETS CONQUER WHEAT. New York: Holt, 1931. 289 p. Illustrated.

> This account of the author's travels in Russia focuses on agricultural problems.

Stuart, Robert C. THE COLLECTIVE FARM IN SOVIET AGRICULTURE. Lexington, Mass.: D. C. Heath, 1972. xx, 254 p.

> This book discusses organizational structure, the role of the kolkhoz in the planned economy, structural changes in the kolkhoz sector, incentives, planning, decision making, pricing, and characteristics of managers. Tables, glossary, bibliography, and index.

──────. "Managerial Incentives in Soviet Collective Agriculture During the Khrushchev Era." SOVIET STUDIES 22 (April 1971): 539-55.

> Topics covered here include shifts in the basis of determination of rewards, the size of income incentives in comparison with the incomes of other members of the collective, and changes in income payments as a managerial incentive. Nine tables.

_____. "Structural Change and the Quality of Soviet Collective Farm Management, 1952-1966." In THE SOVIET RURAL COMMUNITY: A SYMPOSIUM, edited by James R. Millar, pp. 121-38. Urbana: University of Illinois Press, 1971.

> This paper focuses on the changing structure of the kolkhoz and the qualitative improvement of management. Twelve tables.

Swearer, Howard R. "Agricultural Administration under Khrushchev." In SOVIET AGRICULTURE AND PEASANT AFFAIRS, edited by Roy D. Laird, pp. 9-50. Lawrence: University of Kansas Press, 1963.

> The following are discussed: How has the struggle for political leadership affected agricultural administration? What is the condition of the Party in the countryside, and how effectively have Party forces been utilized to step up production? How successful has the post-Stalin leadership been in breathing new flexibility into agricultural administration by cautious decentralization?

Symons, Leslie. RUSSIAN AGRICULTURE: A GEOGRAPHIC SURVEY. New York: John Wiley, 1972. xii, 348 p.

> This book, using the approach of a geographer, is concerned with the development and present characteristics of the man-land relationship and devotes much attention to the physical environment. The structure of Soviet agriculture and the rural population and work force are also discussed. Maps, tables, diagrams, bibliography, and index.

Tang, Anthony M. "Agriculture in the Industrialization of Communist China and the Soviet Union." JOURNAL OF FARM ECONOMICS 49 (December 1967): 1118-34.

> This paper evaluates the Stalinist model of agriculture, examines the successes and failures of agricultural policies, and considers agricultural policies faced by planners. For discussion of this paper, see: Nancy Nimitz. "Discussion: Agriculture in the Industrialization of Communist China and the Soviet Union." JOURNAL OF FARM ECONOMICS 49 (December 1967): 1135-38.

Tchayanov, A. "Agricultural Economics in Russia." JOURNAL OF FARM ECONOMICS 10 (October 1928): 543-49.

> Topics covered here include a brief historical sketch, the theory of peasant farming, and the organization of agricultural economic research.

Tcherkinsky, M. N. "The Position of Russian Agriculture." ECONOMIC JOURNAL 35 (September 1925): 484-90.

> The article surveys the state of Russian agriculture in 1925 and sees it as a result of Soviet agricultural policies since 1917. The major

problem is seen as one of overpopulation of the agricultural sector.

Timoshenko, Vladimir P. "Agricultural Resources." In SOVIET ECONOMIC GROWTH: CONDITIONS AND PERSPECTIVES, edited by Abram Bergson, pp. 246-74. Evanston, Ill.: Row, Peterson, 1953.

    This essay covers climatic limitations, soil limitations, the plans for reforestation, and improved crop rotation and irrigation projects. It is followed by comments by G. B. Cressey.

_____. AGRICULTURAL RUSSIA AND THE WHEAT PROBLEM. Stanford, Calif.: Food Research Institute, 1932. xi, 571 p.

    This study analyzes present conditions of Russian agriculture, particularly grain production, in light of prewar development. Statistical appendix, tables, index, maps, and charts.

_____. "The New Agricultural Policy of Soviet Russia." JOURNAL OF FARM ECONOMICS 13 (April 1931): 280-304.

    This article surveys agricultural policy from attempts at imposing a "socialist organization of agricultural production" through the New Economic Policy and on to collectivization. Tables.

_____. "New Soviet Economic Plan: its Agricultural Aspect." JOURNAL OF POLITICAL ECONOMY 61 (December 1953): 489-508.

    This article reviews the places of agriculture in Soviet economic plans from the first plan for 1928-32 to the fifth plan for 1951-55. Tables.

_____. "The Wheat Problem in USSR." JOURNAL OF FARM ECONOMICS 14 (April 1932): 284-94.

    This article discusses exports of wheat and rye from Russia as far back as the 1890s, statistics of grain production, and possible increases both in yields and in land under cultivation. A single table provides data on exports between 1895 and 1913.

Truog, Emil, and Pronin, Dimitri T. "A Great Myth: the Russian Granary." LAND ECONOMICS 29 (August 1953): 200-208.

    This article analyzes soil, climate, and agricultural policy to conclude that Russia probably never can become a major, dependable producer of food grains. Two maps and seven charts are included.

Tugwell, Rexford G. "Russian Agriculture." In SOVIET RUSSIA IN THE SECOND DECADE. New York: John Day, 1928. xiii, 374 p.

    The author describes the village and the peasant; land organization; Soviet attempts at agricultural improvement; the establishment and

functioning of land banks; rural taxation; agricultural prices; the
management of prices; regional prices; the rural standard of living;
agricultural policy; and agriculture and foreign trade.

Tullis, James F. "The Convergent Trend Between the Agricultural Sectors of
the Economies of the United States and the Union of Soviet Socialist Republics."
JOURNAL OF FARM ECONOMICS 48 (December 1966): 1691-96.

This paper, which received first award in the undergraduate student
essay contest, reviews developments in the agricultural sectors of
the United States and USSR and argues for convergence.

U.S. Central Intelligence Agency. CURRENT PROBLEMS OF SOVIET AGRICULTURE (n.p., n.d.). 32 p.

This report discusses the plenum of January 1961 and the probable
impact on agricultural production. Two tables.

_____. RECENT DEVELOPMENTS IN SOVIET AGRICULTURE (n.p., 1962).
v, 31 p.

Topics discussed include the ranking of agriculture in national
priorities; the roles of Party officials, managers, and technical
specialists in agricultural administration; land use; and the continued low level of collective farm income. The current Party
program is also surveyed.

_____. VACILLATIONS IN THE ORGANIZATION OF SOVIET AGRICULTURE
1953-63 (n.p., n.d.). 23 p.

This paper is concerned with agricultural administration, 1953-63.

U.S. Department of Agriculture. Agricultural Research Service. ECONOMIC
ASPECTS OF SOVIET AGRICULTURE. Washington, D.C.: Government Printing
Office, 1959. 78 p.

Topics discussed include growing conditions; land utilization; organization; crop and livestock production; labor supply and utilization;
mechanization; farm buildings; pricing and procurement; wages; and
living conditions. Map and thirty-four tables.

Venzher, V. G. "Characteristics of the Collective-Farm Economy and Problems
of its Development." EASTERN EUROPEAN ECONOMICS 4, no. 4 (1966):
3-28.

This is translated from V. G. Venzher et al. PROIZVODSTVO,
NAKOPLENIE, POTREBLENIE [Production, accumulation, consumption]. Moscow: Ekonomika, 1965. Topics covered include a
survey of the agricultural situation; collective farm production
and its cooperative nature; features of the collective-farm economy; independent collective-farm planning through forward con-

tracts; marketing problems; and cooperation among collective farms.

Volin, Lazar. "Agrarian Collectivism in the Soviet Union. Pt. I - II." JOURNAL OF POLITICAL ECONOMY 45 (December 1937): 606-33; 759-88.

This article analyzes the policy of collectivization in Russia and its effects from the period of war communism to 1935. Five tables.

_____. "Agricultural Organization." In SOVIET ECONOMIC GROWTH: CONDITIONS AND PERSPECTIVES, edited by Abram Bergson, pp. 275-93. Evanston, Ill.: Row, Peterson, 1953.

The essay concludes that the organization of Soviet agricultural system is in flux.

_____. "The Agricultural Picture in USSR and USA." BULLETIN OF THE ASSOCIATION FOR THE STUDY OF SOVIET-TYPE ECONOMIES 5 (Fall 1963): 2-8.

This is a comparison of Soviet and U.S. agriculture with special attention given to the natural environment and economic and institutional factors.

_____. "Agricultural Policy of the Soviet Union." In COMPARISONS OF THE U.S. AND SOVIET ECONOMIES, U.S. Congress. Joint Economic Committee, pp. 285-318. Washington, D.C.: Government Printing Office, 1959.

This paper deals briefly with the following subjects: collective and state farms; farm giantism; the rise and fall of MTS; household allotment farming; government procurements of farm products; economic incentives and farm labor; capital investment in agriculture and the fertilizer program; planning and management; and the battle for grain-wheat and corn. Tables.

_____. "America Looks at Russian Agriculture." JOURNAL OF FARM ECONOMICS 26 (February 1944): 46-58.

This survey emphasizes the contribution of American agricultural machinery plants, the American concept of large-scale power farming, and American lend-lease to Soviet agriculture. Recovery from the effects of the German invasion is also discussed.

_____. "Khrushchev and the Soviet Agricultural Scene." In SOVIET AND EAST EUROPEAN AGRICULTURE, edited by Jerzy F. Karcz, pp. 1-28. Berkeley and Los Angeles: University of California Press, 1967.

The article discusses Khrushchev's leadership in the area of agriculture; introduction of economic incentives on collectives; the increase in agricultural capital equipment; expansion of land under cultivation; and certain institutional changes.

Russian Agriculture and the Peasantry

_____. "Soviet Agricultural Collectivism in Peace and War." AMERICAN ECONOMIC REVIEW 41 (May 1951): 465-74.

Ideological and economic presuppositions of Soviet agrarian collectivism are explored. The article describes Stalin's success in driving the peasants into collectives at great human and economic cost. For further discussion, see: Evsey D. Domar et al. "The Economy of the Soviet Union--Discussion." AMERICAN ECONOMIC REVIEW 41 (May 1951): 483-94.

_____. "Soviet Agricultural Policy After Stalin: Results and Prospects." JOURNAL OF FARM ECONOMICS 38 (May 1956): 274-86.

Collectivism and attempts to increase output are considered. For further discussion, see: Otto Schiller. "Discussion: The Resources and Performance of Soviet Agriculture." JOURNAL OF FARM ECONOMICS 38 (May 1956): 296-308.

_____. "Soviet Agricultural Policy: Some Selected Lessons." JOURNAL OF FARM ECONOMICS 19 (February 1937): 280-86.

This paper surveys Soviet agricultural policy between 1917 and 1937 and highlights the conflict between the two goals of socialization and increased output.

_____. "Soviet Agriculture Under Khrushchev." AMERICAN ECONOMIC REVIEW 49 (May 1959): 15-32.

Volin looks at developments in Soviet agriculture under Khrushchev. For further discussion, see: Raymond P. Powell et al. "Soviet Economic Trends and Prospects--Discussion." AMERICAN ECONOMIC REVIEW 49 (May 1959): 43-49.

_____. "Stalin's Last Testament and the Outlook for Kolkhozy During the Succession." JOURNAL OF FARM ECONOMICS 61 (August 1953): 291-305.

The last testament referred to is Joseph Stalin. "Economic Problems of Socialism in the U.S.S.R." SUPPLEMENT TO THE CURRENT DIGEST OF THE SOVIET PRESS. October 18, 1952.

_____. A SURVEY OF SOVIET RUSSIAN AGRICULTURE. Washington, D.C.: Government Printing Office, 1951. viii, 194 p. Illustrated.

This survey discusses the natural environment, policy and land tenure, the farm system, government supervision, farming practices, land utilization, crop patterns, livestock, distribution and consumption, foreign trade, and the effects of World War II and reconstruction. Index, tables, and maps.

Vucinich, Alexander. "The Kolkhoz: Its Social Structure and Development." AMERICAN SLAVIC AND EAST EUROPEAN REVIEW 8 (1949): 10-24.

This paper is concerned with the place of the kolkhoz in the Soviet society and with its changing structure and socioeconomic functions.

———. "The Peasants as a Social Class." In THE SOVIET RURAL COMMUNITY: A SYMPOSIUM, edited by James R. Millar, pp. 307-24. Urbana: University of Illinois Press, 1971.

The work of Soviet sociologists regarding the peasantry is reviewed.

Vvedensky, George. "The Soviet Food Industry." STUDIES ON THE SOVIET UNION n.s. 3, no. 3 (1964): 90-97.

This article discusses efforts to increase Soviet food production especially since 1960.

Wadekin, Karl-Eugen. "Kolkhoz, Sovkhoz, and Private Production in Soviet Agriculture." In AGRARIAN POLICIES AND PROBLEMS IN COMMUNIST AND NON-COMMUNIST COUNTRIES, edited by William A. D. Jackson, pp. 106-41. Seattle: University of Washington Press, 1971.

This study is concerned with the portion of total Soviet agricultural output produced by each of three sectors and their specific importance in the years since 1953 and especially since 1962. The paper is followed with a comment by Robert C. Stuart.

———. "The Nonagricultural Rural Sector." In THE SOVIET RURAL COMMUNITY: A SYMPOSIUM, edited by James R. Millar, pp. 159-79. Urbana: University of Illinois Press, 1971.

This paper is concerned with the nonagricultural sector between 1955 and the late 1960s. Tables.

———. THE PRIVATE SECTOR IN SOVIET AGRICULTURE. Edited by George Karcz. Translated by Keith Bush. 2d ed. Berkeley and Los Angeles: University of California Press, 1967. xviii, 407 p.

The chapters contain discussions of the rules governing private holdings; overall performance; size of small-scale producers; the kolkhoz market; the interdependence of private and socialized production; and the policy toward the private sector from 1953 through 1971. The author concludes with a discussion of the "conflict and uneasy coexistence" between the Party and the peasant. Bibliography and indexes.

———. "Soviet Agriculture and Agricultural Policy: Some Regional Features." STUDIES ON THE SOVIET UNION n.s. 3, no. 4 (1964): 52-67.

This paper demonstrates the usefulness of the approach by regions and gives examples of great differences in socialized Soviet agriculture. For further discussion, see the commentary by Fred E. Dohrs, pp. 67-70. Charts and tables for Wadekin's paper follow on pp. 71-98.

_____. "Soviet Rural Society. A Descriptive Stratification Analysis." SOVIET STUDIES 22 (April 1971): 512-38.

>The analysis is based mainly on occupational groups and educational levels as given in the 1954 census, in current statistics, and in other Soviet publications.

Walters, Harry E. "Agriculture in the United States and U.S.S.R." In NEW DIRECTIONS IN THE SOVIET ECONOMY, U.S. Congress. Joint Economic Committee, pp. 473-81. Washington, D.C.: Government Printing Office, 1966.

>An introduction and ten tables providing figures on Soviet and U.S. agriculture make up this paper.

Walters, Harry E., and Judy, Richard W. "Soviet Agricultural Output by 1970." In SOVIET AND EAST EUROPEAN AGRICULTURE, edited by Jerzy F. Karcz, pp. 306-55. Berkeley and Los Angeles: University of California Press, 1967.

>The stagnation in Soviet agricultural output since 1958 is explored. Programs to alter the factors which were responsible for the stagnation are explored; and possibilities for Soviet grain output and yields are evaluated.

Ware, Henry W. "The Collective Farm Peasant Market." JOURNAL OF FARM ECONOMICS 32 (May 1950): 299-306.

>This note surveys the organization and operation of the peasant market and discusses the official attitude towards it, the function which it fulfills, and the degree to which it is a free market.

Wesson, Robert G. "The Soviet Communes." SOVIET STUDIES 13 (April 1962): 341-61.

>The history of Soviet communes are discussed. Two tables provide totals of communes and other social organizations for 1919-33.

Wheatcroft, S. G. "The Reliability of Russian Prewar Grain Output Statistics." SOVIET STUDIES 26 (April 1974): 157-80.

>This work surveys and discusses the corrections applied to Russian grain output statistics by various analysts. Tables.

Whitman, John T. "The Kolkhoz Market." SOVIET STUDIES 7 (April 1956): 384-408.

>This article describes the market's growth from its legal inception in 1932 to the present and its relationship to the state sector of the economy in fields such as retail trade and procurement. Four tables.

Wilber, Charles K. "The Role of Agriculture in Soviet Economic Development." LAND ECONOMICS 45 (February 1969): 87-96.

> This article evaluates Soviet agricultural strategy in relation to the requirements of economic development. Three tables.

Wiles, Peter J. D. "Is the Soviet Agricultural Plan for 1966-70 Reasonable?" In his THE PREDICTIONS OF COMMUNIST ECONOMIC PERFORMANCE, pp. 331-38. Cambridge: At the University Press, 1971.

> In this paper the author uses the "Cobb-Douglas techniques to examine the feasibility of one section of a Soviet-type plan."

Willett, Joseph W. "The Recent Record in Agricultural Production." In DIMENSIONS OF SOVIET ECONOMIC POWER, U.S. Congress. Joint Economic Committee, pp. 95-113. Washington, D.C.: Government Printing Office, 1962.

> Willett surveys the recent trends in agricultural output and presents index numbers of agricultural production, 1950-61, and data on production of major crops and livestock products. Some major new programs to stimulate agricultural growth, changes in agricultural organization, and factors which influence growth are discussed. Tables.

Winner, Irene. "Some Problems of Nomadism and Social Organization Among the Recently Settled Kazakhs; Part I." CENTRAL ASIAN REVIEW 11, no. 3 (1963): 246-67.

> Topics discussed include pre-Soviet Kazakh history and culture, developments in the Soviet period, and the Soviet Settling Programme.

_____. "Some Problems of Nomadism and Social Organization Among the Recently Settled Kazakhs: Part Two." CENTRAL ASIAN REVIEW 11, no. 4 (1963): 355-73.

> This article is concerned mainly with how traditional social organization and customs fare on the collective farms. Two tables.

Wronski, Henri. "Consumer Cooperatives in Rural Areas in the U.S.S.R." In AGRARIAN POLICIES AND PROBLEMS IN COMMUNIST AND NON-COMMUNIST COUNTRIES, edited by William A. D. Jackson, pp. 159-77. Seattle: University of Washington Press, 1971.

> This paper discusses the relation between the Bolshevik party and the cooperative; the maintenance of the cooperative sector; and the various economic activities of the cooperative. It is followed with a comment by Nancy Nimitz, pp. 174-77.

_____. "Peasant Incomes." STUDIES ON THE SOVIET UNION n.s. 3, no. 4 (1964): 123-36.

> Topics discussed here include the effect of the New Agricultural Policy on peasant income in 1954; an early attempt to change policy in 1931; price equalization and wage distribution; development of official policy; the situation in 1958-59, and the cost of state takeover of the collective farm sector. Two tables. See the commentaries by S. S. Kabysh, pp. 136-38, and Werner Klatt, pp. 138-42.

Yakovlev, Y. A. RED VILLAGES: THE 5-YEAR PLAN IN SOVIET AGRICULTURE. Translated by Anna L. Strong. London: Martin Lawrence, n.d. Illustrated. 128 p.

> Written by the People's Commissar of Agriculture, this book discusses large-scale farming, tasks in agricultural development, organizational measures, and the collective farm movement.

Yaney, George L. "Agricultural Administration in Russia from the Stolypin Land Reform to Forced Collectivization: An Interpretive Study." In THE SOVIET RURAL COMMUNITY: A SYMPOSIUM, edited by James R. Millar, pp. 3-35. Urbana: University of Illinois Press, 1971.

> The development of agricultural administration in the Soviet Union in the 1920s and its destruction in 1930-33 are reconsidered.

Zaitsev, Cyril. "The Russian Agrarian Revolution." SLAVONIC REVIEW 9 (March 1931): 547-66.

> The author feels that the agrarian revolution can be understood only by setting it in its broad historical framework. This article examines the last phases of the agrarian revolution and predicts its results.

Zoerb, Carl R. "From the Promise of Land and Bread to the Reality of the State Farm." STUDIES ON THE SOVIET UNION n.s. 6, no. 4 (1967): 89-107.

> This paper appraises the development of the state farm system. Six tables.

_____. "The Pig Gap." STUDIES ON THE SOVIET UNION n.s. 3, no. 4 (1964): 159-63.

> Pig production and slaughter in the private and socialized sectors is noted. Four tables.

_____. "The Virgin Land Territory: Plans, Performance, Prospects." STUDIES ON THE SOVIET UNION n.s. 3, no. 4. (1964): 29-44.

> This is an intensive study of the virgin lands program in Tselinny

Krai in north and northeastern Kazakhstan. The emphasis is on appraising the potentiality of the new lands by comparison with an established farming region analogous in resources and climate. Six tables. For further discussion, see the commentary by Keith E. Bush, pp. 44-51.

Chapter 27

CONSERVATION, NATURAL RESOURCES, AND POLLUTION IN THE SOVIET UNION

Bleyer, B. "The Environmental Economics of the Soviet Union." AMERICAN ECONOMIST 18 (Spring 1974): 124-27.

Environmental problems and policies are discussed.

Bukshtynov, Aleksei D. FOREST RESOURCES OF THE USSR AND THE WORLD. Jerusalem: Israel Program for Scientific Translations, 1960. 65 p.

The forest resources of the USSR are surveyed as to their productivity and composition. The organization of Soviet forestry and forest exploitation are also covered. Bibliography, glossary, and tables.

Bulik, Joseph J. "USSR: The Fifteen-Year Afforestation Plan." LAND ECONOMICS 25 (November 1949): 358-60.

This paper looks at the Soviet plan to add to agricultural land through afforestation. Two tables provide figures on grain acreage and yield for 1913-40 and estimates for the effect of the program on 1970 crops. See also "Comments in Summary," pp. 363-64.

Carey, David W., and Dockstader, Robert A. "Measuring the Extent of Environmental Disruption: A Preliminary Attempt." ASSOCIATION FOR COMPARATIVE ECONOMIC STUDIES BULLETIN 15 (Summer-Fall 1973): 29-50.

In this study the authors sketch environmental disruptions present in the Soviet Union or likely to develop in the future; discuss attempts to control the environment by legislation; estimate the current emissions of water and air pollutants as compared to those in the United States; and predict future trends of water and air pollution and their likely economic impact. For further discussion, see: Victor Perlo. "Two Misleading Articles in the ACES BULLETIN." ASSOCIATION FOR COMPARATIVE ECONOMIC STUDIES BULLETIN 16 (Spring, 1974): 59-66.

Conservation and Natural Resources

Dienes, Leslie. "Issues in Soviet Energy Policy and Conflicts Over Fuel Costs in Regional Development." SOVIET STUDIES 23 (July 1971): 26-58.

>This article deals with the economic evaluation and efficient spatial allocation of fuel and hydrocarbon resources. It examines how such evaluation and costing affect the competitive positions of Soviet regions for industrial development. Three maps and a table.

Fox, Irving K., ed. WATER RESOURCES LAW AND POLICY IN THE SOVIET UNION. Madison and London: University of Wisconsin Press for the Water Resources Center, University of Wisconsin, 1971. viii, 256 p.

>Water resources management in the Soviet Union is evaluated and compared to U.S. practices. The articles included are by both Soviet and American authors. A map of principal river systems is included. Index.

Goldman, Marshall I. "Externalities and the Race for Economic Growth in the USSR; Will the Environment Ever Win?" BULLETIN OF THE ASSOCIATION FOR THE STUDY OF SOVIET-TYPE ECONOMIES 13 (Spring 1971): 19-27.

>Topics covered include cost-benefit analysis; the private property holder; the department-of-public-works mentality; gross national product versus net national welfare; and Soviet advantages in controlling the environment. See also Ignacy Sachs. "Comments," pp. 28-29.

_____. "Pollution Comes to the USSR." In SOVIET ECONOMIC PROSPECTS FOR THE SEVENTIES, U.S. Congress. Joint Economic Committee, pp. 56-70. Washington, D.C.: Government Printing Office, 1973.

>This paper discusses the history of pollution control, the effects of government and ideology on pollution control, and prospects for the future.

_____. THE SPOILS OF PROGRESS: ENVIRONMENTAL POLLUTION IN THE SOVIET UNION. Cambridge, Mass.: M.I.T. Press, 1972. xi, 372 p.

>This survey of Soviet pollution problems discusses environmental protection in the socialist state; water and air pollution; abuses of land and raw materials; problems of Lake Baikal; and conservation and pollution control efforts in the Soviet system. Appendices on conservation and environmental laws. Bibliography and index.

Gubkin, I. M. NATURAL WEALTH OF THE SOVIET UNION AND ITS EXPLOITATION. Moscow: Co-operative Publishing Society of Foreign Workers in the USSR, 1932. 72 p.

>The author examines the natural wealth of the Soviet Union, including coal, oil, natural gas, peat, water and wind power, and forest and mineral wealth.

Conservation and Natural Resources

Harris, Chauncy D. "Industrial Resources." In SOVIET ECONOMIC GROWTH: CONDITIONS AND PERSPECTIVES, edited by Abram Bergson, pp. 163-89. Evanston, Ill.: Row, Peterson, 1953.

> Harris discusses the negative economic qualities of the sheer vastness of the USSR, the energy resources, and metalliferous ores. Comments by M. G. Clard, Dimitri B. Shimkin, and N. W. Rodin follow, pp. 179-89.

Jackson, William A. Douglas, ed., English ed. NATURAL RESOURCES OF THE SOVIET UNION: THEIR USE AND RENEWAL. Edited by I. P. Gerasimov et al. Translated by Jacek I. Romanowski. San Francisco: W. H. Freeman, 1971. xiii, 349 p.

> This Academy of Sciences publication surveys the natural resources of the USSR and discusses conservation of water resources, protection of atmosphere from pollution, and efforts to combat erosion of agricultural land.

Jasny, Naum. "USSR: Law on Measures to Ensure High and Stable Yields in the Steppe and Forest-Steppe Regions." LAND ECONOMICS 25 (November 1949): 351-58.

> This paper looks at the 1948 Soviet conservation plan with respect to artificially-irrigated land, zones with adequate and inadequate precipitation, forest plantings, and rotations. See also "Comments in Summary," pp. 363-64.

Kramer, John M. "Prices and the Conservation of Natural Resources in the Soviet Union." SOVIET STUDIES 24 (January 1973): 364-73.

> This articles focuses on lacks in economic evaluations which have adversely affected the management of resources such as land, water, minerals, and timber. Tables.

Krimgold, Dey Ber. "USSR: Conservation Plan for the Steppe and Timber-Steppe Region." LAND ECONOMICS 25 (November 1949): 336-46.

> This paper looks at the 1948 Soviet conservation plan. A map and two tables provide information of forest planting by forest belt and by district. See also "Comments in Summary," pp. 363-64 and Dimitri Pronin. "'Soil Conservation in the USSR' A Reply by Dimitri Pronin." LAND ECONOMICS 26 (February 1950): 97-99.

Mandel, William M. "The Soviet Ecology Movement." SCIENCE AND SOCIETY 36 (Winter 1972): 385-416.

> This paper examines the history of the ecology movement in the Soviet Union, some recent literature on the movement available in English, and the development of concerned citizens' groups not unlike those in the United States.

Conservation and Natural Resources

Powell, David E. "The Social Costs of Modernization: Ecological Problems in the USSR." WORLD POLITICS 23 (July 1971): 618-34.

>This paper discusses the scope of the pollution problem in the USSR, the causes of pollution, and the remedies which are being tried.

Schwarz, Solomon M. "USSR: The Shelterbelt Program in its Relation to Other Drought Control Projects." LAND ECONOMICS 25 (November 1949): 360-62.

>This paper discusses the 1948 plans to protect agricultural lands with strategically located forest shelterbelts. See also "Comments in Summary," pp. 363-64.

Shimkin, Dimitri B. MINERALS: A KEY TO SOVIET POWER. Cambridge, Mass.: Harvard University Press, 1953. viii, 452 p.

>This book is concerned with reserves, production, and consumption of ferrous metals, nonferrous metals, gold, coal, lignite, petroleum, natural gas, asphalt, and other minerals. Many tables.

_____. "Resource Development and Utilization in the Soviet Economy." In NATURAL RESOURCES AND INTERNATIONAL DEVELOPMENT, edited by Marion Clawson, pp. 155-238. Baltimore: Johns Hopkins Press, 1964.

>This paper outlines the Soviet approach to resource use, discusses the major instruments of resource development and allocation, and evaluates the effects of Soviet management on resources. Possible applications to developed and underdeveloped countries are then discussed. Two maps and a statistical appendix.

Voskuil, Walter H. "Postwar Russia and Her Mineral Deposits." LAND ECONOMICS 23 (May 1947): 199-213.

>This paper considers "only the geographic and natural resource factors and the manner in which these factors form a basis of strength for Soviet isolationism." A map of Scandinavia and the extreme northwest of the USSR is included. Two tables provide figures on iron ore and coal reserves. For a comment, see: Hans Blumenfeld. "Addendum: On Russia's Mineral Resources." LAND ECONOMICS 23 (November 1947): 439.

Vvedensky, George. "Natural Resources and Industrial Potential." STUDIES ON THE SOVIET UNION n.s. 5, no. 1 (1965): 34-46.

>This paper discusses the production and potential of Siberia and the Soviet Far East with regard to fuels, power, metallurgy, chemicals, nonferrous metals, machine building, and gold mining. A table shows Siberian coal reserves.

Zybenko, Roman [O.]. "Fuel and Power Resources." STUDIES ON THE SOVIET UNION n.s. 8, no. 1 (1968): 9-13.

>This short paper concentrates on resources in Soviet Central Asia.

Chapter 28

THE ECONOMIC GEOGRAPHY OF THE SOVIET UNION

Darby, H. C., and Fullard, Harold, eds. ATLAS. VOLUME XIV OF THE NEW CAMBRIDGE MODERN HISTORY. London and New York: Cambridge University Press, 1970. xxiv, 319 p.

> This includes maps on population, economic maps for 1860 and 1913, and maps on mining and industry for 1913 and 1960.

THE PERIOD UP TO 1860

Parker, William H. AN HISTORICAL GEOGRAPHY OF RUSSIA. London: University of London Press; Chicago: Aldine, 1968. 416 p.

> Of significance to the economic historian are chapters on the economic and social geography of Russia in 1600; the economic geography of Russia in 1725, at the end of the reign of Peter the Great; Russia at the beginning of the nineteenth century--agriculture, mining and manufacture; and Russia at the beginning of the nineteenth century--commercial geography. Glossary, index, and maps.

THE PERIOD 1860-1917

A HANDBOOK OF SIBERIA AND ARCTIC RUSSIA. Vol. 1. London: HMSO, 1923? 384 p.

> This volume is as complete as possible up to 1914. It contains a general geographic sketch of the regions, a description of the natural resources; an account of the colonization of Siberia, a description of Siberian railways, and a sketch of Siberian agriculture, the timber industry, and various manufacturing industries. Index.

Krypton, Constantine [G.]. THE NORTHERN SEA ROUTE, ITS PLACE IN RUSSIAN ECONOMIC HISTORY BEFORE 1917. New York: Research Program on the U.S.S.R., 1953. ix, 194 p.

Economic Geography

The book is principally concerned with the social and economic factors which led businessmen and the government of prerevolutionary Russia to pay increasing attention in developing a northern sea route. The author deals with the subject within the general framework of Russia's economic development. Bibliography, index, and foldout map.

THE PERIOD AFTER 1917

Bal'zak, S. S., ed. ECONOMIC GEOGRAPHY OF THE USSR. American edition edited by Chauncy D. Harris. Translated by R. M. Hankin and O. A. Titelbaum. New York: Macmillan, 1949. xiv, 620 p.

This detailed study of Soviet geography deals with natural conditions and natural resources of the USSR; the distribution of productive forces in tsarist Russia; the basic problems in the distribution of the productive forces of the USSR; the population of the USSR and its distribution; the distribution of industry; the distribution of agriculture; the distribution of transport. Maps, tables, and indexes.

Baransky, N. N. ECONOMIC GEOGRAPHY OF THE USSR. Moscow: Foreign Languages Publishing House, 1956. 412 p. Illustrated.

This study discusses general characteristics of the national economy, industrial geography, agricultural geography, and geography of transport. The second part gives a regional survey of the USSR. Maps.

Barr, Brenton M., et al. "Patterns of Urban Spacing in the USSR: Analysis of Order Neighbor Statistics in Two-Dimensional Space." JOURNAL OF REGIONAL SCIENCE 11 (August 1971): 211-24.

An investigation of nearest-neighbor distance relationships among urban settlements in selected Soviet regions is discussed. A map shows the location of sample areas; two tables of data fill four pages.

Cole, J. P., and German, F. C. A GEOGRAPHY OF THE USSR; THE BACKGROUND TO A PLANNED ECONOMY. London: Butterworths, 1961. ix, 290 p.

This book provides an account of the geography of the USSR at the beginning of the 1959-65 seven-year plan. Chapters are devoted to population, transport, agriculture, industry, the economic planning regions, the distribution of productive activities in the USSR, Soviet foreign trade, and the economic race with the United States. Maps.

_____. A GEOGRAPHY OF THE USSR; THE BACKGROUND TO A PLANNED ECONOMY. 2d ed. London: Butterworths, 1970. 324 p. Illustrated.

In the first part the authors discuss technical aspects of the geography of the USSR, its past trends, and future prospects. The second section deals with the relation of the Party to planning and the spatial aspects of planning. The third section describes the physical features in relation to human geography. Finally, there is an overview of the nineteen economic regions. Four appendices, bibliography, maps, and index.

Cressey, George B. HOW STRONG IS RUSSIA? A GEOGRAPHIC APPRAISAL. Syracuse, N.Y.: Syracuse University Press, 1954. ix, 146 p.

This book evaluates people, land, climate, resources, and space as they bear on economic development and political prospects. Cressey discusses the Soviet landscape, mineral resources, pioneering efforts in Siberia, centers of Soviet strength, and Soviet foreign policy. Index.

──────. SOVIET POTENTIALS; A GEOGRAPHIC APPRAISAL. Syracuse, N.Y.: Syracuse University Press, 1962.

This volume briefly appraises material assets and limitations and focuses on three themes: the continentality of the Soviet Union; environmental handicaps such as poor terrain, short growing seasons, and limited rainfall; and the USSR's vast mineral resources. Tables, maps, and index.

──────. "USSR: The Geographic Base for Agricultural Planning." LAND ECONOMICS 25 (November 1949): 334-36.

This paper surveys geography and climatic situation of the USSR and concludes that little can be done to modify its limiting effect on agricultural expansion. For a comment on this paper, see "Comments in Summary," pp. 363-64.

Gray, G. D. B. SOVIET LAND: THE COUNTRY, ITS PEOPLE AND THEIR WORK. London: Adam and Charles Black, 1947. vii, 324 p.

The first part deals with area, physical features, and climate. The second part deals with peoples of the USSR and their history. The third part describes agriculture, industry, transport, and population. The book contains eighty-five photographs, 141 maps, diagrams, and drawings. Index.

Gregory, James S., and Shave, D. W. THE U.S.S.R.: A GEOGRAPHICAL SURVEY. New York: John Wiley, 1944. 636 p.

Part one surveys the USSR in general and contains a chapter on agricultural and industrial development. Part two deals with regional geography, transport, communications, foreign trade, and distribution of population.

Jackson, W[illiam]. A. Douglas. "The Problem of Soviet Agricultural Regionalization." SLAVIC REVIEW 20 (December 1961): 656-78.

> This article is an extensive survey of efforts by geographers to identify agricultural regions in the Soviet Union. Seven maps identify regions by type of agricultural activity and natural vegetation.

Jensen, Robert G., and Karaska, Gerald J. "The Mathematical Thrust in Soviet Economic Geography--Its Nature and Significance." JOURNAL OF REGIONAL SCIENCE 9 (April 1969): 141-52.

> This article is based on L. I. Vasilevskii. "Mathematical Methods in Economic Geography." KRATKAIA GEOGRAFICHESKAIA ENTSIKLOPEDIIA [Short geographic encyclopedia] vol. 5. Moscow: Akademiia Nauk, 1966.

Joore, Georges. THE SOVIET UNION, THE LAND AND ITS PEOPLE. 3d ed. London: Longmans, 1967. xx, 379 p.

> This popular geography includes a description of physical geography, expansion and movement of population, the economic system, and the major natural regions of the Soviet Union. Maps, diagrams, and index. A second edition came out in 1961.

Kish, George. ECONOMIC ATLAS OF THE SOVIET UNION. 2d ed., rev. Ann Arbor: University of Michigan Press, 1971.

> The maps included in this volume locate vegetation zones, air routes, population density, agriculture, land use, mining, industry, and transport systems. Index.

Kolosovskiy, N. N. "The Territorial-Production Combination (complex) in Soviet Economic Geography." JOURNAL OF REGIONAL SCIENCE 3, no. 1 (1961): 1-25.

> This paper first appeared in 1947 and was reprinted in OSNOVY EKONOMICHESKOGO RAYONIROVANIYA [Principles of economic regionalizdat]. Moscow: Gospolitizdot, 1958. Topics covered include the combination of plants and enterprises, cycles of production, territorial-production complexes and regionalization, and application to the cycle method. Four tables.

Krypton, Constantine [G.]. THE NORTHERN SEA ROUTE AND THE ECONOMY OF THE SOVIET NORTH. New York: Praeger, 1956. ix, 219 p.

> This study examines the actual and potential economic role of the Northern Sea Route. It contains chapters on the industries of the north, the limiting factors to development, and a brief section on southern Siberia.

Economic Geography

Lavrishchev, A. ECONOMIC GEOGRAPHY OF THE USSR: GENERAL INFORMATION, GEOGRAPHY OF THE INDUSTRY, AGRICULTURE AND TRANSPORT. Moscow: Progress Publishers, 1969. 379 p.

>The first part describes natural resources and natural conditions, development of the Soviet economy, and population of the USSR and its distribution. The second part deals with industry and gives brief descriptions of metallurgical industry, fuel industry, and light industry. The third part deals with the geography of Soviet agriculture and discusses crop farming and livestock production. The final section deals with transport. Maps and tables.

Lydolph, Paul E. "Schemes for the Amelioration of Soil and Climate in the USSR." In SOVIET AGRICULTURE AND PEASANT AFFAIRS, edited by Roy D. Laird, pp. 204-12. Lawrence: University of Kansas Press, 1963.

>The author discusses theoretical work being done in the field of physical geography in the Soviet Union which eventually may have far reaching effects on agricultural practices and production.

Mellor, Roy E. H. GEOGRAPHY OF THE USSR. London: Macmillan and Co., 1964. xv, 403 p.

>This general geography of the Soviet Union focuses attention on the political-geographical developments of the Russian state as well as on transport problems. Bibliography, glossary, maps, and index.

Nuttonson, M. Y. "USSR; Some Physical and Agricultural Characteristics of the Drought Area and Its Climatic Analogues in the United States." LAND ECONOMICS 25 (November 1949): 346-51.

>This paper studies the reasons for and locations of drought areas in the Soviet Union. For a comment, see "Comments in Summary," pp. 363-64.

Shabad, Theodore. GEOGRAPHY OF THE USSR: A REGIONAL SURVEY. New York: Columbia University Press, 1951. xxxii, 584 p.

>Part one surveys the physical setting, political framework, and economic pattern of the Soviet Union. Part two presents geographic surveys by region and district. Maps, tables, bibliography, and index.

Chapter 29

MANPOWER, LABOR, GOVERNMENT POLICY TOWARDS LABOR, AND TRADE UNIONS

Levine, Irving R. THE NEW WORKER IN SOVIET RUSSIA. New York: Macmillan, 1973. 191 p. Illustrated.

> The first third of the book discusses the condition of Russian workers from the era of Peter the Great to 1917. The remainder discusses the condition of workers under Lenin, Stalin, Khrushchev and the present leaders. Index, bibliography, map, and photographs.

Turin, S. P. FROM PETER THE GREAT TO LENIN: A HISTORY OF THE RUSSIAN LABOUR MOVEMENT WITH SPECIAL REFERENCE TO TRADE UNIONISM. London: P. S. King & Son, 1935. xii, 217 p.

> This has a chronological table, bibliography, glossary, index. Statistics and documents are included in the appendices.

THE PERIOD UP TO 1860

Zelnik, Reginald E. "An Early Case of Labor Protest in St. Petersburg: The Aleksandrovsk Machine Works in 1860." SLAVIC REVIEW 24 (September 1965): 507-20.

> This paper is a case history of peaceful labor protest in Russia in the 1850s and 1860s. Government policy toward these protests is viewed as leading to the more serious labor unrest of the 1870s and 1880s.

_____. LABOR AND SOCIETY IN TSARIST RUSSIA: THE FACTORY WORKERS OF ST. PETERSBURG: 1855-1870. Stanford, Calif.: Stanford University Press, 1971. vii, 450 p.

> The author examines the nineteenth-century Russian worker's part in early industrialization, relates these early experiences of Russian laborers to their subsequent political evolution, and investigates the interaction between the workers' situations and the attitudes and actions of other segments of society before the 1980s. Bibliography, index, and maps.

Manpower, Labor, and Trade Unions

THE PERIOD 1860-1917

Giffin, Frederick C. "The Formative Years of the Russian Factory Inspectorate, 1882-1885." SLAVIC REVIEW 25 (December 1966): 641-50.

    This article surveys the history of the factory inspectorate in Russia and makes some judgments of its effectiveness.

———. "The Prohibition of Night Work for Women and Young Persons: The Factory Law of June 3, 1885." CANADIAN SLAVIC STUDIES 2 (Summer 1968): 208-18.

    This article examines factory system legislation in Russia, the economic environment in which the legislation was passed, and the major proponents of the legislation.

Gliksman, Jerzy G. "The Russian Urban Worker: From Serf to Proletarian." In THE TRANSFORMATION OF RUSSIAN SOCIETY: ASPECTS OF SOCIAL CHANGE SINCE 1861, edited by Cyril E. Black, pp. 311-23. Cambridge, Mass.: Harvard University Press, 1960.

    The author summarizes the evolution of the urban worker.

Gordon, Manya. WORKERS BEFORE AND AFTER LENIN. New York: E. P. Dutton, 1941. 528 p.

    This volume systematically compares a quarter century of Communist achievement since 1917 with Russian progress in the preceding twenty-five years, giving particular attention to the working class. This book compares wages, hours, and food budgets; workers' housing; and dress of workers before and after the Revolution. Other chapters deal with the origin and status of trade unions, factory laws, social security, and the condition of the peasantry. Index.

Hammond, Thomas T. "Lenin on Russian Trade Unions under Capitalism, 1894-1904." AMERICAN SLAVIC AND EAST EUROPEAN REVIEW 8 (1949): 275-88.

    Author discusses Lenin's attitude toward the labor movement of the 1890s, the Social Democrats' support of demands for economic reforms, and the coordination between the economic and political struggles.

"The Living and Working Conditions of Kazakh Craftsmen Before the Revolution." CENTRAL ASIAN REVIEW 10, no. 4 (1962): 343-49.

    Aspects discussed include material and social position; methods of payment; working conditions; division of labor by sex; training of children; cooperation with neighbors; assistants; "guilds"; and customs.

Pospielovsky, Dimitry. RUSSIAN POLICE TRADE UNIONISM: EXPERIMENT OR PROVOCATION? London: Weidenfield and Nicolson, 1971. x, 189 p.

The author appraises the Zubatov movement in Russian trade unionism.

Rimlinger, Gaston V. "The Expansion of the Labor Market in Capitalist Russia: 1861-1917." JOURNAL OF ECONOMIC HISTORY 21 (June 1961): 208-15.

> This article is a review of A. G. Rashin. FORMIROVANIE RABOCHEGO KLASSA ROSSII [The formation of the Russian working class]. Moscow: Izdatel'stvo Sotsial'no-Ekonomicheskoi Literatury, 1958. A table provides figures on the increase in the number of persons working for wages in Russia, 1860-1913.

Rubinow, Isaac M. "New Russian Workingmen's Compensation." BULLETIN OF THE BUREAU OF LABOR 10 (May 1905): 955-59.

> New compensation legislation which took effect on January 1, 1904, is described.

Snow, George E. "The Kokovtsov Commission: An Abortive Attempt at Labor Reform in Russia in 1905." SLAVIC REVIEW 31 (December 1972): 780-96.

> This is an historical study which concludes that the government erred seriously in not implementing Kokovtsov's reform program.

Von Laue, Theodore H. "Factory Inspection Under the 'Witte System': 1892-1903." AMERICAN SLAVIC AND EAST EUROPEAN REVIEW 19 (October 1960): 347-62.

> This article is concerned with factory legislation under Witte and his predecessor, N. C. Bunge.

──────. "Russian Labor Between Field and Factory, 1892-1903." CALIFORNIA SLAVIC STUDIES 3 (1964): 33-65.

> This article surveys low wages in the chief industrial regions, the St. Petersburg district, the central district stretching from Moscow to the east and northeast, the Ukrainian south, and the rural expanses.

──────. "Russian Peasants in the Factory 1892-1904." JOURNAL OF ECONOMIC HISTORY 21 (March 1961): 61-80.

> The topics covered in this article include the relationship between peasants and workers in Russian factories and the exploitation of workers by capitalists.

Walkin, Jacob. "The Attitude of the Tsarist Government toward the Labor Problem." AMERICAN SLAVIC AND EAST EUROPEAN REVIEW 13 (1954): 163-84.

> This article discusses the irrelevance of Marxist concepts to under-

standing the problems of Russian labor under the tsars, the official government policy of "benign neglect" of labor up to 1905, and the changes which occurred in this policy after the 1905 revolution.

Ward, Benjamin. "Wild Socialism in Russia: The Origins." CALIFORNIA SLAVIC STUDIES 3 (1964): 127-48.

This essay studies the origins and growth of the factory committees, associating them with the economic environment in which they operated. Data on wages and prices in 1913-17 are included in tables.

Wolfe, Bertram D. "Gosplan and Zubatov: An Experiment in 'Police Socialism.'" RUSSIAN REVIEW 7 (Spring 1948): 53-61.

This article discusses the efforts of police to control trade unions in Russia about the turn of the century.

THE PERIOD AFTER 1917

Alexandrov, N. "Guarantees of Soviet People's Labour Rights." ECONOMIC AFFAIRS 17 (May 1972): 247-48 and 262.

A polemic stressing how the Soviet trade unions are concerned both with increasing labor productivity and with defending the workers from vestiges of capitalism.

Avrich, Paul H. "The Bolshevik Revolution and Workers' Control in Russian Industry." SLAVIC REVIEW 22 (March 1963): 47-63.

This article discusses the history and politics of workers' control in Russian industry in the years immediately after the Revolution.

Baikalov, Anatole V. IN THE LAND OF COMMUNIST DICTATORSHIP (LABOUR AND SOCIAL CONDITIONS IN SOVIET RUSSIA TO-DAY). London: Jonathan Cape, 1929. 285 p.

The author, who calls himself a Russian Socialist and is hostile toward the Bolsheviks, discusses the working day; wages; unemployment; housing conditions; workers and the control of industrial undertakings; workers and Soviet trade unions; and the peasants and the Soviets.

Barker, Geoffrey R. "A Note on the Productivity of Labour in Industry." BULLETINS ON SOVIET ECONOMIC DEVELOPMENT. Ser. 2. 7 (December 1952): 22-29.

In analyzing the productivity of labor, the author takes into consideration factors which determine the productivity of labor, as well as the means for directing their operation--systems of payment for work, social stimuli, administration, and the application of the law. Tables summarize output per worker per year, 1913-51.

_____. SOME PROBLEMS OF INCENTIVES AND LABOUR PRODUCTIVITY IN SOVIET INDUSTRY; A CONTRIBUTION TO THE STUDY OF THE PLANNING OF LABOUR IN THE U.S.S.R. Oxford, Eng.: Blackwell, 1956. xii, 129 p.

The author analyzes the reasons why the Soviet labor force is so inefficient and discusses some of the ways tried to increase the productivity of labor.

_____. "Soviet Labour." BULLETIN OF SOVIET ECONOMIC DEVELOPMENT. Ser. 2. 6 (June 1951): 1-26.

The author discusses compulsory measures that were taken by the Soviet government to "increase the preparedness and efficiency of the economy" on the eve of the war. Labor discipline, productivity and earnings, "socialist competition" and Stakhanovism, and living standards during the war are examined. The tables are based on Soviet data.

Baykov, Alexander M. "A Note on the Economic Significance of Compulsory Labour in the U.S.S.R." BULLETIN OF SOVIET ECONOMIC DEVELOPMENT. Ser. 2. 7 (December 1952): 30-40.

The author surveys the organization, administration, living and working conditions of compulsory labor in the USSR. He estimates the number of workers engaged in compulsory labor and the approximate percentage of the Soviet labor force which is made up of compulsory labor. Tables.

Beermann, R. "Trade Union Membership of Collective Farmers." SOVIET STUDIES 11 (July 1959): 116-17.

This note discusses an article which appeared in the trade union supplement of Estonian language newspaper.

_____. "Trade Union Problems in Estonia." SOVIET STUDIES 10 (October 1958): 183-88.

This note reviews coverage of trade union activities in the current Estonian press.

Bergson, Abram. "Distribution of the Earnings Bill among Industrial Workers in the Soviet Union, March, 1928; October, 1934." JOURNAL OF POLITICAL ECONOMY 50 (April 1942): 227-49.

This paper deals with methodological problems of measuring, at two separate periods, the distribution of the wage and salary bill among Soviet industrial workers. Five tables.

Manpower, Labor, and Trade Unions

_____. STRUCTURE OF SOVIET WAGES: A STUDY OF SOCIALIST ECONOMICS. Cambridge, Mass.: Harvard University Press, 1944. xvi, 255 p.

> Bergson examines wage variations in the USSR in 1928 and Russia in 1914; Soviet salaries in 1928 and 1934; the distribution of the wage bill among industrial workers in Russia in 1914 and in the USSR in 1928 and 1934; and overall wage administration. Tables and index.

Birmingham University. Bureau of Research on Russian Economic Conditions. "I: Remarks on the Five Year Plan; II: Compulsory Labour in the U.S.S.R." MEMORANDUM NO. 1 (May 1931): 1-19.

> In part one, topics discussed are agriculture, industry, and the cost of production; national income, prices, and the monopoly system; origins of the plan; and summary of recent data. Part two discusses compulsory labor.

_____. "Wages of Industrial Workers in the U.S.S.R." MEMORANDUM NO. 6 (July 1932): 1-24.

> Memorandum discusses the dynamics of real wages, the social level of wages, differentiation of wages, and the influence of the productivity of labor on the level of wages. Table summarizes data.

Bjork, Leif. WAGES, PRICES AND SOCIAL LEGISLATION IN THE SOVIET UNION. Translated by M. S. Michael. London: Dennis Dobson, 1953. 199 p.

> The book covers the following topics: the structure and functions of trade union organization; hours of work and the wage system; labor discipline and conflicts; taxes and state loans; social benefits; and prices of consumer's goods and services. An appendix lists regulations for the trade union organizations which were adopted at the Tenth All-Union Trade Congress.

Brodersen, Arvid. THE SOVIET WORKER; LABOR AND GOVERNMENT IN SOVIET SOCIETY. New York: Random House, 1966. ix, 278 p.

> The book covers the worker in Bolshevik theory and practice, 1917-28; centralized planning for industrialization under Stalin; the formation of the labor force, 1928-55; working conditions and labor productivity under Stalin; and Soviet labor policy after Stalin. Bibliography.

Bronson, David W. "Scientific and Engineering Manpower in the USSR and Employment in R & D." In SOVIET ECONOMIC PROSPECTS FOR THE SEVENTIES, U.S. Congress. Joint Economic Committee, pp. 564-93. Washington, D.C.: Government Printing Office, 1973.

> This paper discusses the stock of engineering and scientific manpower and its allocation to research and development. Tables and charts.

Manpower, Labor, and Trade Unions

_____. "Soviet Experience with Shortening the Workweek." INDUSTRIAL AND LABOR RELATIONS REVIEW 21 (April 1968): 391-99.

Soviet expectations and experiences in changing from a six-day to a five-day work week are discussed. A table provides examples of actual work schedules.

Brown, Emily C. "Continuity and Change in the Soviet Labor Market." INDUSTRIAL AND LABOR RELATIONS REVIEW 23 (January 1970): 171-90.

Topics covered include unemployment; the duty and right to work; lack of statistics; labor shortages; labor supply programs; regional efforts; redundant workers; incentives to release workers; distribution of labor; and the need for employment services.

_____. "Fundamental Soviet Labor Legislation." INDUSTRIAL AND LABOR RELATIONS REVIEW 26 (January 1973): 778-92.

This article examines the content of objectives of the "Fundamental Labor Legislation of the USSR and the Union Republics" enacted in 1970 and the revised "Regulation on the Rights of Factory, Plant and Local Union Committees" enacted in 1971.

_____. "Interests and Rights of Soviet Industrial Workers and the Revolution of Conflicts." INDUSTRIAL LABOR RELATIONS REVIEW 16 (January 1963): 254-78.

This article explores the legal and institutional framework for the resolution of labor conflict in the Soviet Union, the avenues available for the expression of worker dissatisfaction, and the interplay of rights of workers, workers' organizations, and management.

_____. "The Local Union in Soviet Industry: Its Relations with Members, Party, and Management." INDUSTRIAL LABOR RELATIONS REVIEW 13 (January 1960): 192-215.

The author finds that the function of protecting workers' rights and interests is becoming increasingly important, that the unions' power has been expanded, that leadership has become more representative of the rank-and-file, and that these changes stem from policy changes begun in 1957-58.

_____. "A Note on Employment in the Soviet Union in the Light of Technical Progress." SOVIET STUDIES 12 (January 1961): 231-40.

Problems of reconciling efficient utilization of labor with job choice and job security are considered.

_____. "The Soviet Labor Market." INDUSTRIAL LABOR RELATIONS REVIEW 10 (January 1957): 179-200.

This descriptive appraisal of the Soviet labor market in the late 1950s includes the following topics: effects of central planning, wages and manpower allocation, manpower training, recruitment and job choice, and mobility and labor discipline.

_____. "The Soviet Labor Market." In THE SOVIET ECONOMY: A BOOK OF READINGS, edited by Morris Bornstein and Daniel Fusfeld, pp. 141-67. Rev. ed. Homewood, Ill.: R. D. Irwin, 1966.

This is an updating of a previous article with the same title which appeared in INDUSTRIAL AND LABOR RELATIONS REVIEW 10 (January 1957): 179-200. Topics covered include employment and unemployment, planning for labor resources, planned training, job choice and planned placement, organized recruitment, mobility and the turnover problem, and wages and manpower distribution.

_____. SOVIET TRADE UNIONS AND LABOR RELATIONS. Cambridge, Mass.: Harvard University Press, 1966. ix, 394 p.

The book covers the political and economic setting; the labor market; the development, principles, and structure of trade unions; trade union centers; regional trade union councils; labor-management relations and protection of workers; labor disputes; wages and hours in industrial relations; and the industrial relations system. Bibliography.

Bunyan, James. THE ORIGIN OF FORCED LABOR IN THE SOVIET STATE 1917-1921: DOCUMENTS AND MATERIALS. Baltimore: Johns Hopkins Press, 1967. xi, 276 p.

Documents and materials provided refer to the role of labor in the Soviet state; the shift toward labor compulsion; militarization of labor; militarized forms in civilian labor; militarization of the transport system; and the Revolution in crisis. Bibliography and index.

Ceriglia, S. Joseph. WAGES IN THE USSR, 1950-1966: CONSTRUCTION. Washington, D.C.: Government Printing Office, 1967. v, 36 p.

This article makes an extensive search of Soviet sources for information on wages and other income. The author outlines the construction sector and the structure and level of wages. Tables.

Chapman, Janet G. "Real Wages in the Soviet Union, 1928-1952." REVIEW OF ECONOMICS AND STATISTICS 36 (May 1954): 134-56.

Preliminary findings of an investigation aimed at the systematic compilation of real wages data for the years 1928, 1937, and 1952 are examined. Seven tables and an appendix of price relatives are included.

_____. REAL WAGES IN THE SOVIET UNION SINCE 1928. Cambridge, Mass.: Harvard University Press, 1963. xiv, 395 p.

> The first part deals with the retail market and retail prices in the Soviet Union. The second part discusses index number theory; index numbers for price data and for weights of official retail prices in Moscow; and index numbers of the cost of living in the entire urban USSR. The third part surveys wages--money wages, social wages, real wages--living standards, and welfare. Tables, bibliography, and index.

Childs, S. Lawford, and Crottet, A. A. "Wages Policy in Soviet Russia." ECONOMIC HISTORY 2 (January 1932): 442-60.

> Soviet wage policy is traced through the periods of war communism, the NEP, and the First Five-Year Plan (up to 1931). A table summarizes average wage changes between 1924 and January 1931.

Clark, M. Gardner. "Comparative Wage Structures in the Steel Industry of the Soviet Union and Western Countries." INDUSTRIAL RELATIONS RESEARCH ASSOCIATION 13 (December 1960): 266-88.

> The wage structure of integrated iron and steel plants in the Soviet Union and the leading Western countries are compared. Seven tables. See also H. M. Houty and Emily C. Brown. "Discussion," pp. 289-96.

"Collective Agreements in the U.S.S.R." INTERNATIONAL LABOUR REVIEW 66 (November-December 1952): 477-84.

> This article is concerned with the Soviet conception of collective agreements from their reintroduction in 1947 to 1952.

"Conciliation Procedures in Soviet Russia." INTERNATIONAL LABOUR REVIEW 22 (August 1930): 207-20.

> This article discusses the 1928 order concerning conciliation procedures and the procedure before the courts in trade disputes. The organization, procedure, and the legal force of conciliation bodies are sketched.

Conquest, Robert, ed. INDUSTRIAL WORKERS IN THE USSR. New York: Praeger, 1967. 203 p.

> Conquest discusses the economic, political, legal, and social factors which determine the position of the Soviet worker. He considers employment, wages and norms, labor discipline, working hours, leave, and labor protection, and the trade unions. Bibliography.

"The Continuous Working Week in Soviet Russia." INTERNATIONAL LABOUR

REVIEW 23 (February 1931): 157-80.

> This article outlines the history of the seven-hour day and then describes the organization of work under the new system and analyzes the results.

Crottet, A. A., and Childs, S. Lawford. "Trade Unions in the Soviet State." ECONOMIC HISTORY 2 (January 1933): 617-28.

> Relations between the government and the trade unions before the Revolution are summarized. Communist organization, structure, finance, membership, and numbers of trade unions are discussed.

Dallin, David J. THE ECONOMICS OF SLAVE LABOR. Human Affairs Pamphlets, no. 42. Chicago: H. Regnery, 1949. 35 p.

> The pamphlet deals with: slave labor in the Soviet economic system; the organization of Soviet slave labor; working conditions in Soviet camps; the number and location of Soviet labor camps; and some of the long-run effects of slave labor.

Dallin, David J., and Nikolaevsky, Boris. FORCED LABOR IN SOVIET RUSSIA. New Haven, Conn.: Yale University Press, 1947. xv, 331 p.

> This book seeks to present a "natural history" of forced labor in Soviet Russia. It contains eyewitness accounts, discusses the number of camps and prisoners, describes types of camps, and discusses the position of forced labor in the five-year plans.

Deutscher, Isaac. SOVIET TRADE UNIONS. London: Royal Institute of International Affairs, 1950. ix, 156 p.

> This essay analyzes the role of Soviet trade unions, their evolution since the Bolshevik upheaval of 1917, and their functions in the planned economy. It also considers to what extent the Soviet trade unions defend or fail to defend the interests of their members with the employer-state and their relationship with the Communist party.

Dewar, Margaret. "Labour and Wage Reforms in the USSR." STUDIES ON THE SOVIET UNION n.s. 1, no. 3 (1962): 80-91.

> This survey of labor and wage reforms since 1956 concludes that the reforms are progressive but do not represent a new form of society, superior to capitalist society.

De Witt, Nicholas. EDUCATION AND PROFESSIONAL EMPLOYMENT IN THE USSR. Washington, D.C.: Government Printing Office, 1961. xxxix, 856 p.

> This study is an update and a revision of a previous National Science Foundation study entitled SOVIET PROFESSIONAL MAN-

POWER (1955). It focuses on the role of education in the development of professional manpower. Charts, tables, bibliography, and index.

──────. "High-Level Manpower in the U.S.S.R." In NEW DIRECTIONS IN THE SOVIET ECONOMY, U.S. Congress. Joint Economic Committee, pp. 789-816. Washington, D.C.: Government Printing Office, 1966.

Recent developments in Soviet education and manpower training policies, in particular as they effect the supply of specialized professional manpower, are reviewed. Ten tables.

──────. SOVIET PROFESSIONAL MANPOWER: ITS EDUCATION, TRAINING, AND SUPPLY. Washington, D.C.: Government Printing Office, 1955. xxviii, 400 p.

This book discusses the general setting of the Soviet educational system, primary and secondary education, secondary semiprofessional training, higher and professional education, research and advanced degrees, and specialized manpower. Tables, charts, bibliography, and index.

Diatchenko, V. P. "The Financial Problems of Professional Re-training of Personnel in the USSR." PUBLIC FINANCE 24, no. 2 (1969): 391-404.

Topics covered include problems caused by technological progress, the Soviet systems of personnel training and improvement, manpower release and reemployment, and the financing of these programs. Seven tables.

"Dismissal Procedures--III: U.S.S.R." INTERNATIONAL LABOUR REVIEW 80 (August 1959): 173-87.

An extensive survey of dismissal procedures but with no commentary or figures on dismissals or grievances.

Dodge, Norton D. "Fifty Years of Soviet Labor." STUDIES ON THE SOVIET UNION n.s. 7, no. 1 (1967): 1-34.

This paper discusses the various promises made to Soviet labor and the ways in which they were fulfilled. Four tables.

Dogadov, V. M. "Change in the Nature of Soviet Collective Agreements." SOVIET STUDIES 1 (June 1949): 79-84.

This note consists of excerpts from V. M. Dogadov. "Stages in the Development of the Soviet Collective Agreement." Translated from BULLETIN OF THE ACADEMY OF SCIENCES OF THE U.S.S.R. (ECONOMICS AND LAW), 1948-52.

Douglas, Paul H. "Labor Legislation and Social Insurance." In SOVIET RUSSIA IN THE SECOND DECADE, American Trade Union Delegation, pp. 216-38. New York: John Day, 1928.

> The author examines hours of work, rest times, and vacations; the extensive system of social insurance; and the administration of labor laws and social insurance.

──────. "Wages and the Material Condition of the Industrial Workers." In SOVIET RUSSIA IN THE SECOND DECADE, American Trade Union Delegation, pp. 239-52. New York: John Day, 1928.

> The author reviews average wages for manufacturing and mining workers, transportation workers, and agricultural laborers in 1926. He then examines the relative quantity of goods and services that can be purchased with these wages.

Douglas, Paul H., and Dunn, Robert W. "The Trade Union Movement." In SOVIET RUSSIA IN THE SECOND DECADE, American Trade Union Delegation, pp. 189-215. New York: John Day, 1928.

> The following are among the topics discussed: membership; shop committees and union democracy; union-management cooperation; collective bargaining and the fixation of wages; and conciliation and arbitration.

Dunn, Robert W. SOVIET TRADE UNIONS. New York: Vanguard Press, 1928. xix, 238 p.

> Dunn considers the origins and growth of unions; industrial unions; interunion organizations; collective bargaining and labor disputes; relations with the government; and the union's role in production. Index.

Eason, Warren W. "Comparisons of the United States and Soviet Economies: the Labor Force." In COMPARISONS OF THE U.S. AND SOVIET ECONOMIES, U.S. Congress. Joint Economic Committee, pp. 73-93. Washington, D.C.: Government Printing Office, 1960.

> This paper deals with trends in the Soviet labor force, hours of work, and efficiency of the labor force. The author discusses the distribution of the labor force by selected characteristics of the demand for labor, by socioeconomic groups, and by dependency on agricultural and nonagricultural occupations. Statistical data are summarized in five tables.

──────. EMPLOYMENT AND UNEMPLOYMENT IN THE SOVIET UNION. Santa Monica, Calif.: RAND Corp., 1954. 70 p.

> Comprised of four parts, this study in part one outlines the results of the 1926 census. Part two summarizes changes which took place through 1939. Part three gives an account of some of the measures

of the total labor force. Part four compares several measures of employment with those of the labor force and discusses possible indications of unemployment. Tables.

———. "Labor Force." In ECONOMIC TRENDS IN THE SOVIET UNION, edited by Abram Bergson and Simon Kuznets, pp. 38-95. Cambridge, Mass.: Harvard University Press, 1963.

An extensive survey of the qualitative and quantitative factors affecting labor supply in the Soviet Union, this study gives extensive data in the statistical tables. Some of the data go back to the tsarist period.

———. "Population and Labor Force." In SOVIET ECONOMIC GROWTH: CONDITIONS AND PERSPECTIVES, edited by Abram Bergson, pp. 101-25. Evanston, Ill.: Row, Peterson, 1953.

Growth under the five-year plans is summarized and future trends of the population and labor force are explored. Special reference is given to total numbers and the distribution of the labor force by economic sectors. Tables. The paper is followed with a comment by F. Lorimer, pp. 122-25.

———. "Problems of Manpower and Industrialization in the USSR." In POPULATION TRENDS IN EASTERN EUROPE, THE USSR, AND MAINLAND CHINA, pp. 68-88. Proceedings of the 36th Annual Conference of the Milbank Memorial Fund, November 4-5, 1959. New York: Milbank Memorial Fund, 1960.

This paper examines the following topics: the overall supply of labor in quantitative terms, the overall supply of labor in qualitative terms, the recruitment and allocation of labor, and the management of labor in the enterprise and some problems of industrial relation. The main thrust of this paper is the Soviet interest in increasing the efficiency of labor utilization.

"The Eleventh Trade Union Congress." SOVIET STUDIES 6 (October 1954): 162-68.

This note summarizes various aspects of the Congress which took place on June 7-15, 1954.

"The Employment Situation in Russia since the Bolshevist Revolution, I." INTERNATIONAL LABOUR REVIEW 3 (September 1921): 80-96.

This article considers the labor statistics of Russian workers. The paper deals only with factory workers, outlines the causes of unemployment, presents figures on the increase of unemployment, and describes the disintegration of Russian industry.

"The Employment Situation in Russia since the Bolshevik Revolution, II." INTERNATIONAL LABOUR REVIEW 4 (March 1922): 96-110.

This article describes the movement of factory workers away from the nationalized industries into the country and sketches "the measures taken by the Soviet Government . . . to prevent the breakup of Russian factory industries." It also discusses the measures taken to increase productivity and the number of workers.

Fakiolas, R. "Problems of Labour Mobility in the USSR." SOVIET STUDIES 14 (July 1962): 16-40.

This article outlines labor turnover in Soviet industry and considers its dimensions, causes, and financial cost. It concentrates on specific present-day problems of labor mobility in the country. Six tables.

_____. "Work Attendance in Soviet Industry." SOVIET STUDIES 14 (April 1963): 365-78.

Whole-day absence in industry and construction is considered, and the total time lost and the resultant loss of output are analyzed. Four tables.

Feshbach, Murray. "Manpower in the U.S.S.R.: A Survey of Recent Trends and Prospects." In NEW DIRECTIONS IN THE SOVIET ECONOMY, U.S. Congress. Joint Economic Committee, pp. 703-38. Washington, D.C.: Government Printing Office, 1966.

Supply, demand, and utilization of manpower are discussed. Fourteen tables.

Feshbach, Murray, and Rapawy, Stephen. "Labor and Wages." In ECONOMIC PERFORMANCE AND THE MILITARY BURDEN IN THE SOVIET UNION, U.S. Congress. Joint Economic Committee, pp. 71-84. Washington, D.C.: Government Printing Office, 1970.

Labor and wages in the 1950s and 1960s are discussed. Eight tables.

_____. "Labor Constraints in the Five-Year Plan." In SOVIET ECONOMIC PROSPECTS FOR THE SEVENTIES, U.S. Congress. Joint Economic Committee, pp. 485-563. Washington, D.C.: Government Printing Office, 1973.

The authors consider sources and channels of labor supply, employment trends, occupational structure, training, regional distribution, labor turnover, and productivity. Twenty-seven tables.

"The Five-Year Plan and the Regulation of the Labour Market in the U.S.S.R." INTERNATIONAL LABOUR REVIEW 27 (March 1933): 349-77.

Changes in the regulation of the labor market and the policy of the distribution and utilization are discussed.

"Forced Labor in the Soviet Bloc." In TRENDS IN ECONOMIC GROWTH: A COMPARISON OF THE WESTERN POWERS AND THE SOVIET BLOC, by Library of Congress. Legislative Reference Service, pp. 234-46. Washington, D.C.: Government Printing Office, 1955.

>   Aspects discussed include history; "corrective" labor; numbers of forced laborers; economic importance; and restrictions on "free" labor.

Freeman, Joseph. THE SOVIET WORKER; AN ACCOUNT OF THE ECONOMIC, SOCIAL, AND CULTURAL STATUS OF LABOR IN THE U.S.S.R. New York: Liveright, 1932. vii, 408 p.

>   In the first three chapters the author discusses the status of the Russian worker under tsarism, the development of the Soviet economy, and the Soviet planning system. The rest of the book describes present circumstances under which the worker labors and lives. Some topics discussed are trade unions; labor laws; wages and hours; distribution and consumption; forced labor; and the planning of labor. Glossary, bibliography, and index.

Gaenko, F. "Soviet Labour Policy." STUDIES ON THE SOVIET UNION n.s. 3. (December 1960): 83-93.

>   Topics covered include regulations on labor relations, officially recognized labor organizations, and working conditions and job security.

Galenson, Walter. "Industrial Labor Productivity." In SOVIET ECONOMIC GROWTH: CONDITIONS AND PERSPECTIVES, edited by Abram Bergson, pp. 190-224. Evanston, Ill.: Row, Peterson, 1953.

>   This paper examines past trends in Soviet industrial productivity, compares absolute productivity levels in Soviet and American industry, and assesses possible productivity changes in the Soviet Union in the next two decades. The essay is followed by comments by Joseph S. Berliner and M. Gardner Clark.

──────. "Industrial Training in the Soviet Union." INDUSTRIAL AND LABOR RELATIONS REVIEW 9 (July 1956): 562-76.

>   This article surveys Soviet industrial training programs, 1928-54. Topics covered include types of training programs, factory training for new workers, skill upgrading, and vocational education. Tables.

──────. LABOR PRODUCTIVITY IN SOVIET AND AMERICAN INDUSTRY. New York: Columbia University Press, 1955. xiv, 273 p.

>   Part one deals with the concepts and methodology of productivity measurement; part two consists of industry studies; and part three includes summary and conclusions. Tables and bibliography.

_____. "The Soviet Wage Reform." INDUSTRIAL RELATIONS RESEARCH ASSOCIATION 13 (December 1960): 250–65.

This paper discusses the Soviet wage reform between 1956 and 1960. Topics covered include the internal and external wage structures, forms of wage payment, and salaries. Four tables. The paper is followed by H. M. Houty and Emily C. Brown. "Discussion," pp. 289–96.

Golov, A. "Methodology of the Measurement and Planning of Labor Productivity in the U.S.S.R." INTERNATIONAL LABOUR REVIEW 97 (May 1968): 447–64.

The methods of measuring labor productivity discussed here include the cost method, the conventional units of labor method, the "labor" method, and the factor method.

Goodman, Ann S. ESTIMATES AND PROJECTIONS OF SPECIALIZED MANPOWER IN THE U.S.S.R.: 1950–1975. U.S. Department of Commerce. Bureau of the Census. International Populations Reports, Series P-91, no. 21. Washington, D.C.: Government Printing Office, 1970. 50 p.

Full discussion of sources and methodology as well as fifteen tables are included. Paperback.

Grossman, Philip. LABOR SUPPLY AND EMPLOYMENT IN THE USSR, 1950–65. Washington, D.C.: Central Intelligence Agency, 1960. vi, 40 p.

This report summarizes statistics on Soviet manpower and discusses major developments during 1950–59 affecting the labor supply and its utilization, primarily as background for an assessment of probable trends during 1960–65. Twelve tables.

"The Growth of the Working-Class of Turkmenistan up to 1941." CENTRAL ASIAN REVIEW 10, no. 1 (1962): 19–30.

The increase in the labor force from 1921 to 1941 is examined.

Hayenko, Fedor. "The 'Communist Labour' Movement." STUDIES ON THE SOVIET UNION n.s. 5, no. 3 (1966): 46–55.

The conflict between the goals of higher productivity and the protection of worker interests is highlighted.

_____. "Labour Conditions in the Soviet Union." STUDIES ON THE SOVIET UNION n.s. 7, no. 3 (1968): 1–14.

Topics discussed include the wage system, taxation, social security, manpower policy, trade unions, and labor legislation. A table provides figures on average monthly earnings for selected sectors.

_____. "Labour Protection in the Soviet Union." STUDIES ON THE SOVIET UNION n.s. 8, no. 4 (1969): 12-24.

> Labor safety and health standards are discussed.

_____. "Living and Working Conditions at the New Construction Sites." STUDIES ON THE SOVIET UNION n.s. 5, no. 1 (1965): 65-73.

> The construction sites referred to here are in Siberia.

_____. "A Soviet Economist Looks at the Manpower Problem." STUDIES ON THE SOVIET UNION n.s. 5, no. 2 (1965): 89-98.

> This paper consists largely of a translation of E. Manevich. "The Problem of Rational Utilization of Manpower in the Soviet Union." VOPROSY EKONOMIKI, no. 6 (1965). A table shows the distribution of labor resources in Novosibirsk Oblast in Western Siberia in 1962.

_____. "The Soviet Trade Union Movement." STUDIES ON THE SOVIET UNION n.s. 4, no. 4 (1965): 143-49.

> This paper discusses efforts to revive the trade unions as Party tools.

_____. TRADE UNIONS AND LABOR IN THE SOVIET UNION. Munich: Institute for the Study of the USSR, 1965. 150 p.

> The book includes discussions of the great debate of the twenties on the trade unions and the state; the wage system; and labor protection. The USSR statutes on the trade unions are in an appendix. Bibliography.

Hewes, Amy. "Labor Conditions in Soviet Russia." JOURNAL OF POLITICAL ECONOMY 28 (November 1920): 774-83.

> Topics covered include compulsory work; unemployment; the length of the working day; voluntary work; wages; women and child labor; trade unions; nationalization; and cooperatives.

_____. "Russian Wage Systems under Communism." JOURNAL OF POLITICAL ECONOMY 30 (April 1922): 274-78.

> This short paper notes that Soviet wage systems have some capitalistic features.

_____. "Trade Union Development in Soviet Russia." AMERICAN ECONOMIC REVIEW 13 (December 1923): 618-37.

> This article examines the development of trade unions in Russia, 1905-22. Tables include data on wages in selected industries in 1922.

———. "The Transformation of Soviet Trade Unions." AMERICAN ECONOMIC REVIEW 22 (December 1932): 605-19.

> This is an historical account of the redirection of the chief concerns of Soviet trade unions from worker welfare and wages to that of implementing the wage decisions and schemes of state organs for increasing productivity and reducing labor turnover. The growth of the trade unions which accompanied this redirection is also noted.

Hoffding, V. "Labour Conditions in Soviet Russia I. Conditions of Work." SLAVONIC REVIEW 7 (June 1928): 67-76.

> The author examines to what extent workers' positions have improved or deteriorated in comparison with the pre-Bolshevik period.

———. "II. The Living Conditions." SLAVONIC REVIEW 7 (January 1929): 349-60.

> The author discusses how the Soviet government is dealing with the housing problem, workers' insurance, and unemployment.

Hubbard, Leonard [E.]. SOVIET LABOR AND INDUSTRY. London: Macmillan and Co., 1942. xv, 315 p.

> Hubbard examines economic conditions under the tsars; results of the First Five-Year Plan; the rise of Stakhanovism; wages and the organization of labor and industry; labor sources and labor market; trade unions; the standard of living; the planned economy; women in industry; and the industrial and agricultural proletariat.

Hutchings, Raymond [F.] [D.]. "The Ending of Unemployment in the USSR." SOVIET STUDIES 19 (July 1967): 29-52.

> This paper investigates the relation between collectivization and the diminution of urban unemployment in the USSR. Two graphs and four tables.

"Industrial Inspection in Soviet Russia." INTERNATIONAL LABOUR REVIEW 7 (January 1923): 25-37.

> This article outlines the powers and functions of elected inspectors and appointed technical inspectors in Soviet Russia.

Inkeles, Alex. SOCIAL CHANGE IN SOVIET RUSSIA, Russian Research Center Studies, 57. Cambridge, Mass.: Harvard University Press, 1968. xviii, 475 p.

> Twenty-one essays deal with the sociology of the Soviet Union. Of special interest to the economist are essays on social stratification, social mobility, occupational prestige, and ratings of occupations. Bibliography and index.

International Labour Office. LABOUR CONDITIONS IN SOVIET RUSSIA. Systematic Questionnaire and Bibliography Prepared for the Mission of Enquiry in Russia. London: Harrison and Sons, n.d. cxliv, 294 p.

> The book contains information on labor legislation; social welfare; freedom of labor; trade unions; relations between the state and industry; the material situation of the working classes; and agricultural work. Extensive bibliography.

_____. THE TRADE UNION MOVEMENT IN SOVIET RUSSIA. Geneva: P. S. King & Son, 1927. xii, 287 p.

> This volume is divided into three parts. Part one gives an account of the trade union theories preferred by the Russian Communist party. Parts two and three deal with the organization and activities of the trade unions. Tables.

Ivanov, S. A. "International Labor Conventions and the U.S.S.R." INTERNATIONAL LABOUR REVIEW 93 (April 1966): 401-13.

> The author examines the attitude of the USSR towards the standard-setting activities of the International Labor Conventions, which he considers the organization's main function as shown by its record of ratification of conventions and the stand of its representatives in the general conference of the ILO.

_____. "New Codification of Soviet Labour Law." INTERNATIONAL LABOUR REVIEW 108 (August-September 1973): 143-61.

> This paper discusses the reasons for the codification, its place in Soviet labor legislation, its relation to international standards, and its particular features.

Jalnine, V. "Some Recent Development in the Labour Field in the USSR." INTERNATIONAL LABOUR REVIEW 106 (August-September 1972): 191-205.

> This article reviews economic reform undertaken in the USSR in the 1960s, particularly in wages. It analyzes the employment structure and the effect on personal earnings of the increase in labor productivity. It also considers the implications of development in national income distribution for consumption and investment.

Jasny, Naum. "Labor and Output in Soviet Concentration Camps." JOURNAL OF POLITICAL ECONOMY 59 (October 1951): 405-19.

> Topics covered include the 1941 plan; significance of the statistics; economic activities of the NKVD; concentration camp populations; checks for these figures; and the profitability of the camps. For further discussion, see: David A. Redding. "Reliability of Estimates of Unfree Labor in the U.S.S.R." JOURNAL OF POLITICAL ECONOMY 60 (August 1952): 337-40; followed by Naum Jasny. "Comments," pp. 340-42.

Manpower, Labor, and Trade Unions

———. "Peasant-worker Income Relationships: A Neglected Subject." SOVIET STUDIES 12 (July 1960): 14-22.

   Emphasis is on 1952-58.

Kaplan, Norman. EARNINGS DISTRIBUTION IN THE USSR. Santa Monica, Calif.: RAND Corp., 1969. vii, 186 p.

   This study is based primarily on a recent Soviet publication TRUD V SSR (Moscow, 1968). The author derives earnings distributions of three kinds: (1) changes in earnings inequality for various periods in the USSR; (2) United States and USSR comparisons of earnings inequality; and (3) "changes in the direction and degree of asymmetry for both countries." Tables.

Katharine, Duchess of Atholl, M. P. CONSCRIPTION OF A PEOPLE. New York: Columbia University Press, 1931. x, 206 p.

   Among the topics dealt with are forced labor and the First Five-Year Plan; the correctional labor code of 1924; collectivization and the liquidation of the kulaks; compulsory labor for seasonal industries; and conscription of labor for heavy industry. Index.

Kazanskii, A., and Ul'ianova, A. F. "A Great Social Achievement (On the Results of the Transfer of Factory Workers and Office Employees of the USSR to a Shorter Working Day)." PROBLEMS OF ECONOMICS 4 (August 1961): 28-36.

   This is a translation from VESTNIK STATISTIKI, no. 5 (1961). Recent labor reforms are discussed.

Kingsbury, Susan M., and Fairchild, Mildred. EMPLOYMENT AND UNEMPLOYMENT IN PRE-WAR AND SOVIET RUSSIA. Hague, Holland: International Industrial Relations Association, 1931. 132 p.

   This report covers fluctuations in employment and unemployment in prewar Russia and in the Soviet Union. Individual chapters deal with population, employment, unemployment, production, worker productivity, wages, and standards of living.

Kirsch, Leonard. "The Resuscitation of Trade Unions in the U.S.S.R." LABOR HISTORY 12 (Winter 1971): 154-62.

   This article reviews several books dealing with labor and trade unions in the Soviet Union.

———. SOVIET WAGES: CHANGES IN STRUCTURE AND ADMINISTRATION SINCE 1956. Cambridge, Mass.: M.I.T. Press, 1972. xii, 237 p.

   The book contains a brief history of Soviet wage reform and a description of wage determination. Kirsch discusses goals and accomplishments of Soviet wage policy. Charts, tables, bibliography, and index.

Korber, Lili. LIFE IN A SOVIET FACTORY. Translated by Claud W. Sykes. London: John Lane, the Bodley Head, 1933. 280 p.

>This firsthand account, in diary form, concerns a foreign worker's life in Soviet Russia in 1931.

Korsakov, E. "The System of Remuneration in the Soviet Merchant Marine." INTERNATIONAL LABOUR REVIEW 94 (October 1966): 398-414.

>The author discusses wage reforms in 1960 which affected the Soviet merchant fleet. He describes remuneration for responsible personnel under the new system and gives comparative tables showing remuneration for typical offices and ratings before and after the reform.

Kostin, Leonid. "Organisation of Workers' Education in the Soviet Union." INTERNATIONAL LABOUR REVIEW 79 (February 1959): 158-72.

>The emphasis here is on the role of trade unions in workers' education. An organization chart is included.

Koutaissoff, Elisabeth. "Soviet Professional Manpower." SOVIET STUDIES 8 (October 1956): 113-24.

>This article is a review of Nicholas DeWitt. SOVIET PROFESSIONAL MANPOWER--ITS EDUCATION, TRAINING, AND SUPPLY. Washington, D.C.: National Science Foundation, 1955.

Kronsjo, Tom. "Soviet Engineering-Economic Education." ECONOMICS OF PLANNING 2 (December 1962): 184-94.

>This article presents a wealth of information on Soviet education in economics, with its major point being the Soviet efforts to combine a background in engineering with one in economics.

_____. "Tendencies in Soviet Economic Scientific Education." ECONOMICS OF PLANNING 2 (March 1962): 2-20.

>Topics covered include Soviet higher education compared with other countries, the increasing proportion of economics students, basic features of Soviet higher economic education, and cooperation between universities and planning organs, industry, and agriculture. Tables.

"Labour Disputes in Soviet Russia." INTERNATIONAL LABOUR REVIEW 14 (August 1926): 262-68.

>The establishment of conciliation and arbitration organizations in Soviet Russia under the New Economic Policy are discussed. The article contains summary tables of the number of strikes in 1924 and 1925 and the results of the strikes.

"Labour Disputes in Soviet Russia in 1924 and 1925." INTERNATIONAL LABOUR REVIEW 15 (March 1927): 450-54.

> This article discusses the number and magnitude of disputes, their causes, and the procedure for settlement. It also gives a tabular summary of the results of disputes.

"Labour Inspection in Russia in 1925." INTERNATIONAL LABOUR REVIEW 14 (July 1926): 97-102.

> The organization, staff, and work of the inspectorate are discussed.

"The Life of the Kirgiz Miner." CENTRAL ASIAN REVIEW 12, no. 2 (1964): 114-22.

> Aspects discussed include the formation of the working class, life, culture, family and marriage, handicrafts, and public services and culture. A table of workers by nationality, a map, and illustrations of miners' homes are included.

Lozovsky, A., ed. HANDBOOK ON THE SOVIET TRADE UNIONS. Moscow: Cooperative Publishing Society of Foreign Workers in the U.S.S.R., 1937. 144 p.

> The book reviews the history of the Soviet trade union structure and describes the Stakhanov movement; wages and standard of living; social insurance and labor protection; and abolition of unemployment. The relations of women, young people, the Communist party, and the Soviet state with trade unions are examined.

Lungu, Gh. "Population and Labour Force in Eastern Europe and the U.S.S.R.: Structure and Recent Trends." INTERNATIONAL LABOUR REVIEW 91 (February 1965): 135-48.

> After outlining the demography of the countries, the author examines their economically active populations. Trends in the distribution of manpower between agriculture and the nonagricultural sectors and of nonagricultural employment among various branches of economic activity are examined. Ten tables.

McAuley, Mary. LABOUR DISPUTES IN SOVIET RUSSIA, 1957-65. Oxford, Eng.: Clarendon-Oxford University Press, 1969. viii, 269 p.

> The major portion of this study is concerned with two categories of employee-management disputes: disputes over legal rights and disputes over the establishment of working conditions. The first chapters outline the history of labor disputes and discuss the Khrushchev period and policy disputes. Glossary, index, and bibliography.

Manevich, Efim. "The Management of Soviet Manpower." FOREIGN AFFAIRS 47 (October 1968): 176-84.

This article discusses some Soviet manpower problems but asserts that, contrary to some Western opinions, unemployment is not a major problem.

"Manpower." CENTRAL ASIAN REVIEW 1 (April-June 1953): 1-14.

This article concentrates on the training and organization of political personnel and of personnel and labor in the collective farms.

Markus, B. L. "The Abolition of Unemployment in the U.S.S.R." INTERNATIONAL LABOUR REVIEW 33 (March 1936): 356-90.

After describing the employment market in tsarist Russia, the author shows how the transformation brought about by the Revolution has gradually modified the distribution of labor in the USSR. He concludes that unemployment is no longer a problem.

──────. "The Stakhanov Movement and the Increased Productivity of Labour in the U.S.S.R." INTERNATIONAL LABOUR REVIEW 34 (July 1936): 5-33.

The author examines the birth and progress of the Stakhanov movement and the consequences to be expected of it.

Miller, Jacob, ed. "Procedure of Collective Agreements." SOVIET STUDIES 3 (July 1951): 100-103.

This is a translation of questions and answers from a Soviet trade union magazine, V POMOSHCH PROFSOYUZNOMU AKTIVU [To help the trade union aktiv], no. 3 (1951): 42-44.

Minkoff, Jack. "Estimating the Soviet Wage Bill from the Receipts of the Social Insurance System." SLAVIC REVIEW 20 (December 1961): 679-84.

This note discusses the method of estimating the Soviet wage bill indicated in the title. A table presents estimates of the wage bill and average wage magnitudes (1937-58), demonstrating that social insurance tax receipts have represented 6.3 percent of the wage bill.

Moskalenko, G. K. "Collective Agreements in the U.S.S.R." INTERNATIONAL LABOUR REVIEW 85 (January 1962): 18-29.

Collective agreements in Russia, first under the tsars and then under the Soviet government, are examined.

Mots, A. "Industrialisation and Technical Training in the Kazakh S.S.R." INTERNATIONAL LABOUR REVIEW 90 (December 1964): 521-43.

After briefly sketching the history of Kazakhstan's industrialization, Mots shows how dependence for skilled manpower on the more advanced republics of the union has been overcome by comprehensive

Manpower, Labor, and Trade Unions

general education and technical training closely linked to the needs of modern industrial and agricultural production. Six tables.

Nash, Edmund. "Purchasing Power of Workers in the U.S.S.R." MONTHLY LABOR REVIEW 83 (April 1960): 359-64.

Soviet wage-price policy, average earnings in the USSR, and real earnings in the United States and USSR are discussed. Two tables and two charts.

_____. "Recent Changes in Labor Controls in the Soviet Union." In NEW DIRECTIONS IN THE SOVIET ECONOMY, U.S. Congress. Joint Economic Committee, pp. 849-71. Washington, D.C.: Government Printing Office, 1966.

Topics discussed include measures for the relaxation of labor controls, measures concerning labor and living conditions, labor policies as reflected in pronouncements at Party congresses, and problems with implementing labor controls. Two tables.

_____. "Recent Trends in Labor Controls in the Soviet Union." In DIMENSIONS OF SOVIET ECONOMIC POWER, U.S. Congress. Joint Economic Committee, pp. 393-407. Washington, D.C.: Government Printing Office, 1962.

The article summarizes changes in labor controls and working and living conditions in the Soviet Union in the post-Stalin era. He details some of the legislation aimed at improving the working and living conditions of Soviet citizens.

Newth, J. A. "Factors Determining Industrial Wages." SOVIET STUDIES 10 (July 1958): 99-101.

This note reports analytical work done by two Soviet economists. The factors considered are effort involved, skill required, location, and a residual. Two tables.

_____. "Income Distribution in the USSR." SOVIET STUDIES 12 (October 1960): 193-96.

This paper uses the tax reliefs outlined in two of Khrushchev's speeches as a basis for calculating the structure of earned income. Tables.

_____. "The Soviet Labour Force in the Fifties." SOVIET STUDIES 11, no. 4: 363-72.

Article discusses changes in size and composition of the labor force and the significance of these changes. Four tables.

_____. "Soviet Research into Labour Problems." SOVIET STUDIES 10 (October 1958): 188-99.

This note reports on a new Soviet journal, BULLETIN OF SCIENTIFIC INFORMATION: LABOUR AND WAGES, which began publication in 1957.

_____. "Statute on the Rights of Factory and Local Trade Union Committees." SOVIET STUDIES 10 (October 1958): 180-83.

This is an abridged translation from VEDOMOSTI VERKHOVNOVO SOVETA (July 24, 1958).

Nove, Alec. "A Study of Soviet Wages." BRITISH JOURNAL OF INDUSTRIAL RELATIONS 1 (February 1963): 62-72.

This article is largely a critical review of a book in Russian: S. P. Figurnov. REAL'NAYA ZARABOTNAYA PLATS I PODYON MATERIAL'NOVO BLAGOSOSTAYANIA TRUDYASHCHIKHSYA V SSR [Real wages and the raising of material welfare of the working people in the USSR]. Moscow: Social-economic editors, 1960. Tables.

_____. "Wages in the Soviet Union: A Comment on Recently Published Statistics." BRITISH JOURNAL OF INDUSTRIAL RELATIONS 4 (July 1966): 212-21.

This article summarizes in eight tables some recently published Soviet statistics on wages, reviews the accuracy of estimates made before the information was released, and notes the need for additional figures.

Nutter, G. Warren. "Employment in the Soviet Economy: An Interim Solution to a Puzzle." SOVIET STUDIES 12 (April 1961): 376-93.

This note pieces together employment data from many sources. Six tables.

Obukhovich, A. P. "Participation by Workers' Organisations in Planned Social and Economic Development in Byelorussia." INTERNATIONAL LABOUR REVIEW 94 (November 1966): 449-64.

Topics covered include planning machinery and worker participation through trade unions, production conferences, the labor emulation movement, and the voluntary workers' organizations.

"Office Hours Standardized." SOVIET STUDIES 5 (January 1954): 303-7.

This is a translation of an editorial which appeared in PRAVDA on September 1, 1953.

Osipov, B. V., ed. INDUSTRY AND LABOUR IN THE U.S.S.R. London: Tavistock Publications, 1966. viii, 297 p.

> The book is a collection of papers written by Soviet sociologists, social psychologists, demographers, and economists. They deal with social problems connected with the creation of the material and technical bases of communism, problems arising from the development of Communist social relations, and problems of individual development.

Petrov, Vladimir. SOVIET GOLD; MY LIFE AS A SLAVE LABORER IN THE SIBERIAN MINES. Translated by Mina Ginsburg. New York: Farrar, Straus, 1949. viii, 426 p.

> This is a first-person account of life and working conditions of a forced laborer.

Piatakov, A. "Labour Administration by the State and Trade Unions in the U.S.S.R." INTERNATIONAL LABOUR REVIEW 85 (June 1962): 558-72.

> The author discusses the functions of the state and the trade unions in drawing up and administrating labor legislation. He describes the manner in which workers and employees participate in management of the enterprise.

Potichnyj, Peter J. SOVIET AGRICULTURAL TRADE UNIONS, 1917-70. Toronto: University of Toronto Press, 1972. xix, 258 p.

> The book contains chapters on the Soviet view of the role and function of agricultural trade unions; composition of membership in trade unions from 1919 to 1970; trade union finances; the function of trade unions in the areas of labor protection and regulation of working conditions; and union activities in social security and social insurance programs. Bibliography and index.

Price, George M. LABOR PROTECTION IN SOVIET RUSSIA. New York: International Publishers, 1928. 128 p.

> This book is concerned with working conditions, the role of labor unions and government in worker safety and health, social insurance, and medical benefits in the Soviet Union.

"The Problem of Hours of Work in the Soviet Union: I." INTERNATIONAL LABOUR REVIEW 17 (March 1928): 377-89.

> This first part in the study of hours of work deals with the legal regulation of hours of work.

"The Problem of Hours of Work in the Soviet Union: II." INTERNATIONAL LABOUR REVIEW 17 (April 1928): 515-28.

This second part, dealing with the problem of hours of work, considers the eight-hour day and the seven-hour day.

"The Problem of Labour Output in Soviet Russia." INTERNATIONAL LABOUR REVIEW 13 (May 1926): 684-716.

This article discusses the policy of the Supreme Economics Council, whose aim was to reduce production costs through an increase in workers' output. The measures to increase output and initial effects of the August 1924 reforms are discussed.

Prociuk, S. G. "The Manpower Problem in Siberia." SOVIET STUDIES 19 (October 1967): 190-210.

This article reports on problems of colonizing that area and concentrates on the labour situation, a problem for Soviet planners in the period 1962-65.

"Production Risks in Criminal Prosecution." SOVIET STUDIES 6 (October 1954): 191-98.

Excerpts from an article dealing with risks taken by workers on the job and the means taken to reduce them, including prosecution of managers, are translated.

"Proposed Model Collective Agreement for Soviet Industry." INTERNATIONAL LABOUR REVIEW 39 (February 1939): 234-39.

This article outlines the collective agreement drafted for the Stalin Motor Works in Moscow which was based on new wage scales for the automobile industry.

"The Provisions of Work for the Unemployed in the U.S.S.R." INTERNATIONAL LABOUR REVIEW 22 (July 1930): 46-69.

This article examines the organization of employment exchanges in relation to changes in the general economic policy of the government and in the state of the labor market. The registration of the unemployed, the qualification of unemployed workers for retraining, and assistance to the unemployed in the form of work are all examined.

Prudinskii, G. A. "The Concept of Leisure in the USSR." INDUSTRIAL RELATIONS 2 (October 1962): 97-100.

A leading Soviet economist surveys past work and calls for further study of leisure time in the USSR.

Rakitin, G. "Labour Inspection in the USSR." INTERNATIONAL LABOUR REVIEW 104 (October 1971): 289-305.

Rakitin considers the dual nature of the Soviet system of labor inspection--the existence of both state and trade union supervision. He enumerates the various state bodies and trade union bodies involved and describes their respective roles.

"The Recent Evolution of Trade Unionism in the USSR." INTERNATIONAL LABOUR REVIEW 29 (February 1934): 206-22.

Topics covered include the Communist theory of trade unionism, trade union policy before and after 1928, and the transfer of the functions of the Commissariat of Labour to the Central Trade Union Council.

Redding, David A. "Comparison of Volume and Distribution of Nonagricultural Employment in the USSR, 1928-1955, with the U.S., 1870-1952." REVIEW OF ECONOMICS AND STATISTICS 36 (November 1954): 444-50.

Three tables give data for various sectors.

————. "Volume and Distribution of Nonagricultural Employment in the USSR, 1928-1955." AMERICAN SLAVIC AND EAST EUROPEAN REVIEW 13 (1954): 356-74.

This paper provides data on USSR nonagricultural employment and its distribution by broad sectors of the economy, gives "explanatory" comments on employment trends, and describes USSR employment classifications and statistics. A large table provides data and an appendix provides footnotes to the table.

Rimlinger, Gaston V. "The Trade Union in Soviet Social Insurance: Historical Development and Present Functions." INDUSTRIAL AND LABOR RELATIONS REVIEW 14 (April 1961): 397-418.

This article traces the history of the unions' social insurance function, describes the relationship of the social insurance system to union structure, and discusses the extent of the unions' social insurance activities.

Roberts, Benjamin C. TRADE UNIONS AND INDUSTRIAL RELATIONS IN THE SOVIET UNION. London: Workers' Educational Association, 1958. 31 p.

This pamphlet describes the relation of trade unions with the state; the structure of Soviet trade unions; collective bargaining; the incentive wage system; the authority of Soviet management; and social security.

Samuilenko, F. "Stabilisation and Training of Manpower in the Forestry Industry in Byelorussia." INTERNATIONAL LABOUR REVIEW 83 (June 1961): 523-46.

The author describes how, by planning the management and utilization of forest resources, rationalizing and mechanizing work processes, making vocational training available to all, and providing satisfactory conditions of life and work for forestry workers, the Byelorussian authorities have succeeded in creating a permanent skilled and productive labour force for the industry. Six tables.

Schlesinger, Rudolf. "Extension of the Rights of Trade Unions." SOVIET STUDIES 10 (October 1958): 176-79.

This note reviews discussion of the subject in current Soviet publications.

_____. "New Forms of Workers' Participation in Management." SOVIET STUDIES 10 (July 1958): 101-3.

This note reports discussion of this subject in Soviet publications.

_____. "Prolongation of the School Period and the Supply of Skilled Labour." SOVIET STUDIES 10 (July 1958): 104-6.

Soviet concern about the effect of extended education on the supply of labor and efforts to release students for work at least part-time are examined.

_____. "Wages in State Farms and in the Iron and Steel Industry." SOVIET STUDIES 9 (January 1958): 346-52.

This note reviews two articles by V. M. Rabinovich. "The Level of Wages of State-Farm Workers and the Conditions of Their Increase." VESTNIK MOSKOVSKOVO UNIVERSITETA, no. 2 (1957); "Shortening of the Working Day and the Wages Regulation in the Heavy Iron Industries." SOTSIALISTICHESKY TRUD, no. 7 (1957).

Schroeder, Gertrude [E.]. "Industrial Wage Differentials in the USSR." SOVIET STUDIES 17 (January 1966): 303-17.

Topics discussed include the nature of the wage system, trends in average earnings, income inequality, differentials by occupation and by industry, international comparisons, and future trends. Five tables.

_____. "Labor Planning in the USSR." SOUTHERN ECONOMIC JOURNAL 32 (July 1965): 63-79.

This paper covers population projections, labor force plans and results, labor productivity, wages and income, and school enrollments and graduations. Two tables.

_____. "Soviet Industrial Labor Productivity." In DIMENSIONS OF SOVIET ECONOMIC POWER, U.S. Congress. Joint Economic Committee, pp. 141-62. Washington, D.C.: Government Printing Office, 1962.

This article outlines recent trends in labor productivity, both as a whole and for individual industries. Factors which explain recent productivity trends are discussed. The author also compares U.S. productivity with that of the USSR. Nine tables.

_____. "Soviet Wage and Income Policies in Regional Perspective." ASSOCIATION FOR COMPARATIVE ECONOMIC STUDIES BULLETIN 16 (Fall 1974): 3-20.

Schroeder uses reconstructed measures of per capita earnings and of a broader concept including transfers to test movement toward the evening out of regional differentials. Four tables.

Schwarz, Solomon M. LABOR IN THE SOVIET UNION. New York: Praeger, 1951. xviii, 364 p.

Analyzed is the evolution of Russian labor policy--formal, legal, labor policy, and real policy as they constantly adjusted to the goals of official economic policy. Schwarz describes the transformation of the working class, of the labor market, and of the labor relationship and discusses wages, living standards, hours, working conditions, and social insurance.

_____. "On Wage Level in the USSR." AMERICAN SLAVIC AND EAST EUROPEAN REVIEW 14 (1955): 465-80.

This article first comments on Murray Yanowitch. "Changes in the Soviet Money Wage Level Since 1940." AMERICAN SLAVIC AND EAST EUROPEAN REVIEW, April 1955, pp. 195-223. Soviet wage policy and changes in Soviet wage levels are then discussed.

Scott, John. BEHIND THE URALS: AN AMERICAN WORKER IN RUSSIA'S CITY OF STEEL. Boston: Houghton Mifflin, 1942. viii, 279 p.

This is a personal account of a worker's experience and impressions of life and work in Magnitogorsk in the 1930s. Statistical data are in the appendix.

Serge, Victor. RUSSIA TWENTY YEARS AFTER. Translated by M. Shachtman. New York: Hillman-Curl, 1937. xii, 298 p.

The author, a member of the Executive Committee of Communist International, outlines conditions of workers.

"The Seven-Hour Day in Soviet Russia." INTERNATIONAL LABOUR REVIEW 22 (September 1930): 329-57.

This article discusses the history, the working arrangements, the economic and social effects of the new system of hours of work.

Sheehy, Ann. "Labour Problems and Employment in Kazakhstan and Central Asia." CENTRAL ASIAN REVIEW 14, no. 2 (1966): 164-77.

> Sheehy reviews the general employment situation, labor shortages in industry, idle manpower in certain towns, manpower problems in agriculture, seasonal and student workers, and vocational training.

_____. "Secondary Specialized Education in the Central Asian and Kazakh SSR's." CENTRAL ASIAN REVIEW 15, no. 3 (1967): 219-31.

> The emphasis is on the period since 1959. Twelve tables.

Shkurko, A. S. "The Industrial Wage System in the U.S.S.R." INTERNATIONAL LABOUR REVIEW 90 (October 1964): 352-64.

> After explaining the comprehensive basic wage scales applied to all industrial workers in the USSR, the author describes incentive systems in operation and the criteria on which they are based. Other topics include the effects of technological progress on the wage structure and the future evolution of the wage system.

Siegel, Irving H. "Labor Productivity in the Soviet Union." AMERICAN STATISTICAL ASSOCIATION. JOURNAL 48 (March 1953): 65-78.

> The difficulties of computing adequate measures of productivity are discussed and the growth in Soviet labor productivity, as compared with U.S. labor productivity, is examined.

Silde, Adolf. THE PROFITS OF SLAVERY: BALTIC FORCED LABORERS AND DEPORTEES UNDER STALIN AND KHRUSHCHEV. Stockholm: Latvian National Foundation in Scandinavia, 1958. 302 p. Illustrated.

> This book first describes the regions in which forced labor camps were located and then covers the following topics: wages, living conditions, uprisings, and prisons. Index and map.

Smith, Edwin S. ORGANIZED LABOR IN THE SOVIET UNION. New York: National Council of American-Soviet Friendship, 1943. 47 p.

> This pamphlet describes membership in Soviet trade unions, trade union structure, the function of unions, collective bargaining procedures, wages, hours, working conditions, and labor and the war front.

Solovyov, L. "The Reduction of Employees' Working Hours in the Soviet Union." INTERNATIONAL LABOUR REVIEW 86 (July 1962): 31-41.

> The author discusses the settling of the questions of which sector

should have their hours shortened first; what increase in the labor force would be needed; what would be the effects on productivity and wages? Three tables.

Sonin, M., and Zhiltsov, E. "Economic Development and Employment in the Soviet Union." INTERNATIONAL LABOUR REVIEW 96 (July 1967): 67-91.

The authors examine trends in government policy on employment, devoting particular attention to the effects of scientific and technical progress. Eight tables.

Sorenson, Jay B. THE LIFE AND DEATH OF SOVIET TRADE UNIONISM 1917-1928. New York: Atherton Press, 1969. viii, 283 p.

The history of the relations between the trade unions and the Communist party and Soviet government in this period is traced. Bibliography and index.

"Soviet Workers in Germany: Methods of Recruitment and Conditions of Employment." INTERNATIONAL LABOUR REVIEW 47 (May 1943): 576-90.

This article analyzes the regulations issued up to February 1943 concerning Soviet workers in the Third Reich. Topics covered include recruitment, employment conditions, payments and special taxes, savings and wage transfers to the USSR, medical aid, and recruitment of domestic servants in occupied Soviet territory.

Stanley, Emilo J. REGIONAL DISTRIBUTION OF SOVIET INDUSTRIAL MANPOWER: 1940-60. New York: Praeger, 1968. xxiii, 208 p.

This study presents, mainly in a graphic manner, the geographic distribution of Soviet industrial manpower. Graphs, glossary, tables, bibliography, and maps.

"The Statute on Settlement of Labour Disputes." SOVIET STUDIES 9 (July 1957): 99-102.

Major changes in the statute which were made on January 31, 1957, are examined.

Swianiewicz, S. FORCED LABOUR AND ECONOMIC DEVELOPMENT: AN ENQUIRY INTO THE EXPERIENCE OF SOVIET INDUSTRIALIZATION. London and New York: Oxford University Press, 1965. ix, 321 p.

This study is concerned with the 1928-41 period. Part one describes the forced-labor system under Stalin. Parts two and three analyze economic aspects of forced labor in 1928-41. Part four applies the lessons of Soviet experience to underdeveloped and agriculturally overpopulated countries. Twenty-five tables, graph, bibliography, and index.

Manpower, Labor, and Trade Unions

Treml, Vladimir G. "Industrial Employment on the Basis of Soviet Interindustry Data." ASSOCIATION FOR COMPARATIVE ECONOMIC STUDIES BULLETIN 5 (Winter 1973): 12-21.

> This article interprets the recently published large segment of the labor input matrix corollary to the 1959 interindustry flow table, which provides previously unavailable employment data.

"Unemployment in Russia, 1917-1925." INTERNATIONAL LABOUR REVIEW 14 (November 1926): 686-711.

U.S. Central Intelligence Agency. AN EVALUATION OF THE PROGRAM FOR REDUCING THE WORK-WEEK IN THE USSR. Prepared by R. M. Fearn. (n.p., n.d.), 24 p.

> This report discusses the wages and hours program, relation of the program to economic and social problems, and the rationale for the reduction in hours.

_____. LABOR SUPPLY AND EMPLOYMENT IN THE USSR: 1950-70. Washington, D.C.: 1963. 28 p.

> This report presents estimates of the USSR labor force for 1950, 1953, and 1955-70. Seven tables.

_____. UNEMPLOYMENT IN THE SOVIET UNION: FACT OR FICTION? Washington, D.C.: 1966. iii, 24 p.

> Employment policy, the labor market, and nonfarm unemployment are discussed.

Vasudevan, A. "Economic Development with Forced Labour: The Soviet Experience." INDIAN ECONOMIC JOURNAL 13 (January-March 1966): 555-67.

> This article summarizes facts found in S. Swianiewicz. FORCED LABOUR AND ECONOMIC DEVELOPMENT. London: Oxford University Press, 1965. It then discusses the implications of this study for economic planning in India. A table compares trends in per capita consumption in India and the USSR.

"Wages and Currency Reform in Soviet Russia." INTERNATIONAL LABOUR REVIEW 10 (November 1924): 800-824.

> The article deals chiefly with the readjustment of wages to the use of a stable currency. Fiduciary circulation and wage policy before the 1924 reform are discussed.

Wang, C. L. "Setting New Output Norms in Soviet Industry." SOVIET STUDIES 2 (April 1951): 403-12.

> This is a summary of P. Tomashpolsky. "On the Method of Drawing

Up Progressive Norms in Industry." VOPROSY EKONOMIKI, no. 4 (1950): 37-47. A table on work time and norms is included.

Weitzman, Murray S. COMPARISONS OF U.S. AND U.S.S.R. EMPLOYMENT IN INDUSTRY: 1939-1958. International Population Reports. Series P-95, no. 60. Washington, D.C.: Government Printing Office, 1963. iii, 70 p.

An intereconomy comparison of employment in industry is given. Tables and bibliography.

Weitzman, Murray S., and Elias, Andrew. THE MAGNITUDE AND DISTRIBUTION OF CIVILIAN EMPLOYMENT IN THE U.S.S.R.: 1928-1959. International Population Reports. Series P-95, no. 58. Washington, D.C.: Government Printing Office, 1961. v, 193 p.

An integrated set of statistical tables historically depicting the supply and use of human resources in economic activity in the Soviet Union is the focus of this report. Tables and bibliography.

Weitzman, Murray S., et al. "Employment in the USSR: Comparative USSR-US Data." In DIMENSIONS OF SOVIET ECONOMIC POWER, U.S. Congress. Joint Economic Committee, pp. 591-667. Washington, D.C.: Government Printing Office, 1962.

This paper compares USSR employment with U.S. employment. The paper is divided into four parts: (1) general observation on Soviet economics; (2) Soviet employment data and estimates based on Soviet information; (3) Soviet techniques and organizations used in the management of labor supply; and (4) USSR and U.S. estimates for agricultural and nonagricultural employment.

Wiles, Peter J. D. "Average Wages in the U.S.S.R." OXFORD UNIVERSITY. INSTITUTE OF ECONOMICS AND STATISTICS. BULLETIN 15 (September 1953): 327-39.

This article estimates changes in average money wages in the Soviet Union on the basis of official statistics. Data on wages for selected years between 1928 and 1950 are included in four tables. For further discussion, see: Solomon M. Schwarz. "Avèrage Wages in U.S.S.R.: A Rejoinder." OXFORD UNIVERSITY. INSTITUTE OF ECONOMICS AND STATISTICS. BULLETIN 16 (January 1954): 15-17; followed by Peter J.D. Wiles. "A Reply," pp. 18-22.

_____. "A Note on Soviet Unemployment in U.S. Definitions." SOVIET STUDIES 23 (April 1972): 619-28.

This paper goes through a number of calculations to obtain an estimate of unemployment in the Soviet state sector. Eight tables.

Wolfe, Bertram D. "Notes on the Soviet Slave Labor Reform of 1954-55." RUSSIAN REVIEW 15 (January 1956): 57-59.

    Provisions of the reform and the reasons for it are explored.

Yampolsky, M. "The Planning of Labour." SOVIET STUDIES 4 (July 1952): 78-94.

    This is a complete translation of an article under the same title in PLANOVOYE KHOZYAISTVO, no. 5 (1951): 81-91. Three tables.

Yanowitch, Murray. "Changes in the Soviet Money Wage Level Since 1940." AMERICAN SLAVIC AND EAST EUROPEAN REVIEW 14 (1955): 195-223.

    The purpose of this article is to examine the data available on Soviet wages since 1940 for insights into Soviet wage policy and the magnitude of average earnings in recent years. Seven tables provide data on earnings.

_____. "The Soviet Income Revolution." SLAVIC REVIEW 22 (December 1963): 683-97.

    This article is concerned with the money incomes of those classified as workers and salaried personnel. Topics covered include recent trends in Soviet income structure, Soviet income differentials in the future, and the nonequalitarian reduction of income inequality. Numerous data on wages and salaries are included.

_____. "Soviet Patterns of Time Use and Concepts of Leisure." SOVIET STUDIES 15 (July 1963): 17-37.

    Various aspects of Soviet time-use studies are discussed. Three tables.

_____. "Trends in Differentials Between Salaried Personnel and Wage Workers in Soviet Industry." SOVIET STUDIES 11 (January 1960): 229-52.

    Six tables in the text and two in the appendices cover approximately 1928-57.

_____. "Trends in Soviet Occupational Wage Differentials." INDUSTRIAL AND LABOR RELATIONS REVIEW 13 (January 1960): 166-91.

    This article traces occupational wage differentials in the Soviet Union since the First Five-Year Plan and explains changes. Seven tables.

Yanowitch, Murray, and Dodge, Norton T. "The Social Evaluation of Occupations in the Soviet Union." SLAVIC REVIEW 28 (December 1969): 619-43.

    This article presents an extensive survey of Soviet sociological studies on the opinions of Soviet citizens of various occupations. Topics covered include rating and rank-ordering of occupations, parents' views of desirable occupations for their children, and students' career plans. Eight tables.

Zalenko, H. "Vocational and Technical Training in the U.S.S.R." INTERNATIONAL LABOUR REVIEW 80 (December 1959): 489-504.

In this article the chairman of the State Vocational and Technical Training Committee of the U.S.S.R. Council of Ministers describes the organization of vocational training and the principles on which it is based.

Zatsepilin, V. "System of Remuneration in the Coal Mines of the Ukrainian Soviet Socialist Republics." INTERNATIONAL LABOUR REVIEW 82 (September 1960): 251-61.

Wage reforms progressively introduced in the Ukrainian coal mines starting in 1957 are described, and the administrative and technical improvements in the organization of work that preceded and followed it are noted.

Zawodny, J. K. "Grievances and Sources of Tension During Stalin's Regime as Reported by Soviet Industrial Workers." SOVIET STUDIES 14 (October 1962): 158-78.

Topics discussed include work conditions, workers' rights, discipline, regulations, wages, living conditions, and grievances in general. Four tables.

Chapter 30
DEMOGRAPHIC STUDIES

Lewis, Robert A., and Leasure, J. William. "Regional Population Changes in Russia and the USSR Since 1851." SLAVIC REVIEW 25 (December 1966): 663-68.

 This article summarizes the procedures and results of the authors' monograph, POPULATION CHANGE IN RUSSIA AND THE USSR: A SET OF COMPARABLE TERRITORIAL UNITS. San Diego: San Diego State College Press, 1966. Total and urban population figures are given for 1851, 1897, 1926, 1939, and 1959 in a set of comparable territorial units so that regional comparisons can be made over time.

THE PERIOD UP TO 1860

Eaton, Henry L. "Cadasters and Censuses of Muscovy." SLAVIC REVIEW 26 (March 1967): 54-69.

 This is a detailed survey of original source data on the population of Russia in the sixteenth and seventeenth centuries. The author calls for scholarly and systematic publication of these data.

THE PERIOD 1860-1917

Eason, Warren W. "Population Changes." In THE TRANSFORMATION OF RUSSIAN SOCIETY: ASPECTS OF SOCIAL CHANGE SINCE 1861, edited by Cyril E. Black, pp. 72-90. Cambridge, Mass.: Harvard University Press, 1960.

 The author examines the demographic characteristics of Imperial Russia and the Soviet Union since 1861. Socioeconomic characteristics of the population are revealed in indexes.

Leasure, J. William, and Lewis, Robert A. "Internal Migration in Russia in the Late Nineteenth Century." SLAVIC REVIEW 27 (September 1968): 375-94.

 The article describes regional migration patterns and analyzes them primarily in terms of economic differentials. Four maps and six tables.

THE PERIOD AFTER 1917

"The Active Population of the USSR." INTERNATIONAL LABOUR REVIEW 84 (September 1961): 198-203.

> The figures of the 1959 census are compared with those for 1939 to emphasize changes in the last twenty years in the structure of the labor force. Five tables.

Brackett, James W. "Demographic Trends and Population Policy in the Soviet Union." In DIMENSIONS OF SOVIET ECONOMIC POWER, U.S. Congress. Joint Economic Committee, pp. 487-589. Washington, D.C.: Government Printing Office, 1962.

> The author examines present size and composition of Soviet population, development of population under Communist rule, demographic trends through 1980, and Soviet policies relating to population. The article contains extensive statistical data from the U.S. Bureau of the Census and official Soviet statistics.

Brackett, James W., and DePauw, John W. "Population Policy and Demographic Trends in the Soviet Union." In NEW DIRECTIONS IN THE SOVIET ECONOMY, U.S. Congress. Joint Economic Committee, pp. 593-702. Washington, D.C.: Government Printing Office, 1966.

> Topics discussed include population policy, size, age-sex composition, redistribution, ethnic composition, family size and composition, and fertility trends. Thirty-one tables.

Campbell, Arthur A., and Brackett, James W. PROJECTIONS OF THE POPULATION OF THE U.S.S.R.: 1950 TO 1976. U.S. Department of Commerce. Bureau of the Census. International Population Reports. Series P-95, no. 52. Washington, D.C.: Government Printing Office, 1959. vi, 62 p.

> This report estimates the composition of the population of the USSR by age and sex and projects that population to the year 1976. Many tables.

Carson, George Barr, Jr. "A Critical Note on Estimating USSR Population from Election Reports." AMERICAN SLAVIC AND EAST EUROPEAN REVIEW 15 (April 1956): 173-78.

> This article is an evaluation of a method used to estimate Soviet population from numbers of reported election districts. The results of this method are compared with census reports, and some discrepancies are found.

Demographic Studies

David, Henry P. FAMILY PLANNING AND ABORTION IN THE SOCIALIST COUNTRIES OF CENTRAL AND EASTERN EUROPE. A COMPENDIUM OF OBSERVATIONS AND READINGS. New York: The Population Council, 1970. xi, 306 p.

> This work discusses virtually all aspects of population control in the bloc countries, including the Soviet Union. Paperback.

Eason, Warren W. "Population Changes." In PROSPECTS FOR SOVIET SOCIETY, edited by Allen Kassof, pp. 203-40. New York: Praeger, 1968.

> This paper discusses the demographic characteristics of Soviet population growth and the implications of population growth for economic and social change. Eight tables.

_____. THE POPULATION OF THE SOVIET UNION. Washington, D.C.: Washington Council for Economic and Industrial Research, 1955. 78 p.

> This paper surveys the principal characteristics and trends of Soviet population. Eason discusses population distribution by urban and rural areas and the portion of population comprising the labor force. A brief discussion of population trends for a sixty-year period, 1890-1950, is included. Tables.

Feshbach, Murray. "Population." In ECONOMIC PERFORMANCE AND THE MILITARY BURDEN IN THE SOVIET UNION, U.S. Congress. Joint Economic Committee, pp. 60-70. Washington, D.C.: Government Printing Office, 1970.

> Article presents and briefly discusses seven tables providing data on population, birth and death rates, projected population, regional population distribution, and migration.

Grandstaff, Peter J. "A Note on Preliminary 1970 USSR Census Results Concerning Migration." ASSOCIATION FOR COMPARATIVE ECONOMIC STUDIES BULLETIN 16 (Fall 1974): 33-40.

> Two tables provide data on migration between regions.

Guinn, U. K. "A Footnote to the 1939 Census of the USSR." SOVIET STUDIES 14 (April 1963): 421-24.

> Population totals are given for selected administrative districts and cities.

Heer, David M. "Abortion, Contraception, and Population Policy in the Soviet Union." SOVIET STUDIES 17 (July 1965): 76-83.

> This paper reviews Soviet policies regulating population growth since the mid-1950s.

Heer, David M., and Bryden, Judith G. "Family Allowances and Fertility in the Soviet Union." SOVIET STUDIES 18 (October 1966): 153-63.

> This paper investigates the provision of the Soviet system of family allowances, its economic importance to families, its total monetary cost, its differing impact in separate areas of the Soviet Union, and its magnitude compared to family allowance programs in other nations. An estimate of the impact of the program on Soviet fertility is also made. Five tables.

"The Influence of Ethnic Factors on the Territorial Redistribution of Population." CENTRAL ASIAN REVIEW 14, no. 1 (1966): 45-54.

> This article, concerned with Central Asia largely in 1959-64, includes six tables.

Kantner, John F. "The Population of the Soviet Union." In COMPARISONS OF THE U.S. AND SOVIET ECONOMIES, U.S. Congress. Joint Economic Committee, pp. 31-71. Washington, D.C.: Government Printing Office, 1959.

> This paper contains chapters on population and labor supply, fertility and population growth, and basic demographic comparisons between the USSR and the United States. Many tables.

_____. "Recent Demographic Trends in the USSR." In POPULATION TRENDS IN EASTERN EUROPE, THE USSR, AND MAINLAND CHINA, pp. 35-63. New York: Milbank Memorial Fund, 1960.

> The size and composition of the population and mortality and fertility are the focus of this study, which refers generally to the postwar period. A discussion follows the article, pp. 63-67.

Leidy, Frederick A. "Demographic Trends in the USSR." In SOVIET ECONOMIC PROSPECTS FOR THE SEVENTIES, U.S. Congress. Joint Economic Committee, pp. 428-84. Washington, D.C.: Government Printing Office, 1973.

> Topics covered include population changes, trends in vital rates, population redistribution, population policy, and future growth. Tables, charts, and map.

Lorimir, Frank. THE POPULATION OF THE SOVIET UNION: HISTORY AND PROSPECTS. Geneva: League of Nations, 1946. xiv, 289 p.

> This volume notes characteristics and trends of Soviet population. Bibliography, index, and maps in color.

Mazur, D. Peter. "Using Regression Models to Estimate Life Expectation for USSR." JOURNAL OF THE AMERICAN STATISTICAL ASSOCIATION 67 (March 1972): 31-36.

> In this study the Soviet Union serves as a prototype to demonstrate

that basic demographic measures can be reconstructed from scanty data. The author proposes regression models to ascertain the level of births and deaths from sparse information available in official Soviet government publications. Tables and graphs.

Mironenko, Yuri. "A Demographic Survey." STUDIES ON THE SOVIET UNION n.s. 7, no. 4 (1968): 16-27.

This survey is concerned with Soviet Central Asia since 1913. Seven tables.

―――. "The Population." STUDIES ON THE SOVIET UNION n.s. 5, no. 1 (1965): 47-54.

This paper discusses the population of Siberia and the Soviet Far East. Three tables.

―――. "Soviet Population Growth Slowing Down." STUDIES ON THE SOVIET UNION n.s. 4, no. 4 (1965): 95-99.

The reasons for and implications of the declining birth rate are discussed. Two tables.

Newth, J. A. "The First Press Release on the 1959 Census." SOVIET STUDIES 11 (July 1959): 117-23.

Six short tables are included; comparisons are made with selected years between 1939-59.

―――. "The 1970 Soviet Census." SOVIET STUDIES 24 (October 1972): 200-222.

This study of the results of the 1970 Soviet census includes twenty-one tables.

―――. "The Sample Census of Population, August 1957." SOVIET STUDIES 10 (July 1958): 106-10.

This note reports on problems and procedures as discussed in Soviet publications.

―――. "Some Trends in the Soviet Population 1939 to 1956." SOVIET STUDIES 10 (January 1959): 252-78.

Seven tables included in this study. Statistical appendix presents ten pages of tables.

―――. "The Soviet Population: Wartime Losses and the Postwar Recovery." SOVIET STUDIES 15 (January 1964): 345-51.

The note concludes with a three-and-one-half page table of end-of-year population estimates.

_____. "Two Notes on Population: Checks on the April, 1956 Estimate and Children of Pre-school Age in the RSFSR." SOVIET STUDIES 11 (July 1959): 49-60.

> This study includes seven tables. Sources for estimates are discussed in the appendix.

_____. "USSR 1958: Family Size and Fertility." SOVIET STUDIES 12 (January 1961): 288-91.

> This consists of three short tables.

Nove, Alec, and Newth, J. A. "Changes in the Soviet Population." OXFORD UNIVERSITY. INSTITUTE OF ECONOMICS AND STATISTICS. BULLETIN 19 (February 1957): 73-84.

> This article analyzes population changes in the Soviet Union by district for the years 1939-40 and the end of 1955. Data are in tables and a map.

Petrov, Victor P. "Some Observations on the 1959 Soviet Census." RUSSIAN REVIEW 18 (October 1959): 332-38.

> This paper discusses some of the information collected in the 1959 All-Union Census of population.

"The Population of Central Asia and Kazakhstan." CENTRAL ASIAN REVIEW 5, no. 2 (1957): 120-26.

> Six tables and a map are included. The concern is with population changes between 1940 and 1955.

Selegen, Galina V. "Economic Characteristics of the Population in the Soviet Census Questionnaire." SOVIET STUDIES 11 (April 1960): 353-62.

> A table compares economic activities in the 1926 and 1959 census schedules. Topics covered include occupation, economically active population, and social status.

Seton, Francis. "A Note on Estimating the Size of the Soviet Population." SOVIET STUDIES 8 (July 1956): 27-33.

> This note on Soviet population estimates contains four tables, three of which deal with industrial output. Industrial output and per capita output figures are used to obtain population estimates.

Shimkin, Dimitri B. "Demographic Changes and Socio-Economic Forces Within the Soviet Union." In POPULATION TRENDS IN EASTERN EUROPE, THE USSR, AND MAINLAND CHINA, pp. 224-58. New York: Milbank Memorial Fund, 1960.

The author isolates two significant interrelationships: (1) governmental intervention in lowering mortality and (2) the initiating and directing of migration to meet the planned needs for urban labor. The paper is concerned primarily with regional differences in population trends and their correlates. Tables. A discussion follows.

U.S. Central Intelligence Agency. COMPARISONS OF US AND SOVIET POPULATION AND MANPOWER. Washington, D.C.: 1960. 18 p.

Summary data on population and manpower in the United States and in the USSR are given, along with some developments anticipated during the next decade. Charts.

Vogt, Johan. "Population Increase in the Soviet Union." ECONOMICS OF PLANNING 2 (July 1962): 73-86.

This article contains numerous tables of demographic information on the Soviet Union and manipulates the data to estimate the war losses of the Soviet Union and the resulting abnormal age distribution, to calculate the gross reproduction rate, and to compile a life-table for 1958-59. He also discusses the population increase of the 1960s.

Wadekin, Karl-Eugen. "Internal Migration and the Flight from the Land in the USSR, 1939-1959." SOVIET STUDIES 18 (October 1966): 131-52.

This paper uses published Soviet population statistics to study village-to-town migration and inter-regional migration in the USSR. Nine tables.

Chapter 31
HEALTH, EDUCATION, AND WELFARE

Timoshenko, Stephen P. "The Development of Engineering Education in Russia." RUSSIAN REVIEW 15 (July 1956): 173-85.

> This paper reviews the history of and important people involved in the development of engineering education in Russia from the beginning of the eighteenth century.

THE PERIOD 1860-1917

Madison, Bernice. "The Organization of Welfare Services." In THE TRANSFORMATION OF RUSSIAN SOCIETY: ASPECTS OF SOCIAL CHANGE SINCE 1861, edited by Cyril Black, pp. 515-40. Cambridge, Mass.: Harvard University Press, 1960.

> In part one the author discusses the three systems of economic assistance in Russia from 1864 to the October Revolution: state poor relief, local poor relief, and private charity. Part two deals with the period 1917-57 and discusses three types of income maintenance.

Rimlinger, Gaston V. WELFARE POLICY AND INDUSTRIALIZATION IN EUROPE, AMERICA, AND RUSSIA. New York: John Wiley, 1971. ix, 362 p.

> Of particular interest is chapter 7, "Russia from Patriarchalism to Collectivism," which treats social security and insurance from before the Revolution to the post-Stalin period.

Timasheff, Nicholas S. "Overcoming Illiteracy: Public Education in Russia, 1880-1940." RUSSIAN REVIEW 2 (Autumn 1942): 80-88.

> This paper seeks to show that Russia has made steady progress against illiteracy, except when war and revolution have caused disruptions. Five tables.

THE PERIOD AFTER 1917

Abramson, A. "The Reorganisation of Social Insurance Institutions in the U.S.S.R." INTERNATIONAL LABOUR REVIEW 31 (March 1935): 364-82.

This article studies successive transformations undergone by insurance institutions in the USSR, and examines the essential features of the new organization, which is characterized by the abolition of the People's Commissariat of Labour of the USSR and the transfer to the Central Trade Union Council of the administration of social insurance.

_____. "Social Insurance in Soviet Russia." JOURNAL OF POLITICAL ECONOMY 37 (August 1929): 377-99.

Topics covered in this paper include an historical survey, the scope of insurance, benefits, financial resources, and insurance institutions.

Aslanyan, R. G. "Action to Ensure that Soviet Citizens Enjoy Equal Rights and Opportunities." INTERNATIONAL LABOUR REVIEW 100 (December 1969): 551-82.

The author shows how so-called backward republics have developed faster than the USSR as a whole. Measures to increase educational and sexual equality are described, with special reference to equality of opportunity in employment and remuneration. Three tables.

Carey, David W. "Developments in Soviet Education." In SOVIET ECONOMIC PROSPECTS FOR THE SEVENTIES, U.S. Congress. Joint Economic Committee, pp. 594-636. Washington, D.C.: Government Printing Office, 1973.

This paper discusses the structure and administration of Soviet education, developments in education since the mid-1950s, and the contribution of education to Soviet economic growth. Eleven tables and four charts are included.

De Witt, Nicholas. "Education and the Development of Human Resources: Soviet and American Effort." In DIMENSIONS OF SOVIET ECONOMIC POWER, U.S. Congress. Joint Economic Committee, pp. 235-68. Washington, D.C.: Government Printing Office, 1962.

The article includes a detailed diagram comparing the structure of the Soviet Educational System in the pre-reform and post-reform periods with the structure of U.S. education. Graphs and tables.

Goodman, Ann S. "Education." In ECONOMIC PERFORMANCE AND THE MILITARY BURDEN IN THE SOVIET UNION, U.S. Congress. Joint Economic Committee, pp. 85-92. Washington, D.C.: Government Printing Office, 1970.

Five tables provide data on enrollments and graduate totals in the 1950s and 1960s.

Hamilton, Alice. "Science in the Soviet Union; III Industrial Medicine." SCIENCE AND SOCIETY 8 (Winter 1944): 69-73.

> This short paper presents the outstanding successes and omissions of Soviet care of the health of industrial workers.

Hayenko, Fedor. "Social Security in the Soviet Union." STUDIES ON THE SOVIET UNION n.s. 4, no. 3 (1965): 66-78.

> This paper presents an historical survey of the Soviet social system but emphasizes recent developments.

"Health Services in Central Asia." CENTRAL ASIAN REVIEW 3, no. 1 (1955): 45-54.

> Topics covered include history and development, medical education and research, epidemic diseases, tuberculosis, mother and child welfare, organization of health services, and construction.

Lantsev, M. "Progress in Social Security for Agricultural Workers in the USSR." INTERNATIONAL LABOUR REVIEW 107 (March 1973): 239-52.

> The development of social security for USSR agricultural workers is reviewed from the earliest stages of the peasants' mutual aid scheme instituted in 1921 up to the present day. Lantsev describes the different types of benefit available to workers and the manner in which their social security arrangements are financed and administered. Tables.

____. "Social Security in the U.S.S.R." INTERNATIONAL LABOUR REVIEW 86 (November 1962): 453-66.

> This article seeks to give "the ordinary reader an idea of the extent of the social security enjoyed by the citizens of the Soviet Union." Two tables.

Lawrov, V. V. "Socialist System of Financing Public Education: Major Factor of Social Progress of the National Republics of the Soviet Union." PUBLIC FINANCE 21, nos. 1-2 (1966): 170-83.

> Topics covered in this paper include the role of education in economic and cultural development, the system of budget financing, educational financing from state enterprises and cooperatives, the problems of financial planning of education, and educational assistance to developing countries. Three tables.

Lindquist, Clarence B., and Whitelaw, John B. "Teacher Education in the Soviet Union--1962." In DIMENSIONS OF SOVIET ECONOMIC POWER, U.S. Congress. Joint Economic Committee, pp. 307-20. Washington, D.C.: Government Printing Office, 1962.

Health, Education, and Welfare

The following topics are reviewed: teacher supply, organization of teacher education, programs of elementary and secondary teacher education, and the teacher and the national interest.

Madison, Bernice. "Social Services for Families and Children in the Soviet Union Since 1967." SLAVIC REVIEW 31 (December 1972): 831-52.

Topics covered include programs for children living at home or elsewhere and services for unwed mothers, illegitimate children, and juvenile delinquents.

_____. SOCIAL WELFARE IN THE SOVIET UNION. Stanford, Calif.: Stanford University Press, 1968. xxvi, 298 p.

This work discusses social welfare policy formation, 1917-66, and current practices. Bibliography and index.

"Medical Services in Central Asia and Kazakhstan: Part I." CENTRAL ASIAN REVIEW 11, no. 1 (1963): 30-45.

Topics discussed include hospitals, outpatient clinics, doctors, dentists, health resorts, and sanataria. A table gives totals of medical personnel and personnel per capita for the various republics.

"Medical Services in Central Asia and Kazakhstan: Part II." CENTRAL ASIAN REVIEW 11, no. 2 (1963): 114-29.

Topics discussed here are medical research, maternity and child welfare, sanitation, and pharmaceutical services.

Naleszkiewicz, Wladimir. "Financing and Coverage under Social Insurance in Soviet Russia." INDUSTRIAL AND LABOR RELATIONS REVIEW 17 (January 1964): 289-301.

This article is concerned with social insurance as reformed by the "Law on State Pensions," which came into effect on October 1, 1956, and by the statutes on social insurance administration adopted in January 1962 by the Council of Ministers of the USSR and in May 1962 by the All-Union Central Trade Union Councils. Five tables on benefits and budgets are included. For further discussion of this paper, see: Robert J. Myers. "Financing and Coverage under Social Insurance in Soviet Russia" and Wladimir Naleszkiewicz. "Reply." INDUSTRIAL AND LABOR RELATIONS REVIEW 17 (July 1964): 627-29. Author published a similar article entitled "The Present Status of Social Insurance in Soviet Russia." KYKLOS 16 (1963): 483-99.

Noah, Harold J., ed. and trans. THE ECONOMICS OF EDUCATION IN THE U.S.S.R. Praeger Special Studies in International Economics and Development. New York and London: Praeger, 1969. xxii, 227 p.

Health, Education, and Welfare

This book contains papers from a conference which took place in Moscow in 1964. The material covers the economics of education; education training and the increasing of the effectiveness of labor; and questions of the planning of education. Glossary and tables.

Nove, Alec. "Is the Soviet Union a Welfare State?" PROBLEMS OF COMMUNISM 9 (1960): 1-10.

This article compares various aspects of welfare in the USSR with those in selected Western countries and discusses recent policies and the problem of incentives. Several tables.

_____. "Social Welfare in the USSR." PROBLEMS OF COMMUNISM 9 (January-February 1960): 1-10.

Aspects discussed include health, education, social security, holidays, working time, employment reform, wages, and incentives. Tables.

Osborn, Robert J. SOVIET SOCIAL POLICIES: WELFARE, EQUALITY AND COMMUNITY. Homewood, Ill.: Dorsey Press, 1970. x, 294 p.

Topics discussed include values and policies, the Soviet welfare concept, public expenditures and private choices, equality of educational choice, equality and incentives, the urban environment, city communities, and future prospects. Bibliography and index.

Rosen, Seymour M. "Changing Guideposts in Soviet Education." In NEW DIRECTIONS IN THE SOVIET ECONOMY, U.S. Congress. Joint Economic Committee, pp. 817-48. Washington, D.C.: Government Printing Office, 1966.

Aspects discussed include statistics, education reform, and development in programmed learning, audio-visual aids, social studies, indoctrination, and training of foreign students. Statistical appendices. Selected bibliography.

_____. "Higher Education." In DIMENSIONS OF SOVIET ECONOMIC POWER. U.S. Congress. Joint Economic Committee, pp. 269-303. Washington, D.C.: Government Printing Office, 1962.

This article deals with planning and supervision, the production of specialists, and part-time higher education in the USSR. Tables.

Schlesinger, Rudolf. "The New Pension Law (of the USSR)." SOVIET STUDIES 8 (January 1957): 307-16.

This article discusses a new pension law in the context of the Soviet social security system.

Health, Education, and Welfare

Sessa, Pietra. "Social Problems and Social Conditions." In RED ECONOMICS, edited by Gerhard Dobbert, pp. 247-69. Boston and New York: Houghton Mifflin, 1932.

>The author outlines the new types of social legislation and the new forms of social welfare and discusses the real nature of the change, the function of the new forms, and the advantages enjoyed by Soviet workers. The article covers social position of workers; social benefits of workers and their importance; and the standard of living (both material and cultural) of the Soviet worker.

"Social Insurance in the Soviet Union." INTERNATIONAL LABOUR REVIEW 55 (March-April 1947): 261-73.

>This article outlines the working of social insurance in the Soviet Union at the time the article was written.

"Social Insurance in the U.S.S.R., 1933-1937." INTERNATIONAL LABOUR REVIEW 38 (August 1938): 226-42.

>The article examines innovations in social insurance during the period of the Second Five-Year Plan. The scope, financial resources, benefits, and methods of management are surveyed.

Stankiewicz, W. J. "The Development of Different Attitudes to Welfare in Russian and British Socialist Thought: A Note." CANADIAN SLAVONIC PAPERS 2 (1957): 86-97.

>The Russian attitude is seen to be formed largely by Marx and Lenin, while the British attitude is largely one of immediate betterment of the living conditions of labor.

U.S. Department of Health, Education and Welfare. Social Security Administration. THE U.S. SOCIAL SECURITY MISSION TO THE UNION OF SOVIET SOCIALIST REPUBLICS. Washington, D.C.: Government Printing Office, 1972. v, 51 p.

>Topics discussed in this report include the Soviet social security system, social insurance benefits, collective farm workers, and social, welfare, and rehabilitation services. Tables, charts, and maps.

"The Working of Social Insurance in the U.S.S.R." INTERNATIONAL LABOUR REVIEW 28 (October 1933): 539-48.

>This article considers the development of social insurance in the USSR up to 1933 with regard to scope, administration, financial resources, and benefits. Tables.

Chapter 32
WOMEN IN THE SOVIET ECONOMY

Berent, Jerzy. "Some Demographic Aspects of Female Employment in Eastern Europe and the USSR." INTERNATIONAL LABOUR REVIEW 101 (February 1970): 175-92.

    This article is concerned with the economic significance of female employment in Eastern Europe and the USSR since the Second World War and with the main demographic factors affecting such employment. Tables.

Dodge, Norton T. WOMEN IN THE SOVIET ECONOMY--THEIR ROLE IN ECONOMIC, SCIENTIFIC, AND TECHNICAL DEVELOPMENT. Baltimore: Johns Hopkins Press, 1966. xviii, 331 p.

    This book analyzes virtually all factors affecting the participation of women in the Soviet economy from 1917 to the early 1960s. Many tables, bibliography, and index.

"The Employment of Women in Soviet Industry." INTERNATIONAL LABOUR REVIEW 24 (November 1932): 704-7.

    The article summarizes the percentage of Soviet women employed in industry, 1928-31.

Goldberg, Marilyn P. "Women in the Soviet Economy." REVIEW OF RADICAL POLITICAL ECONOMICS 14 (July 1972): 60-75.

    This paper concentrates on the present situation and future prospects of women in the Soviet economy. Regional differences are not discussed, and concern is limited to professional women.

Grunfeld, Judith. "Women's Work in Russia's Planned Economy." SOCIAL RESEARCH 9 (February 1942): 22-45.

    This study looks at employment of women in state enterprises between 1917 and 1941 and concludes that women's opportunities were determined "neither by the Communist conception of women's equality nor by women's need of jobs." Tables.

Kingsbury, Susan M., and Fairchild, Mildred. FACTORY, FAMILY AND WOMEN IN THE SOVIET UNION. New York: G. P. Putnam's Sons, 1935. xxv, 334 p.

> The book describes the status of women in Soviet society. Part one deals with industrial life and part two deals with social life. Part one contains a brief account of workers before the Revolution, describes workers and conditions of work in Soviet Russia, outlines the system of incentives and rewards, discusses the status of women in trade unions and the role of labor protection in Soviet industry, and sketches the collectivization drive. Tables, bibliography, and index.

Moskoff, William. "An Estimate of the Soviet Male-Female Income Gap." ASSOCIATION FOR COMPARATIVE ECONOMIC STUDIES BULLETIN 16 (Fall 1974): 21-32.

> The author shows that even assuming equal pay for equal work, a differential distribution of men and women among branches with different average earnings generate significantly different average earnings for men and women workers. Table.

Nash, Edmund. "The Status of Women in the U.S.S.R." MONTHLY LABOR REVIEW 93 (June 1970): 39-44.

> Topics covered include the growing employment of women, their role as professionals and technicians, working conditions, attitudes toward work, women workers' privileges, and living conditions. A table shows the percentage of women workers in various sectors for selected years between 1928 and 1968.

"The Progress of Women's Employment in the U.S.S.R." INTERNATIONAL LABOUR REVIEW 31 (February 1935): 231-37.

> This short article presents four tables of data on the share of women in various occupations.

Schuster, Alice. "Women's Role in the Soviet Union: Ideology and Reality." RUSSIAN REVIEW 30 (July 1971): 260-67.

> This article surveys the role of women in the economy according to Soviet ideology and in Soviet practice. A table presents the percentages of women among research and professional personnel in 1947, 1950, 1955, and 1959.

Tatarinova, N., and Korshunova, E. "Living and Working Conditions of Women in the U.S.S.R." INTERNATIONAL LABOUR REVIEW 82 (October 1960): 341-57.

> Topics covered include general education and vocational training, employment, and social welfare. Four tables.

"Women in Uzbekistan." CENTRAL ASIAN REVIEW 16, no. 1 (1968): 40-50.

    Progress in education, employment, and public life is discussed.

"Women Workers and Their Protection in Russian Industry." INTERNATIONAL LABOUR REVIEW 20 (October 1929): 512-38.

    The article discusses the extent of the employment of women before and after the Revolution.

Chapter 33
THE CONSUMER AND LIVING STANDARDS IN THE RUSSIAN ECONOMY

THE PERIOD UP TO 1860

Baster, Nancy. "Some Early Family Budget Studies of Russian Workers." AMERICAN SLAVIC AND EAST EUROPEAN REVIEW 17 (December 1958): 468-80.

> This article summarizes studies of two serf households attached to the Urals iron-works and gold mines in 1844. Six tables provide information on the budgets of the peasant households studied.

THE PERIOD 1860-1917

Cazalet, E. A. "The Moujik." ECONOMIC JOURNAL 11 (December 1901): 575-81.

> The moujik is the Russian male peasant. The article sketches his share of the total population, his earnings and standard of living, and his treatment by the government. Tables.

Johnson, William E. THE LIQUOR PROBLEM IN RUSSIA. Westerville, Ohio: The American Issue Publishing Company, 1915. 230 p. Illustrated.

> This book is a muckraking study of the Russian vodka monopoly. It reviews Russian social history and institutional structure and then zeros in on the vodka monopoly, drinking conditions, efforts at reform, and the final overthrow of the monopoly. Tables, index, and foldout map.

Kayden, Eugene M. CONSUMERS' COOPERATION: THE COOPERATIVE MOVEMENT IN RUSSIA DURING THE WAR. New Haven, Conn.: Yale University Press, 1929. xvi, 231 p.

> The author examines (1) cooperative development in Russia; (2) consumers' societies before the war, during the war, and during the Revolution; (3) unions and federations of consumers; (4) the consolidation of consumers' cooperation in Siberia; and (5) the national

federation of consumers' cooperation. Tables.

THE PERIOD AFTER 1917

Aganbegian, A. "Living Standards of the Working People in the USSR and the USA." PROBLEMS OF ECONOMICS 4 (March 1962): 10-24.

> This is a translation from MIROVAIA EKONOMIKA I MEZHDUN-ARODNYE OTNOSHENIIA, no. 10 (1961). It asserts that the USSR will outstrip the United States in real income per capita, consumption, housing, employment, working conditions, social and cultural services, and social security. Tables.

Bergson, Abram. "On Inequality of Incomes in the USSR." AMERICAN SLAVIC AND EAST EUROPEAN REVIEW 10 (1951): 95-99.

> Bergson comments on some information comparing incomes within a selected group of Soviet citizens in 1937.

Bronson, David W., and Severin, Barbara S. "Consumer Welfare." In ECONOMIC PERFORMANCE AND THE MILITARY BURDEN IN THE SOVIET UNION, U.S. Congress. Joint Economic Committee, pp. 93-99. Washington, D.C.: Government Printing Office, 1970.

> This paper discusses trends in consumption and money income in the 1950s and 1960s. Seven tables.

———. "Recent Trends in Consumption and Disposable Money Income in the U.S.S.R." In NEW DIRECTIONS IN THE SOVIET ECONOMY, U.S. Congress. Joint Economic Committee, pp. 495-529. Washington, D.C.: Government Printing Office, 1966.

> This paper is concerned with the period 1950-65. Derivations of indexes is discussed in the appendices. Twelve tables and three charts.

———. "Soviet Consumer Welfare: The Brezhnev Era." In SOVIET ECONOMIC PROSPECTS FOR THE SEVENTIES, U.S. Congress. Joint Economic Committee, pp. 376-403. Washington, D.C.: Government Printing Office, 1973.

> Topics discussed include income, savings, inflation, consumption, food, soft goods, durables, and services. Thirteen tables.

Campbell, Colin D., and Campbell, Rosemary G. "Soviet Price Reductions for Consumer Goods, 1948-1954." AMERICAN ECONOMIC REVIEW 45 (September 1955): 609-25.

> This paper compiles information about the price reductions from translated articles appearing in THE CURRENT DIGEST OF THE

SOVIET PRESS. Topics covered include the factors making price reductions possible, uses of price reductions, price cuts for individual items, and the problem of minimizing inventories. Two tables.

Chapman, Janet G. "Consumption." In ECONOMIC TRENDS IN THE SOVIET UNION, edited by Abram Bergson and Simon Kuznets, pp. 235-82. Cambridge, Mass.: Harvard University Press, 1963.

This paper interprets extensive data on Soviet consumption levels since 1928 and compares real income, wages, and levels and patterns of consumption in the United States and the Soviet Union. Statistical tables.

_____. "Consumption in the Soviet Union." In THE SOVIET ECONOMY; A BOOK OF READINGS, edited by Morris Bornstein and Daniel Fusfeld, pp. 216-27. Rev. ed. Homewood, Ill.: R. D. Irwin, 1966.

This paper traces the effect that the industrialization of the Soviet Union has had on the level and pattern of consumption. A table of selected indicators of consumption for 1928-58 is included.

Chossudowsky, E. M. "De-rationing in the USSR." REVIEW OF ECONOMIC STUDIES 9 (November 1941): 1-27.

This paper analyzes some problems of transition which confront a planned economy when it passes from rationing to a modified freedom of the consumer. It focuses on the transformation the Soviet economy had to make when restrictions on the distribution of consumers' goods were removed.

_____. "Rationing in the USSR." REVIEW OF ECONOMIC STUDIES 8 (June 1941): 143-65.

This paper considers the rationing system which existed in the USSR from the end of 1928 until the beginning of 1935, examines all its aspects, and studies the manner in which that system was superceded. A table notes food rations in April 1930.

"Considering the Consumer." SOVIET STUDIES 5 (January 1954): 307-12.

This is a partial translation of "Study of Demand for Cultural Goods," SOVETSKAYA TORGOVLYA, no. 7 (1953) by K. Akhpolov, the director of the Moscow Trade Group Office.

"The Consumer Co-operative Congress." SOVIET STUDIES 6 (October 1954): 168-69.

This note reviews the concerns of the Congress which took place in Moscow June 29 to August 5, 1954.

The Consumer and Living Standards

"Consumer Goods in Central Asia." CENTRAL ASIAN REVIEW 7, no. 2 (1959): 145-52.

    Aspects discussed include sales organization, supply and demand, availability, quality, luxury goods, household goods, and amenity goods. A table shows the growth in demand for selected consumer goods in Tadzhikistan.

Erro, Imogene. "Catching Up and Out 'Stripping': An Appraisal." PROBLEMS OF COMMUNISM 10 (July-August 1961): 24-30.

    This paper discusses the position of the consumer in the Soviet economy with attention given to textiles, clothing, hosiery, footwear, and durables. Comparisons with the U.S. economy are made. Tables.

_____. "Economic Reform in the Soviet Consumer Industries." In NEW DIRECTIONS IN THE SOVIET ECONOMY, U.S. Congress. Joint Economic Committee. Subcommittee on Foreign Economic Policy, pp. 555-68. Washington, D.C.: Government Printing Office, 1966.

    Experiments in production and distribution of consumer goods are reviewed and the effects of the Kosygin reforms on the consumer sector are discussed.

_____. "Trends in the Production of Consumer Goods." In DIMENSIONS OF SOVIET ECONOMIC POWER, U.S. Congress. Joint Economic Committee, pp. 371-89. Washington, D.C.: Government Printing Office, 1962.

    The author surveys the Soviet production record of textiles, clothing and footwear, and consumer durables. Current growth problems and prospects of light industry are discussed, including materials shortages, low level of technology, investment of capital, and weaknesses in planning and administration. Tables.

Golden, Rachel E. "Recent Trends in Soviet Personal Income and Consumption." In DIMENSIONS OF SOVIET ECONOMIC POWER, U.S. Congress. Joint Economic Committee, pp. 351-66. Washington, D.C.: Government Printing Office, 1962.

    The author is concerned with the slow growth in the supply of goods and services and the simultaneous increase of personal disposable income which resulted in inflationary pressures. This article covers the period 1950-61. Tables.

Golder, Frank A., and Hutchinson, Lincoln. ON THE TRAIL OF THE RUSSIAN FAMINE. Stanford, Calif.: Stanford University Press, 1927. xii, 319 p. Illustrated.

    The book is based on authors' notes which they compiled during their stay in Russia as part of the American Relief Administration program. They attempt to present an objective picture of what they saw in Russia and do not venture any political or social comments. Photographs.

Goldman, Marshall I. "From Sputniks to Panties: Is Economic Development Really that Easy?" BUSINESS HISTORY REVIEW 37, nos. 1-2 (1963): 81-93.

This article analyzes the shifting role of the fashion and consumer goods industries in Soviet Russia's transition from an economy of scarcity to one of greater abundance.

Hanson, Philip. THE CONSUMER IN THE SOVIET ECONOMY. Evanston, Ill.: Northwestern University Press, 1968. ix, 249 p.

This book discusses the effect of Soviet economic development on Soviet citizens as consumers. It summarizes the development of consumption levels over time, as well as discusses the relationship between resource allocation and investment priorities. Indexes.

———. "Soviet Living Standards." OXFORD UNIVERSITY. INSTITUTE OF ECONOMICS AND STATISTICS. BULLETIN 27 (August 1965): 201-27.

Soviet and British living standards in 1964 and 1965 are compared by examining money income, prices, and expenditure patterns. The article is concerned largely with estimation techniques and includes much data in the tables. Appendices discuss price data and expenditure weights and make observations on quality, range, and availability of goods. For further discussion, see the entry below.

Hewett, Edward A. "A Note on Soviet Standards." OXFORD UNIVERSITY. INSTITUTE OF ECONOMICS AND STATISTICS. BULLETIN 31 (February 1969): 55-60.

This note is a comment on previous studies of Soviet living standards conducted by Philip Hanson, Norman Kaplan and Eleanor Wainstein, and Alec Nove. The major concern is with estimation techniques.

Knight, Curtis. "Change in the Soviet Diet." ASSOCIATION FOR COMPARATIVE ECONOMIC STUDIES BULLETIN 10 (Winter 1968): 10-16.

This article presents food balance tables for selected years between 1928 and 1963. All major food items in the diet are covered, with deductions for trade, seed, waste and industrial usage from gross output to arrive at net supply of food for consumption.

"Labour and Living Conditions in Kazakhstan." CENTRAL ASIAN REVIEW 8, no. 3 (1960): 273-79.

Riots over living conditions and agricultural difficulties are discussed.

The Consumer and Living Standards

"Living Conditions in Azerbaydzhan." CENTRAL ASIAN REVIEW 9, no. 1 (1961): 5-15.

> Topics discussed include housing and maintenance, household goods, trade and distribution, repair services, clothing, footwear, food trade and catering, and middlemen. Map.

Lomberg, Doris P., and Turgeon, Lynn. "The Meaningfulness of Soviet Retail Prices." AMERICAN SLAVIC AND EAST EUROPEAN REVIEW 19 (April 1960): 217-33.

> This article compares Soviet prices and wages in an effort to compare the countries' standards of living. Topics covered include a ruble-dollar ratio of disposable income for food, clothing, durable consumer goods, personal care, and recreation; gross family income; taxes; shelter and household operations; medical, dental, and child care; transportation; insurance, contributions, savings, and other expenses; and dollar-equivalent prices. Three tables. For a comment on this paper, see: Alec Nove. "Letter to the Editor." AMERICAN SLAVIC AND EAST EUROPEAN REVIEW 19 (December 1960): 622-23.

London. University. School of Slavonic and East European Studies. THE END OF RATIONING AND THE STANDARD OF LIVING IN THE SOVIET UNION. London: 1935. 28 p.

> This paper discusses the reasons for rationing, the mechanism of rationing, ration scales, reasons for derationing, prices, and effects of derationing. Tables.

Madge, Charles. "Notes on the Standard of Living in Moscow, April 1952." SOVIET STUDIES 4 (January 1953): 229-36.

> This article compares prices in Moscow for consumer goods with prices for similar goods in Birmingham, England. Three tables.

Miller, Jacob. "Note on the Standard of Living in Moscow in 1937." SOVIET STUDIES 4 (January 1953): 237-42.

> This article attempts to evaluate in English prices the material standard of living of an assumed Moscow workingclass family.

Miller, Margaret S. RISE OF THE RUSSIAN CONSUMER. London: Institute of Economic Affairs, 1965. 254 p.

> Part one discusses planning before 1962 and after the 1962 reforms. The 1962 reforms in industry are outlined. Part two deals with agriculture and discusses the 1962 reforms, outlines the tasks in agriculture, and surveys some of the recurrent problems. Part three deals with housing, labor, and internal trade. The book concludes with a brief discussion of consumer sovereignty versus planning.

Moskoff, William. "A Study of Consumer Demand for Leather Footwear in the Soviet Union." MARQUETTE BUSINESS REVIEW 14 (Fall 1970): 134-45.

> This article examines ways in which the demand for leather footwear is studied and attempts to show that the problems which occurred in the distribution network resulted from a planning deficiency. Seven tables.

Nash, Edward. "Purchasing Power of Workers in the Soviet Union." MONTHLY LABOR REVIEW 94 (May 1971): 39-45.

> This article compares the work time required to purchase the seven basic foods during specific years--1928, 1953, 1962, and 1970. A comparison also is made for 1970 between approximate work time required to buy basic consumer goods in Moscow and New York City. Four tables.

Nove, Alec. "The Purchasing Power of the Soviet Ruble." OXFORD UNIVERSITY. INSTITUTE OF ECONOMICS AND STATISTICS. BULLETIN 20 (May 1958): 187-204.

> This paper calculates the purchasing power of the Soviet consumer ruble in terms of sterling. There are a number of tables and a detailed discussion of mathematical techniques used. Appendices discuss price quotations and equivalents and show other calculations.

Oldak, P. WAYS TO INCREASE NATIONAL WELL-BEING. Washington, D.C.: U.S. Joint Publications Research Service, no. 11473, December 8, 1961. 13 p.

> This is a translation from VOPROSY EKONOMIKI, no. 9 (1961). It discusses the reasons why and the means by which the standard of living in the Soviet Union will improve.

Postnikov, S. V. "The Continuous Budget Survey in the U.S.S.R." In FAMILY LIVING STUDIES, pp. 54-66. Geneva: International Labour Office, 1961.

> This article discusses the methods used, coverage of the inquiry, and the results of data on income, expenditure, and consumption of wage earners in the different branches of industry and of salary earners throughout the USSR.

Prybyla, Jan S. "The Soviet Consumer in Khrushchev's Russia." RUSSIAN REVIEW 20 (July 1961): 194-205.

> This study analyzes recent trends in the Soviet citizen's living standards. Two tables provide figures on state budget expenditures, 1956-59, and retail prices in 1958.

Raitsin, V. I. PLANNING THE STANDARD OF LIVING ACCORDING TO CONSUMPTION NORMS. White Plains, N.Y.: International Arts and Sciences

Press, 1969. vi, 69 p.

> This work by a Soviet economist presents information on Soviet consumption patterns and income distribution. Tables. Paperback.

Roellinghoff, Wilhelm. "The Home Market." In RED ECONOMICS, edited by Gerhard Dobbert, pp. 208-24. Boston and New York: Houghton Mifflin, 1932.

> The author discusses Soviet internal trade and transportation and points out that they have not developed in keeping with the rate of industrialization.

Ruban, M. E. "Private Consumption in the USSR: Changes in the Assortment of Goods 1940-1959." SOVIET STUDIES 13 (January 1962): 237-54.

> Eleven tables present figures on production and consumption of consumer goods. An appendix estimates consumption in the agricultural sector.

Rzhanitsina, L. "Public Consumption Funds in the USSR." INTERNATIONAL LABOUR REVIEW 108 (December 1973): 517-35.

> Topics discussed include the general role of public consumption funds, their composition, growth, and sources, the planning and management of these funds, and problems of some specific programs. Tables.

Schroeder, Gertrude [E.]. "Consumption in the USSR: A Survey." STUDIES ON THE SOVIET UNION n.s. 10, no. 4 (1970): 1-40.

> This paper reviews the improvements in Russian living standards over a half-century of Soviet rule. The last eight pages contain two appendices of data tables and notes.

Schultz, T., and Wiles, Peter J. D. "Earnings and Living Standards in Moscow." OXFORD UNIVERSITY. INSTITUTE OF ECONOMICS AND STATISTICS. BULLETIN 14 (September-October 1952): 309-26.

> Topics covered include the cost of a minimum diet in Moscow and in England, earnings and wages, unemployment and social services, and income and household expenditures. There are many tables. Appendices discuss housing conditions and list Moscow prices of selected consumer goods. See also the errata to this article in OXFORD UNIVERSITY. INSTITUTE OF ECONOMICS AND STATISTICS. BULLETIN 14 (November-December 1952): 430. See also the following: G. H. Elvin. "Earnings and Living Standards in Moscow: A Comment." OXFORD UNIVERSITY. INSTITUTE OF ECONOMICS AND STATISTICS 15 (September 1953): 309-14; followed by T. Schultz and Peter J. D. Wiles, "Rejoinder," pp. 315-26.

Schurman, Bernard. "Consumption Trends and the Role of Social Consumption Funds under the Soviet Party Programme." SOCIAL RESEARCH 31 (September 1964): 321-32.

> This paper explores certain aspects of the new Party Programme goals for consumption and analyzes some of the implications of these goals for the social consumption fund.

Skeoch, L. A. "Food Prices and Ration Scale in the Ukraine." REVIEW OF ECONOMICS AND STATISTICS 35 (August 1953): 229-35.

> This paper analyzes price and ration data compiled in Kiev in June and July 1946. Two tables.

Skurski, Roger. "The Buyers' Market and Soviet Consumer Goods Distribution." SLAVIC REVIEW 31 (December 1972): 817-30.

> This paper documents the change from a sellers' market to a buyers' market that occurred in the late 1950s and the resultant change in Soviet trade operations in the 1960s. Five tables present data on Soviet retail trade.

Turgeon, Lynn. "Future Levels of Living in the U.S.S.R." ECONOMICS OF PLANNING 3 (September 1963): 149-65.

> Topics covered include the Twenty-Year Plan for Soviet consumers, prospects for successful fulfillment of this plan, and possible problems. Tables compare Stalin's long range targets with actual output in 1960 and present indexes of actual and planned changes in principal measures of Soviet growth, 1950-80.

———. "Levels of Living, Wages, and Prices in the Soviet and United States Economies." In COMPARISONS OF THE U.S. AND SOVIET ECONOMIES, U.S. Congress. Joint Economic Committee, pp. 319-40. Washington, D.C.: Government Printing Office, 1959.

> This paper contains information on recent and projected developments in Soviet levels of living; a ruble-dollar ratio of disposable income for food, clothing, durable consumer goods, personal care, and recreation; the meaningfulness of Soviet retail prices; and U.S.-Soviet comparisons of consumption. Four tables.

Vogel, Heinrich. "Satisfaction of Consumer Needs." STUDIES ON THE SOVIET UNION n.s. 7, no. 1 (1967): 51-66.

> This paper traces the position of the consumer in the Soviet economy since 1928. Tables.

Wiles, Peter J. D. "Retail Trade, Retail Prices and Real Wages in the U.S.S.R." OXFORD UNIVERSITY. INSTITUTE OF ECONOMICS AND STATISTICS. BULLETIN 16 (November-December 1954): 373-92.

The Consumer and Living Standards

This article examines the official figures which show rapid growth in consumption after the war. For comparison, series are also given for some other main components of the Soviet national income. Appendices discuss the turnover tax and retail trade and the relative weights of state trade, cooperative trade, and kolkhoz trade.

"Workers' Family Budget Enquiries in Soviet Russia." INTERNATIONAL LABOUR REVIEW 20 (October 1929): 568-76.

This article briefly discusses the scope of inquiries into workers' family budgets, the relation of wages to total family income, and expenditures of a worker's family.

Chapter 34
HOUSING AND THE URBAN ECONOMY

THE PERIOD UP TO 1860

Fisher, Raymond H. "Mangazeia: A Boom Town of Seventeenth Century Siberia." RUSSIAN REVIEW 4 (Autumn 1944): 89-99.

> This paper traces the rise and fall of this Siberian fur-trading center. A short table presents figures on the government tithes collected on furs for selected years.

Tikhomirov, M. N. THE TOWNS OF ANCIENT RUSSIA. Translated by Y. Sdobnikov. Moscow: Foreign Languages Publishing House, 1959. 503 p. Illustrated.

> Part one covers the "Economic and Social System of the Towns of Ancient Rus"; part two discusses particular towns by region. Indexes.

THE PERIOD AFTER 1917

Beerman, R. "Legal Implications of the 1957 Housing Decree." SOVIET STUDIES 11 (July 1959): 109-16.

> Among other aspects, the proportion of private to public housing is discussed.

_____. "Privately-Owned Housing: Rents and Evictions." SOVIET STUDIES 10 (July 1958): 103-4.

> This note summarizes M. G. Markova. "The Concept and Practice of the Law of Private Property." VESTNIK LENINGRADSKOVO UNIVERSITETA, no. 5 (1957): 103-15.

Block, Alexander. "Soviet Housing: The Historical Aspect: I. Problems of Amount, Cost and Quality in Urban Housing." SOVIET STUDIES 5 (January 1954): 246-77.

The major contents of this article are the nine statistical tables. The notes and observations are grouped into two sections: the means and sources of information and comparisons of Soviet housing problems with those in the West.

_____. "Soviet Housing: Some Town Planning Problems." SOVIET STUDIES 6 (July 1954): 1-15.

Topics discussed here include size and height of building, giant buildings, quality housing, and landscaping.

"Domestic Housing." CENTRAL ASIAN REVIEW 9, no. 4 (1961): 359-70.

The current situation in Central Asia is discussed.

Frolic, B. Michael. "Decision Making in Soviet Cities." AMERICAN POLITICAL SCIENCE REVIEW 66 (March 1972): 38-52.

This paper is concerned with several aspects of decision making, including budget formulation, the planning process, housing construction and allocation, and the staffing of top urban posts. The present and future of Soviet municipal government are also discussed, and four detailed organization charts are included.

Harris, Chauncy D. CITIES OF THE SOVIET UNION: STUDIES IN THEIR FUNCTIONS, SIZE, DENSITY, AND GROWTH. Chicago: Rand-McNally for Association of American Geographers, 1970. xxviii, 484 p.

This monograph is concerned with 1,247 cities and towns of the Soviet Union of more than 10,000 population for which population data were published in the 1959 census. It stresses the economic functions, size relations, distributional pattern, and growth of these cities.

Herman, Leon M. "Urbanization and New Housing Construction in the Soviet Union." AMERICAN JOURNAL OF ECONOMICS AND SOCIOLOGY 30 (April 1971): 203-19.

Topics covered include the inherited housing problem, the beginning of the current building program, the creation of a construction materials industry, public investment in new urban housing, types of housing ownership, and the housing situation in 1970. Ten tables.

"The Housing Problem in Soviet Russia." INTERNATIONAL LABOUR REVIEW 12 (August 1925): 245-61.

The article outlines housing in Soviet Russia and sketches the government's housing policy to the end of 1921. The prevailing housing conditions of the workers are described, along with the measures taken to remedy the situation.

Kaganovich, L. M. SOCIALIST RECONSTRUCTION OF MOSCOW AND OTHER CITIES IN THE U.S.S.R. New York: International Publishers, 1931. 125 p.

> This book traces the history of Soviet urban development.

Lavrikov, Jurij. "New Forms of Management and Financing of Municipal Economy of Leningrad." PUBLIC FINANCE 27, no. 2 (1972): 227-30.

> This paper discusses the "automated management system" in Leningrad. There is an organization chart of this system.

Letich, Donald G. "Soviet Housing Administration and the Wartime Evacuation." AMERICAN SLAVIC AND EAST EUROPEAN REVIEW 9 (1950): 180-90.

> This article is concerned with the housing problems of workers transported to the East during World War II, with emphasis on their legal status and the safeguards to their housing rights.

May, Ernest. "Cities of the Future." In THE FUTURE OF COMMUNIST SOCIETY, edited by Walter Laquerer and Leopold Labedz, pp. 179-85. New York: Praeger, 1962.

> The author discusses his experiences in the planning of new towns in the Soviet Union in 1929. In 1959 he was invited for a two-week tour of Soviet housing, and he reports the progress that has been made since 1929.

Mequet, G. "Socialist Towns: A New Development of Housing Policy in the U.S.S.R. INTERNATIONAL LABOUR REVIEW 25 (May 1932): 621-45.

> The author outlines housing problems prior to the Five-Year Plan. He concludes by discussing technical and financial difficulties in housing construction.

Mote, Max E. "The Budget of Greater Leningrad." SOVIET STUDIES 19 (October 1967): 245-54.

> This article consists of tables showing annual budgets for the city and for suburbs administratively subordinated to the City Executive Committee for the years 1956-60, with breakdowns by district.

"New Settlements in Central Asia and Kazakhstan." CENTRAL ASIAN REVIEW 11, no. 3 (1963): 234-45.

> New settlements and policies of both the tsarist and Soviet governments are discussed. A map of the area and a table of new urban settlements is included.

Parkins, Maurice F. "Soviet Policy on Urban Housing and Housing Rent." LAND ECONOMICS 29 (August 1953): 269-79.

Housing and the Urban Economy

This paper reviews relevant historical and legal aspects of Soviet urban housing and discusses the problems of housing rent in the Soviet Union. Three tables provide figures on income and rent rates.

Richter, Luba. "Plans to Urbanize the Countryside 1950-62." In SOVIET PLANNING: ESSAYS IN HONOUR OF NAUM JASNY, edited by Jane Degras and Alec Nove, pp. 32-45. Oxford, Eng.: Basil Blackwell, 1964.

This article outlines the history of the official debate, present status, and the long-term plans for urbanization of the countryside.

Schmidt, Hans. "Housing Problems." In RED ECONOMICS, edited by Gerhard Dobbert, pp. 225-46. Boston and New York: Houghton Mifflin, 1932.

Housing problems in the Soviet Union are examined from the viewpoint that the building of socialism and industrialization are parallel developments. The author discusses three factors which "determine the general standard of building and housing activities" and how they function in Russia. The place of housing developments in the Five-Year Plan, the ideal form of dwelling under socialism, and the basis for socialistic town planning are also discussed.

Smith, Williard S. "Housing in the Soviet Union--Big Plans, Little Action." In SOVIET ECONOMIC PROSPECTS FOR THE SEVENTIES, U.S. Congress. Joint Economic Committee, pp. 404-26. Washington, D.C.: Government Printing Office, 1973.

Topics discussed include the housing shortage, new construction, capital investment, and future prospects. Twenty tables.

Sosnovy, Timothy. "Housing Conditions and Urban Development in the U.S.S.R." In NEW DIRECTIONS IN THE SOVIET ECONOMY, U.S. Congress. Joint Economic Committee, pp. 531-53. Washington, D.C.: Government Printing Office, 1966.

Topics discussed include prerevolutionary urban housing, Soviet city planning, housing conditions, economic status of the housing sector, public utilities, and personal services. Fifteen tables.

_____. "Rent in the USSR." AMERICAN SLAVIC AND EAST EUROPEAN REVIEW 18 (April 1959): 174-81.

This brief study of rent concludes that, although housing expenditures in the USSR seem nominal, "in terms of work time expended per unit of dwelling space and in terms of quality," the Soviet worker spends more than an American worker. A table gives percentage of income spent on rent in selected years between 1922 and 1956.

_____. "The Soviet City." In DIMENSIONS OF SOVIET ECONOMIC POWER, U.S. Congress. Joint Economic Committee, pp. 325-45. Washington, D.C.: Government Printing Office, 1962.

    The author investigates the Soviet concept of city planning, housing, public utilities, and the social aspects of inadequate housing.

_____. "The Soviet Housing Situation Today." SOVIET STUDIES 11 (July 1959): 1-21.

    Topics discussed include housing policy, construction, urban housing conditions, types of dwellings, utilities, living space distribution and social groups, quality of construction, and the Seven-Year Plan (1959-65). Tables.

_____. "The Soviet Urban Housing Problem." AMERICAN SLAVIC AND EAST EUROPEAN REVIEW 11 (1952): 288-303.

    This article reviews the state of housing and housing policy in Russia from 1912-14 to 1948.

_____. "Town Planning and Housing." In THE FUTURE OF COMMUNIST SOCIETY, edited by Walter Laquerer and Leopold Labedz, pp. 170-78. New York: Praeger, 1962.

    The author sketches briefly the discussions of the Soviet city held during the 1920s and early 1930s when the Soviets decided on the principle of a "non-urbanized socialist distribution of population" for the future Soviet city. He then reviews what actually happened in thirty years.

Taubman, William. GOVERNING SOVIET CITIES: BUREAUCRATIC POLITICS AND URBAN DEVELOPMENT IN THE USSR. New York and London: Praeger, 1973. xvii, 166 p.

    This book treats the problems of Soviet bureaucratic politics, the role of the Party, company towns, small cities, provincial centers, Moscow, and Leningrad. Glossary, tables, and bibliography.

Chapter 35
REGIONAL STUDIES

Conolly, Violet. SOVIET ASIA. London: Oxford University Press, 1942. 32 p.

    The vast and varied resources of Soviet Asia are surveyed. Conolly gives a geographical sketch, a description of the colonization of Siberia, and the conquest of Central Asia; she then gives a picture of Soviet Asia in the early 1940s.

THE PERIOD UP TO 1860

Baikalov, Anatole V. "The Conquest and Colonisation of Siberia." SLAVONIC REVIEW 10 (April 1932): 557-71.

    This article contains a brief description of the geography of Siberia and an historical account of Russian expansion into Siberia.

Czyrowski, Nicholas L. OLD UKRAINE: ITS SOCIO-ECONOMIC HISTORY PRIOR TO 1781. Madison, N.J.: Florham Park Press, 1963. xi, 432 p.

    In the first part the author describes the land and the people; the characteristics of Ukrainian socioeconomic development; and the social and economic heritage of the prehistoric period. The second part discusses overall economic development; urban centers and their industries; and trade and finance during the Kievan-Galician period (860-1349). The third part deals with the extractive industries; industrial growth; and commercial growth during the Lithuanian-Polish period (1349-1648). The last section deals with the growth of the national economy; trade; industries; commerce; and finance. Name index and maps.

Duran, James A., Jr. "Catherine II, Potemkin, and Colonization Policy in Southern Russia." RUSSIAN REVIEW 28 (January 1969): 23-36.

    This article discusses colonization and settlement policy in southern Russia in the late eighteenth century.

Regional Studies

Foust, C[lifford]. M. "Russian Expansion to the East Through the Eighteenth Century." JOURNAL OF ECONOMIC HISTORY 21 (December 1961): 469-82.

> This article deals with the pre-nineteenth-century history of Siberia.

Gibson, James R. "Russian Occupance of the Far East, 1639-1750." CANADIAN SLAVONIC PAPERS 12 (Spring 1970): 60-77.

> This article chronicles Russian expansion across Siberia and the conquest, settlement, and exploitation of the Russian Far East. Economic emphasis is on the fur trade. Maps indicate routes of expansion.

_____. "The Significance of Siberia to Tsarist Russia." CANADIAN SLAVONIC PAPERS 14 (Autumn 1972): 442-53.

> This article surveys the economic, sociopolitical, and geographical consequences of the incorporation of Siberia into the Russian Empire. Economically, the region was significant as an exporter of furs, source of duties, and state monopolies on trade with China, and as a "frontier region" in which state economic controls were often unenforceable.

Konenko, Konstantyn. UKRAINE AND RUSSIA, A HISTORY OF THE ECONOMIC RELATIONS BETWEEN UKRAINE AND RUSSIA (1654-1917). Milwaukee, Wis.: Marquette University Press, 1958. 257 p.

> The book contains accounts of the conditions of serfdom and precapitalist trade and commerce; postreform agrarian conditions; the development of Ukrainian industry; finance capital in Ukrainian industry; and economic relations between Ukraine and Russia.

Lantzeff, George V. SIBERIA IN THE SEVENTEENTH CENTURY: A STUDY OF THE COLONIAL ADMINISTRATION. Berkeley and Los Angeles: University of California Press, 1943. viii, 235 p.

> This monograph gives an account of the development and growth of colonial institutions in Siberia.

"Nomad Economy in Azerbaydzhan in the First Half of the 19th Century." CENTRAL ASIAN REVIEW 9, no. 2 (1961): 134-43.

> Aspects discussed include nomad areas, nomad populations, land tenure and taxation, and livestock. Map.

"Some Social and Economic Aspects of 16th Century Central Asia." CENTRAL ASIAN REVIEW 12, no. 4 (1964): 265-70.

> Land cultivation, feudal rents, peasants, slave owning, and small traders and craftsmen are examined.

THE PERIOD 1860-1917

Baikalov, Anatole V. "Siberia Since 1894." SLAVONIC REVIEW 11 (January 1933): 328-40.

    The article describes how Siberia become "a flourishing and prosperous country" as a result of the construction of the Trans-Siberian Railway (1892-1900) which gave a great impetus to colonization and the general economic development of Siberia.

"The Development of Kara-Kalpakia after Union with Russia." CENTRAL ASIAN REVIEW 6, no. 1 (1958): 34-45.

    In 1873 this part of the Khanate became part of the Russian Empire. The effects on land tenure, land distribution, agriculture, and class structure are discussed. Map.

Dmitriev-Mamonov, A., ed. GUIDE TO THE GREAT SIBERIAN RAILWAY. St. Petersburg, Russia: Artistic Printing Society, 1900. 520 p.

    This book contains two phototypes, 360 photographs, four maps of Siberia, and three plans of towns. The volume contains detailed accounts of a geographical and historical survey of Siberia; the construction of the Great Siberian Railway; and descriptions of various branch railways.

"Early History of the Transcaspian Railway." CENTRAL ASIAN REVIEW 9, no. 3 (1961): 235-39.

    The origin, construction, maintenance, and workers associated with the railway in the 1880s are discussed.

Lobanov-Rostovsky, A. (Prince). "Russian Imperialism in Asia." SLAVONIC REVIEW 8 (June 1929): 28-47.

    This article describes the origin, evolution, and character of Russian imperialism in Asia.

Pierce, Richard A. RUSSIAN CENTRAL ASIA 1867-1917: A STUDY IN COLONIAL RULE. Berkeley and Los Angeles: University of California Press, 1960. viii, 359 p.

    Of particular interest are parts two and three on urban development, rural colonization, and economic development. Bibliography, index, glossary, and maps.

Poppe, Nikolaus. "The Economic and Cultural Development of Siberia." In RUSSIA ENTERS THE TWENTIETH CENTURY: 1894-1917, by Erwin Oberlander et al., pp. 138-51. New York: Schocken, 1971.

    The article traces the rapid economic development that Siberia

Regional Studies

underwent in the late nineteenth century.

Price, Morgan P. SIBERIA. London: Methuen & Co., 1912. xviii, 304 p. Illustrated.

> This travelog contains interesting chapters on living conditions in the commercial towns, on the post roads, in the provincial towns, and in the villages. Economic conditions and future prospects are also discussed. Four maps.

"Social, Political, and Economic Effects of Russian Influence in Kirgizia (1850-1917)." CENTRAL ASIAN REVIEW 5, no. 3 (1957): 235-46.

> Of interest to the economic historian are sections on administration, class structure and the economy, and Russian economic influence.

Treadgold, Donald W. THE GREAT SIBERIAN MIGRATION: GOVERNMENT AND PEASANT IN RESETTLEMENT FROM EMANCIPATION TO THE FIRST WORLD WAR. Princeton, N.J.: Princeton University Press, 1957. xiii, 278 p.

> Topics covered include the origins of the migration, the peasant in European Russia, migration policy, the railway, Stolypin, and the migration itself. Tables, appendices, bibliography, and index.

"Tsarist Taxation in Central Asia." CENTRAL ASIAN REVIEW 9, no. 4 (1961): 352-58.

> Aspects discussed include treatment of the settled population and the nomads, tax collectors, taxes, and expenditures.

Weinstein, H. R. "Land Hunger and Nationalism in the Ukraine, 1905-1917." JOURNAL OF ECONOMIC HISTORY 2 (May 1942): 24-35.

> This study concludes that land hunger outweighed the demand for political autonomy and cultural freedom in its importance in fostering Ukrainian nationalism.

Williams, D. S. M. "Taxation in Tsarist Central Asia." CENTRAL ASIAN REVIEW 16, no. 1 (1968): 51-63.

> This paper contains a description of the taxation system in tsarist Central Asia based on the relevant sections of the Pahlen Commission's Report. Glossary of terms.

_____. "Water Law in Tsarist Central Asia." CENTRAL ASIAN REVIEW 15, no. 1 (1967): 37-46.

> The effect of government interference on customary irrigation law is examined and found to have been disruptive.

Wright, George F. ASIATIC RUSSIA. Vol. 2. New York: McClure, Phillips & Co., 1902. xii, 291-637 p. Illustrated.

> Of particular interest to the economic historian are chapters 22-25 on social, economic, and political conditions. Bibliography, index, and maps.

THE PERIOD AFTER 1917

"The Agrotown." CENTRAL ASIAN REVIEW 5, no. 1 (1957): 49-54.

> The formation of agricultural townships, rather than small isolated sovkhozes, in Kazahkstan is discussed.

Ali, Agha S. MODERNIZATION OF SOVIET CENTRAL ASIA: AN EXAMPLE OF SOCIALIST CONSTRUCTION. Lahore, India: Punjab University Press, 1964. 102 p.

> Of particular interest to the economic historian is the chapter on the economic development of Central Asia.

"Animal Husbandry." CENTRAL ASIAN REVIEW 2, no. 1 (1954): 85-96.

> This article refers to Kazahkstan in the early 1950s. Map.

Avtonkhanov, Abdurakhman G. "The Underdeveloped Countries in the Soviet Empire." STUDIES ON THE SOVIET UNION n.s. 4, no. 4 (1965): 187-92.

> This paper notes the uneven development and industrial lag of many of the national republics within the USSR. Tables.

Barr, Brenton M., and Bater, James H. "The Electricity Industry of Central Siberia." ECONOMIC GEOGRAPHY 45 (October 1969): 349-69.

> Topics covered include estimated demand for electricity in central Siberia in 1964 and in 1970 by sector, a technique for estimating capacity requirements, the supply of electricity in central Siberia, local industrial growth between 1945 and 1955, large-scale hydroelectric development between 1956 and 1965, prospects for the future, and central Siberia as an electricity-surplus region. A wealth of information is presented in maps, tables, and graphs.

Baykov, Alexander M. "The Location of Heavy Industry in the USSR." OXFORD UNIVERSITY. INSTITUTE OF ECONOMICS AND STATISTICS. BULLETIN 3 (August 1941): 252-56.

> This short article is concerned with the fact that the aim of maximum production has conflicted with the policy of industrial location in the five-year plans. Tables provide figures on the production of coal, oil, iron ore, pig iron, and steel.

Regional Studies

Bone, Robert M. "Regional Planning and Economic Regionalization in the Soviet Union." LAND ECONOMICS 43 (August 1967): 347-54.

> This discussion covers the regional concept, the state of development of the major regions, and a classification of these regions. Two tables.

Bott, Lydia. "Recent Trends in the Economy of Soviet Central Asia." CENTRAL ASIAN REVIEW 13, no. 3 (1965): 199-204.

> Developments in industry and agriculture are discussed. Two tables provide figures on industrial production.

"Budgets, 1956-58." CENTRAL ASIAN REVIEW 6, no. 2 (1958): 159-70.

> This article consists entirely of tables of budget figures for the Central Asian republics.

"Building Materials Industry." CENTRAL ASIAN REVIEW 6, no. 2 (1958): 171-79.

> This article lists projects in Central Asia, such as cement factories, which will produce building materials and their capacities and nearness to completion.

Campbell, Robert W., ed. "Session on the Soviet Economy in Regional Perspective." ASSOCIATION FOR COMPARATIVE ECONOMIC STUDIES BULLETIN 14 (Spring 1972): 14-23.

> This is a summary of a session of the Allied Social Science Association meeting in December 1971 which dealt with the above topic. The article summarizes the papers given and includes tables on the balance of payments of the Ukrainian SSR in 1960 and per capita GNP in Soviet Union republics for the years 1940, 1950, 1960, 1965, and 1969.

"Central Asian Budgets 1953-55." CENTRAL ASIAN REVIEW 3, no. 4 (1955): 323-32.

> Consisting mostly of sixteen tables, this is a compilation of material bearing on the budgets of 1953-55, which has appeared in the Central Asian press. It is supported by interpretive comment where necessary.

Chirovsky, N[icholas]. L. THE UKRAINIAN ECONOMY--ITS BACKGROUND, PRESENT STATUS, AND POTENTIALS OF FUTURE GROWTH. New York: Shevchenko Scientific Society, 1965. 93 p.

> This brief work surveys the various resources of the Ukraine, the extractive industries, manufacturing, and marketing. The author concludes with a discussion of the future possibilities of economic

growth of the Ukraine. Bibliographical references, index, and map.

Conolly, Violet. BEYOND THE URALS--ECONOMIC DEVELOPMENTS IN SOVIET ASIA. New York and London: Oxford University Press, 1967. xx, 420 p.

> Part one discusses the Russian Empire in Asia before the Revolution. Part two outlines the economic development of Central Asia and Kazakhstan under the Soviets, 1917-45. Part three surveys economic development, 1945-60. Select bibliography, index, and maps.

"Cotton-Growing in Central Asia." CENTRAL ASIAN REVIEW 1, no. 3 (1953): 18-27.

> Information on this subject from the Central Asian Press is presented. Map of Tadzhik SSR is included.

Cross, Ralph D. "A Comparative Analysis of Urban-Industrial Growth in the Donestsk and Kuznetsh Basins of the USSR." SOUTHERN QUARTERLY 10 (January 1972): 167-82.

> The emphasis is on the period 1926-70. Five maps and two tables.

"Development of Transport in Northern Kazakhstan." CENTRAL ASIAN REVIEW 4, no. 2 (1956): 114-29.

> This article is concerned with the 1955-57 plan and discusses soil, road, and water transport. Four tables and a map.

"Development of Transport in Northern Kazakhstan." CENTRAL ASIAN REVIEW 6, no. 3 (1958): 281-97.

> Topics discussed include railways, roads, and oblast communications. Map.

Dibb, Paul. SIBERIA AND THE PACIFIC: A STUDY OF ECONOMIC DEVELOPMENT AND TRADE PROSPECTS. New York: Praeger, 1972. xxii, 288 p.

> The book systematically analyzes the Pacific Siberian economy, sector by sector. It deals primarily with the eastern three-quarters of Siberia.

Dienes, Leslie. "Regional Variations of Capital and Labor Productivity in Soviet Industry." JOURNAL OF REGIONAL SCIENCE 12 (December 1972): 401-6.

> This paper includes a map indicating degree of industrialization by region and a table of regional capital and labor productivity estimates for Soviet regions in 1968. The conclusion is that low

Regional Studies

capital productivity in a region is not related to the share of investment allocated to that region.

Dyker, David A. "Industrial Location in the Tadzhik Republic." SOVIET STUDIES 21 (April 1970): 485-506.

This study seeks to explain obvious cases of deviation from economic efficiency in locational patterns. Three tables.

"Electric Power in Kazakhstan." CENTRAL ASIAN REVIEW 6, no. 3 (1958): 298-301.

Plans for expansion of electric power are discussed. Map.

"Electric Power in Uzbekistan." CENTRAL ASIAN REVIEW 1, no. 3 (1953): 28-38.

History and plans for the future are discussed. Two maps.

Frank, Andrew G. "General Productivity in Soviet Agriculture and Industry: the Ukraine, 1928-55." JOURNAL OF POLITICAL ECONOMY 66 (December 1958): 498-515.

The text discusses derivation of the figures which are presented in twelve tables.

Hambly, M. V. "Road vs. Rail--A Note on Transport Development in Tadzhikistan." SOVIET STUDIES 19 (January 1968): 421-25.

This note examines the problem of how to save areas of large-scale development remote from railheads in southwest Tadzhikistan in Central Asia. A table provides figures for freight carried by narrow-gauge railway, water, and road for selected years 1958-65.

"Handbook Issue on Siberia and the Soviet Far East--Geopolitics, Population, Economics." STUDIES ON THE SOVIET UNION n.s. 1, no. 4 (1962): 195 p.

The articles contain many maps, charts, and tables.

Holubnychy, Vsevolod. THE INDUSTRIAL OUTPUT OF THE UKRAINE, 1913-1956: A STATISTICAL ANALYSIS. Munich: Institute for Study of the USSR, 1957. ix, 63 p.

This statistical abstract consists of some 100 tables of figures reflecting the output of the heavy and light industries of the Ukrainian SSR in physical terms during the period 1913-55.

Holzman, Franklyn D. "The Soviet Ural-Kuznetsk Combine: A Study in Investment Criteria and Industrialization Policies." QUARTERLY JOURNAL OF ECONOMICS 71 (August 1957): 368-405.

This paper covers the early history of the industrialization of this region, the controversy over transportation and location of industry, the various stages of investment, 1928-60, and an evaluation of the economic success of the combine. Map and nine tables.

Hooson, David. "The Outlook for Regional Development in the Soviet Union." SLAVIC REVIEW 31 (September 1972): 535-54.

This article first divides the Soviet Union into ten subregions, discusses their general characteristics, surveys their growth in the 1960s, and then discusses their future prospects. Five maps. For further discussion of this article, see the following articles in this issue: Ann Sheehy. "Some Aspects of Regional Development in Soviet Central Asia," pp. 555-63; Stanley V. Vardys. "Geography and Nationalities in the USSR: A Commentary," pp. 564-70; David Hooson. "Reply," pp. 571-73.

"The Hungry Steppe." CENTRAL ASIAN REVIEW 5, no. 1 (1957): 42-48.

The development of this region in Kazakhstan is discussed. Map.

"Irrigation and Water Supplies in Kazakhstan: Projects and Problems." CENTRAL ASIAN REVIEW 12, no. 3 (1964): 198-210.

This article first treats Kazakhstan in general and then the various districts. Two maps.

"Irrigation in Central Asia." CENTRAL ASIAN REVIEW 5, no. 3 (1957): 271-85. Illustrated.

This article surveys Central Asian water resources and discusses irrigation from before the Russian conquest to plans for the future. Two maps and two illustrations. A table listing projected irrigation work in each republic concludes the article.

"Irrigation in Central Asia: Part I." CENTRAL ASIAN REVIEW 8, no. 1 (1960): 44-51.

This article describes water resources and interrepublic irrigation networks. Two maps.

"Irrigation in Central Asia: Part II." CENTRAL ASIAN REVIEW 8, no. 2 (1960): 138-50.

This part describes major irrigation works completed within the last three years or still under construction. Four maps.

Jukes, Geoffrey. THE SOVIET UNION IN ASIA. Sydney: Argus and Robertson, in association with The Australian Institute of International Affairs, 1973. vii, 304 p.

Regional Studies

Of special economic interest are two chapters, one on Soviet Asia, the other on Soviet economic relations with Asian countries. Select bibliography and index.

Keren, Michael. "Industrial vs. Regional Partitioning of Soviet Planning Organization: A Comparison." ECONOMICS OF PLANNING 4, no. 3 (1964): 143-60.

> Two models are developed to establish the thesis that "the relative efficiency of the alternative partitioning depends on the method of planning in use, and that if the present method of planning were to be changed into one based on programming methods, the partition which is now inferior may turn out to be the better one."

Kirsanov, Sergey. "Railway Development." STUDIES ON THE SOVIET UNION n.s. 5, no. 1 (1965): 74-78.

> This paper surveys the rail system in Siberia and the Far East. A map showing existing and planned railroads is included.

Kolarz, Walter. RUSSIA AND HER COLONIES. New York: Praeger, 1952. xiv, 334 p.

> The author describes the working of Soviet colonial policy throughout the USSR and gives examples of the development of a given nationality. Bibliography.

Koropeckyj, I[van]. S. "Industrial Location Policy in the U.S.S.R. During the Postwar Period." In ECONOMIC PERFORMANCE AND THE MILITARY BURDEN IN THE SOVIET UNION, U.S. Congress. Joint Economic Committee, pp. 232-95. Washington, D.C.: Government Printing Office, 1970.

> This paper discusses the reasons for and the development of regionalization, locational objectives, and the geopolitical aspects of location policy. Many tables.

Krypton, Constantine G. "The Economy of Northern Siberia 1959-1965." RUSSIAN REVIEW 19 (January 1960): 47-53.

> This article summarizes the Soviet Union's plans for the economic development of northern Siberia during the 1959-65 Seven-Year Plan.

Laird, Roy D., and Chapell, John E., Jr. "Kazakhstan: Russia's Agricultural Crutch." RUSSIAN REVIEW 20 (October 1961): 326-43.

> This article analyzes the role of the new lands of Kazakhstan in Khrushchev's agricultural policy. A map of the new lands and a table showing grain output in Kazakhstan in 1953-60 are included.

"Land Reclamation in Kazakhstan." CENTRAL ASIAN REVIEW 3, no. 4 (1955): 296-305.

Topics discussed include new immigrants, communications, the plowing campaign, lack of granaries, and degree of progress. Two tables on land reclamation and harvests are in the appendix.

Lebed, A[ndrei]. I., and Yakovlev, B. "The Angarstroy." RUSSIAN REVIEW 14 (January 1955): 50-54.

This short paper discusses the essential features of the Angarstroy hydrotechnical project near Lake Baikal in Siberia.

Mathieson, R. S. "The Soviet Contribution to Regional Science." JOURNAL OF REGIONAL SCIENCE 9 (April 1969): 125-40.

The author recaps the twenty most important references in Soviet literature predating the current "explosion" in regional science writing. He then covers the 1960-68 period under six areas: the search for fundamentals; mathematical-econometric studies; transport net studies; regionalization; territorial complexes; and urban theory studies.

Melnyk, Zinowij L. SOVIET CAPITAL FORMATION: UKRAINE, 1928-1932. Munich: Ukrainian Free Press, 1965. xxvi, 182 p.

This study analyzes financial relations and the flow of capital and fiscal funds between one union republic, Ukraine, and the central USSR government. Tables, bibliography, and index.

Mieczkowski, Z. "The Economic Regionalization of the Soviet Union in the Lenin and Stalin Period." CANADIAN SLAVONIC PAPERS 8 (1966): 89-124.

Particular attention is given to regionalization under war communism, GOELRO regionalization, Gosplan regionalization, and various regionalization practices under Stalin. Comparisons are also made with the tsarist period. Regionalization is seen largely as a statistical convenience, not a means of furthering rational economic organization.

Mikirtitchian, Levan. "Lake Sevan Development Projects in Soviet Armenia." STUDIES ON THE SOVIET UNION n.s. 1, no. 3 (1962): 92-106.

These projects are considered as excellent case studies of the advantages and disadvantages of large-scale economic planning in the Soviet Union.

Miller, Margaret S. "Notes on Industrial Development." CENTRAL ASIAN REVIEW 15, no. 4 (1967): 300-315.

The following aspects of Central Asian industry are discussed: use of capital; capital construction; ferrous metallurgy; research; obstacles to reform; consumer goods; the Party; finance; and labor. For further discussion, see: Margaret S. Miller. "Notes on Industrial

Development." CENTRAL ASIAN REVIEW 16, no. 2 (1968): 159-60.

Newth, J. A. "State Farms in the Kazakh SSR." SOVIET STUDIES 10 (January 1959): 310-12.

> This note discusses the productivity and output of these farms in the 1950s.

North, Robert N. "Soviet Northern Development: The case of NW Siberia." SOVIET STUDIES 24 (October 1972): 171-99.

> The topics discussed in this paper include oil production and movement, natural gas development and expectations, other natural resources, and choices of transport mode. Two tables and three maps.

Nove, Alec, and Newth, J. A. THE SOVIET MIDDLE EAST: A COMMUNIST MODEL FOR DEVELOPMENT. New York: Praeger, 1966. 160 p.

> This study examines the development of Soviet Central Asia and Transcaucasia. A brief introductory chapter describes the history and geography of the region; examines industrial and agricultural developments; and surveys living standards, social services, and finance and growth of services.

"Personal and Maintenance Services in the Central Asian and Kazakh Republics." CENTRAL ASIAN REVIEW 15, no. 1 (1967): 47-56.

> Growth of services, need for services, shortcomings, and future prospects are discussed.

"Private Property Tendencies in Central Asia and Kazakhstan." CENTRAL ASIAN REVIEW 10, no. 2 (1962): 147-56.

> Aspects discussed include housing, vegetable gardens, livestock, and beekeeping.

Prociuk, Stephan G. "The Territorial Pattern of Industrialization in the USSR: A Case Study in Location of Industry." SOVIET STUDIES 13 (July 1961): 69-95.

> This paper discusses the industrial development of Asiatic Russia in comparison with European Russia. Twelve tables.

"Publishing, Printing, and Distribution of Books." CENTRAL ASIAN REVIEW 2, no. 2 (1954): 124-33.

> The output of the Central Asian book publishing industry is discussed.

"Recent Road and Rail Transport Developments in Kazakhstan." CENTRAL ASIAN REVIEW 13, no. 2 (1965): 173-82.

Regional Studies

This article provides a listing of new rail and road routes and discusses aspects of service. Map.

Saushkin, Julian G. "Large Areal Complexes of Productive Forces of the Soviet Union." REGIONAL SCIENCE ASSOCIATION. PAPERS AND PROCEEDINGS 8 (1962): 93-104.

The paper deals with the relationships between labor and material resources in some of the large geographic regions of the USSR.

"Savings and Social Security." CENTRAL ASIAN REVIEW 7, no. 3 (1959): 259-69.

Topics discussed include lotteries, state loans, savings banks, and social security in Central Asia.

Sheehy, Ann. "Irrigation in the Amu-Dar'ya Basin: Progress Report." CENTRAL ASIAN REVIEW 15 (1967): 342-53.

The period covered is from 1963 to mid-1967. A map of the Karshi Steppe irrigation scheme in the Uzbek SSR is included.

_____. "Population Trends in Central Asia and Kazakhstan." CENTRAL ASIAN REVIEW 14, no. 4 (1966): 317-29.

This consists of nine tables. For further discussion, see: Ann Sheehy. "Population Trends in Central Asia and Kazakhstan." CENTRAL ASIAN REVIEW 15, no. 1 (1967): 62-64.

Smolka, H. P. "Siberia: Its Discovery and Development." SLAVONIC REVIEW 16 (July 1937): 60-70.

The author gives a firsthand account of how the Soviets have been developing the vast resources of northern Siberia.

"The Tashkent Oblast." CENTRAL ASIAN REVIEW 6, no. 1 (1958): 46-58.

This article presents available information regarding the population, industry, towns, agriculture, and communications of Tashkent Oblast in Uzbekistan. Map.

Telepko, L. N. LARGE ECONOMIC REGIONS OF THE USSR--SOME PROBLEMS IN TERRITORIAL ORGANIZATION OF THE ECONOMY. Moscow: Institute of Economics, Academy of Sciences USSR, 1963. 198 p.

The book is divided into three sections: (1) the regional organization of the economy; (2) the specialization of large economic regions; and (3) questions dealing with the complex development of these regions.

"Transport in Azerbaydzhan." CENTRAL ASIAN REVIEW 10, no. 2 (1962): 129-46.

> Rail, sea, river, road, and air transport are examined. Map.

Vvedensky, George. "The Major Industries." STUDIES ON THE SOVIET UNION n.s. 8, no. 1 (1968): 1-8.

> Industrial output of Soviet Central Asia is discussed. Seven tables.

Zinam, Oleg. "Soviet Regional Policies: Conflicting Requirements of Specialization and Self-Sufficiency." RIVISTA INTERNAZIONALE DI SCIENZE ECOOMICHE E COMMERCIALI 19, no. 7 (1972): 672-91.

> This paper discusses the history of the Soviet approach to regional policies.

──────. "Soviet Regional Problems: Specialization Versus Autarky." RUSSIAN REVIEW 31 (April 1972): 126-37.

> This paper devotes most attention to the crucial relationship between the central government and major regions of the USSR.

Zybenko, Roman [O.]. "The Economy: Prospects and Problems." STUDIES ON THE SOVIET UNION n.s. 5, no. 1 (1965): 28-33.

> This paper discusses the problems and prospects of the Siberian economy.

Chapter 36
THE FUTURE OF THE SOVIET ECONOMY

Garretson, Robert C. THE ABUNDANT PEACE. Cleveland and New York: World Publishing Co., 1965. xiv, 255 p.

    This study examines trends that may be projected ahead to determine where the economies of the United States and the USSR are going and what kind of problems they will face in the future.

Meyer, A[lfred]. G. "Twenty Years On." In THE FUTURE OF COMMUNIST SOCIETY, edited by Walter Laquerer and Leopold Labedz, pp. 186-96. New York: Praeger, 1962.

    The author discusses the future of the Soviet social system. He assumes an isolated Soviet society and traces the inherent trends makes a projection about Soviet society twenty years hence.

Seton, Francis. "The Soviet Economy in 1967: Forecasts and Reality." In THE PREDICTIONS OF COMMUNIST ECONOMIC PERFORMANCE, edited by Peter J. D. Wiles, pp. 303-8. Cambridge: At the University Press, 1971.

    A table gives annual growth rates for selected sectors.

Zauberman, Alfred. "The Economics of '1980.' " In THE U.S.S.R. AND THE FUTURE: AN ANALYSIS OF THE NEW PROGRAMME OF THE COMMUNIST PARTY OF THE SOVIET UNION, edited by L. B. Schapiro, pp. 103-13. Munich: Institute for the Study of the USSR, 1962.

    Projections for the Soviet economy in 1980 are discussed.

AUTHOR INDEX

In addition to authors, this index includes all editors, compilers, and translators cited in this text.

A

Aboltin, V. 199
Abouchar, Alan 237, 265, 283, 343
Abramov, Viktor 310
Abramovitz, Moses 185
Abramson, A. 28, 71, 416
Abshire, David M. 114, 124, 234
Adam, Jan 238
Adams, Arthur E. 310
Adler-Larlsson, Gunner 112
Aganbegian, A. 426
Akhpolov, K. 427
Alexander, Melinda 272
Alexandorva, Vera 98
Alexandrov, B. 181
Alexandrov, N. 374
Alexinsky, Gregor 10
Algvere, Karl V. 283
Ali, Agha S. 112, 445
Alison, Colin A. 199
Alkhimov, V. 199
Allen, Richard V. 114, 124, 234
Allen, Robert Loring 99, 199-200, 201, 229
Altman, Oscar L. 224
Alton, Thad P. 200
American-Russian Chamber of Commerce 147
Ames, Edward 15, 181, 200, 269

Ammende, E. 15
Anchinhkin, Alexander 21
Anchishkin, I. 57
Anderson, Edgar 200
Anderson, Jeremy 310
Anderson, M.S. 6
Anderson, Olive 223
Andreassen, Knut 181
Andres, Enrike 71
Andrew, I. 201
Andrews, William G. 15
Anisimov, Nikolai I. 311
Antsiferov, Alexis N. 303
Apostol, P.N. 97
Arakelian, A. 257
Arkhimovich, A. 311
Arnold, Arthur Z. 181
Arnot, R.P. 67
Artuikhin, N.E. 57
Asher, Ephraim 128
Aslanyan, R.G. 416
Athay, Robert E. 270
Aubrey, Henry G. 201, 229
Auhagen, Otto 311
Australia Bureau of Agricultural Economics 311
Avrich, Paul H. 374
Avtonkhanov, Abdurakhman G. 445
Azrael, Jeremy R. 257

Author Index

B

Baikalov, Anatole V. 311, 374, 441, 443
Bakalo, Ivan 312
Baker, C.B. 312
Bakhmetov, Boris 71
Balabkins, Nicholas A. 42, 57
Balassa, Bela 129
Balinky, Alexander 57, 72
Ballard, Allen B., Jr. 312
Ballis, William B. 343
Bal'zak, S.S. 366
Bandera, V.N. 57, 238
Banerji, J. 58
Baran, Paul A. 42, 72, 105, 163, 182, 207
Baranov, I. 72
Baransky, N.N. 366
Baritz, Joseph 72, 277
Barkai, Haim 179
Barker, Geoffrey R. 112, 190, 374-75
Barna, Tibor 90
Baron, Samuel H. 39, 42, 281
Barr, Brenton M. 366, 445
Bartol, Kathryn M. 139
Basily, Nikolai A. 58
Bass, Robert H. 312
Basseches, Nikolaus 112
Baster, Nancy 425
Bater, James H. 445
Batra, Raveendra N. 312
Bauer, Raymond A. 58, 283-84
Baumgolts, A.I. 268
Baykalov, A. 303
Baykov, Alexander M. 15-16, 60, 72, 99, 113, 148, 190, 201, 312-13, 375, 445
Beable, William H. 10
Becker, Abraham S. 99, 143, 144, 163-64, 171, 201
Beckhart, Benjamin H. 185
Bednarik, Mojmir K. 224
Beerman, R. 435
Beermann, R. 182, 331, 336, 375
Belkin, V.D. 139
Belov, Fedor 313
Bendix, Reinhard 255
Bennett, M.K. 313

Berent, Jerzy 421
Bergamini, John D. 313
Bergson, Abram 16, 54, 72-73, 113-14, 118, 120, 126, 129, 132, 148, 153, 155, 164-65, 166, 169, 171-72, 209, 210, 217, 239, 267, 271, 325, 332, 351, 353, 363, 375-76, 383, 385, 426, 427
Beriia, L.P. 16
Berkhin, I. 73
Berliner, Joseph S. 58, 73, 119, 130, 148, 182, 201, 229, 257-58, 279, 326
Berman, H.J. 201
Bernard, Jean 202
Bernard, Philippe J. 73
Bernatsky, M.W. 97, 182
Bernstein, S.A. 284
Best, Harry 58
Bickermann, Joseph 16-17
Bieda, K. 131
Bienstock, Gregory 258
Bilimovich, Alexander [Aleksandr] D. 202, 303
Birmingham University. Bureau of Research on Russian Economic Conditions 17, 74, 114, 165, 202, 224, 313, 376
Bjork, Leif 376
Black, Cyril E. 11, 15, 109, 309, 372, 407, 415
Blackman, James H. 238, 271
Blackwell, William L. 107, 108, 255
Bleyer, B. 361
Blitzer, Charles R. 121
Block, Alexander 435-36
Block, Herbert 99
Blum, Jerome 171, 299-300
Blumenfeld, Hans 130, 364
Boddy, Francis M. 24, 74, 114, 166
Boev, V.R. 313
Bogoliepov, Mikhail I. 182
Boles, John J. 202
Bolsover, G.H. 17
Boltho, Andrea 202
Bone, Robert M. 446
Bor, Mikhail Z. 74, 80

Author Index

Borders, Karl 313
Boretsky, Michael 99, 277, 284
Bornstein, Morris 17, 72, 93, 114, 158, 166, 172, 182, 183, 184, 185, 242, 245, 278, 314, 378, 427
Borodaewsky, S.W. 304
Bott, Lydia 446
Boulding, Kenneth 1
Bowers, Robert E. 202
Bowles, Chester 229
Bowles, W. Donald 284-85
Brackett, James W. 408
Brada, Josef C. 203
Bradley, Michael E. 314
Braeker, Hans 203
Braginskii, B.I. 314
Brailsford, Henry N. 17
Brason, Boris L. 58
Bridgeman, John 8
Brodersen, Arvid 376
Bromley, J.S. 6
Bron, Saul G. 114
Bronson, David W. 314, 376-77, 426
Brown, Emily C. 377-78
Brubaker, Earl R. 59, 100, 115, 128, 273, 277-78, 285, 314
Brumberg, Abraham 59
Brutskus [Brutzkus], Boris D. 74, 197
Bryden, Judith G. 409
Buchta, J.W. 24, 278
Budish, Jacob M. 203
Bukharin, N. 59
Bukshtynov, Aleksei D. 361
Bulik, Joseph J. 361
Bunyan, James 378
Burns, Emile 18
Bury, J.P.T. 10
Bush, Keith 74, 265, 285, 315, 355, 359
Butler, Scot 265
Bye, Raymond T. 74
Byrne, Terence E. 18

C

Caiola, Marcello 224
Cairncross, Alec 42

Cameron, Norman 314
Campbell, Arthur A. 408
Campbell, Colin D. 426
Campbell, Malcolm 183
Campbell, Robert W. 1, 18, 43, 82, 115, 130, 134, 148, 166, 173, 183, 238-39, 243, 258, 278, 285, 446
Campbell, Rosemary G. 426
Carey, David W. 315, 361, 416
Carnett, George S. 230
Carr, Edward H. 18, 59
Carson, George Barr, Jr. 408
Carter, Edward C. 100
Carter, James R. 230
Cattell, David T. 239
Cazalet, E.A. 425
Central Statistical Administration 149, 271
Ceriglia, S. Joseph 378
Chaianov, A.V. 315
Chakrabarti, S.C. 115
Chamberlin, William H. 18, 75, 299
Chambre, Henri 23
Chand, Mahesh 158
Chapell, John E., Jr. 450
Chapman, Janet G. 16, 173, 378-79, 427
Charles, K.J. 43
Chase, Stuart 239
Cheng, Chu-Yuan 203
Cherepnin, L.V. 302
Chernomordik, D.E. 268, 271
Chigirin, N. 283
Childs, S. Lawford 379, 380
Chirovsky, Nicolas L. 5, 446
Chossudowsky, E.M. 43, 427
Christoff, Peter 40
Churchward, L.G. 315
Clark, Colin 149, 166
Clark, M. Gardner 102, 285-86, 314, 379
Clarke, Roger A. 150, 237, 315
Clarkson, J.D. 9
Clawson, Marion 364
Clayton, Elizabeth M. 344
Cleinow, Georg 230
Coates, William P. 75
Coates, Zelda K. 75

Author Index

Cohen, Stephen F. 40, 43, 82
Cohn, Stanley H. 100, 115, 124, 130, 166
Cohn, Viktor 278
Cole, J.P. 366
Colm, Gerhard 100
Colton, Ethan 116
Committee on Russian-American Relations 203
Comstock, Alzada 183
Condoide, Mikhail V. 183, 204
Conklin, David W. 239, 316
Conolly, Violet 204, 441, 447
Conquest, Robert 316, 379
Coogan, James 190
Cook, A.C. 75
Cook, Paul K. 240
Cooper, Orah 230
Counts, George S. 19, 75, 87
Couriss, N.J. 12
Crawford, John M. 11
Crawford, Morris H. 206, 230
Crawley, C.W. 10
Cressey, George B. 19, 367
Crisp, Olga 180, 228
Cross, Ralph D. 447
Cross, Samuel H. 76
Crottet, A.A. 379, 380
Crouzet, F. 137
Crowley, Edward L. 297, 334, 335, 342, 346
Czarnomski, F.B. 59
Czyrowski, Nicholas L. 441

D

DaCosta, Eric P.W. 109
Dallin, David J. 380
Dalrymple, Dana G. 287, 304, 315, 316-17
Danielson, Nicolai-on 56
Darby, H.C. 365
Darmstadter, Joel 100
Datar, Asha L. 230
Datta, Amlankusum 116
Daukas, Anthony 286
David, Henry P. 409
Davies, Robert W. 6, 18, 43, 76, 183, 190-91, 238, 240, 278, 286
Davis, Jerome 19

Davletshin, Tamurbek 240, 317
Day, Richard B. 19
De Alessi, Louis 204
Dean, Vera M. 59
Deane, Phyllis 116
Debo, Richard K. 204
De Felice, Frank 286
Degras, Jane 77, 82, 84, 87, 90, 149, 184, 232, 438
Dehn, Wladimir 180
De Lestrade, Combes 304
Dellin, C.A.D. 248
De Madariaga, I. 300
Demaree, Bess 292
DeMaris, E. Joe 184
Denisov, P. 268
Denton, Frederick G. 116
De Pauw, John W. 150, 317, 408
Desai, Padma 150, 230
De Tegoborski, M. Ludvik 6
Deutscher, Isaac 11, 380
Deutscher, L. 43
Devons, E. 60
Dewar, Margaret 204, 380
De Witt, Nicholas 380-81, 391, 416
Diakonoff, V.A. 240
Diamond, Douglas B. 317-18
Diatchenko, V.P. 381
Dibb, Paul 318, 447
Dienes, Leslie 362, 447
Dihkala, Erkki 198
Dinerstein, Herbert S. 318
Djalilov, K.M. 318
Dmitriev-Mamonov, A. 443
Dmytryshyn, Basil 39, 71
Dobb, Maurice H. 19, 44, 60, 77, 101, 116-17, 148, 150, 152, 153, 162, 163, 166, 173, 182, 240-41, 246, 265, 271, 287
Dobbert, Gerhard 60, 112, 183, 184, 205, 244, 262, 420, 432, 438
Dobrin, S. 44
Dobrov, Gennady M. 278
Dobrovolsky, Alexander 318
Dockstader, Robert A. 117, 361
Dodge, Norton D. 381
Dodge, Norton T. 131, 287, 318-19, 405, 421

Author Index

Dogadov, V.M.   381
Dohrs, Fred E.   355
Dolan, Edwin G.   20, 77
Dolensky, N.V.   98
Domar, Evsey D.   103, 215, 319, 354
Dorodmitsyn, A.   80
Douglas, Paul H.   20, 287, 382
Dovring, Folke   319
Dow, Roger   129
Drage, Geoffrey   11
Drew, Ronald F.   300
Drummond, Ian M.   205
Druzhinin, N.   150
Duddington, Natalie   7
Dudinskii, I.   205
Duff, James D.   11
Duimulen, I.   205
Dulles, Allen W.   131, 258
Dumov, D.   314
Dunayevskaya, Raya   44, 47, 51
Duncan, M.W.   205
Dunn, Ethel   300
Dunn, Robert W.   382
Dunn, Stephen P.   300
Duran, James A., Jr.   189, 441
Duranty, Walter   205
Durgin, Frank A., Jr.   319-20
Dyason, J.   12
Dyker, David A.   448

E

Eason, Warren W.   16, 25, 49, 320, 382-83, 407, 409
East, W. Gordon   20
Eaton, Henry L.   407
Ebel, Robert E.   287
Eckstein, Alexander   129, 151, 279, 326
Eddy, George S.   20
Edie (Lionel D.) & Co., Inc. Economics Division   77
Edwards, Imogene U.   271
Edwards, Stephen   225
Efimov, Anatolii N.   21, 78, 117
Eicher, Carl   329
Einzig, Paul   184
Elias, Andrew   2, 404
Elias, Zdenek   251

Ellison, Herbert J.   92, 107, 320
Ellman, Michael J.   78, 143, 241, 261
Elton, G.R.   6
Elvin, G.H.   432
Ely, Richard T.   304
Emelyanov, A.   268
Enden, M.N. de   40
Entner, M.L.   195
Erlich, Alexander   44-45, 117, 288
Erro, Imogene   428
Evenitsky, Alfred   45
Evenko, I.A.   78, 150
Ewing, David W.   258

F

Faas, Vladimir V.   282
Fainsod, Merle   21
Fairchild, Mildred   31, 390, 422
Fakiolas, R.   384
Falkus, Malcolm E.   107, 163, 198
Fallenbuchl, Z.M.   60, 117, 131, 205, 266
Farbman, Michael S.   78
Farrell, John T.   212, 225
Fearn, Robert M.   173, 403
Federov, A.   241
Feiler, Arthur   21
Feiwel, George R.   21, 79, 320
Felker, Jere L.   242
Feller, Arthur   137
Fennell, J.L.I.   6
Ferguson, A.   301
Ferguson, Alan D.   40
Feshbach, Murray   151, 157, 319, 384, 409
Fetter, Frank W.   223
Field, Mark G.   283-84
Figurnov, S.P.   395
Finegold, I.M.   320
First National City Bank of New York   12
Fischer, Louis   117
Fischer, Ruth   21
Fisher, Alan W.   281
Fisher, Harold H.   231
Fisher, Raymond H.   281, 435
Fisher, Richard B.   228
Fiss, Joan   60

Author Index

Fituni, L.A. 206
Fitzgerald, Edward 35
Fitzgerald, Walter 31
Florinsky, Michael T. 12, 21-22
Fokin, D. 206
Foster, E.D. 206
Foust, Clifford M. 28, 195, 442
Fox, Irving K. 362
Frank, Andrew G. 321, 448
Frank, Z. 79
Frankel, Theodore 260
Frederiksen, D.M. 180
Frederiksen, Oliver J. 196
Freeman, J. Fisher 143, 151
Freeman, Joseph 385
Freidman, Elisha M. 22
Friedmann, C.A. 147
Frolic, B. Michael 436
Fuhrmann, Joseph T. 55
Fullard, Harold 365
Fusfeld, Daniel 17, 72, 93, 158, 183, 184, 242, 245, 278, 378, 427

G

Gabor, Andre 116
Gaenko, F. 385
Gaev, A.G. 321
Galenson, Walter 206, 385-86
Gallik, Daniel 191
Gallik, Dimitri M. 51, 79, 288
Gararin, Grigon 321
Garbutt, Paul E. 270
Garretson, Robert C. 455
Garrison, Mark J. 206
Garvy, George 179, 184
Gay, J.E. 198
Gayster, A. 91
Gehrek, Franz 218
Gekker, Paul 173, 184, 225
Genn, Dan H. 258
Gerashchenko, V.S. 191
Gerasimov, I.P. 363
German, F.C. 366
Gerschenkron, Alexander 2, 5, 12, 13, 40, 109, 111, 118, 151, 155, 207, 231, 242, 288, 291, 304, 321
Gibson, James R. 442

Gibson, Roland 278
Giffen, James H. 207
Giffin, Frederick C. 237, 372
Giffler, Milton 152
Gillette, Philip S. 207
Gindin, Sam 242
Ginsburg, Mina 396
Ginsburgs, George 207
Gisser, Micha 118
Gliksman, Jerzy G. 11, 372
Glovinsky, Evgeny 60, 79, 191, 207, 231
Godaire, J.M. 101
Golay, Frank H. 199, 267
Goldberg, Marilyn P. 421
Golden, Rachel E. 428
Golder, Frank A. 428
Goldman, Marshall I. 22, 45, 118, 137, 148, 152, 207, 231, 242, 281, 288-89, 321, 362, 429
Goldsmith, Raymond W. 110
Goldstein, Joseph M. 7
Goldweiser, Alexis 184
Golov, A. 386
Gol'tsev, Aleksandr 167
Goodman, Ann S. 386, 416
Goodstein, Sylvia 105
Gopal, Surendra 196
Gordijew, I. 246
Gordon, Manya 372
Gorlin, Alice C. 242
Goulivitich, Arsene de 12
Goure, Leon 318
Gourvitch, Alexander 61
Grajdanzev, A. 101-2
Grandstaff, Peter J. 409
Granick, David 23, 130, 173, 177, 243, 259, 289-90
Gray, G.D.B. 367
Greenslade, Rush V. 22, 118, 125, 152, 157
Gregory, James S. 367
Gregory, Paul R. 22, 102, 110, 266
Grekov, B.D. 7
Griffiths, M.R.M. 9
Griffits, Franklyn 260
Grigorian, Leon A. 23
Grinko, Grigorii F. 79, 184
Gromyko, O. 80

Author Index

Gross, Hermann 248
Grossman, Gregory 23, 45, 54, 80, 102, 118-19, 125, 148, 153, 173, 185, 208, 239, 243, 244, 266, 272, 279, 290
Grossman, Philip 321, 386
Grunfeld, Judith 421
Grzybowski, Kazimierz 208
Gsovski, Vladimir 61
Gubkin, I.M. 362
Gubsky, N. 61, 304
Guelfat, Isaac 45-46
Guillebaud, Philomena 259
Guinn, U.K. 409
Guins, George C. 61
Gurevich, S.M. 119
Gurko, Vladimir I. 13
Guroff, Gregory 40
Gutmann, Peter 151, 256

H

Haensel, Paul P. 23, 31, 102, 185
Hahn, Werner G. 322
Hajenko, Fedor 290
Hallaraker, Harold 80
Halvorsen, Kjell M. 215
Hambly, M.V. 448
Hamilton, Alice 417
Hammond, Thomas T. 372
Hankin, R.M. 366
Hansen, Alvin H. 119, 131
Hanson, Philip P. 208, 271, 290, 429
Harcourt, G.C. 260
Hardt, John P. 80, 119, 139, 140, 141, 148, 151, 152, 154, 156, 157, 158, 160, 161, 163, 165, 166, 172, 173, 260, 266, 345
Hardy, Jack 64
Harper, Samuel N. 189
Harris, Chauncy D. 201, 322, 363, 366, 436
Harris, Leon 132
Harris, Seymour E. 153
Harvey, Mose L. 102
Hassmann, Heinrich 290
Hathaway, D.E. 326
Haugland, Anton 290
Havelka, Joseph F. 135

Haxthausen, Baron A. von 7
Hayenko, Fedor 386-87, 417
Haywood, Raichard M. 269
Heckscher, Eli F. 217
Heer, David M. 409
Heiss, Hertha W. 208
Heller, A.A. 120
Hellie, Richard 55
Hemy, Geoffrey 291
Hendel, Samuel 61
Henderson, William O. 7, 107-8
Herman, Leon M. 5, 8, 80, 153, 208, 231, 291, 436
Hermonius, E. 223
Hewes, Amy 387-88
Hewett, Edward A. 429
Heyking, A. Baron 13
Heymann, Hans, Jr. 2, 125, 209, 275
Hindus, Maurice 322
Hinsley, F.H. 13
Hirlekar, K.S. 61
Hirsch, Alcan 23
Hirsch, Hans 81
Hodgkins, Jordon A. 291
Hodgman, Donald R. 126, 153, 154, 177, 185, 291
Hoeffding, Oleg 81, 132, 154, 167, 209, 243
Hoeffding, W. 210
Hoffding, V. 388
Hogarth, C.J. 8
Holbik, Karel 231
Holesovsky, Vaclav 167
Hollister, William W. 200
Holt, Robert T. 23, 114, 278, 345
Holubnychy, Vsevolod 46, 65, 154, 174, 448
Holzman, Franklyn D. 16, 24, 81, 174, 177, 185, 187, 191, 210, 214, 225, 448
Home, R.W. 277
Honigsheim, Paul 322
Hooson, David 449
Hoover, Calvin B. 3, 24, 31, 61, 62
Hopkins, J.A. 272
Horvath, Janos 232
Horwitz, Bertrand N. 243, 260, 322

Author Index

Hough, Jerry F. 322
Hourwich, I.A. 13, 198, 305
Hubbard, Leonard E. 186, 291, 323, 388
Hughes, Francis F. 279
Hulicka, Karel 81
Hultquist, Warren E. 323
Hunter, Holland 81-82, 125, 154, 199, 267, 272-73, 275
Huntingdon, W. Chapin 211
Hurt, B. 13
Hutchings, Raymond F.D. 120, 174, 192, 279, 388
Hutchinson, Lincoln 428
Hutt, W.H. 147

I

Ignatieff, Leonid 55
Industrial Labour Office 389
Inkeles, Alex 132, 388
Ischboldin, Boris 39
Iugov, Aron 24, 82
Ivanov, S.A. 389
Ivanov-Mumjiev 89

J

Jackson, Marvin R. 266
Jackson, William A. Douglas 323, 342, 343, 347, 355, 357, 363, 368
Jacobs, Everett M. 323
Jalnine, V. 389
James, Robert Huhn 103
Jasny, Naum 2, 24-25, 46, 62, 82-83, 84, 120, 143, 154-55, 167-68, 174, 291, 320, 323-25, 342, 347, 363, 389-90
Javits, Benjamin A. 62
Jensen, Robert G. 325, 368
Johansen, Leif 139
Johnson, Albert A. 155
Johnson, Alvin 325
Johnson, D. Gale 16, 25, 325-26
Johnson, E.L. 243
Johnson, William E. 425
Johnston, Charles 180, 198
Jonas, Hans 244
Jonas, Paul 118

Joore, Georges 368
Joravsky, David 327
Judy, Richard W. 139, 260, 356
Jukes, Geoffrey 449
Just, C.F. 198
Juviler, P.H. 118

K

Kabaj, M. 260
Kabysh, Simon 327-28
Kachaturov, T.S. 83
Kachorovsky, K.R. 301
Kadomtsev, Boris 97
Kafengauz, B.B. 282
Kaganovich, L.M. 437
Kahan, Arcadius 7, 25, 108, 189, 196, 282, 326, 328-29
Kalvoda, Josef 329
Kamins, Robert M. 186
Kanet, Roger E. 232
Kantner, John F. 410
Kantorovich, L.V. 77, 96
Kantorovitch, V. 279
Kaplan, Norman M. 16, 83, 120-21, 143, 155-56, 168, 174-75, 267, 273, 390
Karaska, Gerald J. 368
Karcz, Jerzy F. 310, 319, 323, 325, 327, 329-31, 332, 334, 340, 342, 343, 353, 356
Karmiloff, G. 83
Karpov, K. 331
Kasdan, Saul 132
Kaser, Michael C. 25, 46, 83-84, 156, 168, 175, 211, 244
Kashtanov, S.M. 189
Kas'ianenko, Vasilii I. 279
Kasitsky, I. 80
Kasparek, Jiri 211
Kassof, Allen 25, 328, 409
Katharine, Duchess of Atholl, M.P. 390
Katkoff, Vladimir 26, 331-32
Kato, Hiroshi 121, 211
Katz, Abraham 244
Katz, Zev 26
Katzenellenbaum, Sakharii S. 180
Kaufman, Adam 47, 291
Kayden, Eugene M. 181, 425

Author Index

Kazakevich, Vladimir D. 103, 121
Kazanskii, A. 390
Keep, J.L.H. 13, 92
Keizer, Willem 62
Kellman, Mitchell 128
Kennan, George 26
Kennard, Howard P. 305
Kerblay, B.H. 211
Keren, Michael 450
Kerner, Robert J. 103
Kershaw, Joseph A. 103, 121, 132, 332
Khachaturov, T.S. 267
Khrushchev, Nikita S. 26, 62, 121, 260
Kihara, Masao 63
Kim, M.P. 121
Kimball, Warren F. 103
King, Arthur E. 203
King, V. 219
Kingsbury, Susan M. 31, 390, 422
Kirchner, Walter 196, 227, 255
Kirsanov, Sergey 450
Kirsch, Leonard 390
Kirschen, E. 79
Kish, George 368
Kishimoto, Shigenobu 175
Kitagawa, Tokusuke 211
Klages, Walter J. 232
Klatt, Werner 232, 332
Klein, L.R. 127
Klein, Sidney 211
Kluck, Mary van 84
Kluichevsky, V.O. 7-8
Knickerbocker, Hubert R. 84, 212
Knight, Curtis 429
Knight, Frank H. 3
Knightsfield, P.F. 77
Knorr, Klaus E. 233
Kochan, Lionel 5
Kochan, Miriam 8
Kohn, Martin J. 84
Kohn, Stanislav 97
Kokovtsev, Vladimir, Count 193
Kolarz, Walter 450
Kolosovskiy, N.N. 368
Kolpakov, B. 156
Konenko, Konstantyn 442
Korber, Lili 391
Korey, William 47

Koropechyj [Koropeckki] [Koropeckyj], Ivan S. 168, 244, 450
Korsakov, E. 279, 391
Korshunova, E. 422
Koshelev, F.P. 122
Kosiachenko, G. 244
Koslow, Jules 299
Kossov, V.V. 144
Kostin, Leonid 391
Kosygin, Alexei 261
Koutaissoff, Elisabeth 26, 282, 391
Kovach, Robert S. 212
Kovalev, N. 139
Kovner, Milton 212
Kozera, Edward S. 63
Kozmin, P.A. 13
Kraev, M. 333
Kramer, John M. 363
Kraval, I.A. 91
Kravchinskii, Sergei M. (Stepniak) 305
Krengel, Rold 132
Kresl, Peter Karl 47
Krimgold, Dey Ber 363
Kronsjo, Tom 391
Krovis, Irving B. 175
Krueger, Constance B. 314, 318, 333
Krylov, K. 333
Krynski, George I. 261
Krypton, Constantine G. 365, 368, 450
Krzhizhanovski, Gleb Maksimilianovich 43
Kucherov, Samuel 333
Kudrov, V. 168
Kuibyshev, Valerian V. 26, 85, 122
Kumar, Krishna T. 128
Kurskii, Aleksandr D. 85
Kutt, Aleksander 333
Kuvshinov, I.S. 85, 333
Kuznets, Simon 16, 126, 132, 155, 164, 210, 325, 383, 427
Kvasha, Ya 245

L

Labedz, Leopold 27, 68, 437, 439, 455

Author Index

Labsvirs, Janis 334
Lagny, Germaine de 8
Laird, Betty A. 335
Laird, Roy D. 297, 299, 323, 324, 326, 329, 334-36, 342, 343-44, 346, 347, 350, 369, 450
Lalan, M. Yves 122
Lamb, Edward 27
Lambert, Paul 63, 85
Lamet, Stefan 292
Landauer, Carl 47
Landreth, Harry 63
Lange, Oskar 27, 47, 85
Lantsev, M. 417
Lantzeff, George V. 442
Lapidus, Iosif A. 47
Laquerer, Walter 68, 437, 439, 455
Laskovsky, Nikolas 245
Laughlin, J.L. 181
Lavelle, Michael J. 175
Lavrikov, Jurij 437
Lavrishchev, A. 369
Lavrov [Lawrov], V.V. 191, 417
Lawton, Lancelot 27
Leasure, J. William 407
Lebed, Andrei I. 273, 451
Lee, Frederic E. 305
Lee, J. Richard 292
Lee, W.T. 151
Leeman, Wayne A. 245, 261
Leeston, Alfred M. 290
Le Fleming, H.M. 270
Leidy, Frederick A. 410
Leites, Kussiel 27
Lembert, Leo 34
Leont'ev, L.A. 47
Leontief, Wassily 48, 86, 280
Lerner, Warren 28
Leroy-Beaulieu, Anatole 301, 305
Letich, Donald G. 437
Letiche, John M. 39, 48
Levasseur, E. 306
Levin, Alfred 40, 237, 301
Levin, C.C. 237
Levine, Herbert S. 25, 28, 86, 122, 143, 144, 265
Levine, Irving R. 371
Lewin, Moshe 82, 336
Lewis, Robert A. 407

Lewitter, L.R. 256
Liaschenko [Liashchenko] [Liastchenko], Peter I. 5, 8, 336
Liberman, Evsei G. 80, 245-46
Lindquist, Clarence B. 417
Lindsay, Franklin A. 28
Lindsay, J.O. 10
Litoshenko, L.N. 133
Littlepage, John D. 292
Lloyd, T. 14
Lobanov-Rostovsky, A. (Prince) 443
Lodge, N.P. 87
Lokshin, Efraim 122
Lomberg, Doris P. 430
London, Kurt 120, 346
London. University. School of Slavonic and East European Studies 430
Long, Neal B., Jr. 133
Lonsdale, Richard E. 246
Lorimir, Frank 410
Lorwin, Lewis L. 28
Lovell, C.A. Knox 247, 336
Lovestone, Jay 63
Lozovsky, A. 392
Lubell, Harold 212
Lubimtsev, N.A. 86
Lungu, Gh 392
Luxenburg, Norman 336
Lydolph, Paul E. 246, 369
Lyons, Eugene 28

M

MacAndrew, Marie-Christine 95, 253
McAuley, Alastair N.D. 337
McAuley, Mary 392
McConnell, John S. 193
McFarlane, B.J. 131, 246, 267
McGraw, Roderick E. 179
McKay, John P. 228, 256
McKitterick, T.E.M. 212
McMillan, Carl H. 213
Macmillan, David S. 196, 227
McNeal, R.H. 9
McRoberts, Samuel 198
Maddison, Angus 28, 133
Madge, Charles 430
Madison, Bernice 415, 418

Author Index

Maggs, Peter B. 337
Makarov, V.L. 140
Maklakov, V. 306
Male, D.J. 337
Malenkov, G. 29
Malevsky-Malevitch, P. 14, 29
Malish, Anton F., Jr. 213
Mandel, William M. 103, 363
Manevich, Efim 387, 392
Manne, Alan S. 297
Manove, Michael 86
Marer, Paul 193, 213, 225
Markham, James W. 292
Markova, M.G. 435
Markowitz, Harry M. 297
Markowski, Stefan 68
Markus, B.L. 393
Marshak, I.I. 87
Marx, Daniel 155
Maslov, P. 150
Masnata, Albert 63
Mason, Edward S. 242
Mathieson, R.S. 451
Matko, D.J.I. 156
Matveev, Laura 13
Mavor, James 8
May, Ernest 437
Maynard, John 337
Mazour, Anatole G. 29, 122
Mazur, D. Peter 410
Meek, Ronald L. 48, 52
Meisel, James H. 63
Melia, Martin E. 301
Mellor, Roy E.H. 369
Melnyk, Zinowij L. 247, 451
Mendershausen, Horst 210-11, 214
Mequet, G. 437
Merrett, Stephen 247
Mertsalov, V. 337
Metzer, Jacob 270
Meyendorff, Alexander F. 87, 97
Meyer, Alfred G. 64, 455
Miall, Bernard 10
Michael, M.S. 376
Michelson, Alexander M. 190
Mickiewicz, Ellen 156
Mieczkowski, A. 247
Mieczkowski, Z. 451
Mikirtitchian, Levan 451
Miklashevsky, Alex 179

Miletsky, Y. 240
Millar, James R. 123, 314, 318, 319, 322, 330, 337-38, 350, 355, 358
Miller, J. 29
Miller, Jack 261
Miller, Jacob 48, 64, 87-88, 247, 261, 268, 338, 393, 430
Miller, Katherine 140
Miller, Margaret S. 64, 88, 110, 123, 186, 193, 223, 262, 338, 430, 451
Miller, Robert F. 338-39
Millikan, Max 117
Mills, Richard M. 339
Milstein, Jeffrey 103
Minkoff, Jack 393
Minnich, Barbara 175
Mins, H.F., Jr. 48
Mintzes, Joseph 175
Mironenko, Yuri 411
Miroshnichenko, B. 88
Mirski, Michael S. 274
Mirsky, D.S. 9
Mitchell, Earl L. 273
Miyashita, Tadao 133
Modig, Carl 119
Modin, Anatoly 144
Molotov, V.M. 88
Monkhouse, Allan 14
Montgomery, Arthur 49
Montias, J.M. 87, 89, 133, 139, 140, 239
Moore, John H. 157
Moorsteen, Richard 156, 157, 161, 268, 293
Moravcik, Ivo 49, 89, 214
Mordvinov, V. 199
Morissens, L. 79
Morozov, Petr Tarasovich 89
Morrison, Rodney J. 193
Morse, W.E. 306
Morton, G. 77, 140
Morton, H.W. 118
Moskalenko, G.K. 393
Moskoff, William 175, 214, 293, 422, 431
Mosley, P.E. 29
Mote, Max E. 437
Mots, A. 393

467

Author Index

Moulton, Harold G. 104
Mowat, C.L. 26
Mstislavsky, P. 268
Mueller, Charles E. 89
Mueller, F.J. 74
Myers, Robert J. 418

N

Nag, Daga S. 233
Naleszkiewicz, Wladimir
 [Naleszkiewicz, Vladimir] 233,
 418
Nansen, Fridtjof 30
Narkiewicz, Olga A. 90, 247, 339
Nash, Edmund 157, 394, 422
Nash, Edward 431
National Bureau of Economic Research
 157
National Industrial Conference Board
 30
Nazaroff, Alexander 293
Nazartsev, N. 339
Nearing, Scott 64
Neetz, Roger E. 339
Nemchinov, V.S. 80, 90, 96, 139,
 140, 248
Neuberger, Egon 214, 248
Newcomer, Mabel 31
Newth, J.A. 157, 176, 339-40,
 394-95, 411-12, 452
Nicholaevsky, Boris I. 340
Nichols, Russell T. 159
Nikolaevsky, Boris 380
Nimitz, Nancy 168, 340-41, 350,
 357
Niwa, Haruki 121, 123, 176
Noah, Harold J. 49, 418
Nodel', V.A. 293
Nol'de, Boris E. 98
Nonomura, Kazuo 30, 186, 341
Nordman, N. 98
Noren, James H. 90, 123
Norman, Conrad 248
Normano, Joas F. 49
North, Robert N. 452
Novak-Decker, Nikolai 341
Nove, Alec 30, 41, 45, 50, 64,
 77, 82, 84, 87, 90, 123-24, 139,
 149, 158, 169, 176, 184, 194,
 215, 232, 248, 268, 341-44,
 347, 395, 412, 419, 430, 431,
 438, 452
Nove, Irene 73, 336
Novozhilov, V.V. 43, 140
Nuti, D.M. 262
Nutter, G. Warren 95, 124-25,
 134, 160, 161, 253, 395
Nuttonson, M.Y. 369

O

Oberlander, Erwin 14, 111, 309,
 443
Obolensky-Ossinsky, V.O. 91
Obraztsov, V. 274
O'Brien, Carl Bickford 39, 301
Obukhovich, A.P. 395
Ofer, Gur 103, 293
Ogden, D. 7
Ohberg, Arne 196
Ohlin, Bertil G. 217
Oi, Walter Y. 344
Okun', S.B. 227
Oldak, P. 431
Olgin, Constantine 49, 51, 140,
 261
Oliver, James H. 248
Olivia, Lawrence J. 9
Opie, Redvers 64
Oppenheim, Samuel A. 249
Ordzhonikidze, Grigori Konstantinovich 43, 140
Organisation for Economic Cooperation and Development. Directorate for Scientific Affairs 280
Osborn, Robert J. 419
Osipov, B.V. 396
Osofsky, Stephen 344
Ostlund, Lyman E. 215
Ostrovityanov, K. 47, 150
Otuis, Brooks 47
Owen, G.L. 215
Owen, L.A. 306
Oxenfeldt, Alfred 65
Ozerov, Sergey 167

P

Paarlberg, Don 31

Author Index

Page, Stanley W. 41
Painter, Priscilla 273
Palubinskas, Feliksas 249, 293
Paquet, Gilles 91
Pares, Bernard 14, 344
Pardigan, Vladimir 186, 249
Parker, William H. 365
Parkins, Maurice F. 437
Parsons, Steven L. 55
Partigul, S. 119
Pashkov, A.I. 39
Pasvolsky, Leo 65, 104
Paul, Eden and Cedar 24
Pavlovsky, George A. 186, 307
Pearce, Brian 45, 50
Pecker, Boris 249
Pejovich, Svetozar 65
Pereslegin, V.I. 187
Perez, Lorenzo L. 128
Perlo, Victor 167, 361
Pervushin, S.A. 137
Pesek, Boris P. 130
Petersen, William 23
Peterson, Howard C. 125
Pethybridge, R.W. 55, 104
Petrov, Victor P. 412
Petrov, Vladimir 396
Petrov, Vsevolod I. 274
Pettibone, Peter J. 194
Phelps, D.M. 294
Piatakov, A. 396
Pickersgill, Joyce E. 187
Pierce, Richard A. 39, 443
Pigou, A.C. 65
Pintner, Walter M. 171, 189
Plaxico, James S. 326
Ploss, Sidney 344
Pogosov, I. 250
Pokrovsky, M.N. 9
Polakov, Walter N. 262
Polanyi, M. 31
Poliakov, M. 226
Poliakov, V. 250
Popluiko, A. 110
Poplyniko, Anatoli 294
Poplyuyka, Anatoli 126
Popov, P.I. 20
Poppe, Nikolaus 14, 443
Poppelmann, Heinrich 262
Portal, Roger 111, 282

Pospielovsky, Dimitry 345, 372
Postnikov, S.V. 431
Poston, M.M. 302
Potichnyj, Peter J. 396
Powell, David E. 364
Powell, Raymond P. 16, 126, 127, 157, 158, 162, 187, 201, 268, 294, 354
Preece, P.F.W. 91
Preobrazhenskii [Preobrazhensky], Evgenii A. 50, 59
Price, George M. 396
Price, J.H. 270
Price, Morgan P. 444
Prince, Charles 226
Probst, A. 250
Prociuk, Stephan G. 91, 397, 452
Prokopovitch, M. 345
Prokopovich, Sergius 91
Prokopovitch, Sergei N. 31
Pronin, Dimitri T. 351, 363
Prudinskii, G.A. 397
Prybyla, Jan S. 65, 126, 215, 233, 345, 431
Pryor, Frederic L. 215, 216
Pshelyaskovskiy, V.I. 91
Pubantz, Jerry 216
Pushkarev, Sergei G. 9, 307
Putman, George E. 31

Q

Queen, George S. 228-29
Quennell, Peter 8
Quigley, John 216

R

Rabinovich, V.M. 399
Rachkov, B. 216
Radkey, Oliver H. 41
Raeff, Marc 9-10
Raffalovich, Alexis 282
Raffalovich, Arthur 14, 98, 190
Ragozin, Z.A. 301
Raitsin, V.I. 431
Rakitin, G. 397
Rao, Subba 176
Rapawy, Stephen 384
Rashin, A.G. 373

Author Index

Raup, P.M. 24, 162, 345
Raupach, Hans 66, 346
Raymond, E.L. 257
Reddaway, W.B. 187
Redding, David A. 274, 389, 398
Reddy, V.V. 111
Reitz, J.T. 104
Reynolds, Lloyd G. 144, 251, 289
Rice, Stuart A. 158
Rich, E.E. 197
Richman, Barry M. 91, 262-63
Richter, Luba 332, 438
Riha, Thomas 302
Rimlinger, Gaston V. 237, 373, 398, 415
Robbins, Richard G., Jr. 307
Roberts, Benjamin C. 398
Roberts, Henry L. 31-32
Roberts, Paul C. 66, 92
Robertson, Wade E. 152
Robinson, Geriod T. 301
Robinson, Joan 177, 319
Rodin, Nicholas W. 294
Roellinghoff, Wilhelm 432
Rogin, Leo 41
Rolph, Earl 105
Romanov, Oslov and I. 268
Romanowski, Jacek I. 363
Rondall, Francis B. 14
Ronimois, Hans E. 66, 92, 195, 216, 250
Ronin, S.L. 91
Roosa, R.A. 256
Roosa, Ruth A. 56
Ropes, E.C. 158, 216-17
Rosefielde, Steven 213, 217
Rosen, J. 294
Rosen, Seymour M. 419
Rosovsky, Henry 86, 185, 256
Ross, Myron H. 288
Rostow, Walt W. 32, 66, 109
Rothschild, K.W. 177
Rothstein, Andrew 32
Roublev, M. 195
Ruban, M.E. 432
Rubinow, Isaac M. 373
Rubinshtein, G. 217
Ruggles, Melville J. 102
Rushing, Francis W. 261, 294
Russell, E. John 346

Ryapolov, Gregory 263
Ryavec, Karl W. 263
Rybcznski, T.M. 187
Rzhanitsina, L. 432

S

Saller, H. 274
Samuilenko, F. 398
Santalov, A.A. 159
Saushkin, Julian G. 453
Scaperlanda, Anthony E. 250
Schaefer, Henry 81
Schaller, W. Neill 326
Schapiro, Leonard B. 32, 68, 328, 455
Scheffer, Paul 32-33
Schiller, Otto 322, 326, 346, 354
Schinke, Eberhard 158, 162, 347
Schlesinger, Rudolf 50, 92, 336, 347, 399, 419
Schmidt, Hans 438
Scholz, Karl 52, 81
Schroeder, Gertrude E. 92, 148, 158, 250-51, 294, 399-400, 432
Schultz, T. 432
Schurman, Bernard 433
Schuster, Alice 422
Schwartz, Harry vii, 26, 33, 63, 104, 148, 152, 153, 159, 162, 163, 166, 217
Schwarz, Solomon M. 41, 105, 251, 263, 364, 400, 404
Scott, John 400
Scott, N.B.S. 50, 217, 233
Sdobnikov, Y. 7, 435
Segal, Louis 159
Selegen, Galina V. 412
Sellakaerts, Willy 263
Selucky, Radoslav 251
Serck-Hanssen, J. 144
Serge, Victor 400
Sessa, Pietra 420
Seton, Francis 33, 126-27, 168, 169, 176, 201, 412, 455
Severin, Barbara S. 426
Shabad, Theodore 295, 369
Shadrin, Nicholas G. 274
Shaffer, Harry G. 33, 82, 263
Shanin, Teodor 307

Author Index

Sharpe, M.E. 251, 264
Shave, D.W. 367
Sheehy, Ann 251, 401, 449, 453
Sheren, Andrew 105
Sherman, Howard J. 34, 92
Sherman, S. 16
Shimkin, Dimitri B. 34, 257, 295, 347, 364, 412
Shipman, Samuel S. 203
Shkurko, A.S. 401
Shotwell, James T. 21
Shuman, Charles B. 348
Shunkov, V.K. 42
Siegel, Irving H. 401
Silde, Adolf 401
Silin, A. 250
Simmons, Ernest J. 40, 41, 45, 301, 313
Singh, V.B. 19, 111
Sinzheimer, G.P.G. 111
Skeoch, L.A. 433
Skerpan, A. 301
Skilling, Gordon H. 260
Skurski, Roger 295, 433
Sladkovskii, M.I. 195
Slusser, Robert M. 194
Smekhov, B. 80, 88
Smirnov, G. 218, 288
Smith, Edwin S. 401
Smith, Enid 324
Smith, Glen Alden 218
Smith, Robert E.F. 302, 348
Smith, Williard S. 295, 438
Smolinski, Leon 74, 93, 251
Smolka, H.P. 453
Snodgrass, John H. 159
Snow, George E. 373
Soboleva, Galina D. 264
Sokolnikov, Grigory 194
Solecki, J. 295
Solovyov, L. 401
Sonim, M. 402
Sontag, John P. 229
Sorenson, Jay B. 402
Sorlin, Pierre 67
Sosnovy, Timothy 438-39
Spechler, Mortin C. 252
Spring Rice, D. 188
Spulber, Nicolas 1, 3, 34, 52, 121, 127, 133, 134, 200, 206, 218

Stalin, Joseph 35, 43, 48, 50, 93
Staller, George J. 160
Stankiewicz, W.J. 420
Stanley, Emilo J. 402
Starovskii, V.N. 134, 160
Starr, Kenneth M. 218
Stavrou, T. 111
Steele, Rodney E. 194
Stenning, H.J. 21
Sterling, J.E. Wallace 13
Sternberg, Fritz 35
Stevens, H.C. 20
Stokke, B.R. 233
Stolte, Stefan C. 93, 218
Stone, N.I. and M. 82
Strauss, Erich 349
Strausz, David A. 349
Strba, Jan 219
Strong, Anna L. 349, 358
Strumilin, Stanislav Gustavovich 49, 50, 94, 137, 150
Struve, Peter B. 11, 16, 98
Stuart, Robert C. 22, 349-50
Studenski, Paul 169
Sumberg, Theodore 105
Supple, Barry E. 109
Suranyi-Unger, Theo 50
Sutton, Antony C. 280
Swanson, E.R. 312
Swearer, Howard R. 252, 350
Swianiewicz, S. 51, 402, 403
Sykes, Claud W. 391
Symons, Leslie 350
Szawlowski, Richard 219
Szczepanik, Edward 341
Szu-k'ai, C. 219

T

Tabacek, Jan 219
Tahir, Pervez 252
Tanaka, Masaharu 55, 56
Tandon, B.C. 35
Tang, Anthony M. 350
T'ang, L.L. 223
Tansky, Leo 233-34
Tarn, Alexander 134
Tarsaidze, Alexander 269
Tatarinova, N. 422

Author Index

Taubman, William 439
Taylor, Alonzo E. 199
Taylor, George E. 234
Tchayanov, A. 299, 350
Tcherkinsky, M.N. 350
Telepko, L.N. 453
Terada, Yataro 219
Tereshtenko, Valery J. 219, 252
Thalheim, Karl C. 14, 111
Thery, Edmond 110
Thompson, A.B. 296
Thompson, David 11
Thompson, James W. 197
Thorner, D. 315
Thornton, Judith G. 94, 127, 130, 160, 169, 215
Thorpe, Willard L. 127
Thumberg, Penelope H. 220
Ticktin, H.H. 156
Tikhomirov, M.N. 435
Timasheff, Nicholas S. 67, 252, 415
Timoshenko, Stephen P. 415
Timoshenko, Vladimir P. 220, 307, 331, 351
Titelbaum, O.A. 366
Tobias, H.J. 305
Tokmakoff, George 307
Tomashpolsky, P. 403
Tompkins, Stuart R. 111
Totomiantz, V.T. 308
Treadgold, Donald W. 5, 299, 308, 444
Treml, Vladimir G. 35, 51, 139, 144–45, 148, 151, 152, 154, 156, 157, 158, 160, 161, 163, 165, 166, 172, 173, 220, 252, 330, 345, 403
Tretheway, R. 302
Truog, Emil 351
Truu, M.L. 35
Tschebotarioff-Bill, Valentine 56, 255, 256, 257, 269
Tschuprow, A.A. 308
Tuckerman, Gustavus, Jr. 51
Tugan-Baranovsky, Mikhail I. 237
Tugwell, Rexford G. 351
Tullis, James F. 352
Turgeon, Lynn 161, 177, 430, 433
Turin, S.P. 35, 94, 171, 220, 371
Turner, Carl B. 48, 52, 252
Turner, John E. 23, 114, 345

Tuve, Jeanette E. 199
Tverskoi, K.N. 274

U

Ul'ianova, A.F. 390
Union of Soviet Socialist Republics. Committee for International Scientific and Technical Conferences 296
U.S.S.R. Council of Ministers. Central Statistical Board 37
U.S. Bureau of the Census 296
U.S. Central Intelligence Agency 161, 352, 403, 413
U.S. Congress. Joint Economic Committee 36, 135, 161
U.S. Department of Agriculture. Agricultural Research Service 352
U.S. Department of Health, Education and Welfare. Social Security Administration 420
U.S. House of Representatives. Committee on Banking and Currency 234
U.S. Joint Publications Research Service 161, 220
U.S. Library of Congress. Legislative Reference Service 135
Ushakov, Serafim 274
Usoskin, M. 188

V

Valentinov (Volsky), Nikolai 264
Valiliev, A. 197
Vardys, Stanley V. 449
Varga, Eugene 67
Vasilevskii, L.I. 368
Vasudevan, A. 403
Vedishchev, A. 253
Vennard, Edwin 296
Venzher, V.G. 352
Vernadsky, George 6, 302
Vernon, Raymond 221
Veverka, Jindrich 161
Vietorisz, Thomas 297
Villari, Luigi A. 14–15
Vinogradov, Vladimir A. 37
Vladimirov, IU.V. 221
Vogel, Heinrich 433

Author Index

Vogt, Johan 413
Volin, Lazar 11, 94, 105, 302, 308, 353-54
Von Laue, Theodore H. 11, 15, 41, 111-12, 373
Von Loewe, Karl 56
VonNeumann, John 140
Vorobyova, A. 261
Voronitsyn, Sergei 280
Vorontsov, V.P. 56
Voskuil, Walter H. 364
Voznesenski [Voznesensky], Nikolai A. 94, 106
Vucinich, Alexander S. 67, 354-55
Vucinich, Wayne S. 302
Vvedensky, George 95, 128, 297, 355, 364, 454
Vyvyan, J.M.K. 10

W

Wadekin, Karl-Eugen 161, 355-56, 413
Waelbroeck, J. 79
Wainstein, Eleanor S. 174
Walden, M. 253
Walkin, Jacob 373
Wallace, P. 118
Wallace, Phyllis A. 125
Walter, Franz 102
Walters, Ellery 37
Walters, Harry E. 356
Wang, C.L. 403
Ward, Benjamin 139, 141, 374
Ward, Harry F. 67
Ward, Richard J. 221
Ware, Henry H. 177, 297
Ware, Henry W. 356
Watstein, Joseph 221, 234, 257
Weinstein, H.R. 444
Weissbort, D. 67
Weissman, Benjamin M. 234
Weitzman, Martin L. 128
Weitzman, Murray S. 404
Weitzman, Phillip 95
Wellington, Stephen 132
Wesolowski, Zdzislau P. 298
Wesson, Robert G. 67, 356
Westergate, H. 27
Westwood, J.N. 270, 275, 282

Wheatcroft, S.G. 147, 356
White, James D. 56
White, William L. 175
Whitehouse, F. Douglas 90, 135, 322
Whitelaw, John B. 417
Whitman, John 309, 356
Wieczynski, Joseph L. 106, 108
Wieth-Knudsen, K.A. 304
Wilber, Charles K. 128, 131, 357
Wilczynski, Josef 67
Wiles, Peter J.D. 33, 37, 52, 68, 93, 123, 162, 177, 323, 332, 357, 404, 432, 433, 455
Willan, T.S. 197, 227
Willett, Joseph W. 357
Willetts, Harry T. 14, 309
Williams, Albert R. 37
Williams, D.S.M. 309, 444
Williams, Ernest W. 275
Willis, H. Parker 181
Wilson, Edward T. 221
Wilson, J.H. 222
Winner, Irene 357
Winterton, Paul 128
Witt, Lawrence 329
Witte, Sergei 15
Wjunow, Boris 321, 343
Wohlmuth, Karl 268
Wolfe, Bertram D. 52, 309, 374, 405
Wootton, Barbara 95
Wright, George F. 445
Wronski, Henri 357
Wyczalkowski, Marcin R. 226
Wyler, Julius 169, 170

Y

Yakobson, S. 197
Yakovlev, B. 451
Yakovlev, Y.A. 358
Yalowitz, Kenneth 235
Yampolsky, M. 405
Yaney, George L. 309, 358
Yanowitch, Murray 53, 400, 405
Yanson, J.D. 222
Yarmolinsky, Abraham 15
Yasnovskiy, N. 288
Yatsunsky, V.K. 108

Author Index

Yedlin, Tova 9
Yezhov, A. 150
Young, Ian 10
Yugow [Yugov], Aron 106, 162
Yurievsky, E. 112
Yurovsky, Leonid N. 188

Z

Zabijaka, Valentine 222
Zagorskii, S.O. 98
Zaitsev, K.I. 98
Zaitsev [Zaitzoff], Cyril 16, 303, 358
Zalenko, H. 406
Zaleski, Eugene 91, 95, 253
Zatsepilin, V. 406
Zauberman, Alfred 41, 49, 53, 68, 96, 140, 141–42, 145, 169, 253, 455

Zavalani, T. 37
Zawodny, J.K. 406
Zdziechowski, Stanislas 222
Zelnik, Reginald E. 371
Zenkovsky, Serge A. 310
Zevin, L. 235
Zhdanko, T. 128
Zhiltsov, E. 402
Zhimerin, D.G. 37
Zimmerman, L.J. 72
Zinam, Oleg 69, 454
Zinov'ev, Grigorii E. 47
Zoerb, Carl R. 358
Zolotarev, V.I. 222
Zverev, A.G. 253
Zybenko, Roman O. 54, 188, 222, 364, 454

TITLE INDEX

This index includes all titles of books which are cited in the text; journals and titles of articles are not included. In some cases the titles have been shortened.

A

ABC of Communism, The 59
Abundant Peace, The 455
Accounting Controls and the Soviet Economic Reforms of 1966 243
Accounting in Soviet Planning and Management 238
Agricultural Labor Force and Population of the USSR, The 320
Agricultural Russia and the Wheat Problem 351
Agricultural Russia on the Eve of the Revolution 307
Agricultural Workers in the U.S.S.R. 316
Aims and Methods of Soviet Planning 74
Alienation and the Soviet Economy 66
American-Soviet Trade Relations: Past and Future 219
Analysis of Soviet Views on John Maynard Keynes, An 48, 52
Annual Economic Indicators for the U.S.S.R. 161
Application of Mathematics in Economic Investigations 96
Asiatic Russia 445
Aspects of Soviet Economy 58
Association of Industry and Trade, 1906-1914, The 256
Atlas. Volume XIV of the New Cambridge Modern History 365

B

Balance Sheet of Sovietism, The 58
Balans Narodnogo Khozyaistva Soyuza SSR 1923-24 Goda 20
Banks, Credit and Money in Soviet Russia 181
Basic Industrial Prices in the USSR, 1928-1950 171
Basic Industrial Resources of the U.S.S.R. 295
Basic Principles and Experience of Industrial Development Planning in the Soviet Union 86
Basic Principles of the Organization of Soviet Agriculture, The 310
Basis of Soviet Strength, The 19
Bauernfrage und Agrarreform in Russland 304
Beginnings of Railway Development in Russia in the Reign of Nicholas I, 1835-1842, The 269
Beginnings of Russian Industrialization, The 107
Behind the Urals 400

Title Index

Best Use of Economic Resources, The 77
Beyond the Urals 447
Bokaro Steel Plant, The 230
Brief History of Russia 9
Broken Earth 322

C

Can Russia Survive? 59
Capital Investment in the Soviet Union, 1924-51 267
Century of Economic Development of Russia and Japan, A 116
Century of Russian Agriculture, A 308
Challenge of Coexistence, The 212
Challenge of Russia, The 20
Cities of the Soviet Union 436
Collective Farming in Russia 334
Collective Farm in Soviet Agriculture, The 349
Commentaries on the Productive Forces of Russia 6
Commercial Relations between Russia and Europe, 1400 to 1800 196
Commercial Russia 10
Commercial Russia in 1904 13
Commercial Yearbook of the Soviet Union, 1925 159
Communism and the Russian Peasant 318
Communist Economic Strategy 123
Communist Trade in Oil and Gas 287
Comparison of 1950 Wholesale Prices in Soviet and American Industry, A 175
Comparisons of US and Soviet Population and Manpower 413
Comparisons of U.S. and U.S.S.R. Employment in Industry 404
Conflict and Decision-Making in Soviet Russia 344
Conscription of a People 390
Consumer in the Soviet Economy, The 429
Consumers' Cooperation 425
Continuity and Change in Russian and Soviet Thought 41
Control Figures for the Economic Development of the U.S.S.R., 1959-65 121

Cost of the War to Russia, The 97
Course in Russian History, A 7
Critique of Russian Statistics 149
Cumulative Book Index, National Union Catalog, The ix, x
Cumulative Subject Index to the Monthly Catalog of U.S. Government Publications 1900-1971 x
Currency Problems and Policy of the Soviet Union 188
Current Problems of Soviet Agriculture 352
Czarism and Revolution 12

D

Der Weizenbau im Sudwestlichen und Centralen Russland unde Seine Rentabilitat 305
Despised and the Damned, The 299
Development of the Soviet Budgetary System, The 190
Development of the Soviet Economic System, The 15, 20, 60
Development of the Soviet Economy: Plan and Performance, The 35
Dollar Index of Soviet Iron and Steel Output 288
Dollar Index of Soviet Machinery Output, 1927-28 to 1937, A 288, 291
Dynamics of Soviet Society, The 66

E

Early History of the Russian Company, 1553-1603, The 227
Earnings Distribution in the USSR 390
Economic Administration and Labor Productivity on a Soviet State Farm 318
Economic Aspects of Soviet Agriculture 352
Economic Atlas of the Soviet Union 368
Economic Background for the Post-War International Trade of the USSR 220
Economic Backwardness in Historical Perspective 109, 111

Title Index

Economic Calculation of the Best Use of Resources 96, 141
Economic Condition of Soviet Russia, The 31
Economic Development in the Soviet Union 115
Economic Development of Russia 1905-1914, The 110
Economic Development of the Soviet Union (Ali) 112
Economic Development of the Soviet Union (Chakrabarti) 115
Economic Factors in the Growth of Russia, The 5
Economic Geography of the USSR 366
Economic Geography of the USSR (American edition) 366
Economic Geography of the USSR: General Information 369
Economic Growth in Japan and the USSR 133
Economic Handbook of the Soviet Union 147
Economic History of Russia, An 8
Economic History of Soviet Russia, An 27
Economic History of the U.S.S.R., An 30
Economic Life of Soviet Russia 24
Economic Methods and the Effectiveness of Production 245
Economic Organization of the Soviet Union, The 64
Economic Performance and the Military Burden in the Soviet Union 36
Economic Planning in Soviet Russia 74
Economic Policy of Soviet Russia 23
Economic Problems of Socialism in the U.S.S.R. 50
Economic Progress of Russia, 1860-1948, The 109
Economic Rationality and Soviet Politics 30
Economic Reform in the Soviet Union 241
Economic Reforms in Eastern Europe: Political Background and Economic Significance 251
Economic Relations between Peking and Moscow 203
Economics of Agriculture, The 310
Economics of Communism, The 65
Economics of Education in the U.S.S.R., The 418
Economics of Slave Labor, The 380
Economics of Socialism, The 67
Economics of Soviet Agriculture, The 323
Economics of Soviet Merchant Shipping Policy, The 270
Economics of Soviet Oil and Gas, The 285
Economics of Soviet Planning, The 73
Economics of Soviet Steel, The 102, 285
Economics of the Russian Village, The 305
Economics of the Soviet Wheat Industry, The 311
Economic Strength of the Soviet Union, The 132
Economic Systems in Action 65
Economic Thought in the Soviet Union 45
Economic Trends in Soviet Russia 24
Economic Trends in the Soviet Union 16
L'economie Sovietique 152
Economy, Management, Planning 21
Economy of the Soviet Union, Past and Present 37
Economy of the U.S.S.R., The 25
Economy of the USSR during World War II 106
Economy, Society, and Welfare 58
Education and Professional Employment in the USSR 380
Ekonomicheskii Raschot Nailuchahego Ispolzovania Resorsov 77, 96
Emergence of Modern Russia, 1801-1917, The 9
Empire of the Tsars and the Russians, The 301
Employment and Unemployment in Pre-War and Soviet Russia 390
Employment and Unemployment in the Soviet Union 382
End of a Revolution, The 35
End of Rationing and the Standard of Living in the Soviet Union, The 430

Title Index

End of the Russian Empire, The 12
Enserfment and Military Change in Muscovy 55
Enserfment of the Russian Peasantry, The 302
Essays in European Economic History, 1789-1914 137
Essays on Soviet Economy 30
Essays on the Soviet Economy 24
Estimates and Projections of Specialized Manpower in the U.S.S.R. 386
Europe in the Russian Mirror: Four Lectures in Economic History 12
Evaluation of the Program for Reducing the Work-Week in the USSR, An 403
Evaluation of the Soviet Profit Reforms, An 316
Experiment of Bolshevism, The 21

F

Factory and Manager in the USSR 257
Factory, Family and Women in the Soviet Union 422
Family Planning and Abortion in the Socialist Countries of Central and Eastern Europe 409
Famine in Soviet Russia, 1919-1923 231
Farm Employment in the Soviet Union 341
Features and Figures of the Past 13
Fiat-Soviet Auto Plant and Communist Economic Reforms, The 234
Finance and Credit 187
Financial and Economic Results of the Working of the Lena Goldfields Co., Ltd., The 284
Financial Program of the U.S.S.R. for 1936 184
Five-Year Plan for the Rehabilitation of the National Economy of the USSR, 1946-50 94
Five-Year Plan of the Soviet Union, The 79
Food Supply in Russia during the World War 98
Forced Labor in Soviet Russia 380
Forced Labour and Economic Development 402, 403

Force Versus Food 312
Foreign Economic Policy of Soviet Russia 233
Foreign Trade Criteria in Socialist Economies 202
Foreign Trade in the U.S.S.R. 222
Foreign Trade of the U.S.S.R. 199
Foreign Trade of the USSR, 1957 220
Foreign Trade of the USSR, 1958 220
Forest Economy in the U.S.S.R. 283
Forest Resources of the USSR and the World 361
Forgotten Class, The 255
Formation of the Russian Working Class, The 373
Formirovanie Rabochego Klassa Rossii 373
Forty Years of Soviet Power in Facts and Figures 37
Foundation of Soviet Strategy for Economic Growth 127
Foundations of a Planned Economy, 1926-1929 18
Freight Transportation in the Soviet Union 275
From Peter the Great to Lenin 371
From the First to the Second Five-Year Plan 35, 79
Fulfilment of the First Five Year Plan, The 88
Fundamentals of Economic Planning 89

G

Geography of the USSR 369
Geography of the USSR, A (1961) 366
Geography of the USSR, A (1970) 366
Geography of the USSR: A Regional Survey 369
Governing Soviet Cities 439
Great Retreat, The 67
Great Siberian Migration, The 444
Growth of Industrial Production in the Soviet Union, The 125, 161
Growth of Soviet Economic Power and Its Consequence for Canada and the United States, The 28

Title Index

Guide to the Great-Siberian Railway 443

H

Handbook of Siberia and Arctic Russia, A 365
Handbook of Soviet Social Science Data 156
Handbook on the Soviet Trade Unions 392
Hearings on Dimensions of Soviet Economic Power 36
Hearings on Soviet Economic Outlook 36
Historical Geography of Russia, An 365
Historical Materialism 43
History of a Collective Farm, The 313
History of Economic Relations between Russia and China 195
History of Russia, A (Kluichevsky) 8
History of Russia, A (Vernadsky) 6
History of Russia, from the Earliest Times to the Rise of Commercial Capitalism 9
History of Russian Economic Thought, A 39
History of Russian Railways, A 270
History of the National Economy of Russia to the 1917 Revolution 5, 8
History of the National Economy of the USSR 5
History of the Russian Non-Marxian Social-Economic Thought 39
Hop Industry of Eastern Europe and the Soviet Union, The 349
How Russia is Ruled 21
How Strong is Russia? 37
How Strong is Russia? A Geographic Appraisal 367
How the Soviet Economy Won Technical Independence 279
How the Soviet System Works 58
Human Life in Russia 15

I

Imperialism and World Economy 47
Imperial Russia 1682-1825 9
Indexes of Soviet Industrial Output 156
Index of Civilian Industrial Production in the USSR, 1950-1961 161
Index of Economic Articles x
India's Economic Relations with the USSR and Eastern Europe, 1953-1969 230
Indices of Soviet Industrial Production, 1928-1954 154
Industrial Development under the Second Five-Year Plan 122
Industrialization of Russia, The 108
Industrialization of Russia, 1700-1914, The 107
Industrialization of Soviet Russia in the First Half Century, The 119
Industrialized Russia 23
Industrial Management in the USSR 257
Industrial Output of the Ukraine, The 448
Industrial Revival in Soviet Russia, The 120
Industrial Revolution in Europe, 1815-1914, The 107
Industrial Revolution on the Continent, The 7, 108
Industrial Russia: The New Competitor 30
Industrial Workers in the USSR 379
Industries of Russia, The 11
Industry and Labour in the U.S.S.R. 396
Industry in the U.S.S.R. 122
In Place of Profit 67
Input-Output and Soviet Planning 143
In Search of Soviet Gold 292
In the Land of Communist Dictatorship 374
Istoriya Khoziaistva Demidovykh V XVIII-XIX vv 282
Istoriya Narodnogo Khozyaystva SSSR 5

K

Kievan Russia 302

Title Index

Kiev Rus 7
Knout and the Russian, The 8
Kratkaia Geograficheskaia Entsiklopediia 368
Krestiane na Rusi i Drevneishikh Vremen do XVII Veka 300
Krushchev's Crop Policy 324

L

Labor and Society in Tsarist Russia 371
Labor in the Soviet Union 400
Labor Productivity in Soviet and American Industry 385
Labor Protection in Soviet Russia 396
Labor Supply and Employment in the USSR, 1950-65 386
Labor Supply and Employment in the USSR: 1950-70 403
Labour Conditions in Soviet Russia 389
Labour Disputes in Soviet Russia, 1957-65 392
Land of Socialism Today and Tomorrow, The 27
Large Economic Regions of the USSR 453
Law of Value and Soviet Economic Planning, The 83
Legal and Practical Aspects of Trade with the Soviet Union, The 207
Leon Trotsky and the Politics of Economic Isolation 19
Life and Death of Soviet Trade Unionism 402
Life in a Soviet Factory 391
Life in Russia under Catherine the Great 8
Liquor Problem in Russia, The 425
Lord and Peasant in Russia, from the Ninth to the Nineteenth Century 300

M

Machines and Men in Russia 117
Magnitude and Distribution of Civilian Employment in the U.S.S.R., The 404
Making of Modern Russia, The 5

Making of the Soviet State Apparatus, The 247
Management Development and Education in the Soviet Union 262
Management in Russian Industry and Agriculture 258
Management of the Industrial Firm in the USSR 259
Managerial Comparisons of Four Developed Countries 259
Managerial Power and Soviet Politics 257
Man and Plan in Soviet Economy 32
Man Versus Systems 310
Marx and Agriculture 316
Materials for the Study of the Soviet System 63
Mathematics and Computers in Soviet Economic Planning 139
Measures of Agricultural Employment in the U.S.S.R. 317
Memoirs of Count Witte, The 15
Minerals: A Key to Soviet Power 364
Modernization of Soviet Central Asia 445
Modern Russia 10
Moscow, 1911-1933 14
Most Unsordid Act, The 103
Muscovite and Mandarin 195
Muscovy Merchants of 1555, The 227

N

Narodnoye Khoziaistvo SSSR 148, 159, 176
National Economic Planning in USSR 78
National Economy of the USSR, The 149
National Economy of the USSR in 1960, The 161
Natural Resources and International Development 364
Natural Resources of the Soviet Union 363
Natural Wealth of the Soviet Union and Its Exploitation 362

Title Index

Nature and Structure of Soviet Agriculture, The 323
Net Cost of Soviet Foreign Aid, The 230
New Currents in Soviet-Type Economies 21
New Directions in the Soviet Economy 36
New Economic Policy, The 71
New Economics, The 45, 46, 50
New Economic Upswing of the U.S.S.R. in the Post-War Five-Year Plan Period, The 119
New Russia 19
New Russia's Primer 87
New Worker in Soviet Russia, The 371
Northern Sea Route, Its Place in Russian Economic History before 1917, The 365
Northern Sea Route and the Economy of the Soviet North, The 368

O

Oil and the Persian Gulf in Soviet Policy in the 1970's 201
Oil Fields of Russia and the Russian Petroleum Industry 296
Oil in the Soviet Union 290
Old Ukraine 441
One Hundred Thousand Tractors 339
On the Further Improvement of Management in Industry and Construction in the U.S.S.R. 260
On the Trail of the Russian Famine 428
Organized Labor in the Soviet Union 401
Origin of Forced Labor in the Soviet State, The 378
Origins of Capitalism in Russia, The 55
Osnovy Ekonomicheskogo Rayonirovaniya 368
L'oural ua XVIII Siecle 282
Outline of Political Economy, An 47

P

Papers on Capitalism, Development, and Planning 60
Peace Problems 98
Peasant Farm Organization 315
Peasant in Nineteenth-Century Russia, The 302
Peasants in Russia from Earliest Times to the XVIIth Century 300
Peasants of Central Russia, The 300
Perehod ot Feodalizma k Kapitalizmu v Rossii: Materialy Vsesoiuznoi Diskusii 42
Petroleum Industry of the Soviet Union, The 287
Piatiletka: Russia's 5-Year Plan 78
Pioneers for Profit 256
Planification de la Croissance et Fluctuations Economiques en U.R.S.S. 91
Planned Economy 72
Planned Economy in Soviet Russia, The 27
Planning and Productivity under Soviet Socialism 129
Planning and the Market in the USSR 72
Planning for Economic Growth in the Soviet Union, 1918-1932 95
Planning in the Soviet Union (Bernard) 73
Planning in the Soviet Union (Strumilin) 94
Planning in the U.S.S.R. 78
Planning of the National Economy of the U.S.S.R., The 85
Planning, Profit and Incentives in the USSR (vol. 1) 251
Planning, Profit and Incentives in the USSR (vol. 2) 264
Planning Reforms in the Soviet Union, 1962-1966 253
Planning the Standard of Living According to Consumption Norms 431
Plan or No Plan 95
Planovoye Khozyaistvo 72
Political Economy; Textbook 50

Title Index

Political Economy of Communism, The 68
Politics of Economic Reform in the Soviet Union, The 244
Politics of Soviet Agriculture, 1960-70, The 322
Population Change in Russia and the USSR 407
Population of the Soviet Union, The 409
Population of the Soviet Union: History and Prospects, The 410
Postwar Outlook for Russian Industry, The 93
Predictions of Communist Economic Performance, The 37
Prices and Production of Machinery in the Soviet Union 1928-1958 161, 293
Primeneniye Matematiki v Ekonomicheskikh Issledovaniyakh 96
Principles of Economic Regionalization 368
Private Sector in Soviet Agriculture, The 355
Production, Accumulation, and Consumption 31
Productivity in Soviet Iron Mining 1890-1960 294
Profits of Slavery, The 401
Progress in the Soviet Union: Past, Present, Future 155
Proizvodstvo, Nakoplenie, Potreblenie 352
Projections of the Population of the U.S.S.R. 408
Prospects for Soviet Economic Growth in the 1970's 122
Prospects for Soviet Society 25

Q

Quality Planning and Price Planning in the Soviet Union 81

R

Readings on the Soviet Economy 24
Real National Income of Soviet Russia since 1928, The 164, 166, 169

Real'naya Zarabotnaya Plats i Podyon Material'novo Blagosostayania Trudyashchikhsya v SSR 395
Real Wages and the Raising of Material Welfare of the Working People in the USSR 395
Real Wages in the Soviet Union since 1928 379
Recent Developments in Soviet Agriculture 352
Recent Economic Developments in Russia 27
Recent Trends in Soviet Trade 209
Record of Soviet Economic Growth, 1928-1965, The 120
Red Economics 60
Red Executive, The 259
Red Phoenix, The 33
Red Villages 358
Regional Distribution of Soviet Industrial Manpower 402
Report to the Nineteenth Party Congress on the Work of the Central Committee of the C.P.S.U. 29
Reprint of Articles Dealing with Russian Trade 198
Results of the Struggle for the Technical Reconstruction of National Economy 26
Retail Prices of Manufactured Consumer Goods in the USSR, 1937-1948 173
Rise and Fall of the MTS as an Instrument of Soviet Rule, The 336
Rise of the Russian Consumer 430
Road Divides--Economic Aspects of the Sino-Soviet Dispute, The 211
Roads to Russia, The 103
Ruble Diplomacy 233
Rural Russia under the Old Regime 301
Russia 198
Russia: A Consideration of Conditions as Revealed by Soviet Publications 32
Russia: A Handbook on Commercial and Industrial Conditions 159
Russia: Between Reform and Revolution 14
Russia: Its Trade and Commerce 14

Title Index

Russia after Ten Years 32
Russia and Her Colonies 450
Russia and Peace 30
Russia and the Imperial Russian Government 12
Russia Enters the Twentieth Century 14
Russia, Her Economic Past and Future 7
Russia in the Economic War 98
Russia in the Era of Peter the Great 9
Russia in Transition 22
Russian Affairs 11
Russian Agriculture: A Geographic Survey 350
Russian-American Company, The 227
Russian-American Trade, a Study of the Soviet Foreign-Trade Monopoly 204
Russian Central Asia 1867-1917 443
Russian Collapse, The 97
Russian Cooperative Movement 305
Russian Currency and Banking, 1914-24 180
Russian Debts and Russian Reconstruction 104
Russian Economic Development since the Revolution 20
Russian Economic Policy in Eastern Europe: Albania, Bulgaria, Czechoslovakia, Hungary, Jugoslavia, Poland, Roumania and Austria 212
Russian Economy, The 35
Russian Empire, Its People, Institutions and Resources, The 7
Russian Factory in the 19th Century 237
Russian Financial System, The 187
Russian Fur Trade 1550-1700 281
Russian Peasant 305
Russian Peasant, The 305
Russian Peasant Movement, 1906-1917, The 306
Russian Peasant Organization before Collectivization 337
Russian Peasantry: Their Agrarian Condition, Social Life, and Religion, The 305
Russian Peasants and Soviet Power 336

Russian Police Trade Unionism 372
Russian Railways, The 270
Russian Realities and Problems 11
Russian Steam Locomotives 270
Russian Workers' Republic 17
Russia, Past and Present 29
Russia's Decisive Year 37
Russia's Economic Front for War and Peace 82
Russia's Export Trade in Timber and the Importance of the Forests of North European Russia 282
Russia's Foreign Trade and the Baltic Sea 195
Russia's Iron Age 18
Russia's Post-War Economy 104
Russia's Productive System 18
Russia's Soviet Economy ix, 33
Russia Twenty Years After 400
Russia under Soviet Rule 58
Russia under the Great Shadow 14
Russia-U.S.S.R. 14
Russo-Persian Commercial Relations, 1828-1914 195

S

Science Policy in the USSR 280
Seasonal Influences in Soviet Industry 120
Second Five-Year Plan 88
Second Five-Year Plan, The 85
Second Five-Year Plan of Development of the U.S.S.R. 75
Selected Comparisons of the Financial Systems of the USSR, Czechoslovakia, Hungary and Poland 193
Sergei Witte and the Industrialization of Russia 112
Service Sector in Soviet Economic Growth, The 293
Seven Years in Soviet Russia 32
Short Geographic Encyclopedia 368
Siberia 444
Siberia and the Pacific 447
Siberia in the Seventeenth Century 442
Sino-Soviet Economic Relations 209
Small-Scale Industry in the Soviet Union 291

Title Index

Social Change in Soviet Russia 388
Social Economic Planning in the Union of Soviet Socialist Republics 91
Socialist Property 37
Socialist Reconstruction of Moscow and Other Cities in the U.S.S.R. 437
Socialized Agriculture of the USSR, The 320, 321, 325, 342
Social Welfare in the Soviet Union 418
Society and Economic Relations 57
Some Problems of Incentives and Labour Productivity in Soviet Industry 375
Soviet Agricultural Program, The 326
Soviet Agricultural Trade Unions, 1917-70 396
Soviet Agriculture 311
Soviet Agriculture: The Permanent Crisis 335
Soviet Agriculture and Peasant Affairs 335
Soviet Agriculture in Perspective 349
Soviet Agriculture since Khrushchev 318
Soviet and Eastern European Trade and Aid to Africa 233
Soviet and East European Foreign Trade, 1946-1969 213
Soviet Asia 441
Soviet Capital Formation 451
Soviet Capital Stock, 1928-1962, The 157, 268
Soviet Challenge to America, The 19
Soviet Chemical Industry, The 291
Soviet Colonialism 202
Soviet Communes 67
Soviet Communism: A New Civilization? 64, 65
Soviet Communism and Agrarian Revolution 335
Soviet Crucible, The 61
Soviet Economic Aid: The New Aid and Trade Policy in Underdeveloped Countries 229
Soviet Economic Controversies 242
Soviet Economic Development 120
Soviet Economic Development: Operation Outstrip, 1921-1965 122
Soviet Economic Development and American Business 114
Soviet Economic Development since 1917 19, 117
Soviet Economic Facts 1917-1970 150
Soviet Economic Growth: A Comparison with the United States 135
Soviet Economic Growth: Conditions and Perspectives 114, 120
Soviet Economic Institutions 67
Soviet Economic Intentions 77
Soviet Economic Performance: 1966-1967 36
Soviet Economic Policy: Early Years 73
Soviet Economic Policy in the East: Turkey, Persia, Afghanistan, Mongolia and Tana Tuva 204
Soviet Economic Power (1st and 2d ed.) 18
Soviet Economic Processes 15
Soviet Economic Prospects for the Seventies 36
Soviet Economic Reform: Progress and Problems 252
Soviet Economics 25
Soviet Economic Statistics 160
Soviet Economic Structure and Performance 22
Soviet Economic Warfare 99
Soviet Economists of the Twenties 46
Soviet Economy, The 34
Soviet Economy; a Book of Readings, The 17
Soviet Economy: A Collection of Western and Soviet Views, The 33
Soviet Economy: An Introduction, The 30
Soviet Economy: Myth and Reality, The 22
Soviet Economy: Structure, Principles, Problems, The 34
Soviet Economy and the War 101
Soviet Economy during the Plan Era, The 24, 168
Soviet Economy during the Second World War 105
Soviet Economy 1940-1965 26
Soviet Economy, 1954-58, The ix

Title Index

Soviet Economy since Stalin, The 33
Soviet Economy Today and Tomorrow (Facts and Figures) 34
Soviet Experiment 58
Soviet Financial System 188
Soviet Financial System, The 191
Soviet Financial System; Its Development and Relations with the Western World 183
Soviet Financial System; What It Is and How It Works 182
Soviet Five-Year Plan and Its Effect on World Trade, The 84
Soviet Foreign Aid 231
Soviet Foreign Trade (Budish and Shipman) 203
Soviet Foreign Trade (Baykov) 201
Soviet Foreign Trade: Organization, Operations, and Policy, 1918-1971 218
Soviet Gold; My Life as a Slave Laborer in the Siberian Mines 396
Soviet Government Grain Procurements, Dispositions, and Stocks, 1945-1963 341
Soviet Industrialization Debate, 1924-1928 45
Soviet Industrialization, 1928-1952 25, 84
Soviet Industrial Production, 1928-1951 153, 154
Soviet Industry (Efimov) 117
Soviet Industry (Koshelev) 122
Soviet Industry (Lokshin) 122
Soviet Institutions and Policies 15
Soviet International Trade in Heckscher-Ohlin Perspective 217
Soviet Labor and Industry 388
Soviet Land: The Country, Its People and Their Work 367
Soviet Logging Industry, The 296
Soviet Management--with Significant American Comparisons 263
Soviet Marketing; Distribution in a Controlled Economy 289
Soviet Metal-Fabricating and Economic Development 290
Soviet Middle East, The 452
Soviet Military Outlays since 1955 99

Soviet Minerals-Fuels Industries, 1928-1958, The 295
Soviet Money and Finance 186
Soviet National Income and Product in 1928 167
Soviet National Income and Product in 1937 165
Soviet National Income and Product in 1965 164
Soviet National Income and Production in 1928 154
Soviet National Income and Product, 1940-48 165
Soviet National Income and Product, 1956-1958 168
Soviet National Income and Product, 1958-62, pts. 1 and 2 164
Soviet National Income 1958-1964 164
Soviet 1956 Statistical Handbook, The 155
Soviet Oil Offensive and Inter-Bloc Economic Competition, The 212
Soviet People and Their Society, from 1917 to the Present, The 67
Soviet Planned Economic Order 75
Soviet Planning: Essays in Honour of Naum Jasny 77
Soviet Planning and Economic Theory 92
Soviet Planning and Labour in Peace and War 101
Soviet Planning and Spatial Efficiency 283
Soviet Planning Today; Proposals for an Optimally Functioning Economic System 78
Soviet Policy in Public Finance 1917-1928 194
Soviet Potentials 367
Soviet Power: Energy Resources, Production and Potentials 291
Soviet Practice in the Classification of Economic Activity 2
Soviet Prices of Producers' Goods 168, 174
Soviet Price System, The 168, 174
Soviet Professional Manpower 380, 381, 391

Title Index

Soviet Quest for Economic Efficiency, The 241
Soviet Quest for Economic Rationality, The 62
Soviet Railways Today 275
Soviet Rural Community, The 338
Soviet Russia: An Introduction 29
Soviet Russia: Legal and Economic Conditions of Industrial and Commercial Activity in Soviet Russia 34
Soviet Russia, 1917-1936 59
Soviet Russia, the Secret of Her Successes 61
Soviets, The 37
Soviets Conquer Wheat, The 349
Soviet Seven-Year Plan, 1959-1965 93
Soviet Social Policies: Welfare, Equality and Community 419
Soviet Society (Economic and Social Structure) 23
Soviet State Planning and Forced Industrialization as a Model for Asia 132
Soviet Statistical System: Labor Force Recordkeeping and Reporting, The 151
Soviet Statistical System: Labor Force Recordkeeping and Reporting since 1957, The 151
Soviet Statistical System: The Continuous Sample Budget Survey, The 150
Soviet Statistics of Physical Output of Industrial Commodities 153
Soviet Strategy for Economic Growth 34
Soviet Taxation 192
Soviet Trade 149
Soviet Trade and Distribution 291
Soviet Trade from the Pacific to the Levant 204
Soviet Trade Unions (Deutscher) 380
Soviet Trade Unions (Dunn) 382
Soviet Trade Unions and Labor Relations 378
Soviet Trade with Eastern Europe, 1945-1949 204

Soviet Transport: Rail, Air, and Water 274
Soviet Transport and Communications 273
Soviet Transportation Experience 272
Soviet-Type Economies, The 18
Soviet Union, The 26
Soviet Union--Paradox and Change 23
Soviet Union and International Economic Cooperation 206
Soviet Union in Asia, The 449
Soviet Union, the Land and Its People, The 368
Soviet Union Today, The 29
Soviet Union Year-Book, 1930 159
Soviet Wages: Changes in Structure and Administration since 1956 390
Soviet Worker; an Account of the Economic, Social, and Cultural Status of Labor in the U.S.S.R., The 385
Soviet Worker; Labor and Government in Soviet Society, The 376
Spirit of Russian Economics, The 49
Spoils of Progress, The 362
Stages of Economic Growth, The 109
State Bank of the U.S.S.R., The 188
State Control of Industry in Russia during the War 98
State of the Soviet Union, The 35
State Planning; Aims, Ways, Results 78
Statistical Abstract of Industrial Output in the Soviet Union, 1913-1955 157
Statistical Handbook of the U.S.S.R. 159
Structure of Soviet Wages 376
Structure of the Soviet Economy, The 145
Studies of Dimensions of Soviet Economic Power 36
Study of the Soviet Economy 34
Success of the Five-Year Plan 88
Supply and Trade in the U.S.S.R. 293
Survey of Soviet Russian Agriculture, A 354
System of Taxation in Soviet Russia, The 193

Title Index

T

Tasks of the Second Five-Year Plan 88
Tentative Input-Output Table for the USSR, A 143
Ten Years of Bolshevic Domination 16
Theory of Peasant Economy, The 315
Theory of Profit in Socialist Economy 246
34th Anniversary of the Great October Socialist Revolution, The 16
Towards an Understanding of the U.S.S.R. 22
Towns of Ancient Russia, The 435
Trade Union Movement in Soviet Russia, The 389
Trade Unions and Industrial Relations in the Soviet Union 398
Trade Unions and Labor in the Soviet Union 387
La Transformation Economique de la Russie 110
Transformation of Russian Society, The 11
Transition from Feudalism to Capitalism in Russia: Materials from the All-Union Discussion 42
Transport Development and Locomotive Technology in the Soviet Union 271
Transport in the USSR 274
Trends in Economic Growth: Comparison 135
Two Systems 67

U

Ukraine and Russia 442
Ukrainian Economy, The 446
Unemployment in the Soviet Union: Fact or Fiction? 403
Unified Transport System of the U.S.S.R., The 274
United States and the Soviet Union, The 203
U.S. and U.S.S.R. Aid to Developing Countries 234
U.S. Social Security Mission to the Union of Soviet Socialist Republics, The 420
United States, the Soviet Union and the Third World, The 231
U.S.S.R.: A Geographical Survey, The 367
U.S.S.R.: An Economic and Social Survey, The 35
U.S.S.R. and the Future, The 32
USSR and the West as Markets for Primary Products, The 215
U.S.S.R. Economy, The 149
U.S.S.R. Economy and the War 103
USSR Industry 149
USSR, Transport and Communications 271
Use of Mathematics in Economics, The 139

V

Vacillations in the Organization of Soviet Agriculture 352
Varieties of Economic Secrecy in the Soviet Union 153
Village Life under the Soviets 313

W

Wages in the USSR, 1950-1966 378
Wages, Prices and Social Legislation in the Soviet Union 376
Was Stalin Really Necessary? 124
Water Resources Law and Policy in the Soviet Union 362
Ways to Increase National Well-Being 431
Welfare Policy and Industrialization in Europe, America, and Russia 415
Western Technology and Soviet Economic Development: 1917 to 1930 280
Western Technology and Soviet Economic Development: 1930-1945 280
Women in the Soviet Economy--Their Role in Economic, Scientific, and Technical Development 421
Work and Authority in Industry 255
Workers before and after Lenin 372
Workers' Paradise Lost 28
Working Principles of the Soviet Economy, The 27

SUBJECT INDEX

This index is alphabetized letter by letter. Underlined page numbers refer to main areas within the subject.

A

Abortion 409
Absenteeism (labor) 384
Academic freedom 48
Academy of Science 280
Accounting practices 22, 243, 249
   in agriculture 345-46
   mechanization of 239
   in national income determination 163, 164, 166, 169, 170
   in planning and management 238, 239
   in statistic gathering 150
   See also Amortization; Bookkeeping; Cost accounting; Financial statements
Act Governing Inventions and Technical Improvements (1941) 279
Administration, economic. See Economic organization and administration
Advertising 292
Aepinus, F.U.T. 277
Afghanistan
   Russian aid to 229
   trade with Russia 204
Africa, Russian aid to 232, 233. See also Underdeveloped countries
Agricultural Bank 331

Agricultural cooperatives. See Cooperatives
Agricultural economics 299, 312, 350
Agricultural education 312, 316
Agricultural geography 350, 365, 366, 367, 368, 369
Agricultural labor 305, 316, 318, 320, 321, 326, 329, 331, 332, 344, 348-49, 350, 353, 376, 382, 389, 393
   hours of labor 333, 339
   productivity of 314, 324, 325, 346
   social security for 417
   statistics 158, 317, 340, 341, 345
   supply of 314
   training of 312
   wages and income 310, 324, 328, 335, 352, 382, 404
   women as 319
Agricultural laws 337, 348
Agricultural machinery and implements 302, 311, 315, 319, 327, 328, 333. See also Tractors
Agricultural machinery industry 84, 105, 292, 352. See also Kharkov Tractor Factory
Agricultural prices 172-73, 174, 176, 314, 315, 326, 328,

Subject Index

    330, 331, 339, 341, 343,
    345-46, 349, 351-52
Agricultural products. See Farm
    products
Agriculture 299
  by subject
    business cycles and 137
    commerce and 348, 351-52,
      354
    comparisons with the U.S. 132,
      134, 135
    costs of production in 341, 343
    credit in 303, 310
    diversification of 128
    finance and investment in 78,
      310, 314-15, 324, 326,
      328, 331, 337-38, 339-40,
      343, 348, 353
    incentives in 73
    national planning in 71, 72,
      73, 74, 75, 77, 78, 79,
      82, 84, 85, 89, 91, 93,
      94, 118, 310
    politics of 322, 325, 334-35,
      342, 345
    private economic activity in
      64, 317, 326, 327, 328,
      336, 340, 343, 344, 346,
      355
    research 323, 350
    and socialist theory 41, 58
    statistics 147, 155, 156,
      157, 158, 161, 162, 167,
      300, 306, 324, 343, 448
    technology in 128, 316, 326,
      335
    World War II and 104, 105
  by time period
    to 1860 7, 8, 9, 10, <u>299-
      303</u>
    1860-1917 10, 11, 12, 13,
      14, 40, 41, 223, 256-57,
      <u>303-10</u>
    after 1917 15, 16, 18, 20-
      21, 22, 23, 24, 25, 26,
      27, 28, 29, 30, 32, 33,
      34, 35, 36, 37, 58, 59,
      60, 62, 64, 65, 71, 72,
      73, 74, 75, 77, 78, 79,
      82, 84, 85, 89, 91, 93,

    94, 104, 105, 110, 113,
    117, 118, 119, 120, 123,
    127, 128, 132, 134, 135,
    147, 155, 156, 157, 158,
    161, 162, 167, 247, 287,
    <u>310-59</u>, 446, 448, 453
  See also Agronomy; Animal hus-
    bandry; Collectivism; Farm
    management; Farm products;
    Gardens; Kolkhozes; Rota-
    tion of crops; Sovkhozes;
    State farms
Agronomy 6, 321, 324, 335, 341,
    351, 369
Air pollution. See Pollution and
    pollution control
Air transport 274, 454
  routes 368
  statistics 271
Albania, trade with Russia 207,
    212
Alcohol. See Liquor industry
Allied Social Science Association
    446
Allocation of resources and materials
    18, 43, 52, 65, 66, 72,
    80, 92, 94, 96, 115, 241,
    <u>265-68</u>, 328, 362, 364
All-Russian Co-operative Bank 181
All-Union Trade Congress (10th) 376,
    418
Aluminum industry and trade 297
American Relief Mission 231, 234
Amortization 53
Amtorg Trading Corp. 203, 217
Amu-Dar'ya Basin 453
Angarstroy Hydrotechnical Project 451
Animal husbandry 302, 310, 323-24,
    340, 445. See also Live-
    stock
Animal products, statistics 158
Animals. See Livestock
Anthropo-geography 365, 366-67
Arab countries, military expenditures
    of 103
Arbitration, industrial 243, 261.
    See also Mediation and con-
    ciliation, industrial
Architecture 286
Armenia 451

Subject Index

Arms race 103
Artels 313, 347
Artisans 55
  decline of 111
Arts 26
Asia
  comparisons with the Russian economy 132
  economic relations with Russia 449-50
  Russian aid to 332
Asia, Soviet 11, 107-8, 128, 241, 251, 287, 293, 327, 349, 364, 401, 411, 418, 428, 437, 441, 442, 443, 444, 445, 446, 447, 449, 450, 451, 452, 453, 454. See also Kazakhstan; Tadzhikistan
Asphalt 364
Association of Industry and Trade 256
Australia, trade with Russia 199
Austria, trade with Russia 212
Autarky 83-84
Automation 277, 280
Automobile industry and trade 234
  production programs 271
Aviation, civil 28
Aviation, international disputes in 211
Azerbaydzhan 430, 442, 454

B

Balance of payments
  to 1860 223
  1860-1917 110, 111, 179, <u>223-24</u>
  after 1917 36, 190, 206, <u>224-26</u>
Balance of trade. See Balance of payments
Balance sheet. See Financial statements
Baltic countries, trade with Russia 216
Baltic Sea, in Russian trade 195
Bank of Assistance for the Nobility 179
Bank of Consumers' Co-operation 181
Banks and banking
  to 1860 10, <u>179</u>
  1860-1917 <u>179</u>-81
  after 1917 21-22, 24, 35, 59, 68, 77, <u>181-88</u>, 228
  See also Agricultural Bank; Gosbank; Land banks; Mortgages; Savings; Soviet Bank for Foreign Trade
Banks and banking, Cooperative 181
Banks and banking, savings 185, 453
Barter. See Exchange economy
Beekeeping 452
Belgium
  comparisons with the Russian economy 10
  investments in Russia 228
Birth and death rates 409, 410-11, 412-13
Blockade 98. See also Embargo
Bokaro Steel Plant 230
Bolsheviks
  agricultural policies of 311-12, 334
  and the cooperative movement 357
  general economic policies and theories 27-28, 34, 40, 98
  labor policies of 376
  "misrule" of 59
  monetary reforms of 184
  technological capabilities of 104
  See also Mensheviks
Bondage. See Serfdom; Slavery
Bonds, tax element of 185
Bonus system 57, 80, 243, 245, 247, 260, 261, 262. See also Incentive programs
Bookkeeping 84
Books, prices 176. See also Publishing industry
Bourgeoisie 255
Bread, prices 190
Bretton Woods Articles of Agreement 226
Brezhnev, Leonid Ilyich 30, 318, 343, 344
Budget, governmental
  to 1860 189
  1860-1917 189-90

Subject Index

after 1917 102, 105, 114, 150, 165, 174, 183, 184, 185, 188, <u>190-94</u>, 343, 431
  See also Finance, public
Budget, household 156, 334, 372
Budget, local 110, 184-85, 437, 446. See also Local government
Builders' Conference (1954) 286
Buildings. See War damage to buildings
Bukhara Railway 270
Bukharin, Nikolai Ivanovich 40, 43, 46, 47
Bulgaria, trade with Russia 212
Buses, production programs 271
Business administration. See Management
Business cycles 137-38. See also Depression, 1929
Businesses, foreign (in Russia). See Investments, foreign
Business law 252. See also Contracts
Byllorussia 395, 399
Byzantine Empire, trade with Russia 197

C

Canada, trade with Russia 204, 214
Capital
  by subject
    allocation of 43, 92
    circulating 191
    comparisons between countries 132-33
    fixed 277-78
    growth of 115
    input and output analysis of 94, 145, 273, 294, 295
    marginal net productivity of 82
    movement of 224, 451
    in national planning 72, 73, 75, 78-79, 88, 91, 266
    scarcity of 45, 131
  by time period
    to 1860 107, 108
    1860-1917 10
    after 1917 25, 31, 33, 43, 45, 72, 73, 75, 78-79, 88, 91, 115, 123, 131, 132-33, 145, 157, 191, 224, 239-40, 241, 247, 277, 428, 447-48, 451
  See also Finance, public; Investments; Money and monetary policy; Profit; Savings
Capital, foreign. See Investments, foreign
Capital goods 16, 77
  prices 174
Capital investments 174, 191, <u>265-68</u>, 279, 314-15
  in agriculture 78, 310, 314-15, 324, 328, 339-40, 353
  productivity as a substitute for 285-86
  time factor in planning of 49
  See also Investments
Capitalism
  by subject
    campaigns against 59
    conflict with state bureaucracies 56
    convergence with communism 68
    decision-making in 114
    development under 49
    failures of 56
    Liberman proposals and 244
    in Marxist thought 41
    in revolutionary thought 39-40
    and socialism 44, 63, 78, 81, 82
  by time period
    to 1860 8, 9, 55, 107, 255
    1860-1917 12, 39-40, 41, 56
    after 1917 21, 34, 44, 45, 49, 58, 59, 63, 64, 68, 78, 81, 82, 114, 244
  See also Entrepreneurship
Capital stock 16, 130, 151, 155, 160, 164, 268, 324
Cargo handling 279-80
Carnegie Endowment for International Peace 12
Cartels 231. See also Trusts, industrial

Subject Index

Catering 430
Catherine II 8, 71, 189, 300, 441
Cattle. See Livestock
Cement industry and trade 95, 283, 446
Census. See Population
Centralization in industry. See Economic organization and administration; Industry and productivity
Central Statistical Administration 155, 157, 163-64
   publications of 158
   See also Economics, statistics
Central Trade Union Council 416
Central Union of Consumers' Cooperatives of the USSR 63
Cereals. See Grains
Charity 415
Chemical industry and trade 30, 72, 84, 287, 291, 294. See also Fertilizers
Chemicals 364
Children
   education 372
   employment 282, 372, 387
   welfare services 417, 418
China
   agriculture and industry in 350
   aid to underdeveloped nations 229
   trade with Russia 195, 203, 206, 209, 211-12, 217-18, 221
   See also Sino-Soviet bloc
Church. See Monasteries; Religion
Cities and towns 453
   war damage to 98
Citrus fruit industry 332
City and town life 55. See also Company towns
City planning 436, 437, 438, 439. See also Housing
Climate and economics 6, 322, 351, 367, 369. See also Rain and rainfall
Clothing and dress 95, 372, 428, 431. See also Fashion
Coal 364
   reserves 362, 364
   See also Lignite
Coal mines and mining

   maps 107-8
   technology in 278
   wages in 406
Coal trade 30, 84, 110, 113
   statistics 151-52, 291, 345
Cobb-Douglas production function 116
Cocoa beans and products, imports 208
Coinage. See Foreign exchange; Money and monetary policy; Ruble
Collective bargaining and agreements 379, 381, 382, 393, 397, 398, 401. See also Arbitration, industrial; Mediation and conciliation, industrial; Trade-unions
Collectivism 3, 16, 18-19, 20-21, 24, 26, 29, 31, 101, 115, 116, 149, 197, 299, 303, 308, 309, 311, 312, 313, 314, 315, 316, 319, 320, 321, 322, 323, 324, 326, 328, 329, 330, 333, 334, 335, 336, 337, 338, 339, 340, 341, 342, 344, 346, 348, 349, 350, 352, 353, 354, 357, 358, 388, 390, 393, 420
   consolidation in 79
   income distribution and 68-69
   management in 258
   marketing statistics of 149
   national income determination under 165
   national planning and 72, 78-79
   role of commune in 40, 67
   role of financial system in 183
   women in 422
   See also Communes; Kolkhozes; Sovkhozes; State farms
Colonial policy
   to 1860 8, 441
   1860-1917 11, 443
   after 1917 202, 218, 450
   See also Imperialism
COMECON 93, 202, 203, 205, 207, 211, 213, 218, 219, 222, 224

493

Subject Index

Commerce
  by country
    Albania 207
    Arab countries 103
    Baltic countries 210
    Byzantine Empire 197
    Canada 204, 214
    China 195, 203, 206, 209, 211-12, 217-18, 221
    Czechoslovakia 211, 219
    Europe 196
    Finland 198
    France 196
    Germany 180, 197, 198, 206, 209-10
    Great Britain 197, 205, 215, 218, 227
    India 196, 229-30
    Iran 205
    Israel 103
    Japan 211
    Latin America 207
    Latvia 200
    Middle East 204
    Persian Gulf area 195, 201
    Scotland 196
    Soviet bloc countries 65-66, 93, 200, 203, 204, 209, 210, 211, 212, 214, 215-216, 218
    underdeveloped countries 125, 199, 214, 215, 231, 232, 233
    United States 196, 197, 198-99, 201, 203, 204, 205, 207, 208, 211, 216, 217, 219-20, 221-22
    Western nations 112, 199, 200, 206, 209, 210, 212, 217, 219, 221, 222, 225
  by subject
    in agricultural products 348, 351-52, 354
    Baltic Sea and 195
    input factors in 295
    national planning and 82, 93, 191
    private economic activity in 64
    specialization in 213
    statistics 147, 155, 161, 200, 208, 211, 220
  by time period
    to 1860 8, 10, 55, <u>195-97</u>, 227
    1860-1917 10, 11, 12, 13, 14, 98, <u>197-99</u>, 229
    after 1917 <u>16, 17</u>, 18, 22, 23, 24, 25, 28, 29, 30, 35, 36, 37, 59, 65-66, 68, 82, 93, 103, 112, 114, 115, 125, 132-33, 145, 147, 155, 161, 184-85, 191, <u>199-222</u>, 229, 230, 231, <u>232, 233</u>, 291, 293, 295
  See also Amtorg Trading Corp.; Balance of payments; Favored-nation clause; Fur trade; Merchants; Shipping; Trade missions; Trade routes
Commerce, internal 17, 23, 99, 221-22, 430, 432
Commercial geography 365, 366, 367
Commercial law 211, 218, 222
Commercial treaties 203, 208, 221. See also Customs unions; Favored-nation clause; Tariff
Commissions, in agricultural marketing 321
Commodities
  classification tables 145
  in national planning 95
  trade data 225
  See also names of specific commodities
Communes 300, 301, 302-3, 304, 305-6, 313, 337, 356. See also Collectivism
Communications
  by subject
    distribution and location of 367
    expenditures for 274
    national planning and 191
    statistics 157, 158
    under the Bolsheviks 104
  by time period

Subject Index

to 1860 107, 108
1860-1917 13, 110, 256-57
after 1917 27, 29, 35, 104, 157, 158, 191, 270-75, 367, 447, 450-51, 453
See also Press; Radio; Telegraph; Telephone
Communism 68
  achievements of 57
  convergence with capitalism 68
  decision-making in 114
  economic foundations of 34
  introduction of after the revolution 66
  and the military 120
  programs and goals of 57, 60
  transition to 33
  See also Bolsheviks; Marxist economic thought; Mensheviks; Socialism; Totalitarianism; War communism
Communist Party
  administrative structure of 240
  agricultural policies and 328, 336, 344, 347, 352
  dissensions in 71-72
  eighteenth congress 27
  ethics of 74
  fifteenth congress 336
  international economic cooperation and 206
  military and 21
  1961 program of 23, 66
  selection of local officials 322
  seventh session 260-61
  trade-unions and 257, 380, 387, 389, 392, 402
  turnover rate of officials 248
  twenty-second congress 63, 83
  See also Politics
Company towns 439
Comparative economics 65, 67, 78, 111, 129-35, 192, 259
  Asia 132
  Belgium 10
  China 133, 134
  Eastern Europe 193
  Germany 10, 130, 132
  Great Britain 130-31, 420, 430, 432

Hungary 193, 248
India 81, 403
Japan 130, 131, 132, 133
underdeveloped countries 131, 133
United States 1, 2, 33, 57, 62, 63, 125, 129, 130, 131, 132, 133, 134, 135, 166, 170, 175, 191, 247, 262, 275, 283-84, 288, 314, 325, 352, 353, 356, 382, 385, 390, 394, 404, 426, 428, 431, 433, 455
Western countries 34, 53, 59, 65, 129, 130, 132, 133, 135, 385
Competition 21, 27, 30, 89-90, 282, 375
Computers
  in economic planning 43, 80, 86, 139-42, 248, 260, 266
  in statistic gathering 156
  See also Cybernetics; Economic models
Concentration camps 389. See also Convict labor; Labor camps; Slave labor
Concessions, expropriation of foreign 280
Conciliation, industrial. See Mediation and conciliation, industrial
Conservation 362, 363. See also Ecology; Environmental economics; Environmental law; Soil conservation; Water resources management
Consolidations 242
Construction industry 25, 62, 102, 113, 286, 294, 296, 384
  costs in 174, 295
  private economic activity in 64
  quality in 439
  wages in 378
  See also Housing
Consumer goods 30, 121, 191, 240, 324, 429, 432, 451
  allocational aspects of 241, 429
  durable 426, 428, 433

495

Subject Index

effect on overall growth 266
non-durable 117, 426
prices of 173, 174, 376, 426-27, 430, 432
production and distribution of 73, 240, 290, 427, 428, 432, 433
rationing of 82, 241
research and planning of 77, 95, 248
statistics 150, 154
wholesale function in 295
World War I and 98
See also Producer goods; Public consumption funds
Consumers 57, 193-94, 241, 430, 433
and the cooperative movement 287, 293, 304, 305, 425-26, 427
role in marketing functions 298
unpredictability of 137-38
and welfare programs 84
Consumption 16, 18, 22, 24-25, 31, 35, 36, 65, 68, 73, 124, 239, 325, 426, 427, 428, 431, 433
compared with the U.S. 426
expenditures for 132-33
of lead and copper 110
levels of 429
output tables 145
patterns of 110
resource allocation and 126
rising expectations of 69
statistics 148, 155, 160-61
of wheat and rye 12
See also Marketing; Prices and price policy; Supply and demand
Contraception 409
Contracts 243, 249-50, 252
Contributions 430
Convict labor 84. See also Concentration camps; Labor camps; Slave labor
Cooperatives 27-28, 32, 63, 67, 303, 308, 345, 387
agricultural 304, 305, 313-14, 346, 357

consumer 287, 293, 425-26, 427
in industry 252
marketing statistics of 149
price and distribution in 65, 287, 333-34
producer 304, 305, 319
during World War I 304
See also Banks and banking, cooperative
Copper, consumption of 110
Corn 310, 322, 328. See also Maize
Corporations, foreign. See Investments, foreign
Cost accounting 238
Cost and standard of living
to 1860 300-301
1860-1917 147, <u>425-26</u>, 444
after 1917 23, <u>24-25</u>, 26, 28, 32, 44, 71, 72, 74, 82, 85, 89, 122, 134, 135, 156, 199, 256-57, 293, 313, 351-52, 375, 379, 387, 388, 390, 392, 394, 400, 401, 406, 420, <u>426-34</u>, 452
Cost-benefit analysis 362
'Cost plus' pricing 176
Cotton growing 309, 447
Council for Economic Mutual Assistance 214-15
Council of Mutual Economic Cooperation 203
Counter-intelligence 104
Crafts 300-301, 392, 442
Credit
by subject
nationalization of 182
rationing of 191
statistics 161
by time period
to 1860 179
1860-1917 <u>179-81</u>, 303, 304, 305
after 1917 21, 31, 123, 161, <u>181-88</u>, 191, 249, 303, 310
See also Debt, national; Finance, public; Government lending;

Subject Index

Investment credit analysis;
Mortgages
Credits, foreign 97, 229, 230
Crimean War, economics of 10, 171, 223
Crops. See Farm products; Rotation of crops
Cultural services
compared with the U.S. 426
demand for 427
national planning and 79, 89
statistics 161
Currency. See Money and monetary policy; Ruble
Customs unions 210. See also Tariff
Cybernetics 140, 260. See also Computers
Czechoslovakia
comparisons with the Russian economy 193
trade with Russia 211, 212, 219

D

Dairy industry 332, 349
statistics 345
Dams. See Dnieperstroi (Dam)
Danielson, Nicolai-on 56
Death rates. See Birth and death rates
Debt, foreign 224
Debt, national 12, 97, 104. See also Finance, public
Decentralization in industry. See Economic organization and administration; Industry and productivity
Decision-making process 244, 258, 259
in agriculture 316, 344, 349
in housing 436
in investment planning 267
in trade-unions 250
Defense policies 1-2, 18, 35, 37, 97-106
expenditures for 99, 100, 101, 102, 107
See also Detente; Disarmament; Foreign policy and relations; Military; Red Army

Democratic centralism 21
Demography
to 1860 407
1860-1917 110, 407-8
after 1917 26, 36-37, 155, 156-57, 347-48, 392, 408-13, 421
See also Fertility, human; Population; Social geography
Dental services, expenditures for 430
Depreciation 238
Depression, 1929 224
De-Stalinization 65-66
Detente 221. See also Peaceful co-existence
Diet 95, 429, 432. See also Food
Diplomacy. See Foreign policy and relations
Diplomatic immunity 218
Disarmament 106
Disaster relief 307. See also International relief
Distribution of goods 57, 59, 63, 65, 74, 117, 186, 241, 286-87, 288, 290, 291, 298, 427, 430
in consumer cooperatives 287
cost of 288, 297
See also Marketing
Division of labor 53
Dnieperstroi (Dam) 118
Donestsk Basin 447
Draft animals 324
Dress. See Clothing and dress
Drought 369
Drug industries. See Pharmaceutical services
Duipsony 46
Duma 306-7
budget rights of 189
first 309
Durable goods. See Consumer goods; Producer goods
Dzerzhiniski, Feliks Edmundovich 43

E

Eastern Europe. See Soviet bloc countries

497

Subject Index

Ecology 363. See also Conservation; Environmental economics; Environmental law; Pollution and pollution control
Econometrics. See Economics, mathematical
Economic assistance. See Foreign aid; Military assistance; Technical assistance
Economic forecasting 45, 46, 120, 121, <u>455</u>
Economic geography 19, 110
  to 1860 365
  1860-1917 110, <u>365-66</u>
  after 1917 19, <u>366-69</u>
  See also Space in economics
Economic growth and development
  to 1860 107-8
  1860-1917 108-12
  after 1917 112-28
Economic history 5-6
  to 1860 6-10
  1860-1917 10-15
  after 1917 15-37
  See also History, Russian
Economic laws 45, 46, 53, 83.
  See also Labor theory of value; Planned (proportional) development, Law of; Value theory
Economic models 83, 87, 89, 90, 121, 123, 127, <u>139-42</u>, 144, 260, 312, 368, 450.
  See also Computers; Economics, mathematical
Economic organization and administration
  to 1860 237
  1860-1917 237
  after 1917 <u>237-53</u>, 263
  See also Economic planning and policy; Industry and productivity; Management
Economic planning and policy
  to 1860 55, 71
  after 1917 2-3, 18, 21, 25, 26, 27, 30, 32, 33, 35, 36, 38, 45, 58, 59, 60, 63, 66, 67, 68, <u>71-96</u>, 107, 115, 117, 118, 125, 127, 137-38, 144, 175, 177, 182, 240-41, 242, 253, 258, 260, 316, 366-67
All-union plan 83
fifteen year plan 103
five year plans 19-20, 22, 27, 44-45, 71, 74, 82, 83, 84, 86, 90, 94, 95, 101, 112, 113, 115, 116, 117, 119, 121, 122, 132, 183, 191, 210, 211, 244, 270, 274, 289, 336, 344, 351, 358, 380, 383, 384
  first 14, 16, 19, 26, 29, 74, 75, 76, 77, 78, 79, 81-82, 84, 87, 88, 91, 92, 93, 114-15, 116, 128, 147, 233, 274, 379, 388, 390, 438
  second 17, 21, 23, 75, 85, 88, 94, 199, 420
  third 29, 287, 292
  fourth 82, 106, 148, 325
  fifth 80, 117, 266
  sixth 76, 326
  seventh 84-85
  eighth 74, 78, 79, 95
  ninth 92, 271
New Economic Policy (NEP) 14, 16, 20, 24, 26, 31, 49-50, 51, 52-53, 57-58, 71, 73, 74, 112, 115, 116, 117, 120, 183, 193, 194, 197, 234, 238, 247, 264, 270, 311, 312, 313, 323, 336, 337, 345, 357-58, 379, 391
1941 plan 87
seven year plan 26, 61, 72, 77, 83-84, 93, 94, 95, 121, 266, 326, 336, 340, 366, 450
twenty year plan 83, 95, 433
two year plan 94
Uzbek economic plan 83
See also Allocation of resources and materials; Computers, in economic planning; Economic models; Economic

Subject Index

organization and administration; Economics, mathematical; Teleological planning
Economics 1-3
  research 1, 2, 83
  statistics 1, 2, 13, 20, 29, 30, 61, 90, 124, 127, 147-62
  study and teaching 1, 40, 44, 48, 50, 51, 59, 391
  See also Agricultural economics; Comparative economics; Macroeconomics; Microeconomics; Rural economics; Seasonal variations (economics); Urban economics
Economics, mathematical 43, 44, 45, 51, 66, 69, 86, 87, 90, 91, 96, 139-42, 312, 451. See also Economic models
Economic sanctions 99, 103. See also Blockade; Embargo
Economics and society. See Society and economics
Economic thought
  to 1860 39, 55
  1860-1917 39-42
  after 1917 42-54
Economists 52
  acceptance of Western theories 48
Education 121, 250, 381, 393, 401, 416-20
  of children 372
  in cooperatives 252
  effect of manpower availability on 399
  of engineers 391, 415
  equality of opportunity in 416, 419
  finance and expenditures 25-26, 31, 417
  higher 419
  of physicians 417
  in post-war reconstruction 100-101
  of scientists 391
  statistics 147, 157, 161, 399
  of teachers 417-18

of workers 391
See also Agricultural education; Foreign students; Industrial education; Professional education; Retraining of the unemployed; Technical education; Vocational education
Educational assistance 232
Efficiency, static. See Inefficiency, static
Egypt, Russian foreign aid to 229
Elasticity of substitution. See Substitution, elasticity of
Electric power industry 34, 296, 445, 448
  inefficiency of 62
  investment in 266
  planning in 75, 83, 91
  statistics 147, 151-52
  technology in 278
Embargo 98. See also Blockade
Employee-management relations. See Labor relations
Employment 379, 382-83, 390, 395, 402
  compared with the U.S. 426
  equality of 416
  factors affecting in cooperatives 319
  full 92-93
  output analysis of 145, 273
  over-full 81
  reform in 419
  services 377, 432
  statistics 148, 161, 398, 403, 404
  technology and 377
  See also Manpower; Unemployed
Engels, Friedrich 41, 49, 56, 257
Engineers 376
  education of 391, 415
Entrepreneurship
  to 1860 255-56, 282
  1860-1917 256-57
  after 1917 257-64
  See also Capitalism; Profit
Environmental economics 361, 362, 367. See also Conservation; Ecology; Pollution and

Subject Index

pollution control
Environmental law 362
Equipment industry and trade 292
  exports 200
  See also Excavating machinery; Machinery industry and trade
Erosion 363
Espionage 215
Ethics 67. See also Political ethics
Ethnic groups 408, 410. See also Minorities
Europe, comparisons with the Russian economy 50, 130-31
Europe, Eastern. See Soviet bloc countries
European Economic Community and COMECON 202
  comparisons with the Russian economy 130-31
  Russian responses to 207, 222
Excavating machinery 278
Exchange economy 92

F

Factor analysis. See Input-output analysis
Factory inspection 373, 388, 392, 398
Factory laws and legislation 372
Factory life 14, 391, 400
Factory system 14, 55, 67, 107-8, 237, 303
  and business cycles 138
  committees in 374
  organization of 18
  See also Economic organization and administration; Industry and productivity; Management
Family allowance programs 409-10
Family size and planning 408, 409, 412
Famines 11, 15, 18-19, 26, 27, 228, 231, 306, 307, 317, 428-29
Farm management 299, 312, 323, 329, 338, 342, 345-46, 349, 350, 352, 353
Farm prices. See Agricultural prices
Farm products 323, 352, 369
  collection of 186
  exports of 199
  marketing and distribution of 78-79, 315, 321, 325, 329, 330, 331, 352-53, 356
  marketing statistics 149, 150
  production comparisons to the U.S. 135
  surpluses 123
  value of 325
  yield statistics 12, 135, 168, 311, 313, 321, 325-26, 329, 330, 331, 332, 336-37, 340, 341, 345, 356, 357
  See also Agricultural prices; Animal products; Grains; Livestock; Rotation of crops; names of individual crops
Fashion 429. See also Clothing and dress
Favored-nation clause 211
Fertility, human 408, 409, 410, 412
Fertilizers 294, 297, 315, 328, 335, 351
Feudal economy 8, 55, 56, 302. See also Manorial system
Field crops. See Farm products
Finance, international
  to 1860 223
  1860-1917 97, <u>223-24</u>
  after 1917 53, <u>224-26</u>
  See also Foreign economic relations
Finance, local 186
Finance, public
  by subject
    national planning and 75, 76, 81, 82, 84, 101
    statistics 147, 155, 161
    and World War II 102, 103
  by time period
    to 1860 8, 9, 107, 108, <u>179</u>, <u>189</u>
    1860-1917 11, 12, 14, 16, 110, <u>179-81</u>, <u>189-90</u>, 256-57
    after 1917 18, 19, 22, 23,

Subject Index

24, 25, 29, 30, 31, 34, 35, 59, 60, 68, 75, 76, 81, 82, 84, 101, 102, 103, 104, 147, 155, 161, <u>181-88</u>, <u>190-94</u>, 243, 451, 452
   See also Budget, governmental; Capital; Credit; Debt, national
Financial statements 240
Finland, trade with Russia 198
Fishing 302
   commercial 274, 290
Five year plans. See Economic planning and policy
Food 31, 72, 84, 110, 288, 355, 426, 430
   consumption data 333
   expenditures for 433
   imports to Russia 199
   prices 104, 171, 175, 433
   in relief work 307
   supply and demand 98, 105, 313, 332
   See also Catering; Diet; Famines
Forced labor. See Convict labor; Labor and laboring classes, compulsory; Slave labor
Foreign aid
   given by Russia 18, 28, 32, 36, 103, 125, 126, 161, <u>229-35</u>
      to Africa 233
      to China 203
      to India 229, 230
      to underdeveloped countries 215, 229, 230, 231, 232, 233, 234, 235
   received by Russia 100, 228-29, 353
   See also Lend-lease program; Military assistance; Technical assistance
Foreign credit programs. See Credit, foreign
Foreign economic relations 17, 25, 33, 232-33
   comparisons with the U.S. 135
   cooperation with Western countries 51
   in post-World War II reconstruction 104
   See also Commerce; Finance, international; Investments, foreign (in Russia)
Foreign exchange, rates 181, 182, 225, 226
Foreign investment. See Investments, foreign (in Russia)
Foreign policy and relations
   to 1860 107-8
   1860-1917 14, 229
   after 1917 17, 25, 26, 32, 35, 99, 202
   See also Colonial policy; Defense policies; Detente; Disarmament; Imperialism
Foreign students, education 419
Foreign trade. See Commerce
Forestry and forest management 11, 283, 361, 399
   reforestation 351, 361, 363
   See also Timber industry and trade
France
   investments in Russia 228
   and Russian economic thought 49
   trade with Russia 196
Freight 273
   rates 272
   statistics 448
   See also Railroads, costs and rates
Fuels. See Coal; Natural gas; Petroleum; Power resources
Fundamental Labor Legislation of the USSR and the Union Republics (1970). See Labor laws and legislation
Fur trade 197, 281, 435, 442

G

Gardens 293, 452
Gas. See Natural gas
Genetics 46
Gentry. See Nobility
Geography. See Agricultural geography; Anthropo-geography; Commercial geography; Economic geography; Physical geography; Political geography; Urban geography

Subject Index

Geological surveys, in economic planning 86
Germany
  comparisons with the Russian economy 10, 49, 130, 132
  trade with Russia 180, 197, 198, 206, 209-10
GOELRO plan 91, 451
Gold 35, 130, 190, 224, 225, 364
  hoarding of 188
  production of 285, 292
  reserves 97, 285
  Soviet theories on 53
Gold mines and mining 364
Gold standard 97, 179, 180. See also Money and monetary policy
Gosbank 158, 180, 182, 183, 184, 185, 186
Gosplan 52, 84, 87, 118, 152, 239, 374, 451
Government borrowing 190
Government expenditures. See Budget, governmental
Government lending 180, 188, 376, 453. See also Credit
Government officials, turnover rate of 249
Government purchasing, of agricultural products 90, 329-30, 333, 341, 353
Grains 190, 317, 331, 336, 339, 344
  exports and imports of 197, 222
  price supports 180
  procurement of 90, 341
  shortages 347
  statistics 24, 147, 328, 329, 332, 351, 356, 361, 450
  See also names of specific grains
Great Britain
  comparisons with the Russian economy 130-31, 192, 420, 430, 432
  investments in Russia 14, 227, 228
  Russian economic thought and 49
  trade with China 195
  trade with Russia 197, 205, 215, 218

Grinevetskii, V. 93
Gross national product 17, 19, 76, 100, 115, 116, 131, 148, 163-70, 182, 446.
  See also Income, national; Net national product
Guilds 372

H

Handicrafts. See Crafts
Hanseatic League 197
Health and medical services 417, 418, 419
  expenditures for 24-25, 31, 430
  research 418
  See also Dental services; Industrial hygiene; Industrial medicine; Physicians
Heavy industry. See Industry and productivity
Heckscher, Eli F. 217
History, Russian 19, 42. See also Economic history
Hop culture 349
Hours of labor 333, 339, 372, 374, 376, 377, 379-80, 382, 385, 387, 390, 395, 396-97, 399, 400, 401, 403, 419
Household goods. See Consumer goods
Housing 30, 31, 60, 372, 374, 388, 430, 435-39
  compared with the U.S. 426
  expenditures for 432
  private and public 435
  statistics 157
  See also City planning; Construction industry; Mortgages; Property
Human geography. See Anthropogeography
Hungary
  comparisons with the Russian economy 193, 248
  trade with Russia 212
Hunting 302
Hydroelectric power. See Electric power industry; Water power

Subject Index

Hygiene, industrial. See Industrial hygiene

I

Ideology and economics. See Communist Party; Marxist economic thought; Politics
Iljushin, I.I. 253
Illegitimacy 418
Illiteracy 415
Imperialism 8, 28, 47, 55, 218. See also Colonial policy
Incentive programs 62, 67, 68-69, 73, 112, 115, 119, 135, 183, 238, 240-41, 246, 247, 250, 251, 258, 259, 260, 262, 263, 264, 314, 324, 325, 335, 338, 342, 344, 345, 349, 353, 375, 377, 398, 401, 419, 422. See also Bonus system
Income, national
  by subject
    comparisons between countries 133, 134, 135
    definition of 164
    distribution and allocation of 163, 389
    indexes 174
    statistics 145, 150, 158, 159, 160-61, <u>163-70</u>
  by time period
    1860-1917 163
    after 1917 16, 24-26, 32, 33, 121, 133, <u>163-70</u>, 174, 376, 389
  See also Gross national product; Net national product
Income, personal 7, 24, 25, 28, 30, 35, 92, 191, 405, 427, 428, 430, 431, 432, 433
  of agricultural laborers 314, 324
  compared with the U.S. 426
  distribution of 41, 65, 66, 68, 128, 394, 400, 426
  of peasants 425
  statistics 148, 156, 158-59, 160-61, 314
  See also Purchasing power

Income tax 191, 192. See also Taxation
Index numbers
  for industrial groups 171-72
  in national income accounting 169
  problems of 175
  theory of 379
  See also Economics, statistics
India
  comparisons with the Russian economy 81, 403
  Russian foreign aid to 229, 234
  trade with Russia 196
Indonesia, Russian foreign aid to 229
Industrial arbitration. See Arbitration, industrial
Industrial associations 250
Industrial cooperation with the West 235
Industrial education 28, 78, 101, 131, 262, 377-78, 384, 385. See also Technical education; Vocational education
Industrial hygiene 387, 396. See also Health and medical services; Industrial medicine
Industrial inspection. See Factory inspection
Industrial machinery, planning needs of 86
Industrial management. See Economic organization and administration; Management
Industrial materials 117
  planning functions and 86, 87, 89
  relationship to labor 453
  supply of 73, 428
  See also Natural resources; Raw materials
Industrial medicine 417. See also Health and medical services; Industrial hygiene
Industrial organization. See Economic organization and administration; Factory system; Management

Subject Index

Industrial products
  demand for 189-90
  prices 172, 176
Industrial relations. See Labor relations
Industrial safety 387, 396
Industry and productivity 5, 137, 365
  by subject
    business cycles and 137, 138
    conflict between private and public sectors 56
    costs of 80, 84, 89, 177, 329-40
    defense and 105
    finance of 123, 186, 190, 193, 221
    influence on income 66
    investment in 60, 265, 266, 267, 268
    local 252
    location and distribution of 82, 101, 102, 103, 117, 244, 365, 366, 367, 368, 369, 445, 447, 448, 450, 452
    Marxist economics and 89
    national planning in 65, 71, 74, 75, 76, 77, 78, 79, 80, 82, 84, 86, 88, 89, 90, 91, 92, 94, 191, 376
    private economic activity in 64
    profit in 123, 239-40, 249
    relationship to modern corporate structure 64
    relationship to retail and whole sectors 293
    relations with the state 389
    research 35
    resource allocation in 94
    size of 81, 249, 250, 251
    social cost of 50
    specialization in 213
    statistics 84, 147, 149, 150, 151, 152, 153, 154, 155, 156, 157, 159, 160, 161, 170-71, 244, 267, 448
    under the Bolsheviks 104
    World War II and 101, 104, 113
    writers' attitudes toward 257
  by time period
    to 1860 6, 7, 8, 10, 55, 107-8
    1860-1917 11, 12, 13, 14, 15, 40, 42, 56, 108-12, 257, 365
    after 1917 15, 16, 17, 18, 19, 20-21, 22, 23, 24, 25, 26, 28, 29, 30, 31, 32, 33, 34, 35, 36, 37, 44, 45, 46, 49, 50, 53, 57, 59, 60, 61, 64, 65, 66, 68, 71, 74, 75, 76, 77, 78, 79, 80, 82, 84, 86, 88, 89, 90, 91, 92, 94, 101, 102, 103, 104, 105, 112-28, 147, 149, 150, 151, 152, 153, 154, 155, 156, 157, 159, 160, 161, 171, 172, 177, 186, 190, 191, 193, 213, 221, 251, 265, 266, 267, 268, 293, 295, 366, 367, 368, 369, 389, 445, 446, 447, 448, 450, 451, 452, 453, 454
  See also Automation; Economic organization and administration; Entrepreneurship; Factory system; Management; Marginal productivity; Small business; Trusts, industrial; names of specific industries
Inefficiency, static 130, 144
Inflation
  to 1860 171
  1860-1917 97, 171
  after 1917 25, 53, 78, 171-77, 426
Inland water transportation 7, 274, 447, 448, 454
Input-output analysis 114, 115, 117, 120-21, 123, 130, 133, 134-35, 139, 140, 143-45, 160, 213, 217, 273, 294, 295, 317, 321, 325-26
Institutions, economic 58
Institutions, public. See Society

Subject Index

and economics
Insurance
  expenditures for 430
  social 24, 32, 112, 300-301,
     372, 382, 386, 388, 392,
     393, 396, 398, 400, 415,
     416, 417, 418, 419, 420,
     426, 453
  state 188
  See also Pensions
Interest 45, 53, 181
International Bank for Economic Cooperation 224
International economic relations. See Foreign economic relations
International finance. See Finance, international
International Institute of Agriculture 154-55
International Labour Office 154-55, 389
International relief 228-29, 231, 234. See also Disaster relief
International Trade Organization 207
Inventory 130, 138
  ratio to sales 293
Investment credit analysis 104
Investments 18, 23, 24-25, 44, 53, 60, 124, 126, 164, <u>265-68</u>
  costs of 168
  long-term 185
  models in decision-making 83
  in national planning 72, 77, 82, 86, 89, 144
  statistics 155, 161
  and World War II 97-98
  See also Capital investments; Interest; Speculation
Investments, foreign (in Russia)
  to 1860 55, <u>227</u>, 255-56
  1860-1917 14, <u>228-29</u>, 256, 257
  after 1917 229-35
Iran, trade with Russia 205. See also Persian Gulf area
Iron and steel industry 23, 30, 55, 62, 102, 110, 113, 132, 282, 285-86, 288, 291, 294

maps of 107-8
statistics 151-52, 445
technology in 278
wages in 282, 379, 399
Iron ore
  imports 198
  reserves 364
Irrigation 328, 351, 363, 449, 453
  law 444
Israel, military expenditures 103

J

Japan
  comparisons with the Russian economy 130, 131, 132, 133
  trade with Russia 211
Job choice 377-78
Job security 377, 385
Joint-stock companies 228
Joint U.S.-USSR Commercial Commission 221-22
Jugoslavia. See Yugoslavia
Juvenile delinquents 418

K

Kara-Kalpakia (khanate) 443
Karshi Steppe Irrigation Scheme 453
Katsenelenbaum,.... 49
Kazakhstan 56, 241, 287, 293, 357, 372, 393-94, 401, 418, 429, 437, 445, 447, 448, 449, 450, 452
Keynes, John Maynard 42, 48, 52, 53
KGB 104
Kharkov Tractor Factory 117-18
Khruschev, Nikita 26, 33, 66-67, 80, 93, 94, 240, 266, 299, 308, 310, 317, 326-27, 329, 330, 332, 334, 335, 340, 343, 350, 353, 354, 392, 394, 431, 450
Kiev 7, 302
Kirgizia 444
Kirschen, E. 79
Kokovtsov Commission 373
Kolkhozes 17, 28, 67, 258, 308,

Subject Index

310, 315, 319, 321, 322,
327, 328, 331, 333, 334,
335, 337, 338, 339-40,
342, 343, 345, 346, 347,
349, 350, 354, 355, 356.
See also Collectivism;
Sovkhozes; State farms
Kosygin, Alexei 30, 238, 244, 428
Kronstadt revolt. See Revolutionary
 movement
Krzhizhanovski, Gleb Maksimili-
 anovich 43
Kulaks 308, 336, 390
Kuznetsh Basin 447, 448-49

L

Labor and laboring classes 371
 by subject
  comparisons with the U.S. 135
  compulsory 375, 376, 378,
   380, 385, 387, 390, 402,
   403
  conditions of 75, 117, 373
  costs associated with 74
  discipline of 375, 377-78,
   379, 406
  distribution of 383
  education of 391
  foreign 224
  inflation and 173
  input factors of 267, 295
  management decisions and 399
  material resources and 453
  national planning and 73, 74,
   75, 76, 78, 82, 86, 91,
   101, 399, 405
  productivity of 89, 134, 374,
   376, 383, 384, 385-86, 388,
   389, 390, 393, 397, 399,
   400, 401, 403-4, 447-48
  recruitment of 73, 377-78,
   383
  rights of 377
  statistics 151, 155, 157, 161,
   383, 403
  turnover 384, 388
  World War I and 97-98
  World War II and 104
 by time period
  to 1860 107, 108, 255, 300,
   301, 371
  1860-1917 11, 12, 13, 14, 15,
   97-98, 237, 270, 372-74
  after 1917 16, 18, 19, 20-21,
   22, 23, 25, 30, 32, 33,
   34, 35, 57, 58, 59, 64,
   68, 73, 74, 75, 76, 78,
   82, 86, 91, 101, 104, 113,
   115, 117, 124, 126, 130,
   134, 145, 151, 155, 157,
   161, 173, 286, 293, 295,
   374-406, 409, 410, 451,
   453
 See also Absenteeism (labor);
  Children, employment of;
  Division of labor; Employment; Hours of labor;
  Leaves of absence; Man-
  power; Office workers;
  Proletariat; Skilled labor;
  Trade-unions; Women, employment of; Working conditions; Workmen's compensation; Unemployment
Labor camps 380, 401. See also
 Concentration camps; Convict labor; Labor, compulsory; Slave labor
Labor disputes 26, 237, 371, 377,
 378, 382, 391, 392, 396,
 402, 429. See also Arbitration, industrial; Collective
 bargaining and agreements;
 Mediation and conciliation,
 industrial; Trade-unions
Labor laws and legislation 22, 377,
 382, 385, 386, 389, 395,
 396. See also Factory laws
 and legislation
Labor mobility 377-78, 383-84
Labor relations 64, 378, 382, 383,
 385, 392, 406
Labor theory of value 41, 43, 47,
 53, 74. See also Value
 theory
Labor-tickets 184
Lake Baikal 362
Lake Sevan 451
Land 324
 abuses of 362

Subject Index

cost of 305
cultivation of 78-79, 442
development and improvement of 313, 315, 343, 353, 450-51
distribution of 443
organization of 351
shortage of 306
Ukranian nationalism and 444
utilization of 352, 354, 368
value of 322
See also Property; Virgin lands program
Land banks 351-52. See also Agricultural Bank
Landlordism 6, 11, 303, 308. See also Rent
Landowners and ownership. See Land tenure and policies; Property
Land settlement 303-4, 308
Land tenure and policies
  to 1860 6, 8, 300, 301, 302, 442
  1860-1917 11, 304, 305, 308, 343, 443
  after 1917 16, 59, 68, 354
  See also Feudal economy; Manorial system
Lange,.... 44, 66
Latin America
  Russian aid to 232
  trade with Russia 207
Latvia
  agriculture 334
  trade with Russia 200
Law
  codes 8, 56, 61, 63-64, 74
  rural 338
  See also Agricultural laws; Business law; Commercial law; Economic laws; Environmental law; Factory laws and legislation; Labor laws and legislation; Labor theory of value; Planned (proportional)-development, law of; Value theory
Lawyers, as a source of economic change 252

Lead, consumption of 110
League of Nations 154-55
Leaves of absence 379
Leisure 397-98. See also Recreation
Lena Goldfields Co., Ltd. 284
Lend-lease program 103, 217, 353
Lenin, Nikolai 9, 40, 41, 43, 44, 45, 49, 52, 55-56, 73, 81, 85, 184, 257, 306-7, 309, 334, 372, 420, 451
Leningrad 437, 439
Less developed countries. See Underdeveloped countries
Lignite 364
Linear programming. See Computers
Liquor industry 282, 288, 425
List, Friedrich 42
Livestock 78-79, 323, 326, 332, 339, 348, 352, 354, 369, 442, 452
  breeding 328
  losses of during World War II 105
  production of 94, 135
  statistics 158, 316, 327, 330, 332, 357
  taxation of 192
  See also Draft animals
Loans. See Credit; Government lending
Loans, foreign. See Finance, international
Local government
  and agricultural policies 342, 344
  and the NEP 71-72, 337
  relations with state farms 339
  role in local industry 239
Location theory 45. See also Industry and productivity, location and distribution of
Locomotives 275
  diesel 271
  electric 271
  production of 62
  steam 270
Logging industry. See Timber industry and trade

Subject Index

Longshoremen 279
Lotteries 453
Lumber. See Forestry and forest management; Timber industry and trade

M

McArthur (Ellen) Lectures 12
McCormick Harvesting Machine Co. 229
Machinery industry and trade 30, 36, 62, 72, 75, 117, 132, 284, 288, 291, 292, 293, 364
  exports in 200
  prices in 171
  statistics 151-52, 154, 161, 218
Machine tool industry 91, 286, 292
  technology in 278
Machine-tractor stations 311, 315, 329, 333, 334, 338, 339, 344, 346, 347, 348, 353
Macroeconomics 15, 17, 57-58, 127, 179, 247. See also Microeconomics
Magnitogorsk 400
Maize 324
Makarov, V.L. 140
Malenkov, Georgi Maksimilianovich 33, 94
Management
  by subject
    accounting in 238
    authority in 398
    development of skills in 22
    ideological antecedents of 242
    influence of in the economy 68
    motivation in 248
    worker participation in 399
  by time period
    to 1860 255-56
    1860-1917 256-57
    after 1917 21, 22, 25, 32, 37, 68, 73, 76, 85, 242, 248, 257-64, 383, 398, 399
  See also Decision-making process; Farm management; Incentive programs; Labor relations;

Personnel management
Manchuria 11
Manganese 291
Mangazeia, Siberia 435
Manorial system 302. See also Feudal economy; Mir
Manpower 32, 36, 49, 86, 384, 386, 387, 391, 393, 397, 401, 413
  distribution and allocation of 376, 377-78, 392, 402
  education in the development of 380-81
  supply and demand 115, 124, 377, 382, 383, 386, 410
Manufacturing. See Industry and productivity
Marginal analysis 145
Marginal productivity 82
Marketing 25, 67-68, 78, 118, 238, 256-57, 288, 289, 293-94
  of farm produce 315, 321, 329, 330, 331, 352-53, 356
  and railroad development 270
  research 249
  See also Distribution of goods
Marx, Karl 41, 53, 56, 257, 316-17, 334, 420
Marxism-Leninism 49
Marxist economic thought 46, 48, 51, 60, 63
  allocation of resources and 52
  capital creation and 45
  capitalism and 41, 56
  deviations from 89
  heavy industry and 89
  income distribution and 41
  influence of Bukharin on 43
  influence of Lenin on 43
  labor and 373-74
  material supply and 66
  national income theory and 167
  national planning and 66, 92
  revisions of 44, 47, 51
  revolution and 74
  service labor and 49
  social classes and 52
  study and teaching of 47-48, 51, 52

Subject Index

See also Communism
Matches 231
Maternal welfare 418
Mechanization. See Automation
Mediation and conciliation, industrial 379, 382, 391. See also Arbitration, industrial
Medical services. See Industrial hygiene; Industrial medicine; Health and medical services; Physicians
Mensheviks 46. See also Bolsheviks
Mercantile system 6, 12, 189
Merchandising. See Marketing
Merchant marine 270, 271, 274
    wages in 391
    See also Shipping
Merchants, writers' attitudes toward 257
Mergers 242
Metal industry and trade 72, 75, 108, 117, 281, 282
    prices in 174
Metallurgy. See Mining and metallurgy
Metals. See Mineral resources
Metal-working industries 243, 282, 289, 290, 297
Microeconomics 15, 57-58, 247, 312. See also Macroeconomics
Middle East, Russian aid to 103-4
Migration, internal 407-8, 409, 413, 450-51
Military
    agriculture and the 301, 348-49
    capital investments and the 265
    claims on resources 36, 72
    communism and the 120
    effect on distribution policies 286-87
    expenditures 25, 32
    strength of the 125
    technology and the 99-100
    See also Defense policies; Red Army
Military assistance 229-30, 232, 233-34
Military service, compulsory 100
Milk. See Dairy industry

Millikan, Max 267
Mineral resources 362, 364
    location and distribution of 365, 367, 368
    See also Coal; Gold; Lignite; Natural gas; Petroleum
Miners 392
    wages 406
Mining and metallurgy 11, 13, 19, 28, 364, 369, 451. See also Coal mines and mining; Gold mines and mining
Ministry of Finance 194
Minorities, treatment of 27. See also Ethnic groups
Mir 299, 304, 308. See also Feudal economy; Manorial system
Miroshnichenko, B. 88
Molotov, V. 27, 79, 88
Monasteries, landownership in 8
Money and monetary policy
    by subject
        Byzantine influence on 197
        demand considerations on 187
        paper money 179, 180, 181, 184, 186-87
        in trade relations 225
    by time period
        to 1860 <u>179</u>, 197
        1860-1917 12, 14, 97, <u>179-81</u>
        after 1917 17, 23, 24, 25, 27, 29, 34, 45, 53, 59, 68, 92, 114, 160-61, <u>181-88</u>, 403
    See also Foreign exchange; Gold standard; Ruble
Mongolia, Outer 192
Mongolia, trade with Russia 204
Monopoly 45, 46, 376
    in foreign trade 212
    in the iron industry 282
Monopsony 46
Morissens, L. 79
Morozhevoe, Autonomous Soviet Republic of 87
Morozov family 255, 256
Mortgages 180
Moscow 439

Subject Index

Moscow Carburetor Works 250
Moscow Economic Conference (1952) 42, 52
Moscow Institute of Economic Research 49
Moscow Narodny Bank 181
Moscow University 51
Most-favored-nation clause. See Favored-nation clause
Motor transport 292, 447
  statistics 271
  See also Automobile industry and trade; Roads; Trucks
Muscovy 56
MVD 104

N

Nakaz 71
Narodniks 39-40, 41-42, 46, 56
Narva (seaport) 197
Nationalization of industry. See Industry and productivity
National product. See Gross national product; Net national product
National security. See Security, national
Natural gas 72, 287, 292, 364, 452
  exports 287
  reserves 362
  statistics 291
Natural resources 120, 126, 363, 364
  allocation of 18, 52, 66, 72, 80, 96, 115, 121, 126
  exploitation of 74, 116
  location and distribution of 46, 366, 369
  reserves 362
  See also Conservation; Industrial materials; Mineral resources; Raw materials
Navigation 6
  international disputes 211
Netherlands, trade with Russia 204
Net national product 148, 164, 362.
  See also Gross national product

New Economic Policy. See Economic planning and policy
New-Narodniks. See Narodniks
New towns. See City planning
Nicholas II 13
NKVD 389
Nobility 7, 8, 9, 179
Nomads, and Soviet economic policies 128, 349, 357, 442, 444
Northern Sea route. See Trade routes
Novozhelov, V.V. 43, 140
Nutrition. See Diet; Food

O

Occupations, social status and 388, 405-6. See also Labor and laboring classes
Ocean transport. See Merchant marine; Shipping
Office workers 395
Ohlin, Bertil G. 217
Oil industry. See petroleum industry and trade
Oil shales 291
Old Believers 255
Ordzhonikidze, Grigori Konstantinovich 43
Organization, economic. See Economic organization and administration
Organization for Economic Cooperation and Development 219
Outer Mongolia. See Mongolia, Outer
Output analysis. See Input-output analysis
Ownership 84. See also Capitalism; Land tenure and policies; Property

P

Pahlen Commission 444
Paris Economic Conference (1916) 98
Participatory management. See Management
Paul I 179, 227

Subject Index

Peaceful co-existence 124, 199, 212. See also Detente
Peasantry 299
  by subject
    controls over 318, 425
    income and wages 312, 324, 330, 333
    institutions of 41
    landowners and 6
    the law and 8, 56
    living standards of 425
    relationships with town laborers 344, 373
    revolution and 39, 306, 307
    self-government of 337
    socio-economic mobility of 307
    under the NEP 71-72
  by time period
    to 1860 6, 8, 9, 10, 56, 299-303, 373, 442
    1860-1917 10, 11, 12, 13, 14, 39, 41, 97-98, 303-10, 372, 425
    after 1917 19, 21, 23, 24, 26, 58, 71-72, 89-90, 312, 313, 315, 318, 322, 323, 324, 327, 330, 333, 335, 336, 337, 340, 341-42, 343, 344, 345, 346, 347-48, 350, 351-52, 354, 355, 356, 357-58, 374
  See also Agricultural labor; Kulaks; Serfdom
Peat 362
Pensions 419. See also Insurance, social
Performance awards. See Incentive programs
Periodicals, prices of 175
Persian Gulf area
  trade with Russia 195, 204
  See also Iran
Personal care, expenditures for 430, 433
Personnel management 250
Pesek, Boris P. 130
Peter the Great 6, 9, 11, 108, 196
Petroleum 364
  reserves 84, 362

  See also Oil shales
Petroleum industry and trade 17, 18, 28, 30, 72, 111, 285, 287, 290, 292, 293, 296, 452
  and East-West relations 209
  in Russian commerce 201, 207, 212, 215, 216, 221, 287
  statistics 151-52, 291
  See also Pipelines
Pharmaceutical services 283-84, 418
Philosophy, Russian 14
Phosphates 231
Physical geography 367, 368, 369
Physicians, education of 417
Pigs 358
Pipelines 271
Planned (proportional) development, law of 90
Platinum 231
Plekhanov, G.V. 39-40, 55-56
Poland
  comparisons with the Russian economy 193
  trade with Russia 212
Police
  budget 194
  trade-unions and 374
  See also KGB
Political ethics 74
Political geography 369, 448
Politics 14
  economics and 19, 21, 29, 36, 64, 81, 108-9, 126, 244, 312, 322, 325, 334-35, 342, 345, 350, 354
  See also Communist Party; De-Stalinization; Duma
Pollution and pollution control 361, 362, 363, 364. See also Ecology; Environmental economics; Environmental law
Pomiestie. See Land tenure and policies
Poor. See Poverty
Poor relief. See Social welfare programs

Subject Index

Population
  by subject
    census of 157, 408, 409, 411, 412
    comparisons with the U.S. 135
    distribution and location of 365, 366, 367, 368, 369, 439
    of farms 324
    percentage of peasants in 425
    projections 399, 408, 410
    rural surplus of 305
    spatial decentralization of 130
    statistics 147, 161, 244, 408
  by time period
    to 1860 10, 407
    1860-1917 13, 110, 305, 407, 425
    after 1917 25, 31, 35, 36-37, 67, 71, 75, 100-101, 130, 135, 147, 157, 161, 305, 313, 320, 324, 347, 350, 366, 367, 368, 383, 390, 399, <u>408-13</u>, 448, 453
  See also Demography; Family size and planning
Portal, Roger 282
Pososhkvo, Ivan Tikhonovich 256
Postal service 271
Potash 231
Potemkin, Grigori Aleksandrovich 441
Poverty 31, 59
Power resources 23, 32, 72, 117, 292, 364, 369
  consumption of 291
  inefficiency in the use of 62
  policy decisions in the use of 295-96
  prices of 172, 174, 362
  statistics 295
  See also Coal; Electric power industry; Mineral resources; Natural gas; Petroleum; Water power; Wind power
Premiums 257-58
Preobrazhenski, Evgenii A. 44, 45, 46
Press, reorganization of 241
Prices and price policy
  by subject
    of books and periodicals 176
    of bread 190
    of consumer goods 173, 174, 376, 426-27
    during World War I 98
    during World War II 104
    economic objectives and 60
    employment and 319
    in foreign trade 200, 210, 211, 214
    fourth five year plan and 82
    of industrial materials 73
    of industrial products 172
    in the iron and steel industry 282
    national income and 165, 169
    national planning and 72, 73, 76, 81, 86, 172
    relationship to costs 248
    relationship to profit 174
  by time period
    to 1860 <u>171</u>, 282
    1860-1917 <u>171</u>, 228, 373
    after 1917 21, 22, 24, 25, 29, 35, 44, 45, 50, 53, 60, 61, 65-66, 68, 72, 73, 76, 81, 82, 86, 92, 98, 104, 114, 124, 153, 156, 160-61, 165, 169, <u>171-77</u>, 182, 190, 210, 211, 214, 220, 225, 226, 240-41, 243, 245, 248, 250-51, 319, 376, 394, 426-27
  See also Agricultural prices; 'Cost plus' pricing; Purchasing power; Retail prices; Wages and wage policy; Wholesale prices
Private enterprise. See Capitalism; Entrepreneurship
Process analysis 297
Producer goods
  effect on economic growth 266
  prices of 174
  See also Consumer goods
Producer's Cooperatives. See Cooperatives

Subject Index

Productivity. See Industry and productivity
Professional education 380-81, 391
Profit 53, 57, 68, 80, 241, 247, 249, 251, 264
  in agriculture 319-20
  effect of prices on 174
  incentives and 245, 246, 260
  maximization of 239-40
  national income and 169
  role of 246, 257-58
  See also Capitalism; Entrepreneurship
Proletariat 11, 39, 41, 388. See also Labor and laboring classes
Property
  law of 317, 435
  private 299, 317, 326, 327, 362
  state 190
  theory of 65
  See also Land; Land tenure and policies
Protestant ethic 12, 256
Publications, statistical 158. See also Books; Periodicals; Publishing industry
Public consumption funds 432, 433
Public health. See Health and medical services
Public officials. See Government officials
Public utilities 22, 438, 439. See also Electric power industry
Public welfare. See Social welfare programs
Publishing industry 452. See also Books; Periodicals
Purchasing power 431

Q

Quality control 252, 258, 282

R

Radio 271
Railroads 11, 17, 72, 83, 84, 111, 210, 255, 269-75, 365, 443, 447, 450, 452-53, 454
  costs and rates 174, 271, 272
  equipment 292
  freight and passenger service 275
  labor productivity of 273
  in marketing development 270
  statistics 271
  See also Locomotives
Rain and rainfall 367. See also Drought
Rand Corporation 2, 148, 214-15
Rationing 16, 28, 82, 99, 104, 245, 427, 430, 433
  of credit 191
Raw materials 117
  abuses of 362
  See also Industrial materials; Mineral resources; Natural resources
Reclamation of land. See Land
Recreation, expenditures for 430, 431. See also Leisure
Red Army, politics and 21. See also Military
Redemption (economics) 181
Reforms, economic. See Economic organization and administration
Regional development and planning 90, 143, 241, 250, 446, 449, 450, 453, 454
  in agriculture 325
  central government and 44, 84, 85, 454
  national income and 168
Regional studies
  before 1860 441-42
  1860-1917 443-45
  after 1917 445-54
Regression analysis 103
Regulation on the Rights of Factory, Plant and Local Union Committees (1971) 377
Rehabilitation services 420
Relief. See Disaster relief; International relief; Social welfare programs; War relief
Religion 14, 305. See also Monastaries; Protestant ethic

Subject Index

Rent 45, 53
   feudal 442
   of houses 437-38
   of land 322
   See also Landlordism
Repair services 430
Reparations 211
Research. See Economics, research; Industry and productivity, research
Rest periods 382
Retail prices 156, 172-73, 176, 177, 294, 379, 430, 431, 433
   indexes of 175, 176
   national income determination and 165
Retail trade 25, 289, 290, 433-34
   procurement in 297-98
   relationship to wholesale and manufacturing sectors 293
   statistics 149
   workers in 297
Retraining of the unemployed 381, 397
Revisionist theories. See Marxist economic thought
Revolutionary movement 8-9
   of 1905 13
   1917-21 21, 46, 51
      economic disintegration during 97
      land settlement and 303-4
      monetary system and 188
      peasantry and 39, 306, 307
      workers and 374
   waning of the ideas of 65
Roads 447, 448, 452, 454. See also Motor transport
Rotation of crops 351, 363
Roumania. See Rumania
Royalties 190
Ruble
   gold convertibility of 224
   value of 170, 186
   See also Foreign exchange; Money and monetary reform
Rumania, trade with Russia 212
Rural economics 10. See also Urban economics

Rural life and conditions 305, 313, 316, 336, 338, 347-48, 356
Russian-American Co. 227
Russian Co. 197, 227
Russo-Chinese Bank 228
Russo-Japanese War, economics of 11, 13, 15
Rye 351
   consumption of 12

S

Safety, industrial. See Industrial safety
Saint Petersburg-Moscow Railway 269
Sales
   ratio to inventory 293
   rewards for 245
Salt manufacture and trade 108
Sanctions. See Economic sanctions
Sanitation 418
Savings 35, 53, 183, 184, 426, 430. See also Banks and banking
Savings banks. See Banks and banking, savings
Science and agriculture. See Agronomy
Science and the economy 26, 28, 33, 34, 78, 80, 93, 126, 277-80, 402
Scientists 376
   education of 391
"Scissors" crisis 20, 27, 89, 112, 115, 116, 117
Scotland, trade with Russia 196
Seasonal variations (economics) 120
Security, national 104
Seed production 321
Serfdom 7, 9, 10, 55, 56, 300, 302, 306, 309
   compared to slavery 129
   emancipation from 9, 10, 11, 107, 301, 302-3, 304, 305-6, 307, 308, 310
   entrepreneurship and 256
   law of 8
   living standards under 425

Subject Index

See also Peasantry; Slavery
Services and service industries 95, 290, 293, 300-301, 392, 426, 438, 452
   statistics 156
Sex discrimination 416
Sheep 347. See also Wool
Shelter belts 364
Shipping 454
   statistics 271
   See also Longshoremen; Merchant marine
Ships, use of foreign 222
Siberia 11, 14, 93, 120, 300, 327, 364, 365, 367, 368, 387, 397, 411, 441, 442, 443, 444, 445, 447, 448, 450, 452, 454. See also Mangazeia, Siberia; Trans-Siberian Railroad
Sino-Soviet bloc 114, 201
   aid to underdeveloped nations 229, 234
   See also China
Skilled labor, use of 131
Slave labor 380, 396, 405. See also Convict labor; Labor camps
Slavery 442
   compared to serfdom 129
Slave trade 281
Small business 245, 291-92
"Smerd" movement 7
Social classes 14, 26, 28, 67, 412, 443, 444
   Marxist thought and 52
   occupational status and 388, 405-6
Social geography. See Anthropogeography; Demography
Socialism
   accumulation theories of 50
   capitalism and 44, 63, 78, 81
   economic theories of 34, 63, 64, 122
   ideological and political aspects of 41, 47
   progress and results of 58
   Soviet views of 61
   See also Communism

"Socialism in one country" concept 19, 51
Social legislation 376. See also Insurance, social; Workmen's compensation
Social mobility 388. See also Labor mobility
Social problems 396, 420. See also Juvenile delinquents
Social security. See Insurance, social
Social statistics 147-62
Social welfare programs
   1860-1917 415
   after 1917 19, 26, 30, 35, 59, 84, 121, 242, 250, 282, 379, 389, <u>416-20</u>, 422, 426, 432, <u>452</u>
   See also Charity; Children, welfare services; Family allowance programs; Maternal welfare; Rehabilitation services
Society and economics
   to 1860 7, 8, 9, 10, <u>55-56</u>, 300-301, 302
   1860-1917 10, 11, 12, 13, <u>56</u>, 108-9, 110, 407
   after 1917 25, 26, 30, 31, 34, 35, 45, 46, <u>57-69</u>, 128, 388
Soft goods. See Consumer goods
Soil conservation 363. See also Erosion
Soil science. See Agronomy
Soviet Academy of Sciences 50
Soviet Bank for Foreign Trade 225, 226
Soviet bloc countries 30
   aid to underdeveloped countries 230, 233
   comparison with Western economies 135
   economic debates in 65-66
   industrial patterns of 117
   peaceful co-existence and 123-24
   trade with Russia 93, 200, 204, 209, 210, 211, 212, 214, 215-16, 218

Subject Index

Soviet Machinery Industry Study of the University of North Carolina 297
Soviet Ministry of Higher Education 51
Soviet Settling Programme 357
Sovkhozes 67, 310, 315, 327, 333, 343, 345, 347, 355. See also Collectivism; Kolkhozes; State farms
Sovnarkhoz 90, 93, 239, 243, 244
Space in economics 367
Space sciences 278
Spanish America. See Latin America
Spasskiy Copper Works 228
Speculation 188, 331. See also Investments
Sputnik. See Space sciences
Stakhanovism 184-85, 375, 388, 392, 393
Stalin, Joseph 29, 43, 46, 47, 48, 49, 52, 66-67, 79, 81, 82, 85, 90, 113, 114, 119-20, 124, 126, 176, 194, 206, 266, 278, 279, 311, 313, 316, 331, 334, 335, 336, 350, 354, 376, 401, 402, 406, 433, 451. See also De-Stalinization
Stalingrad Tractor Plant 287
Stalin Motor Works 397
Standard of living. See Cost and standard of living
State bank. See Gosbank
State farms 78, 299, 311, 313, 314, 318, 320, 328, 333, 337, 339, 345, 348-49, 353, 358, 399, 452. See also Collectivism; Kolkhozes; Sovkhozes
Static inefficiency. See Inefficiency, static
Statistics. See Economic, statistics; Social statistics
Steel industry. See Iron and steel industry
Stolypin, Petr Arkadevich 303, 304, 306, 307, 308, 309
Subsidies 245, 333, 336
Substitution, elasticity of 115, 121

Sugar beets 323
Supply and demand 294, 330, 333
 balance between 266
 of consumer goods 428
 of foodstuffs 332
 of money 187
 in national planning 84, 86
 relation to prices 177
 See also Consumption
Supreme Economics Council 397
Surplus agricultural commodities. See Farm products
Syndicates 18
Synthetic factor shares 115
Sytin, Ivan 257

T

Tadzhikistan 448
Tariff 110, 190, 213. See also Commercial treaties; Commerce; Customs unions; Favored-nation clause
Tariff wars 98, 180, 198
Taxation
 by subject
  of bonds 185
  in cooperatives and collectives 252, 319, 329, 343
  indirect 190
  of livestock 192
  of nomadic populations 442
  rural 351-52
 by time period
  to 1860 <u>189</u>, 442
  1860-1917 <u>189-90</u>, 305, 444
  after 1917 35, 72, 102, 112, 115, 153, 183, 184, 185, <u>190-94</u>, 252, 319, 329, 343, 351-52
 See also Income tax; Turnover tax
Teachers
 education of 417-18
 productivity of 49
Technical assistance 234
 given by Russia 224, 230, 232, 233, 234
 given to Russia 279, 280
 See also Economic assistance; Foreign aid; Military assistance

Subject Index

Technical education 393-94, 406.
　　See also Industrial education; Vocational education
Technology 23-24, 93, 250, 277-80
　in agriculture 128, 135, 316, 326, 335, 352
　economic expansion and 60, 126
　employment and 377, 402
　foreign 22, 257, 316
　in industrial expansion 107, 117
　low level of 428
　military power and 99-100
　retraining and 381
　wages and 401
　See also Science and the economy
Telegraph 271
Teleological planning 46, 77
Telephone 271
Territorial Production Administration 334, 335
Territorial-production complexes 246
Textbooks. See Economics, study and teaching
Textiles 35, 428
Timber
　distribution and location of 366
　exports of 282
　reserves 362
Timber industry and trade 35, 62, 284-85, 296
Time study 405
Timiryazev Agricultural Academy 312
Tobacco trade 196
Totalitarianism 60
Towns. See City and town life; Rural life and conditions; Villages
Tractors 278. See also Agricultural machinery and implements; Kharkov Tractor Factory; Machine-tractor stations; Stalingrad Tractor Plant
Trade. See Commerce
Trade agreements. See Commercial treaties
Trade missions 216
Trade routes 196-97, 365-66, 368
Trade Union Congress (11th) 383
Trade-unions 19-20, 21, 32, 64, 112, 115, 371, 372, 374, 375, 376, 379, 380, 382, 385, 386, 387, 388, 389, 390, 391, 395, 396, 398, 399, 401-2
　capitalism and 374
　control of 63, 257, 389
　decision-making and 250
　education and 391
　finances 153
　government and 380, 387, 392, 402
　labor inspection and 396
　labor legislation and 396
　legal aspects of 395
　police and 374
　regional 252
　rights of 399
　roles of 101
　social insurance and 398
　women in 422
　See also Arbitration, industrial; Collective bargaining and agreements; Guilds; Industrial associations; Labor disputes; Mediation and conciliation, industrial; Voluntary workers' organizations
Transcaspian Railway 443
Transcaucasia 452
Transportation
　by subject
　　comparison with the U.S. 135
　　distribution and location of 366, 367, 368, 369
　　electrification of 274
　　national planning and 71, 79, 84, 191
　　organization of 186
　　in post-World War II reconstruction 104
　　prices in 172
　　statistics 147, 155, 161, 271
　　under the Bolsheviks 104
　by time period
　　to 1860 107, 269
　　1860-1917 12, 13, 14, 256-57, 270
　　after 1917 21-22, 23, 27,

Subject Index

29, 30, 32, 34, 35, 62,
71, 79, 84, 104, 119, 122,
135, 147, 155, 161, 172,
186, 191, <u>270-75</u>, 366,
367, 368, 369, 430, 432,
448-49, 451, 452
  See also Air transport; Automobile industry and trade; Buses; Inland water transportation; Motor transport; Pipelines; Railroads; Roads; Shipping; Trucks
Trans-Siberian Railroad 11, 443
Travel by Soviet citizens 153
Treaties. See Commercial treaties; Favored-nation clause
Trees. See Forestry and forest management; Shelter belts; Timber; Timber industry and trade
Trotsky, Leon 19
Trucks 273
  production programs 271
Trusts, industrial 18, 238. See also Cartels; Monopoly; Syndicates
Tsarskoe Selo Railway 269
Tsentral' noye Statisticheskoe Upravlenie 156
Turkestan 240, 309
Turkey
  Russian aid to 234
  trade with Russia 204
Turner, Frederick Jackson 5-6, 108
Turnover tax 169, 174, 193, 194, 433

U

Ukraine 91, 406, 441, 442, 444, 446-47, 448, 451
Underdeveloped countries 26, 28, 125, 131, 133
  Russian aid to 215, 229, 230, 231, 232, 233, 234, 235
  trade with Russia 199, 214, 215
  use of the Russian economic model 61, 403
Unemployed 61, 374, 377, 383, 387, 388, 390, 392, 393,
403, 404
  assistance for 381, 397
Unions. See Trade-unions
United Arab Republics, Russian aid to 234
United Nations 154-55
United Nations Monetary and Financial Conference. See Bretton Woods Articles of Agreement
United States
  aid to Russia 100, 228-29, 231, 233
  aid to other countries 229-30, 231-32, 234
  investments in Russia 228, 229
  and Russian economic policy 30, 31, 32, 33, 127, 233
  trade with Russia 196, 197, 198-99, 201, 203, 204, 205, 207, 208, 211, 216, 217, 219-20
  See also Comparative economics
Unwed mothers. See Illegitimacy
Urban economics
  to 1860 435
  1860-1917 11, 443
  after 1917 77, 419, <u>435-39</u>, 451
  See also Rural economics
Urban geography 366
Uzbek economic plan. See Economic planning and policy
Uzbekistan 316, 453

V

Vacations 382
Value-added, estimates of in industry 160
Value theory 33, 43, 44, 45, 46, 47, 50, 53, 54, 83, 245. See also Labor theory of value
Village life. See Rural life and conditions
Villages
  agrarian reform and 306, 308, 309
  descriptions of 299, 351-52

Subject Index

self-government of 337
Virgin lands program 311, 313, 317, 320, 331, 335, 339, 358-59
Vital statistics. See Birth and death rates
Vladikavkaz Railway 210
Vocational education 313, 385, 399, 401, 406
    women and 422
    See also Industrial education; Retraining of the unemployed; Technical education
Volsky, Nikolai Vladislavovich 52-53
Voluntary workers' organizations 395
Von Neumann, John 140
Voronstov, V.P. 56
Vygurs 308

W

Wages and wage policy
  by subject
    differentials 405, 422
    influence of productivity on 376
    in the iron and steel industry 282, 379
    national income determination and 165
    in national planning 72, 82, 86, 101
    premium pay 57
    relationship to prices 174
    statistics 148, 156, 158-59, 161, 395
  by time period
    to 1860 300-301
    1860-1917 305, 372, 373, 374
    after 1917 20, 22, 28, 31, 32, 57, 68, 72, 82, 86, 101, 112, 115, 117, 156, 158-59, 161, 165, 174, 282, 374, 375, 376, 378, 379, 380, 382, 384, 385, 386, 387, 388, 390, 392, 393, 394, 395, 399, 400, 401, 403, 404, 405, 406, 419, 422, 427, 430, 432
  See also Agricultural labor; wages and income; Income, personal; Prices and price policy
War and economics. See Crimean War, economics of; Russo-Japanese War, economics of; World War I, economics of; World War II, economics of
War communism 16, 19-20, 21, 27, 65, 74, 90, 92, 112, 115, 116, 117, 121-22, 312, 313, 337, 379
War damage to buildings 98, 296
War materials 98
War relief 100
Water pollution. See Pollution and pollution control
Water power 296, 362, 445, 451
Water resources management 362, 363. See also Erosion
Water supply 449
Weights and measures 10
Western European Economic Community 219
Western nations
  concepts of freedom in 60
  Russian economic policies and 59, 81, 124
  trade with Russia 199, 200, 206, 209, 210, 212, 217, 219, 221, 222, 225
  See also Comparative economics
Wheat 305, 311, 349, 351
  consumption of 12
  exports of 198
  imports of 204, 214
  1933 conference on 202-3
Wholesale prices 114, 172-73, 175, 176
Wholesale trade 290
  in consumer goods 295
  relationship to retail and wholesale sectors 293
Wind power 362
Witte, Sergei Yulievich 13, 40, 42, 111, 112, 228, 309, 373

Subject Index

Women 421-23
  in agriculture 319
  education of 422, 423
  employment of 372, 387, 388, 421, 422, 423
  in post-war reconstruction 101-2
  trade-unions and 392, 422
  wages 422
Wool 347
  imports 199
  statistics 345
  See also Sheep
Working class. See Labor and laboring classes; Office workers; Proletariat
Working conditions 372, 375, 385, 387, 392, 400, 401, 406, 426. See also Rest periods
Workmen's compensation 373
World War I, economics of 12, 13, 15, 17, 27, 28, 97-98, 190

World War II, economics of 32, <u>98-106</u>, 113, 122, 182, 190, <u>211</u>, 219-20, 296, 354, 401, 413, 437. See also Reparations

Y

Yugoslavia
  Russian aid to 229
  trade with Russia 212

Z

Zemstov 14
Zinov'ev, Grigorii E. 47
Zubatov movement 372-73, 374